A New Birth of Freedom

By Harry V. Jaffa

Thomism and Aristotelianism: A Study of the Commentary by Thomas Aquinas on the Nicomachean Ethics (1952)

Crisis of the House Divided: An Interpretation of the Issues in the Lincoln–Douglas Debates (1959)

Equality and Liberty: Theory and Practice in American Politics (1965)

The Conditions of Freedom: Essays in Political Philosophy (1975)

How to Think about the American Revolution: A Bicentennial Cerebration (1978)

American Conservatism and the American Founding (1984)

Original Intent and the Framers of the Constitution: A Disputed Question (1994)

Storm over the Constitution (1999)

A New Birth of Freedom: Abraham Lincoln and the Coming of the Civil War (2000)

Statesmanship: Essays in Honor of Sir Winston Churchill (1982)

Shakespeare's Politics (with Allan Bloom, 1964)

In the Name of the People: Speeches and Writings of Lincoln and Douglas in the Ohio Campaign of 1859 (with Robert W. Johannsen, 1959)

A New Birth of Freedom

Abraham Lincoln and
the Coming of the Civil War

Harry V. Jaffa

ROWMAN & LITTLEFIELD PUBLISHERS, INC.
Lanham • Boulder • New York • Oxford

ROWMAN & LITTLEFIELD PUBLISHERS, INC.

Published in the United States of America
by Rowman & Littlefield Publishers, Inc.
4720 Boston Way, Lanham, Maryland 20706
http://www.rowmanlittlefield.com

12 Hid's Copse Road
Cumnor Hill, Oxford OX2 9JJ, England

British Library Cataloguing in Publication Information Available

Library of Congress Cataloging-in-Publication Data

Jaffa, Harry V.
    A new birth of freedom : Abraham Lincoln and the coming of the civil war /
Harry V. Jaffa.
        p.   cm.
    Includes bibliographical references and index.
    ISBN 0-8476-9952-8 (alk. paper)
    1. United States—Politics and government—1861–1865.   2. Lincoln,
Abraham, 1809–1865.   3. Lincoln, Abraham, 1809–1865. Gettysburg Address.
4. Presidents—United States—Election—1860.   4. Lincoln, Abraham,
1809–1865—Inauguration, 1861.   I. Title.
E459.J34   2000
973.7—dc21   00-031100
                                                                         CIP

Printed in the United States of America

⊖ ^{TM} ·The paper used in this publication meets the minimum requirements of
American National Standard for Information Sciences—Permanence of Paper for
Printed Library Materials, ANSI/NISO Z39.48–1992.

To
Donald and Irmela
Philip and Nancy
Karen and Lawrence
and to
Peter
Nicholas
Kerstin

"And the war came."

Contents

Preface

The present work is the sequel to *Crisis of the House Divided*, promised in the preface of that opus, dated October 7, 1958. That happened to be the hundredth anniversary of the Galesburg debate between Lincoln and Douglas. It was also my fortieth birthday. To the many who reproach me for the length of the interval between the alpha and the omega of this project, I can only reply that it corresponds closely to the distance in time that separated Plato's *Republic* from his *Laws*. One can claim a resemblance to the great without laying any claim to their greatness!

Crisis of the House Divided imitated the disputed question of the Scholastics. "The Case for Douglas" was, in effect, the objections to Lincoln, and "The Case for Lincoln" was, in effect, the reply to those objections. I will not further detail the similarities to the form of the *Summa Theologica*. I only mention these comparisons because *A New Birth of Freedom* is conceived as a commentary on the Gettysburg Address, the commentary being another of the characteristic forms in which Thomas Aquinas delivered his thoughts to the world.

This commentary obviously must be different from that of Thomas on the *Nicomachean Ethics* (the subject of my first book), because a text of Aristotle is virtually a self-contained work, with its meaning altogether within that of the speech by which it is conveyed.[1] The Gettysburg Address, however, is a speech within a drama. It can no more be interpreted apart from that drama than, let us say, a speech of Hamlet or Macbeth can be interpreted apart from *Hamlet* or *Macbeth*. The Gettysburg Address is a speech within the tragedy of the Civil War, even as Lincoln is its tragic hero. The Civil War is itself an outcome of tragic flaws—birthmarks, so to speak—of the infant nation. Thus a commentary on the Gettysburg Address is a commentary on the speeches and deeds that constituted the historical process during the fourscore and seven years preceding it, no less than on the conflict of the war itself.

∾

It may be objected that history is not poetry and that I have confused them. To this I would reply, as I think Lincoln would reply—or rather, as Lincoln in effect did reply—that the place of the necessity in great poetry imposed by the art

xi

of the poet may be occupied by a providential order in history, revealed in the speeches of the tragic hero. Lincoln became the prophetic statesman of a people, like Israel of old, whose failings and sufferings were intrinsic to the uniqueness of their role as a chosen people.

In writing as I have done, I have at every point asked myself how Lincoln would have commented upon his own words and deeds, were he to have had the chance. Unlike Jefferson Davis or Alexander Stephens, Lincoln did not live to write his own *apologia pro vita sua*. My hermeneutics are, so far as I have been able to make them so, those of Leo Strauss. Strauss taught that one must make every attempt to understand a writer as he understood himself. In his own work, Strauss applied this maxim primarily to the greatest authors of the greatest philosophic books. He often observed that those who thought they were wiser about the works of Plato, Aristotle, Xenophon, or Shakespeare than those authors themselves usually succeeded only in exhibiting their own limitations. I have never discovered any reason to think myself wiser than Abraham Lincoln.

According to Strauss, great books are great works of art, and as such they are governed by what he, following Socrates in Plato's *Phaedrus*, called logographic necessity. The smallest details, and especially those small details that appear to be irrelevant to the larger purpose of the work, are often the most important indicators of that larger purpose. Sometimes even more important than the small details of what is said, is what is left unsaid. In the *Republic*, Socrates obtains Glaucon's agreement that in their internecine wars Greeks should not enslave Greeks. Glaucon adds, however, that Greeks should nonetheless continue to enslave barbarians. This proposition Socrates greets only with silence. Elsewhere Socrates says that the best regime may exist in some barbarian place.

In the debates with Douglas, Lincoln reiterates that he is not, and never has been, in favor of bringing about a perfect social and political equality between blacks and whites. He never says that he will not be. And elsewhere he says that the obligation to seek such equality is the same as that imposed by the Savior when he said, "Be ye perfect as your Father in heaven is perfect." Socrates' deference to ordinary Greek prejudices, and Lincoln's to ordinary American prejudices, in no wise proves that either of them shared those prejudices.

Lincoln's life from the repeal of the Missouri Compromise in 1854 until his message to Congress in special session, July 4, 1861, was dominated in its first phase by his debates with Stephen A. Douglas. This phase ended substantially with his inauguration on March 4, 1861. At that point Lincoln was confronted with the legacy of John C. Calhoun and with the power of the argument for state rights and secession based on Calhoun's new political science. This political science claimed to have superseded that of the Founding Fathers, which is to say, of the Declaration of Independence and the *Federalist*. The movement of this book, as of Lincoln's life, is from the debate with Douglas to the debate with Calhoun. The difficulty in characterizing this conflict is that the premises underlying the thought of Douglas and Calhoun are the premises of historicism, positivism, relativism, and nihilism—premises that have become the conventional wisdom of our time. Lincoln's acceptance of the idiom of natural rights and natural law—above all his acceptance of the idea of nature not merely as a record of cause and effect but as a source of moral principles—has become alien to us. Hence it was necessary to challenge the conventional wisdom of the present day to gain a hearing for Lincoln.

∿

A commentary on the Gettysburg Address is necessarily, and above all, a commentary on what is meant by dedication to "the proposition that all men are created equal." The idea compressed within this proposition is called, by Lincoln, "an abstract truth, applicable to all men and all times." It is also said by Lincoln to be the central idea, from which all minor thoughts radiate, of the public opinion upon which the nation was founded. I have found it necessary, in different contexts, to lead the argument again and again from the periphery back to the center, to illuminate the geometrical necessity that, in Lincoln's mind, governed the struggle memorialized at Gettysburg. In doing so, I have not hesitated to repeat either the proposition, abstractly considered, or the structure of reasoning into which it is incorporated. This structure comprehends precisely what James Madison meant in his oft repeated dictum that "compact is the essence of all free government." That maxim of Madison unites his thought and Jefferson's, as it unites the principles of the Declaration and the Constitution. The compact theory and the doctrine of human equality are identical, and I found that the repetition of that identity was essential to compel us to think, as Lincoln thought, that the cause of union was no less metaphysical than moral and political.

I have concluded this volume with what I believe to be a definitive critique of the political science of John C. Calhoun. The Southern argument for secession rested upon the Southern argument for state rights. The Southern argument for state rights rested upon the separation of state rights from natural rights. The separation of state rights from natural rights corresponded exactly, in Calhoun's mind, with the denial of any constitutional standing to the principles of the Declaration of Independence. Since this denial by Calhoun is shared by virtually all of the legal profession today, including nearly all members of the Supreme Court, I thought it particularly important to subject it to rigorous examination. In doing so, I believe I have vindicated not only Lincoln's rejection of the Southern state rights dogma but also the intrinsic validity of the natural rights of the Declaration of Independence, encompassing the proposition that all men are created equal. I hope thereby to promote a climate of opinion in which the alienation from the principles of the Founding Fathers may be overcome, so that we may once again understand the true measure of Lincoln's greatness and through him repossess our inheritance of the genuine blessings of liberty.

The present work will be followed by a concluding volume on the triumph and tragedy of the war years.

1

The Election of 1800
and the Election of 1860

Our popular government has often been called an experiment. Two points in it our people have already settled—the successful *establishing* and the successful *administering* of it. One still remains—its successful *maintenance* against a formidable internal attempt to overthrow it. It is now for them to demonstrate to the world that those who can fairly carry an election can also suppress a rebellion; that ballots are the rightful and peaceful successors of bullets; and that when ballots have fairly and constitutionally decided, there can be no successful appeal back to bullets; that there can be no successful appeal except to ballots themselves, at succeeding elections.

—Abraham Lincoln

Thus Abraham Lincoln wrote, nearing the conclusion of his July 4, 1861, Message to Congress in Special Session. When Lincoln sent this message, Fort Sumter had been attacked (April 12) and had surrendered (April 14). Lincoln had thereupon issued his call for 75,000 troops, instituted the federal blockade of Southern rebel ports, and suspended the writ of habeas corpus. The Civil War had begun.

In his July 4 Message, Lincoln carefully elaborated the reasons why the rebellion had to be suppressed by force of arms. The first and most comprehensive reason was that it presented

to the whole family of man, the question, whether a constitutional republic, or democracy—a Government of the people, by the same people—can, or cannot, maintain its territorial integrity, against its own domestic foes. . . . It forces us to ask: "Is there, in all republics, this inherent and fatal weakness?" "Must a Government, of necessity, be too strong for the liberties of its own people, or too weak to maintain its own existence?"[1]

The epigraph is taken from *The Collected Works of Abraham Lincoln*, ed. Roy P. Basler (New Brunswick, N.J.: Rutgers University Press, 1953), vol. IV, p. 439.

Second, it was necessary, he said, to vindicate the Union against the "ingenious sophism" that "any State of the Union may, *consistently* with the national Constitution, and therefore *lawfully*, and *peacefully*, withdraw from the Union, without the consent of the Union or of any other State."[2] Lincoln held that the alleged constitutional right of secession, as distinct from the natural right of revolution, was a prescription for anarchy. Third, it was necessary, as Lincoln put it in the epigraph of this chapter, to vindicate the principle of free elections. It was necessary to use bullets to establish the right, not of bullets, but of ballots to decide who should rule.

It will, I believe, prove to be true that in Lincoln's mind the idea of a popular government that unites liberty and order, the idea of the Union, and the idea of rule by free elections are one and the same. Their inner unity may be said to resemble the Trinity, the three persons of God in Christian doctrine. But it is important, as in the case of Christianity, to understand the reasons for the distinctions within that threefold unity.

∼

That the legitimate authority of government is founded upon the sovereignty of the people, expressed in free elections under conditions of universal suffrage, is a proposition that is today virtually undisputed in Western civilization. In the world that witnessed the American Revolution, however, it was, to say the least, an idea still struggling to be born. In the world that witnessed the American Civil War, it was an idea whose meaning was fundamentally disputed and whose acceptance was unresolved.[3]

If we are to understand our past as those who lived it understood it, we must free ourselves of any illusion that the kinds of elections we now consider to be the only foundation of legitimate government are the usual or customary foundation of human government. That there "can be no successful appeal" from the ballot box as a means of deciding who shall govern, "except to ballots themselves, at succeeding elections," was the principle by which Lincoln, at the outset of the Civil War, justified the use of force to preserve the Union. But the idea of deciding who should govern by means of a free election by a whole people was something that the world had never known before the American Revolution. Most of mankind has always lived under what we, the heirs of the Founding Fathers and of Lincoln, call tyrannies. These tyrannies have differed among themselves. Recently, for example, we have been instructed in the differences between authoritarian and totalitarian regimes. No doubt this difference matters greatly to those who live under such regimes, just as it mattered during the Roman Empire whether one lived under a Marcus Aurelius or a Nero or Caligula. But it is well to remember that no subjects of the Roman emperors, whether the good emperors or the bad, had anything to say as to who that emperor was. It was the officers of the Praetorian Guard—the "colonels" of the army that ruled the empire of the Caesars—who decided who Caesar would be.

Nor did the phenomenon of appealing to ballots alone in deciding who should govern emerge immediately as a consequence of the American Revolution. Indeed, we know of no example before 1800 of a government in which the instruments of political power passed from one set of hands to those of their most uncompromisingly hostile political rivals and opponents because of a free vote.[4] The electoral contest of 1800 climaxed a decade of party warfare. The election of 1796, the first following the retirement of Washington (whose election had been virtually uncontested), was bitterly fought, but the incumbent party retained office. The political conflict intensified in the next four years, and its rhetoric exceeded in acrimony any in subsequent American political history, including that of the elections preceding the Civil War. Yet when the votes of 1800 (and 1801) had been counted and the election decided according to the forms of the Constitution, the offices were peacefully vacated by the losers and peacefully occupied by those who had prevailed. Nor were any of the defeated incumbents executed, imprisoned, expropriated, or driven into exile, as were the losers in the English civil wars and in the political contests of the Rome of Cicero and Caesar. The defeated Federalists went about their lawful occupations unmolested and for the most part engaged in the same kind of political activity in which their opponents had previously engaged. Again, to the best of our knowledge, this was the first time in the history of the world that such a thing had happened.

It is natural at this point to ask, Why did those who failed to carry the presidential election of 1860 not accept the outcome of that election, as did the defeated Federalists of 1800? This question is necessary and proper. It must be preceded, however, by the question of how the astounding precedent of 1800 itself was established. A break with all previous human history is even more in need of explanation than a break with a precedent of only threescore years. What was it that persuaded or enabled Americans in 1800 to discover in free elections the basis, not merely for choosing a government, but also for choosing a government from one of two bitterly contending parties? More particularly, what enabled them to accept the results of an election in which each of the rival parties charged the other with being subversive of that form of government for which the American Revolution had been fought? Was compliance with the results of the voting in 1800 an acceptance of the idea "that ballots are the rightful and peaceful successors of bullets"? Or was Lincoln in 1861 placing an interpretation upon an event as governed by reason and principle that was in truth merely the fortuitous outcome of prevailing circumstances?

3

The decision for political change heralded by the Declaration of Independence was authorized by a representative legislative body. But can we look upon it in the light of a decision made in consequence of a free election? In a famous letter to Henry Lee in 1825, in which Jefferson went to greater lengths than anywhere else to explain the purposes of the Declaration, he wrote that "with respect to our rights, and the acts of the British government contravening those rights, there was but one opinion on this side of the water. All American whigs thought alike on these subjects."[5] While American Whigs may have thought alike, what of the Tories? In fact, those called Tories in the American Revolution suffered a fate not unlike that customary for defeated partisans throughout the ages. There were many instances of mob violence against them and of the destruction and confiscation of their property. It has been estimated that there were proportionately more refugees from the American Revolution than from the French Revolution. Indeed, British Canada has its origins largely in the emigration thus begun.[6] Few of the émigrés were able to recover, or be indemnified for, their lost property, even though diplomatic attempts were made after the war to provide redress.

From Jefferson's perspective, it would appear that only those who were "American whigs" within his meaning could be considered part of the political universe with respect to which majority rule would be possible. This means that had a plebiscite on independence been possible in 1776, Whigs would (if they could) have excluded Tories from the vote! What constituted an "American whig" was accordingly defined by the statement of principles in the Declaration of Independence, most notably by the passage beginning, "We hold these truths to be self-evident." We may therefore say that from the perspective of the Revolution, a free election can be conducted only among "Whigs"! And the acceptance of the idea of human equality, as that idea was comprehended within "the laws of nature and of nature's God," would appear to be the necessary condition par excellence for defining who might participate in a free election, and hence who might be expected peacefully to abide by its results. Only those can willingly submit to the results of an election who see it as a means of deciding how "to secure these rights." But the rights to be secured, which include "life, liberty, and the pursuit of happiness," are understood a priori to be the equal rights of everyone, those who vote with the minority no less than those in the majority. A community can conduct elections with the expectation that all parties will accept the results only if the elections are preceded by a mutual recognition of the equal rights of the participants. But the rights of the participants in an election are rights under positive law. That the positive law should be one of equal rights can itself be understood as a necessary inference from the antecedent equality that subsists under "the laws of nature and of nature's God."

One cannot imagine the issue that divided the Americans and the British Crown and Parliament being decided by a vote. In effect, this would have meant deciding whether or not to accept the Declaratory Act of 1766, which asserted that

> the King's majesty, by and with the advice and consent of the lords spiritual and temporal, and commons of Great Britain, in parliament assembled, had, hath, and of right ought to have, full power and authority to make laws and statutes of sufficient force and validity to bind the colonies and people of America, subjects of the crown of Great Britain, in all cases whatsoever.[7]

The "American whigs" of 1776 regarded the Declaratory Act to be, in principle, an assertion of a right to exercise despotic power over them. They would have seen a vote to accept it as a vote to accept slavery. Can anyone be asked to vote to enslave himself? Is not the very idea of an election to decide such a question an absurdity? Is it not also evident that someone for whom death is preferable to slavery cannot regard as a fellow citizen someone for whom slavery is an acceptable option? To be a fellow citizen means not only to be able to accept the results of a free election but also to be willing to fight to preserve, protect, and defend the regime of free elections. A community of citizens is a community of those willing to fight for each other. Someone who will not fight for you, when you are willing to fight for him, cannot be your fellow citizen.

∽

A great deal has been written in support of the view that, in the American Revolution, the Americans were fighting primarily and essentially to defend their rights as Englishmen under the positive law of the British constitution. A leading exponent of this point of view is Russell Kirk, who writes:

> Until 1776, protesting Americans had pleaded that they were entitled to the rights of Englishmen, as expressed in the British constitution, and particularly in the Bill of Rights of 1689. But Jefferson's Declaration of Independence had abandoned this tack . . . and had carried the American cause into the misty debatable land of an abstract liberty, equality, fraternity.[8]

Unlike Kirk, Professor Daniel Boorstin, librarian of Congress emeritus and a distinguished scholar of American history, sees no difference between the earlier American arguments and the one set forth on July 4, 1776. The "object" of the Revolution, he writes, "as Thomas Jefferson expounded it in his *Summary View of the Rights of British America* (1774) . . . and then in the Declaration of Independence, was to vindicate the rights of Englishmen under the British Constitution."⁹ Of course, the refusal to accept the Declaratory Act could be understood to mean no more than that the Americans rejected second-class citizenship and that they would have been satisfied with the same kind of representative government enjoyed by the subjects of the Crown in the United Kingdom.

Let us then turn to Jefferson's *Summary View*, to see whether there is continuity or difference in the authoritative arguments of Americans in the Revolution. Above all, let us inquire into the relationship, in Jefferson's understanding, between the rights of Englishmen under the British constitution and the rights of man under the "laws of nature and of nature's God." Let us see how and why, according to Jefferson, the rights of the people were recognized by the British constitution. And let us consider how, or whether, such recognition led to Lincoln's conclusions concerning the role of free elections as a means of deciding who should rule in a popular republic. Is it really possible for ballots to replace bullets in the presence of fundamental differences concerning the purposes of the regime?

∼

The *Summary View of the Rights of British America* was published in August 1774, nearly a year before the beginning of the American Revolution. It was prepared for a meeting of the Virginia revolutionary convention, which was in fact the House of Burgesses, reelected and reconvened after its dissolution by the royal governor. Jefferson hoped that the convention would instruct the Virginia delegates to the Continental Congress to press for the adoption of the *Summary View* by that Congress. It was never actually adopted by either legislative body, being deemed too radical for that moment. But it was ordered to be published, was widely circulated in England as well as America, and came to be regarded, deservedly, as the classic expression of the American cause on the eve of the Revolution. It almost certainly was a major reason that Jefferson was chosen as a draftsman (with John Dickinson) of the Declaration of the Causes and Necessity of Taking Up Arms in July 1775 and a year later of the Declaration of Independence. Indeed, the latter can be regarded as essentially an epitome of the *Summary View*.

The *Summary View* is in the form of a resolution of the Continental Congress, expressing the opinion of all thirteen colonies. We shall speak of it, however, as Jefferson's work and as an expression of Jefferson's views, however much they may, at the time, have been unofficial. Over time, these became the quintessentially American views, which is why Abraham Lincoln looked to Jefferson more than to anyone else for his understanding of the American Revolution.

In addressing the king on behalf of the "colonies," Jefferson refers to the latter, from time to time, as "States." As we shall see, the *Summary View* embodies a Whig view of the British constitution that was in certain respects so radical that its validity would have been conceded by very few Englishmen of Jefferson's generation, and certainly by none of those who were advising the king. Those conservatives who today look to Burke's celebration, in his writings on the French Revolution, of the eighteenth-century British constitution (and of the quasi-feudal social order it encompassed) will not recognize it in Jefferson's "American whig" version. Reading the *Summary View* today, one can sense that the Fourth of July is just around the corner.

It is true that the American demands upon the king are portrayed by Jefferson as authorized by British constitutional law and precedents. But Jefferson's understanding of such law and precedents is distinctively Jeffersonian. At no point is the authority of the British constitution derived from prescriptive or historic right, as distinct from, and opposed to, natural right. Right is prescriptive only insofar as the right that is inherited is itself natural in its genesis and its reason. It is also true that the stated (or prudent) objective of the address is reconciliation. But the tone and manner in which it speaks to the king is one of independence.

The *Summary View* begins by complaining to the king that the "humble application to his imperial throne" made in the past by "his States," acting individually, has gone unanswered. Now the states' "joint address" will be "penned in the language of truth, and divested of those expressions of servility, which would persuade his Majesty that we are asking favors, and not rights." At the beginning of a great tradition, Jefferson thus adopts the language of Union and Liberty (or Equality) as one and inseparable. The king must realize, he says, that it is rights, not favors, for which the "states of British America" ask recognition and redress:

> [T]his his Majesty will think we have reason to expect when he reflects that he is no more than the chief officer of the people, appointed by the laws, and circumscribed with definite powers, to assist in working the great engine of government, erected for their use, and, consequently subject to their superintendence.[10]

To speak of the "chief officer of the people" suggests a republic rather than a monarchy and an office more like America's constitutional presidency than a hereditary monarch. We must also wonder at the bland euphemism in the phrase "appointed by the laws." The laws do not appoint. The laws can only prescribe how someone is to be appointed. Jefferson is here evading rhetorically the fact that this "popular" official is not appointed (or elected) by those for whose sake his office is said to exist.

But how can this hereditary monarch be "subject to [the] superintendence" of the people, when he is neither elected nor removable by any peaceful constitutional process? Jefferson's logic seems to proceed first by attributing (hypothetical) legitimacy to the British constitution and then by recognizing no other ground of legitimacy than the sovereignty of the people. Ergo: the British constitution is based upon the sovereignty of the people! Jefferson seems to be saying that in principle, if not in fact, Britain is a republic under the forms of a monarchy.

Here, according to Jefferson, is how the people had exercised their "superintendence" over their kings during the constitutional crises of the seventeenth century.

A family of Princes was then on the British throne, whose treasonable crimes against their people, brought on them, afterwards, the exertion of those sacred and sovereign rights of punishment, reserved in the hands of the people for cases of extreme necessity, and judged by the constitution unsafe to be delegated to any other judicature.[11]

In 1774, writing as a Whig in the British tradition, Jefferson assumed that it was the natural right of revolution—which here meant plainly the right to kill the king when the people judged him to have become a tyrant—that acted as the inducement to constitutionally correct behavior. Certainly at that time there was no idea on the political horizon of an election of the "chief officer of the people" by the people as the means of assuring that he serve their interests. Not until his inaugural address in 1801 would Jefferson see the right of free election as the normal and peaceable fruit of the right of revolution. But by Jefferson's theory, the right of revolution would forever underlie the right of free election and would supply a compelling reason why governments ought to have such elections as authentic expressions, not only of the people's will, but also of those rights that are the authority for the people's will. That is to say, the wholesome fear of the people by governments would also be a wholesome fear informing the majority in its dealings with minorities.

In Lincoln's first inaugural address, threescore years after Jefferson's, Lincoln would be very careful, while denying any validity to the alleged constitutional right of secession, to insist on recognizing the natural right of revolution. He would concede that there could be occasions on which a minority might be justified in having recourse to that right (as he had once argued on behalf of the Texans' revolt against Mexican misgovernment) if there was a real threat to deprive them of any of their fundamental rights. He would be at great pains, however, to argue that this was not the case in 1861. In the absence of any such threat, the right of revolution gave no moral sanction to secession. On the contrary, the right of revolution, being a right of the people, supported his election by the people. In such a case, the right of revolution became the right of the majority to suppress the rebellion against its legitimate authority.

∼

Expounding the rights of British Americans in their relationship to the rights of those in the mother country, Jefferson reminds the king

> that our ancestors, before their emigration to America, were the free inhabitants of the British dominions in Europe, and possessed a right, *which nature has given all men,* of departing from the country in which chance, not choice, has placed them, of going in quest of new habitations, and of there establishing new societies, under such laws and regulations as to them shall seem most likely to promote public happiness.

What our ancestors had done in coming to America, Jefferson continues, was no different from what their ancestors had done before them. In emigrating to Britain,

> their Saxon ancestors had, *under this universal law,* in like manner, left their native wilds and woods in the North of Europe, had possessed themselves of the Island of Britain, then less charged with inhabitants, and had established there that system of laws which has so long been the glory and protection of that country.[12]

Let us notice first that the British constitution itself arose from "a right [under universal law] which nature has given all men." That right is primarily and essentially a natural right to liberty. It is a right of all men to leave the country "in which chance, not choice, has placed them."[13] Where a man is born may be a matter of chance. Where and how he is to live, however, are (and of right ought to be) matters of choice. But they are not random choices. They are choices guided by reason. In seeking new habitations and establishing new societies, under laws that they have agreed to, men act in such manner as to them "shall seem most likely to promote public happiness." Happiness is the objective good, and therefore the rational good, at which all laws and institutions aim. This is assumed by Jefferson, here and elsewhere, no less than by Aristotle, as it was by American public opinion of the Revolutionary generation.

A great deal has been written to the effect that because the Declaration of

Independence speaks of a right to "the pursuit of happiness," rather than a right to happiness, happiness itself must be something subjective, something each individual should be free to pursue in his own idiosyncratic manner. The implication is that happiness cannot be a goal of public policy, since there is neither an agreement as to what it is nor a means of proving any one opinion on this question to be superior to any other. A free government is therefore looked upon as one that enables each individual to pursue happiness as he thinks fit to do, in as unrestrained a manner as possible. But what is idiosyncratic is private, and Jefferson speaks in the *Summary View* of *public* happiness. The Declaration itself speaks not only of the unalienable right to the pursuit of happiness, with which each individual has been endowed by his Creator, but also of the "safety and happiness" which each people collectively attempts to secure when it institutes new government. Clearly, whatever is uniquely individual in the private pursuit of happiness must be consistent with the public happiness and must fit within its framework.

In a letter in 1819, Jefferson avowed his distrust of an "independent" judiciary as the final authority on the meaning of the Constitution. "Independence can be trusted nowhere but with the people in mass," he wrote, adding that the people "are inherently independent of all *but moral law.*"[14] Likewise, near the end of the *Summary View,* Jefferson tells the king in a most peremptory way that "The great principles of right and wrong are legible to every reader." And again: "The whole art of government consists in the art of being honest."[15] Although Jefferson believed in safeguards against the abuse of power by the people, no less than by anyone else, he also was convinced that the people "in mass" had a greater interest than anyone else in governmental honesty. Lincoln echoed Jefferson's convictions when he asked, in his first inaugural address, "Why should there not be a patient confidence in the ultimate justice of the people?"[16] But however independent of all earthly authorities the people may have been, they were not, according to Jefferson, independent of the "moral law." They too were to be measured against the great standards of right and wrong. Lincoln also made it clear that his confidence in the justice of the people was not unconditional but depended upon their retaining "their virtue and vigilance." One might say that concern with the virtue and vigilance of the people was of the essence of statesmanship, according to Jefferson and Lincoln. In what they understood by a "people," subordination to the "moral law" and the demands of "virtue" was implicit. The people could not promote public happiness if they did not have a due regard for virtue and the moral law in their private lives. No one ever asserted this more categorically than George Washington, in his inaugural address.

[T]he foundation of our national policy will be laid in the pure and immutable principles of private morality . . . since there is no truth more thoroughly estab-

lished than that there exists in the economy and course of nature an indissoluble union between virtue and happiness; between duty and advantage; between
the genuine maxims of an honest and magnanimous policy and the solid rewards
of public prosperity.[17]

As in the tradition of Plato's *Republic*, public virtue, and therefore public happiness, is private virtue writ large.

That the "great principles of right and wrong" were "legible to every reader"
meant that they were knowable to the unassisted reason of any human being of
ordinary, but uncorrupted, intelligence. Certainly they were as legible to peoples
as to kings. And to repeat, there could be no idea of happiness, whether individual or public, inconsistent with virtue and the moral law.[18] While the chance may
have been greater of there being virtue in the people as a whole than in any of the
parts,[19] especially the governmental parts, it is not something guaranteed apart
from the application of the political art, "the art of being honest." In a government of the people, the art of being honest must be the people's art.

∽

The argument of the *Summary View* proceeds:

Nor was ever any claim of superiority or dependence asserted over them by that
mother country from which they had migrated: and were such a claim made, it
is believed his Majesty's subjects in Great Britain have too firm a feeling of their
rights derived to them from their ancestors, to bow down their state before such
visionary pretensions. And it is thought that no circumstance has occurred to
distinguish, materially, the British from the Saxon emigration. America was conquered, and her settlements made and firmly established, at the expense of individuals, and not of the British public. Their own blood was spilt in acquiring
lands for their settlement, their own fortunes expended in making that settlement effectual. For themselves they fought, for themselves they conquered, and
for themselves alone they have a right to hold.[20]

The political independence of America from Britain, in its origins and beginnings,
is absolute and complete and stands upon a footing identical to that of British
independence from the homeland of the Saxons. Some have thought that because
Jefferson speaks here of the "feeling" that the British have for "the rights derived
from their ancestors," the rights in question are emotional attachments to what is
primarily ancestral or historically British. Of course, the particular form of the
British constitution is distinctively British, and its growth is to be traced in British
history. But that constitution arose from the exercise by Britons of "a right which

nature has given to all men," a right under "universal law." The source of all British rights, like all American rights, whether historic, prescriptive, or ancestral, is nature. Indeed, it is nature that attaches us to our families and therefore to our ancestors. But for Jefferson, no less than for Aristotle, what men seek by nature is not the ancestral but the good.[21] After all, neither the Saxon ancestors of present-day Britons nor the British ancestors of present-day Americans left their native lands for any other reason than to better themselves. And therefore no claim or idea of right carries any intrinsic authority if it is contrary to the reason of natural right. That "abstract truth, applicable to all men and all times" that Lincoln said Jefferson had introduced into the Declaration of Independence is already present in the *Summary View*.[22]

In what follows, Jefferson enunciates a theory of the British Empire that also marks a beginning in the American understanding of federalism. It helps us measure the transformations of that understanding that arose in the course of the "fourscore and seven years" that separated the "fundamental act of union of these states" in 1776 from its testing upon the battlefield of Gettysburg.[23]

Jefferson insists, as we have seen, that there is no ground for any assertion of political inferiority or dependence upon the mother country in the origins or growth of the American colonies. He insists equally that no such dependence followed from any assistance given to the colonies in the wars with any of the European empires. Because the American colonies had "become valuable to Great Britain for her commercial purposes," he writes,

> Parliament was pleased to lend them assistance against an enemy who would fain have drawn to herself the benefits of their commerce, to the great aggrandisement of herself, and danger of Great Britain. Such assistance, and in such circumstances, they had often before given to Portugal and other allied states, with whom they carry on a commercial intercourse. Yet these states never supposed that by calling in her aid, they thereby submitted themselves to their sovereignty.

The past support by Great Britain of other states, at war with a common enemy, was not grounds for subjecting those states to her sovereignty. The American colonies were no more subject to British rule because of such aid than was Portugal. Jefferson does not deny the value of this aid, but he makes it clear that Britain gave it because of her commercial interests in the American colonies and that the colonies amply repaid the British by granting them "exclusive privileges in trade." Then Jefferson adds what some might erroneously consider a concession.

> That settlement having been thus effected in the wilds of America, the emigrants thought proper to adopt that system of laws, under which they had hith-

erto lived in the mother country, and to continue their union with her, by submitting themselves to the same common sovereign, who was thereby made the central link, connecting the several parts of the empire thus newly multiplied.[24]

The American colonies, by and large, adopted British laws. But these laws became their laws, not because of any extension of British sovereignty to America, but because the Americans, in the exercise of their natural rights, had judged these laws to be good. They had also submitted themselves "to the same common sovereign," who is now called "the central link" of the empire. We are here confronted with a certain verbal difficulty in that the "common sovereign" is someone altogether without "sovereignty." Jefferson never wavered in the opinion that sovereignty, properly so called, resided only in the people. By Jefferson's account, each of the colonies was inherently independent of Great Britain under "the laws of nature and of nature's God." Yet they became part of an empire "newly multiplied" by reason of their having this "same common sovereign." We may assume, I think, that Jefferson did not think that the colonies had diminished their independence by this voluntary "submission," any more than he would later think that the individual colonies had diminished their independence by forming their own union upon declaring their independence from Great Britain.[25] "Submitting" to this "common sovereign" was consistent, therefore, with that sovereign's subordination to the legislative authority of the people of each colony.

Jefferson's argument points towards such a conception of monarchy as is embodied in the form that the British Empire took more than a century later. He is, in effect, asking dominion status for the colonies—the status accorded, for example, to Canada and Australia in the twentieth century. Such a status was utterly inconsistent with the British constitution in the eighteenth century. It took considerable democratic evolution in the relationships of king and Parliament, and of Parliament and people, before this was possible. Only when the ministers of the Crown (and especially the prime minister) became responsible to Parliament rather than the king, and Parliament became responsible to the people by a genuinely democratic electoral process, could the king be equally king in Great Britain and beyond the seas, without any subordination of the overseas dominions to the government in Westminster. As long as the king in the Parliament in Westminster was the responsible executive head of the British government, or "the chief officer of the people" of Great Britain, he could not be the chief officer of any other people. In the idiom of the British constitution, he could not accept supplies from any place other than the Parliament in Westminster without becoming a threat to the people of Great Britain. It had been the attempts by Charles I and James II to find supplies not voted by Parliament (e.g., ship money, or money supplied by the king of France) that led to their overthrow as tyrants. The American colonists were asking King George to accept supplies voted by colonial legislatures but not by the Parliament in Westminster. In theory, this would enable the king to do things with the money that were not approved by Parliament. As long as the king was the real executive head of the British government and the ministers of the Crown were responsible to him rather than Parliament, this represented a threat of executive tyranny to Great Britain.

Jefferson's demands upon the king, in presupposing a monarchy that reigned but did not rule, presupposed a constitution that Britain would not have for over a century. One might say that it was only after the British constitution had been remodeled to give effect to the American doctrine of popular sovereignty, or after the natural rights to which Americans appealed had in some sense become recognized as the rights of Englishmen, that it was possible for king and Parliament to be free of the dilemma into which Jefferson had cast them. Although Jefferson told the king that the "great principles of right and wrong" were "legible to every reader," the truth is that those principles demanded a transformation of the British constitution that was then beyond the power of any British government. It was, in fact, because the British constitution was a Whig constitution that the British could not accede to the Whig demands of the Americans.[26] Indeed, the appeal to Whig principles implied a transformation, not only of Anglo-American constitutionalism, but also of human government altogether. The effective force underlying those principles is the right of revolution, the right that Lincoln in 1848 called "a most valuable, a most sacred right—a right which, we hope and believe, is to liberate the world."[27] Nothing less was implied by Jefferson in 1774.

∾

The *Summary View* is paradoxical. On the one hand, it lays down principles of legitimacy that are democratic or popular, beyond anything recognizable in the eighteenth-century British constitution. On the other, it holds up that same constitution as an example of political legitimacy. The Glorious (or Whig) Revolution of 1689 had established parliamentary supremacy. But this was very far from the democratic or popular electoral supremacy with which we are now familiar. To resolve this paradox and to understand how Jefferson could have called Great Britain's hereditary monarch "chief officer of the people," we must consider the evolution of the relationship of king, Parliament, and people in the great events of Reformation history.

Among the best sources for deep insight into these events, for us as for Lincoln, are Shakespeare's English histories.[28] His *King John* is set in the thirteenth century—the age of Magna Carta but also of papal supremacy within the Holy

Roman Empire, of which Great Britain was a part. It also foreshadows the great conflicts of the reign of Henry VIII. For instance, when the legate from Pope Innocent demands that the king accept the papal nominee as archbishop of Canterbury, the king answers

> that no Italian priest
> Shall tithe or toll in our dominions,
> But as we, under Heaven, are supreme head,
> So under Him that great supremacy,
> Where we do reign, we will alone uphold
> Without assistance of a mortal hand.
> So tell the Pope, all reverence set apart
> To him and his usurped authority.

One can almost hear the Elizabethan audience cheering this speech, in which the king claims his authority as being independent, not only of the pope, but also of the people of England. At the moment, however, the latter is merely incidental. Consider the response of the pope's legate:

> Then, by the lawful power that I have,
> Thou shalt stand cursed and excommunicate.
> And blessed shall he be that doth revolt
> From his allegiance to an heretic;
> And meritorious shall that hand be called,
> Canonized and worshipped as a saint,
> That takes away by any secret course,
> Thy hateful life.[29]

Surely the boos would have been as loud for the latter speech as the cheers for the former. We see that by medieval Catholic doctrine the pope could excommunicate a king as a heretic, as he had done Henry VIII, and thereby declare him a tyrant whom it was lawful for anyone to kill "by any secret course." Although the dramatic setting is the thirteenth century, the play was performed in 1596, when English fears of another Spanish Armada like that of 1588 were abroad in the land. In the course of the play, the king is forced to reconcile himself with the pope in order to save his throne from domestic enemies. But John nonetheless expressed the Reformation doctrine of the divine right of kings when he said that "we, under Heaven, are supreme head" of the state. In Elizabethan England, that would have been recognized as a doctrine of national independence. In this sense it was democratic doctrine, because Elizabeth, like her father, represented what was a popular and national cause—albeit in a deeply divided nation. Only as the kings of England claimed their mandates directly from God could England free itself from the Holy Roman Empire, the successor (or, as Hobbes would say, the ghost) of the empire of the Caesars.

The attack on the king by the papal legate identifies arbitrary or tyrannical power with disobedience to an alien and priestly autocracy, a power that was, politically considered, much further removed from the people than the king. When King John says that "no Italian priest shall tithe or toll in our dominions," he is far from saying "taxation without representation is tyranny." But in declaring that Englishmen will not be taxed by foreigners, he is taking a long stride in that direction. The doctrine of tyrannicide put forth by the papal legate was invoked to maintain the authority of a universal church over a national church and of a universal empire over a national state. In this context the doctrine of tyrannicide was, from the point of view of Englishmen, in the service of alien authority, and hence of tyranny; and the doctrine of the divine right of kings was in the service of national independence, and hence of popular freedom. We must therefore take notice of how tyrannicide and the divine right of kings would have to reverse their roles in the seventeenth century before Whig doctrine might begin to function in the sense recognized by eighteenth-century Americans.[30]

In the sixteenth century, the Tudors and Parliament stood together and used the doctrine of divine right to their advantage in their struggle for national independence against the papacy and Spain (including the continental empire of the Habsburgs). In the seventeenth century, the Stuarts also invoked the doctrine of divine right, but now for the purpose of enhancing monarchical prerogative and independence of the Crown from Parliament. In this conflict, Parliament claimed, and Jefferson (abiding by the British Whig tradition) appears to have agreed, that it stood closer to the people than the Stuart kings. In the struggle between the Stuarts and Parliament, "divine right," the ally under Henry VIII and Elizabeth I of the cause of Protestantism and national independence, reversed its role and became the ally of "popery" and the continental Catholic powers, Spain and France.

In the *Summary View*, the right of the people to rule themselves appears primarily as the right of revolution, which includes the right to kill tyrants. It is clear enough today that the right of revolution has evolved into the right of free elections, although that evolution is not unambiguous within the framework of British history. It is not unambiguous because the political conflicts from which the British constitution evolved were indissolubly intertwined with sectarian religious conflicts. Looked at in their own right, the constitutional victories that are hailed as milestones of British Whig constitutionalism are victories of religious sectarians. Henry VIII's "victory" over the pope and William of Orange's "victory" over his father-in-law, James II, were seen as victories of Protestantism no less than of civil liberty. They were victories in which Catholic Englishmen could hardly be said to share.[31] These victories differed from the victory of the Whigs of the American

Revolution, whose creed, expressed in the Declaration of Independence, was that of a nonsectarian party of natural right. From Jefferson's own point of view, sectarian religious questions were not susceptible to decision by voting, because the rights of conscience were beyond political rule altogether.[32] Jefferson's attitude in the *Summary View*, in which he still affects to be a British Whig, places much greater weight upon the right of revolution than the right of free election. That is because he abstracts a nonsectarian doctrine of natural right from actual political conflicts that, in their religious aspects, could not be resolved by voting. Yet this nonsectarian doctrine culminates in the right of a people to be governed only by free elections. Clearly this was impossible in eighteenth-century Britain, in which the Church of England was looked upon as the cornerstone of parliamentary supremacy and political freedom, practically considered. We must look back in British history to understand why.

In the eighteenth century, although Parliament did not elect the king, the king remained both the de facto and the de jure head of government. The ministers of the Crown were appointed by the Crown (as they are to this day), but they remained responsible to the king, and not (as today) to the House of Commons and through the Commons to the universal suffrage of the people. Throughout the eighteenth century, the king's ministers needed the confidence of Parliament to carry on the government and carry out the king's policies, but they could not (as now) be dismissed by a vote of the House of Commons. As Jefferson indicated, the only constitutional precedent for the removal of a king who was in fundamental disagreement with Parliament was to exert "those sacred and sovereign rights of punishment, reserved in the hands of the people . . . for cases of extreme necessity."

Here is the language of the Act Erecting a High Court of Justice for the Trial of Charles I, passed by the Commons in 1649:

> Whereas it is notorious that Charles Stuart, the now King of England . . . hath had a wicked design totally to subvert the ancient and fundamental laws and liberties of this nation, and in their place to introduce an arbitrary and tyrannical government . . . [and] hath prosecuted it with fire and sword . . . against Parliament and kingdom; whereby the country hath been miserably wasted, the public treasure exhausted, trade decayed, thousands of people murdered . . .

The resemblance is hardly coincidental between this indictment and the indictment of George III in the Declaration of Independence for "having in direct object the establishment of an absolute Tyranny over these States." Also striking is the fact that the accusations against Charles are contained in the act establishing the court that is to try him. It is in fact a bill of attainder. And it is a foregone conclusion that the court will, as it did, "adjudge . . . the said Charles Stuart . . . a tyrant, traitor, murderer and public enemy to the good people of this nation [and that he] shall be put to death by the severing of his head from his body."[33] That Parliament should use attainders (and ex post facto laws) in pursuit of its quarrel with Charles I shows that the rule of law was no more honored by the one side in the English civil wars than by the other and that the issues that divided the parties were no more susceptible to decision by election than by jury.

If the victory of Parliament over Charles was a victory of "the good people" over a tyrant, as both Cromwell and Jefferson (for different reasons) supposed, it proved nonetheless to be in certain respects a Pyrrhic victory, because it was a victory on the Caesarian model. Cromwell governed through Parliament, but it was a Parliament purged and brought to heel by his New Model Army. The experience of Cromwell went a long way to discredit the idea of pure republicanism, or republicanism with an elected executive, in Great Britain. If Charles I was a tyrant, his nemesis did not appear to be any less so—certainly not to Jefferson. Tyrannies may be established upon the authority of the people no less than the authority of kings. Writing of Parliament in the *Summary View*, Jefferson observes: "History has informed us, that bodies of men as well as of individuals, are susceptible of the spirit of tyranny."[34] And in a memorable passage of the *Notes on Virginia*, Jefferson would write: "An *elective despotism* was not the government we fought for."[35] Not only in Restoration Britain but also in Whig Britain after the Glorious Revolution, hereditary monarchy appeared to be a safeguard against democratic tyranny. The king would be commander in chief, but he would depend upon Parliament for every shilling of support for the army and navy.

With the Restoration, England was determined to keep the powers of the purse and the sword separated. It was in the aftermath of Cromwell that purchase of military commissions was instituted. This seemingly irrational practice (which lasted until after the Crimean War) served to assure the country that the officer class would be drawn from the propertied class and would not consist of adventurers who might expect their fortunes from the booty of the conquests of their commander—whether that commander was a popular leader like Cromwell or a hereditary monarch. (The British experience explains why the president of the United States, as commander in chief, must be a civilian and why all appointments to the higher ranks of the armed services must be consented to by the Senate. This consent is the American equivalent of purchase.)

In 1689, King James II had been locked in a struggle with Parliament that closely resembled his father's. When it appeared that he would lose the contest in the field (and with it his head), he fled to the hospitable dominion of the Catholic king of France, where he established a government in exile at St. Germains. Parliament thereupon declared the throne vacant and further declared that William and Mary, James's Protestant daughter and son-in-law, had succeeded to that throne. According to Parliament, James had abdicated, and it had merely declared who, as next of kin, was to succeed him. This was the form in which parliamentary supremacy was achieved.

The crisis that culminated in the Glorious Revolution was precipitated by the birth of a son to Mary of Modena, James II's second wife. Mary, like Catherine of Aragon, was a Spanish princess and a Catholic. It was certain that the child, James Francis Edward, later known as "the Old Pretender," would be raised as a Catholic. As a male heir, he would take precedence of his half-sisters, Mary and Anne, whose mother, James's first wife, had been a Protestant and had raised her daughters as Protestants. Protestant England had endured their king's unmistakable (although not openly professed) Catholicism, so long as they thought it would end with his death. Now, however, they were faced with the prospect of an indefinite succession of Catholic kings, who might attempt to return England to submission to the Catholic Church and to the Catholic European empire. For the great majority of Englishmen, including the weightiest interests of the realm, this was intolerable.

Here we must pause to remind ourselves how profoundly religious were the great political questions that dominated British constitutional development before the American Revolution. We must look back to Henry VIII's break with Rome and to the Act of Supremacy of 1534, by which the king of England became the head of the Church of England. Although the king did not exercise sacerdotal power himself, he appointed those who did. Thus Henry had provided for his divorce from Catherine of Aragon, after the pope (under the control of the Habsburgs and of Spain) had refused it to him. For a successor of Henry VIII to acknowledge papal supremacy would, in effect, deny the legitimacy of the church of which he was the head. It would call into question the apostolic rights of every bishop consecrated under the authority of the Crown since 1534. Even more important, it would call into question the vested rights of the most powerful class of property holders in the realm. It would do so because Henry VIII, following the example of William the Conqueror some five hundred years earlier, had distributed to his supporters the properties of the monasteries that he had confiscated. In the bestowal of these vast possessions, the king had created a new aristocracy or oligarchy whose very existence was tied to the Church of England he headed.

The property confiscated by Henry VIII after his break with Rome supported the titles (and thereby the political influence) of a majority of the seats in the House of Lords. With this influence went the control of many (sometimes most) of the seats in the House of Commons. It should be remembered that until the late nineteenth century, there were no secret ballots in the elections to the Commons. Voting took place under the eyes of powerful (and often titled) landlords, whose tenants would be loath to disregard the wishes of their social superiors and propertied patrons.

The Spanish Armada of 1588 was the climactic event of the reign of the first Queen Elizabeth. It was an attempt by King Philip II of Spain to seize the throne of England, on the grounds that Elizabeth was a usurper and that the crown belonged to Philip in virtue of his deceased wife Mary, Elizabeth's half-sister and predecessor. Mary had been the daughter of Catherine of Aragon. Elizabeth was the daughter of Anne Boleyn, whom Henry had married after divorcing Catherine. From the Catholic point of view, all of Henry's marriages after the one to Catherine were null and void, and any children of such marriages illegitimate. But the birth of a son to James II's second wife, Mary of Modena, threatened to undermine if not undo the entire constitutional development of Great Britain that had been built upon Henry VIII's break with Rome. In driving out the king in 1689 and replacing him with his Protestant son-in-law and daughter, the Parliament was, from Jefferson's Whig point of view, once again exerting those "sacred and sovereign rights . . . reserved in the hands of the people for cases of extreme necessity." But Jefferson never even hinted that for English Whigs of 1689 the cause of national independence and political and religious freedom was identified with the particular form, or any of the particular doctrines, of Church of England Protestantism.

$\sim$

In the *Summary View* Jefferson rebuts the claim of the British Parliament, as a representative body, to give law to the Americans.

> Can any one reason be assigned why 160,000 electors in the island of Great Britain should give law to four millions in the states of America, *every individual of whom is equal to every individual of them* in virtue, in understanding, and in bodily strength? Were this to be admitted, instead of being a free people, as we have hitherto supposed . . . we should suddenly be found . . . slaves.[36]

Here is the doctrinal ground of the American Revolution in its purest form—a ground that owes nothing to British history or the rights of Englishmen. When Jefferson writes of "four millions" of Americans, he refers to every man, woman, and child, black and white, free and slave. "Every individual" of these four millions, he says, is equal to "every individual" of the electors of Great Britain in respect to those attributes by which human beings are said to be entitled to participate in human government. No boundaries arising from class, sex, race, religion, or ethnic identity have any standing in opposition to the rights of human beings as human beings.

We might wonder why the same 160,000 electors, who are said to have no right to give the law to 4 million Americans, should have any more right to give the law to the more than 10 million in Great Britain. Jefferson's disparagement of the unrepresentative character of the British Parliament vis-à-vis America is no less an indictment of the oligarchic character of that same Parliament vis-à-vis Great Britain. By implication, Jefferson has established the most radical imaginable democratic franchise as the test of political legitimacy. For if every American is equal to every British elector, is not every Briton equal to every British elector? And is not every American (male and female, free and slave) also equal to every other American? Jefferson knew perfectly well that none of the "free and independent legislature(s)" of "the States of America" had electors equal to the adult population it represented, not even to its free white male adult population. But he is establishing here a standard for America, Britain, and the world for all future time. We see therefore that the proposition "that all men are created equal" is the premise of the American Revolution before it ever began.

Lincoln, in his speech on the *Dred Scott* decision in 1857, confronted the argument of Chief Justice Roger B. Taney and Senator Stephen A. Douglas that the authors of the Declaration of Independence had not meant to include Negroes in the proposition of universal human equality, on the evidence that "they did not at once actually place them on an equality with the whites." "This grave argument," said Lincoln, "comes to just nothing at all, by the other fact, that they did not at once, or ever afterwards, actually place all white people on an equality with one another." Lincoln did not then say who were the whites excluded from the privileges of equality. However, in one of the earliest announcements of his political views, in the *Sangamo Journal* on June 13, 1836, Lincoln had said, "I go for admitting all whites to the right of suffrage, who pay taxes or bear arms, (by no means excluding females)." Certainly the largest class of excluded "equals" were women, and Lincoln at the age of twenty-seven is on record as favoring female suffrage. Speaking in 1857, however, he said he understood that the authors of the Declaration "meant simply to declare the *right*, so that the *enforcement* of it might follow as fast as circumstances should permit."[37] Jefferson himself, in his famous diatribe against slavery in *Notes on Virginia*, speaks of the "execration" with which a statesman would be loaded, "who, permitting one half the citizens thus to trample on the rights of the other, transforms those into despots, and these into enemies, destroys the morals of the one part, and the *amor patriae* of the other."[38] For Jefferson to write in the 1780s of slaves as "one half the citizens" of Virginia—that is to say, citizens by natural right, if not by positive law—is certainly extraordinary. But it is consistent with his reference in 1774 to the whole population of America as the equals, by right of nature, to the electors of Great Britain.

Jefferson addresses slavery and the slave trade in the *Summary View* itself. Attacking the Crown for its complicity with this atrocious crime, he writes:

> For the most trifling reasons, and, sometimes, for no conceivable reasons at all, his Majesty has rejected laws of the most salutary tendency. The abolition of domestic slavery is the great object of desire in those colonies where it was unhappily introduced in their infant state. But previous to the enfranchisement of the slaves we have, it is necessary to exclude all further importations from Africa. Yet our repeated attempts to effect this, by prohibitions, and by imposing duties which might amount to a prohibition, having been hitherto defeated by his Majesty's negative; thus preferring the immediate advantage of a few British corsairs, to the lasting interests of the American States, and to the rights of human nature, deeply wounded by this infamous practice.[39]

No one can write properly about the American Civil War without taking note of the fact that Jefferson, in 1774, declared the "abolition of domestic slavery" to be "the great object of desire" in the American colonies. There can be no question that this passage was of surpassing importance in forming the mind and soul of Abraham Lincoln. The word "abolition" did not have the significance in 1774 that it had in the 1850s, when "abolitionists" represented the most radical form of antislavery opinion—an opinion distinguished by its contempt for the Constitution and for constitutional limitations upon antislavery action. Abraham Lincoln was never an abolitionist in this later sense, since he did not believe that there was any federal jurisdiction over slavery in any of the states in which it was lawful and insisted upon the federal obligation to enforce the fugitive slave clause of the Constitution, however infamous that clause might appear in light of "the rights of human nature." Still, Jefferson used the strongest word known to him in describing the "great object of desire" of his countrymen. The word "abolition," not "emancipation," is linked to the word "enfranchisement" in his very next sentence. In the context, this need have meant no more than emancipation. Yet the word can also mean, and often did mean, equality of political rights as well as personal freedom. Jefferson's choice of words, much stronger than the case required, is then consistent with his later reference to slaves in Virginia as "one half the citizens."

Throughout the *Summary View*, Jefferson frames his argument, as he will in the Declaration of Independence, upon the distinction between the natural human right to freedom and the natural human wrong of despotism or tyranny. But despotism and tyranny are synonymous with slavery. In his contemptuous contemplation of the subjection of the American people to the electors of Great Britain, he wrote that in such a case, "we should suddenly be found the slaves, not of one, but of 160,000 tyrants." And again: "[D]oes his Majesty seriously wish, and publish it to the world, that his subjects should give up the glorious right of representation . . . and submit themselves the absolute slaves of his sovereign will?"[40] Nowhere in Jefferson's argument is there any ground for a distinction in principle between "domestic slavery" and that slavery whose imposition by the British Crown and Parliament is being so stoutly resisted. Indeed, after the Revolution, as Jefferson saw his countrymen fall below the level of his expectations with respect to what he had said was their "great object of desire" in 1774, he wrote:

> What a stupendous, what an incomprehensible machine is man! who can endure toil, famine, stripes, imprisonment, and death itself, in vindication of his own liberty, and, the next moment, be deaf to all those motives whose power supported him through his trial, and inflict on his fellow men a bondage, one hour of which is fraught with more misery than ages of that which he rose in rebellion to oppose.[41]

Much has been written about Jefferson himself being laggard, later in life, in his efforts against slavery. But in Jefferson the draftsman and spokesman for the American people in the American Revolution, the man of whom Lincoln would say that he "was, is, and perhaps will continue to be, the most distinguished politician of our history,"[42] there was never the least equivocation as to slavery's injustice and immorality.

As we have seen, Jefferson demanded to know what possible reason there could be for the 160,000 electors of Great Britain to give law to 4 million Americans who were in every respect their equals. We now take note, not merely of Jefferson's radically democratic premises, but also of his rejection of any of the medieval elements of representation that still prevailed in British constitutionalism. He is at pains, not only to derive the rights of Americans from the example of the Saxon emigration to Britain, but also to deny any authority or legitimacy from the Norman Conquest. What he says about the Normans is intended to preclude any ascription of legitimacy to feudal ideas of property or representation. Above all, he is at pains to deny that any title to property in the American colonies originates in grants or charters of the kings.[43]

> Our Saxon ancestors held their lands, as they did their personal property, in absolute dominion. . . . Feudal holdings were therefore but exceptions out of Saxon laws of possession, under which all lands were held in absolute right. These, therefore, still form the basis or groundwork of the Common Law, to prevail wheresoever the exceptions have not taken place. America was not conquered by William the Norman, nor its lands surrendered to him or any of his successors.

In America, all possessions were held "in absolute dominion" and "in absolute right." Jefferson concedes, however, that there are grounds for exceptions—a concession he immediately withdraws:

> Our ancestors, however, who migrated hither, were laborers, not lawyers. The fictitious principle that all lands belong originally to the King, they were early persuaded to believe real, and accordingly took grants of their own lands from the Crown. And while the Crown continued to grant for small sums and on reasonable rents, there was no inducement to arrest the error. . . . But his Majesty has lately taken on him to advance the terms of purchase and of holding. . . . It is time therefore . . . to declare that he has no right to grant lands of himself. From the nature and purpose of civil institutions, all the lands within the limits which any particular society has circumscribed around itself, are assumed by that society, and subject to their allotment only. This may be done by themselves assembled collectively, or by their legislature, to whom they may have delegated sovereign authority; and, if they are allotted in neither of these ways, each individual of the society may appropriate to himself such lands as he finds vacant, and occupancy will give him title.[44]

One cannot exaggerate the importance of Jefferson's assertion that the rights of property in America are rights descended from "our ancestors" who were "laborers." Jefferson here follows precisely the argument of John Locke in his *Second Treatise of Civil Government*. One cannot imagine a more effective way of presenting ancestral right as identical with natural right. The right grounded in labor is understood to confer upon the property-producing individual the authority to legislate with his fellows for the protection of their joint and several properties. Or they may delegate this sovereign authority to a legislature that they regard unquestionably as representing them. Laws governing property must emanate from individuals whose dominion over the property is "absolute." But the individual's dominion over his property is absolute because, and in the same sense that, his dominion over his body and soul is absolute. In short, the natural right to property (and the legislative power emanating therefrom) is grounded in the natural right to own one's self. For the king to claim that he is the source of the right to the lands carved out of the wilderness by others is an absurdity. Jefferson's Lockean understanding of property—above all, his understanding that personal freedom, personal property, constitutional government, and the rule of law all originate in the natural right to own one's self—was inherited directly by Lincoln and was the rock upon which his biblical house was built.

It cannot be repeated too often that, according to Jefferson, the king was "no more than chief officer of the people, appointed by the laws . . . to assist in working the great machine of government, erected for their use." The only ground of the king's authority in America is the utility to Americans of the king's executive power. That utility may be found in executing the laws required for the protection of property. By nature, property itself is understood to reside first and foremost in the persons of individual human beings. The natural rights to life, liberty, and property are ultimately one and the same. If one man could rightfully own another, he could rightfully own the product of that other's labor. If this were possible in any case, it would be in the case of the British king. It is upon the denial that it is possible in any case that Jefferson denies it to the king. It is upon his insistence that it is an impossibility in nature that one man can rightfully own another that the entire argument of the *Summary View* depends.

We turn now to the *Summary View*'s eternally memorable peroration. In his exordium Jefferson had addressed the king "in the language of truth . . . divested of . . . expressions of servility," that is to say, in language consistent with the truth of human equality. He returns now to that same theme, expressing himself, he says, with

> that freedom of language . . . which becomes a free people, claiming their rights as derived from the laws of nature, and not as the gift of their chief magistrate. They know, and will therefore say, that Kings are the servants, not the proprietors of the people.

One might suggest that Jefferson recognizes here the legitimate inequality that arises between a people and its servants. If anyone is inferior, it is the king. But Jefferson is explicit that he is asserting the equal rights of human nature under the laws of nature. The prescriptive, inherited, or historical rights of Englishmen have nothing whatever to do with the justice of the American cause. "The great principles of right and wrong," as noted before, are accessible to man as man, by virtue of the reason that defines man's nature. Jefferson warns the king not to sacrifice one part of his empire "to the inordinate desires of another." He agrees that Britain and America might concede special commercial privileges to each other. But such agreements must not "exclude us from going to other markets to dispose of those commodities which they cannot use, nor to supply those wants which they cannot supply." What follows is cosmic drama:

> Still less let it be proposed that our properties, within our own territories, shall be taxed or regulated by any power on earth but our own. The God who gave us life, gave us liberty at the same time: the hand of force may destroy, but cannot disjoin them. This, Sire, is our last, our determined resolution.[45]

The "shot heard round the world" some eight months later was, in truth, the reverberation of Jefferson's fiery eloquence. We must not, however, be so carried away by that eloquence as to fail to attend to what is intrinsic to his argument. The pronouncement that "Our properties . . . shall [not] be taxed or regulated by any power on earth but our own" is a continuation of the argument against British trade regulations that arbitrarily limited the ability of Americans to buy in the cheapest, and sell in the dearest, markets. These regulations reduced arbitrarily the value of Americans' products, and therewith the value of their labor. To reduce the value of a person's labor is to reduce the value of his life and freedom. When someone joins with others with whom he has previously joined himself in civil society to tax or regulate their joint or several properties, he and they are presumed to be acting together for their own purposes through the instrumentality of their own government. Even then, however, as Jefferson said in his inaugural address, government should "not take from the mouth of labor the bread it has earned."[46]

In taxation by authentic representation, there is no necessary diminution of rational freedom. Taxes levied otherwise must be either by fraud or by force. Since Jefferson has exposed the fraud, it can henceforth occur only by force. From such force, however, no right can result, because the original ground of property is as inalienable as the rights to life and liberty. You can kill an innocent man, but as long as he lives, you cannot take away his right to defend himself. It is equally unreasonable to say—in words Lincoln would use to characterize the essence of slavery—"You work; I'll eat." As Lincoln would repeat after Jefferson, the hand that earns bread has the natural right to put that bread into its own mouth. To be taxed by anyone except one's self, acting together with one's fellow citizens, is no different from having an alien predator come between the bread in your own hand, the product of your own labor, and your own mouth. Slavery, of course, is nothing but taxation without representation carried to its ultimate extreme.

∾

Jefferson's doctrine, which is the American doctrine in its purest form, is a doctrine of natural rights under natural law, owing nothing of its intrinsic character to "the rights of Englishmen." Whatever is to be commended in the British constitution is owing to its harmony with nature. Nature, not positive law, is the source of the rights that positive law exists to secure and render more valuable to their possessors.

By the same doctrine, the rights that governments exist to secure belong a priori to human individuals. This is emphasized when Jefferson compares American individuals to individual British electors. Such individualism detracts in no way from the understanding of man as a social (as well as a rational) animal.

Human individuals manifest their gregariousness by forming societies, which enact laws to attempt to secure their rights as human individuals. But the "public happiness" of which Jefferson speaks in the *Summary View* is an expression of the social nature of these same individuals. Individual rights become valuable only insofar as they result in a good society—a society in which man's moral and intellectual virtues can find their fullest measure of opportunity. There is in Jefferson none of that radical individualism that sees the rights of the individual transcending and opposing the moral demands of a good society. The opposition between the demands of society and the rights of the individual, so familiar in our time, arose only as those rights were no longer understood to be natural rights subject to the natural law.

It is in the defining characteristics of the doctrine of natural rights under natural law, the doctrine of the naturally right or just, that we must seek the relationship of the principles of revolutionary republicanism to free elections. In the Whig historical perspective of the *Summary View*, we see the British people exerting their sovereign right to self-government only by extreme actions in civil wars, in which offending monarchs are either executed or driven into exile. Whig constitutionalism of the Jeffersonian kind emerged full-blown in the Glorious Revolution. But its great antecedent was in the famous Petition of Right of 1628. Charles I had consented "not to levy taxes without the consent of Parliament, not to imprison his subjects without due cause being shown, not to billet soldiers in private homes, and not to put civilians under martial law." The authors of the Petition "somewhat incorrectly [claimed] . . . the precedent of Magna Carta."[47] In doing so, they initiated (or perhaps continued) the practice of presenting or disguising natural right as customary or historical right. Nevertheless, in the *Summary View*, and later in the Declaration of Independence, these constitutional precepts reappear solely as violations of the sovereignty of the people, and hence of natural right.

The English Civil War that began in 1642 ended with the death of the king in 1649. For refusing, in the judgment of Parliament, to be bound by the principles of the Petition of Right, Charles was executed as a tyrant. On his side, and with equal reason, Charles denied the jurisdiction of the high court that tried him. This court was unprecedented in English law and had in fact been created by the so-called Rump Parliament, a Parliament that had been purged by Cromwell's officers. Cromwell is reported to have said, "I am as much for government by consent as any man, but where will you find consent?"[48] Free elections to decide the questions that divided Cromwell and the king were clearly out of the question. Elections are not held to decide who will be the executioner and who the victim. The bill of attainder used by Parliament against Charles was, even in Jefferson's view, a legitimate instrument of the sovereignty of the people in dealing with the king. But a bill of attainder, like an ex post facto law, is lacking in the elements of impartiality that we associate with a judicial process. It can be justified, not as a legal process, but—like tyrannicide—as an act of self-defense by the people, in circumstances in which there is and can be "no common judge."

The American Constitution provides just such a common judge as the British constitution lacked. The impeachment process provides for the constitutional removal from office of the president, the vice president, and all "civil officers of the United States." Moreover, if someone is removed from office for "treason, bribery, or other high crimes and misdemeanors," he is still subject to indictment and trial by the ordinary courts of law, in which all the guarantees of a fair trial apply. The prohibition in the Constitution of 1787 of bills of attainder and ex post facto laws assumes that no questions shall ever arise for which a proper court or forum is not available. The reason for this assumption is that in the American Constitution, the sovereignty of the people is expressed unequivocally in the Preamble and not merely implied, as it is even in the British Whig constitutionalism of the *Summary View*. There are no holders of office who are not elected by the people, whether directly or indirectly, or who are not appointed by those that have been elected. It is assumed that no question can arise as to who is or shall be sovereign, such as dominated British constitutional conflicts from Henry VIII (if not earlier) to William and Mary. But in those conflicts, the question of who should be sovereign was always inextricably intertwined with the question of what the religion of the sovereign ought to be. *Cuius regio eius religio*—which may be translated to mean "the religion of the king determines the religion of the kingdom"— was the motto of the Reformation. In British Whig constitutionalism, this came to mean that it was the sovereign right of the people to determine the religion of the king. But in Article VI of the American Constitution, which antedates the guarantees of religious freedom in the First Amendment, it is provided that "no religious test shall ever be required as a qualification to any office or public trust under the United States." Instead, before entering upon his duties, the president or any other officer is offered the alternative of an "oath or affirmation." Thus it would appear that under the American Constitution the people are competent to resolve, by peaceful political means, all their political differences. This is plausible because questions of sovereignty and religion have been removed from politics. Unburdened by the great questions that burdened British constitutional history, the American people might safely abide by the rule of constitutional majorities— majorities that leave inviolate the equal rights of minorities.

Our review of Jefferson's American understanding of an emergent Whig constitutionalism in Great Britain must impress anyone with the tenuousness of the idea of free and uncoerced elections replacing violent exertions of the right of revolution. We must remember that the *Summary View*, while looking back to revolutionary violence as the chief vehicle for securing the people's rights within the framework of British constitutional history, looked forward to the Declaration of Independence as the greatest of all such exertions on behalf of these same rights. Thereafter, Jefferson himself was slow to recognize election as a replacement for revolution. His aphorisms on the subject of the latter are notable. Here are some of them:

> The tree of liberty must be refreshed from time to time with the blood of patriots and tyrants. It is its natural manure.[49]

> I hold that a little rebellion, now and then, is a good thing, and as necessary in the political world as storms are in the physical.[50]

> The spirit of resistance to government is so valuable on certain occasions, that I wish it to be always alive.[51]

And on Shays's Rebellion:

> God forbid we should ever be twenty years without such a rebellion. . . . If [the people] remain quiet under such misconceptions, it is a lethargy, the forerunner of death to the public spirit.[52]

The latter three passages are from the year 1787, when Jefferson was in Paris and when the gathering storm of the French Revolution—in Jefferson's eyes, a most necessary cathartic—was about to vent itself upon the world.

Jefferson's reaction to Shays's Rebellion contrasts remarkably with the reactions of Washington, Madison, Hamilton, and other leading Founders. For them, that rebellion proved a catalyst for the Convention that framed the Constitution of 1787, a document that had no more urgent purpose than to provide security for property against popular passions. Property was being endangered in the states by the people seeking relief from debt, either through the legislature or by mob action. But despite his reaction to Shays's Rebellion, no one was more committed than Jefferson to the security of property under the rule of law, in popular no less than in other kinds of government. Jefferson always believed that the people are the origin of all the just powers of government and that it is by the majority alone that the people can act. But in keeping with his view that "An elective despotism was not the government we fought for," Jefferson believed with the other Founders in the danger of majority tyranny. The rights of minorities, meaning the rights of individuals, were no less inviolable by the people than by kings. And he thought that popular governments were subject to corruption and that resistance to corruption might be manifested in resistance even to popular governments.

The right of revolution, which underlay all the people's rights, might then be manifested either in violent resistance to corrupt or tyrannical governments or in the institution and maintenance of popular governments deriving their just powers from the consent of the governed. In the 1790s, Jefferson was frequently of two minds as to whether the government instituted as a result of the ratification of the Constitution deserved loyalty as an embodiment of the people's (and the majority's) rights or whether it deserved resistance for having usurped powers never given to it by the people.

The transformation of the right of revolution into the right of free election really began with Jefferson's own party's victory in 1800. We are reminded that Lincoln's first great speech, the Lyceum speech of January 27, 1838, had as its theme the particular importance in a popular government of reverence for the laws. Lincoln stressed the necessity of obeying even bad laws while working for their repeal or reform, because disobedience to bad laws engenders a habit of lawlessness that easily turns into mob rule. And when law cannot protect persons and property, men will turn away from the rule of law to despotism for their security. Indeed, Lincoln's understanding in this speech of the dangers of lawlessness for popular government, or of the inexorable connection between anarchy and tyranny, was substantially the same as the one that animated those who called for the Constitutional Convention of 1787.

$\sim$

The tension between the right of resistance to unjust government and the duty to "preserve, protect, and defend" the Constitution may be better understood in light of the issues that divided Americans in their first experience of the Constitution. It was in the 1790s that the precedents were established whereby almost all great political differences in American history have resolved themselves into constitutional controversies. In Washington's first administration, Jefferson and Hamilton fell out over the question of whether Congress had the power, under the Constitution, to charter a bank. Jefferson objected that this was not among the congressional powers enumerated in the Constitution. Nor was it, he thought, among those powers described in the "necessary and proper" clause of Article I, section 8, which grants nonenumerated powers that are "necessary and proper" for carrying into execution any of the enumerated powers.

For Jefferson, a nonenumerated power, to be "necessary and proper," must be such that the enumerated power could not be carried out without it. Here is the heart of Jefferson's mode of constitutional interpretation, as set forth in February 1791, which has been known ever since as the doctrine of strict construction:

I consider the foundation of the Constitution as laid on this ground—that *all powers not delegated to the United States, by the Constitution, nor prohibited by it to the states, are reserved to the states, or to the people* (10th amend.). To take a single step beyond the boundaries thus specially drawn around the powers of Congress, is to take possession of a boundless field of power, no longer susceptible of any definition.[53]

Hamilton replied with the doctrine of implied constitutional powers, or what has come to be called liberal construction. According to Hamilton, the powers of the government of the United States were sovereign powers. In the enumeration of congressional powers, the people intended that Congress should choose the most efficacious means of carrying out the purposes for which the powers were delegated to it. Jefferson had admitted that the "necessary and proper" clause authorized powers not expressly enumerated. From this point, Hamilton proceeded as follows:

It is conceded that *implied powers* are to be considered as delegated equally with *express ones.* . . . The only question must be, in this, as in every other case, whether the means to be employed, or in this instance the corporation to be erected, has a natural relation to any of the acknowledged objects or lawful ends of the government. Thus a corporation may not be erected by Congress for superintending the police of the city of Philadelphia, because they are not authorized to *regulate* the *police* of that city. But one may be erected in relation to the collection of taxes, or to the trade with foreign countries, or to the trade between States, or with the Indian tribes; because it is the province of the federal government to *regulate* those objects and because it is incident to a general *sovereign* or *legislative* power to *regulate* a thing, to employ all the means which relate to its regulation to the best and greatest advantage.[54]

One might reduce the difference in constitutional interpretation between Hamilton and Jefferson to the difference they assign to the word "necessary" in the "necessary and proper" clause. For Jefferson, it means that without which the power in question cannot be exercised at all. For Hamilton, it means that without which the power in question cannot be exercised "to the best and greatest advantage." There is no difference between them regarding the fact that Congress cannot employ powers not delegated by the people through the Constitution, or that the assumption of powers not delegated constitutes usurpation, or that usurpation is of the essence of tyranny and demands resistance.

The government of the United States in 1791 was unique both in the fact that it was a government wholly popular in its principles and in the fact that it allowed for a distinction—wholly unknown to the British constitution, then or since—between the law of the Constitution and the statute law of Congress. Article VI of the Constitution declares that "This Constitution and the laws of the United States, which shall be made in pursuance thereof . . . shall be the supreme law of the land; and the judges in every state shall be bound thereby, any thing in the constitution or laws of any state to the contrary notwithstanding." In 1791, Hamilton and Jefferson differed as to whether a bill chartering a national bank was "in pursuance" of the Constitution. Americans have since differed as to whether measures such as protective tariffs, internal improvements, wage and hour regulation, and public accommodation legislation were in pursuance of the Constitution.[55] Anyone who is convinced that a given measure is not in pursuance of the Constitution is authorized by that fact to think that the measure is not a law and that he is not bound to obey it. Whether it is prudent for him to act on this opinion depends upon circumstances. If he is alone in his opinion, or nearly alone, he can do little until he persuades others to join him. But it is important to understand that civil disobedience, or disobedience to a law that one does not believe has been passed in pursuance of the Constitution, cannot of itself be regarded as disloyalty to the Constitution. This is all the more true because the Constitution itself does not say how one can discover when a law is in pursuance of it. Much of American history is the tale of attempts, by one means or another, to resolve controversies as to what is in pursuance of the Constitution.

If an individual's discontent with a law is shared with a majority or a large minority of his fellow citizens, they may join together to resist it or to have the law repealed or declared unconstitutional in the courts. The best example in our own time of how these processes are related to each other is provided by the civil rights movement that culminated in the Civil Rights Acts of 1964 and 1968. Here civil disobedience, court action, political action, and finally legislative action all conspired to produce an outcome that, in all likelihood, would not have come to pass without all of them. These same elements, in differing proportions, have been present in all the great political movements and controversies in American history, including anti- (and pro-) slavery, temperance (and repeal), women's suffrage (and its sequel, equal rights), and pro- (and anti-) abortion.

Let us return for the moment to that pristine conflict between Hamilton and Jefferson concerning the constitutionality of the bill chartering the first Bank of the United States, a conflict centering in Talmudic fashion on the meaning of the word "necessary." Jefferson thought that powers acquired by Hamilton's mode of construing the Constitution were usurped, and usurpation meant tyranny. Hamilton denied that the powers in question were usurped and thought that Jefferson's strict construction prevented the government from employing those measures that were to "the best and greatest advantage" of the people. Hamilton thought that an ineffective government would breed discontent and discredit the cause of popular government. In fact, Hamilton considered strict construction to be a rearguard action by anti-Federalism to return to the weak government that characterized the Articles of Confederation. In this opposition of Hamilton and Jefferson (who was joined by Madison in the ensuing partisan battle), each claimed an unblemished devotion both to the Constitution and to the cause of popular government. We can see, however, that someone distrusting Hamilton's motives (as Jefferson certainly did) might think that the greatest "advantage" of the bank consisted in the patronage it placed in the hands of the secretary of the treasury and his friends—patronage that would subvert the republican virtue of influential classes of citizens and of their representatives in Congress. Since it was apparently by similar means that the British king sought control of Parliament, and since Hamilton was known to be an admirer of the British system,[56] Jefferson and Madison denounced Hamilton's policies as attempts to introduce the substance of monarchy under the forms of republicanism.[57] Yet it takes no great astuteness to surmise that Jefferson, while denying that the question of the utility (as distinct from the constitutionality) of the bank was at issue, did in fact disagree with Hamilton as to that utility. It is an oft told tale that Jefferson and Madison, when in office, discovered the utility and constitutionality of measures (including the bank) that they had fought on constitutional grounds when in opposition. They did not, however, simply retract their earlier views. What they said later was that the people, by the views of those they had elected and reelected to office, had in their wisdom legitimated the constitutionality of such measures. It is not cynicism that leads us further to notice that the people, while electing and reelecting to Congress representatives who accepted banks, tariffs, and other measures previously denounced by Jefferson and Madison, also elected and reelected Jefferson and Madison to the presidency. Measures that were suspect when promoted by those whose loyalty to the republican form of government was suspect were no longer subject to such suspicions.

The opposition engendered by Hamilton's fiscal policies in the 1790s was mild when compared with the divisions that ensued upon the passage of the Alien and Sedition Acts in June and July of 1798. These acts were followed by the resolutions of the Kentucky and Virginia legislatures in November and December of the same year, and a further resolution adopted in Kentucky in February 1799. These protests presented the already familiar argument about strict construction as a constitutional requirement of the Tenth Amendment. They also introduced, as a necessary inference from the doctrine of strict construction, a theory of civil liberty as the ground of the legitimacy of the political process. If we understand the Kentucky and Virginia Resolutions as Jefferson and Madison understood them at the time, the defense of state rights and the defense of civil liberty formed part of a single argument. Looked at in the light of nearly two centuries, however, they stand at the headwaters of two divergent trends in American political and constitutional history. The defense of state rights against "numerical majoritarianism" and the "tyranny of the majority" became in time a defense of slavery and, after that, of Jim Crow. Paradoxical as it may be, in its association with "state rights," the argument against "tyranny" became the argument for "despotism," notwithstanding the fact that these two words at bottom mean the same thing. For Jefferson and Madison, however, the rights of the states, as of all legitimate civil societies, were grounded in the natural rights of individuals, as proclaimed in the Declaration of Independence and the bills of rights of the states. The rights of the states and the condemnation of slavery were part of the same doctrine. To understand the election of 1800, we must not read back into it the opposition between state rights and civil liberties that may be said to have begun (as Lincoln saw it) in the nullification crisis of 1828 to 1833.

~

The Kentucky and Virginia Resolutions defined for Jefferson's and Madison's Republican Party, which would be victorious in the upcoming national election of 1800, the issues of that election. In doing so, they were in some measure anticipating the national party platforms of the post-1832 "second American party system." These later platforms were the work of national nominating conventions, which were themselves meetings of delegations from state party conventions. In the absence of such party machinery, state legislatures played this role in 1798 and 1799. In defining and publicizing the issues in the upcoming elections, they were preparing the means by which the country could form and express the countrywide opinions that culminated in a countrywide election.

On the one hand, the publication and distribution of the Kentucky and Virginia Resolutions facilitated the process of majority consensus. This in itself laid the groundwork for all future free elections. On the other hand, by attributing to the opposition a design of despotism similar to the one that the Declaration of Independence had attributed to the British king and Parliament, the resolutions left open the inference that the people's sovereignty, expressed in and by their organization in states, might be exercised in revolutionary resistance rather than electoral change. This ambiguity in the legacy of the resolutions explains why, at one and the same time, they laid the foundation for peaceful change by national elections and furnished arguments that justified rejecting the results of these elections.

We will have occasion to return to the fact that these same resolutions were looked on by South Carolina in 1832 as supplying the precedents justifying its

Ordinance of Nullification. We will also observe their similar role in 1860 and 1861 with respect to the ordinances of secession that preceded the formation of the Confederacy. Nullification, backed up by the threat of secession, was understood by its advocates to express the principle of resistance to oppression found in these resolutions. As we have observed in the *Summary View*, the essence of political conflict as seen by Americans in the period of the Revolution was the conflict between the rights of the people and government usurpation of those rights. Political evil consisted in the attempts by governments to turn from the common good of the ruled to the private advantage of the rulers.[58] The idea of deep-seated differences between equally sincere partisans of the people's rights, with free elections as the sufficient means for resolving those differences, was an idea whose time had certainly not come, if indeed it can be said ever to have come.

We recall Jefferson's admonition to the king in the *Summary View* that "The whole art of government consists in the art of being honest." It was followed by this assurance:

> Only aim to do your duty, and mankind will give you credit where you fail. No longer persevere in sacrificing the rights of one part of your empire to the inordinate desires of another. . . . Let no act be passed by any one legislature, which may infringe on the rights and liberties of another.[59]

We have already observed that it was constitutionally impossible for the king in 1774 to take Jefferson's view of his "honest" duty. Apart from this, however, one would be hard-pressed to find, in any major episodes of Jefferson's political career, instances in which he credited with honesty those opposed to his strongly held political opinions. Nor did the change from British monarchy to American republicanism of itself change greatly Jefferson's view of the nature of political conflict. To anticipate: Jefferson and Madison, in the Kentucky and Virginia Resolutions, saw the federal Congress usurping rights belonging to the states and the people of the states in a manner closely paralleling what Jefferson had charged Parliament with doing to the colonial legislatures before the Revolution. Jefferson, in the Kentucky Resolutions, declares explicitly that the fact that the president and the Congress were elected, and were thus "the men of our choice," did not lessen the tyrannical character of their usurpations. An elected government has no more moral or legal right to arrogate authority or employ powers not delegated to it by the people through the Constitution than a nonelected government. The use of such powers is inconsistent with the constitutional limitations intended to harmonize the rule of the majority with the rights of the minority. When a freely elected government usurps authority, it too may by this fact invite resistance. Moderation and compromise are justly regarded as the hallmarks of popular government. Fidelity to the

Constitution, however, is understood to be the ground of moderation and compromise. How can there be moderation and compromise with respect to the
ground of moderation and compromise? When contending parties see each other
as pursuing policies unauthorized by the Constitution, what ground is there for
moderation and compromise? This is the dilemma presented by the republicanism
of the American Revolution.

The Kentucky and Virginia Resolutions opened a debate that has never
ended, as to whether constitutional differences can be regarded as political differences to be resolved within the political process by debate and compromise followed by elections. Calling one's opponent's position unconstitutional implies a
right to invoke resistance grounded in the right of revolution, which is first and
foremost a natural right. One need not go outside the positive law to do this, of
course, since reminding the electorate of the ultimate recourse of resistance may
itself rally one's supporters and intimidate one's opponents. We today tend to
think that the use of free speech, freedom of association, the right of petition, and
political campaigns culminating in free elections by secret ballot are the only
means by which to protest the measures (actual or prospective) of a government
with which we disagree. Such was the opinion expressed by Lincoln in his first
inaugural address: "Why should there not be a patient confidence in the ultimate
justice of the people? Is there any better or equal hope in the world?"[60] But Lincoln in 1861, like Jefferson in 1801, was speaking as the victor in a just-conclud-
ed electoral contest. The precedents provided by Jefferson and Madison in 1798,
before their electoral triumph of 1800, are not unambiguous on this question. Nor
can we say that Lincoln would have regarded as legitimate a government based
upon the electoral victory of a party committed to the extension and perpetuation
of slavery.[61]

Before turning to the texts of the Kentucky and Virginia Resolutions, we
would note the symmetry of two notable forms of political resistance to alleged
usurpations. In 1798, the Republicans discovered that it was the right of the states
to contest, on constitutional grounds, the measures of a Federalist Congress and
president. In 1803, the Federalists discovered a right to contest, on constitutional grounds, the measures of a Republican Congress and president. The latter discovery was embodied in the doctrine of judicial review, as set forth by Chief Justice John Marshall in Marbury v. Madison. We will later examine the inner
resemblance of state rights and judicial review as alternative modes of resisting
alleged assumptions of usurped powers.[62] Here we would only alert ourselves to
the fact that both state rights and judicial review were arrayed against Lincoln
and the Union in the crisis of 1860–61.

∾

The first of nine resolutions put forth by Kentucky on November 16, 1798, reads:

> Resolved. That the several States composing the United States of America, are not united on the principle of unlimited submission to their general government; but that by compact under the style and title of a Constitution for the United States and of amendments thereto, they constituted a general government for special purposes, delegated to that government certain definite powers, reserving each State to itself, the residuary mass of right to their own self-government; and that whensoever the general government assumes undelegated powers, its acts are unauthoritative, void, and of no force: That to this compact each State acceded as a State, and is an integral party, its co-States forming, as to itself, the other party: That the government created by this compact was not made the exclusive or final judge of the extent of the powers delegated to itself; since that would have made its discretion, and not the Constitution, the measure of its powers; but that as in all other cases of compact among parties having no common Judge, *each party has an equal right to judge for itself, as well of infractions as of the mode and measure of redress.*[63]

That the states are not united "on the principle of unlimited submission to their general government" is true because no citizen of any state, any more than of the United States, is united with any other citizen "on the principle of unlimited submission." Unlimited submission is characteristic only of despotism; all legitimate government is nondespotic and is therefore limited government.

Throughout the Kentucky Resolutions, Jefferson echoes the language of the Revolution. The claim of the king and Parliament in the Declaratory Act of 1766, "to bind the colonies and people of America, subjects of the crown of Great Britain, *in all cases whatsoever*,"[64] was the core of the attempt, as the Declaration of Independence put it, "to reduce them under absolute despotism." The usurpation by the general government of powers not delegated by the Constitution, as alleged by the Kentucky Resolutions, is said to represent an attempt "to bind the States . . . *in all cases whatsoever*, by laws not made with their consent."[65]

Jefferson appeals throughout the Kentucky Resolutions to the principles of "compact," the Constitution itself being a particular compact.[66] The idea of compact is at the heart of American constitutionalism. It is at the heart of the philosophical statesmanship that made the Revolution, of which the Constitution is the fruit.[67] In the most fundamental respect, compact is an inference from the proposition "that all men are created equal." If men were by nature unequal— that is to say, if some were born with saddles on their backs, and others booted and spurred—then it would be naturally right for those with the boots and spurs to ride those with the saddles. It is because there is no such inequality within the human species that legitimate government arises from compact or consent.

In 1860–61, the "seceding" states also referred to the Constitution as a compact. From their peculiar understanding of its meaning, they found justification, not only for slavery, but also for their withdrawal from the Union. That understanding differed fundamentally from Madison's and Jefferson's, in that it severed the connection between human equality and the requirement of consent. They might consistently, even if erroneously, have denied both equality *and* consent; but they could not consistently demand the benefit of being ruled only by their own consent while denying that other human beings shared in that human nature that is the original and necessary justification for the requirement of consent. It is therefore of the highest importance that we understand the term "compact" as an expression of the doctrine of the Declaration of Independence and as the essence of the philosophical and constitutional statesmanship of the Revolution. This is the sense in which Jefferson and Madison understood it in 1798–99, a very different sense from that in which it was used by South Carolina and her spokesmen in the debates surrounding nullification and secession from circa 1831 to 1861.

Madison's language in the key Virginia resolution closely resembles Jefferson's above.

> That this assembly doth explicitly and peremptorily declare that it views the powers of the Federal Government as resulting from the compact to which the states are parties, as limited by the plain sense and intention of the instrument constituting that compact; as no further valid than they are authorized by the grants enumerated in that compact; and that in case of a deliberate, palpable, and dangerous exercise of other powers not granted by the said compact, the states, who are partners thereto, have the right and are in duty bound to interpose for arresting the progress of the evil, and for maintaining within their respective limits the authorities, rights, and liberties appertaining to them.[68]

In Madison's "Report of 1799–1800," which was the answer of the Virginia House of Delegates to the replies of several states to the Virginia Resolutions, he remarked: "The authority of constitutions over government, and of the sovereignty of the people over constitutions, are truths which are at all times necessary to be kept in mind."[69] These "truths" must "be kept in mind" because they are direct inferences from the nature of compact, a concept that is equally central to both sets of resolutions. That the Constitution of 1787 is itself a compact remains obscure, however, until we understand that the constitutions of the states, which are said to be parties to the federal constitutional compact, are compacts themselves, and the results of compacts. First and foremost it is necessary to understand the original compact, which is not one of states but of individual persons and which removes those persons from the "state of nature" into civil society. Thus the Bill of Rights of Massachusetts declares that "The body-politic is formed by a voluntary association of individuals; it is a social compact by which the whole people covenants with each citizen, and each citizen with the whole people, that all shall be governed by certain laws for the common good."[70]

We observe that the language of the Kentucky Resolutions, "that to this compact [the Constitution] each State acceded as a State . . . its co-States forming, as to itself, the other party," exactly parallels that of Massachusetts when it declared that the body politic is formed when each citizen voluntarily "covenants" with the whole people, and the whole people with each citizen. In other words, in forming the "more perfect Union" of the Constitution, each state played the same role that each individual played in forming the compact that removed him from the state of nature. As each individual person placed himself under government in forming the social compact that resulted in a body politic, so each individual state placed itself under government in entering into the federal constitutional compact. In both cases, the government is limited by the terms of the compact in what it might rightfully do. But with respect to the objects for which each compact was entered into, the result of the compact is, in the fullest sense, a government. According to the Kentucky Resolutions, "the government created by this compact [viz., the Constitution] was not made the exclusive or final judge of the powers delegated to itself." But Jefferson meant no more by this than he meant in the Declaration of Independence when he said that "whenever any form of government becomes destructive of these ends [viz., 'to secure these rights'], it is the right of the people to alter or abolish it." Obviously the government itself cannot be the judge of whether it has become destructive of its proper ends. There must be a standpoint outside of government from which the people can judge whether it ought to be altered or abolished. Similarly, there must be such a standpoint from which each individual person can make such a judgment. In the Kentucky Resolutions, a state is presented as examining the actions of the government of the United States in the same way that any people or person always has the right to examine and judge whether his government has become destructive of the ends for which it was established. But what is the role of elections and electoral processes (including impeachment and amendment) in implementing such judgments?

Each of the original thirteen colonies was regarded as a body politic formed by and from such a compact or contract as that described in the Massachusetts Constitution. We recall that Jefferson, in the *Summary View*, wrote that "America was conquered, and her settlements made and firmly established, at the expense of individuals, and not the British public." These same individuals, who were also members of families and communities of families, and whose blood, toil, tears, and sweat produced the pristine settlements in the wilderness, joined together in "voluntary association" to constitute the civil societies that came to be called the colonies. These became eventually the "independent states" of the United States. But it is to the first or fundamental compact, which removed individuals from the state of nature, that we must look to discover the original meaning of "compact" in the vocabulary of Revolutionary republicanism. This original compact was made by men who, in the wilderness, were not subject to any government until they formed governments for themselves. It is this compact that determines the qualities (especially limited government and the rule of law) that are intrinsic both to the state constitutions and the federal Constitution of 1787. For it is the nature of the compact that removes men from the state of nature that determines the nature of any subsequent compact.

Throughout his life, Jefferson spoke with perfect consistency and unfailing passion of the rights of man as the only legitimate foundation of government: "The equal rights of man, and the happiness of every individual, are now acknowledged to be the only legitimate objects of government."[71] And again: "Nothing is unchangeable but the inherent and inalienable rights of man."[72] Jefferson meant by such statements neither more nor less than did Madison when he declared (as he did throughout his life) "that all power in just and free government is derived from compact." And again: "Of all free government, compact is the basis and essence."[73]

The foregoing are taken from Madison's essay entitled "Sovereignty," one of a number of his later writings opposing the South Carolina nullifiers and especially the use made by these nullifiers of the Kentucky and Virginia Resolutions. In the same essay, Madison shows how ever present the compact theory of government was to Americans of the Revolutionary generation and how necessary it was to their self-understanding:

> At the period of our Revolution it was supposed by some that it dissolved the social compact within the Colonies, and produced a state of nature which required a naturalization of those who had not participated in the Revolution. The question was brought before Congress at its first session by Dr. Ramsay, who contested the election of William Smith, who, though born in South Carolina, had been absent at the date of independence. The decision was, that his birth in the Colony made him a member of the society in its new as well as its original state.[74]

That there was a "state of nature" prior to civil society was never doubted.[75] It belonged to the common coin of political discourse in the Revolutionary generation. The question addressed here was whether the state of nature had recurred because of the separation from Great Britain. According to Dr. Ramsay, it had done so. Therefore the political community into which William Smith had been born had been dissolved, and a different one, of which he was not a member, had been constituted in its place. This reminds us of the question that Aristotle addresses near the beginning of the third book of the *Politics*: Should a democracy pay the public debts of the tyrant that the democracy has overthrown? Is the political community (polis) the same or different when it changes from a tyranny into a democracy? What is it that makes for sameness and difference in the identities of political communities? Aristotle's answer is that it is the form of government or the constitution (*politeia*) that gives a political community its identity. When such a community changes from, let us say, a tyranny or an oligarchy into a democracy, it is no longer the same, any more than a chorus is the same when it changes from a tragic into a comic chorus.[76] Madison, in the "Report of 1799–1800," repeats the basic argument of Jefferson's *Summary View*, asserting:

> The fundamental principle of the Revolution was, that the colonies were co-ordinate members with each other, and with Great Britain, of an empire, united by a common executive sovereign, but not united by any common legislative sovereign. The legislative power was maintained to be as complete in each American parliament, as in the British parliament. And the royal prerogative was in force in each colony, by virtue of its acknowledging the king for its executive magistrate, as it was in Great Britain, by virtue of a like acknowledgment there. A denial of these principles by Great Britain, and the assertion of them by America, produced the Revolution.[77]

When Madison writes that each colony recognized the king for its executive magistrate, he does so from the Whig point of view (as articulated in the *Summary View*), which sees the executive in light of the doctrine of legislative supremacy. This means, in brief, that the king is the agent of the people, who have chosen him as their chief executive magistrate. The people are not instruments for carrying out the will of the king.[78] And what Madison says about the completeness of the legislative power in each colony before the Revolution implies that the sovereignty of the people was the established principle in each colony before as well as after the Revolution. Hence there had not been any recurrence of "the state of nature."

The proposition that the legislative power was as complete in each colonial parliament as in the parliament of Great Britain masks an underlying difference between the British constitution (then and now) and an emergent American constitutionalism. In Great Britain, the king (or queen) in Parliament is the legal sovereign, the lawfulness of whose acts may not be called into question in any other place. There is consequently no such thing as an unconstitutional act of Parliament. In America, only the people are legally sovereign. The act of the people in

41

establishing the Constitution and their subsequent acts in amending it may not be called into question by any other body in any other place.[79] Thus every legislature, executive, and court of law, whether state or federal, can rightfully exercise only such powers as are delegated or permitted to it by the Constitution. Furthermore, since every citizen is a party to the compact that created his state of residence and every state is a party to the constitutional compact, any citizen may challenge any act of government that he regards as unauthorized by either of those compacts.[80]

That powers that are regarded as usurped, even by a lawfully elected body, may be resisted is inherent in the American political tradition from the outset, as seen in the right to "alter or abolish" tyrannical governments in the Declaration of Independence. It is clear that resistance to tyranny is a natural right of the people collectively. But the Declaration sees that collective right as itself the result of the compact of human individuals who, being equal by nature, are in a state of nature prior to the compact. These individuals became a "people" by the compact that removed them from the state of nature with respect to each other, although it did not remove them from the state of nature with respect to other peoples or to individuals not party to their compact.

A people consists of human persons who have been formed by their own voluntary agreement into a civil society. It is they who may be said to have the right, under certain circumstances, to "alter or abolish" governments, which has come to be called the right of revolution. But a people is not any chance assemblage. Their fidelity to "the laws of nature and of nature's God" in 1776 made the American people, according to the Declaration, "the good people of these colonies." A *good* people may change a bad government. But what of a bad people? Does sovereignty, in the sense of legitimate political power, belong to a bad people as well as a good people? As we shall see, to Madison or Jefferson this would be absurd. The compact theory presupposes a people that is good in the sense that it is united by the morality inherent in "the laws of nature and of nature's God." This morality defines in principle the rights and duties in virtue of which minorities and majorities can accept the decisions of the ballot box.

That the powers usurped by an elected legislature should be resisted in and by the electoral process—that is to say, by "throwing the rascals out" in the next election—may be the mode that now appears most desirable and most compatible with republican principles. But that depends upon the circumstance that neither side in a contest believes, or has reason to believe, that its political opponents intend to use the power of government, gained by election, to deprive it of its equal natural rights. Indeed, no one can accept as a fellow citizen anyone who does not see the process of voting as a means to implement the equal rights of everyone. Before the votes are counted, it must be understood that the winner represents those who voted against him no less than those who voted for him. Above all, the president of the United States, the commander in chief of the armed forces, who has the ultimate responsibility for the security of the entire nation, is the representative of every citizen. If such an understanding does not prevail, as it obviously did not in 1860, then the political process envisaged by the Declaration of Independence and the Constitution cannot function.

At the time of the Kentucky Resolutions in 1798, a nonelectoral right of resistance appears to have been as prominent in the mind of Jefferson as it had been in the *Summary View* and the Declaration two decades earlier. Whether the same should be said of Madison and the Virginia Resolutions of 1799 remains to be seen. Certainly it would appear that before 1800, both Jefferson and Madison were more concerned to deny legitimacy to the Alien and Sedition Acts than to affirm majority rule as the arbiter of grave political and constitutional differences under the republican form of government.

The Kentucky and Virginia Resolutions, by their contribution to the electoral victory of the Republicans in 1800, contributed to the unprecedented world-historical event we noted at the outset: the peaceful and nonpunitive replacement in the offices of government of one party by its bitterest political rivals, on the basis of a free decision by a whole people at the ballot box. Likewise, as we have noted, both judicial review and civil disobedience have been, at one time or another, elements in the electoral process, since they have been means of focusing the attention of voters upon the issues to be decided. But once one concedes that even a lawfully elected government may govern unconstitutionally, one must concede that free elections, in and of themselves, do not confer final legitimacy.[81] It is against this background that we will later consider Lincoln's defense of the Union cause in his Message to Congress on July 4, 1861, as a defense of the principle of free elections.

We recall that before the Revolution, King George III was regarded by American Whig doctrine as no more than the "chief officer of the people" in each colony, "appointed by the laws" and subject to the people's "superintendence." The very act of declaring independence was the joint act of the several political societies represented in the Continental Congress. It was the joint act of the several peoples who had severally formed themselves into their respective bodies politic, and who by that joint act had become the "one people" of the Declaration. So far were they from dissolving themselves by their act of independence, as Dr. Ramsay had suggested, that the very act of declaring independence presupposed their undissolved corporate presences. The Congress clearly decided correctly in rejecting Dr. Ramsay's view of the matter.

Let us now turn to Madison's essay "Sovereignty" for its account of that original compact by which individuals in a state of nature bring civil government into existence. It is by this compact that the natural freedom and independence of each individual is transformed into the sovereignty of the people, acting by its majority. It was by virtue of such popular sovereignty that citizens of the several colonies declared their independence of Great Britain and their union with each other, adopted the Articles of Confederation, and later replaced those Articles with the "more perfect union" of the Constitution.

Madison writes:

> To go to the bottom of the subject, let us consult the Theory which contemplates a certain number of individuals as meeting and agreeing to form one political society, in order that the rights, the safety, and the interest of each may be under the safeguard of the whole. The first supposition is, that each individual being previously independent of the others, the compact which is to make them one society must result from the *free* consent of every individual.[82]

Civil society, or the body politic, is a *voluntary* association. The first and most fundamental characteristic of a free society arises from the first and most fundamental characteristic of the social compact. No one is a member who does not join of his own will, and no one who does not join of his own will is a member. This means that whoever does not join has no inherent right to claim the benefits of membership. Nor does the political community have any inherent right to claim his obedience. The supposition mentioned by Madison, that each individual had been independent prior to the compact, means that there had been no relationship of governing or being governed between them. That is to say, in the state of nature, and by nature, each individual is equal in authority to every other, no one having more claim to the obedience of another than another has claim to obedience from him. It is only by virtue of each person's recognition of this equality in those with whom he contracts to form a civil society that such a civil society can be formed.

The divine government of the universe, so prominent in the Declaration of Independence and other documents of the Founding, does not arise from the voluntary agreement of men to be governed by God's providence. Nor does the human government of the lower orders of creation depend upon the voluntary agreement of dogs or horses or cattle. But there is no such difference between man and man as there is between man and God, on the one hand, or man and beast, on the other, that would make the government of one man by another the natural and involuntary consequence of the differences between them. This is not to deny the fact of human differences or to minimize the importance of some of these differences, especially those involving wisdom and virtue, for government. But whatever differences there may be, they do not constitute a rightful ground for the assertion of the authority of one man over another until voluntary agreement has authorized legitimate government itself. It is one thing to say that one man is wiser than another. It is a different thing to say that such wisdom confers a right to rule on the one side or a duty to obey on the other.[83]

The compact theory explains how legitimate political authority can arise among men and why such authority is consistent with human nature. Nature is the involuntary cause of the fact that we are human. But being human, we can only be governed justly by other human beings on the basis of our voluntary agreement. Of course, authority can arise in many ways other than compact. Conquest is the most common. But force of itself can never give rise to right. Some men may demand obedience on the ground of their alleged godlike superiority or because of the alleged inferiority of others. But these demands are pronounced to be fraudulent. No one can rightfully demand obedience of another, however plausible his claims to superior ability, until he has proved that his ability will be devoted, not to exploiting, but to benefiting the other. Only the compact guarantees that the rulers will rule in the interest of the ruled.

The voluntary association that becomes a body politic is intended to place "the rights, the safety, and the interest of each . . . under the safeguard of the whole." That the whole can safeguard each better than each can safeguard himself is the first and most evident rational ground for the voluntary action of each in agreeing to become a member of a political society. Moreover, the equality that is presupposed among the compacting or contracting parties extends necessarily to the equality of the safeguards to which each is entitled as a result of his membership. No one can say that he is joining the community so that *his* life, or *his* property, or *his* family members will enjoy greater safety than anyone else's. To say that is tantamount to saying, "You risk your life to protect me, but I won't risk mine to protect you." No one makes a contract in which the risks are unequal and the profits equal, or in which the risks are equal and the profits unequal. No contract can be valid except upon the basis of the equality of the contracting parties. This does not mean that there may not be privileged positions within society. The president of the United States may be accorded greater security than other citizens. Apart from the fact that he may be in greater danger than others because of his position, the importance of his security is due to the importance of his function as chief executive, and especially as commander in chief of the nation's armed forces. That is to say, whatever privileges we accord to the president are due to his importance to us. Whatever is unequal in the structure of authority in a free society is in the service of the equal rights of all. In an army, the life of the general is not more precious than the life of the private. But the necessities of command, upon which the safety and effectiveness of the entire army depend (just as the safety of the nation depends upon its armed forces), require that the general remain out of the line of fire. This is the core meaning of "equality under the law" in a free society.

But how does unanimous and free consent turn itself into the active safeguard of the equal rights of individuals by government? Madison continues:

> But as the objects in view could not be attained, if every measure conducive to them required the consent of every member of the society, the theory further supposes, either that it was part of the original compact that the will of the majority was to be deemed the will of the whole, or that this was a law of nature, resulting from the nature of political society itself, the offspring of the natural wants of man.
>
> Whatever be the hypothesis of the origin of the *lex majoris partis,* it is evident that it operates as a plenary substitute of the will of the majority of the society for the will of the whole society; and that the sovereignty of the society as vested and exercisable by the majority, may do anything that could be *rightfully* done by the unanimous concurrence of the members; the reserved rights of individuals (of conscience for example) in becoming parties to the original compact being beyond the legitimate reach of sovereignty, wherever vested or however viewed.[84]

The requirement of unanimity of consent in the establishment of a body politic follows necessarily from the recognition of the natural equality of mankind and is necessary if the society is to be free. But the requirement of unanimity of consent to the measures of the government would defeat the purposes of those whose consent established it. Indeed, if such unanimity were possible, government itself would be unnecessary. (Recall Madison in the fifty-first *Federalist*: "If men were angels, no government would be necessary.") What then can be the ground for the legitimate action of government? The only possible answer is that "the will of the majority [must] be deemed the will of the whole." According to Madison, this might be regarded either as implicit in the original compact or as itself "a law of nature." We would suggest that the two alternatives are actually one and the same. Majority rule is a necessary consequence of the compact because a government, no less than an individual, if it is to preserve itself (or those for whom it acts), must be capable of being moved by a single will. That will cannot be the will of a minority, since that would imply a greater original right to rule in some of the original contracting members than in others. If such natural inequality existed, then legitimate government would arise from it, rather than from compact. No one needs the prior consent of his dog in order to become its master! Dogs recognize human beings as their natural superiors. Any such claim by man with respect to man, however, is a fraud.

Jefferson, in his first inaugural, says that it is a "sacred principle" that "the will of the majority is in all cases to prevail." In calling this principle sacred, Jefferson meant that minority rule is inconsistent with the primordial equality that underlies the original compact. No will other than that of the majority can be legitimate. Although the minority itself has no right to rule, it nonetheless has rights that limit the discretion of the majority in ruling. The majority may not prevail where it has no right to prevail. In Jefferson's memorable words, the will of the majority "to be rightful, must be reasonable," and the minority must "possess their equal rights, which equal laws must protect, and to violate which would be oppression."[85] The purpose of majority rule is to protect the equal rights of all. Whenever that proposition is not credible, free or constitutional government—government based on compact—breaks down. The rights of the minority must be seen as equal to the rights of the majority *because they are the same rights.* When the government acts to protect life, liberty, and property, the majority and the minority may differ as to how that protection may best be accomplished. But the majority may not deliberately pursue a policy of placing at risk the life, liberty, and property of the minority while safeguarding their own. This would violate the fundamental equality that was a necessary condition of the original compact.[86]

Free governments differ from unfree both in the equality of the security they provide to the rights of all citizens and in the security from interference they provide for what Madison calls "the reserved rights of individuals." These, he says, are "beyond the legitimate reach of sovereignty, wherever vested or however viewed." Madison here gives only the example of the rights of conscience. What he means by conscience is well represented by the opening words of the First Amendment: "Congress shall make no law respecting an establishment of religion, or prohibiting the free exercise thereof." We may also recall Jefferson's similar pronouncements in the *Notes on Virginia* in 1782:

> The error seems not sufficiently eradicated, that the operations of the mind, as well as the acts of the body, are subject to the coercion of the laws. But our rulers can have no authority over such natural rights, only as we have submitted to them. The rights of conscience we never submitted, we could not submit. We are answerable for them to our God. The legitimate powers of government extend to such acts only as are injurious to others.[87]

Of course, the operations of the mind extend to subjects other than those of conscience. In the Statute of Virginia for Religious Liberty of 1786, Jefferson wrote that "our civil rights have no dependence on our religious opinions, any more than our opinions in physics or geometry."[88] The persecutions of Galileo and Giordano Bruno were no doubt in Jefferson's mind, as were the innumerable immolations of religious martyrs. It is notorious that Jefferson remarked, in this context, that "it does me no injury for my neighbor to say there are twenty gods, or no God. It neither picks my pocket nor breaks my leg."[89] Some have taken this to suggest a purely materialist or even Hobbesian attitude toward religion and morality. In fact, it represents only Jefferson's hostility to sectarian conflict within the political arena, which only diminishes the necessary and just influence of religion upon the morals of the people. In his inaugural address, Jefferson speaks of his fellow citizens as

> enlightened by a benign religion, professed, indeed, and practiced in various forms, yet all of them inculcating honesty, truth, temperance, gratitude, and the love of man; acknowledging and adoring an overruling Providence, which by all its dispensations proves that it delights in the happiness of man here and his greater happiness hereafter.[90]

Nor must we ever forget Jefferson's apostrophe, in *Notes on Virginia*, concerning the relationship between the rights with which mankind has been endowed by the Creator and the providential order. Here is the source and archetype of Lincoln's second inaugural:

> And can the liberties of a nation be thought secure when we have removed their only firm basis, a conviction in the minds of the people that these liberties are of the gift of God? That they are not to be violated but with his wrath? Indeed I tremble for my country when I reflect that God is just; that his justice cannot sleep forever; that . . . an exchange of situation [between masters and slaves] is among possible events; that it may become probable by supernatural interference! The Almighty has no attribute which can take side with us in such a contest.[91]

Certainly Jefferson never believed for a moment that such thoughts as these ought to be coerced by law. Nevertheless, there seems little doubt that if Jefferson's neighbor said that there is no God, he would be saying what, on Jefferson's own authority, would tend to undermine the "only firm basis" of the "liberties of a nation." It would then be up to Jefferson to reason him out of such an opinion.

Madison, we noted, defined the limits of majority rule when he said that the majority "may do anything that could be *rightfully* done by the unanimous concurrence of the members." Madison himself emphasized the word "rightfully." Clearly, the rights of conscience and other reserved rights of individuals, being beyond the reach of sovereignty, are beyond the reach of the majority, even if there is not a single dissenting vote. An establishment of religion, for example, would be just as wrong in a community in which everyone belonged to the same faith as in one characterized by religious pluralism.

But Madison's limitation of majority rule does not refer *only* to reserved rights. As we have noted, Jefferson says that the people are independent of all "but moral law." If the "only firm basis" of the liberties of a nation is the "conviction in the minds of the people that [they] are of the gift of God," then respect for the rights of others ought to be looked upon as a duty to God. Not rights alone but the reciprocal relationship of rights and duties forms the "moral law" that a people, individually and collectively, must obey, if they are to expect "the blessings of liberty" from a "God [that] is just." Implicit in the natural rights doctrine of the Declaration of Independence is the rule laid down in the New Testament: "Therefore all things whatsoever ye would that men should do to you, do ye even so to them: for this is the law and the prophets."[92] As Jesus' admonition is addressed to all humanity, present and future, it presupposes necessarily, and as a self-evident truth, "that all men are created equal."[93] The following aphorism of Edmund Burke is one of which Churchill was fond: "The effect of liberty upon a people is that they may do as they please. We must see what it pleases them to do, before we risk congratulations."[94] There is here no ground for difference between Jefferson and Burke (nor between them and Abraham Lincoln).

We have seen that according to Madison, the principle of majority rule resulted "from the nature of political society itself, the offspring of the natural wants of man." In a letter to Daniel Webster, Madison repeated his familiar maxim: "It must not be forgotten that compact, express or implied, is the vital principle of free governments as contradistinguished from governments not free; and that a revolt against this principle leaves no choice but between anarchy and despotism."[95] The "natural wants" of mankind lead properly to, or seek their fulfillment in, compact and free government. Their denial leads to despotism or anarchy. What are these "natural wants"? It is important to understand "rights" and "wants" as two aspects of a single phenomenon. The two most celebrated statements of why men enter civil society, next to the Declaration of Independence itself, are the Bills of Rights of Virginia and Massachusetts, adopted in 1776 and 1780, respectively. By the first, it is affirmed

> That all men are by nature equally free and independent, and have certain rights, of which, when they enter into a state of society, they cannot by any compact deprive or divest their posterity; namely, the enjoyment of life and liberty, with the means of acquiring and possessing property, and pursuing and obtaining happiness and safety.

By the second it is said that

All men are born free and equal, and have certain natural, essential, and unalienable rights; among which may be reckoned the right of enjoying and defending their lives and liberties; that of acquiring, possessing, and protecting property; in fine, that of seeking and obtaining their safety and happiness.[96]

In these documents, as in the Declaration of Independence, safety and happiness are the alpha and omega of political life. To say that someone has a right to life is to say that he has a natural desire or want to preserve his life. All rightful authority is founded upon recognition of this desire or want as a right, and no authority can be rightful that does not recognize it and is not consistent with it. The right to life would be worthless, however, for someone without the liberty to acquire the means—that is to say, property—by which to defend and preserve it. And the right to acquire property would mean very little unless it resulted in secure possession. But life, liberty, and property together are not ends in themselves. In the Virginia and Massachusetts Bills of Rights, as in the Declaration, safety is the first of the ends or purposes of political life, but happiness is the end for which life, liberty, and property are wanted. Liberty and property come to sight as means to the preservation of life, but their enduring worth is in the service, not of mere life, but of the good or happy life. The natural wants or rights of man from which society springs are not random but ordered. And it is the natural order of these wants, directed toward their corresponding natural ends, that constitutes the architectonic principles of a society arising out of compact, properly understood.

In the foregoing, we have given an account of that compact that is the central idea in the Kentucky and Virginia Resolutions. This idea is nowhere articulated in the resolutions themselves, because the public to which they were addressed took the idea for granted. This moreover is the same compact that Madison, throughout his life, declared to be "the vital principle of free government." From this account we see that a free election, properly so called, can only decide questions for a people united by the terms of such a compact. No election, however free, can *rightfully* decide questions "beyond the legitimate reach of sovereignty, wherever vested or however viewed." Nor can even unanimous consent *rightfully* authorize what is inconsistent with the "great principles of right and wrong."

But suppose differences of opinion arise as to whether policies or institutions are, or are not, beyond "the legitimate reach of sovereignty," or whether proposed measures are, or are not, consistent with the "great principles of right and wrong"? What right does a majority have to insist upon its opinion? Obviously, the legitimate right of the majority to rule ought not to be a pretext for its ruling beyond the boundaries or against the principles authorized by the compact. On the other hand, what right does a minority have to declare that the majority is usurping powers not granted and therefore that the enactments in question are null and void? What assurance can there be that the minority is not using the doctrine of reserved powers as a pretext to obstruct the rightful will of the majority? Does the possibility that the majority may abuse the doctrine of majority rule or that the minority may abuse the doctrine of minority rights affect the intrinsic validity of these doctrines? Is a regime combining majority rule and minority rights at best a hypothetical, but not a practical, possibility?[97] "Our popular government has often been called an experiment," said Lincoln at the outset of the Civil War.[98] The conflict of 1861 is already visible in the dilemmas of 1798.

∼

The Kentucky Resolutions differed materially from those of Virginia, adopted a month later. These differences will be discussed in their proper place. For the moment we wish to look at them as joint expressions of the Republican partisanship that triumphed in the election of 1800 and as glosses upon the idea of a free election as the authoritative means, within a free society, for resolving partisan differences.

The towering historic significance of these resolutions arises not only because of their role in the election of 1800, and not only because of the uniqueness of this election in the history of free government, but also because they were used by South Carolina in 1833 to justify its claim of a right to nullify the tariffs of 1828 and 1832. The doctrines generated by the nullification crisis went on to become the ground of the right of secession claimed in 1860–61 by the eleven states that came to form the Confederacy, all of which refused to accept the results of the election of 1860. The importance of these resolutions arises further from the fact that those who drafted them, Jefferson and Madison, were, respectively, the author of the Declaration of Independence and the Father of the Constitution, as well as being the party chiefs of the coalition that carried the 1800 election. As political victors in that first watershed election, they went forward to two terms each as president of the United States. To understand why their electoral triumphs proved ambiguous must be at the heart of any attempt to understand the causes of the Civil War.

∼

In returning to the Kentucky Resolutions, we are struck by their inner and essential resemblance to the *Summary View,* as well as to the Declaration of Independence. Their dominant theme is the right of the people to resist oppression. Although they culminated in a free election that changed the government, it is not unambiguous that such a result was anticipated. The resemblance of the language of the Kentucky Resolutions to that of the *Summary View* suggests forcing the government to change rather than changing the government. And the resemblance to the Declaration of Independence suggests overthrowing the government if it does not change.

Jefferson writes in the initial resolution that the states had constituted "a general government for special purposes." We are reminded that *every* civil society arising from individual consent fits this description. Because individuals cannot adequately protect their lives, liberties, and properties, severally and separately, they combine to form government. In like manner, the states forming the Union could never have gained their independence severally and separately. Nor could the governments of the states, after independence, have provided the security, foreign or domestic, desired by their citizens without the Union. But the Union, under the Articles of Confederation, did not have powers adequate to fulfill the purposes for which it was formed.

We might compare government under the Articles to a hypothetical state constitution in which the government had the authority to levy taxes but not the power to collect them. The "advantage" of such a constitution would be that each individual could decide for himself whether the tax being levied was for a purpose within the government's delegated powers, in accordance with the compact.[99] The disadvantage is that as soon as one person refused to pay his taxes, either everyone else would refuse to pay until the recalcitrant paid, or everyone else would combine to use force against the recalcitrant. Strange to say, it was this latter alternative that Jefferson envisaged under the Articles, as in the following letter written from Paris during the Constitutional Convention:

> It has been so often said, as to be generally believed, that Congress have no power by the confederation [viz., under the Articles] to enforce anything, e.g. contributions of money. It was not necessary to give them that power expressly; they have it by the law of nature. When two nations make a compact, there results to each a power of compelling the other to execute it. Compulsion was never so easy as in our case, where a single frigate would soon levy on the commerce of any state the deficiency of its contributions.[100]

Jefferson writes in 1787 of the relationship of each state to the other states under the Articles of Confederation as that of "two nations" which have made "a compact." In the Kentucky Resolutions of 1798, as we have seen, he writes that each state had "acceded" to the "compact" of the Constitution of 1787, "its co-States forming, as to itself, the other party" and that these parties had "no common Judge." By the idiom of the compact theory, having "no common Judge" means being in a state of nature. But Jefferson in 1787 also said that each of these compacting parties, "by the law of nature," had "a power of compelling the other to execute it." That of course follows from the premise that where there is "no common Judge," the "executive power" of the law of nature remains with each.[101] Jefferson was saying in 1787, as he would a decade later, that a government under a constitution might be made to function as it was intended to function. The right of nature, under the natural law, here appears as an implicit element of the constitutional order. There is no question but that in this, Jefferson tended to obscure—with dire consequences after his death—the distinction between nullification and secession as constitutional rights under the positive law, and nullification and secession as manifestations of the right of resistance to intolerable oppression under the natural law.

In 1787, Jefferson declared the right of the government of the Union to use compulsion on a state that failed in its constitutional obligations. In 1798, he implied the right of a state to use compulsion against the government of the Union should it fail in its constitutional obligations. Considering the later appeal by the nullifiers and secessionists to the authority of Jefferson in the Kentucky Resolutions, one should note that this appeal to natural right was a justification of the use of force *by either side* upon the other. From the perspective of Jefferson's 1787 letter, the right of coercion of the Union by a state has no more constitutional standing than the coercion of a state by the Union.

This relationship of mutual coercion between each state and the general government was what Jefferson envisaged in the first resolution of Kentucky. When men are under government, they have a common judge. This is not the case in the state of nature, where a dispute over property ownership, for example, can be settled only by the parties to the controversy, and more often than not by force. In the state of nature, there is no impartial way to decide whether someone is rightfully defending his own or attempting unjustly to take what is another's. But the jurisprudence of a civilized people—that is to say, a people voluntarily formed into government by compact—is designed to secure objectivity and fairness in both criminal and civil procedures. For this reason, judges should be independent both of the parties in controversy and of the political branches of government. Juries are selected with a view to their independence, not only of the parties in controversy, but also of preconceived opinions concerning the facts that they are called on to determine. Everyone knows that unfailing perfection in such procedures is not to be expected and that from time to time there will be miscarriages of justice. But failings are reasons for correcting errors and striving for greater perfection, not for overturning the system that provides for the administration of justice. Of course, when such a system is systematically and notoriously perverted by bribery, intimidation, or other malfeasance, the system itself may no longer answer the purposes for which it was established. But until that moment it cannot be said that men have "no common judge."

What has been said about the administration of justice applies equally to the process of legislation. Madison writes in the tenth *Federalist* that

> No man is allowed to be a judge in his own cause because his interest would certainly bias his judgment, and, not improbably, corrupt his integrity. With equal, nay with greater reason, a body of men are unfit to be both judges and parties at the same time; yet what are many of the most important acts of legislation, but so many judicial determinations, not indeed of the rights of single persons, but concerning the rights of large bodies of citizens?

Where men are judges in their own causes is precisely what is meant by the state of nature, because there is "no common judge." But consider the case of a majority faction, defined by Madison in the same tenth *Federalist* as "united and actuated by some common impulse of passion or of interest, adverse to the rights of other citizens, or to the permanent and aggregate interests of the community."[102] In such a case the state of nature may be said to have recurred, as surely as in a judicial system in which judges and juries may be bribed with impunity. In the forty-seventh *Federalist*, Madison asserts that "No political truth is . . . of greater intrinsic value" than that "The accumulation of all powers, legislative, executive, and judiciary, in the same hands, whether of one, few, or many, and whether hereditary, self-appointed, or elective, may justly be pronounced the very definition of tyranny."[103] In *Federalist* 48, Madison cites the passage we have previously discussed in the *Notes on Virginia*, in which Jefferson declared that "An elective despotism was not the government we fought for." Jefferson had pointed out that Virginia's constitution of 1776, to which he took such exception (and under which he had held the office of governor), was one that

> laid its foundation on this basis, that the legislative, executive, and judiciary departments should be separate and distinct, so that no person should exercise the powers of more than one of them at the same time. *But no barrier was provided between these several powers.*[104]

These passages in the *Federalist* (including the quotation of Jefferson) recognize that tyranny may arise from republican election as well as from nonrepublican modes of choosing governments. But nowhere is it declared or acknowledged that the only or proper response to the tyranny of elected officials is to vote them out at the next election. The sole recognized response to usurpation of authority, whether by elected or nonelected officials, is—in one form or another—resistance.

The tyranny of the majority, exercised through the electoral and legislative process, can apparently endanger the equal natural rights of the citizens as much as the subornation of justice in the judicial system: "When a majority is included in a faction, the form of popular government . . . enables it to sacrifice to its ruling passion or interest both the public good and the rights of other citizens."[105] Madison is best known for his theory of the extended republic as the means for preventing such tyranny. He discovers the remedy first of all in the distinction he draws between democratic and republican government, the former being one in which the people meet "in person," the latter being one in which they act through "representatives and agents."[106] The latter can comprehend much larger territories and populations in which a greater diversity of interests, passions, and opinions can be found. And the greater this diversity, the less the likelihood of a homogeneous majority being formed that is dangerous to the rights of minorities. In the federal republic of the United States, Madison writes, "all authority . . . will be derived from and dependent on the society . . . [while] society itself will be broken into so many parts, interests and classes of citizens, that the rights of individuals, or of the minority, will be in little danger from interested combinations of the majority." But Madison's argument does not depend altogether upon this social and economic fragmentation for the defense of individual and minority rights.

> In the compound republic of America, the power surrendered by the people is first divided between two distinct governments, and then the portion allotted to each subdivided among distinct and separate departments. Hence a double security arises to the rights of the people. The different governments will control each other, at the same time that each will be controlled by itself.[107]

Separation of powers, in which ambition counteracts ambition and the interest of each officeholder acts as the guardian of the constitutional rights of his place, is the means by which governments control themselves. Federalism, by which the power surrendered by the people is divided between two distinct governments, provides the means by which the "different governments will control each other."

In the *Federalist*, the control exercised by the states over the federal government is said to arise from the fact that

> each of the principal branches of the federal government will owe its existence more or less to the favor of the State governments, and must consequently feel a dependence, which is much more likely to beget a disposition too obsequious than too overbearing towards them. On the other side, the component parts of

the State governments will in no instance be indebted for their appointment to the direct agency of the federal government.[108]

One can hardly imagine how the Madison of the *Federalist* would have responded, except with incredulity, had it been suggested to him that in less than eleven years he himself would declare that it was necessary for the states to "interpose" their authority to prevent the transformation of the United States "into an absolute, or, at best, mixed monarchy." Yet the formal possibility is nonetheless considered in the *Federalist*:

> [A]mbitious encroachments of the federal government on the authority of the state governments would not excite the opposition of a single State, or a few States only. They would be signals of general alarm. Every government would espouse the common cause. A correspondence would be opened. Plans of resistance would be concerted. One spirit would animate and conduct the whole. The same combinations, in short, would result from an apprehension of the federal, as was produced by the dread of a foreign yoke; and unless the projected innovations should be voluntarily renounced, the same appeal to a trial of force would be made in the one case as was made in the other.[109]

Except that the Kentucky and Virginia Resolutions did not quite represent a "general alarm," this is a remarkable anticipation of those two states' reactions to the Alien and Sedition Acts. But it is the improbability of such "encroachments," not the manner of resistance to them, that is the dominant theme of this paragraph in the forty-sixth *Federalist*:

> But what degree of madness could ever drive the federal government to such an extremity? In the contest with Great Britain, one part of the empire was employed against the other. The more numerous part invaded the rights of the less numerous part. The attempt was unjust and unwise; but it was not in speculation absolutely chimerical. But what would be the contest in the case we are supposing? Who would be the parties? A few representatives of the people would be opposed to the people themselves; or rather one set of representatives would be contending against thirteen sets of representatives, with the whole body of their common constituents on the side of the latter.[110]

Here Madison does not foresee the possibility of such strongly held differences of constitutional interpretation as those that divided Jefferson and Hamilton in 1791 concerning the Bank of the United States. He did not apparently foresee that one man's "necessary and proper" lawmaking might become another man's usurpations. The plausibility of these rival views of the Constitution surely indicated that they called for debate and voting and not the exercise of resistance founded in the right of revolution. That Madison, even in the *Federalist*, foresaw resistance, is all the more surprising when we remember that he was at that very moment in the midst of the struggle over ratification, in which both sides professed devotion to the principles of the Revolution. Yet the Anti-Federalists saw the proposed Constitution as an encroachment upon the rights of the states and the people, while the Federalists saw it as a means for rectifying the weaknesses of a government radically inadequate for securing those same rights.

Madison's rhetoric in the forty-sixth *Federalist* is also remarkable for seeing the hypothetical conflict between the federal government and the states under the Constitution as not different in kind from the recent "contest with Great Britain." Although Madison denies any probability of such a conflict, he anticipates the Jefferson of the Kentucky Resolutions in seeing potential usurpations by constitutionally elected officials to be as dangerous to liberty as the usurpations of the British Crown and Parliament. And this, notwithstanding the fact that Americans had no agency in choosing their British rulers nor any constitutional means of vetoing their actions or removing them from office!

Like Jefferson in 1798, the Madison of the forty-sixth *Federalist* foresees the same kind of resistance by the people to their own elected officials as to the agents of the British Crown and Parliament. And he assumes the same unanimity of the people in resisting the "ambitious encroachments" of their own representatives that Jefferson attributed to "all American whigs" during the Revolution. In the extraordinary means of resistance described in *Federalist* 46, the role of free elections in deciding political-constitutional differences, to which Lincoln will appeal in 1861, is not visible.[111]

∿

The Virginia Resolutions are a confession by their author that the "inventions of prudence" he had celebrated in the fifty-first *Federalist*,[112] as promising an exemption from the abuses of power that had plagued previous republican governments had failed.[113] Let us now examine the precise charges by both Kentucky and Virginia with respect to those failures. Our initial citations will be to Virginia.

The Alien and Sedition Acts were condemned on two counts: first, for violating the principles of American federalism, as distinctly and expressly set forth in the Tenth Amendment, by usurping powers that are reserved by the Constitution to the states or to the people; and, second, for subverting "the general principles of free government." The Alien Act was said to subvert these general principles "by uniting legislative and judicial powers to those of the executive," and the Sedition Act "because it is leveled against the right of freely examining public characters and measures, and of free communication among the people thereon, which has ever been justly deemed the only effectual guardian of every other right."[114]

The Alien Act was thus condemned as violating the constitutional principle of separation of powers in a way that *Federalist* 47 said might "justly be pronounced the very definition of tyranny." Madison was at pains, in that number of the *Federalist*, to refute the objection that the Constitution insufficiently separated the powers of government. In fact, he argued, a partial agency of each department in the powers of the others was necessary to make the separation effective. But the principle of separation of powers is intrinsic to free government and belongs to it by its very nature.

In like manner, the Sedition Act, by violating the Constitution's protection of free speech, also violated a principle that is natural or intrinsic to free government. Freedom of speech is presented here not as an end in itself but as an indispensable means to all the ends of free government.[115] As rights indispensable to the functioning of free government, freedom of speech and of association require and impose obligations that are antecedent to positive law and that must be fulfilled if free government is to exist.

In response to such abuses of power, the Virginia Resolutions appear on their face to contemplate measures far less drastic than those anticipated in *Federalist* 46:

> [I]n case of a deliberate, palpable, and dangerous exercise of other powers not granted by the said compact [viz., the Constitution], the states, who are parties thereto, have the right and are in duty bound to interpose for arresting the progress of the evil, and for maintaining within their respective limits the authorities, rights, and liberties appertaining to them.[116]

Madison later insisted that it was the "states" (plural) whose collective constitutional right to "interpose" he had in mind, and not that of a single state (as South Carolina would claim in its 1832 Ordinance of Nullification).

"Deliberate, palpable, and dangerous" puts us in mind of "the long train of abuses" in the Declaration of Independence. But it also reminds us of the "prudence" in the Declaration that dictates that governments "should not be changed for light and transient causes." We are obliged to remember that the Alien and Sedition Acts enacted in 1798 would expire in 1801 and that congressional and presidential elections would be held even before then. Although the Kentucky Resolutions, unlike the Virginia Resolutions, asserted a right of "each state . . . to judge for itself as well of the infractions as of the mode and measure of redress," this right was asserted not as a constitutional right but as a "natural right." As such, it was a manifestation of the right of revolution that underlies all free government. The Kentucky Resolutions end more tamely than they began, asking "co-states" to join in denouncing the Alien and Sedition Acts and "requesting their repeal at the next session of Congress." Considering the contempt Jefferson had poured on the "men of our choice" for their "tyranny" in the body of the resolutions, not to mention the threats of "revolution and blood," this conclusion may seem somewhat lame.[117] Similarly, the end of the Virginia Resolutions contains no appeal to the allegedly tyrannical Congress to reverse itself but calls on other states to join "in declaring . . . that the acts aforesaid are unconstitutional" and to cooperate "in maintaining unimpaired the authorities, rights, and liberties reserved to the states respectively or to the people."[118] Exactly what form this cooperation was to take is left deliberately and necessarily obscure. It was necessarily obscure because the case itself—the case of a freely elected government enacting laws alleged to be destructive of free government—was unprecedented. Madison's most pregnant comment on the Virginia Resolutions, in the "Report of 1799–1800," was that they were "expressions of opinion, unaccompanied with any other effect than what they may produce on opinion, by exciting reflection." Such effect, he hopes, "may lead to a change in the legislative expression of the general will."[119] In short, both Jefferson and Madison seem in the end to have expected the Kentucky and Virginia Resolutions to alter the offending behavior of Congress either by electoral pressure or by electoral change. In this, they point to elections as the mode of resolving questions that had hitherto been resolved, if they were resolved at all, only by revolution.

Yet elections are not, in and of themselves, an alternative to "blood and revolution." The threat or menace of revolution remains an integral element of the pressure brought to bear in and through the electoral process. That threat or menace, however, consists less in the fear of the force that might be brought to bear than in the reminder of the role of the right of revolution in the theory on which the American Revolution was grounded. In the forty-third *Federalist*, Madison justified the departure of the Constitutional Convention from the instructions of the Congress of the Articles of Confederation by an appeal "to the transcendent law of nature and of nature's God, which declares that the safety and happiness of society are the objects at which all political institutions aim, and to which all such institutions must be sacrificed."[120] The appeal by the *Federalist* for the adoption of the Constitution of 1787 is in part an appeal to the law of nature against the positive law of the then existing constitution, the Articles of Confederation. The *Federalist* itself appears as campaign literature in an electoral process, the process of ratification, and as such was meant to produce only an effect on opinion, by exciting reflection. Its appeal to the right of revolution is purely peaceful and rational. Madison in the *Federalist* legitimates subsequent appeals, such as those in the Kentucky and Virginia Resolutions, against the very government whose adoption he is recommending. These appeals are at once revolutionary, threatening, peaceful, and rational. The natural right of revolution, we may say, is the right whose recognition and understanding are supremely necessary if "reflection and choice" are to replace "accident and force" in the government of mankind. The appeals to this right in 1798 were laying a foundation for an unprecedented transfer of power by free election.

◇

Jefferson's inaugural address of 1801 is a commentary on what he and the American people had learned in the election of 1800 about the nature of elections as the arbiter of deep divisions among the citizens of a free polity and as a rational and legitimate mode of transferring power without violence. As we observed at the outset, that election was unique in human history. In the Revolution, the differences between American Whigs and Tories were decided by the sword. In the struggle over ratification of the Constitution, differences were fought out within the ratifying conventions, and those struggles differed from state to state. There was no nationwide referendum, although there emerged something like a nationwide consensus once the Constitution went into effect, especially after the adoption of the Bill of Rights. Henceforth, the kinds of differences that appeared in the debates over ratification reappeared as differences over the interpretation of the Constitution and in that way contributed to the rise of parties.

Jefferson speaks as follows of this world-historical event of 1800:

> During the contest of opinion through which we have passed, the animation of discussion and of exertions has sometimes worn an aspect which might impose on strangers unused to think freely and to speak and to write what they think; but this being now decided by the voice of the nation, announced according to the rules of the Constitution, all will, of course, arrange themselves under the will of the law, and unite in common efforts for the common good.[121]

Certainly no one had contributed more to the "animation of discussion" than Jefferson himself. Yet we find him here tactfully deprecating that "aspect" of such animation as it might appear to "strangers" unaccustomed to the turbulence of freedom. As we have noted, the party warfare of the 1790s was as bitter as our nation has seen. Both sides presented their differences as if they were the same kinds of differences that divided American Whigs and Tories in the Revolution. Nothing illustrates that better than the passages in the Kentucky Resolutions that so closely resembled the Declaration of Independence. In present-day parlance, both parties presented the contest as a zero-sum enterprise in which the advantages of one side were losses to the other. From this viewpoint, ballots can never really substitute for bullets. In the sarcasm that Jefferson in the Kentucky Resolutions had poured on the "men of our choice," he went far toward belittling ballots. Now, however, to use one of his own metaphors, he is merely a new pilot putting the republican ship on an opposite tack.

If losing an election is like losing a war, then those who lose the election will retain the option of going to war—which was, of course, what happened in 1861. Jefferson's inaugural address had as its purpose, as Lincoln's would in 1861, to convince the American people that in losing the election, no one had lost a war. He presented the election of 1800 as a contest to decide which of two competing parties represented the majority. He reminded the country that under their compact it had been agreed in advance that the majority would rule and that the minority was morally bound to accept such rule. He also reminded the majority, which was his own party and which he more than anyone else represented, that its rule was limited and that the principle of majority rule in no way sanctioned violations of the equal rights of the minority. We repeat the celebrated—but ambiguous—passage: "All, too, will bear in mind this sacred principle, that though the will of the majority is in all cases to prevail, that will, to be rightful, must be reasonable; that the minority possess their equal rights, which equal laws must protect, and to violate which would be oppression."[122]

Prior to the 1800 election, each side had accused the other of intentions incompatible with the safety of their equal rights. The Federalists had called the Republicans "democrats," implying thereby a kinship to the Jacobins of the French Revolution, whose Committee of Public Safety had ruthlessly guillotined and expropriated anyone they called "enemies of the people." The Republicans had called the Federalists "monocrats," implying a kinship with the crowned heads of Europe who were even then conspiring to restore the French monarchy in defiance of the will of the French people. Jefferson in his inaugural is at great pains to repudiate these characterizations (including his own).

> Let us, then, fellow-citizens, unite with one heart and one mind. Let us restore to social intercourse that harmony and affection without which liberty and even life itself are but dreary things. And let us reflect that having banished from our land that religious intolerance under which mankind so long bled and suffered, we have yet gained little if we countenance a political intolerance as despotic, as wicked, and capable of as bitter and bloody persecutions.[123]

We are put in mind here of Lincoln's poignant appeal to friendship at the end of his first inaugural address, sixty years later. And we note the kinship of this passage with the following in the *Nicomachean Ethics*:

> Friendship seems to hold political communities together, and lawgivers to care
> more for it than justice; for unanimity seems to be something like justice, and this
> they aim at most of all, and expel faction as their worst enemy; and when men are
> friends they have no need of justice, while when they are just they need friend-
> ship as well, and the truest form of justice is thought to be a friendly quality.[124]

Aristotle's "unanimity" and Jefferson's "one heart and one mind" remind us that
an original unanimous agreement is the foundation of the compact and of majority rule. That is to say, the majority may do only those things that have, in principle, been agreed to in advance by everyone.

According to the Whig theory of the American Revolution, the ground of
friendship among republican citizens is to be found in the nature of the social
compact, "by which the whole people covenants with each citizen and each citizen with the whole people, that all shall be governed [by the majority] by certain
laws for the common good." These words from the Massachusetts Bill of Rights of
1780, which we have cited before, were written by John Adams, the man Jefferson defeated for the presidency in the election of 1800 (having himself defeated
Jefferson in 1796). Adams and Jefferson had been close friends during the Revolution, and the correspondence in which they would one day record the resump-
tion of that friendship is one of the precious legacies of the American people. The
poignancy of their separation by the party battles of the 1790s underlies the noble
passage on restoring harmony and affection in Jefferson's inaugural. Among the
others divided by the politics of the 1790s were Hamilton and Madison, foremost
among the promoters of the Constitutional Convention and principal coauthors
of the *Federalist*. The party warfare divided men who had fought shoulder to
shoulder in the Revolution, and it is essentially the principles of the Revolution,
the principles of unanimous consent embodied in the social compact, to which
Jefferson appeals in arguing for the restoration of friendship. Their differences, he
is saying, ought to be looked upon as arising within the boundaries of these common principles.

Jefferson's classic formulation of the relationship between majority rule and
minority rights appears on its face as a conundrum. When men are passionately
opposed to each other, the majority sees the minority as obstructing its sacred
right to prevail, and the minority sees the majority as bent upon violating its
equally sacred inviolable rights. Who is to define the equal rights of the minority
and the limits of majority rule? Jefferson's answer is contained in his Aristotelian
appeal to unanimity and friendship. In writing that friends "have no need of justice," whereas just men "need friendship as well," Aristotle alludes to the saying
that friends have all things in common. Legal justice is to be found in the "thine"
and "mine" marked out by the laws of private property. But a true friend regards

his own property as being as much at the disposal of his friend as of himself. No amount of wealth can dispense with someone's need for friends; indeed, says Aristotle, one of the principal reasons for wanting wealth is to place it at the disposal of friends. Without that friendly feeling that transcends justice, there can be no true community, and without true community, justice goes against the grain of men's inclinations. When human beings come into conflict, passion blinds them to what they have in common, and reason must be restored to its throne. In the political process, there is no arbiter between majority and minority. Unless the conditions exist by which they can be brought to an agreement among themselves, free government is not possible. The problem is to secure those conditions.

The difficulty presented by this appeal to friendship and community is that the American republic, under the Constitution, is a community of communities, a nation of states. Can the bonds of human fellowship that extend outward from the family to the tribe and to the collection of tribes that was the ancient city—which is what Aristotle, like all ancient lawgivers, had in mind—extend as far as the experiment of American republicanism required? Yet Aristotle himself identifies the origin of civic friendship in the philanthropy that nature has planted in us as members of our species, with respect to which, it can be said, "all men are created equal."

> [P]arent seems by nature to feel it for offspring and offspring for parent, not only among men but among birds and among most animals; it is felt mutually by members of the same race, and especially by men, whence we praise lovers of their fellow men [literally, philanthropists]. We may see even in our travels how near and dear every man is to every other.[125]

When we sit at home, we think of races and nations far distant as if they were beings of a different kind. But when we travel, we discover the humanity that is in fact common to all members of our species. That is to say, however limited by time and place the number of our actual friends, we should look upon all men as potential friends. American citizenship draws upon the unity of man's humanity for the unity, the *e pluribus unum*, of a nation of states.

Aristotle regards unanimity (literally, "oneness of mind") as the good, greater than justice, that draws men towards justice. Similarly he regards faction as the evil, equal and opposite to unanimity, that drives men to injustice. But what about the celebration of "faction" in *Federalist* 10 and 51? Does not Madison's acceptance of faction as a normal and necessary attribute of a free society place American republicanism on an entirely different footing from Aristotle's classical republicanism?

First, let us notice that Madison agrees with Aristotle that "the violence of faction" has been the bane of republics: "The friend of popular governments never finds himself so much alarmed for their character and fate, as when he contemplates their propensity to this dangerous vice." The Madison of the tenth *Federalist* would say, however, that the appeal to friendship to moderate factionalism in previous republics has never succeeded. It is the reconstitution of republicanism through the combination of representation and federalism that will enable better motives to succeed. The extended republic will comprehend such a "variety of parties and interests" as to make a majority faction improbable. This invention of prudence, however, is not conceived as a replacement for friendship or, in general, for better motives but rather as a means to make it possible for such motives to prevail. Hence the ending of *Federalist* 10: "In the extent and structure of the Union . . . we behold a republican remedy for the diseases most incident to republican government. And according to the degree of pleasure and pride we feel in being republicans, ought to be our zeal in cherishing the spirit, and supporting the character of federalists."[126] Considering the extraordinary attention that the tenth *Federalist* has received in the literature of American political science, Madison's reference to the "diseases" of republican government bears special notice. The medical analogy, which he shares with Lincoln as well as Aristotle, reminds us that removing disease is only a condition for healthy activities. It does not by itself tell us what health is.

We anticipate the progress of Jefferson's argument in noting what is perhaps the best-known sentence in his first inaugural: "We are all republicans—we are all federalists."[127] We see this foreshadowed at the end of the tenth *Federalist,* where the solution to the problem of faction is said to lie in the multiplication of factions that takes place in the extended republic.[128] In short, the interdependence of republicanism and federalism not only serves to control faction but also becomes a ground for promoting friendship among the citizens.

It is true that the meaning of federalism and republicanism as party labels was not in 1787 what it had become in 1801, after a decade of bitter political conflict under the new constitution. In the interval, the idea and function of a political party had taken a different shape and form. From being virtually synonymous with faction (as in Washington's Farewell Address), "party" became for the Republicans an organization of citizens against monarchism and other forms of antirepublicanism, and thus the antithesis of faction. Those who were "partisans" in this post-1800 Jeffersonian and Madisonian sense did not think of themselves as permanently organized to choose candidates, frame platforms, and conduct campaigns—in short, to conduct the political business of the republic. This became true of what has been called the second (or two-party) American party system that came into being after 1832. But the arguments against the Alien and Sedition Acts were not arguments as to which of two (or more) alternative policies ought to be pursued. They were arguments from principles that could not be compromised if the United States was to retain the republican form of government guaranteed to each of the states by Article IV of the Constitution. The Republican Party of 1800 had been called into existence, according to its own understanding of itself, to save the Republic from an attempt to "change its republican form." If its victory put an end to that danger, it would put an end as well to the need for the party. Political parties were not yet seen as permanent features of the political system, because the questions that produced them in the 1790s were not thought to be permanent features of political life.

In his inaugural, Jefferson places his disagreement with the Alien and Sedition Acts in this light:

> During the throes and convulsions of the ancient world, during the agonizing spasms of infuriated man, seeking through blood and slaughter his long lost liberty, it was not wonderful that the agitation of the billows should reach even this distant and peaceful shore; that this should be more felt and feared by some and less by others; that this should divide opinions as to measures of safety.

Henry Adams remarked on the exuberant delight among the Federalist wits in noting how Jefferson's "spasms" turned into "billows."[129] Here, however, is Jefferson's recognition (absent from the Kentucky Resolutions) that American reaction to the French Revolution was responsible for the division of opinion that centered upon the Alien and Sedition Acts. He admits that these acts might be regarded, whether wisely or not, as "measures of safety." They need not then have been regarded, as Jefferson regarded them in the Kentucky Resolutions, as merely willful usurpations of powers not granted by the compact. The divisions in American opinion that followed the French Revolution would be repeated by similar divisions more than a century later, following the Bolshevik Revolution. Whether measures limiting the liberties of alleged sympathizers with Jacobinism or with Communism are subterfuges to suppress freedom or are expressions of legitimate concern for security is a never ending debate. Jefferson here indicates that both points of view are possible and implies that he himself had gone too far in attributing only antirepublican motives to those who had promoted the Alien and Sedition Acts. Hence, he continues,

> every difference of opinion is not a difference of principle. We have called by different names brethren of the same principle. We are all republicans—we are all federalists. If there be any among us who would wish to dissolve this Union or to change its republican form, let them stand undisturbed as monuments to the safety with which error of opinion may be tolerated where reason is left free to combat it.[130]

The bulk of the opposition, then, were honest citizens, even if they were mistaken. They differed with Republicans over what the public safety required, but they were not for that reason antirepublican. Jefferson in his inaugural is extending the hand of friendship to his defeated rivals. In so doing, however, he is shrewdly inviting them to become his fellow partisans in a more broadly based party, thereby isolating the more radical and uncompromising Federalists. The election just ended was extremely close. By embracing the "uncorrupted" Federalists, Jefferson was helping to assure that the next election would not be close—as it was not.[131] With the ascendancy of Republicanism, the electoral process was gaining a dignity in Jefferson's eyes that it did not have in 1798. Then, his Kentucky Resolutions poured scorn upon "the men of our choice" and held out the threat of "blood and revolution." Now, the right of revolution begins to recede into the background. We begin to perceive in elections the authority that Lincoln invoked when he said there could be no appeal from the decision of ballots, except to ballots themselves, at future elections.

Jefferson speaks of those who differ in opinion but not in principle as opposed to those who would dissolve the Union or change its republican form. Of the latter he says, in a memorable phrase that bears much repetition, "let them stand undisturbed as monuments of the safety with which error of opinion may be tolerated where reason is left free to combat it." Civil libertarians of a later age have invoked this passage as testimony to the proposition that First Amendment rights to free speech must encompass "freedom for the thought we hate." Whatever the merits of this proposition, Jefferson's words here lend no support to it. Jefferson is supporting the view that the victors in the election should not persecute the losers, which is essential to the idea of replacing bullets with ballots. But Jefferson is all the while isolating those whose thought he hates, rendering their thought more impotent by the very fact of tolerating it. Toleration of antirepublicanism is therefore a dictate of prudence rather than the recognition of a right.

Jefferson says that error may be tolerated where reason is left free to combat it. The republican cause is grounded in reason, antirepublicanism in unreason. Human beings are by nature rational and political beings; hence republicanism is the natural consequence of the emancipation of human reason. The Alien and Sedition Acts were predicated upon the hypothesis that the government had to protect itself by jailing or deporting certain of its critics. But Jefferson says that this is absurd: The critics would have little influence against the natural affinity of a free people for a free government. "The republican is the only form of government which is not eternally at open or secret war with the rights of mankind," he had written in 1790.[132] A republican government has every reason to have confidence in the loyalty of its citizens, because they can have no rational interest in any other kind.

I know, indeed, that some honest men fear that a republican government cannot be strong; that this government is not strong enough. But would the honest patriot, in the full tide of successful experiment, abandon a government which has so far kept us free and firm, on the theoretic and visionary fear that this government, the world's best hope, may possibly want energy to preserve itself? I trust not.

Jefferson's rhetorical question became anything but rhetorical in 1861, as illustrated by the passage from Lincoln that stands as the epigraph to this chapter. For Jefferson, the victory of republicanism—and the isolation of antirepublicanism—in the election of 1800 was a sufficient rebuke to the doubters. "I believe this, on the contrary, the strongest government on earth. I believe it is the only one where every man, at the call of the laws, would fly to the standard of the law, and would meet invasions of the public order as his own personal concern." Jefferson does not contemplate a rebellion by disgruntled monarchists. There was no need to suppress them because there was no need to fear them. If there were need, the people would fight to preserve a government that they recognized as embodying their will. "Sometimes it is said that man cannot be trusted with the government of himself. Can he, then, be trusted with the government of others? Or have we found angels in the forms of kings to govern us? Let history answer this question."[133] These words echo constantly in the speeches of Abraham Lincoln. The rule of masters over slaves and that of kings over peoples are but two varieties of what he called "the same old serpent." Both presuppose that the nature of the ruler differs from the nature of the ruled, as the nature of the horse differs from the nature of the rider. Although the threat in the Kentucky Resolutions that the policies of antirepublican Federalists might "drive these states into revolution and blood" was not borne out by events, this section of the inaugural must remind us of Jefferson's far more portentous prophecy, in the *Notes on Virginia*, of a civil war arising from the sin of domestic black slavery.[134]

The interest that citizens of a republic have in their own freedom from monarchical or despotic rule does not extend automatically to an interest in the emancipation of those over whom they themselves may rule despotically. In 1786 Jefferson lamented the failure of Congress to outlaw slavery in a bill for the organization of the Western Territory—an omission that was in fact repaired the next year in the great Northwest Ordinance. Furthermore, as we have already noted, Jefferson fully recognized that domestic black slavery in America was of a higher order of evil than the slavery denounced in the revolt against the tea tax or the stamp tax.[135] Someone may ask, then, why Jefferson made no direct reference in his inaugural address to that negation of the compact, which clearly represented the ultimate challenge to the idea of a natural right to freedom and the ultimate danger to republicanism. Here we might apply to Jefferson (as we might in some respects apply it to Lincoln himself) the following excerpt from Lincoln's eulogy of Henry Clay:

> He was ever, on principle and feeling, opposed to slavery. The very earliest, and one of the latest public efforts of his life, separated by a period of more than fifty years, were both made in favor of gradual emancipation of the slaves in Kentucky. He did not perceive, that on a question of human right, the negroes were to be excepted from the human race. And yet Mr. Clay was the owner of slaves. Cast into life where slavery was already widely spread and deeply seated, he did not perceive, as I think no wise man has perceived, how it could be at *once* eradicated, without producing a greater evil, even to the cause of human liberty itself.[136]

When Jefferson delivered his first inaugural, the Northwest Ordinance had settled the slavery question insofar as it was a federal question. And for Jefferson and Clay and Lincoln—and indeed for everyone except the most radical abolitionists—the status of slavery within each state was placed by the Constitution exclusively within the jurisdiction of that state. Slavery does not have the overt prominence in Jefferson's inaugural that it would have in Lincoln's. There were no urgent political questions concerning slavery in 1801, as there would be following the repeal of the Missouri Compromise in 1854. Absent a federal question, for Lincoln and for Jefferson, the proper forum for the discussion of emancipation was within each of the states in which it was a lawful institution. Once Illinois (following the decree of the Northwest Ordinance) had outlawed slavery within its borders, Lincoln's duties with respect to slavery as a citizen of Illinois were, as he saw them, at an end.

The ultimate importance of the question of slavery, however, can hardly be said to have been absent from Jefferson's inaugural. When he spoke of "infuriated man, seeking through blood and slaughter his long lost liberty," the reference, although ostensibly to the French Revolution, certainly put his hearers in mind of dangers closer to home. Elsewhere, including in *Notes on Virginia*, Jefferson had warned repeatedly that if the slaves in America were not emancipated by their masters in a timely and opportune way, emancipation would come about by a different agency and through unimaginable violence and suffering. Yet the ultimate and all-encompassing reason why the slaves had to be freed, for Jefferson and for Lincoln, was that the denial of their natural rights would equally justify the denial of those rights to their masters. Jefferson and Lincoln both held that there was no power in human reason to justify the enslavement of one human being that would not equally justify the enslavement of any other. Conversely, there was no power in human reason that could justify the freedom of one man that would not equally justify the freedom of any other. It was the appeal to these rights that formed the core of the case presented to a "candid world" in the Declaration of Independence. One could not consistently address the world, which included all the races of mankind, in the name of these rights while restricting their application. Yet on the eve of the Civil War, those who maintained that slavery was a positive good declared that freedom belonged by nature to some but not to others. The followers of Senator Stephen A. Douglas did not say that slavery was a positive good but regarded it as a matter of moral indifference, subject to the sacred right of "popular sovereignty." Lincoln would climb to the prominence that enabled him to become president by insisting that there was no such middle ground as Douglas proposed to occupy, between declaring slavery a positive good and declaring it evil.

Nearing the end of his days, Jefferson replied to a young lady correspondent, Fanny Wright, that the subject of her letter to him, on ways and means to bring about emancipation, "has been through life that of my greatest anxieties." "The march of events," he added, "has not been such as to render its completion practicable within the limits of time allotted to me; and I leave its accomplishment as the work of another generation."[137]

When Jefferson in his inaugural asked if there were angels in the form of kings to govern mankind, his rhetorical question applied to any human being who would govern another without his consent, to slave owners no less than to crowned heads. The problem of human government arises from the fact that the nature of rulers and the nature of the ruled is one and the same. That "all men are created equal" means not only that all men have been equally endowed with certain rights by their Creator but also that they have been endowed by that same Creator with a nonangelic nature. The myth that those who govern are, or may be, of a nature superior to those they govern is the root of tyranny. "All men are created equal" contains in itself the first principle of the rule of law and of constitutional government: that those who live under the law share in making the law and, conversely, that those who make the law live under the law. This signifies, however, that elections are not merely means by which it is decided who shall rule. It signifies that those who win elections shall be limited in their authority by the rule of law, protecting the equal rights of the minority and preserving the possibility of the minority becoming the majority in a future election.

In the last of their joint debates of 1858, Lincoln defined the issue between himself and Stephen Douglas as follows: "He contends that whatever community wants slaves has a right to have them. So they have if it is not a wrong. But if it is a wrong, he cannot say people have a right to do wrong."[138] Jefferson had denounced the divine right of kings as a fraud. Lincoln picked up where Jefferson had left off, in telling the people themselves—a harder task—that they had no more right than kings to rule others without their consent. For both Jefferson and Lincoln, a regime in which the majority alone may rule is nonetheless a regime sharply circumscribed by a moral order. This moral order, ordained by God and discovered by reason, must be obeyed by the majority itself, in order that the power to govern be the right to govern. These are the criteria by which elections rightfully become the peaceful successors to revolutions.

Jefferson's inaugural address paid a respect to the electoral process that Jefferson himself had not hitherto shown to "the men of our choice." Of course, now Jefferson and his party were the ones who had been chosen! This must not, however, be understood cynically. In commending a process that had issued in his own political success, Jefferson was not merely praising the people for choosing him. He was also praising his electoral opponents for accepting the results of the election. He therefore took pains to assure them that his government was dedicated to their rights no less than to those of their fellow citizens. But the famous assertion, "We are all Federalists—we are all Republicans" was a two-edged sword. It linked their mutual acceptance of each other as fellow citizens to the fact that "every difference of opinion is not a difference of principle." Elections may properly decide only between those whose differences of opinion are *not* differences of principle. Jefferson's confidence in ballots as the peaceful successors of bullets rested upon the assumption that those who would dissolve the Union or change its republican form represented so small a threat that they might safely be tolerated. The threat was small because the people had an overwhelming interest in preserving their Union and its republican form. The enemies of Union and republicanism would have to be enemies of the people themselves. How could these enemies make headway against Union and republicanism in a popular election?

For Jefferson, the virtue and strength of republicanism or of the principles of a free society consisted above all in the fact that "error of opinion may be tolerated where reason is left free to combat it." This passage in the inaugural reminds us of the great peroration in the Virginia Statute of Religious Liberty, declaring

> that truth is great and will prevail if left to herself, that she is the proper and sufficient antagonist to error, and has nothing to fear from the conflict, unless by human interposition disarmed of her natural weapons, free argument and debate, errors ceasing to be dangerous when it is permitted freely to contradict them.[139]

It was Jefferson's belief in the power of truth in the free political marketplace of ideas, in a republican regime, that gave confidence to his belief in future free elections strengthening the foundations of such a regime. It was his belief that this truth was accessible to the people, that it was compelling in its own right, and that it was so evidently in their interest to believe it that it would not be possible to deceive them into abandoning it.

"We hold these truths to be self-evident" is an assertion at once of a necessity and of a freedom inherent in reason and nature. It implies a freedom in the mind to apprehend truth, and a necessity in nature, a necessity external to the mind, that determines what the truth is. In the last analysis, freedom is the ability to be determined by the truth.

A free society is a fellowship—a unanimity, or oneness of mind—of those who recognize these self-evident truths as the basis of their social and political relationship, within which they can resolve their differences peacefully by debate, discussion, and free elections. Jefferson's inaugural testifies to the existence of this unanimity sufficient to validate this peaceful process. It also testifies to the continuing necessity for such unanimity if the process is to continue. The refusal of the South to accept Lincoln's election in 1860 is testimony to the fact that such unanimity was not then present. Lincoln's inaugural address in 1861, as we shall in due course present it, undertook to prove by Jefferson's criteria that there was no more just cause to reject his election than to reject any other election, including Jefferson's, that had preceded it.

The revolt against Lincoln's election suggests that Jefferson's optimism concerning the future of the popular consensus in favor of Union and republicanism had not been justified. Jefferson had said that there was no threat to safety from "error of opinion . . . where reason is left free to combat it" and that truth had nothing to fear "unless by human interposition disarmed of her natural weapons." But what precisely are the conditions in which reason is "free"? And when is truth "disarmed"? Are not political campaigns for electoral supremacy precisely the times when the still small voice of reason is least heard, when passion and demagoguery obscure reason?

The fact that Lincoln's name or the names of his party's electors were not even allowed on the ballots of ten states in the 1860 election suggests a public mind in those states very different from the one Jefferson praised in his inaugural. How could a people bred in the cause of Union and republicanism have come to such a pass? Suffice it for the present to say that the seceding states justified their secession on the ground that it was the free states, and not themselves, that had rejected the Union under the Constitution. They appealed fundamentally to the right of revolution in the Declaration of Independence as one that had endowed them with a natural right to withdraw from a government to which they no longer consented. But they claimed as well a right of secession under the positive law of the Constitution from which they were withdrawing. A difference had arisen concerning both the laws of nature and of nature's God and the human law, the Constitution, grounded upon it. What those differences were, how they arose, and by what arguments the attempt was made to justify them we must presently inquire. And then we must see how Lincoln in responding to them applied the arguments he had learned from Jefferson.

2

The Declaration of Independence,
the Gettysburg Address, and the Historians

All honor to Jefferson—to the man who, in the concrete pressure of a struggle for national independence by a single people, had the coolness, forecast, and capacity to introduce into a merely revolutionary document, an abstract truth, applicable to all men and all times.
—Abraham Lincoln

To ask whether the natural rights philosophy of the Declaration of Independence is true or false is essentially a meaningless question.
—Carl Becker

Since the Civil War, in which the Southern States were conquered, against all historical logic and sound sense, the American people have been in a condition of political and popular decay. . . . The beginnings of a great new social order based on the principle of slavery and inequality were destroyed by that war, and with them also the embryo of a future truly great America.
—Adolf Hitler

"We hold these truths to be self-evident, that all men are created equal, that they are endowed by their Creator with certain unalienable Rights, that among these are Life, Liberty, and the pursuit of Happiness." The nation dedicated to this proposition has now become, no doubt partly as a consequence of this dedication, the most powerful and prosperous of the nations of the earth. Does this nation in its

---

The epigraphs are taken from Letter to Pierce and Others, April 6, 1859, in *The Collected Works of Abraham Lincoln*, ed. Roy P. Basler (New Brunswick, N.J.: Rutgers University Press, 1953), vol. III, p. 376; Carl Becker, *The Declaration of Independence: A Study in the History of Political Ideas* (New York: Harcourt Brace, 1922), p. 277; Adolf Hitler, 1933, in *The Voice of Destruction*, by Hermann Rauschning (New York: Putnam, 1940), pp. 68–69; and Leo Strauss, *Natural Right and History* (Chicago: University of Chicago Press, 1953), p. 1.

maturity still cherish the faith in which it was conceived and raised? Does it still hold those "truths to be self-evident"?

—Leo Strauss

Aristotle begins the second book of his *Politics* with an apology. His purpose, he says, is to consider what form of political community is best for those most able to live according to their desire. That is to say, he wishes to discover the form of government that is best for mankind, everywhere and always. But he does not wish to be thought to be doing so merely to display his own cleverness. For this reason, he undertakes to examine the merits of those actual governments that are thought to have just claims to the highest excellence, as well as those that exist only in the writings of others.[1]

Aristotle will prove by his analyses that no regime exists, either in speech or in deed, that deserves to be called best. Lacking such a model of excellence, there cannot be political science, properly so called. Aristotle, the son of a physician, believed that a genuine political science must be able to distinguish between political health and disease as much as medical science must be able to distinguish between bodily health and disease.

The literature on Abraham Lincoln and the American Civil War is virtually boundless. Yet nowhere does one find in that literature the kind of diagnosis of the pathology that afflicted the American body politic of that era that Aristotle, or an Aristotelian political scientist, might recognize. Yet Lincoln's own analysis was remarkably Aristotelian. In the course of his debates with Stephen A. Douglas, Lincoln characterized slavery as a cancer that could not immediately be excised without causing the patient to bleed to death. Like any cancer, however, it could not be permitted to spread without also causing the death of the patient.[2] In medically diagnostic terms, Lincoln proposed preventing the extension of slavery into any new territories (from which new states might be formed). Once slavery was irreversibly confined to the states where it already existed, he thought measures could be pursued within those states for the gradual reduction and elimination of this cancer. What those measures might be, he did not at once propose. Under the pressure of events, all his efforts had to be concentrated upon preventing the growth of the malignancy. Indeed, at the center of his task was the necessity of convincing his fellow countrymen that slavery was indeed a morally pathological condition, as opposed to a matter of moral indifference (as Douglas held) or a positive good (as the disciples of John C. Calhoun maintained). For Lincoln, the criterion for distinguishing between healthy and diseased bodies politic was the difference between despotic and free government recognized by the Declaration of Independence. This difference, in Lincoln's understanding, was as surely grounded in nature as the difference between health and disease in the human body.

A half century ago, the title of the leading biography of Lincoln's Illinois rival was *The Eve of Conflict: Stephen A. Douglas and the Needless War*.[3] Although it expressed what was in some respects a selective partisanship with respect to Douglas, it did not differ materially in its "needless war" thesis from the work of James Garfield Randall, who was then widely regarded as a Lincolnophile and who remains the leading academic Lincoln biographer. Nor did it differ in this respect from any of the notable Civil War scholarship of the interwar period.[4]

On the eve of secession Lincoln wrote to his old Whig comrade, Georgia congressman Alexander Stephens (soon to become vice president of the Confederacy): "You think slavery is *right*, and ought to be extended; while we think it is *wrong* and ought to be restricted. That I suppose is the rub. It certainly is the only substantial difference between us."[5] According to Lincoln, the Civil War was above all a dispute about whether slavery was right or wrong. By the canons of revisionist historiography, fundamental differences of opinion concerning right and wrong cannot be decided by any rational process. Revisionist historians thus approached the Civil War convinced a priori that they understood the questions facing the American people of that period better than Lincoln or any of his contemporaries. They were convinced that they knew, as Lincoln and his fellow citizens did not, that to ask whether slavery was right or wrong was to ask, in the words of Carl Becker, an "essentially meaningless question." And they concluded that to go to war over a difference of opinion that could not be settled by any rational means was essentially foolish.[6]

Becker's book *The Declaration of Independence: A Study in the History of Political Ideas* remains the most influential and, in most respects, the finest scholarly work ever written on its subject.[7] Becker was a master craftsman of his guild. His gracefulness and lucidity have a charm that marks a bygone age of academic writing. But except for its elegance, it is difficult to realize that this work was published in 1922. Despite the enormous number of books on American history written in the last seventy-five years, Becker's perspective on the natural rights philosophy has remained unchanged and unchallenged in the mainstream of the academic world. So far as I know, for example, no historian who has written about the Civil War has seriously asked whether Lincoln's belief in the truth of the Declaration can be accepted, not merely as emotionally evocative and persuasive, but as philosophically sound. Neither has anyone inquired as to whether it was intrinsically reasonable to believe, as Lincoln did, that the principles of the Declaration form the ground for distinguishing the healthy from the pathological in the body politic.[8] But if the question as to whether the philosophy of the Declaration is true or false is essentially meaningless, then questions as to whether slavery is right or wrong or whether freedom is better than despotism are equally meaningless.

It is not our immediate purpose to inquire whether Becker's declaration is itself true or false. What we do say now, however, is that no account of the Civil War can claim historical authenticity that does not undertake to explain why Lincoln and his antagonists believed as they did. Nor, in the final analysis, can such an account withhold judgment concerning the validity of those contrary and contradictory beliefs. For if what Becker asserts is the incontrovertible truth of the matter, then the conviction upon which Lincoln defended his policy of preserving the Union and justified his entire life (not to mention his death, and the deaths of 600,000 other Americans) was a delusion. The conclusion of the honest historian in such a case would be that the Civil War was the consequence of that delusion, a "tale told by an idiot, full of sound and fury, signifying nothing."[9]

If Becker is correct about the erroneousness of belief in the truth of the Declaration of Independence, then Lincoln's analogy between slavery and cancer is false. We would have to say that this analogy is merely indicative of Lincoln's emotional reaction to something he disliked. It would have no more objective validity than the lament for the destruction of slavery by Adolf Hitler, to whom "the falsities of liberty and equality" were as pathological as slavery was to Lincoln.[10] The struggle between slavery, on the one hand, and liberty and equality, on the other, would become merely a struggle between differing preferences, neither of which could be shown to be objectively superior to the other. This struggle would appear much as the struggle in Lilliput between "Little-enders" and "Big-enders" appeared to Gulliver. Here the question arises whether all struggles that are ostensibly between right and wrong do not appear in this light, at least until one chooses sides. But choosing sides, in such a case, can mean nothing more than blinding oneself to the indifference of reality or of the nature of things to one's preferences. The historical revisionists who regarded the Civil War as "needless" did so on the assumption that there was no real ground, in "the laws of nature and of nature's God," for the conviction of Lincoln and his contemporaries as to the injustice of slavery. They were certain that from the abolitionists to the advocates of the positive good of slavery, those who asserted a ground of truth for their moral preferences were laboring under delusions. They therefore condemned, whether explicitly or implicitly, those politicians on either side of the Mason and Dixon Line who inflamed the uncompromisable moral passions of the electorate.

The historical revisionism that prevailed in the first half of the twentieth century was replaced in the second half, largely but not entirely, by a viewpoint that regards slavery as unquestionably and unqualifiedly evil.[11] But the change from the earlier revisionism is more apparent than real. Like their predecessors, scholars of more recent years see the distinction between good and evil as rooted, not in nature and reason, but in the passions. The earlier revisionists, whose hero was

Stephen A. Douglas, thought that sensible statesmanship would always work for the subordination of moral questions to matters of interests, and consequently for the peaceful accommodation of conflicting interests. In this respect, they preserved something of the rationalist tradition they otherwise rejected. They were at least governed in their thinking by the idea of what a reasonable person would do when confronted by uncompromisable differences over the morality of slavery. Their successors, however, have substituted commitment for reasonableness (in any sense of that word) as the norm by which human actions are to be judged. Our latter-day writers, who generally detest Douglas, are by and large committed to the moral superiority of the antislavery cause. For them, the impotence of reason to decide moral questions does not mean, as the earlier revisionists concluded, that moral questions should be ignored, bypassed, or compromised. It means rather that a full-blooded and passionate commitment should be made to the position one regards as moral. Since reason cannot speak against their moral commitment, there is no reason for them to moderate their passionate feelings about slavery. (By the same token, of course, reason does not speak against the proslavery cause or provide any ground to moderate the passions of those committed to it.)[12] But both the earlier revisionists and their successors despise those whose moral judgments are governed by what the Declaration of Independence refers to as the "dictates of prudence."

The meaning of prudence, in the context of the politics of the antebellum United States, may be gathered from this passage in Lincoln's Peoria speech of 1854: "Much as I hate slavery, I would consent to the extension of it rather than see the Union dissolved, just as I would consent to any GREAT evil, to avoid a GREATER one."[13] A morality governed by prudence is largely beyond the ken of our latter-day abolitionist historians. For them, prudential compromises in dealing with slavery are regarded as mere excuses for inaction.[14] They have much in common with Chief Justice Roger Taney, who in the *Dred Scott* decision of 1857, declared that the Signers of the Declaration of Independence could not have regarded slavery as wrong, since they did not abolish it—ignoring the fact that, in any event, they had no power to abolish it! For such historians as these, the portrayal of a "racist" American Founding is a necessary preamble to the disavowal of any authority to the principles of the Revolution, notably those enshrined in the Declaration.

As partisans of the antislavery cause, latter-day historians approve of Lincoln's role in destroying slavery but do not for a moment consider that his reasons for believing slavery wrong might be true. Their endorsement of Lincoln is limited to the fact that he finally adopted a policy the abolitionists had always advocated. They might applaud him more were they to think that his scruples about using his power were insincere and that he was merely opportunistic. That he took seriously a moral duty to abide by the limits the Constitution placed upon federal (and presidential) authority in dealing with slavery was something they themselves cannot take seriously. That his reasons for abiding by those constitutional limits and the reasons for his moral condemnation of slavery were ultimately the same is also something they can never take seriously. Yet for Lincoln, the wrongness of slavery and the wrongness of arbitrary power *are* one and the same. This is what we must understand if we are to understand Lincoln as he understood himself, which is to say, if we are to understand what is most important about the Civil War.

∼

The present work is intended to be what, in medieval literature, would be called a Great Commentary. Its text, as the title indicates, is the Gettysburg Address. The Gettysburg Address, as we know, has been read and recited countless times by Boy Scouts and Girl Scouts, by schoolchildren of all ages, by visitors to the Lincoln Memorial, by politicians, citizens, and scholars. As Soviet tanks were crushing the Hungarian revolution of 1956, the final message of the Hungarian freedom fighters, broadcast on the Free Hungarian Radio, was a reading of the Gettysburg Address. The reading was not completed when it was cut off to the sound of gunfire. Some forty years later, however, the Soviet tanks are gone, and the reading of the Gettysburg Address will have resumed. We can say once again that Lincoln's words, and Jefferson's, have proved more powerful than tyranny and despotism.

In all the literature of the world, perhaps only the Sermon on the Mount and the Lord's Prayer have been repeated so often or have evoked such feelings of reverence and piety as has the Gettysburg Address. It is astonishing, therefore, to reflect that nowhere in the writings of American historians, or in scholarly literature generally, has there been any systematic attempt to understand the connection between the beginning and the ending of the Gettysburg Address. Nowhere do we find a discussion of the intrinsic and (in Lincoln's mind) necessary relationship between the liberty and equality that are said to have attended the birth of the nation and that form of government that, it is said, shall not perish from the earth. That there might be any such relationship has been rejected implicitly by the acceptance of the thesis popularized by Carl Becker. If it is meaningless to ask if there is any truth to the proposition to which, Lincoln tells us, the nation was dedicated, then it must be equally meaningless to ask why the kind of government ensuing from that dedication should long endure. Freedom fighters, however, whether in Budapest or in Tiananmen Square, have fortunately understood intuitively what scholars have declared to be unknowable.

~

For Abraham Lincoln, the terrible sacrifices exacted upon the battlefield of Gettysburg, and upon ten thousand other battlefields of the Civil War, could be vindicated only by "a new birth of freedom." Lincoln called upon "us the living" to be dedicated to "the unfinished work" thus far advanced by the "honored dead." Lincoln made clear what that work was when he said that the nation, at its conception, had been dedicated to the proposition "that all men are created equal." The war had come because many Americans had turned their backs on this defining axiom, some calling it a "self-evident lie," others arguing that it applied only to "superior races." For its defenders, slavery was far from being an anomaly, an evil temporarily entailed upon the new Republic from its colonial past. Instead it became a "positive good," and they devoted themselves to strengthen, perpetuate, and extend it. Lincoln and members of his party had been elected to office because, in light of what they held to be the self-evident truth of the Declaration of Independence, they thought slavery a great moral wrong, whose extension into newly organized territories and into the states to be formed from those territories should be prevented by law. Restricted thus, they believed, slavery would be placed, lawfully and constitutionally, "in course of ultimate extinction."

By September 1862, Lincoln was convinced that he could not fulfill his constitutional oath to preserve the Union unless he acted to destroy slavery in those states and parts of states that were in rebellion against federal authority. The Emancipation Proclamation progressively deprived the Confederacy of a vast reservoir of slave labor, which had enabled many more Southern whites to serve in the Confederate ranks than would otherwise have been possible. It also added great numbers of emancipated slaves to the ranks of the Union armies, as well as giving them the greatest of all incentives to fight. Notwithstanding the Proclamation's exceptions and exemptions, which proved temporary, it destroyed the viability of the institution of chattel slavery in the whole Union. In issuing the Proclamation, Lincoln acted from military necessity. In the Gettysburg Address, Lincoln called upon the nation to ratify what had been done, not simply because it was necessary, but because it was good. The Gettysburg Address, it should be understood, was more than an exercise in ceremonial propriety: It was a political speech intended to gain support for the Thirteenth Amendment. Military necessity had enabled the federal government to do lawfully what the Constitution hitherto had prevented it from doing. For that government to have acted against slavery in the states except under the exigencies of the war would—according to Lincoln's understanding of the Constitution—have meant usurping powers to which the people of the United States had not given their consent. It would thus, he thought, have defeated the very ends of human freedom. It would not do, as Lincoln warned in his Lyceum speech in 1838, to emancipate slaves by enslaving freemen. This had been the path marked out by those great destroyers of republics, Alexander, Caesar, and Napoleon. Lincoln was determined to avoid it.

The Gettysburg Address presupposes the truth of the great proposition set forth originally in the Declaration of Independence. We repeat, however, that according to the most justly famous book ever written about the Declaration, this presupposition is false. But the author of that book, Carl Becker, did not think that Jefferson and Lincoln were fools for believing in the great proposition. Rather he believed that they, like all human beings always, asked questions that History compelled them to ask, and that History made certain answers seem so plausible as to delude them into believing those answers to be true. This, Becker thought, reveals to us the limitations under which Jefferson and Lincoln labored. They were "men of their time," just as we are men of our time.[15] The underlying assumptions that determined the fundamental character of their thinking were bound up in the climate of opinion of their age. What Lincoln and Jefferson thought were abstract truths, transcending time and place, were in fact illusions created by the time and place in which they lived. One is bound to ask, however, as apparently neither Becker nor his countless epigones ever did, why the thought that all such thought is an illusion is not itself an illusion.

∾

The Gettysburg Address is the consummate epitome of a quarter-century of Lincoln's thought and expression. In the same 1859 letter in which Lincoln called the great proposition of human equality "an abstract truth, applicable to all men and all times," he also declared that the "principles of Jefferson are the definitions and axioms of free society."[16] Lincoln, like the generation of the Founding, believed that those principles were grounded in reason and nature. The Founders did not for a minute think that their convictions were a matter of historical fate, blind faith, or mere will. While they did hold some opinions as a matter of faith, they were confident that these opinions were in harmony with the teachings of unassisted human reason.

That all men are created equal meant, at the very least, that it is a fact open to observation by anyone at any time that whatever the conventions of any society, human beings are not distinguished from each other by nature in the way that the rider is distinguished from his horse. The subjection of the horse to the rider is according to nature. It is not arbitrary, and we do not say that the horse is a slave. Nature has made no such distinction between man and man. For one man to claim the obedience of another in the same way that he claims the obedience of an irrational animal is arbitrary and against reason and nature. Who should rule ought not, therefore, to be decided unilaterally by any king or elite whatsoever but by those who are to be ruled.

If no one is by nature a ruler, then all human beings are a priori, or by nature, nonrulers of each other. Although legitimate political authority does not arise immediately from nature, it does arise according to nature, when it arises from consent (otherwise called, as we have seen in chapter 1, the social compact or contract). Such consent, however, is not an act of the will alone. It does not mean acquiescence in any political relationship whatever. It must be rational and must reflect the mutual acknowledgment of the rights of each by all and of all by each. Anyone claiming political authority in his own right or alleging that he has received it from God is attempting a fraud. Such claims are the ground only of despotism. As Aristotle says in the *Politics*, despotic institutions have as their purpose the selfish advantage of the rulers; legitimate or free government exists for the equal advantage of all who are ruled. There is therefore no reason or obligation, other than the effect of mere force, why anyone should obey a law or command by another unless it rests in some intelligible way upon his own informed consent. Political constitutions have as their natural ends the safety and happiness of the people to be governed by them. They ought to be designed, not only to secure these ends, but also to prevent political power from being perverted to any other ends. This was Jefferson and Lincoln's "common sense of the subject." This is what "the natural rights philosophy of the Declaration of Independence" meant to them. They did not conceive how reason could be employed, except by sophistry, to render the truth of such a teaching meaningless.

That the truth of that common sense might be denied, and in fact had been denied throughout human history, was perfectly well known to Jefferson and Lincoln and to their contemporaries who shared their convictions. But this did not lessen their confidence in the evidence or reasoning, the philosophical teaching, that led them to such conclusions. The motives of those who, from time immemorial, had supported despotism were as transparent as they were unjust.

Both the Declaration of Independence and the Gettysburg Address were born of wars in which their principles had been challenged in debate no less than in battle. Who prevails on the battlefield never tells us who (if anyone) had justice on his side. Who (if anyone) in a debate may be said to have truth on his side is an even more difficult matter, since competent judges of truth are rarely, if ever, the judges of the debates. Jefferson, as we saw in chapter 1, had great confidence in the power of truth to prevail, "unless by human interposition disarmed of her natural weapons, free argument and debate." But how often has truth not been so disarmed?

We are reminded of the opening scene of Plato's *Republic*. Socrates and

Glaucon, having gone down to the Piraeus to watch the festival, prepare to return to Athens. Polemarchus observes that they are leaving and asks Socrates if he does not see how many of them there are. Socrates answers that he does. "Well, then, either prove stronger than these men or stay here," Polemarchus says. Socrates asks if there is not another possibility, namely, that he persuade them to let him and Glaucon go. Polemarchus asks, "Can you persuade us if we don't listen?" Glaucon answers, "There's no way."

There are many reasons why human beings cannot be persuaded, a refusal to listen being prominent among them. Refusing to listen itself has many forms, some of them friendly (as in the instance just given) and some of them unfriendly. It may refer to ignorance, or inability to understand. Ignorance, in turn, may be either invincible or remediable. Socrates in the *Republic*, having been compelled to remain, compels his compellers to listen to a dialogue on justice. In that dialogue one interlocutor is compelled, at first against his will but later willingly, to admit that justice is not the interest of the stronger. More precisely, he is compelled to admit that justice is not the interest of those whom he had mistakenly regarded as the stronger. Only those who know what is truly in their interest are truly stronger, and only those who know the truth about their interests know what is truly in their interest. And such truth must transcend their interests in order to be truly their interests.

Socrates is challenged to prove that it is better to be the victim of a tyrant than to be a tyrant. The conclusion, of course, is that it is better to be neither. But the victim of the tyrant suffers less evil than the tyrant, on the basis of the argument that justice is the health or true interest of the soul and that it is at least as much in anyone's interest to have a healthy soul as to have a healthy body. The soul of the tyrant is diseased (that is to say, dysfunctional), because he is the victim of the tyranny of his passions over his reason. The rule of law—of reason unaffected by passion, according to Aristotle—compels us to pursue our own interest only by rational means, that is to say, by means consistent with the equal rights of others. By preventing us from injuring others, the law makes it possible for us to have others as friends. In acting consistently with the rights of others and in not injuring others, we are habituated to virtue. By becoming good, we are enabled to be friends of the good, and having good friends is the most indispensable of the means to happiness.

The tyrant, subjecting others, cannot be a friend. Although surrounded by others pretending to be his friend, he is without friends. But without friends, life is not worth living. Once we understand this, upon which our well-being depends, we understand our interest in the rule of law. We understand as well why it is against our interest to become tyrants as why it is in our interest to prevent tyrants from ruling us. That is the argument of Plato as well as Aristotle. It is the argument of the American Revolution, the Declaration of Independence, and the Gettysburg Address. Yet it is an argument held in almost no esteem today. How is that possible?

The answer is that in our time, truth has been disarmed by the opinion that reason is impotent to know what is just or unjust, right or wrong, true or false. If there is no truth, or if the truth is beyond the power of the human mind to know, then free argument and debate as means of arriving at the truth are meaningless. Truth is thereby disarmed of her natural weapons a priori. This challenge to the principle of a free society is one that neither Jefferson nor Lincoln anticipated. Nonetheless, we assert categorically that the common sense of the subject as it appeared to Jefferson and Lincoln, although it has been denied by the mainstream of Western thought for more than a century, has not been refuted. Confronted with the statement of principles beginning "We hold these truths to be self-evident," most writers, even the most learned, assume that what follows are merely the subjective opinions of a bygone age, possessing no more truth for us than anything else that may be agreeable to our passions. From this perspective, there can be no ground for denying that justice is the interest of the stronger, in the sense that Thrasymachus originally intended. From this perspective, Socrates may forever remain in the Piraeus, but there will be no dialogue on justice. The dialogue on justice, however, represents the highest form of what Jefferson, in his first inaugural, called that "social intercourse, that harmony and affection, without which liberty and even life itself are but dreary things." The Civil War, bitter and harsh as it was, was nonetheless understood on both sides to be in the service of that friendship that makes common citizenship, and thereby justice and the rule of law, possible. As we shall see, each side accused the other of being false to such friendship. But every sacrifice made on either side of that conflict would become vain if the dialogue on justice that accompanied it were to be pronounced meaningless.

⤳

Leo Strauss, commenting after the Second World War on the fate of the self-evident truths of the Declaration of Independence, cites as authoritative a German scholar who said that by "abandoning the idea of natural right, and through abandoning it, German thought has 'created the historical sense,' and thus was led eventually to unqualified relativism." Strauss continues:

> What was a tolerably accurate description of German thought twenty-seven years ago would now appear to be true of Western thought in general. It would not be the first time that a nation, defeated on the battlefield and, as it were,

annihilated as a political being, has deprived its conquerors of the most sublime fruit of victory by imposing on them the yoke of its own thought.[17]

The victory of historicism and relativism, culminating in nihilism, over the natural law and natural rights doctrine of the Declaration and the Gettysburg Address actually occurred long before the date assigned to it here by Strauss. That victory is certainly apparent in Carl Becker's book in 1922. In fact, the attack on the natural rights philosophy had its beginnings in the reaction to the French Revolution and in the formation of the Holy Alliance that defeated Napoleon.[18] That alliance declared its opposition to the alleged "rationalism" of the French Revolution and the "abstractions" by which the "philosophes" had condemned the institutions of feudalism, monarchy, and established churches in the ancien régime. After Waterloo a new breed of philosophes, those of the Holy Alliance, attempted in every way to depreciate the doctrine of the rights of man and of government by consent in favor of loyalty to throne and altar—to the right of kings to rule directly by the grace of God and the right of established churches to anoint kings.

Becker presents a brilliant précis of how opposition to the French Revolution transformed the dominant focus of European political thought from one of natural to one of historic rights.

> The effectiveness of the historic rights philosophy was . . . precisely in this, that it encountered the natural rights philosophy on its own ground, and refuted it from its own premises. Admitting that rights were founded in nature, it identified nature with history, and affirmed that the institutions of any nation were properly but an expression of the life of the people . . . the cumulative deposit of its experience, the resume of its history. It implied that every people has, therefore, at any given time, the social order which nature has given it, the order which is on the whole best suited to its peculiar genius and circumstance, the order which is accordingly the embodiment of that freedom which it has achieved and the starting point for such further freedom as it may hope to attain.[19]

Remembering that Becker represents the very highest level of academic sophistication, we are obliged to point out why it is a fallacy to say that the historical school refuted the natural rights philosophy from its own premises, by identifying nature with history. The idea of nature as a standard is the idea of an unchanging ground of changing experience. To identify nature with history is to identify the unchanging with the changing, or to alter the meaning of nature into its opposite. This is a substitution of meanings, not a refutation. A refutation would have to take the form of a demonstration that there is no unchanging ground of human experience. Merely to deny that there is a permanent nature is not to prove that it does not exist, any more than to deny the existence of God proves that God does not exist. To the best of our knowledge there has been no such proof, either by the historical school of the nineteenth century or by any other school at any other time.[20] The most that can be said for Becker is that he assumes that since the dominant philosophical schools have gone from nature to history as the ground of understanding and judgment, they must have done so for a sufficient reason. In that he is simply mistaken.

The most sophisticated form of the metamorphosis of natural rights into historic rights was Hegel's. In the course of the nineteenth century, it became the prevailing doctrine of liberals no less than conservatives. There were left-wing as well as right-wing Hegelians, the most famous of the former being Karl Marx and the most famous of the latter, certainly for our purposes, being John C. Calhoun. Historic rights were held by Hegel to be rational, and each successive "synthesis" of the antecedent "thesis" and "antithesis" was believed to move mankind to a higher level of rationality. The conflicts in the historical process were driven entirely by men's passions, not their reason. Philosophers did not arrive at the truth by abstract reasoning, as Plato and Aristotle had mistakenly believed, but by discovering, through long and exacting study, the design in events caused by the great nonphilosophical agents of historical change, such as Napoleon, Bismarck, and Lincoln. The victors in great wars were instruments of "the cunning of history," which used them for rational ends that formed no necessary part of the victors' own conscious intentions. Becker wrote:

> "The most indifferent arguments are good when one has a majority of bayonets," Bismarck assured his contemporaries; and contemporaries celebrated his work when he made the German Empire by 'iron and blood' . . . and in the New World it was not by the sweet reasonableness of Congressional debate, but by force of arms, that freedom was conferred upon the slave.[21]

From this perspective, Lincoln was no less a man of iron and blood than Bismarck, and the victory of the Union cause and its justice were but two terms for the same thing. From the point of view of the historical school, no meaningful distinction can be drawn between the "is" and the "ought." Accordingly, Lincoln's greatness did not stem from the reasons for his policy but from his historical destiny or success. Here we may see why Becker found the question of the truth of the Declaration a matter of such little moment. If Washington and Lincoln commanded "a majority of bayonets," it mattered little whether the arguments of the Americans against the British, and of the North against the South, were "indifferent." There is a double irony here, in that the admiration of Lincoln in the later nineteenth and twentieth centuries is on the same grounds upon which slavery itself had been defended: the identification of the ought with the is. The Union had proved itself right because it was stronger than the Confederacy, just as masters had been right by being stronger than the slaves.

When the spirit of the Holy Alliance crossed the Atlantic in the early 1830s, the defense of the ancien régime was replaced by the defense of slavery. It is easy to see how the identification of nature with history, or of the ought with the is, could lead Southerners to interpret the defense of their peculiar institution as a defense of their legitimate historic rights and therefore their freedom. The articulation of the defense of slavery and the Confederate cause was above all the work of John C. Calhoun. Like his European counterparts who attacked the doctrine of the rights of man, Calhoun—as we shall show in chapter 7—was influenced decisively by Rousseau and Hegel. In Calhoun, moreover, we will not only see natural rights transformed into historical rights, with the latter becoming the rights of positive law; but we will also see the denunciation of the appeal from the positive law to the natural law, so characteristic of the American Revolution, as being itself immoral.[22] In short, we will see in Calhoun the generation of the most powerful forces that today dominate the intellectual life, not only of the United States, but also of the Western world generally. We will see that if ever there was a nation annihilated politically on the battlefield that nonetheless imposed the yoke of its thought upon its conquerors, it was the Confederacy.

~

In proof of the foregoing, we submit in evidence the testimony of the present chief justice of the United States, William Rehnquist. In his celebrated essay "The Notion of a Living Constitution," Rehnquist advocates what is currently called a jurisprudence of original intent, whereby the Constitution should be interpreted according to the intent of those who framed and ratified it. In itself this is unexceptionable and perfectly traditional. Aristotle said that the intention of the legislator is the law. And James Madison wrote that he concurred

> in the propriety of reasoning to the sense in which the Constitution was accepted and ratified by the nation. In that sense alone it is the legitimate Constitution. And if that be not the guide in expounding it, there can be no security for the consistent and stable, more than for a faithful exercise of its powers. If the meaning of the text be sought in the changeable meaning of the words composing it, it is evident that the shape and attributes of the government must partake of the changes to which the words and phrases of all living languages are constantly subject. What a metamorphosis would be produced in a code of laws if all its ancient phraseology were to be taken in a modern sense![23]

86

Like Madison, Rehnquist takes issue with those who hold that the Constitution, as a "living organism," should "evolve" over time and that judges should discover an evolving meaning in its words. Such new meaning would be adapted to the exigencies of the present, unencumbered by what the same words meant when they were accepted by those who ratified the document.

In properly denying any authority to this evolutionary view, however, Rehnquist sets forth a doctrine even more alien to that of the framers and ratifiers of the Constitution. The advocates of the "living constitution," he says,

> [i]gnore . . . the nature of political value judgments in a democratic society. If such a society adopts a constitution and incorporates in that constitution safeguards for individual liberty, these safeguards do indeed take on a generalized moral rightness or goodness. They assume a general social acceptance neither because of any intrinsic worth nor because of any unique origins in someone's idea of natural justice, but instead simply because they have been incorporated in a constitution by a people.[24]

As we shall see, Rehnquist's "original intent" has less in common with the intent of those who ratified the Constitution than with the intent of those who "de-ratified" it in 1860–61. The Civil War was fought between two different conceptions of what constituted the "original intent" of the framers and ratifiers. The seceding states asserted that they were acting in defense of the constitutional principles of 1787, which they claimed the free states had abandoned. The heart of the Southern understanding of the Constitution consisted in the denial that any moral distinction could be drawn between the safeguards of individual liberty in the Constitution and the safeguards of slavery. By their account, all parts of the Constitution were of equal moral, no less than of equal legal, obligation. To denounce slavery as immoral, as the Republican Party and its successful candidate for president in 1860 had done, was to repudiate the moral obligation of those parts of the Constitution that recognized and protected the institution of slavery. More than that, it was to destroy the moral partnership in the Constitution that was the basis of the friendship, the true ground of common citizenship, between the sections.

Rehnquist, it might at first appear, is merely endorsing the idea of popular sovereignty, as did Jefferson and Lincoln. Unlike them, however, he finds no antecedent ground for the people's choice of a free constitution other than the mere fact of its adoption. If "safeguards for individual liberty" have no "intrinsic worth," then they have no greater intrinsic worth than safeguards of slavery, and no moral distinction can rightfully be drawn between them. No theme was more pronounced in the justifications of secession issued by the seceding states in 1860–61 than the denunciation of the free states and the free soil movement for regarding one set of constitutional safeguards as less moral or worthy of respect than others.

It is clear, therefore, that Rehnquist's jurisprudence of original intent has more in common with Calhounian or Confederate original intent than with that of the Founders or Lincoln. Yet his view is not identical with the Calhounians'. The Calhounians did not believe that constitutional safeguards were lacking in "any intrinsic worth." They believed in the positive good of slavery, and indeed of all the provisions of the Constitution, as they understood them. With slavery as its foundation, they believed that they could build an edifice of freedom and virtue surpassing the glories of Greece and Rome. Rehnquist's views are very different. For him, intrinsic worth as a concept has no foundation in reason. If safeguards of liberty have no such worth, then neither has liberty itself, or even life. In Rehnquist, we can observe that historical right has been transformed into unmitigated positivism or indeed into nihilism. He accounts for constitutional morality by saying that constitutional safeguards "take on a generalized moral rightness or goodness" when they "assume a general social acceptance." Constitutional safeguards or laws that have in themselves no intrinsic worth, and therefore no moral goodness, "take on" (whatever that means!) the aspect of morality by being accepted. But how can "acceptance" transform what has no moral worth into what is morally worthy? Or if acceptance can perform this miracle of *creatio ex nihilo*, can it not do so equally for anything, slavery or genocide included? Clearly acceptance has nothing in common with that "consent of the governed" from which are derived the "just powers of government," according to the Declaration of Independence. Jefferson's "great principles of right and wrong," which "are legible to every reader," are antecedent to all positive law. Rehnquist, however, cannot read anything except the laws that have already been laid down. He can therefore see no moral reason why any one set of laws should be adopted over any other, for example, the American Constitution over the constitution of the Third Reich.

Rehnquist writes:

> Beyond the Constitution and laws in our society, there is simply no basis other than the individual conscience of the citizen that may serve as a platform for the launching of moral judgments. There is no conceivable way in which I can logically demonstrate to you that the judgments of my conscience are superior to the judgments of your conscience, and vice versa.[25]

At first glance, Rehnquist appears to be saying here that we must obey the Constitution and the laws of our society because beyond them or outside them there is nothing but an anarchy of individual opinions as to what is right or wrong, just or unjust. Actually what he says is that there is no basis in reason for any opinions as to what is right or wrong, just or unjust, either in the Constitution and laws of our society or outside them. If no individual conscience is more rational than any other, how can any collective conscience be more rational than any other? A collective conscience becomes merely another name for superior force. This means that there is nothing in the power of reason to support the view that the moral judgment of a Washington or a Lincoln is superior to that of any absolute monarch, not to mention that of a Hitler or a Stalin.

On July 4, 1776, the American people asserted a right to that "separate and equal station" to which, they said, they were entitled by "the laws of nature and of nature's God." They acted by and through a representative assembly, the Congress of the United States. That was the platform from which they launched a moral judgment heard round the world. The laws to which they appealed were certainly not those of "our society," because the obligation of all hitherto existing laws had been dissolved, and a new source of obligation was being put into place. Chief Justice Rehnquist, as a member of the Supreme Court of the United States, derives his judicial authority from the American Constitution, which derives its authority from the American people. But the American people, according to the record of their own acts and deeds, derive their authority from a source superior to themselves. The voice of the people can reasonably be thought to be the voice of God, insofar as the people acted conscientiously in accordance with those rights with which they believed their Creator had endowed them. That is why they appealed in 1776 "to the supreme judge of the world for the rectitude of our intentions."

Rehnquist's alternative of either obeying the Constitution and the laws or being subjected to an anarchy of individual consciences is a false alternative. "The great principles of right and wrong" were legible before 1787, as they were before 1776. Those principles of lawful behavior, or of the laws of nature, instructed the American people before they adopted the Constitution. The American people were bound by their consciences, individually no less than collectively, by the terms of the social compacts that had already united them in their several states and by which they were further united, first into a union, and then into a more perfect union.

Rehnquist asserts without argument—as received wisdom, as an article of faith that it never occurs to him to doubt—that the laws of nature, which the Founders and Lincoln held to be principles of moral judgment, are mere "value judgments," none of which can be said to be supported by reason. Again, we hear Carl Becker saying that to ask whether the moral judgment of the king of Great Britain or that of the Continental Congress is right is an essentially meaningless question. But the entire Declaration of Independence is a logical demonstration, first, that tyranny and despotism are immoral; second, that the acts of the British king and Parliament have been despotic and tyrannical; and third, that in throwing off their duty to the king, the Americans are acting conscientiously in accordance with an intrinsically rational law that is a higher source of obligation than the law of Great Britain. In dismissing "someone's idea of natural justice," Rehnquist simply ignores the historic argument of the American people. Of this argument there is no attempted refutation, merely denial.

Rehnquist's nihilism might seem so thin and casual as to be insignificant, except for the fact that he is, after all, chief justice. What is received wisdom according to a personage of his eminence will also be the received wisdom in the legal and historical professions. It is in fact a somewhat radicalized version of the position represented by Becker, transmitted inelegantly, but in essentials unmodified, over a period of some eighty years.

We repeat that original intent, in Rehnquist's sense of the term, had its source, not in the thought of the Revolution or of the Founding, but in the repudiation of that thought by John C. Calhoun.[26] In Calhoun's rejection of the Declaration of Independence, in his substitution of prescriptive historical right for natural right, we find a constitutional jurisprudence that places safeguards for slavery on the same moral level as any other constitutional safeguards. Although Lincoln and his party never denied the moral obligation to implement fully the legal guarantees of slavery in the Constitution, they insisted nevertheless upon a distinction between the Constitution's compromises and its principles. Yet the South, on the eve of the Civil War, declared that any attempt at moral discrimination between or among the different parts of the Constitution was destructive of that political friendship upon which a common citizenship depended. The echo of Calhoun in the words of the present chief justice is evidence that the Confederacy is alive and well and that the Union victory at Appomatox has not been accompanied by any ascendancy of the principles of the Gettysburg Address.

∿

The historical school of the first half of the nineteenth century had attempted, in part, to reincorporate Aristotle into political philosophy by insisting that the truth about man's nature was not (as the Enlightenment had supposed) something abstract but something that could be discovered only by examining it in its concrete manifestations within actual political communities. There were no such things as human rights or natural rights belonging to human individuals apart from the particular rights recognized in the laws of particular communities. Each political community, in virtue of its history and development, shaped the characters of those who lived within it and formed them into the kind of human beings that they were. There was no humanity possessed of a nature apart from these particular manifestations. No one, therefore, could claim a right by saying that nature entitled him to it. All rights were by-products of the development of each society. The freedoms of speech, religion, association, and all other such freedoms of the Anglo-American political tradition could be claimed only within that tradition, and only by reason of the particular stage of maturity and political development arising from the unique circumstances of Anglo-American history. The idea that these freedoms or rights belonged by nature to any human beings anywhere—for example, to primitive savages or to the servile subjects of Asiatic despotisms, with their completely different life experiences and traditions—was considered absurd.

By nature, Aristotle had said, man was a political animal, and the political community was prior to the individual.[27] A man's individuality was not a self-subsisting reality but something that belonged to him in virtue of his partnership in civil society. He could make no claim that was unrelated to his ability to perform a function that contributed to the larger good of the political order. What was lacking in this Hegelianized Aristotelianism, however, was Aristotle's doctrine of the best regime, that unique form of political community that is intrinsically or naturally best for man as man, everywhere and always.[28] From the classical Aristotelian perspective of the best regime (or the perfectly healthy regime, in the analogy between medical science and political science), any actual regime might be judged more or less defective or more or less excellent. Action to remedy or improve it might thereby be recommended. The historical school rejected Aristotle's best regime for the same reason that it had rejected natural rights—because it represented a nonhistorical judgment concerning the human condition. Aristotle, like Jefferson and Lincoln, believed that fundamental principles were timeless and placeless, which meant that they existed outside of history. He believed that the human good, like health, was determined not by history but by nature, and he had no difficulty in judging primitive tribes barbaric and inferior or in judging Asiatic despotisms to be at war with human virtue. He understood as well as nineteenth-century historicists that the contingent circumstances or historical fate that governs the lives of particular peoples determine, to a very great extent, their chances for excellence and happiness. But he did not think, as neither Jefferson nor Lincoln thought, that what constituted excellence or happiness or what was the nature of human virtue or human rights was dependent upon those circumstances.

The historical school saw no need for a doctrine of the best regime, because it was confident that the historical process itself was essentially a controlled movement toward an ever more perfect human condition. In essence, this meant that the best regime was intrinsic to the historical process. It might in fact be called "the end of history," implying both senses of the word "end"—the termination of a series of events and the ultimate fulfillment of a purpose. No nineteenth-century thinker expressed belief in the irreversibly determined upward movement of history more than John C. Calhoun:

> The application of gunpowder to the art of war, has forever settled the long conflict for ascendancy between civilization and barbarism, in favor of the former, and thereby guarantied that, whatever knowledge is now accumulated, or may hereafter be added, shall never again be lost.

Calhoun was confident that the progressive mastery "of the laws that control the great agents of the material world" could only contribute to the moral and political improvement of the condition of mankind. It would be impious to doubt this, he said since it would be to suppose

> that the all-wise and beneficent Being—the Creator of all—had so constituted man, as that the employment of the high intellectual faculties with which he has been pleased to endow him, in order that he might develop the laws that control the great agents of the material world, and make them subservient to his use—would prove to him the cause of permanent evil—and not of permanent good.[29]

Calhoun accepted Hegel's belief that history is the unfolding of the mind of God. Belief in progress thereby came to be the essence of piety.

For Calhoun, as for most of his contemporaries, the conquest of nature by modern science, making the laws of the material world subservient to human use, became the supreme manifestation of God's goodness. It became the heart of their Christianity, or of revealed religion generally. But the same facts that were the ground of Calhoun's piety were the ground of Karl Marx's atheism.[30] The "high intellectual faculties" with which God had endowed man, according to Calhoun, and with which he was accomplishing the conquest of nature were the very reason why, according to Marx, God had become superfluous. In fact, according to Marx, it was because men had prayed to God for the good things of this world—health, wealth, and freedom—that they had so long neglected the cultivation of those same "high intellectual faculties."[31] While Calhoun would thank God for the ever increasing benefits resulting from the application of scientific methods to human needs, Marx would point out that men's prayers were being answered by relying on the use of their own unassisted human reason. Science could then be seen either as God's means of answering men's prayers or as the true reality that the idea of God had only obscured. As the nineteenth century progressed, as the prestige of science grew and scientific discoveries seemed more and more to be the answers to men's prayers, the presence of God seemed to become ever more identical with the presence of Science. At the same time the line between piety and atheism became ever more indistinguishable.

Calhoun, no less than Rousseau, was aware that material progress did not in itself constitute moral and political progress. He insisted that all the great progress made in the natural sciences and in harnessing the laws of material nature for human well-being would come to naught without good government. In *A Disquisition on Government*, he set forth the scientific formula that he believed he himself had discovered, that would assure the conversion of material into moral and political well-being. The political science in Calhoun's *Disquisition* plays the same necessary role in supporting the idea of progress that the doctrine of proletarian revolution plays in Marx's writings. According to Marx, the progress of science intensifies the historical class conflict, in part because it magnifies the quantity of goods that are the objects of human envy and avarice. But Marx believed it to be a scientific truth that human avarice and envy were rooted, not in human nature, but in the institution of private property. To abolish private property by a communist revolution is to emancipate human nature from the thrall of the selfish passions imposed upon it by the institution of private property. Thereafter, all advances in productivity flowing from science would redound equally to the advantage of all. Calhoun's principle of the "concurrent majority"—by which certain minorities are given a veto power over actions of the government—is likewise said to transform factional strife in society into harmony and mutual advantage. As presented by Calhoun, it neutralizes and brings into unity the otherwise uncontrollable conflicts of interests, in much the same way that the abolition of private property is thought to do by Marx. But we must notice the remarkable fact that these two exemplary mid-nineteenth-century representatives of the idea of progress presuppose, as if they are axiomatic truths—truths upon which their entire systems depend—propositions that directly contradict each other. For Calhoun, it is the proposition that the human being is so constituted "that his direct or individual affections are stronger than his sympathetic or social feelings." This, he says, is a fact "as unquestionable as is that of gravitation, or any other phenomenon of the material world."[32] For Marx, the abolition of private property changes what Calhoun says is unchangeable, in transforming man's innate egotism into altruism.

As we observed, Calhoun thought it impious (or unthinkable) to suppose that the great causes of material progress could end in "permanent evil." But from the foregoing argument, it appears that belief in God's goodness depends upon the correctness of the argument of Calhoun's own *Disquisition*. More precisely, God's goodness and the continuity of progress depend not only upon the scientific validity of the argument of the *Disquisition* but also upon its adoption by Calhoun's fellow citizens as the basis of their Constitution. Even more precisely, as we shall see in chapter 7, it depends upon the replacement of the political science of the *Federalist* by the political science of the *Disquisition*.

It is equally the case that the plausibility of Marx's atheism depends upon the conviction that human beings are by nature altruistic. For Marx, it is only after the abolition of private property that human nature will stand revealed for what it truly is. With the release of human nature from the bondage of class struggle and of the egotism it imposes, universal harmony will follow. If spontaneous cooperation and voluntary sharing under communism do not replace the competitive acquisitiveness of capitalistic society, then on Marx's own premises the fruits of science will not automatically redound to man's well-being, and history as progress will not be vindicated. In that case, the argument for atheism, along with the argument for communism, will have failed. In like manner, any failure of Calhoun's equally utopian expectations would constitute a refutation of his pious identification of God's goodness with the idea of Progress.

From such considerations we see how extremely tenuous the belief in History as Progress was, even in its most optimistic heyday. We see moreover that two of the most outstanding representatives of that belief, from either end of the political spectrum, rested their optimism upon premises that directly contradicted each other. The somber theology of Lincoln's second inaugural address, as we shall see, is the epitaph of the utopian belief in progress that so dominated the mid-nineteenth century.

~

Hegel's "cunning of history," by which the rational ends of human civilization were supposedly advanced without any rational foreknowledge of those ends by the makers of the great events of history, was the tacit ground of the optimism equally of Calhoun and of Marx. Both, like Hegel, believed that they looked back upon the course of human history and were able to descry therein a rational purposefulness of which even philosophers had not hitherto been aware. They believed this was possible because, unlike their predecessors, they lived in proximity to that absolute moment when the purpose of all previous history would stand revealed. Because of this, they could be rational or scientific concerning the actions necessary to promote the completion of the historical process, and thereby the human good, as none of their predecessors could have been.

The idea of progress led Hegel, Marx, and Calhoun radically to depreciate the role of reason in all of their predecessors, whether statesmen or philosophers, to none of whom the rationality of history itself had been vouchsafed.[33] Reason was truly manifest only in the absolute moment wherein history as progress was revealed. The scope and importance of reason as a means of access to truth, or of guiding human life toward human fulfillment, was thereby immeasurably degraded, except within the infinitesimal boundaries of the absolute moment. But questions were inevitably raised about that moment. By what right had the historical school exempted itself from the relativism that it attributed to everyone else? It was Nietzsche who argued—conclusively, it appeared—that this absolute moment was at least as great an act of self-deception as any that the historical school had attributed to mankind in former ages. It is of some importance that Carl Becker, in his account of nineteenth-century philosophy, mentions Hegel but not Nietzsche. Had he considered Nietzsche's critique of the historical school, he could not have erred as he did in thinking that the historical school had refuted the natural rights school.

Nietzsche's proclamation that "God is dead" meant, among other things, that Science now promised everything for which mankind had once turned to God. Unlocking the secrets of nature would unlock the mystery of creation, the mystery for which God was no more than a symbol. The piety professed by Calhoun now collapsed into atheism. Why continue to praise God for what man's unaided powers alone can accomplish? The progress of Science meant that mankind now had the power, and the responsibility, of a God who created ex nihilo. To be possessed of such power meant that man, like God, was beyond good and evil. Mankind did not need nature or reason to discover the standards by which human life ought to be lived; he could now invent his own principles, along with the means to satisfy them. Mankind, or any man who understood the true condition of mankind and commanded the resources of Science, could now play God or, what amounted to the same thing, become the tyrant of the universe he created. Those superscientists Hitler and Stalin come to mind.

Although political megalomaniacs are the most conspicuous end products of this reasoning, they are not necessarily the most characteristic. Atheistic nihilism transforms the "bourgeois" and highly moral individualism of the American Revolution into something entirely different. That older individualism was based on the idea of unalienable rights endowed by man's Creator. Such rights were not unconditional. They were to be exercised only in accordance with the laws of nature and of nature's God, which were moral laws. Rights and duties were in a reciprocal relationship. But the nature revealed by modern science—the unconditional basis of the belief in Progress—was that of mindless matter, a source of power to be commanded, not a source of morality to be obeyed. From here on, "rights" would be understood as the unconditional empowerment of the individual to do as he pleased. Self-realization became the code word for the new morality. The human self, however, was no longer understood to be made in the image of God, since God was dead. Self-realization was in fact only the correlate of the new atheism. As there could no longer be any distinction between man and God, which distinction is as fundamental to the Declaration of Independence as to the Bible, there could be no distinction between base and noble desires. All desires were understood to be created equal, since all desires were seen as originating in that highest of all authorities, the self-creating self. Each human being was to be his own God, obeying only those restrictions that were enforced upon him by the fact that he was not yet himself the universal tyrant. In time, however, Science would enable everyone to act as if he were the universal tyrant.

As these doctrines were filtered through the intellectual establishment of modern liberal regimes, of which Chief Justice Rehnquist is a typical representative, the emancipation from morality was itself seen as moral progress, and the opponents of that emancipation were seen as the reactionary enemies of both freedom and morality. The essence of the new Liberalism was to make each human being, as far as possible, a universal tyrant within his own world, commanding all the pleasures possible in that world, and emancipated from everything except those limits upon his power that Science had not yet conquered. Thus would the return to a Garden of Eden—but one in which there would be no forbidden fruit—be accomplished.

Although the historical school represented the last attempt to preserve some form of rationalism in political philosophy, a certain post-Hegelian simulacrum of historical reason reappeared in the form of Darwinism. Becker's evidence is testimony to the fact that the most enduring and powerful form of historicism has been that of evolution. Thus Becker writes that

> the fruitful discoveries of natural science, particularly the great discovery of Darwin, were convincing the learned world that the origin, differentiation, and modification of all forms of life on the globe were the result of natural forces in a material sense; and that the operation of these forces might be formulated in terms of abstract laws which would neatly and sufficiently account for the organic world, just as the physical sciences were able to account for the physical world. When so much the greater part of the universe showed itself amenable to the reign of a purely material natural law, it was difficult to suppose that man (a creature in many respects astonishingly like the higher forms of apes) could have been permitted to live under a special dispensation. It was much simpler to assume one origin for all life and one law for all growth; simpler to assume that man was only the most highly organized of the creatures (the missing link would doubtless shortly be found), and to think of his history accordingly, as only a more subtly negotiated struggle for existence and survival.[34]

To think of human history as "only a more subtly negotiated" version of the sur-vival of the fittest is, however, to be trapped ineluctably in self-contradiction. It means, on the one hand, to assert that reason can be nothing more than an instrument of self-preservation. If that were true, all knowledge would be a form of power. Earlier ways of knowing would be made obsolete by later ones, for the same reason that gunpowder made obsolete the bow, the catapult, and the sling-shot. What is called knowledge would be desired only as a means to being the fittest in the struggle for survival. Any given adaptation to this end would be des-tined to be superseded in the course of evolutionary change. The theory of nat-ural rights, which served as a fighting faith in the American Revolution, would be superseded by other theories in the same way that the muzzle-loading musket has been superseded by the breech-loading rifle and the machine gun. But the theory of evolution, which condemns the theory of natural rights to the dustbin of his-tory, cannot exempt itself from the imperatives of this perspective. Either it rep-resents a phase in the evolutionary struggle of mankind, or it does not. If it does, it too is destined for the dustbin. If it makes a claim to truth independent of evo-lutionary history, then the mind is not the prisoner of history that the theory itself asserts. In that case, there can be no presumption against the natural rights phi-losophy as superseded by history, evolutionary or otherwise.

In fact, Becker believed evolution to represent a higher form of understand-ing than the natural rights philosophy of the Declaration of Independence. He saw it as a "unified field theory" that reduced natural and human history to a sin-gle set of causes. But this is a "scientific" test of validity, not an evolutionary or historical test. And it is a fallacious test, because in it Becker had exempted the mind of the philosopher or scientist from the "field" that was to be "unified." He fell into the same fatal dualism that has characterized all the descendants of that first of modern philosophers, the Cretan who said that all Cretans are liars!

In the simplicity with which he falls into this trap of dualism, Becker testifies nonetheless to the overwhelming power of Darwinism upon the intellectual life of Western man in the later nineteenth and early twentieth centuries. The class struggle central to Marx's doctrine came to be viewed less as a manifestation of Hegel's dialectic than of Darwin's account of the competition of organic life for survival. The race struggle, central to the doctrines of Chamberlain and Gob-ineau—out of which Hitler's notions of Aryan supremacy emerged—came also to be seen as no more than an inference from Darwin's teaching.

What deserves particular notice in Becker's summary of Darwinism is the twofold denial, first, of any fundamental distinction between natural history and human history, and, second, of any fundamental distinction between force and right. Thus: "In a universe in which man seemed only a chance deposit on the surface of the world, and the social forces no more than a resolution of blind force, the 'right' and the 'fact' were indeed indistinguishable; in such a universe the rights which nature gave to man were easily thought of as measured by the power he could exert."[35] The doctrine of the last sentence, that might makes right, certainly enlisted Hitler and Stalin among its disciples, along with many others. It denies any legitimacy to the distinction between noble failure and base success, a distinction fundamental to the idea of human dignity as enshrined in the tradition of biblical and classical ethics, no less than in the Declaration of Independence. What Becker writes here constitutes as well an endorsement of Calhoun's theory of the concurrent majority, by which only those minorities that are powerful enough to obstruct the will of the majority are entitled to the veto power. Hence Southern slaveholders had minority rights, but Southern slaves (or free Negroes) had none. From this perspective it is not so much meaningless as rhetorical to ask if the philosophy of the Declaration is true or false. It is false!

Yet Becker can still write about the need of man to justify himself, as if such justification represented a quest for a transhistorical truth or justice and as if "the social process" was something other than "a resolution of blind force."

> When honest men are impelled to withdraw their allegiance to the established law or custom of the community . . . they seek for some principle more generally valid, some "law" of higher authority. . . . They formulate the law or principle in such a way that it is, or seems to them to be, rationally defensible. To them it is "true" because it brings their actions into harmony with a rightly ordered universe, and enables them to think of themselves as having chosen the nobler part . . . in order to serve God or Humanity or a force that makes for the highest good.[36]

Becker refers to those appealing to higher law as "honest men." But from this perspective, Hitler and Stalin were no less honest than Jefferson and Lincoln. The only truth to any version of the higher law is whether it contributes to the victory of the party espousing it. By assimilating all behavior to evolution, Becker is saying that whatever beliefs appear to motivate human beings—whether in God, humanity, natural law, the class struggle, or Aryan supremacy—are merely instrumental mechanisms in the evolutionary process, enabling men to find within themselves and their cohorts resources for proving stronger than their enemies. Although these beliefs appear true to their adherents, Becker does not for a moment entertain the possibility that one or another of them is actually true, apart from being believed and apart from contributing to the struggle of a human organism in its contest for predominance with other such organisms.

∾

Carl Becker's book on the Declaration, first published in 1922, was reprinted in 1942 with an introduction dated September 14, 1941. This introduction, and the time that it was written, casts a large shadow across the argument of the book, and in particular across Becker's thesis concerning the meaninglessness of the question as to the truth of the doctrine of the Declaration. September 14, 1941, was less than three months after Hitler launched his attack upon the USSR and less than three months before Pearl Harbor. This was the very apogee of Hitler's success. It was the moment when, to all the world, the establishment of the Thousand Year Reich appeared imminent and certain. Hardly anyone doubted that the fall of the USSR was impending and was as certain as the fall of France in 1940. Once that occurred, Hitler, in partnership with Japan, would be master of the entire Eurasian continent, and the fall of Britain could not much longer be postponed. At that point the naval resources of the United States would be no match for the Axis, and the United States would no longer be able to defend itself. Nothing could then stand against the domination of the world by Hitler and his allies. Becker thought that the reprinting of his book might be particularly pertinent "just now, when political freedom, already lost in many countries, is everywhere threatened." At such a time, he believed, "the readers of books would be more than ordinarily interested in the political principles of the Declaration of Independence."[37]

In 1941, Becker returned to the Declaration, not as an academic exercise, but as an instrument in the fight against tyranny. In the crisis of that year, it was not a meaningless question to ask whether Hitler's Third Reich was an evil empire. Nor did Becker then doubt that the principles of the Declaration represented the goodness of political freedom as much as the evil of tyranny was represented by the Third Reich. He wrote: "Certainly recent events throughout the world have aroused an unwonted attention to the immemorial problem of human liberty." According to Dr. Johnson, "when a man knows he is to be hanged in a fortnight, it concentrates his mind wonderfully." The prospect of Hitler's imminent victory concentrated Becker's mind in 1941 in a way that it had not been concentrated in 1922. If the problem of human liberty is "immemorial," might not the principles of human liberty also be immemorial? And if they are immemorial, as the Declaration maintains, then they are not historical or time-bound, as Becker had maintained twenty years before.

> The incredible cynicism and brutality of Adolf Hitler's ambitions, made every day more real by the servile and remorseless activities of his bleak-faced, humorless Nazi supporters, have forced men everywhere to re-appraise the validity of half-forgotten ideas, and enabled them once more to entertain convictions as to the substance of things not evident to the senses.[38]

Twenty years earlier Becker had written approvingly of the historicist and evolutionary theory that, as it turned out, was at the heart of National Socialism. Then he had appeared persuaded that "the origin, differentiation, and modifications of all forms of life" might best be understood as "the result of natural forces in a material sense." And he had dismissed the notion that "man . . . could have been permitted to live under a special dispensation."[39] Now, however, it is precisely to such a dispensation that he appeals, desperate at the prospect of Nazi victory.

"Liberty, equality and fraternity," as well as the "inalienable rights of man"—that is to say, rights grounded, not in changing history, but in unchanging nature—are said by Becker in his 1941 introduction to be "phrases, glittering or not, that denote realities—the fundamental realities that men will always fight for rather than surrender."[40] What in 1922 had been fundamental illusions have now become "fundamental realities"! As an epigone of modern science, Becker had earlier given short shrift to an alleged reality grounded in "the substance of things not evident to the senses." But now his previous view of "the social process" as "no more than a resolution of blind force" might appear as an endorsement of Hitler's belief in "the triumph of the will."

No one writing in 1941 about the crisis of freedom could use the words "fight rather than surrender" without invoking the spirit of Winston Churchill. Clearly, it was only Churchill who in 1941 could have led Becker to hope against all odds that the darkest hour of the defenders of freedom might yet prove to be their finest hour: "we shall fight on the beaches, we shall fight on the landing grounds, we shall fight in the fields and in the streets, we shall fight in the hills, we shall never surrender."[41] Churchill showed indeed that "the substance of things not evident to the senses" might fearlessly engage the most naked materialism. In World War II, and in the Cold War that followed it, the doctrine that might makes right confronted the doctrine that right makes might, and in both cases the latter won. Yet there was no *necessity* that caused it to win. Nothing in the idea or theory of evolution could explain why freedom triumphed over tyranny. The very idea of human freedom, embodied in the Declaration of Independence, requires that we act according to the right, without being able to know that the right will triumph. That same idea requires that we act on the conviction that noble failure is better than base success, so that, win or lose, we shall have taken the better part.[42] This contrasts with both the Nazi belief in the triumph of the will and the Communist belief in the historically predetermined victory of the revolutionary proletariat. Neither of these tyrannical causes can justify failure, any more than evolutionary theory can justify organisms that become extinct in the struggle for survival.

In 1941 Becker hoped that the principles of the Declaration might, as in 1776 and in 1863, arm the cause of right and freedom. But the "incredible cynicism and brutality" of the Nazis was no illusion, and neither could it be an illusion to think that those resisting Hitler had chosen the nobler part.

In 1922, Becker's last words about the Declaration of Independence were a strange mixture of admiration and condescension. It was, he wrote,

> founded upon a superficial knowledge of history . . . and upon a naive faith in the instinctive virtues of human kind. Yet it was a humane and engaging faith. At its best it preached toleration in place of persecution, goodwill in place of hate, peace in place of war. It taught that beneath all local and temporary diversity, beneath the superficial traits and talents that distinguish men and nations, all men are equal in possessing a common humanity; and to the end that concord might prevail on earth instead of strife, it invited men to promote in themselves the humanity which bound them to their fellows, and to shape their conduct and their institutions in harmony with it. . . . This faith could not survive the harsh realities of the modern world.[43]

The beginning and the end of this passage represent condescension. Is it not clear, however, that the words in between represent a political faith that, in Becker's own mind, is independent of time and place? Could he really have believed that the superiority of toleration to persecution (or of freedom to slavery) was founded upon "a superficial knowledge of history" or "a naive faith in the instinctive virtues of human kind"? Does the most profound knowledge of history teach us to deny that "beneath all local and temporary diversity . . . all men are equal in the possession of a common humanity"? This was what Lincoln incorporated into the Gettysburg Address as the central idea of political freedom from which all its minor thoughts radiated. To say that this, as a rational faith, could not survive the harsh realities of the modern world is to say that there is no intrinsic reason to prefer toleration to persecution, goodwill to hate, peace to war. In 1922, when Becker praised the identification of force and right in evolutionary doctrine, it was before he knew that it would be the creed of Adolf Hitler. It was before he knew that National Socialism would come to represent the Darwinian and scientific historicism that he thought had superseded the doctrines of the Declaration. But in 1941 he could not repeat what he had said on this score at the same time that he called upon the democracies not to surrender to the Thousand Year Reich.

Becker's case against the Declaration in his 1922 book is implicitly repudiated in his 1941 introduction. Yet there is no evidence that he had thought through the meaning of that repudiation. Had he done so, he would have rewritten the book, or written another book—which it apparently never occurred to him to do. Becker's central reason for rejecting the natural rights philosophy was his belief that it had been refuted by the historical school, which "identified nature with history." But nature, as we have observed, refers to the unchanging ground of changing experience. To identify the unchanging with the changing is to identify what is the same with the different, or the like with the unlike. The different manifestations of man's humanity in no way disprove the proposition that "all men are equal in the possession of a common humanity." It would be difficult to credit a man of Becker's sophistication with so simple an error in logic were it not for the fact that the historical profession has for more than seventy-five years so unvaryingly followed his example.[44]

∾

Becker prefaces his book on the Declaration with four epigraphs that declare in advance his disbelief in the truth of the document to which he has given such devoted labor. These epigraphs define, perhaps better than his text, the climate of opinion within which his mind moved and within which American historiography has moved ever since. The first two, taken from Pascal's *Pensées*, are:

> But what is nature? Why is custom not natural? I greatly fear that this nature is itself only a first custom, as custom is second nature.

> We need not feel the truth that law is but usurpation; it was introduced without reason, it has become reasonable; it is necessary to cause it to be regarded as authentic, eternal, and to conceal the beginning of it, if we do not wish it to come soon to an end.

We take up the latter of these epigraphs first. We note that the *Pensées* were published around 1670, when Europe was still wracked by religious wars emanating from the breakup of feudalism and the Holy Roman Empire, as well as by the rise of Protestantism, capitalism, nationalism, and democracy. When Pascal says "law is but usurpation," he is anticipating what Tom Paine will say about feudal law in the *Rights of Man*. The feudal order was founded upon conquest, the feudal nobility being in its origins nothing more than the heads of the gangs that ruled in their localities following the barbarian invasions and the dissolution of the legal order of the ancient Roman Empire. Feudal services were what the chieftains, who differed little from the capos of the latter-day mafiosi, exacted from their followers in exchange for the protection that they received as members of the gang. The lawfulness of their titles, some hundreds of years later, was nothing but the effect of long possession.[45]

In chapter 1 we saw that Jefferson, in his *Summary View*, denied legitimacy to the feudal regime introduced into England by the Norman Conquest. Jefferson considered the authentic or Whig constitution as emanating from the Normans'

Saxon predecessors. This pristine order had resulted, not from conquest, but from the voluntary actions of a free people. According to Hamilton's memorable words in the first *Federalist*, however, "It has been frequently remarked that it seems to have been reserved to the people of this country, by their conduct and example, to decide the important question, whether societies of men are really capable or not of establishing good government from reflection and choice, or whether they are forever destined to depend for their political constitutions on accident and force."[46] Hamilton and Lincoln would certainly have agreed with what Pascal says about the law, as a description of the ancien régimes of Europe, before the Glorious Revolution of 1689 in Great Britain and the American Revolution of 1776. But they would also say that the distinction between law as usurpation (or as despotic) and law as reasonable implies the necessity of the truth of the distinctions enshrined in the Declaration of Independence. What Pascal says is that law, which begins as force, may yet become what is right by becoming what is reasonable. What the Declaration says is that a people, in throwing off rule that has become unreasonable and tyrannical, may institute new government that is nontyrannical and in accordance with reason. Nothing in what Pascal says prevents force that is not usurpation, or what came to be called the right of revolution, from being used in the service of the institution of free government. That such may never have happened before, or that such a government may have no precedent in the human record, does not mean that it is not possible.

The words *novus ordo seclorum* on the great seal of the United States, with "1776" subscribed beneath them, indicates the American conviction that the principles of the Declaration of Independence had their first actual institution by a people in the American Revolution. In view of the fact that Pascal wrote a century before the American Revolution, there is no reason to think that the Signers of the Declaration would not have agreed with Pascal, or Pascal with the Signers. What Pascal says may be paraphrased as follows: "All actual governments have their origins in injustice. But these governments, over time, have achieved a degree of decency that makes it desirable that their laws be obeyed. It is necessary therefore to conceal by myths the reality of these origins, if the reasons for obeying such governments are not to be undermined." Becker assumes as a matter of course that the Declaration is merely another myth of origins, invented to justify a regime that is not intrinsically justifiable. But this assumption is gratuitous. It is worth noting, moreover, that the Declaration, while justifying the actions of the rebelling colonies, did not assume or declare that they were establishing a new order that completely or sufficiently exemplified the criteria to which they appealed. The Preamble to the Constitution speaks only of "a more perfect Union." According to Lincoln, the Declaration meant to establish "a standard maxim for free society" that, although "never perfectly attained," might yet be "constantly approximated," thereby "augmenting the happiness and value of life to all men everywhere."[47] This would not be possible unless the doctrines of the Declaration really are what they professed to be. The fact that throughout human history the origins of regimes have, for good reasons, been shrouded in myths does not mean that "these truths" are myths. Becker, in citing this passage of Pascal, imputes to it a meaning that it cannot bear.

In fact, Pascal himself assumes the existence in his own mind of something like the truths of the Declaration when he distinguishes law that is "usurpation" from law that "has become reasonable." In so doing, he further assumes that in becoming reasonable, the law conforms to a standard that is "authentic" and "eternal." Pascal here implies what Lincoln meant when he spoke of a truth "applicable to all men and all times."

～

We turn now to the first of Pascal's two aphorisms employed by Becker. It is evidently meant to call into question the credibility of the idea of nature as a source of norms of human conduct. "But what is nature?" Pascal asks. "Why is custom not natural?" He greatly fears, he says, "that this nature is itself only first custom, as custom is a second nature."

Clearly his fear is unjustified. Aristotle observed that fire burns the same way both here and in Persia but that the things regarded as just and unjust differ everywhere.[48] The doubt of nature as a source of the principles of human conduct begins, not by doubting the existence of nature, but by doubting that human laws or morals can be other than conventional. It begins by doubting that law or morality can be called good or bad with reference to any unchanging principles outside human will or human enactment.[49]

Aristotle starts from the premise that those physical relationships that are invariable attest to the existence of causes that can properly be called natural. If a stone is thrown upwards a hundred times, it will fall downwards the last time exactly as it did the first time. The stone (like fire) cannot become "accustomed" to acting in a way different from the way in which nature determines it to act.[50] A stone cannot have a second nature. But neither can it have a first custom!

Aristotle says that human beings are not determined by nature to be either good or bad. To say that human behavior is not predestined by causes outside the human will (as the behavior of a stone is determined), however, is not to say that there is no human nature. The Declaration of Independence assumes what is affirmed at the outset of Jefferson's Virginia Statute of Religious Liberty: "Almighty God hath created the mind free." When Jefferson presented "these truths" as "self-evident" in the Declaration, he did so on the assumption that a disinterested human intelligence—one free to accept or reject, on the basis of unassisted human reason, any propositions presented to it—would recognize them for what they were. Human beings are not compelled to think this or that and therefore are not determined to act thus or so. A free society is in harmony with the nature of man because it recognizes that the human good arises from human freedom. It recognizes, quoting again from the Virginia Statute, "that truth is great and will prevail if left to herself . . . unless by human interposition disarmed of her natural weapons, free argument and debate."[51]

Human freedom relates first and foremost to the freedom of the mind.[52] But a free society, while not employing any form of compulsion, is not indifferent to how its members act or how they think, as is shown by this famous passage in the Northwest Ordinance: "Religion, morality, and knowledge, being necessary to good government and the happiness of mankind, schools and the means of education shall forever be encouraged."[53] Like other animals, man needs food and is driven by a natural necessity to find it. Such a necessity is not mindless like that that makes a stone fall to earth, but it is a necessity nonetheless. No one is compelled, however, to decide to earn his food by honest labor rather than to steal it from someone else. The choice between these two modes of acquisition is one that at some point everyone must make. Enslaving another man to save oneself the pain of labor is of course a form of stealing. That the distinction between stealing and earning corresponds to the distinction between vice and virtue is hardly arbitrary or merely conventional.

Other animals are either carnivorous or herbivorous, and they hunt or graze according to their nature. But human beings are allowed by their nature to make choices, and the quality of those choices determines the quality of their lives. Whatever in human life is involuntary, like breathing, is not subject to the distinction between virtue and vice.[54] Unlike a stone, a human being, by repeatedly acting honestly, will become honest, and by repeatedly acting dishonestly, will become dishonest. The necessities of man's nature determine the conditions within which he may become either good or bad. What he has become accustomed to doing determines his character. Custom can be called second nature only because nature cannot be properly called first custom.

Becker's display of Pascal's aphorism is evidently meant to commend the ostensible truth of what today is called cultural relativism. There is of course no question as to the human propensity to identify one's own customs with what is intrinsically or naturally just. Indeed, it is precisely because of this that the Declaration of Independence, which is addressed to all mankind, rests its case upon a universal standard. It rests legitimate government upon the consent of the governed. A free people does not have its laws or institutions imposed upon it from outside or above. Human freedom is consistent with an apparently limit-less variety of laws and customs. Yet all these laws and customs, to be legitimate, are within boundaries prescribed by nature. Consent that is blind to the reality of man's nature does not give rise to the just powers of government. The great proposition of human equality, the central idea of the Gettysburg Address as of the Declaration, means at the very least that those consenting to government recognize the humanity that they and their fellow citizens share with all men everywhere. It means that they recognize that human beings are neither beasts nor gods. It means therefore that no one has a right to govern other human beings as God may be said rightfully to govern the world or as human beings may be said rightfully to govern the beasts of the field. It means that laws are right-fully for the benefit of the governed, not of the government. It means that those who live under the laws should share in making them and that those who make the laws must live under them. Consent cannot of itself legitimate tyrannical government or the tyranny of barbarous customs based upon superstition. Human freedom is itself an aspect of nature. When properly consulted by rea-son, nature therefore directs the use of human freedom and enables us to dis-tinguish its proper from its improper uses.

∿

The third of Becker's four aphorisms, from Thomas Burnett's *Essay upon Gov-ernment*, contemplates the changes in the British constitution wrought by the civil wars of the seventeenth century:

> As to the late Civil Wars, 'tis pretty well known what Notions of Government went current in those Days. When Monarchy was to be subverted, we know what was necessary to justify the Fact; and then, because it was convenient for the pur-pose, it was undoubtedly true in the Nature of Things, that Government had its original from the People, and the Prince was only their Trustee. . . . This was the doctrine that was commonly received, and the only doctrine relish'd in those times. But afterwards, when Monarchy took its place again . . . another Notion of Government came into Fashion. Then Government had its original entirely from God, and the Prince was accountable to none but Him. . . . And now, upon anoth-er turn of things, when people have a liberty to speak out, a new set of Notions is advanced; now passive obedience is all a mistake, and instead of being a duty to suffer Oppression, 'tis a Glorious Act to resist it: and instead of leaving Injuries to be redressed by God, we have a natural right to relieve ourselves.

We might call this the political theory of the Vicar of Bray. The Vicar, the hero of the famous anonymous ballad, adopts in turn the doctrines of the successive (and successful) protagonists in the English civil wars—Cromwell, Charles II, and William of Orange—and manages thereby to keep his place. The refrain goes:

And this is law, I will maintain,
Unto my dying day, sir,
That whatsoever king shall reign,
I will be Vicar of Bray, sir!

Becker's belief in the relativism of all moral and political truth rests upon the assumption that, because we can see that men's doctrines serve their interests, therefore the meaning of the doctrines is to be found in the interests they serve. It does not take a course in logic to see that this is a non sequitur. The Vicar of Bray is an amusing scoundrel who professes to believe whatever the government of the day declares is true. His only "interest" is in his place. He certainly is not worried by his conscience or by the judgment of God. From Becker's perspective, the deadly serious men who fought the English civil wars, the American Revolution, and the American Civil War did so from motives that were not essentially different from the Vicar's, however unconscious of that fact they may have been. But neither Oliver Cromwell nor William of Orange nor George Washington nor Abraham Lincoln was a Vicar of Bray! There is no reason to doubt that these great leaders believed they were fighting for causes that were just, and that in so doing they were subordinating their interests to their duties. How can anyone say a priori that they were mistaken as to their own motives? For Becker to reduce a Cromwell or a Lincoln to a common denominator with the Vicar of Bray, thereby denying the reality of the difference between knaves and heroes, is to destroy the very distinctions that constitute the phenomena of history.

According to Burnett, "When monarchy was to be subverted" it became "necessary to justify the fact." He implies that those who wished to overthrow the king sought justification after the fact as a means to this end. Because it was "convenient" for this purpose, "it was undoubtedly true in the Nature of things that Government had its Original from the People, and the Prince was only their Trustee." The words "undoubtedly true" have all the mockery of a police investigator listening to the alibi of a hardened criminal. Here we have Becker's judgment concerning the intrinsic validity of "the laws of nature and of nature's God" invoked by the Declaration of Independence. What is true "in the nature of things" is merely what is convenient for purposes that have nothing to do with either nature or truth. "Truth" becomes merely a euphemism for what men believe, or say they believe, in order to persuade (or deceive) others for basely interested reasons. Once again, we must apply Becker's standard to himself and ask, what is his interest that causes him to proclaim this doctrine as true?

107

Is it really out of the question, however, that some men in seventeenth-century England, or in eighteenth- or nineteenth-century America, compared and contrasted the doctrine of the divine right of kings with that of popular sovereignty and asked themselves, "Which is right?" Is it not possible that at least some men, at all times, have taken with full seriousness the thought that God distinguished them from brute creation for no less a purpose than to live by their rational perceptions of the just and the unjust? How can we say that men's interests generate their opinions when some men, at least, decide what their interests are only after they have decided what those interests ought to be? One of the conspicuous features of the Declaration of Independence is the appeal of its Signers "to the supreme judge of the world for the rectitude of our intentions." Becker would have us believe that they were either deluded or insincere. Yet their confidence in their rectitude was an assurance, in their own minds, that their intentions had been determined by no interests apart from the cause they had set forth out of "a decent respect to the opinions of mankind." The rectitude of that cause was in its conformity with the self-evident truths proclaimed in the Declaration, truths emanating from the laws of nature and in accordance with what they believed to be the divine government of the universe. Their confidence in this rectitude was the ground of their "firm reliance on the protection of divine Providence." Justice defined their interest, armed them in the struggle, and was the ground of their faith in victory.[55]

To say that the doctrine of the divine right of kings was convenient for advancing the cause of monarchy or that the doctrine of popular sovereignty was convenient for overthrowing monarchy does not tell us anything about the truth of these doctrines. The case for popular sovereignty in the seventeenth century was a less sophisticated version of the argument, advanced supremely by the Declaration of Independence, that all legitimate government rests upon the consent of the governed. Both the divine right of kings and the rule of masters over slaves violated that doctrine. The great antebellum debate over slavery pitted those who believed slavery to be an evil—or at best a necessary evil—against those who declared it a positive good, a benefit to both the slaves and their masters. It was a familiar saying of Abraham Lincoln that "although volume upon volume is written to prove slavery a very good thing, we never hear of the man who wishes to take the good of it, by being a slave himself!"[56] So far as I know, such a man has not yet been found. Still, one might reply to Lincoln that the goodness of slavery for natural slaves is not disproved by his observation. How does one weigh the interest of an individual or a people in ruling himself or themselves against the interest of that same person or people in being ruled by his or their natural superiors? If we say that the claim to natural superiority is a ruse to advance the selfish interests of the would-be rulers, we beg the question. Calling an assertion of natural superiority merely self-interested can be met by the counterassertion that the denial of such a claim is also self-interested. A natural slave may prefer his unrestrained liberty, like an unbroken stallion. But that does not mean his preference is justified.[57] The interest of the master in slavery and the interest of the slave in freedom do not tell us what we need most of all to know about slavery and freedom. Someone might reply to Lincoln that horses do not seek the good of being trained by horse trainers. The real question is whether the natures of masters and slaves differ as much as the natures of horse trainers and horses. If they do, then slavery may in fact be good for slaves, whether they know it or not. Likewise, mastery would be good for the master class, whether its members know it, like John C. Calhoun, or whether, like Lincoln, they do not. Can we not then ask whether some human beings differ in nature from others in such degree or kind as to make their slavery just, whether they consent to it or not?[58] This at bottom is the question that Carl Becker declares is meaningless, and it is this question we must be prepared to answer.

Now it is undoubtedly true, as Becker maintains, that many if not most of those holding that slavery was an evil came to have a political interest in that opinion. But does having such an interest disqualify someone from having an objective understanding of whether slavery is good or evil? Would Becker have us say that a black slave such as Frederick Douglass, arguing against the morality of slavery, is merely an interested party and that his argument is to be discounted because of that interest? Is not the fact that he advances arguments in his cause, whether the arguments are sound or unsound, proof that he is *Homo sapiens* and therefore that he possesses the same nature as John C. Calhoun, who advanced the positive good theory of slavery?[59] As we shall see, the Becker thesis about the meaninglessness of the question of whether reason can decide the truth or falsity of a doctrine is a denial that man really is *Homo sapiens*. Reason is only a surrogate or proxy for the subrational or nonrational. That man really differs from the beasts is essentially an illusion. We have here another example of Becker's denial, embodied in the first epigraph from Pascal, that man has a nature.[60]

The repeal of the Missouri Compromise wrenched Abraham Lincoln from political obscurity. His advocacy of the policy of excluding slavery from all federal territories, although it failed to make him a United States senator, served eventually to make him president. Are we to say that Lincoln's reasons for thinking slavery morally wrong are to be discounted because he presented them in political campaigns?[61] Should Lincoln have advanced his arguments "with one, two, or three, but never publicly,"[62] so as to maintain the purity of his interest in unsullied truth? There is reason to believe that Lincoln wrestled long and hard in private with the question of the morality of slavery, as he had with the question of free will and predestination. Having come to a conclusion, however, he could not let the matter rest there. Moral arguments point to moral obligations. Lincoln could advance the antislavery cause only by gaining political advantage for the antislavery argument. Certainly there is an abstract interest, perhaps the highest of all human interests, in knowing whether an argument is true. But when the truth relates to questions of right and wrong, of just and unjust, then it also relates to how one ought to act. Whether we act justly or unjustly determines whether we ourselves become just or unjust.[63] At that point an interest in truth is joined inescapably to an interest in justice.

In his Peoria speech of October 16, 1854, Lincoln compared Senator Douglas's argument for the right of white settlers to decide in favor of slavery, if they wished to do so, with

> the old argument for the "Divine right of Kings." By the latter, the King is to do just as he pleases with his white subjects, being responsible to God alone. By the former, the white man is to do just as he pleases with his black slaves, being responsible to God alone. The two things are precisely alike; and it is natural that they should find similar arguments to sustain them.[64]

Similar remarks about the divine right of kings are repeated throughout Lincoln's speeches. In his Chicago speech of July 10, 1858, for example, he attacks Douglas for "this idea of 'don't care if slavery is voted up or voted down.'"

> Those arguments that are made, that the inferior race are to be treated with as much allowance as they are capable of enjoying; that as much is to be done for them as their condition will allow. What are these arguments? They are the arguments that kings have made for enslaving the people in all the ages of the world. You will find that all the arguments in favor of king-craft were of this class; they always bestrode the necks of the people, not because they wanted to do it, but because the people were better off for being ridden. That is their argument, and this argument of the Judge is the same old serpent that says you work and I eat, you toil and I will enjoy the fruits of it. Turn it whatever way you will—whether it come from the mouth of a King, as an excuse for enslaving the people of his country, or from the men of one race as a reason for enslaving the men of another race, it is all the same old serpent.[65]

In this, as in so much else, Lincoln was the heir of Jefferson. The latter's most famous expression on this theme was in a letter declining an invitation from the mayor of Washington, D.C., to a great celebration of the fiftieth anniversary of the Glorious Fourth. As we know, this turned out to be the very day on which Jefferson and his Revolutionary cohort, John Adams, would undergo their apotheoses. But Jefferson made the day memorable, not so much by his death, as by the immortal words he penned for it. Concerning the Declaration of Independence, he wrote:

> May it be to the world, what I believe it will be, (to some parts sooner, to others later, but finally to all), the signal of arousing men to burst the chains under which monkish ignorance and superstition had persuaded them to bind themselves, and to assume the blessings and security of self-government. That form which we have substituted, restores the free right to the unbounded exercise of reason and freedom of opinion. All eyes are opened, or opening, to the rights of man. The general spread of the light of science has already laid open to every view the palpable truth, that the mass of mankind has not been born with saddles on their backs, nor a favored few booted and spurred, ready to ride them legitimately, by the grace of God. For ourselves, let the annual return of this day forever refresh our recollections of these rights, and an undiminished devotion to them.[66]

I have quoted so much of the foregoing because it enshrines so much of Lincoln's legacy from Jefferson. In the "annual return of this day," Jefferson places that mark of traditional ceremony on the Fourth of July upon which Lincoln would build his conception of political religion. In making it the day upon which the citizens would be reminded of the reasons for their enjoyment of the blessings of freedom, Jefferson anticipates the way in which Lincoln would speak of the Fourth as if it were the American Passover. This is the day on which, in a phrase of Henry Clay that Lincoln often repeated, the cannon "thunders its annual joyous return." This is the day on which Americans are reminded of their ancestral liberation from the tyranny of the "Pharaohs" of inequality and despotism, to the "blessings and security of self-government" and the "unbounded exercise of reason and freedom of opinion." Only as each successive generation is reminded of, and instructed anew in, "the rights of man" can the blessings of liberty be perpetuated.

The central metaphor employed by Jefferson, and continued by Lincoln, is that centering upon that "old serpent," the doctrine of the divine right of kings. Jefferson certainly encountered it in Sidney's *Discourses Concerning Government*, where we read:

> Man therefore must be naturally free. . . . God only, who confers this right upon us, can deprive us of it: and we can no way understand that he does so, unless he had so declared by express revelation, or had set some distinguishing marks of dominion and subjection upon men; and, as an ingenious person not long since said, caused some to be born with crowns upon their heads, and all others with saddles upon their backs.[67]

The idea that a departure from the principle of mankind's natural equality would require an "express revelation" was also transmitted to Jefferson by Locke, as can be seen from the following celebrated passage from chapter II of *The Second Trea-tise of Government*:

> there being nothing more evident[68] than that creatures of the same species and rank, promiscuously born to all the same advantages of nature and the use of the same faculties, should also be equal one amongst another without subordination or subjection; unless the lord and master of them all should, by any manifest dec-laration of his will, set one above another, and confer on him by an evident and clear appointment an undoubted right to dominion and sovereignty.

This is also the precursor of the magnificent irony of the Continental Congress in the Declaration of the Causes and Necessity of Taking Up Arms, of July 6, 1775.

> If it was possible for men who exercise their reason to believe that the divine Author of our existence intended a part of the human race to hold an absolute property in, and an unbounded power over others, marked out by his infinite goodness and wisdom, as the objects of a legal domination never rightfully resistible, however severe and oppressive, the inhabitants of these colonies might at least require from the parliament of Great Britain some evidence, that this dreadful authority over them had been granted to that body.[69]

Returning to the horses-and-riders metaphor, we find that Sidney (himself soon to be martyred to the cause of republicanism) was paraphrasing from a speech delivered on the scaffold by Colonel Richard Rumbold, June 26, 1685. Rumbold is reported to have said, "I am sure there was no Man born marked of God above another; for none comes into the World with a Saddle on his Back, neither any Booted and Spurr'd to Ride him."[70]

The idea of human equality is encapsulated in the idea that no such distinc-tion arises between man and man as there is between man and horse, such as to make one man by nature the ruler of another. A purist might object, of course, that if human beings are not born with saddles on their backs, neither are horses. This great foundational metaphor of free government rests upon the assumption that horses are by nature suited to be ridden by men—for which purpose saddles and bridles on the one and boots and spurs on the other are appropriate and fit-ting augmentations of nature. The form and function of a horse mark it as useful for certain human purposes, and in serving these purposes, the horse serves ends that we deem higher than those of which the horse's nature is in itself capable. The rule of man over horse is not arbitrary, because it is in accordance with nature. The horse cannot argue that it ought not to be enslaved. The horse is not denied the right of consent, because it is incapable of consent, as consent is humanly understood. The horse cannot enter into a contractual relationship of any kind, although the well-trained horse does willingly obey its master. But every normal adult human being can make a contract—that is to say, voluntarily do something for someone else, now or in the future, in exchange for the other person doing something for him, now or in the future. And it is against nature, as it is against reason, for one human being to subject another to his will for no other cause than that by which a horse is brought to obey its rider. Since a black slave in antebellum America was held as a chattel, like a horse or any other cattle, he was held as if he belonged to a subhuman species. This was against the objective order of nature, and therefore against reason, and therefore unjust. It is precisely such an argument that Becker dismisses as meaningless.

Adam Smith, near the beginning of *The Wealth of Nations*, remarks that no one ever saw two dogs trade bones. A little dog with a big bone and a big dog with a little bone do not exchange bones on the basis of a comparison, in their minds, of their respective sizes with the sizes of their bones. The exchange, if it does take place—probably because the big dog takes the big bone from the little dog—is not based upon the principle of comparative advantage. Yet every normal adult human being, when asked to do something voluntarily, is in effect asked to do it for the sake of some advantage to himself. This is because, as Aristotle declared long ago, every voluntary human action necessarily aims at some good. Necessity and freedom are joined in this fact. Every human action necessarily intends something that the agent believes to be advantageous to himself. Even someone who deliberately sacrifices his life, like a soldier who throws himself on a grenade to save his comrades, does so for what he believes to be a greater good. We call an action voluntary when we think that it is the agent's own opinion that decides on the good for which he acts. The banker who promotes industry by lending money and the bank robber who discourages industry by stealing money each acts according to what appears good to him. They may have identical motives, in the sense that each intends to enrich himself by what he does. But the banker, in the ordinary course of his vocation, will have reason to believe that he promotes the enrichment of others as well as himself, while the robber knows very well (without caring) that he tends to impoverish others by his actions.

Our understanding of the difference between the banker and the bank robber turns upon our recognition of human freedom as an aspect of human nature. The banker lends money upon terms that are agreed to voluntarily by the borrower.[71] The borrower believes that his profit from the use of the money will be greater than the interest he pays the banker. The banker believes that the money he is lending will earn as much as or more than if he were not to lend it at all, or lend it to someone else. Each acts upon the principle of comparative advantage that underlies all voluntary exchanges, and each expects to gain thereby—as much as the two dogs, had they been able to reason, might have expected each to have a bone better for him as the result of a trade. All voluntary exchanges or contracts, whether implicit or explicit, are expressions of human nature, and as such contribute to a common good and friendship among those who participate in them. By equal reason, all exchanges that are imposed by force (or that result from fraud), whether that of the bank robber or of the despot or tyrant, are violations of human nature and contribute to enmity rather than friendship. Since men need friendship for their well-being at least as much as they need material goods, to impose on others by force is, whether one understands it or not, to act against one's deepest interest. As all "just and free government is derived from compact," so is it an objective expression of the principle of comparative advantage arising from human nature.

The doctrine, as characterized by Burnett, that "Government had its original from the People, and the Prince was only their Trustee" was and is rooted in the idea that "the People" itself is a voluntary association. Like all contractual relationships, it comes into being as an expression of the principle of comparative advantage. What is given up, when the original social contract is formed, is the natural right that each individual has to act without the permission of anyone else, to use such force as he may possess to protect his life, liberty, and property. What is gained is the collective force of the whole people in protecting the life, liberty, and property of each. This collective force is disposed by something called government. And this government, as we have seen, must a priori act by the majority, as the rational substitute for the unanimous consent that brought civil society into existence, but which cannot govern it. Civil society, we say, legislates by the majority, as the surrogate of the whole. In exactly the same sense, the executive, as the surrogate of society, enables it to act. "Prince" (or monarch), as much as "president," is simply the name of an office deemed useful by the people in enabling government to serve their purposes. Exactly what form the executive is to take—whether it is to be singular or plural, hereditary or elective—is a secondary matter that lies within the discretion of the people. It was clear from Jefferson's Whig perspective in the *Summary View* that he was addressing the king as if he were essentially a republican executive.

The radical core of the binding connection between human reason, human freedom, and human nature in the compact (or contract) theory of government is supremely expressed—as Lincoln expressed it at Gettysburg—in the idea of man's natural equality. Consider also the following by President Calvin Coolidge, speaking in Independence Hall in 1926, commemorating the 150th anniversary of the Declaration of Independence:

The idea that the people have a right to choose their own rulers is not new in political history. It was the foundation of every popular attempt to depose an undesirable king. This right was set out with a good deal of detail by the Dutch when as early as July 26, 1581, they declared their independence of Philip of Spain. In their long struggle with the Stuarts the British people asserted the same principles, which finally culminated in the Bill of Rights, deposing the last of that house and placing William and Mary on the throne. In each of these cases, sovereignty through divine right was displaced by sovereignty through the consent of the people. Running through the same documents, though expressed in different terms, is the clear inference of inalienable rights. But we should search these charters in vain for an assertion of the doctrine of equality. This principle had not before appeared as an official political declaration of any nation. It was profoundly revolutionary.[72]

I believe that Coolidge was correct in maintaining that in the Declaration the doctrine of equality was for the first time officially joined with the doctrine of popular sovereignty. This also marked the first time that a nation declared that the rights in virtue of which it asserted its own independence were rights it shared with all men everywhere. But the idea of popular sovereignty attained full logical coherence and moral force only when it was firmly grounded in the idea of human equality. Those forming a civil society by means of a compact can do so only in virtue of their prior recognition of each other's equal humanity. In forming the community, no one can consistently reserve more right to himself than he allows to another or claim any right a priori to any offices of profit or honor.

Unlike Carl Becker, Coolidge believed that "It was in the contemplation of these truths that the fathers made their declaration and adopted their constitution."[73] In consideration of the foregoing, how can Becker—how can anyone— think that the doctrine of popular sovereignty is no more than a self-serving rationalization of a nonrational desire to overthrow monarchy? Or think it no more intrinsically justifiable than the divine right of kings?

∽

In the epigraph from Burnett, we also read that "afterwards, when monarchy took its place again . . . another Notion of Government came into Fashion. Then Government had its original entirely from God, and the Prince was accountable to none but him." What Burnett had in mind here was the end of the Cromwellian commonwealth and the restoration of monarchy under Charles II. Cromwell's rule, however, although it had "its Original from the people," ended in a military dictatorship like that of Julius Caesar. Lincoln, in his Lyceum speech of 1838, spoke of "Alexander, Caesar, and Napoleon" as the three great destroyers of republics. The example of Cromwell, like that of Caesar, and like the later example of Napoleon—who loomed large and recent on Lincoln's horizon—shows how the principle of popular rule can be used to subvert popular rule. "Monarchy took its place again," in Burnett's chronicle of the English civil wars, because republicanism had been discredited by Cromwell's authoritarianism. The forces that defeated and beheaded Charles I were those of Parliament, a representative body that revolted against the king because he attempted to raise taxes without its consent. But Cromwell transformed himself from the servant of Parliament into its master. He became what Caesar had become in relation to the Roman senate, after crossing the Rubicon. These examples, to be followed by that of Napoleon, illuminate a problem endemic to popular government: appeals to the rights of the people can become the pretext or occasion for a military dictatorship or tyranny. For Jefferson, as for all the Founding Fathers, popular rule was inseparable from the rule of law. The idea that "An elective despotism was not the government we fought for"[74] epitomizes the spirit of the Founding as much as "Taxation without representation is tyranny." From the outset of his career, Lincoln recognized slavery as a danger to the cause of free government, in part because of the denial of the human rights of the slaves, but equally because of the temptation to overcome that denial by governing without the consent of the governed. The evil of slavery lay not only in slavery itself but also in the temptation to abandon the rule of law in adopting a Caesarian solution to the problem of slavery.[75] It was Lincoln's determination to deal with slavery only by constitutional means that made his task so extraordinarily difficult.

After Cromwell's death, the restoration of a chastened monarchy seemed preferable to the Commonwealth. Indeed, the rule of a Charles II, unwilling to challenge Parliament's authority as his father had done, seemed closer to the rule of law than the rule of Parliament dominated by Cromwell. Although the divine right of kings was held in official esteem, Charles's rule was acceptable only so long as it did not assert the claims of divine right in such a way as to challenge the great vested interests of the realm.

When James II succeeded his brother, he failed to observe his brother's caution. The pretensions of monarchy took a strange and anomalous turn. James was a not-so-secret Catholic. As king, however, he was also head of the Church of England. The Church of England, since the time of Henry VIII, had taught the doctrine of passive obedience to the monarch. It needs to be repeated that the doctrine of the divine right of kings was a different doctrine in the Reformation than it had been in medieval political theory. When popes contested ultimate authority with emperors, secular rulers ruled by divine right only so long as they did not come into fundamental conflict with the popes. It was the sacramental authority of the popes, administered through their appointed bishops, that endowed emperors and kings with divine right. As we saw in the case of Shakespeare's King John, if the pope excommunicated a rebellious king, he became an outlaw and was pronounced to be a tyrant who might lawfully be assassinated. When Henry VIII broke with Rome and became head of the Church of England, however, it became a cardinal doctrine of that church that as the king could not excommunicate himself, neither could he ever be regarded as a tyrant.[76] That meant unconditional or passive obedience to the king under all circumstances, as Burnett says.

The doctrine of passive obedience, as a feature of the emended doctrine of the divine right of kings, was revealed as self-contradictory when James II showed an intention of returning the Church of England to its former obedience to Rome. For the church to obey the king passively would be to give up the very ends for which passive obedience had been preached. Those ends included the preservation of the rights of property that had resulted from Henry VIII's expropriation of the monasteries. The validity of a huge proportion of the titles to real property in England in 1689, including the property of the Church of England, depended upon the validity of Henry VIII's break with Rome.

It was decisive for the future of popular government, and fatal to the cause of the divine right of kings, when in 1689 the bishops of the Church of England abandoned passive obedience and joined in the struggle against the head of their church. James was driven from the throne and replaced by his Protestant daughter Mary, together with his Protestant son-in-law William of Orange. Although the kings (and queens regnant) of England would henceforth, as hitherto, be heads of the Church of England, the title to the throne would be decisively parliamentary. Passive obedience would no longer be seriously considered, because the right of the people, as represented in Parliament, would have replaced the divine right of kings once and for all.

∼

The last of the four epigraphs encapsulating Carl Becker's thesis as to the meaninglessness of the question of the truth of the Declaration of Independence is:

The [French] constitution of 1795, like all of its predecessors, is made for Man. . . . I have seen, in my time, Frenchmen, Italians, Russians, etc.; I even know, thanks to Montesquieu, that one may be a Persian: but as for Man, I declare I never met him in my life; if he exists, it is without my knowledge.

The author quoted is De Maistre, and the quotation is from a book published in 1875, from the irredentist French right, protesting against popular sovereignty and favoring the divine rights claimed by the ancien régime. The quotation is repeated in the last paragraph of Becker's last chapter, "The Philosophy of the Declaration." This fourth epigraph repeats the thesis of the first—namely, that there is no such thing as human nature. We may therefore say that Becker's book, a book about the civil document that above all others asserted the rights of human nature, begins and ends with a denial of human nature. And we should note that, however unwittingly, Becker is quoting with approval a member of the same political sect that would say, in 1940, "Better Hitler than Blum."

The first two epigraphs, from Pascal, were presented by Becker to let us know that nature is nothing but deep-seated custom, something that we wish to regard as eternal because we do not wish it to come to an end. In other words, the origin of the idea of nature is in man's will rather than his reason, and it represents human wishes rather than any truth independent of those wishes. From this perspective "nature," which seems to stand in opposition to "culture," is in fact only culture in disguise. This means, in effect, that such a principle as that the just powers of government are based upon the consent of the governed is no more than a temporary aspect of a changing culture.

The epigraph from De Maistre supports this thesis by denying any reality to the universal "man," as opposed to the particular human beings bearing national appellations, such as Englishmen or Frenchmen. This is an epistemological thesis about human thought and reason. To say that one has met Englishmen and Frenchmen, but not man, is as much as to say that one has met German shepherds and Great Danes, but not dogs. Every common noun—man, horse, dog, tree, chair, house—is a universal predicated of an infinite number of possible particulars.

All language, all reasoning, is constituted by, and is about, common nouns. "Dog" is a common noun or universal, and "Fido" is a particular. In calling Fido a dog, we recognize the universal in the particular. We recognize Fido as a member of a species, however exceptional a dog we may think him to be. If we told someone, "We have a Fido," and not "We have a dog named Fido," he would not know what we were talking about (unless he guessed that Fido was a dog). Intelligible speech is not possible without common nouns, and every common noun is a universal.

The most fundamental of the assumptions underlying the American political tradition is not set forth in the Declaration of Independence. Rather, it is to be found in the magisterial exordium of the Virginia Statute of Religious Liberty, in the assertion that "Almighty God hath created the mind free." When the Declaration says, "We hold these truths to be self evident," it assumes that the minds holding the truths do so on the basis of that metaphysical freedom asserted in the

Virginia Statute. We must understand precisely in what that metaphysical freedom of the mind consists, because the moral and political freedom asserted on behalf of mankind is grounded in it. Without this metaphysical freedom, moral and political freedom would be meaningless. And that freedom is, primarily and essentially, the freedom by which human minds perceive the universals in the particulars by which they denominate anything denominated by a common noun.

While every individual (or actual) dog has a particular size, form, and color, the idea of the dog—the universal—has no material or sensible attributes whatever. The idea or the universal expressed by every common noun is itself entirely immaterial. The idea of the dog, perceived in every dog, is an abstraction from every possible dog. Sensible reality can become intelligible reality in our minds only in virtue of ideas that are themselves entirely abstracted from any sensible qualities. We cannot begin to think about dogs until we have separated "what it is to be a dog" in our minds from every actual or individual or particular dog. When, therefore, I say that Fido is a dog, I am also saying that there are an infinite number of possible dogs, each different in some respect from Fido, that are equally dogs. When I say that anyone is an Englishman or a Frenchman, I do not imply that anyone is either more or less a human being in virtue of being either French or English. I am recognizing an infinite number of possible human beings, each different from the other, but every one as human as the other. Man is the only species that employs common nouns as its medium of communication, and it is in this sense that man alone possesses language or speech. This is what is meant primarily and essentially by the identification of man as *Homo sapiens*. This identification is assumed by the Declaration of Independence in holding certain propositions to be true. Of course, Englishmen do speak a language different from Frenchmen, although common nouns, which can be translated from one language into another, play the identical role in every human language. For all human languages, notwithstanding their differences, are equally human.

When De Maistre says he has seen "Frenchmen" but does not know that "Man" exists, he is talking the purest nonsense. "Frenchman" is itself a compound of the noun "man" and the adjective "French." If there were no noun, there could not be an adjective. Of course De Maistre has never seen "man," but for the same reason that he has never seen "dog" or "cat" or "tree" or "horse." Since every common noun stands in the same relationship to every possible particular that it may characterize, the idea expressed by the common noun has no color, form, or size. It is perfectly immaterial, and therefore is apprehended by the mind in abstraction from all sensible qualities. It is this freedom of the mind from matter, when it thinks the universal, that constitutes the metaphysical freedom of the mind. The mind can think, in the human sense, only because it can abstract or separate what is intelligible from what is sensible. The mind of man, when it thinks, is emancipated from the matter about which it thinks. It is the purely abstract character of every common noun that enables the mind to think and to convey in language what it thinks. This is the metaphysical freedom of the mind that underlies all the other freedoms that we, as the heirs of Thomas Jefferson, hold dear. It explains why the Declaration of Independence, in saying "We hold these truths to be self-evident," supposes that there is nothing illusory about the truths so held.

When the Declaration asserts that all men are created equal, it is asserting what is in one sense not merely a truth but a truism. All human beings are equally human beings, in the same sense that all dogs are equally dogs, and all chairs are equally chairs. Anything denominated by any common noun partakes equally in the class characteristics referred to by that noun. If we say then that the Constitution, being based upon the principles of the Declaration, is color blind, we say what must be true because the idea of man is color blind. It is color blind because every common noun is lacking color or any other sensible quality. Dogs and chairs, as dogs and chairs, are not white dogs and chairs or black dogs and chairs. And human beings, as human beings, are not white or black human beings, or human beings of any other color.

The Declaration not only holds certain things to be true but holds them to be true because self-evident. This too is a truism. Every common noun is known by induction, not deduction. From seeing many particulars, the mind forms the judgment that these particulars fall into different classes. It distinguishes living things from those that are not living. It distinguishes plants from animals, and it distinguishes different kinds of plants and different kinds of animals. It sees that all men are animals but not all animals are men. It sees that all dogs are animals but not all animals are dogs. Some animals are dogs, and some animals are men, but no man is a dog, and no dog is a man. It sees that Socrates is a man, but not all men are Socrates. The common nouns or universals fall into divisions and subdivisions that are genera, species, and varieties. Experience, or inductive reason, constantly revises, corrects, and improves upon the accuracy of these classifications. But no experience in recorded history (and certainly none since Socrates, Plato, and Aristotle) has ever revised in any fundamental way the distinction between the human, the subhuman, and the superhuman. The distinction between man, beast, and God, as set forth in the first book of Aristotle's *Politics*, remains the framework of the thought of the Declaration of Independence, and the differences between man and beast, on the one hand, and man and God, on the other, remain self-evident and definitive. For that reason, we know that any attempt of human beings to rule other human beings, as if the former were gods, and the latter beasts, is wrong. That is why the rule of law—ruling and being ruled in turn—is the only intrinsically just arrangement by which human beings can rule one another. This is a permanent truth, and one in no way dependent upon its recognition. The truths enshrined in the Declaration are no more dependent upon their recognition for their truthfulness than the truths about the relationship of the three angles of the triangle.

~

We believe that we have examined, and found wanting, every serious argument of contemporary historical scholarship to deny or disparage the intrinsic significance or validity of Lincoln's assertion that the United States was founded upon and dedicated to "an abstract truth, applicable to all men and all times." To ask if such an assertion is credible or not, so far from being a meaningless question, is the question that must be answered above all others if meaning is to be found in the work of the Founding Fathers and in the lives and deaths of those who, with Lincoln, kept that work from perishing. We may therefore now approach the Civil War with the full seriousness demanded by Lincoln's contention that it represented a test of whether any nation, founded upon such truth, might endure.

We must face the reality, however, that in the long experience of mankind, the self-evident truths of the Declaration of Independence had never, before 1776, been the basis of the experiment of popular self-government. This in itself is sufficient to raise the question of whether it was utopian to think that mere abstract truth could serve as the basis of an actual political regime. It is to ask the question that Plato himself asked, but did not answer, of whether natural right could become political right. We may be confident that James Madison had the Socratic tradition in mind when he wrote that "A government deriving its energy from the will of the society, and operating, by the reason of its measures, on the understanding and interest of the society . . . is the government for which philosophy has been searching and humanity been fighting from the most remote ages."[77] In 1838, Lincoln said of the Founding Fathers, "Their ambition aspired to display before an admiring world, a practical demonstration of the truth of a proposition, which had hitherto been considered at best no better than problematical; namely, the capability of a people to govern themselves."[78] That proposition had become even more problematical when on July 4, 1861, Lincoln asked whether there was not "in all republics, this inherent and fatal weakness," that any government must "of necessity be [either] too strong for the liberties of its own people, or too weak to maintain its own existence."[79] In this, Lincoln was asking whether the idea of self-government was not in fact utopian and whether it might after all be true that, in Jefferson's words, "man cannot be governed but by a rod of iron."[80] Certainly the conditions for the success of the American experiment in self-government were more propitious than any that had existed in previous human history or that were likely to occur in any imaginable future. Hence it was anything but improbable that if the experiment failed here, it was not likely ever to succeed elsewhere.

Concerning the *novus ordo seclorum*, however, we must ask why, if its principle was accessible to human reason at any time, it required so many centuries before its political embodiment was attempted. It was certainly plausible to maintain, as Calhoun and other defenders of slavery did, that all great societies of the past, like those of Greece and Rome, were built upon a foundation of human slavery. But slavery itself was only the most radical form of the inequality that predominated in all governments, ancient and modern, before the American Revolution.[81]

It is certainly an oversimplification to reduce all political theories to the equal rights of mankind, on the one hand, and the divine right of kings, on the other. Yet as we saw above, this was Lincoln's perspective. As a stump orator, which he was through much of the 1850s, he did not deliver academic lectures on the history of political doctrines. Within the rough vernacular of the political arena, however, Lincoln penetrated, as nearly as anyone has ever done, to the heart of the problem of the great alternatives within the human condition. The divine right of kings, as Lincoln understood it, might have been a shorthand expression for many different forms of human oppression, but it was one that the American people and many other peoples, then and since, have easily understood.

We must understand that the alternatives faced by the American people in 1776 were not between what today would be misnamed "secular humanism" and divine right. The doctrine of natural law and natural rights enshrined in the Declaration is a doctrine of natural *and* divine right. On May 27, 1776, the citizens of Malden, Massachusetts, resolved that they were

> confirmed in the opinion, that the present age would be deficient in their duty to God, their posterity and themselves, if they do not establish an American republic. This is the only form of government which we wish to see established; for we can never be willingly subject to any other King than he who, being possessed of infinite wisdom, goodness, and rectitude, is alone fit to possess unlimited power.[82]

The American people, in declaring themselves independent of Great Britain and of any mortal power, did so in accordance with laws of nature that were God's laws, to which they declared themselves subject in the very act of independence. Jefferson's metaphor of horses and riders stressed the absence of any natural difference between man and man, such as there is between man and beast, that would justify rule without consent. But the distinction between man and beast was no more fundamental than that between man and God. Just as the irrationality of beasts marks them out as fit subjects for mankind, so too do the inherent limitations in human nature mark out the reasons why it is inconsistent with God's creation to entrust a God-like authority to any man or men. The rule of law, ruling and being ruled in turn, is as naturally fitting to the relationship of man and man as are subjection and obedience to the relationship of man and horse. As rational beings, men are superior to beasts. In human beings, however, reason is easily and often subordinated to passion. Hence the distance between man and God is as politically relevant to answering the question of who should rule as the distance between man and beast. Because of the difference between man and God, "No man is allowed to be a judge in his own cause."[83]

For the Founding Fathers and for Lincoln, the attempt to find the nearest earthly approximation to divine rule, to "reason unaffected by desire," is by means of the rule of law. The republican form of government, embodying the rule of law, is grounded in the idea of human equality. The proposition that all men are *created* equal implies, as we have said, a right that is both natural and divine. This is given emphasis in the assertion that all human beings are endowed *by their Creator* with the rights that belong to them by nature. Republican government understands itself to be in accordance with a natural order that is itself in harmony with the divine government of the universe.[84] It does not differ in the least from the divine right of kings with respect to the divine origin of political right. It differs only in asserting the unalienable presence of that right equally in every human individual and in denying that it has any greater inherent or a priori presence in any particular persons, be they called kings, nobles, senators, or ruling classes, however defined. This principle of right is in no way disturbed by the fact that among barbarians or savages it cannot become the actual source of the powers of government. Unless the people understand what might justly be demanded, of themselves no less than of others, in recognition of their equal natural rights, the rights will be ineffective. It cannot be emphasized too often that the doctrine of the Declaration requires a people who can appeal truthfully and sincerely to the supreme judge of the world for the rectitude of their intentions. According to Jefferson and Lincoln, failure to respect the rights of others may disqualify one for the protection of one's own rights and expose one to the wrath of the God who is their source. Although the rights of man exist wherever man exists, the existence of a people sufficiently enlightened, and having the courage and the means to act on them, may be rare. However rare such a people, the rights themselves, under the laws of nature, provide the ultimate standard by which men and nations are to be judged.

Steeped as we are in the republican tradition, it is difficult to realize that throughout the Christian centuries, the distance between man and God was seen as reason to draw the opposite conclusion from that drawn by the people of Malden, Massachusetts, in 1776 and by Americans ever since. Although everyone knew that kings were no less mortal, no less subject to human frailty, than other human beings, it was thought that human government required that they be endowed by doctrine and ceremony with a stature that placed them so far above their subjects that their subjects would look upon them with an awe and reverence befitting the direct representatives of God. The distance between man and God was to be paralleled, at least symbolically, by the distance between monarchs and their subjects. What was true of the distance between kings and subjects would also be true of the distance between ruling classes and their inferiors. The inequality of man and God was accordingly thought to be the reason for the inequality of man and his rulers. It was this latter view that prevailed in the Christian West until the American Revolution. Nor was a pre-Christian philosophic equivalent lacking. Corresponding to the divine right of kings, we find in Plato's *Republic* that the citizens are to be taught the "noble lie" that the souls of the three classes of men are mixed, respectively, with gold, silver, and bronze. The subordination of the lower to the higher will then be accepted as in accordance with nature and/or the will of the gods.

Thus we see that the inequality between man, beast, and God has been the source of two diametrically different doctrines of the proper relationship between man and his government: the doctrine that human government requires inequality as its principle, and the doctrine that it requires equality. Emancipated as we now are from the assumption that it is meaningless to ask where the truth lies, we must attempt to discover the cause or causes of this difference.

Certainly we can agree with Carl Becker that to understand political history, one must recognize that the interests in conflict in the political arena are not always represented by the doctrines put forward to justify them. The Vicar of Bray may indeed be more typical than a Jefferson or a Lincoln. But that some men are scoundrels does not mean that all men are scoundrels or that the only non-scoundrel is the one who says all men are scoundrels! Nor does it mean that men are always dominated, whether knowingly or unknowingly, by interests or passions that have nothing to do with the reasons by which they say (and believe) they are guided. Nor does it mean that to be sincere, one must always put forward the best or truest argument in support of one's cause. Sometimes the best argument is the least persuasive, and the most persuasive argument is far from being the best. That those who dissemble often do so in the cause of injustice does not mean that those who dissemble may not do so in the interest of justice. In war, said Churchill, the truth is so precious that it should not go abroad except with a bodyguard of lies. But wars are often won or lost, or caused or prevented, by what one does in time of peace. It is therefore a perfectly non-Machiavellian insight that there is no time in which the truth may not require a bodyguard of lies. This certainly complicates the task of discovering the truth and of distinguishing the just from the unjust dissemblers, but it does not affect our responsibility to distinguish the just from the unjust or the true from the false.

There is an infinite variety of circumstances in which truth and falsehood, justice and injustice come into conflict, and their relationship is as varied as those circumstances. That variety, however, is unintelligible if one starts from the assumption that it is meaningless to ask what is true and what is just. For it is not the case that all truth is relative except the truth that all truth is relative. The intrinsic wrongness of tyranny and the intrinsic rightness of free government, as they are distinguished in the Declaration of Independence, are beacons of truth not affected by circumstances. The question of how, when, and whether such truth may be made the ground and basis of government, however, is governed by dictates of prudence, as the Declaration itself says. We must not, then, be misunderstood to say that the cause of legitimate government can be advanced only by the arguments in the Declaration.

We remind the reader of the appeal to both English patriotism and the divine right of kings in Shakespeare's *King John*. In our discussion of that play in chapter 1, we saw that the divine right of kings served the popular cause, while the doctrine of tyrannicide actually promoted tyranny. The infinite changeability of political circumstances makes it impossible to predict accurately what the relationship will be between the logic inherent in a political doctrine and the effect it will have with respect to justice or injustice in a particular time and place. A great deal depends upon the motives of the political actors. Good doctrines can be used by bad men for bad ends, and bad doctrines by good men for good ends. In the case of King John, we may even say that a bad man appealed to a bad doctrine for a good end. That is to say, from a perspective that is outside of history, we can see that King John promoted a good end, even if it was no part of his intention to do so. Perhaps the last word on the relationship of mutable circumstances to immutable purposes is that of Winston Churchill, in his essay "Consistency in Politics":

> [A] Statesman in contact with the moving current of events and anxious to keep the ship on an even keel and steer a steady course may lean his weight now on one side and now on another. His arguments in each case when contrasted can be shown to be not only very different in character, but contradictory in spirit and opposite in direction; yet his object will throughout have remained the same. His resolves, his wishes, his outlook may have been unchanged; his methods may be verbally irreconcilable. We cannot call this inconsistency. The only way a man can remain consistent amid changing circumstances is to change with them while preserving the same dominating purpose.[85]

125

The argument that justifies the wise statesman's "dominating purpose" is the only one that can tell us of the justice of his cause. Yet the interest of justice may require that this argument not appear publicly, or even that it be concealed from all his contemporaries.

Perhaps there is no better illustration of how the mutability of circumstances affects the utility of truth than Macaulay's account of the Toleration Act of 1689.

> The Toleration Act approaches very near to the idea of a great English law. To a jurist versed in the theory of legislation, but not intimately acquainted with the temper of the sects and parties into which the nation was divided at the time of the Revolution, that act would seem to be a mere chaos of absurdities and contradictions. It will not bear to be tried by sound general principles. Nay, it will not bear to be tried by any principles, sound or unsound. The sound principle undoubtedly is, that mere theological error ought not to be punished by the civil magistrate. This principle the Toleration Act not only does not recognize, but positively disclaims. Not a single one of the cruel laws enacted against nonconformists by the Tudors or the Stuarts is repealed. Persecution continues to be the general rule. Toleration is the exception. . . . These are some of the obvious faults which must strike every person who examines the Toleration Act by that standard of just reason which is the same in all countries and in all ages. . . . That the provisions which have been recapitulated are cumbrous, puerile, inconsistent with each other, inconsistent with the true theory of religious liberty, must be acknowledged. All that can be said in their defense is this; that they removed a vast mass of evil without shocking a vast mass of prejudice.[86]

We must notice, first of all, that Macaulay's praise of the Toleration Act is premised upon the assumption that he himself knows "that standard of just reason which is the same in all countries and in all ages." He seems to have been of the same mind as Lincoln when Lincoln spoke of "an abstract truth applicable to all men and all times." Macaulay also spoke of "the true theory of religious liberty," according to which "mere theological error ought not to be punished by the civil magistrate." In this Macaulay is saying no more than Jefferson in the Virginia Statute of Religious Liberty, itself informed by John Locke's *Letters on Toleration*. In truth, the Glorious Revolution of 1689 was conducted largely by men who had known Locke and who were familiar with the doctrines of both his *Letters* and his *Second Treatise of Government*. Yet they were wise enough to know that in the face of "a vast mass of prejudice," the true purposes of civil and religious liberty could not be stated openly without jeopardizing those purposes. According to Macaulay, the Toleration Act could advance the cause of religious liberty, to the extent to which it was then possible, only by disavowing any intention to do so. In like manner, we will see Lincoln in the 1850s disclaiming any intention to make voters or jurors of Negroes. Given the vast mass of prejudice with which Lincoln was confronted, it would have been destructive of the antislavery cause for him to say anything else. That the true theory of religious liberty was recognized in Macaulay's England in the mid-nineteenth century was due in large measure to the fact that it had been disavowed in 1689. Likewise, Negroes have voting rights and serve on juries today owing in large measure to the fact that Lincoln in the 1850s disavowed any intention to make them voters or jurors.

In both these cases we discern the principles on which statesmen acted—in 1689 and in the 1850s—from the direction in which they moved events, in the ends implicit in that direction, and in the reasons by which those ends are vindicated. In the one case, the true theory of religious liberty and, in the other, the true theory of civil liberty were vindicated. The validity of those theories, we believe, is timeless and independent of all circumstances. The true statesman, however, chooses among the alternatives actually before him: the lesser evil or the greater good. In order to make such choices, he must have clearly before the eye of his mind the distinction between the unconditionally good and the unconditionally evil. It is such an unconditional understanding that is presented to us, as to civil and religious liberty, by the Declaration of Independence and the Virginia Statute of Religious Liberty.

∾

The divine right of kings, in the comprehensive sense of the right to rule others without their consent, predominated within Western civilization until the American Revolution. To have done so for nearly eighteen hundred years after the birth of Christianity would make it appear that civilized mankind, with the possible exception of a few philosophers, had during all that time lived in ignorance of the rights announced in the Declaration of Independence. The divine right of kings must therefore have had a plausibility not easily visible today. We must understand that plausibility in order to take the measure of the magnitude of the change in human consciousness achieved in the American Founding—and thus the magnitude of the stakes at risk in the American Civil War.

As a prologue to understanding the origin and nature of a doctrine that held such power over mind and imagination in the history of the Christian West, we would invite further attention to divine right monarchy as presented in Shakespeare's English histories. Although Shakespeare presents us with such monarchy in all its human failings, there does not, on the horizon of the plays, appear to be any alternative theory of political obligation. That is to say, although the divine right of kings is never a sufficient title to rule, it appears always to be a necessary one. And Shakespeare's English histories present us with an almost unbroken spectacle of civil war.

We do not assume that Lincoln's understanding of civil war was drawn from his reading of these plays. However, when we recall that Lincoln himself equated the divine right of kings and the positive good theory of slavery, the probability of such a correlation seems high. In the middle of the Civil War, Lincoln wrote to a prominent Shakespearean actor that

> Some of Shakespeare's Plays I have never read, whilst others I have gone over perhaps as frequently as any unprofessional reader. Among the latter are Lear, Richard Third, Henry Eighth, Hamlet, and especially Macbeth. I think nothing equals Macbeth. It is wonderful.[87]

Earlier in the same letter, Lincoln had said that for one of his age, he had seen very little of drama and that the "first presentation of Falstaff I ever saw was yours here last winter or spring." What he had seen acted and what he had read in private are certainly not the same, but on the basis of this we may add *Henry IV, Part I*, to the list given above. Lincoln's fascination with *Macbeth* is clearly due to its theme of the relationship of wrongdoing and retribution, and the kinship with his own second inaugural is obvious.[88]

Let us begin in medias res, with the episode in *Henry V* on the night before the battle of Agincourt, when the disguised king meets two common soldiers, Bates and Williams, who are pessimistic about the coming battle. The forces of the French outnumber the English many times over, and the French troops are fresher, better equipped, and fighting on their own ground. His proper person concealed, the king attempts to solace his discomfited men, although he has nothing to say to contradict the grim reality of their position: "methinks I could not die any where so contented as in the king's company—his cause being just, and his quarrel honorable." To this Williams answers, "That's more than we know." But Bates replies, "Ay, or more than we should seek after; for we know enough, if we know we are the king's subjects: if his cause be wrong, our obedience to the king wipes the crime of it out of us."[89] This is what the king wishes to hear and what he wants his men to believe. In elaborate scholastic fashion, Henry reinforces this conviction by arguing that each man must answer to God for whatever sins he may have committed. The king is not responsible for his subjects' personal salvation, but neither are the subjects responsible for the justice of the king's cause. The subject's duty to the king is unconditional and is not dependent upon the justice of the king's cause.

We, unlike Bates and Williams, would be the more persuaded by Henry's skillful dialectics if we were not conscious all the while, as was Henry himself, that the crown he holds was stolen by his father from its rightful owner. We are reminded, moreover, that unlike the ancient city, where each citizen's soul has no destiny apart from that of his city, in the Christian world order each man's eternal destiny is separate from that of his country. It is a matter between himself alone and his God. And that God is no more the God of his nation than of any other nation. Bates and Williams understand that they can go to hell, even if the king's cause triumphs and that they can go to heaven even if it fails. This disjunction between the fate of the individual and the fate of his city is the core of Machiavelli's indictment of Christianity.

In his soliloquy after the dialogue, the king justifies the subordination of his subjects on the ground that it is a burden or sacrifice that he bears on their behalf: "What infinite heart's ease must kings neglect, That private men enjoy!" And again:

> No, not all these, thrice gorgeous ceremony,
> Not all these, laid in bed majestical,
> Can sleep so soundly as the wretched slave,
> Who, with a body filled and vacant mind,
> Gets him to rest, cramm'd with distressful bread;
> Never sees horrid night, the child of hell . . .
> And, but for ceremony, such a wretch,
> Winding up days of toil and nights with sleep,
> Had the forehand and vantage of a king.
> The slave, a member of the country's peace,
> Enjoys it; but in gross brain little wots
> What watch the king keeps to maintain the peace,
> Whose hours the peasant best advantages.[90]

Here is the positive good theory of monarchy and slavery in almost precisely the form in which Lincoln characterized it. Kings, Lincoln said, "always bestrode the necks of the people, not that they wanted to do it, but because the people were better off for being ridden."[91] Among the many ironies of this soliloquy is the fact that the "slaves" in Henry's bedraggled army have hardly eaten or slept. And the king, for whom they are about to go into battle, has hardly kept the peace. It is in large measure Henry's and his father's ambition that has kept England in a constant state of turmoil. Neither in *Henry V* nor in any of the English history plays, with the possible exception of *Henry VIII*, do we see any surcease from war. The crown is always being contested, and there is no peaceful way of deciding the contest. The king's peace is an illusion. Lincoln, a profound reader of Shakespeare, must have seen English history through Shakespeare's eyes as virtually one long civil war, with little if any relief from the violent alternations of tyranny and anarchy.

At Agincourt, Henry and his army are engaged in a foreign adventure contrived by Henry (and conspired in by the archbishop of Canterbury) to repress the quarreling factions at home and consolidate his hold upon the crown his father had usurped. In his prayer before the battle, Henry asks the "God of battles" to steel his soldiers' hearts and to "think not upon the fault My father made in compassing the crown!" This "mirror of all Christian kings" tells God that he has reinterred Richard's body and that five hundred aged pensioners send prayers twice daily for the release of Richard's soul from purgatory. Yet he confesses that his penitence "comes after all," that is to say, while he remains in unyielding possession of the fruit of his father's crime. His belief (like Hamlet's) in the heaven, hell, and purgatory of medieval Catholicism appears to be perfectly genuine. He must assume therefore that the fate of his own soul, or his father's, will not be different from Richard's. Yet he never considers, even for a moment, relinquishing the crown to lessen the pains of purgatory, if not of hell. This certainly belies the attempt in his soliloquy, only a few moments earlier, to persuade himself that his subjects benefit more from his rule than he himself.

Henry's claims upon the French crown are even more doubtful than his claims upon the crown of England. They are certified to him by the archbishop of Canterbury by a pious fraud, one that has less piety and more fraud than Henry's penitence for the murder of Richard. The motive for the fraud lies even more with the church than with Henry. The archbishop desires to gain the king's favor in opposing a law that threatens to confiscate a major part of the church's wealth. Henry and the church need each other. The church needs Henry's protection for its property, and Henry needs the church to certify that he is anointed by heaven.

In the great Saint Crispin's Day speech with which Henry leads his badly outnumbered army into battle, he speaks of that army thus:

> We few, we happy few, we band of brothers;
> For he today that sheds his blood with me
> Shall be my brother; be he ne'er so vile,
> This day shall gentle his condition.[92]

"Slaves with vacant minds" are now a "band of brothers," and Henry is an eminently democratic monarch. Valor in battle takes precedence of class distinctions. An aristocracy of merit points beyond inherited rank and gives new meaning to nobility and gentlemanship. We see Henry, the son and heir of a usurper, gaining legitimacy as he gains popularity—a popularity that Richard, a genuinely legitimate king, did not know how to achieve. Henry becomes legitimate by a refounding in which he shares his own upward mobility with those who help him to achieve it. Henry's credibility as king results, not from inheritance, but from performance. And that performance consists especially in his ability to destroy his enemies, no less by skill in deception than by open force.[93]

Having asked God to steel his soldiers' hearts, Henry undertakes to do it himself. In his speech before the battle, on the day of a Christian saint, we hear no allusion to God or Christian doctrine, nothing about the fate of the soul (as in his dialogue with Bates and Williams), and nothing about the justness of his cause. Rather we hear about the honor and glory the soldiers can win for themselves. In particular, Henry tells how each veteran will in old age remember "with advantages, what feats he did that day." Yet when the victory is actually won, not only is all the credit given to God, but precisely the kind of boasting he had promised his soldiers is, at least for the time being, sternly forbidden.

> Come, go we in procession to the village:
> And be it death proclaimed through our host
> To boast of this, or take the praise from God Which is His only.[94]

The more wonderful the victory seems, or the more it is attributable to God and not to God's Englishmen (or Englishman!), the more Henry's possession of the crown will appear to be of divine right. Here one might compare Henry V's attribution of providential intervention with that of Richard II. Before the battle in which he will be dethroned by Bolingbroke, Richard expresses the doctrine of the divine right of kings in its purest form.

> Not all the water in the rough rude sea
> Can wash the balm from an anointed king;
> The breath of worldly men cannot depose
> The deputy elected by the Lord:
> For every man that Bolingbroke hath prest
> To lift shrewd steel against our golden crown,
> God for his Richard hath in heavenly pay
> A glorious angel: then, if angels fight,
> Weak men must fall; for heaven still guards the right.[95]

Richard thinks that God will give him the victory whether or not he has made adequate preparations. Henry V takes into far greater account how much "the breath of worldly men" enters into election by the Lord. If angels do indeed fight, it will not be in their proper persons but by how they may nerve the arms of soldiers. It is precisely in nerving the arms of his men that Henry (unlike Richard) excels. Henry acts on the principle that God helps those who help themselves and afterwards attributes his success to God as a confirmation of the righteousness of his (not very righteous) cause.

All of Shakespeare's English history plays, but particularly the cycle that begins with *Richard II* and concludes with *Henry V*, turn about the problem of political legitimacy. Because the question of who ought to rule is always in dispute, English history, seen from the perspective of these plays, is dominated by civil war. Divine right is recognized as a necessary, but never a sufficient, condition of legitimacy. In *Richard II*, civil war resulted from the fact that Richard, although indubitably an anointed king, lives a corrupt and luxurious life, surrounded by courtiers who are detested outside the court. To support these parasites, he needs money and is tempted to take it by confiscating his subjects' property. But there is no constitutional way of getting rid of an anointed king, and indeed no way at all except usurpation and murder. Government can be changed only by an exercise of what Jefferson would call the natural right of revolution. Although this right is not recognized by its proper name, and will not be so recognized until 1689, it operates by natural necessity. The doctrine of tyrannicide might have operated at least as an aspect or surrogate of the right of revolution, except that in the Christian Middle Ages it was, as we have seen, mainly an instrument to enable popes to bring emperors or kings to heel. The genuine doctrine of tyrannicide had its origin in classical republicanism, and it became an instrument of the popular cause only in the seventeenth century, with the revival of the republican tradition. In the cycle of plays beginning with *Richard II*, the division of authority between king and pope, as seen earlier in *King John*, has disappeared. Albeit somewhat anachronistically, what we see in the Bolingbroke saga is the Reformation doctrine in which all divine right is concentrated in the king.

Henry Bolingbroke pursues his feud with Richard with incomparable skill and absolute ruthlessness. His son continues the war against his father's enemies, now his enemies, with perhaps even more cunning and, if possible, even less moral scruple. It would have been impossible for the Bolingbrokes to have had Machiavelli himself as a counselor and to have fashioned a policy in which morality and religion were more completely subordinated to purely political ends. Yet not for a moment does either father or son doubt the sovereignty of God or that their own souls are destined for heaven, hell, or purgatory. The doctrine preached to Bates and Williams, as summarized by Williams, is that it is certain that "every man that dies ill, the ill [is] upon his own head—the king is not to answer it." Yet the same doctrine would have concluded that, even as each subject is responsible to God for his particular ending, so also is the king. If we look again at the soliloquy on the eve of Agincourt in which the king asks God "to think not upon his father's fault in compassing the crown," we find him admitting that his penitence "is nothing worth." Yet what worries him is only what effect this will have upon God's disposition toward the coming battle. Having told God how piously he has acted toward the fate of Richard's immortal soul, he says nothing whatever about his own. He asks God's grace only for the battle to retain the crown that has been usurped. In giving all praise to God for the victory after it comes, he evidently thinks that God must have answered his prayer, notwithstanding the moral shortcomings he had admitted. Evidently God does not judge harshly the departures from the moral law that successful princes must pursue to be successful.[96] This must then be of the essence of what makes Henry V the "mirror of all Christian Kings."

Richard had attempted to confiscate Bolingbroke's estate, and Henry raised a revolt against him that was joined by others who felt threatened by Richard. But those who helped Bolingbroke dethrone Richard did not necessarily wish to make him king, particularly as he was not the next in line according to the rules of inheritance, which are also the rules of divine right. These rules are never questioned by anyone, even when necessity seems to drive men to break them. The only way Henry IV and Henry V can legitimate the overthrow of a legitimate king is by becoming legitimate kings themselves. They can only do this by being victorious over their enemies, foreign and domestic, and passing the crown from father to son, until the memory of the origin of their rule is obscured both by the success of that rule and by the passage of time. A mandate of heaven descends eventually upon a reigning monarch, if he is successful enough, long enough. Of course if we traced the origin of Richard's title, or the title of any king, far enough back in time, we would find that it too originated in conquest. The same is true of the origin of the right of any people to the land they possess. The children of Israel, for example, were possessed of their land by divine right, because it was promised to them by God. But they took possession by conquest nonetheless. From this perspective, the Bolingbrokes' success is no more than an act of refounding. As we shall see, the ministry of the Gospels outside the boundaries of ancient Israel—that is to say, the ministry that transformed a Jewish sect into Christianity—was itself made possible only by the conquests of Caesar. The Gospel of man's salvation could not be preached to the world until Caesar had prepared the world for its reception. Christ's kingdom not of this world depended upon Caesar's kingdom in this world. We might say that Jesus' separation of morality from politics, making each man's salvation a personal matter between himself and God, depended upon Caesar's subjection of morality to politics. In Shakespeare's English histories, and in particular his history of the "mirror of all Christian kings," we see individual morality emancipated from politics, and politics emancipated from individual morality. Yet we see in the person of Henry V the doctrine of the morality of personal salvation in the next world and the morality of political necessity in this world combined in the same person. We do not see anywhere on the horizon of these histories any resolution of the tension between these two moralities. We see such a resolution only as we see the Signers of the Declaration of Independence appeal to the supreme judge of the world for the rectitude of their intentions.

The great victory at Agincourt is followed by the marriage of Henry and a French princess. The crowns of England and France, having been united by Mars, will now be united by Venus. In the presence of this dazzling success, endorsed by both public opinion and the church, Henry is now securely on the throne. But at the end of the play, the Chorus reminds us that Henry lived only a short time after the events in the play, and that the hypothetical union of the crowns of England and France proved illusory and a disaster to both nations. Henry's conquest at Agincourt in the end only aggravated the factional struggle at home that had been temporarily suppressed. The civil war that followed, the War of the Roses, was crueler than any that had preceded it. England was in every respect worse off in the aftermath of Henry V's successes than it had been because of Richard II's failures. Divine right monarchy seems to be consistent only with constant oscillation between anarchy and tyranny, with civil war, or something like Hobbes's state of nature, as the ever recurring condition.

The three parts of *Henry VI*, which record this lamentable descent into anarchy, are followed by *Richard III*. With the possible exception of Iago, its central character is the most villainous in Shakespeare.[97] Richard III's death on Bosworth Field leads to the reign of Henry VII and the Tudor dynasty, which by judicious marriages ends the War of the Roses. *Henry VIII*, said to be Shakespeare's last work, and written after Elizabeth's reign, is a celebration of the events leading up to the birth of Elizabeth, for whom a glorious reign is prophesied. There can be no question as to the glory of Elizabeth's reign, whose crowning glory was the work of Shakespeare himself. The Elizabethan era in England, with the burst of national energy that followed the defeat of the Spanish Armada—like the burst of energy of Periclean Athens following the defeat of the Persians at Marathon—comprehended some of the loftiest achievements of the human soul in all recorded history. Yet we cannot list among those achievements political stability that extended beyond the reign itself.

It is true that during four centuries, beginning at least with Magna Carta, the organism of parliamentary democracy was slowly being formed within the womb of medieval monarchy. Yet the birth of the institutions of popular government awaited the passing of the divine right of kings and the transfer of the idea of sovereignty from kings to people. It is sufficient here to note that just as one peak of divine right monarchy is reached in the reign of Henry V, so another is reached in the reign of Elizabeth. But as the earlier peak is followed by the War of the Roses, so the second peak is followed, after Shakespeare's death, by another civil war. Cromwell's victory over Charles I appears initially to be a definitive victory of popular sovereignty over the divine right of kings. But Cromwell's republicanism ended in a military dictatorship, which in turn led to a restoration of the British monarchy. It required one more revolution, the Glorious Revolution of 1689, to end once and for all the pretensions of the Stuarts to divine right. But it required the American Revolution to identify the sovereignty of the people with the rule of law, in which the will of the majority can prevail only as it comports with the equal rights of the minority. The seemingly endless series of civil wars in England came to an end only as the divine right of kings was replaced by the God-given right of the people to rule themselves. Unfortunately, one more civil war, the greatest of them all, was required to confirm this right of the people.

～

Of all the revolutions in human consciousness, perhaps none is greater than that by which it came to be perceived that the source of all political authority, properly so called, is the divine right or rights with which each individual has been endowed by his Creator, and that governments have no lawful powers except those granted to them by the governed. Certainly for more than a millennium and a half of the history of the Christian West, the prevailing opinion was that political authority descended from the top down, from God to kings and rulers, and that the obligation of the ruled was simply to obey.

Before the people's right to govern themselves could be recognized, the right of the nation to govern itself had to be established. As we shall see, this right was embodied in kings before it was embodied in the people. Before tyranny could be defined, from the people's point of view, as "taxation without representation," it was necessary to vindicate the principle that political authority was inherent in the nation. Only later could it be maintained that the political authority inherent in the nation was itself inherent in the people and not in the king.

To explain why this was so we must consider that from the end of the Roman republic until the rise of the modern nation-state, the political life of Western civilization was dominated by the Roman Empire, pagan and Christian. The latter was a transformation of the former. This transformation was marked first by the extension of Roman citizenship to the provinces sometime in the third century. It was followed about a century later by the establishment of Christianity. The universalization of Roman citizenship was the culmination of a process that began in Rome's most remote past. We find this account of Rome's origins in the work of Fustel de Coulanges:

> The origin of Rome and the composition of its people are worthy of remark. . . .
> The Roman race was strangely mixed. . . . Thus at Rome all races were associated and mingled; there were Latins, Trojans, and Greeks; there were, a little later,
> Sabines and Etruscans. . . . Rome did not seem to be a single city; it appeared like
> a confederation of several cities, each one of which was attached by its origin to
> another confederation. [98]

Bearing in mind the importance of the Roman model for the American Founding, this multiethnic character is striking.[99] The motto of the United States, e pluribus unum, has always referred to a unity in diversity more fundamental than the union of the states. This unity was discovered in "the laws of nature and of nature's God," by which "one people" could arise from many hitherto existing nations, ethnic identities, races, and creeds. In comparing and contrasting the imperial federalism of Rome with that of the United States, we must notice how ancient Rome's ethnic diversity served the cause of Rome's conquest of the ancient world. Fustel de Coulanges writes:

> The Roman population was then a mixture of several races, its worship was an assemblage of several worships, and its national hearth an association of several hearths. It was almost the only city whose municipal religion was not isolated from all others. . . . There was hardly a people it could not admit to its hearth.

The core of American diversity, and the reason why there was no people America could not, in principle, "admit to its hearth," was not, however, the accident of the "association of several hearths" but the abstract or philosophic truth of the Declaration of Independence. On the other hand,

> Rome was the only city that understood how to augment her population by war. The Romans pursued a policy unknown to the rest of the Graeco-Roman world; they annexed all that they conquered. They brought home the inhabitants of captured cities, and gradually made Romans of them. At the same time they sent colonies into the conquered countries, and in this manner spread Rome everywhere; for their colonists, while forming distinct cities, in a political point of view, preserved a religious community with the metropolis; and this was enough to compel the colonies to subordinate their policy to that of Rome, to obey her, and to aid her in all her wars.[100]

While Rome understood how to augment her population by wars and conquest, the United States understood how to accomplish this by voluntary immigration, fueled by the attractions of freedom.[101] The Statue of Liberty symbolizes the difference.

This process of Rome's development, of imperial conquest and religious syncretism, underlies the later belief that the secular history of Rome constituted part of the sacred history of Christianity. It was believed to be Rome's providential destiny to form the universal empire, which was the necessary preparation for the reception of the universal religion. Although Christianity postulates the equality of all human souls in the eyes of the one God, the empire was brought into existence by the legions of Rome and by a regime that recognized all gods in the interest of subjecting their peoples, or votaries, to the authority of Rome. Caesarism, a popular military despotism, destroyed the balance of Rome's mixed or republican constitution by destroying the senate and the patrician class. It thereby destroyed all rule of law, overthrowing all republican equality between government and the governed within Rome, while institutionalizing the greatest inequality between the conquerors and the conquered. Yet Caesarism presented itself as the most democratic of regimes, because Caesar's power was ostensibly exercised entirely for the benefit of the people. Lincoln's warning, in his Lyceum speech of 1838, against Caesarism, against the transformation of a republic into a military despotism "in the name of the people," is a fundamental element of his constitutionalism. Caesar's founding of his power upon the demos, or common people, anticipated the Gospel celebration of the poor and dispossessed. Although Caesar's regime represented the greatest possible inequality between rulers and ruled, it nonetheless prepared the way for the celebration of the most egalitarian of all regimes, at first in the next world, but later in this one.

The extension of imperial Roman citizenship in the third century marked the termination of a process that began more than a millennium before, in the founding period of republican Rome. The universalization of Roman citizenship meant also the end of the ancient city and the ancient world. If every citizen was a Roman citizen, then Rome was not one political regime among many, it was *the* regime for the government of mankind. It was not a political regime, because a political regime, properly so called, is always one of many. A citizen of republican Rome, such as the tragic hero of Shakespeare's *Coriolanus*, understood his very being in its contradistinction to non-Romanness. He wished to see Rome elevated in power and glory over non-Roman cities. Yet the political ambition of a Roman citizen was an ambition to compel recognition of his city's superiority, and of his own superiority in his city's service. It was a demand for recognition by competent and, in the last analysis, disinterested judges of virtue. This in turn implied a standard for the judgment of political things that was in itself transpolitical. In Shakespeare's *Coriolanus*, we see the necessity of Aufidius, the great warrior of Corioli, as a proving ground of the Roman hero's claim to highest honor. Notwithstanding the fact that these two men have dedicated themselves to killing each other on the battlefield, there is a kind of friendship between them, based upon the need of each for the other's recognition. Notwithstanding the fact that each is an alien enemy of the other, together they form a class by themselves. Coriolanus's claim to the highest honors in Rome depends upon the worthiness of the foe he must vanquish. The paradox that each, in a certain respect, has more in common with the other than either has with his fellow countrymen points to a self-contradiction intrinsic to political life. It points to the necessity of a noncontradictory form of friendship that is not political. The City of God (which of course by this-worldly standards is a noncity) will prove to be cosmopolitan.

Caesar's empire, when in its own self-understanding it has become universal, and thus when it has nothing outside itself except barbarism and disorder by which to distinguish itself, will have nothing against which to define itself. Rome will cease to be a city or a political community. Rome's conquest of the world will end in the world's conquest of Rome. This is the original, nonbiblical meaning of the end of history. There will not be another Coriolanus or Aufidius. The day of the godlike ancient hero will be gone forever.[102] Nor can there ever again be another Caesar. Caesar has brought down to earth, so to speak, the transpolitical regime towards which all previous political regimes point. A contest of pride in a world of inequality will be replaced by contests of humility in a world of equality.[103]

The eventual transformation of Caesar's empire into the City of God, or into the worldly foreshadowing of the City of God, meant the end of the kind of heroic virtue recognized by the ancient city. It also meant that the noncontradictory or transpolitical form of friendship, towards which the virtue of the ancient city pointed as something beyond itself, was now intrinsic to political life as redefined. Thus what appears as the extension of Roman citizenship in the third century actually marked the end of Roman citizenship, as it marked the end of Rome as a republican city that triumphed over other cities and in which law meant ruling and being ruled. This end of Roman citizenship had been foreshadowed when Caesar crossed the Rubicon, and political power passed from the Senate and people of Rome to the commander of the legions.

Ancient Israel, founded in the desert by Moses, with laws given by God, set itself apart from all Gentile peoples. For Israelites, no less than for Romans, to be a citizen meant to be politically different. But if Rome became the world, then all ground of political difference, and all ground of citizenship, dissolved. The plurality of gods in the pagan world of antiquity corresponded to the plurality of cities or independent governments, each with its own god or gods as the putative source of its laws. Whatever skepticism philosophy had eventually wrought in the private beliefs of the citizens of the ancient cities, according to public doctrine all cities were governed by laws that had been given, whether directly or indirectly, by gods. Plato's *Laws* begins when the Athenian Stranger asks the Cretan and the Spartan, "A god, is it, or some human being . . . who is given the credit for laying down your laws?" To this the Cretan replies: "A god, stranger, a god—to say at any rate the most just thing. Among us Zeus, and among the Lacedemonians, from whence this man here comes, I think they declare that it's Apollo."

Because God or the gods were held to be the ultimate source of all law in the ancient world, the question of political obligation, as we understand it, never arose. In the *Antigone*, the conflict between Antigone and Creon is a conflict between the gods of the family, which command her to give her brother proper burial, and the gods of the city, which command Creon to leave him unburied as a traitor to the city. In Plato's *Apology of Socrates*, Socrates is convicted of corrupting the young by teaching them not to believe in the gods of the city and of introducing new gods. For an Athenian, to believe in gods different from the city's gods meant to be attached to alien gods, the sources of alien laws, and hence to be disloyal. The crime of which Socrates was accused was not essentially different from that of worshiping the golden calf in Exodus. At one point in Socrates' trial, Meletus accuses Socrates of atheism. But atheism, which in this context meant philosophy, is itself understood more as a species of infidelity to the city than as any merely theoretical disbelief. What is crucial is the identification of piety with lawfulness, and of lawfulness with justice. Impiety is thus identified either with lawless anarchy or with treasonable correspondence with the gods and laws of another city.

Most Americans will be familiar with the idea of divine legislation in the Old Testament. The laws of the Israelite political community, formed in the desert after the escape from slavery in Egypt, are given to Moses by God. Although the God of Israel eventually is seen by believers to differ from all other gods, being alone truly God, he comes to sight as the lawgiver of a particular city. In this characteristic respect, this particular city, ancient Israel, does not differ from ancient Crete, Sparta, Thebes, Athens, Carthage, or Rome. It is also characteristic of ancient cities or polities that their gods are seen as their defenders. The story of Exodus is the story of how a nation of slaves, without arms of its own, was led to freedom by the power and might of its God. But the story of how the God of Israel led his people out of Egyptian bondage is in itself also typical of the relationship of the god of any ancient city to the freedom of its people, a freedom depending upon its ability to defeat its enemies in war.[104] When an ancient city was defeated in war, the usual result, over many centuries, was the slaughter of all adult males and the enslavement of the women and children. (As civilization progressed, the males would also be enslaved rather than slaughtered.) The defeat of an ancient city meant the defeat of its gods. In the contest before Pharaoh, the God of Israel was vindicated, first by Moses' victory over the Egyptian magicians and then by his victory over the military forces of Pharaoh, in the escape through the Red Sea into Sinai. By delivering the Israelites from slavery, God possessed himself of a people, and the people possessed themselves of a God. Gradually, in the course of the Old Testament, it appeared that the God of Israel is not the God only of Israel but the only God, the God of all peoples, the God of the universe, which he alone created. The uniqueness and universality of God is shown, in part, by the fact that unlike the gods of other cities, neither he nor his people disappear from the stage of history when subjected to defeat in war. Alone among ancient peoples, the Jews did not become clients of the gods of their conquerors, even when they had been carried into captivity or were dispersed among foreign lands. Alone among ancient peoples, the Jews have survived.

In Lincoln's 1838 address to the Young Men's Lyceum of Springfield, he mentioned Alexander, Caesar, and Napoleon as the three great destroyers of republics. Alexander destroyed the independence of the Greek cities, and Caesar carried his work to completion by Rome's imperial domination of the world of classical antiquity. In Shakespeare's *Julius Caesar*, we witness Caesar thrice rejecting the kingly crown. Although Caesar's self-denial is supposed to prove his humility, we, like Shakespeare's audience, are aware that he is in fact rejecting a lesser for a greater title. The name of Caesar ("Kaiser," "Czar") will become the title for the emperor of the world, not a king but a ruler of kings, a king of kings. We must bear in mind that it was during the reign of Caesar Augustus, the first imperial Caesar, the heir of the great Julius, that Jesus was born and carried on his ministry. Like Caesar, he too became known as a King of Kings, although of a kingdom said not to be of this world. Yet the political history of Western man for the next millennium and a half was dominated, especially in the High Middle Ages, by the contest for preeminence between emperors and popes, the two ultimate forms of rule in the post-classical world. As we shall see, the solution to the problem of that relationship of emperor and pope, or of Caesar and Christ, was only discovered in the American Revolution and the American Founding, in the separation of church and state.

The process by which Rome (understood as it understood itself) became, not one city, but the world was also the process by which a Roman citizen became a citizen, not of Rome, but of the world. It was also the process by which Caesar became the name of the emperor, not of Rome, but of the world. In the first centuries following the battle of Actium—which decided that Augustus Caesar, and not Mark Antony, would be Caesar—the divinization of the emperor proceeded along lines familiar to the ancient world: from victors to heroes to gods. But the divinization of the emperor was only an intermediate step. As has been said, Rome was no longer one city among many. As the "eternal city," it could not be ruled by a mortal god. The gods of ancient cities were mortal in this decisive respect: the cities that worshiped them could be defeated, and the gods might disappear from the stage of history with the cities that had been their votaries. Only a transcendent God whose rule of the universe was unchallengeable, since he was the only God, corresponded with Rome's supposedly unchallengeable rule of the human world.

Most of us are familiar with the passage in the New Testament in which the Pharisees seek to "entangle" Jesus by asking whether it was lawful to pay taxes to Caesar. And there are few of us who have not marveled at Jesus' shrewd and perfectly ambiguous reply: "Render therefore to Caesar the things that are Caesar's, and to God the things that are God's." [105] Since the American Revolution, the Jeffersonian principle that it is against natural right for any government to intervene between a man and his God has come to be widely accepted, certainly among Americans, as the authentic interpretation of Jesus' reply to the Pharisees. The distinction between the things of Caesar and the things of God has placed the authority of Jesus behind the separation of church and state. It is no objection to this interpretation of Jesus' saying to direct attention to the absurdity of identifying the American republic with "Caesar," even if it is only for the limited purpose of distinguishing church and state.

Once upon a time, every American schoolchild memorized the following passage of Patrick Henry's speech on the Stamp Act: "Caesar had his Brutus; Charles the First his Cromwell; and George the Third ['Treason' cried the Speaker]—*may profit by their example. If this be treason, make the most of it.*"[106] The American Revolution reversed the dominant Western tradition, which had been antirepublican and monarchical. The earlier tradition was well represented by Dante, who in his *Divine Comedy* located those heroes of republicanism, Brutus and Cassius, in the innermost circle of hell, with Judas, the betrayer of Christ. Contrast with this the motto of the State of Virginia, adopted in the Revolution, *sic semper tyrannis*, which was testimony to the virtue of the enemies of Caesar. This, alas, is what John Wilkes Booth is said to have cried out as he jumped onto the stage of Ford's Theatre, having slain the greatest enemy of tyranny the world has ever known. However misapplied, it was not a sentiment with which Lincoln (any more than Jefferson or Henry) would have disagreed. But we should bear in mind that if Booth misapplied it, so also had the medieval popes, who used it as a means of bending kings and emperors to their wills. As we saw in Shakespeare's *King John*, the doctrine of tyrannicide had been misused, as an instrument of despotism, long before the assassination of Abraham Lincoln.

American republicanism, arising in a world of Christian monotheism, was not, however, purely classical. Although Americans would have placed Brutus in heaven rather than hell, they would have left Judas where Dante put him. If they accepted separation of church and state, it was because they were persuaded that the true teaching of the Gospel required that, as in the ministry of Jesus, no political rewards or punishments influence the soul in its contemplation of the requirements of eternal salvation. And they were persuaded that disagreements as to the requirements for felicity in the next world should not prevent agreements concerning the common good in this world. Paying taxes in a republic was a duty, but not for the reasons Jesus may have had for paying taxes to Caesar. In the Roman province in which Jesus lived, one paid taxes to Caesar because the alternative was to be crucified—Rome's all-purpose punishment. In America, one paid taxes because the government, under "the laws of nature and of nature's God," had been authorized to govern by the vote of the people themselves. The government that taxed Americans, provided it was acting within its constitutional authority, was implementing the taxpayers' own God-given rights.

When Jesus referred to "Caesar," his interlocutors did not understand him to refer to "state" as opposed to "church." They knew, as Jesus knew, that the distinction between God and Caesar would have made little sense in any ancient city in any earlier age, whether to Romans in pre-Caesarian Rome or to Jews in the Jerusalem of David or Solomon. To the contemporaries of Jesus it was a distinction that applied essentially to the regime under which they lived, in which the power of Caesar's legions was as despotic as it was irresistible. It was also the case, however, that Caesar's interest in the provinces, apart from insistence upon the recognition of Roman hegemony, included little more than receiving taxes. Caesar's rule, although inflexible on the matter of taxes, was on the whole tolerant of (or indifferent towards) the customs, and in particular the religious customs, of the different nations that had been conquered and incorporated into the empire. Jesus knew that Caesar left him, as a Jew, to his own God, just as he left all the peoples of the empire to their own gods.

This blandly tolerant (because indifferent) despotism could not, however, survive indefinitely. Mankind had hitherto been divided into many cities, with their many laws and many gods. But after Rome conquered the ancient world and Caesar conquered Rome, there was but one city, and there could be but one paramount law and, with equal reason, but one God. There was something of a providential inevitability in the process by which, once citizenship and law had been universalized, the one God would become the God of the one city, and the worship of this God would become the only form of worship sanctioned by such a city.

If Rome was not one city among many, the deity of the emperor could not remain that of one god among many. The Hebraic conception of Deity fitted the conception of an eternal city or empire ruled by an eternal God as no pagan conception of deity could. The God of Israel had given laws for a particular people, who believed themselves to be the chosen people of their God. But if the God of Israel was in truth the One God, then he was equally the God of every other people. The God of Israel, now recognized as the God of the Gentiles no less than of the Jews, ceased to be the legislating God who was the God of Moses. Although the God of the Jews could become the God of the Gentiles, the laws of Moses, fitted peculiarly for the Jews, could not become the laws of every people. Such a God might continue to be the source of all legitimate authority but not the direct source of municipal law. He could not be conceived as giving different particular laws for every particular people, as he had done when he was regarded primarily as the God of his chosen people. The laws given to Moses were not regarded as adapted to the peculiar characteristics of the Jews. On the contrary, the peculiar characteristics of the Jews were understood to be the result of their adaptation to

God's laws.[107] The God of a universal empire might, however, provide the sanction for the authority of a human emperor. This emperor might parcel out his authority, in virtue of a kind of imperial federal franchise, to the kings or nobles or magistrates who ruled the subdivisions of his empire. Roman law, like the federal law of the American Union after 1787, would be the paramount law with respect to "interstate commerce" and other matters of general interest (especially that of keeping the peace), while law would remain municipal with respect to matters that were essentially domestic and internal. The Roman Empire was for many centuries a highly efficient political organism in adapting itself to the requirements of universalism and cosmopolitanism, on the one hand, and local self-government, on the other. But authority was always understood as a devolution downward from the emperor, never upwards from the people.[108]

The Christian God transformed the messianic conception of the particular salvation of the Jews, by means of obedience to the Torah or Law, into the universal salvation of mankind by means of faith. It bears repetition, however, that not only the Jews but all ancient peoples identified God or gods as the source of law. By accepting Jesus as the Messiah, any human being, of any race or nation, might now find entrance into the Kingdom of God without reference to the particular people (or family) to which he belonged or to what laws he obeyed. As the primacy of law was replaced by the primacy of faith, so did felicity in the next world replace felicity in this world as the ultimate human and political concern. God's promises to Abraham, one should recall, referred only to his descendants' prosperity in this world. With Christianity, the Kingdom of God, a kingdom not of this world, replaces the empire of this world as the central human concern. As life in this world came increasingly to be seen as preparation for the life to come, the government of this world came increasingly to be seen as ministerial to the requirements of the City of God. As the City of God was of necessity monarchical in character, so the empire of this world, as a reflection of that greater empire, was seen as indefeasibly monarchical. Here, in the Christian centuries of the Roman Empire, was the inner bond connecting the idea of legitimate rule with the divine right of kings.

Although Jesus declared that his kingdom was not of this world, once Christianity was established as the sole religion of the universal (catholic) empire, all the kingdoms of this world were seen as depending upon that other kingdom for their legitimacy. In fact, the dominant tradition within Western Christianity, which we find expressed in Aquinas, Dante, Shakespeare, and numerous others, held that the secular history of Rome reflected God's providential order no less than the sacred history of the Jews. It was necessary to the fulfillment of God's purposes that Caesar preside at the birth of a universal empire if mankind were to be offered salvation by a universal Savior. A world of many flourishing and independent cities with many gods, the world of Plato's *Republic* and Aristotle's *Politics*, could not have been a vessel for the reception of the Gospel of Jesus Christ.

Because of this, the authority of Caesar came to be seen as nearly, or more than nearly, sacramental in character. Although Jesus himself, in his response to the Pharisees, clearly distinguishes God's authority from Caesar's, we find his disciples identifying the two. We find this in the New Testament, long before the extension of Roman citizenship to the provinces in the third century or the establishment of Christianity in the fourth century. Indeed, this identification of the authority of God and Caesar occurs at a time when Christians were being subjected to terrible persecution. Here is Saint Paul, in his Letter to the Romans: "Let every person be subject to the governing authorities. For there is no authority except from God, and those that exist have been instituted by God. Therefore he who resists the authorities resists what God has appointed, and those who resist will incur judgment."[109] In later centuries—as, for example, when Richard II said that not all the water in the sea could wash the balm from an anointed king—consecration by a deputized representative of the Lord was necessary for a king to appear possessed of divine right. According to Paul, however, nothing more was needed for the possession of such right than the possession of power. Men are seen as "subjects" of government, not as citizens. Nor is there any suggestion of Aristotle's distinction between just and unjust governments, nor of the right to kill tyrants, recognized by both Aristotle and Cicero.

Paul continues:

> For rulers are not a terror to good conduct, but to bad. Would you have no fear of him who is in authority? Then do what is good, and you will have his approval, for he is God's servant for your good. But if you do wrong, be afraid, for he does not bear the sword in vain; he is the servant of God to execute his wrath on the wrongdoer.[110]

Except for the reference to the sword (rather than the rod), Paul might be speaking of the relationship of parents and children. One would think that the love and care of governments for the well-being of their subjects was as natural as that of parents for their children and that the phenomenon of tyranny never existed. The reference to "rulers" is generic, implying that we have no more choice of our rulers than of our parents, or that there is no more need to choose the one than the other. It was Christian doctrine that God loved the world and that the death of Jesus on the Cross was testimony of that love. But to suppose that the Emperor Nero loved mankind as God did is supposing something entirely different. Yet we do not find visible here an alternative to the regime of Caesar, any more than to the regime of God.

The same doctrine is contained in the first Epistle of Peter:

Be subject for the Lord's sake to every human institution, whether it be to the emperor as supreme, or to governors as sent by him to punish those who do wrong and to praise those who do right. For it is God's will that by doing right you should put to silence the ignorance of foolish men. Live as free men, yet without using your freedom as a pretext for evil; but live as servants of God. Honor all men. Love the brotherhood. Fear God. Honor the emperor.[111]

The fundamental purpose of government seems to be moral education, as it is in Aristotle's *Politics*. But the imperial moral preceptor when Paul and Peter wrote was the Emperor Nero, the incarnation of every vice ever attributed to pagan man or pagan god.[112] We can see in the doctrine of submission to authority in Paul and Peter the archetype of the doctrine preached by Henry V. We can see in it also the separation of the morality of the ruler from the morality presumably demanded of his subjects. The tension within the persona of the "mirror of all Christian kings" is already present in the persona of the pagan emperor as seen through the eyes of Paul and Peter.

In these epistles, to live as a free man does not mean, as in Aristotle (or Jefferson or Lincoln), to participate in ruling. To live as a free man means to live as a servant of God who at the same time obeys and honors the emperor. Here we see the apparent acceptance of Caesarian despotism, not only as the universal empire preparing the way for the universal religion of the Messiah, but also as the final form of human government, as indeed the "end of history." That the Caesarian empire should be the final form of human government agreed, of course, with the Christian expectation of the imminent second coming of the Messiah, followed by the resurrection of the dead, the Last Judgment, and the end of this world.

The imperial regime accepted by Paul and Peter, apparently without qualification, resembles the government of the family, or perhaps more precisely the government of children, rather than political government. It is subject to Aristotle's objection, at the beginning of the *Politics*, to those who fail to distinguish the different forms of rule and do not see that a republic, a kingdom, and a family differ, not in number, but in kind. Paul and Peter do not envisage the least participation in government by the governed, or anything resembling the rule of law. We find, therefore, the apparently complete depreciation of the political as a continuing concern of human life. The responsibility of the ruled to the rulers is unconditional. The rulers are responsible to God alone, although nothing is said as to why or how the rulers are qualified, either by character or by intelligence, for this vocation. Above all, nothing is said as to why the rulers will think themselves obliged to rule righteously in the interest of their subjects, rather than tyrannically in their own selfish interest. Here then is the doctrine of divine right in its purest form.

～

More than a millennium after the Epistles of Paul and Peter, the most comprehensive as well as the most exalted justification of the divine right of kings appeared in Dante's treatise *On Monarchy*.[113] Dante's work is of particular interest to us, in part because its argument for the uncontrolled rule of one man over the entire world represents the furthest distance possible from the doctrine enshrined in the Declaration of Independence. But it is of interest also because of its resemblances to, as well as its differences from, the central ideas of America's Founding.

The Declaration of Independence, equally with *On Monarchy*, assumes that the divine government of the universe supplies the paradigm for the right government of man by man. According to the Declaration, the divine government embodies distinct and distinguishable legislative, judicial, and executive functions,[114] and the American people identified their understanding of human constitutionalism with what they believed was the constitution of the universe. As we have already noted, however, they took their bearings from the *difference* between man and God. The government of the universe might be monarchical, and the one God might properly exercise all three functions, because God and God alone is possessed of "infinite wisdom, goodness and rectitude." But the American people, while proclaiming "In God We Trust," considered it impious to think that such confidence might be placed in humans. They did not, like Paul and Peter, think that the moral authority of God could be found in the autocratic rule of any king or ruling class. They refused, therefore—as we saw in the resolution of the citizens of Malden, Massachusetts, in 1776—to be subject to any other king than God.[115]

In America, as Tom Paine said, only the law is king. Likewise Jefferson, in the Kentucky Resolutions, thundered that

> it would be a dangerous delusion were a confidence in the men of our choice to silence our fears for the safety of our rights: that confidence is everywhere the parent of despotism: free government is founded in jealousy and not in confidence. . . . In questions of power then let no more be heard of confidence in man, but bind him down from mischief by the chains of the Constitution.[116]

One can hardly imagine a greater distance than the one separating this from Paul and Peter, not only with respect to the source of authority, but also with respect to confidence in those exercising governmental power, however legitimate. We have seen that the framers of the Constitution held that placing the legislative, executive, and judicial powers of government in the same hands is "the very definition of tyranny."[117] Dante, on the contrary, took the perfection of God's monarchical rule as a model for human imitation. In doing so, he appears to be providing a justification, on the basis of unassisted human reason, for the doctrine we observed in the Epistles. Dante's emperor is thought to be above the ordinary human passions, even as God is above such passions. The goods for which men envy and strive against each other are already subject to his dominion. What unsatisfied ambition can he have? Of whom can he be jealous or envious? His only passion, by Dante's account, would be that perfection of his government that would make him appear as what he really is: God's representative on earth, the kingly reflection of the King of Kings.

The *Federalist*'s analysis of faction, particularly in numbers 10 and 51, parallels a similar underlying analysis in Dante. Their opposite conclusions proceed from curiously corresponding premises. Both see the problem of faction as central to the political problem. Both see the ineffectiveness of virtue in controlling envy, greed, and hatred. But what the extended republic under the proposed constitution is to the *Federalist* in controlling the virulence of faction, the unimpeded rule of the Roman Emperor is to Dante. Both see the importance of human freedom. Both see a world in which genuine freedom, which is rational freedom, is submerged by the tyrannical power of the uncontrolled passions. But Dante is committed, a priori, to what we might call a solution from above, placing all authority in the hands of *one*, even as the Founding Fathers were committed to a solution from below, with all authority emanating from and being responsible to the *many*.

It might indeed be said, from the perspective of the Becker thesis, that Dante's contention on behalf of monarchy only reflected the historical necessities of his interests in the historical circumstances in which he found himself. It is certainly true that the option open to the Founding Fathers in eighteenth-century America was not open to Dante in fourteenth-century Italy. The reverse also is true. Dante's argument for absolute monarchy would not only have been anathema to Jefferson; it would also have been politically irrelevant. Nonetheless it would have resonated in Jefferson's soul in at least one respect: it was directed against the political pretensions of the papacy. Its object was to free the authority of the emperor from any political submission to the pope. In his demand for the independence of the emperor from papal political authority, Dante anticipated the Reformation doctrine of the divine right of national kings that we saw in Shakespeare's *King John*. His doctrine differed from that of the Reformation, in which national kings were also the heads of national churches, in that he did not claim ecclesiastical authority for the emperor. He did not contest the pope's claim to head the church, or the church's right to prescribe the doctrinal or sacramental ground of salvation. None of these prerogatives, however, entitled the pope to guide or control the emperor's political rule—any more, we might add, than Paul or Peter thought of themselves as having any ultimate authority over their emperor.

The rootedness of Dante's *On Monarchy* in the particular political quarrel between pope and emperor in fourteenth-century Italy does not mean that whatever claims it makes to eternal truth or justice are simply reducible to Dante's historical circumstances and necessities. As we have previously observed, the limits of action are not the limits of thought. The limits of action may, however, impose limits upon the manner in which the thought that directs action is expressed. Dante was born into a world that was dominated politically by parties allied with either pope or emperor, and his political fortunes were cast with the imperial party. He was exiled from his native city of Florence by the defeat of his friends, and his only hope of returning depended upon the overthrow of his enemies. His tract on monarchy was certainly designed to contribute to the fortunes of his party. Despite appearances, it was anything but purely theoretical. In this sense, it was calculated to play a role similar to that of Locke's *Two Treatises of Government* with respect to the fortunes of the Whigs in the constitutional struggle between Parliament and James II that culminated in the Glorious Revolution of 1689. Historical circumstances certainly played a major role in determining what arguments might be useful in persuading Dante's contemporaries, in the one case, or the contemporaries of William of Orange, in the other. But what is persuasive is not the same as what is true.

In Dante's world, the political claims of Catholic Christianity were of necessity paramount. No arguments that did not assume the validity of these claims would have been politically relevant. Conversely, before Caesar's Rome, during the golden age of the Roman republic, the political claims of Catholic Christianity would have had no hearing on their merit. Indeed, the message of the Gospels itself would have been almost entirely unintelligible in a world in which each city had it own gods. The period of the political vigor and independence of Sparta, Crete, and Athens was the period when their own laws, and their own gods, were paramount. Only Caesar's conquest of these cities, and of their gods, opened the souls of the citizens to a different God. The Christianity of Dante's world, like the Gospels themselves, recognized that the catholicism of Caesar's empire was indispensable for the catholicism of Christ's ministry. Thus, Dante regarded God's providence to be as manifest in Caesar's empire as in Christ's ministry. In *On Monarchy*, Dante's explorations of Roman history and poetry (especially Virgil) to prove the divinity of Caesar's mission resemble nothing so much as the parallel passages in the synoptic Gospels in which testimony from the Old Testament is brought forward as prophetic proof that Jesus was the Messiah. Caesarism is therefore accounted by Dante as the providential correlate of Christianity. Caesar ministers to Christ in the same way that, according to Aristotle, practical wisdom ministers to theoretical wisdom.[118] Here, of course, theoretical wisdom is subordinated to theological wisdom as defining the ultimate end of human life. Both theoretical and theological wisdom are "higher" than practical wisdom, but neither gives commands to it. Practical wisdom gives its commands *for the sake of* the higher wisdom but is not governed by it. Likewise, according to Dante, the emperor serves the pope and the church but is not governed by them. For the pope to attempt to govern the emperor would destroy the efficacy of the emperor's service to the church. Neither pope nor emperor can do his proper work well if either interferes with the work of the other.

According to Dante, the necessity of the independence of the political sphere from religious authority is attested by the paradoxical fact that the Christian purpose of Caesar's conquest of the ancient world would not have been realized had Rome been governed by Christian doctrine. That is to say, if Caesar had been Christian, he would not have conquered.[119] The disorder of Dante's political world, by Dante's own account, is rooted in the usurpation of political authority by the popes. We find in this a remarkable prefiguring of Jefferson's argument in the Virginia Statute of Religious Liberty. In the *novus ordo seclorum*, for the state to serve the cause of religion, the churches must be divested of all political patronage and there must be no religious test for office. When church officials seek office, or when offices depend upon church officials, both state and church are corrupted. The purity of religion is defiled and the purpose of government is perverted.[120] Jefferson's argument may not appear on the surface to be Dante's, because on the surface Dante offers no challenge to the authority of the church on purely religious grounds. The wars of the Reformation lie just over the horizon. Those wars convinced wise statesmen, like the American Founding Fathers, that any interference either by religion with politics or by politics with religion could lead only to civil war. Dante's argument in *On Monarchy*, despite its absurd elevation of imperial pretensions, points nonetheless toward the separation of church and state, which separation was the indispensable condition for the revival of republicanism. Majority rule was impossible unless it could be combined with minority rights. This combination could not occur until those participating in voting did not divide along sectarian religious grounds.

The emancipation of the emperor from the pope, by the argument of Dante's *On Monarchy*, represented a long step away from the identification of the gods and the law that was the Christian world's inheritance from the ancient city. In fact, Christianity itself had broken the connection between the gods and law. What remained was the connection between God and the political authority that gave the sanction to law—or to be more precise, the connection between God and emperor. The Reformation, however, broke up the Holy Roman Empire, effectively ending the claims to universal authority equally of pope and of emperor. Divine right monarchy survived in the claims of the kings—notably, for our purposes, the kings (and queens) of England—who now headed their national churches. What remained was that further revolution that transferred the divine authority of law from kings to people.

The preparation for the final transformation of the ancient city into the modern state is also to be found in the New Testament. In Mark we read:

> There came then his brethren and his mother, and, standing without, sent unto him, calling him. And the multitude sat about him, and they said unto him, Behold, thy mother and thy brethren without seek for thee. And he answered them, saying, Who is my mother, or my brethren? And he looked round about on them which sat about him, and said, Behold my mother and my brethren! For whomsoever shall do the will of God, the same is my brother, and my sister, and mother.[121]

The family of blood becomes the family of faith. The New Testament begins, in the first chapter of Matthew, by tracing the genealogy of Jesus through thrice fourteen generations, from Abraham to Joseph the husband of Mary, the mother of Jesus. The argument in favor of Jesus as the Messiah depends upon his being of the seed of Abraham, by whom God's promises to Abraham are to be fulfilled. In Jesus, we see the community of blood transformed into a community of faith. Through Jesus, God's promises to Abraham become promises to all mankind. In respect to those promises, it can now be said "that all men are created equal."

This was celebrated in the following famous passage from Lincoln's Chicago speech of July 10, 1858:

> Now it happens that we meet together once every year, somewhere about the 4th of July. . . . In every way we are better men, in the age, and race, and country in which we live, for these celebrations. But after we have done all this, we have not yet reached the whole. There us something else connected with it. We have, besides these men—descended by blood from our ancestors—among us, perhaps half our people who are not descendants at all of these men; they are men who have come from Europe—Germans, Irish, French, and Scandinavians—men that have come from Europe themselves, or whose ancestors have come hither and settled here, finding themselves our equals in all things. If they look back through this history to trace their connection with those days by blood, they find they have none; they cannot carry themselves back into that glorious epoch and make themselves feel that they are part of us; but when they look through that

old Declaration of Independence, they find that those old men say that "We hold these truths to be self-evident, that all men are created equal," and then they feel that that moral sentiment taught in that day evidences their relation to those men, that it is the father of all moral principle in them, and that they have a right to claim it as though they were blood of the blood, and flesh of the flesh, of the men who wrote that Declaration, and so they are.[122]

Within the American political tradition, Lincoln transmutes the latter-day immigrants from the ethnically divided nations of the Old World into members of the same family, united by the transcendent faith in human equality. That faith is the faith of the same ancestral "fathers" he will celebrate in the Gettysburg Address. Indeed, in saying that they are of the same flesh and the same blood, he uses the very idiom of transubstantiation.

The late M. E. Bradford, a resolute foe of Abraham Lincoln and defender of the cause of the Confederacy, wrote that "there is no man equal to any other, except perhaps in the politically untranslatable understanding of the Deity."[123] That all men are equal in the sight of God has been the unassailable premise of Judeo-Christian ethics. That this premise is "politically untranslatable" was a tenable inference from the belief that the Caesarian despotism of postrepublican Rome represented the end of history. We have seen that such a belief followed from the supposition that Caesar's conquest of the ancient world was a providential provision for the preaching of the Gospel of Jesus Christ throughout that world, and that the end of the world was imminent. On the other hand, if the temporal end of the world is not imminent, then there is no reason to think that the temporal empire of the Caesars is the final form of human government and that it will not be susceptible to the passing away to which all things are susceptible that have come into being. That Caesar's conquest of the ancient world may have been a necessary prelude to the preaching of the Gospel throughout that world does not mean that an imperial despotism was the best form of human government. To say, as Bradford said, that the equality of souls in the sight of God is politically untranslatable is to say that God never intended the equality he saw to be seen by man. This is an impossible assertion.

That the equality of human souls in the sight of God ought to be translated into a political structure of equal political rights has come to be regarded as the most authentic interpretation of the Gospel itself. Slavery, and the imposition of all arbitrary forms of inequality of man by man, has come to be seen as demeaning to the souls of God's creation, and therefore demeaning to God. This view was set forth with matchless eloquence in 1910 by Bourke Cockran, the leading lay spokesman for the Catholic Church in America at the turn of the century.

The essential principles of democracy were not first formulated in our Constitution, nor in our Declaration of Independence, nor in the English Bill of Rights, nor in Magna Carta, nor in the institutes of King Alfred, nor in any monument of human wisdom, evolved from human experience. They were first revealed by the Divine Author of Christianity when he taught that all men are brothers, children of the same father, equal heirs to the same immortal heritage beyond the grave. As the political institutions under which men live always reflect the beliefs they cherish, a government built on the principle that all men are equal in the eye of the law resulted inevitably from the general acceptance of the religious doctrine that all men are equal in the sight of God.

While democracy was the inevitable, it was not the immediate fruit of Christianity. But this only shows that men find it easier to accept a truth than to regulate their lives by it. It took less than four centuries to convert pagan temples into Christian churches, but it took eighteen centuries for the religious beliefs of Christians to bear fruit in political institutions of freedom. Still, from the first hour when the tongues of fire descended upon the heads of the Apostles, it was inevitable that if civilization became Christian, two results must follow—the substitution of free labor for slave labor in industry, and the erection of free institutions on the ruins of despotic institutions in government. Here on this soil Christianity has finally borne these, its capital and inevitable fruits. Here the spiritual equality of all men taught by Jesus Christ on Lake Galilee is embodied in a government based upon the political equality of all men. Here labor is not a degrading task reluctantly performed under fear of the scourge by a wretched slave who is a chattel, but a voluntary enterprise cheerfully undertaken and loyally discharged by the free man who is a sovereign. Never was a system vindicated by results so beneficent—peace, abundance, happiness have blessed the nation which acknowledges no sovereign but the citizen and tolerates no slave but the felon.[124]

Whether the doctrine of equality in the Gospels was knowable by unassisted human reason as a doctrine of the natural law, apart from divine revelation, is not a question that needs to be decided here. (Cockran himself only says that it was "first formulated" in the Gospels.) That the doctrine of the Declaration of Independence is alone fully consistent with the "inevitable" result of the Gospels and that slavery is as inconsistent with Christianity as with the republicanism of the Founding Fathers are as certain to this son of the Catholic Church as they were to Abraham Lincoln.

We have, we believe, explained why the inertial force of the doctrine of the divine right of kings was as powerful as it was, why eighteen centuries were needed for it to be replaced, and why the intrinsic rationality of the regime of popular self-government is in no way gainsaid by the difficulties in the way of its acceptance or the obstacles in the way of its implementation.

3

The Divided American Mind on the Eve of Conflict: James Buchanan, Jefferson Davis, and Alexander Stephens Survey the Crisis

Between the acting of a dreadful thing
And the first motion, all the interim is
Like a phantasma, or a hideous dream.
The genius and the mortal instruments
Are then in council; and the state of man,
Like to a little kingdom, suffers then
The nature of an insurrection.

—William Shakespeare

The Civil War, the Gettysburg Address tells us, was a test whether popular government would survive or perish. This reflection upon the whole of human history is so familiar that its breadth and depth have almost been lost to us. We repeat the words of Bourke Cockran from the end of our last chapter, that "it was inevitable that if civilization became Christian, two results must follow—the substitution of free labor for slave labor in industry, and the erection of free institutions on the ruins of despotic institutions in government." We have already seen a present-day defender of the Southern cause declaring that the equality proclaimed by Christianity was "politically untranslatable." The Civil War was as much a war between differing versions of Christianity (or about the teaching of the Bible) as it was about slavery and the Constitution. The division between the Northern churches and the Southern churches may be compared to the division between Protestants and Catholics in the wars of the Reformation.

We have seen that it was only under certain defined conditions that popular sovereignty, rightly understood, could replace the divine right of kings and that free elections could replace the exercise of the right of revolution. Those conditions required that there be no religious tests for office and that separation of

---

The epigraph is taken from *Julius Caesar*, act II, scene 1.

church and state removes questions of sectarian religious belief from the political arena. In his first inaugural address Jefferson proclaimed that "we are all federalists, we are all republicans" and that "not every difference of opinion is a difference of principle." But it was clear that some differences of opinion *were* differences of principle, and that in the presence of such differences among a sufficiently numerous body of citizens a government combining majority rule with minority rights would not be possible. During the party warfare of the 1790s, the Republicans had called their opponents "monocrats," a pejorative corruption of "monarchists," implying that they were votaries of monarchy. In his inaugural, Jefferson acknowledged that the party of John Adams and Alexander Hamilton was not antirepublican. But it was clear nonetheless that the differences of republicans and antirepublicans could not be settled by voting.

In the years following the American Revolution, in the Western world generally, the identification of Christianity with popular government, or with free political institutions, was far from a settled matter. It was far from a settled matter in America, even after the adoption of the Constitution of 1787 and the peaceful transfer of political power in the election of 1800. Despite the apparent success of the American experiment in the early years of the nineteenth century, the defeat of Napoleon was followed by a wave of reaction in Europe against the French Revolution and against the identification of Christianity with the cause of popular government. The insistence that the equality of human souls in the eyes of God was "politically untranslatable" is an expression of that reaction. Indeed, it is the core of the defense of the ancien régime against the rising tide of democracy. The Holy Alliance that had defeated Napoleon, and which ruled Europe in his aftermath, continued to link Christianity with the principle of the divine right of kings, as well as with a rigidly hierarchical society in which status was determined mainly by birth. It is against this background of European reaction against the rights of man that the Gettysburg Address must be read.

For white Americans, the antebellum period was one in which society was becoming ever more democratic and egalitarian. Paradoxically, it was also a period in which Negro slavery was rapidly growing and gaining power, both economically and politically. Nowhere in Europe, or indeed in the entire world, was personal status more completely determined by birth than in American slavery.[1] In the period before the Civil War, manumission became legally impossible in virtually all the slave states. In nearly all, it was made a felony to teach a slave to read or write. As theories of racial inequality came increasingly to dominate public discourse in the South, greater efforts were made to suppress evidence of Negro talents or ability. If, as was often said, slavery was a school for barbarians, it was not a school in which success was measured by the progress of the students. Most important of all, it was not a school from which anyone was permitted to graduate.

Whether Christianity condemned or endorsed slavery was one of the great issues that divided Americans on the eve of the Civil War. Because the Northern and Southern churches divided over the question, the Civil War took on many of the characteristics of a religious war. It was well understood in the period of the Founding that the free exercise of religion and the separation of state and church were indispensable adjuncts of a regime of majority rule and minority rights.[2] When the slavery question took on the dimensions of a religious question, the entire experiment in free government was thereby at risk. This risk was compounded, as we shall see, by the fact that throughout the nineteenth century, modern Science (with a capital "S") was becoming an authority parallel to, and sometimes indistinguishable from, biblical religion. But it was an authority in direct opposition to the moral reasoning of equality embodied in the Declaration of Independence and to the Bible seen as a document recording God's will that mankind should be free.

Although Abraham Lincoln did not belong to any church, he constantly appealed to the Bible—along with the Declaration—as a source of moral authority, and never more so than when he said, "As I would not be a *slave*, so I would not be a *master*. This expresses my idea of democracy. Whatever differs from this, to the extent of the difference, is not democracy."[3] The first sentence is clearly an application of that Golden Rule that, according to Jesus, was the sum of the law and the prophets. The second and third sentences indicate that the ethical core of biblical religion is identical with the rational principle of popular government— that is to say, of the Declaration. Lincoln's axiom assumes the coincidence of equality, rightly understood, as the principle of Christianity and of free government. But this assumption was rejected by the Christian churches of the antebellum South, no less than by its political leaders.

The political theology that governed the Southern cause—the antithesis of Abraham Lincoln's—is expressed authoritatively and concisely in the following passage from a speech of Jefferson Davis, delivered to the Democratic State Convention, Jackson, Mississippi, July 6, 1859.

It was said of the members of a once powerful family which gave kings to Europe that they "learned nothing and forgot nothing." If we credit antislavery agitators with sincerity, such would seem to be their condition. Though investigation and experience have disproved the assertions and refuted the theories on which their movement commenced, they neither learn the correction nor forget exploded errors unsubstantially founded upon the popular phrases which they have brought into disrepute by constant misapplication. A declaration of rights made by bodies politic is construed as an essay upon the individual relations of man to man. Arguing to their own satisfaction for the unity in origin of the races of man, they draw thence the conclusion of his present equality. If the premises be correct, the conclusion is surely a *non sequitur* and the student of facts as they exist in our time will not be disturbed in his inquiries. As to him, it matters not whether Almighty power and wisdom stamped diversity on the races of men at the period of creation, or decreed it after the subsidence of the flood. It is enough for us that the Creator, speaking through the inspired lips of Noah, declared the destiny of the three races of men. Around and about us is the remarkable fulfill-ment of the prophecy, the execution of the decree, and the justification of the lit-eral construction of the text.

The judgments of God are not as those of man. To the former all things are accommodated, and the fate of the subject is thereby his nature, but the victim of man's decree rebels and struggles against his condition.

When the Spaniards discovered this continent and reduced the sons of Shem to bondage, unsuited to that condition they pined and rapidly wasted away in unproductive labor. The good Bishop Las Casas, with philosophical humanity, inaugurated the importation of the race of Ham; they came to relieve from an unnatural state the dwellers in tents, and to fulfill their own destiny, that of being "servants of servants." In their normal condition they thrived, and by their labor the land was subdued and made fruitful. The West India Islands became marvels for their productiveness and so continued until man, assuming to reverse the working of nature's laws, gave to the black a boon he could not utilize or esti-mate save as it brought him slothful or vicious indulgence, and thus remanding him to barbarism robbed him of the plenty, the comfort and the civilization with which in servitude he was blessed.[4]

Here is as lucid a confrontation as one could possibly wish of the opposing prin-ciples animating the opposing presidents in the war that was about to begin.

Davis begins by remembering what had been said of the émigrés of the French Revolution: They could forget nothing, namely, their undeserved and socially use-less privileges; and they could learn nothing, namely, that their fellow countrymen would no longer tolerate the continuance of those privileges. Lincoln reduced the essence of slavery to the formula, "You work, I'll eat." That formula certainly characterized the relationship of the French monarchy and aristocracy to the body of French society on the eve of the Revolution of 1789. That it might be applied with greater propriety to slave owners than to "antislavery agitators" never occurred to Davis.

Davis charges that the antislavery movement misapplied "a declaration of rights made by bodies politic" to "the individual relations of man to man." He alludes here to the declarations of rights made by eight of the original thirteen states in their first constitutions after independence. The best known and most influential were those of Virginia and Massachusetts. But the most famous of all, made jointly by all thirteen states, was the Declaration of Independence. Accord-ing to Davis, the equality proclaimed therein was one of communities, not individuals. The authors of the Declaration did not, he thought, intend to say that all human beings were equal but rather that the thirteen states asserting independence and the government of Great Britain, each representing a collective whole, were legally and morally equal. Yet this view is directly contradicted by Jefferson himself when he asks, in the *Summary View*, whether "any one reason [can] be assigned why 160,000 electors in the island of Great Britain should give law to four millions in the states of America, *every individual of whom is equal to every individual of them* in virtue, in understanding, and in bodily strength."[5] Nothing could be more definitive of the fact that, by the political theory of the American Revolution, the rights declared by the American colonies were, primarily and essentially, the rights of individuals.

As discussed in chapter 1, James Madison held that "compact" is the basis of all free government. And the primordial compact, according to the "common sense of the subject" for all of the Founding Fathers, is one of individuals consenting unanimously to form themselves into a political community. The equality of peoples, or of political communities, is derivative from the original equality of individuals, each one of whom is endowed by his Creator with unalienable rights. The rights of communities to which Davis refers are derived from these God-given rights of individuals. As we saw in our discussion of Carl Becker in chapter 2, it was the historical school that found the rights of individuals to be those recognized in the laws of the society into which the individuals happened to be born. According to the historical school, free-born citizens were endowed by God and the Constitution with the rights of freemen, but those born into slavery were by the same token destined by God and nature for slavery. Davis, in asserting that the equality of the Declaration applies only to communities and not to individuals, identifies nature with history, committing the same non sequitur as Becker and the historical school. The irony and inconsistency of this will be compounded when, as president of the Confederate States of America, Davis appeals to the "consent of the governed" in the Declaration for the justification of secession. By the logic of the Declaration, however, the consent of the governed can become a moral and political imperative only in virtue of the antecedent equal rights of human individuals.

Davis justifies his rejection of human equality by reference to the Bible. Let us then review the biblical text which Davis says requires "literal construction." It is from Genesis 9:18–28.

And the sons of Noah, that went forth of the ark, were Shem, and Ham, and Japheth: and Ham is the father of Canaan. These are the three sons of Noah: and of them was the whole earth overspread. And Noah began to be a husbandman, and he planted a vineyard. And he drank of the wine, and was drunken;

157

and he was uncovered within his tent. And Ham, the father of Canaan, saw the nakedness of his father, and told his two brethren without. And Shem and Japheth took a garment, and laid it upon both their shoulders, and went backward, and covered the nakedness of their father; and their faces were backward, and they saw not their father's nakedness. And Noah awoke from his wine, and knew what his younger son had done unto him. And he said, Cursed be Canaan; a servant of servants shall he be unto his brethren. And he said, Blessed be the Lord God of Shem; and Canaan shall be his servant. God shall enlarge Japheth, and he shall dwell in the tents of Shem; and Canaan shall be his servant.

Davis recognizes that the antislavery party starts from the premise that Adam and Eve are the common parents of us all and that therefore the Lord "hath made of one blood all nations of men."[6] Whether "diversity" was stamped upon the races of man in the Creation or after the Flood, it unquestionably followed, according to Davis, from the curse and the blessing pronounced by Noah after he "awoke from his wine." The curse is upon Canaan, the son of Ham. We leave it to others to comment upon the strange fact that, although the offense is that of the father, the curse is upon the son. Noah says that Canaan shall be "a servant of servants . . . unto his brethren." He does not say, however, that all the descendants of Canaan, for all future time, shall be "servants of servants," nor that Canaan himself shall be a "servant of servants" to anyone other than "his brethren."

Although Shem and Japheth together covered their drunken father in the approved manner, only Shem is blessed, or more precisely, only "the Lord God of Shem" is blessed. Japheth shall be "enlarged" and dwell in the tents of Shem, and Canaan will also be his servant. Clearly, Canaan can serve both his brethren only if they live together. Without attempting anything like Talmudic exegesis—although this story certainly calls for it—it seems probable that it is linked to the fact that Canaanites occupied the promised land before the children of Israel. For the Israelites to take possession, they had first to conquer (and either kill or enslave) the Canaanites. The curse of Canaan (like the myth of autochthony in Plato's *Republic*) would provide moral justification for such conquest. But any attempt to link the Canaanites of the Bible with American Negro slaves is pure fantasy. For one thing, the Canaanites were not black.

According to Davis, Noah's prophecy declared the destiny of the three races of men. But how are these three to be identified among the nations of the modern world? When the Spaniards discovered America, Davis says, they "reduced the sons of Shem to bondage." But if the Native Americans (or Indians) were the sons of Shem, who were the Spaniards? If we are to take Noah's words with the literalness of Davis, then the sons of Shem should be the masters, not the quondam slaves. Davis says nothing of the sons of Japheth, but they would at best represent a secondary or auxiliary master class. In any event, it makes no sense at all to suggest that the Spaniards were sons of Japheth and that they had at one time enslaved the sons of Shem. Nor is it accurate to say that the sons of Shem (referring to the Indians), unsuited to bondage, "pined and rapidly wasted away in unproductive labor." In fact, they were swept away by diseases brought by their conquerors, to which they had no immunity.[7]

One hardly knows whether to laugh or weep at this theological justification of slavery. Before laughing, one must remember that hundreds of thousands of men (on both sides of the Civil War) met violent deaths because of it. One must therefore ask seriously how Davis thought he knew that black slaves imported from Africa were descendants of Ham. Davis says that the nature of a race is decreed by God and its fate determined by its nature. In other words, those born to be slaves must be slaves, and those intended to be free must be free. If freemen are enslaved, or slaves freed, these are miscarriages of nature and of the divine will and are destined to end in disaster. But what of the slavery of the Jews in Egypt, which God intervened to bring to an end? And why was the Christian Messiah born of their stock?

The slavery of the ancient Mediterranean world—which lasted for more than a thousand years—was mainly that of whites, and these slaves, or many of them, were highly efficient in their offices. In fact, the slaves of ancient Greece and Rome performed some of the most exalted offices of society, as well as the most menial. There were resident philosophers, poets, teachers, doctors, bankers, and estate managers among them. In fact, the condition of slavery was not considered a badge of natural inferiority. The ranks of the slaves were recruited from those captured in battle, and a prince or princess in one country might become a slave in another. There was no necessary connection such as Davis supposed between inferiority of birth and slavery. Ancient slavery would not then have been possible if, as Davis believed, slaves had to be recruited from those supposed to be descendants of Ham and Canaan.

We must also wonder why Davis, as a Christian, did not think that the redemptive power of Jesus Christ, although sufficient for the original sin of Adam and Eve, could not extend to the supposed offense of Ham, and how he could suggest that Christianity had been benevolently "diffused" among the slaves, when all the ethical principles of Christianity were violated by slavery. Slaves were held in bondage, not as human persons, but as chattels. There was no legal marriage, and therefore no adultery as defined in the seventh commandment. Slave children and slave parents were equally the property of their masters, and thus the duties of parents and children, commanded by God, were not capable of fulfillment. As Jefferson noted, the commandment against stealing could hardly have had much meaning to those from whom everything was taken.[8] If slave owners were Christian, then it would have to follow that the slaves were subhuman, because the commandments to do unto others as you would have them do unto you and to love one's neighbor as one's self were inconsistent with human slavery. That is why the long antebellum debate over slavery resolved itself, as Lincoln repeatedly emphasized, essentially into the question of whether the Negro was a human being.

Ignoring again the slavery of the ancient world, Davis uses the example of the West Indies to illustrate his view of the providential necessity by which slavery and freedom are related. According to Davis, the West Indies prospered under slavery, but emancipation brought ruin in its wake. What happened there would happen here if the abolitionists had their way. According to Davis, the blacks are natural slaves who prosper under slavery and fall into dissoluteness and penury under freedom. The miserable condition of free blacks in the North is said to be further testimony to this truth, as well as to the fact that "history . . . exhibits the negro in all times as the subservient race."[9]

As to the failure of West India's economy under freedom, one can only observe that in the whole history of mankind the difficulty of establishing institutions of political freedom has been extraordinary. And of all transitions, the leap from slavery to freedom has been the most extraordinarily difficult. The Lord led the children of Israel out of servitude in Egypt toward the promised land. But not a single one of those who left Egypt, including Moses, reached that destination. According to the old saying, it was easier to get the Jews out of Egypt than to get Egypt out of the Jews. Forty years were spent in the wilderness, during which the Israelites received a radically new code of laws that rooted out the slavish habits of subservience and dependence engendered by despotism. They learned to obey God and no one else. These laws transformed them into a tightly organized political community of hardened desert warriors, led by able officers, who could fight their way into the land that they had been promised. God did not give them this land as an indulgent parent who would spoil the child. His only free gift was the laws, by which they acquired the virtue to deserve his favor. And he kept them in the desert until all the traces of Egypt had vanished, and only the discipline of the law remained. It is as foolish as it is dishonest to blame slaves for acting slavishly or to think that the effects of slavery will vanish with the causes that produced them.

While all conditions of slavery have some things in common, they nevertheless differ widely among themselves. Ancient slavery differed from American slavery—as Jefferson observed in the *Notes on Virginia*—in that there was no racial stigma attached to it, and slaves, when emancipated, could disappear into the ranks of freemen.[10] American Negroes, whether free or slave, carried the stigma of racial inferiority, which stigma increased dramatically (as a by-product of evolutionary theory) in the course of the nineteenth century. Davis even blames the

Negroes themselves for accepting this stigma, as if they had been given any chance to repudiate it.

> At no time has he ["the negro"] asserted his equality by separating himself from the master race, to establish an independent community of his own. In the Northern states where a false sentiment has prevailed, and the greatest efforts have been made by enthusiasts to raise the negro to social equality, he is still subjected to such odious discrimination, as persons fit to be free would not for a day voluntarily endure.

Davis uses examples of English and French emigration from the Old World to further disparage American Negroes: "For far less cause the Puritans embarked for the inhospitable shores of New England, and the Huguenots penetrated the swamps of Carolina, with no sustaining aid to guide them."[11] How much "less cause" the Puritans and Huguenots had may be inferred from Jefferson's comment, which we discussed in chapter 1, that man is a "stupendous" and "incomprehensible machine" for his ability to endure hardship and death to vindicate his own freedom and then inflict more miserable bondage on his brethren than he has ever known.[12] Nothing better measures the distance of Jefferson Davis from Thomas Jefferson than a comparison of their declared opinions on slavery. Whatever animadversions on the intellectual faculties of Negroes may be found in the *Notes on Virginia*, none is presented as a justification of slavery. In the world of the Founding Fathers, whose fundamental principles Jefferson articulated for all the world and for all time, no one answering to the description of a human being is excluded from the proposition of human equality. In that world, no one had any more right than anyone else not to be enslaved. In that most fundamental of respects, all men are created equal.

The most evident difference in the conditions of Puritans and Huguenots fleeing persecution in their original homelands and American Negroes is that the former had not been slaves. Like the ancient Israelites entering Canaan, they were extremely close knit communities, bound together by their own versions of the same law that Moses had brought down from Mount Sinai. Davis does not reflect on this difference. Nor does he consider how relatively few white Europeans were spirited enough to immigrate to the American wilderness to escape from discrimination or tyranny. By his own criterion, perhaps 99 percent of white Europeans were no more fit for freedom than American Negroes. Moreover, the great majority of Davis's fellow citizens, or their ancestors, immigrated to America only after communities had been established in that wilderness.

In his derogatory comment regarding the free Negroes of the North, Davis does not consider that subjection to "odious discrimination" is no more conducive than slavery to the prodigiously focused communal energy exhibited by the ancient Israelites in the wilderness and by their latter-day descendants (Jewish and Christian) in America. We might here interject the observation that, since Davis's lifetime, we have seen political organization to resist "odious discrimination" by the descendants of the antebellum slaves and the antebellum freemen perhaps as remarkable as that of the Puritans and Huguenots. It is noteworthy that the political capacity for freedom, whose absence among Negroes Davis declared in 1859, appeared in due course in the black community in the same way that it appeared earlier in the white communities of Puritans and Huguenots, namely, in their churches.[13] There is also no question but that the inspiration in all three cases came from the Bible, not only in the story of Moses, but also in the conviction that Jesus' death on the cross promised emancipation from slavery and from odious discrimination as much as from other manifestations of original sin. The Bible that was read in the black churches was one in which the message of eternal salvation was inseparable from the message of freedom in this world. Indeed, the political theology of the black churches during the civil rights movement was indistinguishable from that of Lincoln's second inaugural address, of which we will speak at length later. The development of that theology, and of the social and political organization required to give it full effect, took no more time for black Americans than for Puritans or Huguenots. And it is at least a question whether the latter did so in conditions as difficult as those of American slavery or of its successor, Jim Crow.

The subculture of American Negroes is perhaps the most deeply rooted of all American subcultures, since most black Americans are descended from ancestors who were on the North American continent long before those of the great majority of white Americans. And the blood of many of them is, in truth, mingled with that of the great white families of the colonial and Revolutionary periods. The achievements of this subculture, both in slavery and in freedom, are among the most exalted in the human record. It is to be doubted whether any expression of the human spirit transcends the Negro spiritual.

> Go down, Moses,
> Go down to Egypt land,
> And tell old Pharaoh,
> To let my people go.

Although he did not hear them, the slaves were singing this, and many other songs of freedom, when Jefferson Davis made his contemptuous estimate of their humanity. The Exodus was beginning even then, although Davis did not know it.

Davis's strictures on Negro inferiority continue, with reference to the American Colonization Society:

> But speculative philanthropy imagined that if a colony were established in the land of his forefathers, the African would there exhibit his capacity for self-government. With this view, in 1816, a Colonization Society was formed. Its purpose was the transfer of the free blacks from the United States to the coast of Africa, and the benign promise was the diffusion among their barbarian brethren of the civilization and Christianity which these colonists had acquired through servitude in America.

The founder of this society was James Monroe, for whom Liberia's capital city of Monrovia is named. Among its enthusiastic supporters were Thomas Jefferson, James Madison, Henry Clay, and Abraham Lincoln.

> The experiment was made under the most favorable circumstances. The colonists had been trained in industry and order, and were, it must be inferred from the circumstances, of the best class of their race. The Society embraced in its lists of members many of the first men of our country, and the zeal with which their purpose was pursued would have won success if it was attainable.[14]

Davis here makes a pardonable error. The circumstances that make for success are not those he describes. It is not merely that individual habits of industry, frugality, temperance, and honesty are required for communal success. There must also be a spirit of cooperation, mutual assistance, and self-sacrifice for a higher purpose.

The American Colonization Society did indeed represent "speculative philanthropy," because the initiative came from white Americans trying to solve the problem of black slavery, not from the black but from the white point of view. It was not supported by the kind of indigenous religious community that sustained the Puritans and the Huguenots and later the civil rights movement. Indeed, it could not be so supported in the antebellum United States, because no such communities were permitted among the slaves. The guardians of the institution of slavery were alert to every imagined sign of incipient organization, as if it were the prelude to servile insurrection and slaughter. Davis speaks of the Christianity that the "slaves had acquired through servitude in America." It is true that a class of Negro preachers was permitted to develop, and to this day a large proportion of the black professional classes is descended from these preachers. But they were carefully monitored lest they utter the subversive abolitionist doctrines of the genuine Bible. Their real ministries were largely underground, where alone the revolutionary freedom of "Go down, Moses" could be preached.

The importance of the American Colonization Society is not to be measured

163

by its essential impracticability or by the failure of Liberia as a colony. At a time when abolitionism was looked upon, even in the North, as no better than Jacobinism, atheism, and anarchism combined, support for colonization offered a respectable means of being antislavery. Lincoln sincerely believed in its feasibility. But even if he did not, it would have been an almost indispensable position for him to adopt, as a means of maintaining his nonabolitionist antislavery credentials.[15] Without those credentials, neither he nor the abolitionists could in the end have succeeded.

There is a further and deeper reason why colonization failed and why all subsequent attempts to return Americans of African descent to Africa, even those originating solely within the black community, have failed. That reason is that the overwhelming majority of these Americans regard their destiny to be in the United States.[16] They were, after all, sold into slavery originally by black tribesmen, who captured them in order to sell them, and who slaughtered the ones they did not sell. No resentment of slavery, however profound, engendered any love of a mythical African homeland. To have asked them to return to Africa was not unlike asking American Jews whose parents or grandparents fled czarist or Stalinist tyranny to return to Russia. However involuntary their emigration from Africa, American Negroes, whether free or slave, have always seen America itself as the only promised land. Both Christianity and the Declaration of Independence embodied promises to all men. They saw no better or equal hope anywhere else, and certainly not in Africa. The truth is that the slaves, ignorant and illiterate as they may have seemed, were far from unintelligent. The Bible that they heard about—even if they were not allowed to read it—contained stories that convinced them that the same God that had freed the children of Israel would free them. Jefferson Davis might have thought this to be mere credulity. Yet it certainly compared favorably with his own absurd reading of the story of Noah.

While slavery meant Egypt, and slavemasters meant Pharaoh, America itself remained the promised land. The slaves knew that it was not in Africa, Europe, or anywhere else that a nation had been founded upon the self-evident truth that all men are created equal. It was their destiny to cross over Jordan here, and to make their decisive contribution to the human story here, by partaking of that new birth of freedom that alone could vindicate the cause of all human beings everywhere.

∽

A rebuttal of Jefferson Davis on Negro inequality by Abraham Lincoln may be found in the following fragment, "On Slavery," which has a tentative date of October 1858:

Suppose it is true, that the negro is inferior to the white, in the gifts of nature; is it not the exact reverse of justice that the white should, for that reason, take from the negro, any part of the little which has been given him? "*Give to the needy*" is the Christian rule of charity; but "*Take from him that is needy*" is the rule of slavery.

PRO-SLAVERY THEOLOGY

The sum of pro-slavery theology seems to be this: "Slavery is not universally *right*, nor yet universally *wrong*: it is better for *some* people to be slaves; and in such cases it is the Will of God that they be such."

Certainly there is no contending against the Will of God; but still there is some difficulty in ascertaining, and applying it, to particular cases. For instance, we will suppose the Rev. Dr. Ross has a slave named Sambo, and the question is, "Is it the will of God that Sambo shall remain a slave, or be set free?" The Almighty gives no audible answer to the question, and his revelation—the Bible—gives none—or, at most, none but such as admits of a squabble, as to its meaning. No one thinks of asking Sambo's opinion on it. So, at last, it comes to this, that *Dr. Ross* is to decide the question. And while he considers it, he sits in the shade, with gloves on his hands, and subsists on the bread that Sambo is earning in the burning sun. If he decides that God wills Sambo continue a slave, he thereby retains his own comfortable position; but if he decides that God wills Sambo to be free, he thereby has to walk out of the shade, throw off his gloves; and delve for his own bread. Will Dr. Ross be actuated by that perfect impartiality, which has ever been considered favorable to correct decisions?

But slavery is good for some people!!! As a good thing, slavery is strikingly peculiar, in this, that it is the only good thing which no man ever seeks the good of, *for himself*.

Nonsense! Wolves devouring lambs, not because it is good for their own greedy maws, but because it is good for the lambs!!![17]

Lincoln's approach to Christianity, and to biblical religion altogether, is striking in its difference from that of Davis. Davis, we recall, said that it mattered not whether God "stamped diversity on the races of men" at the Creation or after the Flood. The key words here are "stamped diversity," which contradict "created equal" in the Declaration of Independence. They also contradict Davis's own interpretation of the Declaration, when he said that the word "equal" referred to human communities. If diversity is stamped on "the races of men," then they cannot, in Jefferson's or Lincoln's sense, have equal rights, for they would not be equally human. But Davis also contradicts the New Testament's assertion that the Lord "hath made of one blood all nations of men." He even contradicts his own rhetoric, albeit unconsciously: At the beginning of his speech he told his fellow citizens that their "responsibility embraces all the hopes which depend upon the demonstration of man's capacity for self-government."[18] But if the potentiality for self-government is "man's," then it must belong to the descendants of Ham as well as of Shem.

Lincoln avoids such capricious sectarianism. While on notable occasions appealing to the authority of the Bible, his ethical precepts are drawn from reason no less than revelation. In no case does Lincoln make any use of the Bible incompatible with either the letter or the spirit of the "no religious test" clause or the First Amendment of the Constitution. He begins his fragment "On Slavery" from a generally admitted principle, the rule of charity, that could hardly be disputed by any Protestant or Catholic. Nor is the teaching in question any less Jewish than Christian, although in the present case he is addressing a Protestant divine.

Throughout the slavery controversy, Lincoln is careful to avoid contesting the question of the equality or inequality of the races "in the gifts of nature." Given the overwhelming prejudices of white America, North as well as South, it would have been senseless for him to do otherwise. He is at great pains, however, to argue that this question is irrelevant to the question of the justice or injustice of slavery. To have contended for anything more than freedom would only have endangered whatever prospects for freedom there might have been. Yet careful analysis of Lincoln's many references to the intelligence or abilities of Negroes shows amazingly little actual concession to the prejudices of his contemporaries, even while seeming not to contradict them.[19]

There was no argument, Lincoln was fond of saying, that could justify the enslavement of Negroes that could not also justify the enslavement of whites. When the leading proslavery theorist of the antebellum South, George Fitzhugh, published *Cannibals All!* Lincoln was delighted to point out that it was an argument for *slavery*, not black slavery. And Calhoun's "positive good" argument, to which we shall return, found slavery to be beneficial to the North by controlling the burgeoning conflict between free labor and capital. It did so, in part, by threatening to break strikes with slaves. In short, Southern slavery tended to reduce Northern white workers to the class of slaves.

In beginning the fragment above "Suppose . . . the negro is inferior," Lincoln, like Socrates, is reasoning from the premises that are generally accepted. In so doing, he does not at all concede the truth of those premises. It is notable that Davis's reference to "diversity" in the story of Noah and his sons is a denial of a single human nature. Lincoln's argument assumes a single human nature. On that assumption, the natural rights of whites must also be the natural (but not necessarily the civil or political) rights of blacks.

Turning to the recognition that "there is no contending against the will of God," Lincoln quietly and piously moves the argument from revelation to reason. The Bible gives no such direct answers as Dr. Ross and Jefferson Davis think it does. Unless we know the answers of reason, we cannot know the answers of revelation. Lincoln is prompted by the same thought that prompted Madison to write in the tenth *Federalist*, "No man is allowed to be a judge in his own cause, because his interest would certainly bias his judgment, and, not improbably, corrupt his integrity."[20] The interest in slavery that biased Dr. Ross and Jefferson Davis was one they shared with a majority of the citizens of the slave states. To be biased or corrupted by such interest is an attribute of human nature, which in itself permits of no distinction within mankind. Even if it were true that there are some human beings of such great virtue that they are capable of rising above the partiality of their nature, how could we discover who they were? Would not anyone making a claim to such virtue be a fraud? Said Madison in the fifty-first *Federalist*, "If angels were to govern men, neither external nor internal controls on government would be necessary."[21] The slave owners of America required both internal and external controls on their own government to protect them from tyrannical rule by each other. Why should whites, who would not trust themselves to govern each other without such controls, dispense with such controls in their government of Negroes?

Lincoln contemplates the Rev. Dr. Ross considering whether it is the will of God that Sambo remain a slave or be set free. But, says Lincoln, no one thinks of asking Sambo's opinion. This is Lincoln's most devastating critique of the proslavery position. By reason of the self-evident truth that Sambo is capable of having an opinion, his status as a human being is established. As Aristotle remarks, only man has speech, and only man can indicate the beneficial and the harmful, the just and the unjust. All assertions of "diversity" among the different descriptions of human beings as a ground for asserting a difference in their natural rights founder on the fact that the sole defining attribute of man as a species is his capacity for speech or reason. No difference of intelligence or of the skill with which reason or speech are employed is a ground for asserting different natural rights in those possessed of reason or speech. This becomes clear when we consider that the Declaration of Independence is first and foremost an assertion of the principles of political obligation *from the point of view of those being asked to obey*. It was exactly from this point of view that the Continental Congress, in its Declaration of the Causes and Necessity of Taking Up Arms, asked the British Parliament by what manifest declaration of the will of God they had been granted an unbounded authority, not rightfully resistible, over the colonies.[22] What greater evidence was there that God intended Sambo to obey Dr. Ross, than that God intended the colonies to obey the king and Parliament of Great Britain? What greater *reason* was there—other than that the colonists were armed and Sambo was not—for Sambo to obey Dr. Ross?

Human beings may submit to a power they cannot resist. But submitting to compulsion is not submitting to authority. An authority, properly so called, is someone whose commands we recognize as carrying with them *obligation*. And obligation, according to the Declaration, arises from the consent of the governed in accordance with "the laws of nature and of nature's God." Dr. Ross's and Jefferson Davis's attempt to ground slavery on the authority of Scripture is precisely what the Continental Congress rejected with scorn in 1775, in terms that applied not only to themselves but to all mankind. It is with the same scorn that Lincoln rejected the proslavery argument as the antebellum debate was reaching its climax.

~

Lincoln's two inaugural addresses serve as prologue and epilogue of the Civil War. The first tells us why there should have been no war. The second tells us that the war was necessary because of man's sinfulness and God's justice. Lincoln's first inaugural has many of the qualities of a chorus in a Greek tragedy. It is the voice of reason in a world governed by passion. There would not have been a war if reason and moderation could have ruled. But they could not. The Civil War was a tragedy precisely because each side saw reason enough to fight and neither could see any ground for compromise in its reason. But it was not only the case that neither could see a ground of compromise: There was no ground of compromise between slavery seen as right and slavery seen as wrong.

If there was one moment, however, when a word of compromise might have averted war, it was when Lincoln was confronted with the Crittenden Compromise. This would have extended the latitudinal line of 36 degrees 30 minutes—the southern border of Missouri—to the Pacific Ocean. Slavery would have been "forever" banned from all the territory north of that line, with the implication that it might be permitted south of it. In his Peoria speech of 1854, Lincoln had said, "Much as I hate slavery, I would consent to the extension of it rather than see the Union dissolved, just as I would consent to any GREAT evil, to avoid a GREATER one." Yet on December 11, 1860, he wrote to a Republican in Congress:

> Entertain no proposition for a compromise in regard to the *extension* of slavery. The instant you do, they have us under again; all our labor is lost, and sooner or later must be done over. Douglas is sure to be again trying to bring in his "Pop. Sov." Have none of it. The tug has to come & better now than later.

One week later he wrote to another Republican:

> I am sorry any republican inclines to dally with Pop. Sov. of any sort. It acknowledges that slavery has equal rights with liberty, and surrenders all we have contended for. Once fastened upon us as a settled policy, filibustering for all South of us, and making slave states of it, follows in spite of us, with an early Supreme Court decision, holding our free state constitutions to be unconstitutional.[23]

Why was Lincoln unwilling in 1860 to make a concession he had considered in 1854? The answer turns upon the distinction, in Lincoln's mind, between a great and a greater evil. Neither in 1854 nor in 1860 would he consent to the dissolution of the Union. In 1860, there were two alternatives to dissolution: the extension of slavery, and war. In 1854, Lincoln had in mind the Compromise of 1850, which he had described as a system of equivalents, in which the contending parties had made a series of concessions to each other, trading each measure granted for another gained. If the North did not then insist upon the exclusion of slavery from the Utah and New Mexico Territories, it was because California was admitted as a free state. If it agreed to a new Fugitive Slave Law, it was because the slave trade was banished from the District of Columbia. The boundaries of Texas, a slave state, were reduced—the northern boundary to the Missouri line— but Texas's debt was paid by the United States. And so it went. No concession could be considered in separation from its accompanying equivalent. But the vote in the election of 1860 was not a vote for a compromise or a system of equivalents. The question of whether slavery would be restricted, once and for all, to the states in which it already existed or be allowed to extend into the national territories had reached an impasse that the legislative process could not resolve. The election itself was the only mode—other than civil war—by which the deadlock in the political system could be broken. And Lincoln's election represented a clear and decisive victory for the antislavery cause.

As Lincoln saw it, to compromise after the 1860 election in the matter that the election had decided would have meant nothing less than abandoning the electoral process as a means of resolving political differences. Of course, on the other side of the political divide, it appeared that the election had placed one section of the country in the position of a permanent minority. We have previously quoted Lincoln on July 4, 1861, to the effect that once a majority has spoken constitutionally with ballots, "there can be no successful appeal back to bullets," but only "to ballots themselves, at succeeding elections."[24] But if the election of 1860 had decided against the extension of slavery once and for all, there could be no future appeal to ballots to reverse that decision.

Lincoln tried to limit the explosiveness of the territorial question by insisting that he had no inclination or intention of interfering with slavery in the states where it existed. But the South never took his disclaimers at face value. Why?

∼

To comprehend the mind of the nation on the eve of the Civil War, in "the great secession winter," we turn to the public statements of the three men who represented the highest political authority of the divided nation during this crisis.

We turn first to the incumbent but outgoing president, James Buchanan, elected in 1856 but not renominated by the Democratic Party in 1860. His fourth and last annual message to Congress was delivered on December 3, 1860. One should bear in mind that this message came three full months before Lincoln's inauguration on March 4, 1861. During that interim, the seven states of the Deep South seceded, and six of them established their own union as the Confederate States of America and inaugurated their own president, Jefferson Davis. Moreover, with only two exceptions, they took over all the dockyards, arsenals, and other property of military utility of the old Union. All this was accomplished peacefully and without even threatened interference by the government of which James Buchanan remained the executive head. It is impossible to grasp the full measure of the difficulties Lincoln faced without grasping the extent to which Buchanan had effectively cooperated with the Southern disunionists.

⌁

President Buchanan begins his message by observing that no economic distress had contributed to the present difficulties: "[N]o nation in the tide of time has ever presented a spectacle of greater material prosperity than we have done. . . . Why is it then that discontent now so extensively prevails, and the union of these States, which is the source of all these blessings, is threatened with destruction?"[25] His answer was that

> The long continued and intemperate interference of the northern people with the question of slavery in the southern States has at length produced its natural effects. The different sections of the Union are now arrayed against each other and the time has arrived, so much dreaded by the Father of his Country, when hostile geographical parties have been formed.
>
> I have long foreseen, and often forewarned my countrymen of the now impending danger. This does not proceed solely from the claim on the part of Congress or the territorial legislatures to exclude slavery from the Territories, nor from the efforts of different States to defeat the execution of the fugitive slave law. All or any of these evils might have been endured by the South, without danger to the Union, (as others have been), in the hope that time and reflection might apply the remedy. The immediate peril arises, not so much from these causes, as from the fact that the incessant and violent agitation of the slavery question throughout the North for the last quarter century has at length produced its malign influence on the slaves, and inspired them with vague notions of freedom. Hence a sense of security no longer exists around the family altar. This feeling of peace at home has given place to apprehensions of servile insurrections. Many a matron throughout the South retires at night in dread of what may befall herself and her children before the morning.

According to Buchanan, the causa causarum of the sectional crisis is antislavery agitation. Not the aggressiveness of the proslavery party in demanding a federal slave code for the territories, not fanaticism concerning the enforcement of the Fugitive Slave Law, but the repeated expression of antislavery opinion is the source of all the danger to the Union. Curiously, this agrees with what Lincoln himself had said in his Cooper Institute speech in February 1860:

Will they be satisfied if the Territories be unconditionally surrendered to them? We know they will not. In all their present complaints against us, the Territories are scarcely mentioned. Invasions and insurrections are the rage now. Will it satisfy them if, in the future, we have nothing to do with invasions and insurrections? We know it will not. We so know because we know we never had anything to do with invasions and insurrections; and yet this total abstaining does not exempt us from the charge and the denunciation.

The question recurs, what will satisfy them? Simply this: We must not only let them alone, but we must somehow convince them that we do let them alone. This, we know by experience, is no easy task. We have been so trying to convince them from the very beginning of our organization [the Republican Party], but with no success. In all our platforms and speeches we have constantly protested our purpose to let them alone; but this has had no tendency to convince them. Alike unavailing to convince them, is the fact that they have never detected a man of us in any attempt to disturb them.

These natural and apparently adequate means all failing, what will convince them? This, and this only: cease to call slavery *wrong*, and join them in calling it *right*. And this must be done thoroughly—done in *acts* as well as in *words*. Silence will not be tolerated—we must place ourselves avowedly with them. Senator Douglas' new sedition law must be enacted and enforced, suppressing all declarations that slavery is wrong, whether made in politics, in presses, in pulpits, or in private. We must arrest and return their fugitive slaves with greedy pleasure. We must pull down our Free State constitutions. The whole atmosphere must be disinfected from all taint of opposition to slavery, before they will cease to believe that all their troubles proceed from us.[26]

The agreement of Buchanan and Lincoln in the foregoing passages demonstrates the degree to which free government, in all its dimensions, was at risk. The "long continued and intemperate interference" with which Buchanan charged "the Northern people" consisted primarily and essentially in saying that slavery was wrong. To cease that interference meant to cease calling it wrong. But how can a free society stop its citizens from expressing their most deeply held convictions? According to Buchanan, it would have been both dangerous and irresponsible to read aloud and in public either the Declaration of Independence or the story of Moses in Egypt. In the refusal of the Northern people to accept such restrictions upon their freedom of speech lay their responsibility for the crisis. One wonders how Buchanan imagined the American Revolution could have come to pass if Patrick Henry, had curbed his tongue, lest his slaves discover what he was saying about freedom. What Buchanan demanded of the North in 1860 was no less impossible than a demand upon the South at that time to cease and desist defending slavery.

Buchanan complained that antislavery agitation in the North had inspired Southern slaves with "vague notions of freedom." Considering the prevailing censorship in the slave states of both speech and writing with regard to antislavery opinion, it is difficult to understand how Northern agitation could produce such effects.[27] Southern postmasters had cut off any delivery of abolitionist literature, and itinerant speakers, if they were discovered, were lucky to get off with no more than a tarring and feathering. Most slaves were illiterate, and in the decade before the Civil War it was made a felony in most of the slave states to teach a slave to read. On the other hand, "vague notions of freedom" in the slaves did not need abolitionism to stir them. The white South was not a feudal society in which status was decided by birth. On the contrary, except for the slaves, it was radically egalitarian and animated in a high degree by upward social mobility. To look every day upon freedom and to be denied it was the most powerful of all inspirations. And among the institutions of freedom, none was more potent than the religion of the Bible. That Christianity taught equality no less than the Declaration of Independence was something no power on earth could keep the slaves from discovering. One must wonder how Buchanan could have imagined that, with or without antislavery agitation, the slaves would not be inspired with a desire for freedom. To be excluded from the equality and liberty open to everyone else was like looking up into heaven from the place below! Perhaps Lincoln's best comment on these charges against Northern antislavery agitation was the following: "If a slave runs away, they overlook the natural causes which impelled him to act; do not remember the oppression or the lashes he received, but charge us with instigating him to flight. If he screams when whipped, they say it is not caused by the pain he suffers, but he screams because we instigate him to outcrying."[28]

Lincoln had addressed Southern fears of slave insurrection in his Cooper Institute speech:

Occasional poisonings from the kitchen, and open or stealthy assassinations in the field, and local revolts extending to a score or so, will continue to occur as the natural results of slavery; but no general insurrection of slaves, as I think, can happen in this country for a long time. Whoever much fears, or much hopes for such an event, will be alike disappointed.

172

Slaves were chattels by law but human persons by nature. The "natural results of slavery" arose from the unnaturalness of slavery, especially slavery in a land of freedom. Lincoln continued:

> Slave insurrections are no more common now than they were before the Republican party was organized. What induced the Southampton insurrection, twenty-eight years ago, in which at least three times as many lives were lost as at Harper's Ferry?

And again:

> John Brown's effort was peculiar. It was not a slave insurrection. It was an attempt by white men to get up a revolt among the slaves, in which the slaves refused to participate. In fact, it was so absurd that the slaves, with all their ignorance, saw plainly enough that it could not succeed.[29]

Despite these facts, Buchanan continued to play on irrational Southern fears of insurrection, as if the source of danger were not slavery itself but Northern antislavery opinion. We return to his 1860 message to Congress:

> Should this apprehension of domestic danger, whether real or imaginary, extend, and intensify itself, until it pervades the masses of the southern people, then disunion will become inevitable. Self-preservation is the first law of nature, and has been implanted in the heart of man by his Creator, for the wisest purpose; and no political union, however fraught with blessings and benefits in all other respects, can long continue, if the necessary consequence be to render the homes and firesides of nearly half the parties to it habitually and hopelessly insecure. Sooner or later the bonds of such a Union must be severed.

Buchanan's reference to the danger as "real or imaginary" is remarkable. Until this point he had not as much as hinted that it might be the latter. Certainly the "remedy" could not be the same for an imaginary as for a real danger. Lincoln's diagnosis showed that it was in fact imaginary. Yet every word of Buchanan's message has been a justification of, and encouragement to, secession.

Buchanan then denies the consequences of his own argument: "It is my conviction that this fatal period has not yet arrived; and my prayer to God is, that he would preserve the Constitution and the Union throughout all generations." "Let us take warning in time," he continues, "and remove the cause of danger." But how is the cause of danger to be removed? Buchanan returns to his single-minded philippic against the expression of antislavery opinion:

It cannot be denied that for five and twenty years the agitation at the North against slavery has been incessant. ...This agitation has ever since been continued by the public press, by the proceedings of state and county conventions, and by abolition sermons and lectures. The time of Congress has been occupied in violent speeches on this never-ending subject; and appeals, in pamphlets and other forms, indorsed by distinguished names, have been sent forth from this central point and spread broadcast over the Union.

It is difficult to recall, in all of human history, a more fatuous pronouncement in the midst of a great crisis by a responsible holder of high office.[30] How could Buchanan have thought that silence could suddenly fall on a subject that had for a quarter of a century dominated public discussion in all the party and political institutions of the country? How could he have thought that the conflict between freedom and slavery could be ended simply by asking people to stop talking about it? Not only is this Buchanan's proposed solution, but it is one he believes could be easily implemented!

How easy would it be for the American people to settle the slavery question forever, and to restore peace and harmony to this distracted country. . . . All that is necessary to accomplish the object, and all for which the slave states have ever contended, is to be let alone and permitted to manage their domestic institutions in their own way. As sovereign states, they and they alone are responsible before God and the world for the slavery existing among them. For this the people of the North are not more responsible, and have no more right to interfere, than with similar institutions in Russia or Brazil.

This passage is disingenuous almost beyond belief. The Republican Party and its successful candidate for president had reiterated that they had no intention of interfering in any way with the domestic institutions of the slave states. Indeed, during the course of his debates with Douglas in 1858, Lincoln had made an observation almost identical to Buchanan's, saying that as a citizen of Illinois, he had no more responsibility for slavery in South Carolina than for serfdom in Russia. In his first inaugural address, Lincoln would quote from the Republican platform: "That the maintenance inviolate of the rights of the States, and especially the right of each State to order and control its own domestic institutions according to its own judgment exclusively, is essential to that balance of power on which the perfection and endurance of our political fabric depends. . . ."[31]

The furor over slavery in American politics, from the repeal of the Missouri Compromise in 1854 until secession in 1860–61, focused upon the status of slavery in the territories.[32] But it was impossible to say why slavery ought to be kept out of the territories without saying why slavery was bad. While rejecting altogether the principle of human equality as set forth in the Declaration of Independence, the South nonetheless demanded "equality" for their "peculiar" kind of property in the territories. They did so on the ground that to discriminate between the property of free-state settlers and slave-state settlers *in the territories* was to discriminate against the constitutional equality of the slave states themselves. Only by this course of reasoning could it be argued that the Republican Party was attacking the slave states. It was true, however, that the status of slavery in the territories involved the question of the status of slavery in the Union. It was well understood on all sides that the dynamics of slavery and of freedom were such that the expansion of the one meant the contraction of the other.

In the *Dred Scott* decision of 1857, Chief Justice Taney had held that there was no power under the Constitution, either in Congress or in a territorial legislature, to exclude slavery from a territory. Indeed, he said that Congress's only power over slavery in the territories was the power, "coupled with the duty," of protecting the slave owner in his rights. It was this interpretation of the Constitution that the Southerners demanded be recognized as the only possible meaning of the Constitution, binding upon all sections and parties. Without the unqualified acceptance of Taney's dicta, they said, the compact or contract by which they were joined to the North had been breached, ending any mutual obligation to remain in the Union. Taney's dicta became "rights" that were inviolable by majorities. But as Lincoln repeatedly pointed out, these same dicta contained premises that could logically lead to the further conclusion that there was no power under the Constitution for any *state* to exclude slavery. If it became accepted doctrine that slavery could not be constitutionally excluded from either territories or states, the nation would indeed become "all slave." It was precisely to prevent such an outcome that the Republican Party nominated Lincoln and that the nation elected him to the presidency. Yet Buchanan might have lived the last four years of his life in China for any sign or suggestion of recognition of this fact.

It is true that Lincoln's election, by ensuring that slavery would not be extended to any territory, and thus that no more slave states would be added to the Union, destined the slave states to become an ever smaller fraction of an expanding Union. The possibility existed, therefore, that at some time in the future, three-fourths of the states would be free states. At that point it would become possible for the free states to amend the Constitution to abolish slavery without the consent of the slave states. But this was a very remote possibility. Even today, the fifteen former slave states are more than the one-fourth of the fifty states needed to block an amendment to the Constitution. Still, the possibility of becoming a permanent minority within the Union on a matter that, in the Southerners' view, had come to constitute their most vital interest was a forbidding prospect. Every year henceforth they would become a relatively smaller minority, less able to resist what was in their view a tyrannical majority. And although there was never a hint in any of Lincoln's speeches that action against slavery in the slave states, when it came, would be anything but action by the people of the states themselves, pressure on these states to adopt plans of gradual and compensated emancipation would surely increase as the slave population was confined to its existing limits. Furthermore, as the slave population grew, and as there were no new territories or states to which the surplus slaves might be sold, the economic pressure for emancipation would grow.

Although Buchanan remained stubbornly blind to it, any reasoning person could see that the debate over slavery in the territories was about much more than the territories alone. It was about the future and character of free government and about the republican form of government guaranteed to each of the states by the federal Constitution. In 1776 the Continental Congress, in the name of "one people," had pronounced certain truths to be self-evident. These truths were the justification of American independence. But they could not justify this independence without at the same time justifying the liberty of all human beings. Americans had become the "one people" of the Declaration of Independence only by recognizing the universality of the rights they claimed as their own. When Taney said that Negroes, under the Constitution, had no rights that white men were bound to respect, he was denying the rights of all Americans. This raised the question of whether Americans were still "one people." It was agreement on the truths in the Declaration that made the people one. Without such agreement, there was no basis for that civic friendship of which Jefferson spoke so movingly in his inaugural address. Without it, there was no unanimous consent from which to derive the "just powers of government" or to mark out the boundaries between majority rule and minority rights.

In speaking of self-preservation as the first law of nature, Buchanan had invoked the right of revolution, the ultimate right to which all other claims must yield. Thus James Madison, in the forty-third *Federalist*, had justified the framers' unauthorized departure from the then existing Constitution—the Articles of Confederation—by appealing "to the absolute necessity of the case; to the great principle of self-preservation; to the transcendent law of nature and of nature's God, which declares that the safety and happiness of society are the objects at which all political institutions aim, and to which all such institutions must be sacrificed."[33] But Buchanan, having given the strongest argument possible for whatever measures the South might deem necessary in the present crisis, by justifying their alleged fears for their safety, abruptly shifts his argument to denying the conclusions he had drawn.

And this brings me to observe that the election of any one of our fellow-citizens to the office of President does not of itself afford just cause for dissolving the

Union. This is especially true if his election has been effected by a mere plurality and not a majority of the people, and has resulted from transient and temporary causes, which may probably never again occur.

In fact, Lincoln's majority appeared to be anything but transient. There were four parties in the contest of 1860, but the Republicans had large majorities in states that held a majority in the electoral college. That is, even if all the non-Republican votes in every state were combined in favor of a single fusion candidate, Lincoln's electoral college majority would still have been decisive. Furthermore, the fact that Lincoln received only 39 percent of the popular vote count in the nation is misleading. There were no Republican electors in ten of the eleven states that later made up the Confederacy, and so no Republican votes were counted in those states. That over one hundred thousand Southern men joined the Union army in the Civil War is ample reason to believe that there would have been a substantial number of Republican voters in those ten states, had there been any means for them to register their votes.[34] Insofar as the fears of the South centered upon becoming a permanent sectional minority in electoral divisions concerning slavery, those fears were entirely justified. Yet Buchanan continued:

> In order to justify a resort to revolutionary resistance, the federal government must be guilty of "a deliberate, palpable, and dangerous exercise" of powers not granted by the Constitution. The late presidential election, however, has been held in strict conformity with its express provisions. How, then, can the result justify a revolution to destroy this very Constitution? Reason, justice, a regard for the Constitution, all require that we shall wait for some overt or dangerous act on the part of the President elect, before resorting to such a remedy.

Here Buchanan uses the language of the Virginia and Kentucky Resolutions, employed to denounce the Alien and Sedition Acts of 1798, which language had been repeated by South Carolina to denounce the tariff of 1828. On both previous occasions, the protesting parties reminded their fellow citizens of the right of revolution as an ultimate recourse but did not appeal to that right. Although there was some ambiguity about this, especially in the Kentucky Resolutions, nullification was by and large looked upon as a constitutional remedy intended to prevent the execution of the law or laws that were said to be unauthorized by the Constitution. It was not intended to destroy the Constitution.

Buchanan's appeal on the South's behalf to the law of self-preservation—like Madison's appeal in the forty-third *Federalist*—is an appeal to a law higher than any constitution. Southern discontent was not motivated by any alleged exercise of powers not granted, as in the cases of the Alien and Sedition Acts in 1798 and the "Tariff of Abominations" of 1828. Rather was it motivated by the refusal to exercise a power allegedly granted: the power of Congress to protect the rights of slave owners in the territories. More generally, it was motivated by the belief that the ground of this refusal was a moral condemnation of slavery and that such moral condemnation made impossible the civic friendship that was the necessary condition of common citizenship.

Having thus said nearly everything necessary to justify the breakup of the union, Buchanan now calls for its preservation:

> It is said, however, that the antecedents of the President elect have been sufficient to justify the fears of the South that he will attempt to invade their constitutional rights. But are such apprehensions of contingent danger in the future sufficient to justify the immediate destruction of the noblest system of government ever devised by mortals? . . . After all, he is no more than the chief executive officer of the government . . . and it is a remarkable fact in our history that, notwithstanding the repeated efforts of the anti-slavery party, no single act has ever passed Congress, unless we may possibly except the Missouri Compromise, impairing in the slightest degree the rights of the South to their property in slaves. And it may be observed, judging from present indications, that no probability exists of the passage of such an act by a majority of both houses, either in the present or the next Congress.

As we have seen, however, the South's deepest fear of a design to reduce it under what it considered absolute despotism lay in a future in which a steady accession of free states would reduce the slave states to less than one-fourth the number needed to block an amendment abolishing slavery. Only if enough slave states could be added to preserve a sectional balance could the South, in its own mind, find safety within a future Union. Buchanan's arguments against the "rashness" of immediate secession are contradicted not only by his justification of fears of servile insurrection but also by the electoral arithmetic of Lincoln's election, which marked, in all probability, the end of any addition of slave states to the Union. This "containment" of slavery could only forecast that "ultimate extinction" that Lincoln had declared, in the House Divided speech, to be the ultimate end of his policy—as it had been of the Founding Fathers. The ability of the slave South to resist this "ultimate extinction" could only grow weaker with the passage of time. Prudence could only dictate immediate separation, whether as an exercise of the admitted right of revolution or of a supposed constitutional right of secession.

Buchanan then turns to the theory of popular sovereignty in the territories:

> Only three days after my inauguration the Supreme Court of the United States solemnly adjudged that this power [to prohibit slavery in a territory] did not exist

in a territorial legislature. Yet such has been the factious temper of the times that the correctness of this decision has been extensively impugned before the people, and the question has given rise to angry political conflicts throughout the country. Those who have appealed from this judgment of our highest constitutional tribunal to popular assemblies, would, if they could, invest a territorial legislature with power to annul the sacred rights of property. This power Congress is expressly forbidden by the federal Constitution to exercise. Every state legislature in the Union is forbidden by its own constitution to exercise it. It cannot be exercised in any state except by the people in their highest sovereign capacity, when framing or amending their state constitution. In like manner it can only be exercised by the people of a territory, represented in a convention of delegates, for the purpose of framing a constitution preparatory to admission as a state of the Union. Then, and not until then, are they invested with power to decide the question whether slavery shall or shall not exist within their limits. This is an act of sovereign authority and not of subordinate territorial legislation. Were it otherwise, then indeed would the equality of the states in the territories be destroyed and the rights of property in slaves would depend not upon the guarantees of the Constitution, but upon the shifting majorities of an irresponsible territorial legislature. Such a doctrine, from its intrinsic unsoundness, cannot long influence any considerable portion of our people, much less can it afford a good reason for a dissolution of the Union.

Someone reading this paragraph more than a century and a third after it was written, and lacking the necessary instruction in what we might call the metaphysics of the territorial question, would be perplexed as to what the president was talking about. The unnamed doctrine whose "intrinsic unsoundness" he deprecates is that of "popular sovereignty" as espoused by Senator Stephen A. Douglas. Douglas had been the author and chief sponsor of the Kansas–Nebraska Act of 1854, which had repealed the Missouri Compromise of 1820 as being

inconsistent with the principle of non-intervention with slavery in the States and Territories, as recognized by the legislation of eighteen hundred and fifty . . . it being the true intent and meaning of this act not to legislate slavery into any Territory or State, nor to exclude it therefrom, but to leave the people thereof perfectly free to form and regulate their own domestic institutions in their own way, subject only to the Constitution of the United States.[35]

Douglas had insisted that these provisions of the Kansas–Nebraska Act had left it to the settlers in Kansas and Nebraska to decide for themselves, through their territorial legislatures, whether to include slavery among their "domestic institutions." But the alleged "non-intervention" by Congress with slavery in the territories and states in the 1850 compromise did not—or at least did not unambiguously—leave it to the territorial legislatures to decide on the status of slavery. As Buchanan said, all that was distinctly and expressly left to the people of the territories in the 1850 legislation was the right, when the territories were admitted to the Union as states, to do so as their constitutions "may prescribe at the time of their admission." But the 1850 compromise said nothing as to the status of slavery in those same territories *during the territorial period.* In fact, the legislation of 1850 touched on this question only by declaring that any dispute concerning the right to property in slaves during the territorial period could be appealed directly from the highest court of the territory to the Supreme Court of the United States. Thus Congress itself in 1850 set in motion the process by which the attempt was made (in *Dred Scott* in 1857) to have the status of slavery in the territories decided by the Supreme Court.[36] When the Kansas–Nebraska Act spoke of leaving the people of the territory "perfectly free to form and regulate their domestic institutions in their own way," it may indeed have intended that territorial legislatures decide the fate of slavery during the territorial period. But there was no language even approximating that in the 1850 legislation. By insisting that the 1854 law was carrying forward a policy enshrined in its predecessor, Douglas rendered that policy equally doubtful in both. In this, Buchanan's complaint is justified.

Although Buchanan spoke of the "intrinsic unsoundness" of popular sovereignty, Douglas persistently claimed that it had not only been enacted into law in 1854 but also proclaimed as official doctrine in the Cincinnati Platform of the Democratic Party of 1856, upon which Buchanan himself had been elected, that

> the American Democracy recognize and adopt the principles contained in the organic laws establishing the Territories of Kansas and Nebraska as embodying the only sound and safe solution to the "slavery question" upon which the great national idea of the people of this whole country can repose in its determined conservation of the Union—non-interference by Congress with slavery in the States or Territories, or in the District of Columbia.[37]

As Buchanan noted, however, three days after his inauguration the Supreme Court "solemnly adjudged" that popular sovereignty, no less than congressional exclusion of slavery from the territories, was unconstitutional. This decision, had it been accepted as a political rule, would have excluded from the ballot in 1860 not only the Republican Party that elected Lincoln but also the Democratic Party that had (after the secession from it of the seven states of the Deep South) nominated Douglas. That is to say, it would have effectively disfranchised three-quarters of the voters of the free states. In this light, how could Buchanan attribute to "the factious temper of the times" the refusal to accept "the correctness of this decision"?

In fact, when Buchanan said that Congress was "expressly forbidden by the federal Constitution" to exercise the power to exclude slavery from the territories, he echoed the language, not of the Constitution itself, but of Chief Justice Taney in *Dred Scott*. He is simply reflecting the most rabidly proslavery opinions and treating them as if they were the only opinions eligible for consideration.

Next Buchanan turns to the Fugitive Slave Law and to the attempts to resist its enforcement by several of the states. This 1850 law, unlike the right to carry slaves into a territory, was indeed founded upon an "express provision" of the Constitution (Article IV, section 2, paragraph 3). It was much more stringent than its predecessor of 1793 and had been carried out unflinchingly by Presidents Fillmore, Pierce, and Buchanan himself since its enactment. The position Buchanan sets forth in this regard is not different in its essentials from that of Abraham Lincoln or the Republican Party. It was not a matter in dispute between any of the parties in the 1860 presidential election. As Buchanan himself notes, the state laws attempting to interfere with the reclaiming of fugitives had in every case been overridden by federal authority. As a practical grievance, the presence of these laws was essentially moot. To the South, however, their very existence was intolerable simply as an expression of antislavery opinion. Buchanan nonetheless demanded "that the State legislatures . . . repeal their unconstitutional and obnoxious enactments. Unless this shall be done without unnecessary delay, it is impossible for any human power to save the Union." This was a perfectly gratuitous aggravation of sectional antagonism. Lincoln and the Republican Party in Congress had no authority over free-state legislatures, and Buchanan's demand was one that he knew could not possibly be met.

Although it was undoubtedly true that the Fugitive Slave Law was constitutional in principle, it was not necessarily so in its manner of operation. The personal liberty laws passed by free-state legislatures were designed, in part, to prevent the law being used as a pretext to kidnap free Negroes into slavery. Yet Buchanan saw no moral or legal justification for any attempt by a free state to protect the rights of freemen who happened to be black:

> The southern States, standing on the basis of the Constitution, have a right to demand this act of justice from the States of the North. Should it be refused, then the Constitution, to which all the States are parties, will have been willfully violated by one portion of them in a provision essential to the domestic security and happiness of the remainder. In that event, the injured States, after having first used all peaceful and constitutional means to obtain redress, would be justified in revolutionary resistance to the government of the Union.

Having thus thoroughly justified the South in the exercise of the natural and inherent right of revolution, Buchanan turns to the question of secession as a constitutional right. Given the aforesaid justification, one would think that the question of whether secession was a legal right under the Constitution was a minor distinction of no great practical importance. Yet in fact, Southern opinion laid great weight upon the doctrine that secession by each state, deratifying its membership in the Union by the same procedures as had ratified it, was sanctioned by the Constitution. It is entirely possible that secession might not have occurred at all if this were not believed to be the case. As we shall see, Buchanan's argument in this regard is absolutely impotent in its conclusions. Although nominally denying the constitutional thesis put forth by the secessionists, its real effect is to deny in advance any possibility of effective action against secession by his successor.

> I have purposely confined my remarks to revolutionary resistance, because it has been claimed within the last few years that any State, whenever this shall be its sovereign will and pleasure, may secede from the Union in accordance with the Constitution, and without any violation of the constitutional rights of the other members of the Confederacy. That as each became parties to the Union by the vote of its own people assembled in convention, so any one of them may retire from the Union in a similar manner by the vote of such a convention.

If, however, "the other members of the Confederacy" have "willfully violated" constitutional rights "essential to the domestic security and happiness" of the slave states, why are not the slave states—by the very nature of the law of contracts—released from their mutual obligations under the Constitution? Buchanan continues:

> In order to justify secession as a constitutional remedy it must be on the principle that the federal government is a mere voluntary association of states, to be dissolved at pleasure by any one of the contracting parties. If this be so, the Confederacy is a rope of sand, to be penetrated and dissolved by the first adverse wave of public opinion in any of the states. In this manner our thirty-three states may resolve themselves into as many petty, jarring, hostile republics, each one retiring from the Union without responsibility whenever any sudden excitement might impel them to such a course.

This passage is almost enough to make one a Confederate sympathizer! Where now are the Southern states who, "standing on the basis of the Constitution," had "a right to demand this act of justice from the states of the North"? How were the aggrieved slave states to enforce this right within the Union if they were now a permanent minority, with no rational prospect of ever obtaining redress by the political process? What better way to indicate the distance of their action from any merely "sudden excitement" than to call constitutional conventions, to exert the full deliberative sovereignty of each state? In fact, the Union was a "voluntary association," by virtue of its contractual basis. But a compact to form a government, like a marriage, although entered voluntarily, does not leave the contracting parties free thereafter to do as they please. Nor did the Southern secessionists ever say that it did. As we shall see, they alleged the same causes to justify secession that Buchanan gave as justifying revolution.

In what follows, Buchanan cites the authority of President Jackson, quoting this passage from Jackson's proclamation of January 1833 against the nullifying ordinance of South Carolina:

> The right of the people of a single state to absolve themselves at will and without the consent of the other states from their most solemn obligations, and hazard the liberty and happiness of the millions composing this Union, cannot be acknowledged. Such authority is believed to be utterly repugnant both to the principles upon which the general government is constituted, and the objects which it was expressly formed to attain.

Since Lincoln would rely heavily upon this Jacksonian precedent, it is important to understand how Buchanan's use of it is—or is not—justified.

In 1833, South Carolina was claiming the power to nullify a federal tariff law, that is to say, to prevent the collection of duties on goods imported from abroad into the ports of South Carolina. South Carolinians well understood that no other state would pay the duties if South Carolina did not. They expected that their action would thus compel the other states, using the convention mode for amending the Constitution (as provided in Article V), to rule on the constitutionality of the law that South Carolina disputed. If three-fourths of the states agreed to the law, then South Carolina would, presumably, consent to obey it. However, if one-fourth of the states plus one refused, then it could not be constitutionally enforced. This was an application of John C. Calhoun's famous doctrine of the concurrent majority, concerning which we will speak at length later. It was Calhoun's alleged improvement upon the political science of the *Federalist* as a means of preventing the tyranny of the majority. It was presented as a political process within the Union, as a means of guaranteeing that majority rule would be consistent with minority rights. Jackson, however, considered nullification an unconstitutional interference with the properly expressed will of the majority, and secured the Force Bill from Congress, which would have enabled him to send an army to South Carolina to collect the tariff. At the same time, however, Congress lowered the tariffs. At this point South Carolina withdrew its nullifying ordinance, after which the Force Bill was withdrawn. Both sides claimed victory, and the underlying issues presented by Calhoun's doctrine of state rights remained unresolved.

When Jackson issued his 1833 proclamation, he and Calhoun (who had been his vice president) had become the deadliest of enemies. Although, as we have seen, nullification was conceived by Calhoun (and South Carolina) as a constitutional political process, Jackson brushed this argument aside as inconsequential and spoke as if nullification and secession were one and the same. Although closely related, they were not the same, since nullification was intended to be a process by which the collective sovereignty of the people of all the states could be brought to bear upon the determination of a disputed constitutional question. The nullifying state was conceived as a full partner within the Union in this process.[38] However, if a nullifying state was overridden by three-fourths of its co-states, then it was—as Calhoun's theory developed—still left with the option of seceding.

Between 1833, when he took the lead in formulating the South Carolina doctrine, and his death in 1850, Calhoun became the prophet of the positive good theory of slavery and the Moses of states' rights constitutionalism. Ten years after his death, he had achieved an unrivaled authority in the slave South. Taney's opinion in *Dred Scott*, which asserted that the right conferred by a state to own a slave was a right carried by the owner beyond the jurisdiction of the state itself, was purely Calhounian in the sense that the positive good theory of slavery completely divorced the concept of state rights from that of natural rights. Moreover, it was Calhoun's anti–natural rights reformulation of the doctrine of state sovereignty and state rights that left the "marriage" of state and Union (accomplished by the ceremony of ratification) without any agreed definition of what constituted fidelity to that relationship. In the absence of such a standard, ratification did indeed resemble a marriage in which the subjective feelings of each partner became the grounds upon which each partner might decide whether or when the marriage might be dissolved. A state could deratify the Constitution and secede from the Union by the same process by which it had ratified and joined. By analogy, marriage would not be a permanent commitment but one in which marriage and divorce were, so to speak, the forward and the reverse of the same machinery. Buchanan, by endorsing the Calhounian theory of state rights as it related to slavery in the territories, was, whether he knew it or not, endorsing Calhoun's theory of the relationship of the states to the Union. This theory was fully compatible with the idea of secession as a constitutional right.

Here is Buchanan's comment on the passage from President Jackson's 1833 proclamation:

> It is not pretended that any clause of the Constitution gives countenance to [the theory of a right of secession]. It is altogether founded upon inference, not from any language contained in the instrument itself, but from the sovereign character of the several states by which it was ratified. But is it beyond the power of a state, like an individual to yield a portion of its sovereign rights to secure the

remainder? In the language of Mr. Madison, who has been called the father of the Constitution, "It was formed by the states—that is, by the people in each of the states acting in their highest sovereign capacity, and formed consequently by the same authority which formed the state constitutions."

Buchanan ignores, or is perhaps altogether innocent of, the fact that there are two radically different theories of what constitutes sovereignty involved here. No two figures in American history have ever stood in greater opposition to each other on the interpretation of American constitutionalism than did Madison and Calhoun in the nullification crisis. Madison was the last authority to whom Buchanan, with his anti-antislavery posture, was entitled to turn at this juncture in his message.

When Buchanan speaks of the power of a state "like an individual to yield a portion of its sovereign rights to secure the remainder," he is referring to the "compact" theory, which Madison called the basis of all free government and which we explored at length in chapter 1. In that theory, however, to speak precisely, it is not the rights themselves that are yielded but only their *exercise*. For good reason, the rights themselves are called "unalienable" by the Declaration of Independence. The exercise of those rights can be resumed at any time that the government to which one has yielded that exercise is unwilling or unable to do so in one's behalf. Accordingly, as a member of civil society, one cannot, in the ordinary course of events, execute justice upon someone who has stolen one's property or assaulted one's person. One must have recourse to the police and the courts of law established by civil society. But if at the time of the theft or the assault, the government can offer no protection, then the state of nature has recurred, and one resumes the exercise of the rights one has otherwise yielded to the government. In such an event, one has the natural and legal right to use sufficient force to defend one's person and property. At that moment, to the extent that the positive law is in harmony with the natural law, the natural law becomes part of the positive law.

Under slavery, the positive law denied the slave the right to defend himself against the theft of his property in the fruit of his labor and against the violence to his person that might be committed with impunity by his master. But the sovereign rights to life, liberty, and property are inseparable from one's being. That is to say, they are inseparable from one's nature as a human being, despite what any positive law might assert. Like so many of his generation, and other generations, Buchanan did not see that these rights could not belong to the masters unless they also belonged to the slaves. If, as he had said earlier, self-preservation was the first law of nature, then slavery was a threat to the self-preservation of the white South, because it was first and foremost a threat to the self-preservation of the black South. If slavery was a threat to the security of the white South, then extending and strengthening slavery was hardly the solution to that threat. It is a curious fact about the antebellum controversy concerning the enforcement of the Fugitive Slave Act that no one ever, to our knowledge, declared an obligation on the part of the *slaves* to obey the law of slavery. The slaves themselves had no obligation inconsistent with the natural law, even if everyone else was said to be under an obligation to the positive law. A good citizen, as distinct from someone who obeys the law only out of fear of punishment, normally recognizes obedience to law as both morally right and in his own best interest. But this obedience is attenuated, if not annulled, when the rights for the sake of which one might—under the law of nature—compact or consent to government are rendered less rather than more secure by the government itself. It is a measure of Buchanan's moral imbecility that he could justify the resistance of the South on the basis of the natural law of self-preservation but could see no justification for resistance to slavery.

The states that would attempt to secede and form a new union in 1861 would appeal again and again to the passage in the Declaration of Independence that says, "whenever any form of government becomes destructive of these ends [natural rights], it is the right of the people to alter or to abolish it, and to institute new government." These words refer to the right of revolution, and what Buchanan is denying at this point is a constitutional right. But can a constitutional right stand in the way of a revolutionary right? It certainly did not do so in 1776. In language closely resembling what Lincoln would say three months later, Buchanan added that the Constitution "was intended to be perpetual, and not to be annulled at the pleasure of any one of the contracting parties." A strange comment for someone to make who has just indicted the free states for causing Southern matrons to fear that they and their children might be murdered! To annul for cause is not to annul at pleasure. Nevertheless, Buchanan continues:

> The old Articles of Confederation were entitled "Articles of Confederation and perpetual union between the States"; and by the thirteenth article it is expressly declared that "the articles of this confederation shall be inviolably observed by every state, and the union shall be perpetual." The preamble to the Constitution of the United States having express reference to the Articles of Confederation, recites that it was established "in order to form a more perfect union." And yet it is contended that this "more perfect union" does not include the essential attribute of perpetuity.

Here we must look again, and with utmost circumspection, upon the question of the perpetuity of both the Articles and the Constitution that succeeded them. This is all the more necessary because Lincoln will use virtually the same language as Buchanan, connecting the perpetuity of the Articles with the more perfect Union of the Constitution. Lincoln himself will tell us that "perpetuity is implied, if not expressed, in the fundamental law of all national governments."[39] This is as much as to say that all the governments that have ceased to exist did so notwithstanding the aforesaid perpetuity. And cannot as much be said of the government of the Articles? We must observe that the Constitution does not tell us that the "more perfect Union" is the same Union that existed previously. We may therefore ask whether the old Union was dissolved and a new and more perfect one put in its place, or whether it was endowed with greater perfection without first having been dissolved. How this question is resolved will depend upon whether the Union under the Articles was itself dependent upon the ratification of the Articles, or whether there was not another and primordial ground of Union that the Articles themselves were intended to effectuate.

Since Buchanan has, however inconsistently, invoked the authority of James Madison, let us look at this question through the eyes of the Madison of the *Federalist*. First let us note the following: To say that the Union under the Constitution of 1787 was the same Union as that of the Articles requires that one explain an undoubted anomaly. That anomaly consisted in the fact that under Article VII of the Constitution, the new government was to come into being with the ratification of only nine of the thirteen states. That meant that the four nonratifying states would remain outside the newer Union. Theoretically, they were still under the Articles. But the government of the Articles had ceased to function. Were they then merely independent states, under none of the obligations derived from the advantages of union? For Confederate constitutionalists in 1860–61, Article VII of the Constitution proved irrefutably that the Union of the Articles had been dissolved and a new Union formed by the ratification of the Constitution by nine states. It meant that the ratification of the Constitution constituted a deratification of the Articles of Confederation. For them this was an authoritative precedent for their own actions. Their acts of secession, by conventions elected for no other purpose than to exert the full sovereignty of the people of the states, fulfilled all the criteria for legitimacy that had attended the simultaneous dissolution of the Union of the Articles and the institution of the new government of the Constitution. Here in essence is the strongest of all the arguments for the South's asserted right of secession, whether as a natural right, a constitutional right, or as a peculiar compound of both.

Buchanan had quoted the Articles of Confederation to the effect that "the union shall be perpetual." The full sentence (from Article XIII) reads as follows: "And the Articles of this confederation shall be inviolably observed by every state, and the union shall be perpetual; nor shall any alteration at any time hereafter be made in any of them; unless such alteration be agreed to in a congress of the united states, and be afterwards confirmed by the legislatures of every state."[40] Here as well are the words of Article VII of the Constitution of 1787: "The ratification of the conventions of nine states, shall be sufficient for the establishment of this Constitution between the States so ratifying the same." The Constitution clearly became the supreme law of the land by a breach of the Articles of Confederation unauthorized by anything in that document. This replacement of one constitution by another did not take place by the conquest of war, as did the replacement of the law of Great Britain by the law of the Continental Congress. It took place by a peaceful process, acquiesced in by all the parties principally concerned. And yet it was as much an expression of the full sovereignty of the people, otherwise called the right of revolution, as was the repudiation of the law of Great Britain on July 4, 1776.

Here is what James Madison had to say on this subject in the forty-third *Federalist*:

> Two questions of a very delicate nature present themselves on this occasion. 1. On what principle the confederation, which stands in the solemn form of a compact among the States, can be superceded without the unanimous consent of the parties to it? 2. What relation is to subsist between the nine or more States ratifying the Constitution, and the remaining few who do not become parties to it?

We have previously quoted Madison answering the first question in terms of "the absolute necessity of the case," "the great principle of self-preservation," and "the transcendent law of nature and of nature's God, which declares that the safety and happiness of society are the objects at which all political institutions aim, and to which all such institutions must be sacrificed." He continues:

> Perhaps also an answer may be found without searching beyond the principles of the compact itself. It has been heretofore noted among the defects of the Confederation, that in many of the States, it had received no higher sanction than a mere legislative ratification. The principle of reciprocality seems to require, that its obligation on the other States should be reduced to the same standard. A compact between independent sovereigns, founded on ordinary acts of legislative authority, can pretend to no higher validity than a league or treaty between the parties. It is an established doctrine on the subject of treaties, that all the articles are mutually conditions of each other; that a breach of any one article is a breach of the whole treaty; and that a breach committed by either of the parties absolves the others; and authorizes them, if they please, to pronounce the treaty violated and void. Should it unhappily be necessary to appeal to these delicate truths for a justification for dispensing with the consent of particular States to a dissolution of the federal pact, will not the complaining parties find it a difficult task to

answer the MULTIPLIED and IMPORTANT infractions with which they may be confronted? The time has been when it was incumbent on us all to veil the ideas which this paragraph exhibits. The scene is now changed, and with it, the part which the same motives dictate.[41]

The Gettysburg Address begins with the biblical "fourscore and seven years," invoking the authority of "our fathers" as presiding at the birth of the nation in 1776. In so doing, it presumed to put a period to an issue that had divided Lincoln and Douglas in 1858, and North and South in 1860–61. During the joint debates, Douglas stated repeatedly that we existed as a nation (or Union) only by virtue of the Constitution. But if the Constitution made the Union, and ratification made the Constitution, then both Constitution and Union (which would be dated from 1789, not 1776) could be dissolved by the same process (deratification or secession) by which they were brought into existence. Madison's reference above to the "dissolution of the federal pact" seems to justify this view of the ratification process. On the other side, Lincoln's argument for the indissolubility of the Union depended upon the premise that it was formed, not by the Constitution nor by the Articles, but by the event of July 4, 1776. Without this assumption, the argument against secession as a constitutional right does indeed fall to the ground. That is why Calhoun's reformulation of the doctrine of state rights had as its necessary foundation the denial of any authority to July 4, 1776, as the time of the formation of the Union. For Calhoun, that date was the occasion for the independence of thirteen separate (not united) states, which at that moment became as legally independent of each other as of Great Britain.[42] For Calhoun, the statement of principles at the beginning of the Declaration of Independence had no authority whatever for the constitutions, state or federal, that followed upon it.

To repeat, the argument that the Union that became operative in 1789 was wholly dependent for its existence upon the ratification process, and that the ratification process was therefore competent to dissolve the union that had preceded it, is the heart of the argument for secession as a constitutional right. And the strongest foundation for this argument is to be found in Madison's forty-third *Federalist*. We must accordingly confront it without equivocation.

We begin by observing that Madison, in the passage we have quoted, employs two separate and distinct lines of argument, the first based upon the natural law, the second upon the positive law. He appeals first to that same law of nature to which Buchanan appealed at the outset of his message to Congress. The imbecility of the government under the Articles, which formed the particular theme of the early numbers of the *Federalist*, leaves no doubt that it did not adequately secure those rights for which civil societies are formed and governments instituted. It was time, therefore, "to alter or to abolish" it, and to institute "new government." This, however, is an argument for exercise of the right of revolution, not for secession as a constitutional right.

Next, however, Madison observes "that in many of the States [the Articles] had received no higher sanction than a mere legislative ratification." Of course, the Articles were adopted in the midst of a bitter war, to help meet the harsh exigencies of that war. There was no leisure to elect ratifying conventions or debate the merits of a new constitution. By Madison's own argument, the legitimacy of the Articles must be sought, at least in part, in the necessities from which they arose, as well as in the means by which they were ratified. Now, however, the Articles that were forged in the crucible of war had demonstrated their inadequacy to meet the exigencies of peace. Not the means by which the Articles were adopted, but the ends which they no longer serve, are the reasons for abandoning them. However, in emphasizing the importance of the difference between mere legislative ratification and ratification by constitutional convention, Madison brings into view the distinction between the delegated authority of the people and the sovereign authority of the people. In so doing he is adumbrating the distinction between ordinary statute law and the law of the Constitution. This distinction, unknown to the British constitution, was soon to assume overwhelming importance in American law.

According to Madison, mere legislative ratification seems to reduce the Union under the Articles to a "compact between independent sovereigns" that "can pretend to no higher validity than a league or treaty between the parties." Madison does not actually say that the states that formed the compact of the Articles were "independent sovereigns." What he says is that one might draw that conclusion if one does not search "beyond the principles of the compact itself." Nor does he say that searching within the compact is sufficient to define the nature of the Union. Later we will see that how one understands the Constitution will depend utterly upon principles, not stated in the Constitution, that one brings to bear upon its interpretation. And it will be those principles, not the Constitution itself, that determine the nature of the Union.

Madison suggests that the Articles of Confederation, looked at in and of themselves, imply an alliance but not a genuine union. The second of the Articles reads, "Each state retains its sovereignty, freedom, and independence, and every power, jurisdiction, and right, which is not by this confederation expressly delegated to the United States in Congress assembled."[43] Calhoun and his descendants, in 1860–61 and ever since, have taken these words to mean that each state retains its unqualified and undivided sovereignty. Many have taken the Tenth Amendment of the Constitution as a reaffirmation of this Article, despite the fact that the Tenth Amendment does not repeat the word "expressly" before the word "delegated." In any event, what each state retains is what remains *after* what has been delegated and not what existed before such delegation. In this light, the crucial difference between the Articles and the Constitution is that under the former, Congress did not have any means of executing its laws except by the instrumentalities of the state governments. The Articles resembled a league formed by treaty, in that the Union had no real government to carry out its decisions. This in itself seems to be in full agreement with the Calhounian or Confederate thesis that the Declaration of Independence resulted in thirteen separate sovereignties, and not one. It directly contradicts Buchanan and Lincoln.

We must notice, however, that in the passage we have quoted of the forty-third *Federalist*, Madison begins with a justification based upon "the law of nature and of nature's God," reproducing almost exactly words contained in the first sentence of the Declaration of Independence. Madison thereby tells us that the reason for abandoning the Articles is of the same order of urgency as the abandoning of the British constitution. In 1776, however, there was no right to appeal to, other than the natural right of revolution. The British constitution did not admit of a right of secession.[44] In 1787, withdrawal from the Articles might be legally justified, because the Articles did not provide for a government in the full and proper sense. Under the "established doctrine on the subject of treaties," it was possible to establish a right less drastic than the right of revolution, drawn from positive law as distinct from natural law. The positive law here is the law of federalism, but of pre-*Federalist* federalism. Prior to the Constitution of 1787, "federalism" referred exclusively to those relationships that were founded upon treaties between independent sovereigns. A government "partly federal, partly national" was unknown before the *Federalist* itself.[45] That the Articles of Confederation represented an essentially treatylike union is shown by the fact that it had neither executive nor judicial branches and that there was no means, other than voluntary compliance by the states, for carrying out the decisions of its Congress. Each state could decide, therefore, for whatever reason, not to abide by a decision of the Congress. It was the essential incompetence of the government under the Articles that justified secession from it. This could hardly be the justification for secession under the Constitution. Or more precisely, it could hardly be a justification for secession if the Union proved itself a true government by successfully treating secession as rebellion. Buchanan is thus perfectly correct in drawing from Madison the inferences that he does against a constitutional right of secession.

To understand the Civil War, it is necessary to grasp the fact that Calhoun and the South had rejected the *Federalist*'s redefinition of federalism. For them the Union under the Constitution, notwithstanding its greater intimacy, remained in the decisive respect a treaty between sovereigns. They rejected the concept of dual sovereignty or dual federalism that Buchanan invoked, according to which sovereignty was divided between states and nation. By this Madisonian under-standing, the government of the United States was a genuine government, with all the legislative, executive, and judicial instrumentalities for carrying into effect the powers granted it by the Constitution. It was as sovereign within its own juris-diction as the states were within theirs. In ratifying the Constitution, the people of the states acted by means of conventions chosen to exert their full sovereign authority. In those conventions, the people gave the same authority to the gov-ernment of the Union that they had given to the governments of their respective states. The government of the Union and the governments of the states had the identical foundation in the sovereignty of the people, being distinguished rather by their different jurisdictions. Calhoun rejected this concept of dual federalism because it implied dual sovereignty, and he denied that sovereignty could be divided.[46] He is reported to have likened sovereignty to chastity, in that neither could be surrendered in part. In his mind, "partly federal" was as much a solecism as "partly pregnant." When Buchanan asked if a state could not, like an individ-ual, surrender a portion of its sovereignty, he was invoking the *Federalist's* charac-terization of our constitutional government as "partly federal, partly national," which was repudiated by all those who (following Calhoun) believed that seces-sion was a constitutional right.[47]

The seeds of the *Federalist's* conception of dual federalism and dual sover-eignty may be found in resolutions of the Revolutionary colonial legislatures in 1776, authorizing their delegates to the Continental Congress to vote for inde-pendence. A number of these resolutions called for independence *and* union.[48] While calling for union, however, they reserved their "internal police" or "inter-nal affairs" to the governments of their own legislatures. That the union resulting from independence was to be a genuine government, and not a mere alliance rest-ing upon a treaty relationship, was implicit in the process by which the Conti-nental Congress itself acted as an agent of all the people of all the colonies in pro-viding a general government that nonetheless left each state free to govern itself internally. How the line was to be drawn between the internal government of each state and the common government of the union was certainly not perfectly known then. It is not perfectly known today, and can never be known perfectly. The drawing and redrawing of that line has been a never-ending preoccupation. There is no question, however, as the *Federalist* makes clear, that leaving the draw-ing of the line entirely to the states, as under the Articles of Confederation, had led to a kind of anarchy. But if the central government could execute its undoubt-ed laws with its own agents, how could any state obstruct that execution, except by insurrection and rebellion?

In 1825, Madison and Jefferson together maintained that the Declaration of Independence was not only the *first* of the "best guides" to the principles of the governments both of Virginia and of the United States but also the "act of Union of these states."[49] It is this view of the origin of the Union and of the United States as a nation that Lincoln maintained in his inaugural and immortalized in the Gettysburg Address. But if the Declaration was the primordial instrument of Union, both legal and moral, then the ratifications of both the Articles of Confederation and the Constitution took place within a framework provided by that instrument. Is this view of Madison and Jefferson in 1825, and later of Lincoln, consistent with Madison's earlier justification, in the forty-third *Federalist*, of the breach of the Articles by the new Constitution?

Having set forth the reason for regarding the Articles as no more than a treaty, rather than the frame of a common government, Madison says that a breach of any article by any of the parties authorizes the others to pronounce the treaty violated and void. He alludes to the numerous failures of the states to carry out their obligations under the Articles as "delicate truths" that it had hitherto been "incumbent on us all to veil." That is to say, mutual recriminations would hitherto have been useless. But these same facts are no longer recriminations. They are reasons to change the frame of government altogether. Madison suggests that the failures of the states to carry out their obligations under the Articles justified "a dissolution of the federal pact." But would real or alleged failures of the states to carry out their obligations be less obnoxious under the new Constitution than under the Articles? Would not such failures, if they concerned matters touching the most vital interests, also justify "a dissolution of the federal pact"?

Buchanan has already said that the failure of the free states to repeal the laws allegedly obstructing the enforcement of the Fugitive Slave Law would certainly lead to the dissolution of the Union. He implies that this dissolution would result from the right of revolution. How does the "doctrine on the subject of treaties" differ in this from the doctrine concerning the kind of contractual relationship represented by the Constitution? Let us assume that one of the states is attacked by a foreign power and the federal government (or the representatives of the other states in Congress) refused to defend it. Would that not constitute a failure of the government of the Union that would release the state in question from its obligations under the Constitution? Would not that state then have both the moral and the legal right to make a treaty of alliance with a foreign government (something forbidden by the Constitution) in order to provide for its defense? Would not a state doing this be exercising a right arising from the law of self-preservation, the transcendent law of nature? Would it not be in essence what the states that ratified the Constitution of 1787 did, without, however, first troubling themselves to withdraw from the Articles of Confederation?

Here let us recall the second of the "two questions of a very delicate nature" posed by Madison in the forty-third *Federalist*: Where did the nine states that abandoned the Articles and ratified the Constitution leave the four states that did not? Madison says that this question

> is one of those cases which must be left to provide for itself. In general, it may be observed, that although no political relation can subsist between the assenting and the dissenting States, yet the moral relations will remain uncanceled. The claims of justice, both on one side and on the other, will be in force, and must be fulfilled; the rights of humanity must in all cases be duly and mutually respected; whilst considerations of a common interest, and above all the remembrance of the endearing scenes which are past, and the anticipation of a speedy triumph over the obstacles to re-union, will, it is hoped, not urge in vain MODERATION on one side, and PRUDENCE on the other.[50]

To say that the question "must be left to provide for itself" is a tactful or prudent way of saying that it presents a problem that cannot easily be decided by recourse to the principles hitherto invoked. Why this is so may perhaps be seen by returning to the question of the perpetuity of the Union. Both Buchanan and Lincoln take a stand on the language of "perpetual Union" in the Articles, and maintain that as the Union under the Constitution is said to be "more perfect," it can hardly have had less of the attribute of perpetuity than its predecessor. But the perpetuity of the Articles did not prevent the Constitutional Convention from bifurcating the Union into "assenting and dissenting states" by the ratification process. Is the more perfect Union the same Union? Considered as a political union, it cannot be the same if "no political relationship can subsist" between the ratifying and nonratifying states. Yet, Madison says, "the moral relations . . . remain uncanceled." That is to say, the moral union continues, even if there is a hiatus in political union. Because the interruption must of necessity be regarded as temporary, means of fulfilling the political obligations must be found, even in the absence of a common political government. And indeed, Article VI of the Constitution declares that "All debts contracted and engagements entered into, before the adoption of this Constitution, shall be as valid against the United States under this Constitution, as under the Confederation." It is notable that the Constitution makes no provision for distinguishing between the debts of the "assenting and dissenting" states. Under the Constitution, all the debts of all the states of the Union of the Confederation will be honored, those of the four no less than those of the nine. It is also noteworthy that number XII of the Articles of Confederation closely resembles Article VI of the Constitution in accepting responsibility for the debts of the United States before the adoption of the Articles. Thus "the United States" as a singular responsible moral and political personality, which is to say as a union, is continuous from July 4, 1776.

Madison's argument in the forty-third *Federalist* resolves itself into the doctrine that the United States is, first and foremost, a moral union, in which the "claims of justice . . . must be fulfilled" and "the rights of humanity . . . duly and mutually respected," even apart from the particular and immediate form of its political government. This, however, implies a common understanding of what constitutes such claims and such rights. Where is that common understanding set forth? Can there be any more authoritative statement than the document from which all the acts of deeds of the United States are dated? Is it not there that we see the rights of humanity as the ground of the claims of justice? It is clearly Madison's thesis that such claims and rights can, except for a brief intermission, be properly and conveniently fulfilled and respected only by a political union. Political union is therefore a moral necessity. That is why Madison considers the breach arising from the ratification of only nine states as being only temporary. But he also sees it as a breach only of political union in the immediate governmental sense, not of the deeper moral union that defined the original political union, and from which all subsequent forms of political union derived.

Madison sees reunion arising expeditiously from "MODERATION on one side, and PRUDENCE on the other." Prudence, we recall, is the intellectual virtue that discovers the means to the ends of the moral virtues and functions within a framework of common ends. The Declaration of Independence proclaims that "life, liberty, and the pursuit of happiness" are the ends for which governments are instituted *because* they are rights belonging to human beings under the laws of nature. The obligations of prudence and the moderation with which they ought to be undertaken arise from the deference human beings pay to each other when they recognize the bonds between them under these laws. The "common interest" and the "remembrance of . . . endearing scenes which are past" evoke the great historical memory of the Revolution, fought under the banner of the great Declaration. What Buchanan has said about slavery, and his endorsement of the Southern position on state rights, has negated the doctrines of that Declaration and thoroughly undermined the power of reunion upon which Madison relied in 1788. Between the positive good theory of slavery, which is the driving force behind Calhoun's conception of state rights, and the categorical denunciation of tyranny and despotism that informed the Union at its inception, there is very little common moral ground.

Although the breach in political union effected by Article VII of the Constitution may have been temporary, it was nonetheless necessary. The ratification process embodied in that article corresponds closely with the logic of the compact theory. We recall that Buchanan himself used the language of this theory, in stark inconsistency with his endorsement of Calhoun's doctrine of state rights, when he said that "a state, like an individual," can consent to be governed by a stronger government in order to enjoy greater safety. The states, in forming their more perfect Union in 1787, stood in a relationship to each other similar to that in which individuals stand when they transform their relationship from that of the state of nature to that of civil society. In that transformation, there must be unanimous consent. It is this unanimous consent that legitimates majority rule. It is this unanimous consent that defines the rights that each and every one possesses, which rights define and limit the role of the majority in governing. And it is this unanimous consent that defines the moral nature of the moral union that is the foundation of political union. We remember that according to Madison's essay *Sovereignty*, the limits of majority rule are prescribed by whatever might be done *"rightfully"* by "unanimous concurrence."[51] Unanimity limits the sphere of government, and of majority rule, to those purposes for which human beings surrender the exercise of their natural rights. That excludes from the sphere of government "the reserved rights of individuals," such as conscience. But unanimity itself is limited by the requirement of rightfulness. Unanimous consent is a prescription for justice between the consenters. It cannot, however, authorize violations of the "rights of humanity" of those outside the political community by authorizing what is intrinsically wrong—for example, slavery or predatory wars. It is obvious, on the other hand, that what is concurred in unanimously (or nearly so) can hardly be subjected to constitutional restraint, however unrightful, in a government based upon the opinion of the governed. This is why the opinion of the governed, in a government deriving its just powers from the consent of the governed, must be enlightened. By Madison's premises, the opinion of the governed must itself be governed by the claims of justice and the rights of humanity. This means as well that the claims of justice belong to "persons," and not citizens merely. Justice between fellow citizens arises from the attempt to make secure the rights that they possessed before their unanimous consent made them fellow citizens. The bonds that united them under "the laws of nature and of nature's God" provided the principles by which their rights under those laws became the principles of legitimate government. Without the recognition of the antecedent laws of nature, there can be no enlightenment informing consent, no state rights consistent with human rights, no just powers of government arising from the consent of the governed.

The provision that the Constitution become operative between nine ratifying states was actually a provision, not for breaching the principle of unanimity, but for guaranteeing it. According to that social compact that is the basis of all free government, unanimous consent of itself authorizes majority rule. It does not authorize minority rule or rule by extraordinary majorities, which would permit a minority veto of majority rule. The majority may, of course, impose upon itself a requirement of extraordinary majorities in the operation of its government. This the Constitution does when requiring three-fourths majorities in the Senate for treaties, two-thirds majorities in both houses for submitting amendments to the states, and three-fourths majorities of the states for the ratification of amendments.[52] These are prudential devices to promote consensus on vital questions, limitations imposed upon the majority by itself, and, as such, reflections of the majority principle. The Articles, however, by requiring three-fourths for ordinary legislation and unanimity for amendments, did not reflect that principle. Under the compact theory, the whole purpose of unanimity a priori is to enable it to give way to majority rule a posteriori.

To assert the obvious, if civil society is formed by the free consent of each of its individual members, anyone whose free consent is not given is not a member. But what is the position of those "dissenting" at the moment civil society is formed? If we think of a frontier society, are they to wander off into the wilderness? Undoubtedly, this must sometimes have occurred. Such dissenters may go looking for others with whom they are in greater sympathy (especially in regard to religious persuasion) to form another independent political society. But the refusal of a dissenting minority to adhere to the decision of an assenting majority to form a civil society cannot impede or delay the decision of the latter, for this is what they are authorized to do by the law of nature. If the dissenters remain in the vicinity, however, they will have the incentive of this very same law—the law of self-preservation—to join, later if not sooner. This was precisely the position in which Article VII of the Constitution left the "dissenting" states. Unlike individuals, they could not move out of the neighborhood, and all in time ratified the Constitution, making consent unanimous. The provision that three-fourths of the states might hereafter adopt amendments to the Constitution rests upon that previously given unanimous consent to accept amendments so ratified. Article VII then followed closely the reasoning of the compact theory, first, by not allowing dissenting individuals, whether individual persons or individual states, to prevent the formation of the more perfect Union; and second, by assuring that the government of this Union, resting upon unanimous consent of every state, would embody the full moral authority of the principle of majority rule.

We note in concluding this segment of our commentary on Buchanan's Message to Congress that although Buchanan was correct in denying any constitutional right of secession, his denial was stultified by his earlier acceptance of the Calhounian theory of state rights, by which secession, as an act of revolution, could certainly be justified. By calling self-preservation the first law of nature in his denunciation of antislavery agitation as the danger to the Union—not thinking for a moment that slaves were entitled to the benefits of this law—Buchanan placed himself squarely on the side of the South.

After exploring the question of secession as a lawful right under the Constitution, Buchanan turns to the issue of the duty of the president: "What . . . is the responsibility and true position of the Executive? He is bound by solemn oath, before God and the country, 'to take care that the laws be faithfully executed,' and from this obligation he cannot be absolved by any human power." Here is an admirable precedent that Lincoln will indeed follow. But how, under the Constitution, is the president to fulfill his duties in the circumstances of such a crisis as that impending in 1860–61?

> [W]hat if the performance of his duty, in whole or in part, has been rendered impracticable by events over which he could have exercised no control? Such, at the present moment, is the case throughout the State of South Carolina, so far as the laws of the United States to secure the administration of justice by means of the federal judiciary are concerned. All the federal officers within its limits, through whose agency alone these laws can be carried into execution, have already resigned. We no longer have a district judge, a district attorney, or a marshal in South Carolina. In fact, the whole machinery of the federal government has been demolished, and it would be difficult, if not impossible, to replace it.

Buchanan turns to a 1795 law that authorizes a president to call forth the militia, and then the army and navy, to support the federal marshal in the execution of a civil or criminal process. But what can he do when there is no federal marshal, and where "even if there were such an officer, the entire population would constitute one solid combination to resist him"? It is up to Congress, he says, to amend the present laws or to enact new ones sufficient "to overcome united opposition in a single state, not to speak of other states who may place themselves in a similar attitude." This, however, raises a further question: "Has the Constitution delegated to Congress the power to coerce a state into submission which is attempting to withdraw or has actually withdrawn from the Confederacy?"

Having boldly and uncompromisingly asserted the inescapable duty of the president to see to it that the laws are faithfully executed, Buchanan then says, first, that Congress must afford him the necessary means, and, second, that the Constitution has withheld those means from Congress.

> After much serious reflection, I have arrived at the conclusion that no such power has been delegated to Congress or to any other department of the federal government. It is manifest, upon an inspection of the Constitution, that this is not among the specific and enumerated powers granted to Congress; and it is equally apparent that its exercise is not "necessary and proper for carrying into execution" any one of these powers.

This assertion is astonishing, in that Buchanan himself has just told us that the operation of the Constitution in South Carolina has been obstructed by the resignation of federal officials and by the solid opposition of the citizenry. In existing conditions, no one will accept appointment to the vacated places because of physical danger. Only by force to overcome the obstructions can the laws be faithfully executed in South Carolina (or, hereafter, in other seceding states). Buchanan continues: "Without descending to particulars, it may safely be asserted that the power to make war against a state is at variance with the whole spirit and intent of the Constitution." This is surely a truism. A more profound truism, however, was that the indefinite extension of slavery, as required by the doctrine of state rights enshrined in the *Dred Scott* decision, was at war with the spirit and intent of the Constitution. Yet Buchanan had endorsed it.

> In the nature of things, we could not, by physical force, control the will of the people and compel them to elect senators and representatives to Congress, and to perform all the other duties depending upon their own volition and required from the free citizens of a free state as a constituent member of the Confederacy.

But the choice confronting Buchanan is not between the use and nonuse of physical force. Unless one or the other side recedes, as Lincoln will make clear, it is between the successful obstruction of the rule of law by physical force and the successful upholding of the rule of law by physical force.

Buchanan himself has argued that secession was unlawful and that to concede otherwise would make the Union "a rope of sand." He has said that the federal Constitution, to the extent of its delegated powers, "is as much a part of the constitution of each state . . . as though it had been textually inserted therein." By reason of the supremacy clause in Article VI—which says that the Constitution is "the supreme Law of the Land . . . any thing in the constitution or laws of any State to the contrary notwithstanding," and which each state had ratified— "secession" would be as much an abrogation of the authority of a state constitution as of the federal Constitution. There is, moreover, no difference in principle between "secession" of an individual from the "compact" of a state constitution and "secession" of a state from the "compact" of the federal Constitution. Secession was in effect a denial that the government of the United States, within its constitutionally defined sphere, had ever been the actual government of the people of each state. South Carolina in 1860 was not, as in 1833, attempting to obstruct the operation of a single federal statute alleged to be unconstitutional. It was, rather, acting as if federal officials had been agents of a foreign government who had hitherto been permitted within the borders of South Carolina by a treaty now rescinded. "The fact is," Buchanan continued, that our Union rests upon public opinion, and can never be cemented by the blood of its citizens, shed in civil war. If it cannot live in the affections of its people it must one day perish. Congress possesses many means of preserving it by conciliation, but the sword was not placed in their hands to preserve it by force.

We must remember that it was Buchanan, not Lincoln, who first faced actual secession. And no appreciation of the task facing Lincoln is possible unless we grasp the magnitude of the burden placed upon him, not only by the fact of secession, but also by this assertion of constitutional impotence by his predecessor in office.

Buchanan was correct, of course, in saying that the Union rested upon public opinion. But it rested there because, like every free government, it was based upon "compact," or upon that unanimous consent by which majority rule is authorized. As we have seen, such consent had been forthcoming at the national, no less than at the state, level. But government cannot operate by unanimous consent. As Lincoln will say, to abandon rule by constitutional majority leaves only tyranny or anarchy as alternatives. And Buchanan has conceded that Lincoln's election had been a perfectly regular expression of the will of a constitutional majority. Moreover, as Buchanan also well knew, the Constitution authorizes Congress to suspend the writ of habeas corpus "when in cases of rebellion or invasion the public safety may require it." Clearly the Constitution contemplated just such a contingency as "secession" when it used the word "rebellion," and it just as surely contemplated using the sword to suppress it.

In the eleventh volume of *The Works of James Buchanan*, there is an addendum to the text of his Fourth Annual Message to Congress, in the form of a letter by Buchanan's biographer, George Ticknor Curtis, to the Philadelphia *Times*, dated August 20, 1883. Curtis defends Buchanan against the charge of impotence by saying that he distinguished between coercing a state and coercing individuals within a state. This is an important distinction. It is by virtue of this distinction that we know the conflict as the "Civil War" and not "the War between the States." For anyone who, like Buchanan (or Lincoln), denied that secession was legally possible, there could be no war between the states as such. What occurred was rebellion against the lawful authority of the Union. Why then did Buchanan speak of making war against a state (or states) when he himself had just concluded that a state could not secede?

Curtis argues that those who demanded that Buchanan coerce a state would have had him, for example, forcibly disperse the Massachusetts legislature to prevent it from passing a personal liberty law. Similarly, it would have had him forcibly disperse the South Carolina convention that voted secession. But that is nonsense. No one contemplated using force against those engaged in peaceable assembly, whether a Northern state legislature or a Southern state convention. As far as the personal liberty laws were concerned, they were for the most part effectively nullified by the federal courts. But where federal marshals were obstructed—whether by mobs or state officials—in carrying out federal court orders with regard to fugitive slaves, federal force was used against them. This in fact occurred in Massachusetts. With the breakdown of the federal judicial system in South Carolina, however, Buchanan simply threw up his hands. Curtis claims that Buchanan asked the Republicans in Congress to cooperate with him in drafting legislation to give him the authority to deal with secession. But the annual message rules out such legislation a priori.

Buchanan says that Congress cannot preserve the Union by force but only by conciliation. This may be accomplished, he thinks, by an "explanatory amendment" defining "the true construction of the Constitution" on three points:

> 1. An express recognition of the right of property in slaves in the states where it now exists or may hereafter exist.
> 2. A recognition of the duty of protecting this right in all the common Territories throughout their territorial existence, and until they shall be admitted as states into the Union, with or without slavery, as their constitutions may prescribe.
> 3. A recognition of the right of the master to have his slave, who has escaped from one state to another, "delivered up" to him, and of the validity of the fugitive slave law enacted for this purpose, together with a declaration that all state laws impairing or defeating this right are violations of the Constitution, and are consequently null and void.

The first of these proposed provisions was essentially noncontroversial and would in fact be proposed by Lincoln himself in his first inaugural. As for the third, Buchanan himself recognized that it was essentially superfluous:

> It may be objected that this construction of the Constitution has already been settled by the Supreme Court of the United States,[53] and what more ought to be required? The answer is, that a very large proportion of the people of the United States still contest the correctness of this decision, and never will cease from agitation and admit its binding force until clearly established by the people of the several states in their sovereign character.

The right of a master to have his escaped slave restored could hardly be made more explicit than it already was in Article IV of the Constitution. But the Fugitive Slave Act of 1850 was challenged in the free states on grounds other than the rights of masters as set forth in Article IV. That act declared that affidavits submitted by "claimants" were all that was necessary to establish the identity of alleged fugitives, and that no Negro accused of being an escaped slave could testify in his own behalf or summon witnesses. The personal liberty laws passed in free states, insofar as they were designed to prevent free men or women from being carried into slavery, were not in violation of Article IV.

In *Dred Scott*, the Supreme Court held that constitutionally, Negroes were "beings of an inferior order . . . and so far inferior that they had no rights which the white man was bound to respect; and that the negro might justly and lawfully be reduced to slavery for his benefit."[54] Free-soil opinion might have been willing to accept the Court's decision (in *Ableman v. Booth* in 1859) asserting the supremacy of federal law over state laws attempting to nullify the right of slave owners to reclaim fugitive slaves. But it was not willing to accept the enslavement of free men or women as an incidental by-product of the Fugitive Slave Law. To establish the identity of a runaway slave solely on the basis of the testimony of the slave owner, or of witnesses summoned by the slave owner, violated every principle of justice known to Anglo-American jurisprudence and enshrined in the Bill of Rights. That Buchanan, like Southern opinion generally, failed to recognize this can only be attributed to the premise laid down in *Dred Scott*—the premise that being reduced to slavery was a "benefit" to a Negro and that as no harm was done thereby, no legal process was necessary to prevent it. Buchanan's idea of conciliation or compromise was therefore utterly stultified by his assumption that free Negroes, like slaves, had "no rights which the white man was bound to respect."

The second of the three points in Buchanan's proposed "explanatory amendment" reveals still more of his moral bankruptcy. The absolute political center of the intersectional firestorm was the demand for federal protection of the right to hold slaves "in all the common territories throughout their territorial existence." The Democratic Party had split asunder at its Charleston convention in May of 1860, precisely because the majority, who eventually nominated Douglas, would not vote for such protection. The Southerners bitterly resented the characterization of what they demanded as a "slave code," although that is what it was. They insisted that what they asked for was simply neutrality toward the property of the citizens from the different states migrating to the territories. They would not concede that there was anything "peculiar" about slave property that entitled anyone to discriminate against it. And they denied that they were asking for more protection for their property than they were willing to extend to anyone else's. That is what they meant by "equality." Buchanan here is thus endorsing the demands of the Southern rump of the Democratic Party that had been overwhelmingly defeated, first within the party and then at the general election. His idea of restoring "peace and harmony among the States" was to surrender the fruits of electoral victory to the threats of secession and civil war.

In the balance of his message, Buchanan has some eloquent things to say about the Union. He calls it "the grandest temple which has ever been dedicated to human freedom since the world began." How that could be reconciled with perfect moral neutrality toward the phenomenon of human slavery is difficult to understand. Yet he continues: "The slavery question, like everything human, will have its day. I firmly believe it has reached and passed its culminating point. But if, in the midst of the existing excitement, the Union shall perish, the evil may then become irreparable."

For Buchanan, the "slavery question" is simply one of many political questions that excite the passions and disrupt civic friendship. That slavery, unlike any other political question, challenges the principle upon which republican government is founded, the principle upon which the rights of all the citizens of every state is grounded, seems never to have crossed his mind. This in itself conveys to us the magnitude of Lincoln's task. Buchanan, after all, was a highly educated man, prominent in public life for nearly four decades. Although his electoral strength in 1856 had been predominantly Southern, in 1860 he no longer had a political motive for such an uncompromising endorsement of the slaveholding interest. Unlike Chief Justice Taney, whose rabidly proslavery opinion in *Dred Scott* he adopted completely, Buchanan continued to reject secession and was loyal to the Union cause in the ensuing war. His rejection of secession was important, since it meant rejecting one implication of the Calhounian doctrine of sovereignty. Unfortunately, he did not reject another implication of that doctrine, by which the sovereignty of the states endowed slave property with a right in the territories equal to all other forms of property. But even his rejection of secession was negated by his finding of constitutional impotence to prevent it. At this great moment of crisis, when he still held the executive power of the United States, he spoke and acted altogether in the interest of slavery.

∼

Like Buchanan, Jefferson Davis had had an exceptionally distinguished career. As a West Point graduate, he was a contemporary of Robert E. Lee. During the Black Hawk Indian War of 1832, he was a minor officer of the regular army at the same time that Abraham Lincoln was an inconspicuous officer of Illinois volunteers, although they did not meet. He was elected to Congress in 1844 but resigned the following year to serve in the Mexican War, in which he distinguished himself at the battle of Buena Vista. In 1847 Mississippi sent him to the U.S. Senate. In 1851 he resigned from the Senate to run for governor, but lost. In 1853 he became secretary of war in the cabinet of Franklin Pierce. In 1857, at the end of the Pierce administration, he reentered the Senate, where he remained until January 21, 1861, when he received notification of the secession of Mississippi and bade his colleagues farewell. Less than a month later, on February 18, 1861—exactly two weeks before Abraham Lincoln was inaugurated president of the United States—Davis was inaugurated provisional president of the Confederacy. A year later, on Washington's Birthday in 1862, he was inaugurated as its regularly elected president. For a generation, Davis had been a prominent political figure on the national stage. As secretary of war and as U.S. senator, he had been a major actor in the national drama as it drew to its climax. The contrast of his public stature with Lincoln's was almost as great as Buchanan's.

Davis's Farewell Address to the U.S. Senate began: [55]

> I rise, Mr. President, for the purpose of announcing to the Senate that I have satisfactory evidence that the state of Mississippi, by a solemn ordinance of her people in convention assembled, has declared her separation from the United States. Under these circumstances of course my functions are terminated here. . . . It is known to Senators who have served with me here that I have for many years advocated as an essential attribute of state sovereignty, the right of a state to secede from the Union.

Davis explained that he would be bound by the action of his state, even if he disapproved of it. In fact, he said, he advocated and endorsed it. He then contrasted nullification with secession, pointing out that the former was a constitutional process within the Union and designed to preserve it.

> Secession belongs to a different class of remedy. It is to be justified upon the basis that the states are sovereign. There was a time when none denied it. I hope the time may come again when a better comprehension of the theory of our government, and the inalienable rights of the people of the states, will prevent any one from denying that each state is a sovereign, and thus may reclaim the grants which it has made to any agent whomsoever.

It is notable to what extent all sides agreed that, in the regime of the American Founding, practical wisdom depended upon "comprehension of the theory of our government." It was with respect to such theory that President Buchanan had only recently articulated what Madison meant when he called the Constitution "partly federal, partly national." When the people of each state ratified the Constitution, they affirmed certain powers and functions as belonging to the United States and forbade certain powers and functions to the states. The several peoples of the several states, with respect to the powers and functions of the government that was common to them all, formed, therefore, a single people with a single government. They were not a single people with respect to those powers and functions reserved by the Constitution to them alone as the people of their respective states. As citizens of their respective states, they were, with respect to the sphere allotted to them by the Constitution, perfectly independent of the people of other states. In framing or amending their state constitutions, they were entirely free to adopt whatever form of republican government seemed best to them, subject only to those limitations placed equally upon all the states by the Constitution. It followed from this divided sovereignty that the people of a state could no more secede from the Union than the people of a county, or indeed an individual citizen, could secede from a state. That the Union stood in the same relationship to a state as a state to a county was one of Lincoln's contentions, and we can see here how accurately it fits the theory that Buchanan, citing Madison, had endorsed. Davis, on the other hand, inherited Calhoun's theory of undivided state sovereignty, which meant that an individual citizen was bound by his promise to his state but not by his promise to the nation. And this notwithstanding that his promise to the nation entailed his commitment to the supremacy clause in Article VI of the Constitution. Nowhere does Davis confront or even recognize Madison's theory of divided sovereignty.

As we saw when we examined the compact theory in chapter 1, the Madisonian theory of sovereignty is itself a feature or aspect of the theory of natural rights that are in accordance with the "laws of nature and of nature's God" encapsulated in the Declaration of Independence. In his farewell speech to the Senate, Davis offers an interpretation of the Declaration that, in his mind, supports his theory of state sovereignty. We will find it remarkable, not only in how it differs from Madison's and Jefferson's, but also in how it differs from that of his mentor, John C. Calhoun. Davis says:

> It has been a conviction of pressing necessity, it has been a belief that we are to be deprived in the Union of the rights which our fathers bequeathed to us, which has brought Mississippi into her present decision. She has heard proclaimed the theory that all men are created free and equal, and this made the basis of an attack upon her social institutions; and the sacred Declaration of Independence has been invoked to maintain the position of the equality of the races.

The attack upon Mississippi's "social institutions" means that the citizens of that state are threatened with deprivation of "rights which our fathers bequeathed to us." Davis does not specify which rights are so threatened, but it is apparent that he refers to the asserted equal rights of slavery and freedom in the territories. The territorial dispute, however, is only the focus of the generalized moral conflict over slavery. The unanimity underlying a system of majority rule and minority rights in the government of the Union has been disrupted by the difference concerning slavery, and those who differ on this question can no longer remain friends and fellow citizens. Davis presents the question, Who has disrupted the Founding consensus? Is it those who are proslavery, or those who are antislavery, who have violated the unanimous consent that governed the period of the Revolution and the forming of the Constitution?

Davis, like Chief Justice Taney in *Dred Scott* and like many of the Southern legislatures and secession conventions, takes his stand on his interpretation of the Declaration, and especially his understanding of the proposition that later became the thematic center of the Gettysburg Address:

> That Declaration of Independence is to be construed by the circumstances and purposes for which it was made. The communities were declaring their independence; the people of those communities were asserting that no man was born— to use the language of Mr. Jefferson—booted and spurred to ride over the rest of mankind; that men were created equal—meaning the men of the political community; that there was no divine right to rule; that no man inherited the right to govern; that there were no classes by which power and place descended to families, but that all stations were equally within the grasp of each member of the body politic. These were the great principles they announced; these were the purposes for which they made their declaration; these were the ends to which their enunciation was directed.

With the exception of seven interpolated words—"meaning the men of the political community"—the foregoing might been taken from a speech of Abraham Lincoln.

Like Madison and Jefferson in 1825, but unlike the man who was otherwise his mentor, John C. Calhoun, Davis here considers the Declaration as a guide to the republican principles of American government. We have seen in chapter 2 that it was the Declaration's purpose to reverse a millennium and a half (at least) of the divine right of kings. There can be no doubt that the Declaration condemned any idea of an "inherited right to govern" or of "classes by which power and place descended to families." No one doubted that it affirmed the principle "that all stations were equally within the grasp of each member of the body politic." All these hallmarks of republicanism were negations of the British constitution from which the Founding Fathers broke in 1776. The British constitution, whose Parliament had in 1766 declared its lawful right to bind the people of America "in all cases whatsoever," belonged to a quasi-feudal social structure. Its monarchy, if no longer one of divine right, was nonetheless hereditary, and the office of the Crown was not a station within the grasp of anyone outside the royal family. The great estates of the realm were entailed, and the power and place of primogeniture or birth gave a radically unequal influence to the distribution of wealth and honors. The monarchy and aristocracy together constituted a preponderant portion of the governing establishment of Great Britain. British society was rigidly hierarchical, with the royal family at the apex, and with dukes, earls, viscounts, barons, knights, and commoners ranked in order below. Moreover, there was an established church, and religious tests for office.

Although Davis will assert a "sacred duty to transmit unshorn" the "rights we inherited" from "our fathers," it was nonetheless the case that those fathers themselves had not inherited the rights they transmitted. The equal civil and political rights of the republican regime they founded were derived, not from the quasi-feudal British monarchy, but from the natural rights that Davis denounces. It is true that colonial society had begun the process of leveling before the Revolution, but that very process represented a repudiation of traditional British institutions. This is not to say that there were not important elements of American constitutionalism that were inherited from the British constitution. As we saw in our analysis of the *Summary View*, American Whigs before independence identified with British Whigs and respected the British constitution because it had itself incorporated many elements of the rights of the laws of nature. But the features of American republicanism that Davis singles out as the "great principles" of the Founding are those that are distinctive in reflecting the principle of equality and in distinguishing American republicanism from the inequalities in the government and society of Great Britain. Davis wants to preserve the inheritance from "our fathers." But those fathers did not simply preserve the inheritance from their fathers. On the contrary, as Aristotle would say, they chose the good over the ancestral.

There was one institution in the American colonies in 1776 that was more unequal than any that distinguished the more privileged from the less privileged in Great Britain. Indeed, it was more unequal than any in the ancien régimes in which authority descended upon the people from the divine right of kings. That institution was chattel slavery. Because Britons of even the lowest social classes enjoyed a high degree of personal liberty, there was much more social mobility in Britain than the formal distinctions of rank and class would indicate. The vitality of the British constitutional order, what distinguished it from France (and the Continent) before 1789, was the frequency with which the upper classes were recruited from those below. Fortunes created by trade bought themselves rank. Old titles become threadbare were recruited by marriages with new wealth. Although Britain had nothing like the social mobility of white America, neither did it have anything as inflexible in its immobility as American slavery. And as it was the immobility of the classes in France that caused the French Revolution, it was the immobility of slavery that caused the Civil War. Whatever might once have been said in favor of limiting the freedom of slaves newly imported from Africa, on the grounds of their unpreparedness for the responsibilities of a free society, there was no such justification for applying the same limitations to their children, grandchildren, or descendants to the furthest generation. Nor was there any justification for denying freedom to those of proven intelligence, virtue, talent, and ambition. Nothing measures better the distance between the cause of the Union and the cause of the Confederacy than Davis's condemnation to perpetual slavery of all of African descent by the lunatic label of "the degenerate sons of Ham." The airtight cage of fixed status in which slaves were confined generated pressure that became intolerable. The only means by which the South could see a reduction of such pressure was by the expansion of slavery into new lands. But that expansion, while it might have reduced the pressure for emancipation upon the white South, would have only strengthened the hold of slavery upon the slaves themselves and made their cage even tighter.

The problem Davis raised, but did not face, was how he could claim the "great principles" of the American Revolution to be a general equality of rights and privileges within the community, while denying absolutely and completely any claim to such rights by the four million slaves. His presumed answer is to be found in his claim that "all men are created equal" refers only to the equality of the communities asserting independence in 1776.

In a historic speech on his "resolutions concerning the relations of the states" of May 8, 1860, Davis is at some pains to expound the thesis that the meaning of "equality" in the Declaration of Independence refers only to "community independence."

> The government of the United States is a compact between the sovereign members who formed it; and if there be one feature common to all the colonies planted upon the shores of America, it is desire for community independence. It was for this the Puritan, the Huguenot, the Catholic, the Quaker, the Protestant left the land of their nativity, and guided by the shadows thrown by the fires of European persecution, they sought and found the American refuge of civil and religious freedom. Whilst they existed as separate and distinct colonies they were not forbearing towards each other. They oppressed opposite religions. They did not come here with the enlarged idea of no established religion. The Puritans drove out the Quakers; the Church of England men drove out the Catholics. Persecution reigned through the colonies, except, perhaps, that of the Catholic colony of Maryland; but the rule was persecution. Therefore I say the common idea, the only common idea, was community independence—the right of each independent people to do as they pleased in their domestic affairs.[56]

Davis says that the various religious communities from which the thirteen colonies sprang "sought and found the American refuge of civil and religious freedom," and in the next breath he claims that "persecution reigned throughout the colonies." But these colonists could not have sought religious freedom if they themselves continued to practice persecution. If their one idea was "community independence," then such independence must have meant no more than to persecute without being persecuted! There is in such "community independence" not even a suggestion of those principles of equal rights that even Davis, in his Senate farewell speech, said those same communities announced on July 4, 1776.

Davis says that while they were "separate and distinct," the colonies "were not forbearing towards each other." If it was true that as independent colonies they practiced bigotry and oppression, then only in and through union did they discover the meaning of "civil and religious freedom." Civil and religious freedom could not therefore have any necessary connection with "community independence." By Davis's own testimony, "the enlarged idea of no established religion" became a principle of American civil order only as community independence was qualified by community interdependence. Hence "the right of each independent people to do as they pleased in their domestic affairs" could not be an unlimited right. If an independent people engage in religious persecution, how can they form a union with another people of a persuasion that they persecute? Above all, how can any independent people or peoples form republican governments, governments in which there is majority rule and minority rights, if they believe in the persecution of those who differ from them in their religious beliefs? In fact, community independence meant, on Davis's own showing in his Senate farewell speech, (1) no divine right to rule; (2) no inherited right to govern; (3) no classes by which power and place descended to families; and (4) all stations equally within the grasp of each member of the body politic. Are these principles not elements of that "republican form of government" that, under the Constitution, the United States guarantees to each of the states of the Union? Are they not, in fact, inferences from a more fundamental principle, namely, that all men are created equal? Does not the republican guarantee imply a boundary within which the variety of state institutions is limited? And is not such a boundary a limitation upon state sovereignty? How could the Constitution guarantee to each state a republican form of government if a state could secede from the Union in order to adopt a nonrepublican form?

That slavery is a nonrepublican institution is proved by Davis's own four criteria. First, as we have seen, Davis maintains that the right to enslave Negroes is derived from the curse of Ham placed in the mouth of Noah by God. That is certainly an allegation of a divine right to rule. Second, the power of masters to govern slaves was inheritable, as property. Third, the right to govern slaves belonged to white people as a class, without regard to any other qualification. And fourth, no "stations," that is to say, no positions of influence, profit, or honor, were within the grasp of any member of the servile class.

Among the features of Davis's exposition of the Declaration is his citing Jefferson to the effect "that no man was born booted and spurred to ride over the rest of mankind." As a reader of the previous chapter will recognize, this is not an exact quotation, but it is sufficiently so. No metaphor has ever better conveyed the idea that "all men are created equal" refers to mankind as a species and that no man is good enough to govern another man without the other's consent. Davis himself, like Jefferson, applies the metaphor to "mankind" as a species. Davis must have known Jefferson's condemnation of slavery in both the *Summary View* and the *Notes on Virginia*. How then can he pretend that the author of the Declaration was not antislavery? The word "chattel" (as in "chattel slavery") is derived from "cattle" and refers to the subrational order of creation. To call black human beings chattels is to deny that they are part of "mankind." Yet even according to Davis's perverse theology, they shared a common descent from Adam and Noah.

Davis asserts, perfectly gratuitously, and in contradiction of his own premises, that none of the principles he finds in the Declaration of Independence had "reference to the slave." Here is his argument:

> [H]ow happened it that among the items of arraignment made against George III was that he endeavored to do just what the North has been endeavoring of late to do—to stir up insurrection among the slaves? Had the Declaration announced that the negroes were free and equal, how was the Prince to be arraigned for stirring up insurrection among them? . . . When our Constitution was formed, the same idea was rendered more palpable, for there we find provision made for that very class of persons as property; they were not put upon the footing of equality with white men—not even upon that of paupers and convicts; but, so far as representation was concerned, were discriminated against as a lower caste, only to be represented in the numerical proportion of three fifths.[57]

As we saw in a similar charge by Buchanan, the idea that "the North" was trying to stir up insurrection among the slaves was without any real foundation. But we also recall, prominent in the *Summary View*, Jefferson's assertion that "the abolition of domestic slavery" was a "great object of desire" in the colonies; his complaint about the king's preventing colonial attempts to end the slave trade; and his characterization of that trade as an "infamous practice," contrary to "the rights of human nature."[58] Everyone knows that a similar denunciation of the crown and of the slave trade was deleted by the Continental Congress from Jefferson's original draft of the Declaration of Independence. Nevertheless, the principle by which slavery and the slave trade were to be condemned remained in the Declaration. Like religious intolerance, slavery was part of the inheritance of the colonies that was rejected in principle by the Founding. But it was, especially in the Southern colonies, so interwoven with all the institutions of society, and especially with the institution of private property, that it could not be easily abolished. We recall again the wise words of Bourke Cockran, "that it is easier for men to accept a truth, than to regulate their lives by it."[59] But Davis, like Taney in *Dred Scott*, implies that by not abolishing slavery, the Founding Fathers showed that they had no moral objection to it and that they had not therefore included Negroes in their postulate of human equality.

Davis asks how it was that if Negroes were free and equal, King George was denounced in the Declaration for stirring up insurrection among them. The answer, of course, is that freedom and equality are natural rights, not civil rights. According to Jefferson, slavery existed among the Americans largely because of the action of the crown. For the king to have been complicit in the importation of slaves into America and then to have attempted to use them in a war against their masters merited condemnation in its own right. In no way did such condemnation imply a justification of slavery itself. As Jefferson's strictures in the *Notes on Virginia* show, and as Lincoln's statesmanship was to prove, the highest interest of the slaves themselves was always in the vindication of the principles of the Declaration. It was hardly remarkable that a nation of slaveholders, upon declaring independence, did not at once abolish slavery. What was remarkable— perhaps more remarkable than any other event in human history—was that a nation of slaveholders declared that all men are created equal and thereby made the abolition of slavery a moral and political necessity. It was athwart this consummation that Jefferson Davis now took his stand.

Davis also grossly misrepresents the purpose of the Constitution's compromises in regard to slavery. In the Constitution, he says, "we find provision made for that very class of persons as property." Yet those who were slaves are never referred to in the Constitution as anything but "persons," a characterization that is perfectly neutral as to race or sex. That some of these persons were slaves was something arising from state law, not from the Constitution itself.[60] In Article I it is said that representatives shall be apportioned among the several states, according to their respective numbers. In addition to all free persons—including free persons of color—three-fifths of all other persons were to be counted.[61] According to Davis, the three-fifths clause was evidence that the slaves were regarded "as a lower caste." But those who so regarded them did not want them counted as three-fifths! The slave owners wanted the slaves counted as five-fifths, and those in the North who were opposed to them did not want slaves counted at all. The three-fifths proportion was therefore a compromise. It added to the number of representatives from the slave states in Congress and, equally important, it added to their votes in the electoral college. In 1860, the additional votes given to the cause of slavery by the presence of four million slaves in a nation of approximately thirty-one million was not inconsiderable.

The paradox of calling the same human beings persons and property brings the cause of the Civil War into the sharpest focus. A person by definition is a being possessed of a rational will. A chattel by equal definition is a piece of movable property without a rational will. Because a horse or a dog lacks a rational will, its owner is responsible for any damage or injury it may cause. But slaves were held as responsible for their own actions, as were their masters, under the criminal codes of the slave states. The slave owners, in seeking to have the slaves counted as five-fifths, were asserting that they were full human beings. At the same time, by claiming the right to their labor as chattels, they were asserting them to be subhuman. How the slaves could be both was something that Jefferson Davis and his friends never explained.

Perhaps the most devastating testimony against Davis's interpretation of the Declaration of Independence comes, not from any free-soil source, but from John C. Calhoun, the loftiest of all authorities for the Confederate cause. Calhoun was the great discoverer of the pure doctrine of undivided state sovereignty and of the state rights that depended thereon. He was at once the philosopher–king and the Moses of the Tablets of nullification and secession. Yet Calhoun saw the doctrine of equality in the Declaration, not as referring to "community independence," but as referring to human equality in the same sense as Jefferson. He denounced it as the most false and dangerous of errors, but he did not doubt that it meant what it said. The equality of communities of men is certainly implied in the Declaration, but it is derived from the primordial equality of the human beings who agree voluntarily to form those communities.

In a speech on the Oregon Bill in 1848, Calhoun had the following to say about the proposition that all men are created equal:

> We now begin to experience the danger of admitting so great an error to have a place in our declaration of independence. For a long time it lay dormant; but in the process of time it began to germinate, and produce its poisonous fruits. It had strong hold on the mind of Mr. Jefferson, the author of that document, which caused him to take an utterly false view of the subordinate relation of the black to the white race in the South; and to hold, in consequence, that the former, though utterly unqualified to possess liberty, were as fully entitled to both liberty and equality as the latter; and that to deprive them of it was both unjust and immoral.[62]

Nothing could be more straightforward. The Declaration of Independence, said Calhoun, meant that slavery was unjust and immoral and that blacks were as fully entitled to the benefits of liberty and equality as whites. The antislavery movement, for which Davis, like Buchanan, denounced the Northern free states, was in fact the "poisonous fruit" of the Southern slaveholder who composed the

Declaration! Nothing could more sharply contradict Davis's thesis that the equality of the Declaration refers to the equality of "communities" and not of human persons. It also contradicts Davis's claim to stand in the tradition of "our fathers."

Calhoun implies that the doctrine of human equality was somehow a personal aberration of Thomas Jefferson. Yet Jefferson himself, as we have seen, regarded the Declaration as an expression of "the American mind." Nor is there a shred of historical evidence that anyone devoted to the patriot cause, either in or outside the Continental Congress, regarded it differently. Yet Davis continued to invoke the Declaration by identifying the right of secession with the right to be governed only with one's own consent. He did so notwithstanding its complete inconsistency with slavery, and especially with the alleged biblical authority for condemning "the degenerate sons of Ham." He did so notwithstanding the fact that consent in the Declaration is the reciprocal of equality, which is to say that consent is a requirement for the just powers of government only because all men are created equal. Davis himself saw this when he cited the Jeffersonian metaphor that horses, but not men, are born to have saddles on their backs.

Jefferson's metaphor was consistent only with the understanding of equality as applying to all individuals within the human species and not merely to communities of individuals. Davis thus had no ground whatever to identify the right of secession with the principles of the Revolution, as he did in this conclusion of his Senate farewell speech:

> Then, Senators, we recur to the compact which binds us together; we recur to the principles upon which our government was founded; and when you deny them, and when you deny to us the right to withdraw from a government which, thus perverted, threatens to be destructive of our rights, we but tread in the path of our fathers when we proclaim our independence, and take the hazard. This is done not in hostility to others . . . but from the high and solemn motive of defending and protecting the rights which we inherited, and which it is our solemn duty to transmit unshorn to our children.

The question of whether the election of Abraham Lincoln threatened in any way the rights that Davis, or any other American citizen, inherited from his "fathers," will become central to Lincoln's first inaugural address.

Davis wanted to appear as the guardian of the same ancestral tradition that his mentor Calhoun had repudiated. In order to present himself as the pure embodiment of his Revolutionary forebears, Davis invented a synonym for "created equal"—"community independence"—that was entirely spurious.

≈

An even more powerful witness against Davis, as well as against Calhoun's view of Jefferson as an aberration, is Alexander Stephens. Stephens, a former representative from Georgia, was a fellow Whig with Lincoln in Congress from 1847 to 1849. Like Lincoln, he had opposed the war with Mexico and did not want to see the slavery question reopened by the expansion of federal territory. Also like Lincoln, he supported the Compromise of 1850. But he parted company with Lincoln in supporting the Kansas–Nebraska Act, which repealed the Missouri Compromise. Stephens later denounced Stephen Douglas as a turncoat, after the latter's break with Buchanan over "popular sovereignty" in Kansas. From the time of the Lecompton fight over Kansas, he was firmly in the ranks of the "solid South" in the defense of slavery.

Stephens also, however, made the most powerful of all Southern speeches against secession, on the floor of the State Convention of Georgia in 1861. In this speech, he listed the many advantages the South had enjoyed in the Union, showing that the numbers of federal offices held by Southerners were far out of proportion to the number and size of the Southern states. Typical of the data he brought to bear is the following:

> While three-fourths of the business which demands diplomatic agents abroad is clearly from the free states, from their greater commercial interest, yet we have had the principal embassies so as to secure the world markets for our cotton, tobacco, and sugar on the best possible terms. We have had a vast majority of the higher offices of both army and navy, while a larger proportion of the soldiers and sailors were drawn from the North. Equally so of clerks, auditors and comptrollers filling the executive department, the records show for the last fifty years that of the three thousand thus employed, we have had more than two-thirds of the same, while we have had but one-third of the white population of the Republic.

And again:

> We have had sixty years of Southern presidents to their twenty-four, thus controlling the executive department. So of the judges of the Supreme Court, we have had eighteen from the South, and but eleven from the North; although nearly four-fifths of the judicial business has arisen from the free states, yet a majority of the Court has always been from the South.

In showing how privileged the position of the South had been in the years since the adoption of the Constitution, Stephens also reminds his hearers that Lincoln's election represents a probable end of that privileged position. In doing so, he reminds us how much the slaveholding South resembled the French aristocracy on the eve of the Revolution. But to repeat, Stephens in this speech is uncompromising in denouncing the folly of secession: "What reason can you give to the nations of the earth to justify it? . . . What right has the North assailed? What interest of the South has been invaded? What justice has been denied? And what claim founded in justice and right has been withheld?" Stephens here eloquently anticipates Lincoln's first inaugural on the irrationality of secession. And he is unequivocal that secession means war, and that war would bring devastation for which there would be no compensation. In such a war, moreover, he warns that "*the vindictive decree of a universal emancipation...may reasonably be expected.*" No one could have been more prescient.[63]

But despite his opposition to secession, Stephens was a disciple of Calhoun's theory of sovereignty, according to which he was bound by Georgia's decision to leave the Union when the vote in the convention went against him. Because he had been such a strong unionist, and because it was thought he would help secure the loyalty of others who had been of his persuasion, he was chosen vice president of the Confederacy at the same time that Davis was chosen president.

Stephens's greatest claim to fame is his two-volume masterpiece, *A Constitutional View of the Late War between the States*, published between 1868 and 1870. It is certainly the best of all the apologies for the Confederacy. One can say of it that it is the book that John C. Calhoun might have written. It is, like Calhoun's own works, a brilliant exhibition of flawless deductive reasoning from unexamined premises. Of those premises, it is Calhoun's conception of undivided sovereignty, and of state rights grounded upon such sovereignty, that is foremost. Pursuing the theme of Calhoun's *Disquisition on Government*, Stephens in retrospect saw the Civil War, which he of course called the War between the States, as an attempt to preserve constitutional government from the tyranny of the majority. Slavery as such is hardly noticed. In this, Stephens's *Constitutional View* was in remarkable agreement with the pro-Confederate position taken by Lord Acton in an essay apparently written early in 1861.[64] Acton was one of the most celebrated of nineteenth-century liberals, and yet he saw the Civil War entirely through the eyes of Calhoun. Slavery he considered only as an excuse for the North to impose its tyranny upon the South. That a European liberal of Acton's stature should take such a view of the war tells us a great deal of the difficulty Lincoln faced in gaining the goodwill of those abroad—even those dedicated in their own minds to the cause of freedom.

Stephens, after the war, would pick up the argument where Acton had left it. For this reason it is all the more important to see Stephens's defense of the Confederacy in a speech he delivered in Savannah, Georgia, two months after his speech at the Georgia convention but before the war had begun. Nothing is said in this speech of state rights, or of the tyranny of the majority, or of the South as a permanent minority within the "old Union." The distinction of the Confederacy is said to consist solely and exclusively in its foundation in slavery.

This speech of Stephens, which we will quote at some length, was delivered on March 21, 1861. The time deserves particular notice. Stephens and Davis had been inaugurated on February 18 and Lincoln on March 4. The firing on Fort Sumter was twenty-two days into the future. It was a time of tremendous suspense—a time when, in Shakespeare's words, the genius and the mortal instruments of the nation were still in council. President Buchanan had denounced secession but had also said that there was no power under the Constitution to coerce the Southern states. Lincoln had echoed Buchanan on secession but had as yet taken no decisive action to prove where he stood on the question of coercion. Stephens is silent on his previous opposition to secession. Whatever his inner doubts or trepidations, he speaks of the Confederacy as an accomplished fact, a government destined to endure. Now if ever was the moment to tell the world at large the strongest reason why it should endure. In a sense, this was the high-water mark of the Confederacy, and Stephens's speech, more than any other, is the Gettysburg Address of the Confederate South.

This address has come down to us as the Cornerstone speech. Like Lincoln's House Divided speech, it is known by the words of the Bible it evokes: "The stone which the builders rejected has become the head of the corner" (Psalm 118:22). In the New Testament, the "cornerstone" is Jesus himself.[65] Stephens's pronouncement that slavery is the cornerstone of the Confederacy takes on its full meaning only in the light of this comparison. The Cornerstone speech has received only cursory notice in most of the literature on the Civil War. It is seldom, if ever, found in documentary collections. Yet no utterance of the time reveals more fully the inner truth about the impending conflict.

The new [Confederate] Constitution has put at rest forever all agitating questions relating to our peculiar institution—African slavery as it exists among us—the proper status of the negro in our form of civilization. This was the immediate cause of the late rupture and present revolution. Jefferson, in his forecast, had anticipated this as the "rock upon which the old Union would split." He was right. What was conjecture with him is now a realized fact. But whether he fully comprehended the great truth upon which that rock stood and stands, may be doubted. The prevailing ideas entertained by him and by most of the leading statesmen of the time of the formation of the old constitution, were that the enslavement of the African was in violation of the laws of nature: that it was wrong in principle, socially, morally, and politically. It was an evil they knew not well how to deal with, but the general opinion of the men of that day was, that somehow or other, in the order of Providence, the institution would be evanescent and pass away. This idea, though not incorporated in the Constitution, was the prevailing idea at the time. The Constitution, it is true, secured every essential guarantee to the institution while it should last, and hence no argument can be justly used against the constitutional guarantees thus secured, because of the common sentiment of the day. Those ideas, however, were fundamentally wrong. They rested upon the assumption of the equality of the races. This was an error. It was a sandy foundation, and the idea of a government built upon it; when the "storm came and the wind blew, it fell."[66]

Unlike Calhoun, Stephens does not single out Jefferson alone for holding the opinion that slavery is wrong. On the contrary, Jefferson's ideas were (as Lincoln maintained) the "prevailing ideas [of] . . . most of the leading statesmen" of the founding. This flatly contradicts nearly every public defense of secession as motivated by the desire to abide by the "compact" embodied in the "old Constitution." More profoundly, it contradicts the crucial assumption underlying Taney's opinion in *Dred Scott*, the assumption that "at the time of the Declaration of Independence, and when the Constitution of the United States was framed and adopted . . . [Negroes were] regarded as beings of an inferior order . . . and so far inferior that they had no rights which the white man was bound to respect." It was this false historical assumption that enabled Taney to say that no black person, whether free or slave, could be a citizen of the United States. It was this same assumption that determined Taney's judgment that there was no constitutional basis for distinguishing slave property from other kinds of property, and thus that slave property was entitled to the same protection in federal territories as other kinds of property—that slavery, in effect, followed the flag. In 1860, the South had consolidated politically under the banner of this interpretation of the "old Constitution." They expended boundless moral indignation against the Republicans, and even Douglas Democrats, who dared to question the literal identification of Taney's opinion with the Constitution itself. That Lincoln and the Republican Party intended to deprive them of their constitutional right to extend slavery was the driving force behind secession. Yet according to Stephens, the assumption underlying all this, upon which Davis (following Taney) relied, was absolutely false.

Stephens says that among the prevailing ideas of the men of the time of the formation of the "old Constitution" was the idea that "in the order of Providence, the institution [of slavery] would be evanescent and pass away." Nothing that Lincoln had said before his election had enraged the South more, or done more to move them towards secession, than his insistence in the House Divided speech upon a policy directed toward the "ultimate extinction" of slavery. Yet throughout the Lincoln–Douglas debates and in the Cooper Institute speech, Lincoln repeatedly asserted, against Douglas no less than against the proslavery South, that the Founding was predicated upon the expectation that slavery was morally wrong and would eventually disappear. In the House Divided speech itself, Lincoln was

217

careful to say that he *expected* the house to cease being divided and that he *expect-ed* slavery to disappear. He stated repeatedly that he would do nothing against slavery in the states where it existed by law. Stephens, in saying that the Founding Fathers believed that "in the order of Providence, the institution [of slavery] would be evanescent and pass away," accurately captures both the letter and the spirit of Lincoln's speeches. Above all, Stephens vindicated Lincoln's claim that his policy intended no more than to restore the policy of the Founding Fathers. Had Lincoln himself written these passages in the Cornerstone speech, they could not have gone further in justifying him.

Stephens also said, as did Lincoln, that the Constitution secured to slavery "every essential guarantee . . . while it should last." Again, the last phrase empha-sizes Stephens's (and Lincoln's) belief that the framers of the Constitution regard-ed slavery as a transient phenomenon. In granting security to slave property, the framers (according to Stephens) saw no inconsistency with their fundamental conviction that slavery was an evil and that it was destined to ultimate extinction. But although evil, it was a necessary evil within the framework of their nation-building task. And there was, Stephens says, nothing in these guarantees of slave property inconsistent with "the common sentiment of the day," that is to say, with antislavery sentiment. Here we touch the very nerve of Davis's (and Taney's) belief that the guarantees granted to slavery in the Constitution meant that the framers could not have believed slavery morally wrong.

In the second of his "Relations of States Resolutions" of May 8, 1860, Davis set forth the following:

> That negro slavery, as it exists in fifteen states of this Union, composes an impor-tant portion of their domestic institutions, inherited from their ancestors, and existing at the adoption of the Constitution, by which it is recognized as consti-tuting an important element in the apportionment of powers among the states; and that no change of opinion or feeling on the part of the non-slaveholding states of the union, in relation to this institution, can justify them, or their citi-zens, in open or covert attacks thereon, with a view to its overthrow; and that all such attacks are in manifest violation of the mutual and solemn pledge to pro-tect and defend each other.[67]

Central is the assertion that "no change of opinion or feeling on the part of the non-slaveholding states" can justify attacks on the institution of slavery. Here Davis is undoubtedly echoing Taney in Dred Scott: "No one, we presume, sup-poses that any change in public opinion or feeling, in relation to this unfortunate race . . . should induce the court to give to the words of the Constitution a more liberal construction in their favor than they were intended to bear when the instrument was framed and adopted."[68] No one, North or South, was contending against the thesis that courts ought to interpret the Constitution, insofar as possible, according to the meaning of its words in the minds of those who framed and ratified it. The conflict was over that meaning. Taney assumed that the Declaration of Independence was an authentic witness of the framers' beliefs. And he confessed that, had the Declaration and the Constitution been contemporary documents—that is to say, contemporary in 1857—then "all men are created equal" would have included the Negro. But he denied that the Signers of the Declaration in 1776 had ever contemplated that Negroes were among the "men" comprehended by "all men are created equal." This is what Davis also maintained by insisting that equality referred only to "communities" and not to human beings as such.[69] Taney wrote: "It is difficult at this day to realize the state of public opinion in relation to that unfortunate race, which prevailed in the civilized and enlightened portions of the world."[70] He attempted to maintain this thesis by evidence that, at every point, failed to do so.[71] Lincoln, in his speech on Dred Scott, refuted Taney, concluding that "It is grossly incorrect to say or assume, that the public estimate of the negro is more favorable now than it was at the origin of the government."[72]

One piece of evidence Lincoln did not use in his refutation of Taney's claim that opinion in 1857 was more favorable toward the humanity of Negroes than opinion at the Founding relates to a Maryland trial in 1818 of a Methodist minister named Jacob Gruber.[73] Gruber had spoken at a camp meeting at Hagerstown on "the national sin."

> About twenty-six hundred white people were in the audience and over four hundred negroes were on the outskirts of the crowd. The bold evangelist attacked slavery as being inconsistent with the Declaration of Independence and criticized the slave trade as inhuman and cruel. Consequently, he was indicted by the grand jury for attempting to incite slaves to rebellion. So incensed were the people of Hagerstown that the counsel for the defense . . . secured the removal of the case to Frederick.

The Reverend Mr. Gruber's sermon was precisely the kind of inflammatory speech that President Buchanan (and Jefferson Davis) had denounced as responsible for the sectional crisis. It was the kind of speech that the proslavery South denounced as a betrayal of the constitutional compact and used to justify secession. Here is the successful speech to the jury by Gruber's counsel, calling for his acquittal:

> Any man has a right to publish his opinions on that subject [slavery] whenever he pleases. It is a subject of national concern, and may at all times be freely discussed. Mr. Gruber did quote the language of our great act of national independence, and insisted on the principles contained in that venerated instrument. He

did rebuke those masters, who, in the exercise of power, are deaf to the calls of humanity; and he warned them of the evils they might bring upon themselves. He did speak with abhorrence of those reptiles, who live by trading in human flesh, and enrich themselves by tearing the husband from the wife—the infant from the bosom of the mother: and this I am instructed was the head and front of his offending. Shall I content myself with saying he had a right to say this? That there is no law to punish him? So far is he from being the object of punishment in any form of proceeding, that we are prepared to maintain the same principles, and to use, if necessary, the same language here in the temple of justice, and in the presence of those who are the ministers of the law. A hard necessity, indeed, compels us to endure the evil of slavery for a time. It was imposed upon us by another nation, while we were yet in a state of colonial vassalage. It cannot be easily or suddenly removed. Yet while it continues it is a blot on our national character, and every real lover of freedom confidently hopes that it will be effectually, though it must be gradually, wiped away; and earnestly looks for the means, by which this necessary object may best be attained. And until it shall be accomplished: until the time shall come when we can point without a blush, to the language of the Declaration of Independence, every friend of humanity will seek to lighten the galling chain of slavery, and better, to the utmost of his power, the wretched condition of the slave.

Such was Mr. Gruber's object in that part of his sermon, of which I am now speaking. Those who have complained of him, and reproached him, will not find it easy to answer him: unless complaints, reproaches and persecution shall be considered an answer.[74]

If Gruber's trial had been in Illinois in 1858, instead of Maryland in 1818, one might have guessed that his attorney had been Abraham Lincoln. There is not a word in this defense that is not fully consistent, nay that is not identical with Lincoln's arguments of the 1850s. Even the rhythm and phrasing of the speech are Lincolnian. Nor is this an attorney acting merely in the interests of his client. He says that he is willing himself to maintain in court the same principles in the same language that Gruber had used. This is the purest confirmation of Alexander Stephens's characterization of the antislavery convictions of the Founding.

One of the charges against the legitimacy of Lincoln's election in 1860 was that the Republican Party was a sectional party. Like Lincoln, Gruber's attorney says that the subject of slavery is national and that those at fault are those who would limit, not those who would promote, its discussion. Second, he assumes without question that the principles of the Declaration of Independence apply to all mankind, to the slaves no less than to their masters. Third, he says, as Lincoln (following Jefferson) would also say, that slavery "was imposed upon us by another nation." It was not an institution freely chosen by a free people but an evil deeply·entrenched, and one that "cannot be easily or suddenly removed." From this perspective, which is also that of Lincoln and Alexander Stephens, the guarantees of slavery in the Constitution are in no way to be construed as representing moral approval. This is in flat contradiction to the doctrine of *Dred Scott*, by which constitutional morality demanded recognition of slave property as being as deserving of protection as any other kind of property. This doctrine of the equality of property as defined by positive law, as opposed to the equality of man as defined by natural law, became the heart of the justification of secession. Finally, Gruber's attorney maintained, as did Lincoln and Stephens, that the policy implicit in the Declaration, as well as in the framing and ratifying of the Constitution, was one that looked to the passing away or the ultimate extinction of slavery. Only when this "blot on our national character" is removed will we be able, he says, to "point without a blush to the language held in the Declaration of Independence." Now the reader will be interested to learn the identity of Gruber's attorney, the author of these noble and just sentiments, these Jeffersonian and Lincolnian sentiments, so eloquently and even beautifully expressed. His name was Roger Taney.[75]

How can we account for this *peripeteia*, this turning around, from absolutely antislavery to absolutely proslavery, in the soul of the chief justice? Such changes are not uncommon over a period of nearly forty years. What is astounding, however, is that Taney could, in the face of his own earlier opinion, characterize the change that had come over the country as the direct opposite of what it actually had been. We would not assail the chief justice merely for changing his opinion. A similar change had come over John C. Calhoun, who began his political career both as a nationalist and as a votary of the doctrine of natural rights. As a defender of his version of state rights, Calhoun would later pour all his scorn and contempt upon natural rights. But Taney, in his *Dred Scott* opinion, did not denounce the natural rights philosophy. On the contrary, by saying that it was difficult in 1857 to realize the state of opinion concerning that "unfortunate race" at the time of the ratification of the Constitution, he implied that contemporary opinion, including his own, was favorable to the Negro's humanity but that he was constrained by his obligation to the intentions of those who framed and ratified the Constitution to interpret it as they would have done. This implication that Taney did not, in the abstract, think differently of slavery than he had in 1818 has not been sufficiently noted. The question remains, however, if Taney was not as proslavery as his opinion suggests, why did he go to such lengths in falsely representing the opinions of the framers and ratifiers? It is clear from his speech on behalf of Jacob Gruber that the doctrine he proclaimed in 1818 was what he then believed was the doctrine of the Founding Fathers. There is no more powerful witness against the Taney of 1857 than the Taney of 1818.[76]

Returning now to the Cornerstone speech, we find that Confederate vice president Alexander Stephens will not only annihilate the defense of Confederate independence put forth by Confederate president Jefferson Davis, but he will also put forth a defense diametrically different:

Our new government is founded upon exactly the opposite idea [to the idea of equality in the Declaration]; its foundations are laid, its corner stone rests upon the great truth that the negro is not equal to the white man. That slavery—subordination to the superior race, is his natural and normal condition. This, our new Government, is the first, in the history of the world, based upon this great physical and moral truth. This truth has been slow in the process of its development, like all other truths in the various departments of science. It has been so, even amongst us. Many who hear me, perhaps, can recollect well, that this truth was not generally admitted, even within their day. The errors of the past generation still clung to many as late as twenty years ago. Those at the North who still cling to these errors, with a zeal above knowledge, we justly denominate fanatics.[77]

Stephens again contradicts Taney in *Dred Scott*. That the Confederacy is founded upon "exactly the opposite idea," that idea being racial inequality, means that the "old Constitution" of "the fathers" was founded upon the equality of the races. "Our new government" is new in a double sense: It is new in its existence and new in its principles. So far is it from having its roots in ancestral wisdom that it rests upon that species of human knowledge, modern science, whose relentless advance renders obsolete if not foolish everything that it leaves behind. "The errors of the past generation," the belief in human equality foremost among them, "still clung to many as late as twenty years ago." "Our fathers," who framed and ratified the Constitution of 1787, must therefore have dwelt in darkness. In a memorable passage in his "Circular to the States" of 1783, George Washington proclaimed that "The foundation of our empire was not laid in the gloomy age of ignorance and superstition, but at an epoch when the rights of mankind were better understood and more clearly defined than at any former period."[78] According to the new enlightenment proclaimed by Stephens, Washington's supposed enlightenment, reflected in the Declaration of Independence, was itself an "age of ignorance and superstition." There can be no merit, then, in Davis's justification of Confederate independence as treading in the path of Washington.

Stephens continues to expound the new science of race, and its role in defining the Confederate Constitution.

In the conflict thus far, success has been on our side, complete throughout the length and breadth of the Confederate States. It is upon this, as I have stated, our actual fabric is firmly planted; and I cannot permit myself to doubt the ultimate success of a full recognition of this principle throughout the civilized and enlightened world. As I have stated, the truth of this principle may be slow in development, as all truths are, and ever have been, in the various branches of science. It was so with the principles announced by Galileo—it was so with Adam Smith and his principles of political economy—it was so with Harvey and his theory of the circulation of the blood. It is stated that not a single one of the medical profession, living at the time of the announcement of the truths made by him, admitted them. Now they are universally acknowledged. May we not therefore look with confidence to the ultimate universal acknowledgment of the truths upon which our system rests? It is the first government ever instituted upon principles of strict conformity to Nature and the ordination of Providence, in furnishing the materials of human society. Many governments have been founded upon the principles of certain classes; but the classes thus enslaved, were of the same race, and in violation of the laws of nature. Our system contains no such violation of nature's laws. The negro, by nature, or by the curse against Canaan, is fitted for that condition which he occupies in our system. The architect, in the construction of buildings, lays the foundation with the proper materials, [first] the granite, then comes the brick or the marble. The substratum of our society is made of the material fitted by nature for it, and by experience we know that it is best, not only for the superior, but for the inferior race that it should be so. It is indeed in conformity with the ordinance of the Creator. It is not for us to inquire into the wisdom of His ordinances, or to question them. For His own purposes He has made one race to differ from another, as He has made "one star to differ from another star in glory." The great objects of humanity are best attained when conformed to His laws and decrees, in the formation of governments, as well as in all things else. Our Confederacy is founded upon principles in strict conformity with these laws. This stone which was first rejected by the first builders "is become the chief stone in the corner" in our new edifice. The progress of disintegration in the old Union may be expected to go on with almost absolute certainty. We are now the nucleus of a growing power, which, if we are true to ourselves, our destiny, and high mission, will become the controlling power on this continent. To what extent accessions will go on in the process of time, or where it will end, the future will determine.[79]

This remarkable address conveys, more than any other contemporary document, not only the soul of the Confederacy but also of that Jim Crow South that arose from the ashes of the Confederacy. From the end of Reconstruction until after World War II, the idea of racial inequality gripped the territory of the former Confederacy—and not only of the former Confederacy—more profoundly than it had done under slavery. Nor is its influence by any means at an end. Stephens's prophecy of the Confederacy's future resembles nothing so much as Hitler's prophecies of the Thousand-Year Reich. Nor are their theories very different. Stephens, unlike Hitler, spoke only of one particular race as inferior. But the principle of racial domination, once established, can easily be extended to fit the convenience of the self-anointed master race or class, whoever it may be.

In this last selection from the Cornerstone speech, Stephens expresses the belief that success has been completely on the side of the Confederacy. This was some weeks before Fort Sumter, and before the depth of the differences between Lincoln and Buchanan had yet been revealed. But Stephens's optimism rested not on how Lincoln and the old Union would respond in the immediate crisis but upon the conviction that the government of the Confederacy was built "upon principles of strict conformity to Nature and the ordination of Providence." Thus, he thinks, it must grow ever stronger, while the old Union will disintegrate because it had been built upon the denial of those principles.

Stephens compares the great scientific discovery in regard to the Negro to the discoveries of Galileo, Adam Smith, and Harvey. He does not name the discoverer of Negro inferiority, nor does he even hint at what evidence had supported this great discovery. One can only surmise that Darwin's *Origin of Species*, published in 1859, may have been on his mind. Yet there is nothing in that work bearing directly upon the question of Negro equality.[80] It is noteworthy that Stephens groups Adam Smith's work, which is social science, with the other two, which belong to natural science. As we shall see, John C. Calhoun, in his *Disquisition on Government*, claimed to be pushing back the frontiers of political science upon the model of physical science, as represented by Galileo. Stephens uses Harvey, the discoverer of the circulation of the blood, a biologist rather than a physicist, for his main example. But Harvey's discovery had no bearing upon any political question dividing a whole country. The indiscriminate grouping of physics, biology, and economics reveals the mid-nineteenth-century faith in science in its most comprehensive and naive form. Lest we be unfair to Stephens, however, we remind the reader that Carl Becker, the epitome of twentieth-century academic sophistication, unhesitatingly credited social Darwinism with embodying the unifying principle of all the sciences, whether nonhuman or human.

Although Stephens's main argument is grounded squarely on the alleged authority of science, he refers in passing to the same biblical text upon which Davis built his justification of slavery: "The negro, by nature, or by the curse of Canaan, is fitted for that condition which he occupies in our system." It is an interesting inference from Stephens's mode of reasoning that it apparently required a discovery of science to reveal the truth within the Bible. After all, the generation of the Founding Fathers, who certainly knew the story of Noah and his sons, nonetheless believed in the equality of the races. But whether we look to the president or the vice president of the Confederate States of America, or whether we look to their appeals to the authority of the Bible or of science, or to some peculiar combination of the two, for the justification of Negro slavery, we can find nothing more than what Lincoln found in the ruminations of Dr. Ross: "Non-sense! Wolves devouring lambs, not because it is good for their own greedy maws, but because it is good for the lambs!!!"

~

In chapter 1, we saw in Jefferson's *Summary View* that the foundation of the rights of Britons in Great Britain, no less than of the king's subjects in British America, were the natural rights of man. But Jefferson Davis rejected natural rights as having any bearing upon constitutional rights. Here is one of his strictures on the subject:

> I do not propose to argue questions of natural rights and inherent powers; I plant my reliance upon the Constitution which you have all sworn to support. . . . When the tempter entered the garden of Eden and induced our common mother to offend against the law which God had given her through Adam, he was the first teacher of that "higher law" which sets the will of the individual above the solemn rule which he is bound, as a part of every community, to observe.[81]

We pause to observe that by this reasoning, positive law is the higher law. Here is the essence of the historical school, as characterized in chapter 2. If the positive law is the higher law, then whatever inequalities are found in that positive law, including slavery, contain obligations against which no individual has a right to appeal. This, of course, contradicts what Davis said in his Senate farewell speech about the equality proclaimed in the Declaration for the "communities" by whom it was issued. Although Davis opposed natural rights and natural law when they were invoked on behalf of the Negro, he did not hesitate to invoke them himself for his own purposes.

The following remarks are excerpted from Davis's comments on a bill for federal funding of schools in the District of Columbia. He opposed the bill in part because black children might attend:

> I do not choose to argue with anyone who thinks it proper to assert the equality of the negro and the white man. The man who makes the assertion may prove to me his equality with the negro. He proves to me no more; and I accept his argument only for so much. . . .
>
> In this District of Columbia you have but to go to the jail and find there . . . the result of relieving the negro from that control which keeps him in his own healthy and useful condition. It is idle to assume that it is the want of education; it is the natural inferiority of the race. . . . Why, then, this attempt in the District of Columbia to overturn the laws of nature, as declared by all the knowledge which we possess, revealed and historical?[82]

225

Irony aside, if one of Davis's white fellow senators can prove to him "his [the white fellow senator's] equality with the negro," then Davis cannot say that he accepts his argument "only for so much." Proofs of the allegedly upward equality of the Negro with the white man or of the allegedly downward equality of the white man with the Negro are equally proofs of equality. Only one example is needed. Any single dog or any single horse proves the inequality of their species with the human species. It is self-evident that there is no such difference between or among human beings.

Here Davis does not hesitate to decry an alleged attempt "to overturn the laws of nature." His identification of the positive law with the natural law extends only to the positive law that accords with his preconceptions. According to Davis it did not require a Galileo or a Harvey (or a Darwin) to discover the natural inferiority of the Negro. All that was necessary was a visit to the District of Columbia jail! One wonders why such a simple experiment had been beyond the powers of the Founding Fathers.

That the differences between human beings, as distinct from the differences between species, are natural and not cultural cannot be proved by any such examples. Jefferson noted that those who were themselves property, and who were denied all the advantages of acquiring or possessing property, could hardly be expected to respect the laws regarding property.[83] One also wonders what Davis thought of Moses, who killed an Egyptian overseer who was beating a slave.

≈

Another episode from the same Senate debate casts further light upon the differences over slavery that gripped the nation.

> Mr. Wilson [Senator from Massachusetts]. The natural equality of all men I believe in, as far as rights are concerned. So far as mental or physical equality is concerned, I believe the African race inferior to the white race.
>
> Mr. Davis. "Natural equality" would imply that God had created them equal, and had left them equal, down to the present time. Is that what the Senator means?
>
> Mr. Wilson. I mean this, Mr. President; I believe in the equality of rights of all mankind. I do not believe in the equality of the African race with the white race, mentally or physically, and I do not think morally. I do not believe in the equality of the Indian race with us; but upon the question simply of equality of rights, I believe in the equality of all men of every race, blood, and kindred.
>
> Mr. Davis. When the Senator says "equality of rights" does he mean political and social rights—political and social equality?—because what "rights" mean is a thing to be determined afterwards. All men have a right to just so much as belongs to them, so much as has been conceded to them by the Creator or by the

political institutions of the country. I wish to know whether, when he denies the equality between the races, or objects to the argument which imputes the theory of equality of the races, he means political and social equality?

Mr. Wilson. I believe that every human being has the right to his life and to his liberty, and to act in this world so as to secure his own happiness. I believe, in a word, in the Declaration of Independence; but I do not, as I have said, believe in the mental or moral or physical equality of some of the races, as against this white race of ours.

Mr. Davis. Then the Senator believes and he does not believe, and he changes his position so rapidly . . . that it is impossible to tell what he does believe. He believes in the Declaration of Independence, and intimates that he means by that all men are equal; but he immediately announces that there is a difference between the two races.

Mr. Wilson. Well, Mr. President, I believe there are a great many men in the world of the white race inferior to the Senator from Mississippi, and I suppose there are quite a number superior to him; but I believe that he and the inferior man and the superior have equal natural rights.

Mr. Davis. I suppose the Senator knows what he means, I take it for granted he does; but it is impossible to get it from his language.[84]

This remarkable exchange reminds us of Churchill's observation, with respect to some of the difficulties arising during the conferences of the Anglo-American Joint Chiefs during World War II, that the British and Americans were two great nations divided by a common language! Here the Declaration of Independence meant two very different things to the two senators, one from New England and the other from the Deep South. And because they did not understand the words of the Declaration in the same way, neither understood what the other was saying.

In the course of the Lincoln–Douglas debates, Lincoln repeatedly denied that he had any intention to bring about the political or social equality of the Negro and the white man. He made this denial because Douglas was pressing hard to identify Lincoln with a racial egalitarianism that he knew was anathema to public opinion in Illinois in 1858. Lincoln was demanding the same kind of recognition of the Negro's rights as Senator Henry Wilson in the foregoing dialogue. To have asked for more would not have been to gain more but rather to lose everything. In 1858 the opinion was almost universal, in antislavery no less than in proslavery circles, that the Negro was inferior to the white man in moral and intellectual faculties. In fact, Lincoln never went so far as Wilson in embracing this common view. Lincoln's characteristic expression was, "Certainly the negro is not our equal in color—perhaps not in many other respects." The only inequality that was "certain," according to Lincoln, was color. Only the prejudices of his audiences would find a judgment of Negro inferiority in such an assertion. Yet Lincoln would continue, in a phrase that, with minor variations, he repeated endlessly: "still, in the right to put into his mouth the bread that his own hands have earned, he is the equal of every other man, white or black." The contrast between the ambiguity of what Lincoln says about Negro inequality and the unambiguousness of what be says about Negro equality is striking.

Senator Wilson was arguing from premises very close to Lincoln's, but without the same felicity. He needed to distinguish more clearly than he did the difference between natural rights, the unalienable rights with which we are endowed by our Creator, and political rights, such as voting and serving on juries, which depend upon the positive laws of civil society. Davis said that "all men have a right to just so much as belongs to them," but he did not think that the laws, either of God or man, require that black men have a right to anything except what white men decide to allow them. The allegedly just powers of the black man's government are not derived from the black man's consent. And Davis can see no connection whatever between this judgment and that of the British Parliament when it declared that it had the right to bind the colonies "in all cases whatsoever."

It has often been asked how Lincoln thought the black man could ever put into his mouth the bread that his own hand had earned if he had no share in making the laws regarding the acquisition and possession of property. The answer, of course, is that one must go from slavery to freedom before one can go from freedom to citizenship—which is as much as to say that there had to be a Thirteenth Amendment before there could be a Fourteenth Amendment. Only after one had succeeded in gaining recognition of the black man's natural rights could a discussion of his civil or political rights even begin. Such a beginning, as we shall see, only came in the very last months of Lincoln's life. But Lincoln's life is what made that beginning—and everything good that has come after that beginning—possible.

In 1860 Senator Wilson, like Lincoln, could not ask for recognition of more than the black man's natural rights. But he showed in dramatic fashion that his argument, like Lincoln's, applied ultimately to all rights, civil and political no less than natural. He said he supposed that there were many of the white race who were inferior to Senator Davis, as well as many who were superior. Yet he thought that all these had the same natural rights. He did not say, although nothing in reason forbade him to say it, that all these also were entitled to the same civil and political rights. Why then should black men who were the senator's inferiors, not to mention those who were his superiors, not also have the same civil and political rights? The same questions, incidentally, might have been asked concerning women. But the time had not yet come for that.

That one man can run faster than another is no reason to prevent the latter from entering the race. Indeed, until the race is run, how do we know who can run faster?[85] In comparing the known inequalities among whites to the alleged inequalities between blacks and whites, Wilson illuminates the logical and moral irrelevance of the distinction of the races in considering the principles of republican government. Nevertheless, this topic could not be addressed in the pure light of reason and nature, because public opinion, North or South, would not permit it. Even Wilson, as radical an antislavery man as could be found in Congress in 1860, prefaced his remarks to Davis by a standard form disclaimer of any belief in the mental or physical equality of the races.

∾

Lincoln was inaugurated after seven states had seceded and six of them had formed the Confederate States of America. Although four more states would eventually join the Confederacy, the official argument for secession was already writ large in the record. It is sufficient for our present purposes to give the official justifications of South Carolina.

South Carolina adopted two documents, an Address to the People of the Slaveholding States and a Declaration of the Causes of Secession (also styled the Declaration of Independence of South Carolina).[86] The former is an almost perfectly Calhounian denunciation of the tyranny of the majority that the free states are allegedly attempting to impose upon the slave states. Until it is far along, one would suppose that South Carolina's greatest grievance was still the tariff of 1828. Echoes of Calhoun's "Remonstrance and Protest" of that year abound, especially those portions in which Calhoun claimed to prove that the tariff put money into the pockets of Northern merchants that had been taken out of the pockets of Southern planters. That the tariff of 1828 had given way in the compromise measures of 1833 is unremembered. Parallels are drawn, however, between the attempt of the British Parliament "to bind the colonies in all cases whatsoever" and the impending tyrannical Northern rule of the South. South Carolina sees no difference between "taxation without representation" by Parliament and taxation by a majority of the U.S. Congress. If, they say, they can be outvoted on issues involving what they consider to be their greatest interests, their position is no better than if they are not represented at all.

One wonders what has happened to James Madison's argument, especially in *Federalist* 10 and 51, that the "extended republic" of the Union will embrace such a large variety of interests that a tyrannical majority will not be formed. As the Address to the People of the Slaveholding States proceeds, we find that South Carolina in fact concedes that in all respects except one the diversity of interests in the North and the overlapping of such interests with a similar variety in the South would prevent any homogeneous (and hence potentially tyrannical) majority. The exception is slavery, which can lead to a consolidation cutting across this diversity, giving the members of the now homogeneous antislavery majority a common interest in plundering the South.

> The people of the North have not left us in doubt as to their designs and policy. United as a section in the late Presidential election, they have elected as an exponent of their policy one who has openly declared that all the States of the United States must be made free States or slave States. . . . If African slavery in the Southern states be the evil their political combinations affirm it to be, the requisitions of an inexorable logic must lead them to emancipation. If it is right to preclude or abolish slavery in a Territory, why should it be allowed to remain in a state? The one is not at all more unconstitutional than the other, according to the decisions of the Supreme Court of the United States. . . . Brute numbers with them is the great element of free government. A majority is infallible and omnipotent. "The right divine to rule in kings" is only transferred to the majority. The very object of all constitutions, in free, popular governments, is to restrain the majority. Constitutions, therefore, according to their theory, must be the most unrighteous inventions, restricting liberty . . .[87]

This purely Calhounian understanding of the controversy that led up to the Civil War would become the essential thesis of Alexander Stephens's aforementioned postbellum defense of the Confederate cause. Nothing could be more revealing than the identification of antislavery opinion with that very same "divine right of kings" with which Lincoln identified slavery.

Much of the argument of the address, taken at face value, would not have been rejected by Lincoln or the Republican Party. It is not true, however, that the purpose of constitutions in free governments is to restrain the majority. Their purpose is rather to make majority rule compatible with minority rights. According to the compact theory, the majority is the surrogate for the whole community, which has unanimously agreed that the voice of the majority shall be taken as the voice of all. Unanimous consent underlies majority rule and sets the boundaries within which it must operate. Constitutions in free governments are designed to assure majorities that operate within those boundaries. But free governments must be able to act. And if the majority cannot act, the government cannot act, and the very purpose of government is denied. Lincoln and his party would denounce as strongly as South Carolina the doctrine of "brute numbers." The real question between them is not whether numbers alone can rule. The real question is: What are the constitutional boundaries to majority rule? And following that: Have the free states breached those boundaries? Or, conversely, have the slave states refused to accept the rule of the majority within those boundaries?

On December 24, 1860, South Carolina catapulted the South into rebellion when it issued its Declaration of the Causes of Secession or Declaration of Independence. This imitation of the Declaration of 1776, and its appeal to the authority of that earlier document, is deliberate and self-conscious. What is repeated, and what is omitted, is then of the highest interest. After reviewing the American Revolution, South Carolina's declaration speaks of

> the two great principles asserted by the Colonies, namely, the right of a State to govern itself, and the right of a people to abolish a government when it becomes destructive of the ends for which it was instituted. And concurrent with the establishment of these principles was the fact that each Colony became and was recognized by the mother country as a free, sovereign, and independent State.[88]

South Carolina cites, loosely but with substantial accuracy, some of the language of the original Declaration. That Declaration does say that it is the right of the people to abolish any form of government that becomes destructive of the ends for which it was established. But South Carolina does not repeat the preceding language in the earlier document:

> We hold these truths to be self-evident, that all men are created equal, that they are endowed by their Creator with certain unalienable rights, that among these are life, liberty, and the pursuit of happiness. That to secure these rights, governments are instituted among men, deriving their just powers from the consent of the governed.

It is only with this prelude that the Declaration of 1776 proclaims the right to revolution. The people do not have an indiscriminate or uncontrolled right either to establish or to abolish governments. They have a right to abolish only those governments that become "destructive of these ends." "These ends" refers to the security of equal natural rights. It is only for the sake of the security of these rights that legitimate governments are instituted, or that governments may be altered or abolished. And governments are legitimate only insofar as their "just powers" are derived "from the consent of the governed." All of the foregoing is omitted from South Carolina's declaration, for obvious reasons. In no sense could it have been said that the slaves in South Carolina were governed by powers derived from their consent. Nor could it be said that South Carolina was separating itself from the government of the Union because that government had become destructive of the ends for which it was established. South Carolina in 1860 had an entirely different idea of what the ends of government ought to be from that of 1776 or 1787. That difference can be summed up in the difference between holding slavery to be an evil, if possibly a necessary evil, and holding it to be a positive good.

South Carolina's case against the free states focuses first of all on their alleged noncompliance with their constitutional obligation (under Article IV) to return fugitive slaves. They list the names of fourteen free states that "have enacted laws which either nullify the acts of Congress, or render useless any attempt to execute them." After citing the Preamble of the Constitution, South Carolina concludes:

> We affirm that those ends for which this government was instituted have been defeated, and the government itself has been made destructive of them by the action of the non-slaveholding States. These States have assumed the right of deciding upon the propriety of our domestic institutions, and have denied the right of property established in fifteen of the States, and recognized by the Constitution; they have denounced as sinful the institution of slavery; they have permitted the open establishment among them of societies whose avowed object is to disturb the peace and to endanger the property of the citizens of other States.[89]

No grievance loomed larger in the rhetoric of secession than the alleged refusal of the free states to comply with the Fugitive Slave Law of 1850. We observe, however, that this complaint was directed against the free states and not against the federal government. The latter had passed the 1850 law, which could hardly have been more stringent, in order to satisfy Southern complaints against the inadequacy of the previous (1793) law in enforcing the fugitive slave clause of the Constitution. The assertion that personal liberty laws in the free states had nullified the acts of Congress for the rendition of fugitive slaves or rendered useless the attempts to execute these acts is simply false. In fact, as we have previously noted, the federal courts, and especially the Supreme Court, had declared unconstitutional any attempts by the states to nullify the Fugitive Slave Law of 1850.

The decisive moment in the challenge within the free states to the enforcement of the 1850 law came in 1854, in the case of Anthony Burns. Burns had escaped from Virginia by stowing away on a ship to Boston. He made the mistake of writing to his brother, who was still a slave, and whose owner intercepted the letter and headed north to reclaim the fugitive. A "vigilance committee" in the city of Boston attempted to prevent the recapture, and violence resulted. The confrontation was finally resolved when President Pierce ordered marines, cavalry, and artillery to Boston, where they joined state militia and local police. Although the owner seemed ready to sell Burns, the U.S. attorney refused to sanction such a solution. It appeared that the president was determined to see that the law was upheld, and upheld in the most publicly visible way in the very cockpit of abolitionism. Burns was marched to the city wharf surrounded by troops, placed on board ship, and returned to slavery.[90] So much for the allegation that the free states had made it impossible for the federal government to execute the Fugitive

Slave Law. Both Presidents Pierce and Buchanan, elected in 1852 and 1856, were determined supporters of the Fugitive Slave Law, and President-elect Lincoln had repeatedly and unwaveringly reaffirmed his conviction that it would be his constitutional responsibility to sustain it.

South Carolina's declaration charges the free states with "having encouraged and assisted thousands of our slaves to leave their homes, and those who remain have been incited by emissaries, books, and pictures, to servile insurrections."[91] During the debates with Lincoln, Douglas had insisted repeatedly that slavery could not exist a day or an hour without local police regulations to support it. Whether this was strictly true, it was certainly true that all the slave states had elaborate police and intertwined social institutions to prevent slaves from running away or conspiring for any other purpose. We recall the river patrol in *Huckleberry Finn*, which caused the runaway Jim to hide under the raft, holding his breath, as Huck told lies. If "thousands" of slaves had escaped from South Carolina, it would have been because of a breakdown in this system of repression and not because of the activities of abolitionists.[92] One need only look at a map of the United States and see the enormous distance between South Carolina's borders and the nearest free state. In fact, we doubt that anything done or said in any free state was responsible for one single slave escaping from any one of the states of the Deep South in the decade before the Civil War. Among the paradoxes of the period was that the loudest complaints concerning fugitive slaves came from the Deep South, from which escape to freedom was virtually impossible. The fewest complaints came from the border slave states. Of the five such states—Missouri, Kentucky, Virginia, Maryland, and Delaware—only Virginia seceded. And it seceded last, after the firing on Fort Sumter, not for any of the reasons given by South Carolina, but because it opposed Lincoln's call for troops and the policy of coercion.

The most thorough academic study of the enforcement of the Fugitive Slave Law from 1850 to 1860 is Stanley W. Campbell's *Slave Catchers*.[93] In a summary table at the end of the book, the total number of fugitive slave cases for that eleven-year period is given as 332. Of these, 191 came before a federal tribunal, resulting in 157 slaves being sent back in the custody of their owners. The number rescued from federal custody during this period was 22, and the number that escaped was 1. But the most devastating refutation of the charge of thousands of slaves escaping owing to free-state infidelity to constitutional obligations is that

The census report [of 1860] shows that notwithstanding all the controversies upon the subject of the fugitive slave law and its enforcement, from 1850 down to 1860, there was less percent escapes of fugitive slaves than at any former period of the Government. The report states: "The number of slaves who escaped from their masters in 1860 is not only much less in proportion than in 1850, but greatly reduced numerically. . . . [T]he number of escapees has been gradually diminishing to such an extent that the whole loss to the southern states from this cause bears less proportion to the amount of capital involved than the daily variations which in ordinary times occur in the fluctuations of State or Government securities in the city of New York alone. From the tables annexed it appears that while there escaped from their masters 1,011 slaves in 1850, or 1 in each 3,165 in bondage (being about one thirtieth of one percent), during the census year ending June 1, 1860, out of 3,949,557 slaves, there escaped only 803, being 1 to about 5,000, or at the rate of one fiftieth of one per cent."[94]

These facts must have been as well known to the South Carolinians who issued their Declaration of the Causes of Secession at the end of 1860 as to anyone else. It is quite possible that the census report was not perfectly accurate or did not tell the whole story. It is possible that there were thousands of runaways who went unreported. But it is also probable that the great majority of these never got very far and were returned to their owners without ever entering into statistical computations. And if the actual figure of losses was two- or three-fiftieths of 1 percent, it was still insignificant.[95] Nor is there any reason to doubt that the number of successful escapes from slavery was declining steadily after the enactment of the 1850 law. The crescendo of Southern denunciation of the free states over fugitive slaves rose continuously as the reality of their grievance declined. There is a paranoid quality to these protests that bears a striking resemblance to the Nazi denunciation in the 1930s of an alleged Jewish conspiracy or the Stalinist denunciation of counterrevolutionary conspiracies at the Moscow show trials of 1936.

The South Carolina declaration rails against the free states for the unbearable presumption of having "denounced as sinful the institution of slavery." But that state's own Senator Hammond, only two years earlier, had said that this was precisely what nearly everyone in the South had thought less than a quarter century earlier. As to permitting "the open establishment of societies, whose avowed object is to . . . endanger the property of the citizens of the other states," Senator Hammond had also boasted that the strength of the slave system had grown vastly and that the value of each individual slave had doubled in the period that had seen the rise of abolitionism in the North.[96]

We come at last to that complaint of South Carolina that alone can be said to have substance:

A geographical line has been drawn across the Union, and all the states north of that line have united in the election of a man to the high office of President of the United States, whose opinions and purposes are hostile to slavery. He is to be entrusted with the administration of the common government because he has declared that that "government cannot endure permanently half slave, half free," and that the public mind must rest in the belief that slavery is "in the course of ultimate extinction."[97]

Lincoln had indeed spoken these words. This was the head and front of Lincoln's offense. The territorial question, around which everything else revolved, was seen by the South, as indeed it was by Lincoln, as the question that would decide the ultimate fate of slavery in the Union. Lincoln called for slavery's "ultimate extinction" in the House Divided speech, at the beginning of his campaign for the Senate against Douglas in June of 1858. And there can be no doubt that Lincoln regarded his election in 1860 as a decision by the American people with respect to the alternatives set forth in that speech. South Carolina, followed eventually by ten other slave states, refused to accept that decision. And they believed they had a moral right, a constitutional right, and a natural right to reject it.

~

Jefferson Davis was inaugurated as President of the Provisional Government of the Confederate States of America on February 18, 1861. His inaugural address is remarkable only in the degree to which, as in the case of South Carolina's declaration, it mimics the rhetoric of the great Declaration of July 4, 1776.

> I enter upon the duties of the office to which I have been chosen with the hope that the beginning of our career as a Confederacy may not be obstructed by hostile opposition to our enjoyment of the separate existence and independence which we have asserted, and, with the blessing of Providence, intend to maintain. Our present condition, achieved in a manner unprecedented in the history of nations, illustrates the American idea that governments rest upon the consent of the governed, and that it is the right of the people to alter or abolish governments whenever they become destructive of the ends for which they were established.

Ignoring his own rejection of the results of the presidential election of 1860, Davis takes pains to assert, not only that it is the principles of the Declaration of Independence that are being followed, but also that it has been by "a peaceful appeal to the ballot box" that the states forming the Confederacy have proceeded.

> In this they [the States] merely asserted a right which the Declaration of Independence of July 4, 1776 had defined to be inalienable; of the time and occasion for its exercise, they, as sovereigns, were the final judges, each for itself. . . . The

right solemnly proclaimed at the birth of the States . . . undeniably recognizes in the people the power to resume the authority delegated for the purposes of government. Thus the sovereign States here represented proceeded to form this Confederacy, and it is by abuse of language that their act has been denominated a revolution.[98]

Davis here shapes the issue that will be paramount in the dialectical confrontation with Abraham Lincoln that is to come. The right to alter or abolish governments is unalienable, according to Jefferson's Declaration, only because the rights with which all men have been equally endowed by their Creator are unalienable. Davis, like South Carolina, demands respect for the conclusion, while ignoring the premises.

4

The Mind of Lincoln's Inaugural and the Argument and Action of the Debate That Shaped It—I

I hold, that in contemplation of universal law, and of the Constitution, the Union of these States is perpetual.

—Abraham Lincoln

When Lincoln took the oath of office from Chief Justice Taney on March 4, 1861, he entered upon the stage of history, not as a minor politician from a western state, but as the central protagonist in a world-historical drama. Never, perhaps, since the drama that began in Bethlehem, had someone risen from so low an estate to play so high a role in deciding the fate of mankind.

How the stage was set for this entrance must now preoccupy us. Since Lincoln's election, the sectional conflict had moved with ever increasing velocity and force. To contemplate Lincoln's inaugural address, we must try to remove from memory everything that came after it. We must ourselves feel something of the uncertainties that Lincoln felt to understand how his words reflected his awareness of these uncertainties. Seven states had seceded. Six of them had formed the Confederate States of America. They had sworn in a provisional president and vice president and elected a congress. All the U.S. government arsenals, forts, and military equipment in these states, with two exceptions—one in Charleston harbor and one in Florida—had been seized. The Confederate government was fully operational; indeed, it was far more operational than the government of the Continental Congress at the outset of the American Revolution. The United States, moreover, had declared its independence in 1776, a full year after the war had begun. When Lincoln was inaugurated, the Confederacy was not only a going concern, it was at peace. Clearly, however, any attempt to coerce the seceded states back into the Union would be met by force. From the Confederate point of

---

The epigraph is taken from *Julius Caesar,* act II, scene 1.

view, any such attempt would be seen as an act of unprovoked aggression. Perhaps this was how Europe might be brought to view it. Opinion in the North was itself divided on this issue. No less an antislavery personage than Horace Greeley counseled, "Let our erring sisters depart."

Critical to the future, as seen from the perspective of March 4, 1861, was the fact that although seven of the fifteen slave states had seceded, eight had not. The border states were Delaware, Maryland, Virginia, Kentucky, and Missouri. Between the Deep South and the border states lay the middle tier: North Carolina, Tennessee, and Arkansas. If none of these other slave states joined the Confederacy, its continued independence might come to be regarded as quixotic or pointless. But it would also then have been impossible to attempt any form of coercion across those states. Nothing would drive the unresolved slave states into the Confederate camp faster than an expressed resolve to bring the seceded states back into the Union by force. If all of the slave states joined the Confederacy, on the other hand, the Union was doomed. Lincoln is reported to have said that he hoped that God was on the side of the Union, but that without Kentucky there was no hope at all.

In composing his inaugural, Lincoln had to articulate the cause of the Union and of the overriding importance of the elected government of the Union taking possession of the offices to which it had been elected. He had to do so in a manner calculated to make his fellow citizens willing to fight for this government, without actually conceding that it would be necessary to fight. It was indispensable, because of the eight slave states still in the Union, that he present himself as no less an apostle of peace than of union. He must not give any countenance to the charge of aggression. He must declare the indissolubility of the Union and yet declare his pacific intentions at one and the same time. Although he could not say so, Lincoln certainly knew that the Union would not be preserved without war. But for him to say so at this juncture would probably make it impossible to win such a war. The tension between these two imperatives, which set the parameters within which the speech had to be composed, is obvious.

In addition to the danger of tipping the trembling balance between unionist and secessionist forces in the eight slave states, there was another reason for Lincoln to exhibit a pacific demeanor. He had virtually no military forces at his disposal in the capital city. Washington was encompassed by the slave states of Maryland on three sides and Virginia on the fourth. Before the District of Columbia could be reinforced from the free states of the North, the militias of either of these slave states might have overrun the capital. Lincoln's predecessor, President Buchanan, had declared that both secession and coercion were unconstitutional. But the secession of seven states, whether legal or illegal, was an accomplished fact. Whether coercion was possible depended upon what the people of the free states and border states were willing to do. Lincoln did not and could not know, as he stood up to speak, what support there would be for a policy of coercion if nothing else could preserve the Union. Thus he had to give heart and soul to a policy that might lead to coercion without actually threatening to coerce.

Commentaries on the Civil War tend to emphasize the superior means of the North in terms of population, industrial resources, and commercial wealth. They tend to assume that there was an inevitability in the outcome of the war, because of the weight of these superior assets. It is certainly true that as this weight was brought to bear, it played a great part in determining that outcome. But it is a great error to think that the outcome was in any sense foreordained. It must be remembered that in the American Revolution, the disparity in population, wealth, and military assets between Great Britain and the colonies was at least as great as that between North and South. That this disparity did not determine the outcome was due, at least in part, to the powerful "American" party among British Whigs. The Howe brothers, who commanded both the land and naval forces of Great Britain through the early years of the Revolution, had (like Edmund Burke) been partisans of the American cause in Parliament. Part of the reason they were appointed to their commands was to gain Whig support for a Tory policy. In great measure, the American Revolution was a civil war within the Anglo-American Whig political order. When one side is more united than its adversary, the outcome is not decided by the comparable resources available.[1] Great Britain never prosecuted the war against the Americans the way it would prosecute the war against Napoleon, largely because the Americans were never a threat to Britain's survival. Similarly, the Confederacy tried to present itself as no threat to the Union of the North. Its leaders spoke in terms of merely seeking independence on the same principles as their Revolutionary forebears. It appointed commissioners who, although Lincoln would not receive them, were ready to negotiate a peaceful resolution of competing claims to the joint possessions of the states under the Constitution of 1787. Both in seceding from the "old" Union and in forming a new one, the Confederacy asserted all its rights as grounded in the proposition that the just powers of government are derived only from the consent of the governed. They declared an indefeasible right to withdraw their consent from—"to alter or abolish" —any government that no longer secured the rights for which, in their view, it had been instituted. On the same ground, they claimed an indefeasible right to institute a new government. Taking their stand upon a simulacrum of the Declaration of Independence, whose language they imitated even as they rejected its fundamental premise, they convinced themselves of the justice of their cause and believed they had good hope of persuading others, North as well as South, and abroad as well as at home.

239

In considering Lincoln's situation, we must also understand that in the Civil War, victory for the North meant conquering the South. Anything less than the extinction of the Confederate government meant victory for the South. No Confederate armed force loyal to a Confederate government could be left standing. If we measure the resources at the disposal of the two sides from this perspective, any advantage of the North shrinks into virtual insignificance. If we consider the vast geographical area that comprised the eleven states of the Confederacy, an area greater than the contiguous Northern states, we see that, just as in the American Revolution, the task of conquering, as compared with that of not being conquered, was immensely greater. It was to this immensely greater task that Lincoln had to devote all the resources of his leadership and statesmanship.

~

Aristotle complains of the Sophists that they thought of politics as identical with rhetoric.[2] Implicit in this criticism is the necessity of understanding the harsh realities that do not yield to speech or persuasion.[3] At one point during the Civil War, Lincoln replied to critics that wars are not won by shooting rosewater through cornstalks. Lincoln did not make the mistake of the Sophists. His silences are as notable as his speeches, and to understand the latter, one must also understand the former. Of his public silences, none is more impressive than that which extended from before his nomination until his inauguration. Since such a thing would be entirely incomprehensible today, we must take careful note of it.

Lincoln's prepresidential political career falls into two distinct parts. In the first part, before 1854, Lincoln was a Whig and was a follower rather than a leader. We need say no more about this part here.[4] From the moment of the repeal of the Missouri Compromise in 1854, Lincoln began an essentially new career, a "second sailing" shaped entirely by the controversy over slavery in the territories. Between 1854 and 1860, he gave four major speeches in which he developed and set forth the arguments in virtue of which he became the political leader of the antislavery cause and president of the United States. They are: (1) the Peoria speech, on the Repeal of the Missouri Compromise, October 16, 1854;[5] (2) the speech on the *Dred Scott* decision, Springfield, June 26, 1857; (3) the House Divided speech, delivered at the close of the Republican State Convention at Springfield, June 16, 1858; and (4) the Address at Cooper Institute, New York City, February 27, 1860. Of course, Lincoln gave many hundreds of speeches besides these four. Almost every one of them had something distinctive in it whose absence would have left us poorer in our appreciation of Lincoln's mastery of the vernacular of American politics and of his flexibility and versatility before a variety of audiences. Nevertheless, the structure of his life and argument, seen in relationship to the shifting scenes of a rapidly changing political world, is contained in these four speeches. A notable fact about these speeches is that each of them is directed against, and is a reply to, a preceding speech by Senator Stephen A. Douglas. The seven joint debates between Lincoln and Douglas were essentially spun from the controversial assertions of the House Divided speech, especially Lincoln's charge of a conspiracy involving the "four workmen"—Senator Douglas, Presidents Pierce and Buchanan, and Chief Justice Taney—to make slavery lawful throughout the Union. In the course of the joint debates, however, Lincoln also drew extensively from arguments he had set forth in the Peoria and *Dred Scott* speeches. In like manner, at Cooper Institute, Lincoln's argument both reinforces, and is reinforced by, the earlier speeches. We will see that Lincoln's first inaugural address, however much adapted to its particular occasion, has a similar character, exhibiting no break in continuity of thought or reason with what he had said before.

The span between Lincoln's last major prepresidential utterance and his first as president, however, is notable. The Cooper Institute speech was delivered on February 27, 1860. The inaugural was March 4, 1861. That is an interval of one year and six days. Of course it is not the case that Lincoln made no speeches whatever during this interval. After Cooper Institute, he made a New England tour, with brief but gradually lengthening speeches at Providence, Rhode Island; Manchester, New Hampshire; and Hartford and New Haven, Connecticut. The New Haven speech was on March 6, 1860. Everything in these speeches is repeated or adapted from Cooper Institute, although some of Lincoln's impromptu commentaries on his own text are priceless. We interpolate just one such:

> If the Republicans, who think slavery is wrong, get possession of the general government, we may not root out the evil at once, but may at least prevent its extension. If I find a venomous snake lying on the open prairie, I seize the first stick and kill him at once. But if that snake is in bed with my children, I must be more cautious—I shall, in striking the snake, also strike the children, or arouse the reptile to bite the children. Slavery is the venomous snake in bed with the children. But if the question is whether to kill it on the prairie, or put it in bed with other children, I think we'd kill it![6]

There is one more speech on record in the spring of 1860, reported in a Bloomington, Illinois, newspaper of April 10, 1860, as having been given "On Tuesday evening last."[7] No other public speech is recorded until Lincoln left Springfield for Washington on February 11, 1861, the day before his fifty-second birthday.

The Republican National Convention of 1860 met in Chicago on May 16. Three days later Lincoln was nominated. After accepting the nomination, he adopted a policy of official silence, which extended throughout the campaign and after the election. Silence during the campaign was in accordance with established custom, although it was a custom breached by Douglas, many of whose speeches were directed less at his own election than at warning the South against secession. During the campaign, Lincoln referred all queries as to his views to his published statements.

Apart from Lincoln's nomination, the decisive event of the political year of 1860 came before the Republicans met and determined not only the outcome of the presidential election but also the sequence of events that followed it. The Democratic convention met in Charleston on April 23. The story of this convention, its breakup, and its reassembly into rival conventions, nominating rival candidates on rival platforms, has been well told many times.[8] Suffice it for our purposes to note that the majority in the Charleston convention would have nominated Douglas, but the two-thirds rule prevented them from doing so. The price that the Deep South would have exacted for Douglas's nomination was the adoption of a plank in the party platform guaranteeing federal protection of slave property in the territories. This the Douglasites could not accept, as no candidate who hoped to carry a single free state could have accepted it. The seceders from the national convention, who would become the seceders from the Union after Lincoln's election, later nominated John C. Breckinridge in a separate convention held in Baltimore in June. The national convention also adjourned until June, at which time it also reassembled in Baltimore and nominated Douglas. This breaking up of the Charleston convention in April had given the Republicans, who met in May, the strongest reason to believe in the victory to come in November.

The first two planks in the convention that nominated Breckinridge summarize the sectional conflict within the Democratic Party and within the nation.

> 1. That the government of a Territory organized by an act of Congress is provisional and temporary; and, during its existence, all citizens of the United States have an equal right to settle with their property in the Territory, without their rights, either of person or of property, being destroyed or impaired by Congressional legislation.
> 2. That it is the duty of the Federal government, in all its departments, to protect, when necessary, the rights of persons and property in the Territories, and wherever else its constitutional authority extends.[9]

Both these resolutions embody doctrines that were presumably certified as true constitutional law by Chief Justice Taney's opinion in *Dred Scott.* Slavery is not mentioned in either. The second resolution, however, was a direct inference from the following in Taney's opinion:

And no word can be found in the Constitution which gives Congress greater power over slave property, or which entitles property of that kind to less protection than property of any other description. The only power conferred is the power coupled with the duty of guarding and protecting the owner in his rights.[10]

These were perhaps the most fateful words ever pronounced from the bench of the high court. From the point of view of the Deep South, and not of the Deep South alone, these words of Taney were, for all practical purposes, the words of the Constitution itself.

Southerners were indignant at the characterization of the second resolution as a "slave code," insisting that it asked for nothing more than recognition of the equal right to equal protection of all forms of property. The Southern argument for the recognition without distinction of all property in the territories mimicked Lincoln's argument for the recognition without distinction of all human persons in the territories. The difference between the two sides consisted in the fact that the South either saw property rights as defined exclusively by positive law or saw Negro slavery as in accordance with natural and divine law. This latter position we saw set forth with greatest boldness by Alexander Stephens, while Jefferson Davis was at one moment a legal positivist denying natural rights and at another an advocate of Stephens's "scientific" version of natural law. Both Stephens and Davis, however, agreed that, science or not, slavery was decreed by "the curse of Canaan." Lincoln also invoked the Bible, as when he said that God had ordained that man should earn his bread by the sweat of his own face. But Lincoln also knew, as he once remarked, that there was always a "squabble" as to what the Bible meant. On another occasion, Lincoln said that

the free states carry on their governments on the principle of the equality of men. We think slavery is morally wrong, and a direct violation of that principle. We *all* think it wrong. It is clearly proved, I think, by natural theology, apart from revelation. Every man, black, white, or yellow, has a mouth to be fed and two hands with which to feed it—and that bread should be allowed to go to that mouth without controversy.[11]

Lincoln saw property rights as having an origin, prior to positive law, in nature—in the original right that every human being possessed to own himself, and consequently to own the fruit of his own labor.[12] Although there is no evidence that Lincoln read Locke's *Second Treatise of Civil Government*, his views correspond closely to the labor theory of value expounded in the fifth chapter of that work. During the Civil War, he will take pains to elaborate the relationship of the property rights originating directly in labor and those of capital derivative from it.[13]

Although Lincoln kept almost complete public silence during the period between his election and his inauguration, behind the scenes he was extremely active in thwarting all attempts at compromise on any of the fundamental issues that he believed had been decided by the election. The movement and temper of his influence may be seen in his response to the famous Crittenden Resolutions of January 16, 1861. The second (of six) of these resolutions declared that Congress had no power to abolish slavery in places under its exclusive jurisdiction situated within slave states. The third declared that Congress should not abolish slavery in the District of Columbia so long as slavery remained lawful in Maryland and Virginia. Nor should slavery be abolished in the District without the consent of the slave owners of the District nor without compensation for any slaves emancipated. The fourth prohibited Congress from interfering with the interstate slave trade. The fifth declared that it would be the duty of Congress to provide that slave owners who had been prevented by violence or intimidation from reclaiming their fugitive slaves should be recompensed by the United States. The sixth declared that all the articles of the Constitution containing guarantees of slavery were to be unamendable and provided especially that "no amendment shall be made to the Constitution which shall authorize or give to Congress any power to abolish or interfere with slavery in any of the States by whose laws it is, or may be, allowed or permitted." This last resolution corresponded to one of the planks in the Republican platform and was therefore hardly controversial. (The idea of "unamendable amendments" would be strange, however, for those whose idea of state sovereignty embraced the right of secession.) Numbers 2, 3, and 4 concerned matters of minor irritation of no substantial import, although the idea of recompensing the owners of escaped slaves faced two overwhelming objections: that it might encourage interference with the enforcement of the fugitive slave law; and that it wrongly assumed that Congress possessed the constitutional power to buy and emancipate slaves. Such a power would run counter to the very assumption that Congress had no lawful power to interfere with slavery in the slave states.

It was only the first of the Crittenden Resolutions that went to the heart of the crisis. It proposed that

> In all the territory of the United States now held, or hereafter acquired, situated north of the latitude 36 degrees 30 minutes, slavery or involuntary servitude, except as punishment for crime, is prohibited while such territory shall remain under territorial government. In all the territory south of said line of latitude, slavery of the African race is hereby recognized as existing, and shall not be interfered with by Congress, but shall be protected as property by all the departments of the territorial government during its continuance.[14]

The final stipulation of this resolution, repeating the language of the 1850 Territorial Acts for Utah and New Mexico, provided that whenever any territory, north or south of the line, contained sufficient population for statehood, it might be admitted into the Union with or without slavery, as its constitution might provide.

The proposal to extend the Missouri Compromise line to the Pacific, forbidding slavery north of the line and permitting it south of the line, was the final and only proposal that could have averted the Civil War. Had Lincoln thrown his influence behind it, it almost certainly would have passed the Congress. But he threw his full weight into opposition. The *New York Herald* of January 28, 1861, attributed the following language to the president-elect:

> I will suffer death before I will consent or advise my friends to consent to any concession or compromise which looks like buying the privilege of taking possession of the Government to which we have a constitutional right; because, whatever I might think of the merit of the various propositions before Congress, I should regard any concession in the face of menace as the destruction of the government itself, and a consent on all hands that our system shall be brought down to a level with the existing disorganized state of affairs in Mexico. But this thing will hereafter be, as it is now, in the hands of the people; and if they desire to call a convention to remove any grievances complained of, or to give new guarantees for the permanence of vested rights, it is not mine to oppose.[15]

To yield, whether in whole or in part, what had been gained by the election because of the threat of secession would be as fatal to the cause of free government as secession itself. If the constitutional majority cannot rule without yielding after the election to those who had opposed it in the election, the government of the United States will, Lincoln said, be reduced to the level of Mexican anarchy. He recognized, however, that there are other constitutional processes by which the people could, if they wished, alter the results of elections; they could do so by constitutional amendments, and especially by the convention mode of making such amendments.[16] Any such decision emanating authentically and constitutionally from the will of the people Lincoln would be obligated to accept. Absent an amendment to the Constitution, however, Lincoln's binding mandate was from the 1860 election, and no ulterior motive, such as preserving the Union without secession or war, could justify him in bargaining away that mandate.

The foregoing attributed statement is Lincoln's only published statement during this "deadly hiatus" between his election and his inauguration, when the secession of the Deep South was going forward. But Lincoln was active behind the scenes. In a letter of December 15, 1860, to John Gilmer of North Carolina, Lincoln explained why he thought any public declarations by him would be interpreted as a sign of weakness. His positions on all disputed matters, and above all the question of slavery in the territories, were fully set forth in the volume of his joint debates with Douglas (to which Lincoln provided page references), as well as in the Republican platform. For him to repeat now what he had said before the election, as if it needed justification, would only, he wrote,

> make me appear as if I repented for the crime of having been elected, and was anxious to apologize and beg forgiveness. To so represent me, would be the principal use made of any letter I might now thrust upon the public. My old record cannot be so used; and that is precisely the reason that some new declaration is so much sought.

And again:

> On the territorial question, I am inflexible, as you see my position in the book. On that, there is a difference between you and us; and it is the only substantial difference. You think slavery is right and ought to be extended; we think it is wrong and ought to be restricted. For this, neither has any just occasion to be angry with the other.[17]

Whether or not the occasion was just, all the anger of the sectional conflict was concentrated upon the difference between those who thought slavery right and those who thought it wrong. Lincoln's Cooper Institute speech was his definitive statement concerning the passions that attended that difference. It had been published in pamphlet form and was widely distributed. Historians, commenting on Lincoln's prolonged public silence in this period, have failed to give him credit for the voice with which he had spoken in his earlier speeches. Seeing with the benefit of hindsight the approaching carnage of the war, they think Lincoln should have done something—anything—rather than allow the crisis to proceed without any intervention whatever. They cannot accept what Lincoln accepted, namely, that nothing more within the compass of human wisdom could be said, other than what had been already said, to prevent the impending conflict. Unlike the Sophists whom Aristotle criticizes, Lincoln, who is perhaps the greatest master of political speech the world has ever seen, understood its limits. He knew at what point speech had to be accompanied by deed if the paramount purposes of speech itself were not to be sacrificed. The purposes for which Lincoln had been elected were embodied in his speeches before the election. Now the task was to make good the results of that election. Now he had to be silent until the moment when, provided with the powers of the office, he could speak and act as the chief executive and commander in chief described and defined in the Constitution.

The most notable defense by a Southerner of a Unionist position during this interregnum was that of Alexander Stephens. We have cited previously, not only

Stephens's Cornerstone speech of March 21, 1861, delivered when he was vice president of the Confederacy, but also the fact that before his state of Georgia seceded, Stephens was a vigorous opponent of secession. On November 30, 1860, Lincoln wrote to Stephens that he had "read, in the newspapers, your speech recently delivered (I think) before the Georgia Legislature, or its assembled members. If you have revised it, as is probable, I shall be much obliged if you will send me a copy." Stephens replied on December 14 "that he had not revised the speech but that newspaper reports were substantially correct."[18] The speech that Lincoln requested is assuredly an American classic. It seems at first glance to be entirely opposed to what Stephens would say three months later in the Cornerstone speech. Yet analysis will show no real contradiction.

Stephens argues to the Georgia legislature that the proslavery cause can still flourish within the Union. Prudence dictates that there be no secession by the slave states until there has been an open act of aggression against their constitutional rights. But he does not think this will happen, especially if Southern congressmen and senators keep their places. Lincoln cannot have anyone in his cabinet that the Senate does not approve, and (absent secession) the Democratic Party will have a controlling majority in the Senate. Here is an excerpt from Stephens's exordium:

> My object is not to stir up strife, but to allay it; not to appeal to your passions, but to your reason. Good government can never be built up or sustained by the impulse of passion. . . . That people should disagree in republican governments upon questions of public policy, is natural. That men should disagree on all matters connected with human investigation, whether relating to science or human conduct, is natural. Hence in free governments parties will arise. But a free people should express their different opinions with liberality and charity, with no acrimony toward those of their fellows when honestly and sincerely given.[19]

Such words are hardly open to criticism. We are reminded, however, of Jefferson's inaugural, in which he announced "we are all federalists, we are all republicans" and said that not every difference of opinion is a difference of principle. Could the same be said now about the differences between the advocates of expanding and the advocates of restricting slavery?

Stephens says that a free people should express their differences with liberality and charity, but a community governed by liberality and charity is a community governed by shared principles of right and wrong. Such principles were, of course, set forth in the Declaration of Independence. Stephens's speech, however conciliatory and pro-Union, nonetheless assumes an understanding of right and wrong corresponding to John C. Calhoun's doctrine of state rights, in opposition to the doctrine of human rights encompassed by the Declaration. On the question of secession as it was then before the Georgia legislature, he asked,

> Shall the people of the South secede from the Union in consequence of the election of Mr. Lincoln to the Presidency of the United States? My countrymen, *I tell you frankly, candidly and earnestly, that I do not think that they ought*. In my judgment the election of no man, constitutionally chosen to that high office, is sufficient cause for any State to separate from the Union. . . . But it is said Mr. Lincoln's policy and principles are against the Constitution, and that if he carries them out it will be destructive of our rights. Let us not anticipate a threatened evil. If he violates the Constitution, then will come our time to act. . . . The President of the United States is no emperor, no dictator—he is clothed with no absolute power. He can do nothing unless he is backed by power in Congress. The House of Representatives is largely in the majority against him. In the Senate he will also be powerless. . . . He will be in the condition of George III . . . who had asked the whigs to appoint his ministers and was compelled to receive a cabinet utterly opposed to his views; and so Mr. Lincoln will be compelled to ask of the Senate to choose for him a cabinet. . . . Then how can Mr. Lincoln obtain a cabinet which would aid him, or allow him to violate the Constitution?

Wise and prudent as these words may be, Stephens still stands upon the Calhounian ground of state equality, which meant the legal equality within the Union of those who affirmed and those who denied the morality of slavery. In practice, this meant that the free states had no constitutional right to prevent the extension of slavery. Thus Stephens does not question the allegation that Lincoln's principles are "against the Constitution." He merely doubts that Lincoln will be able to act on his principles.

> I say to you . . . as a Georgian, I never would submit to any Black Republican *aggression* upon our constitutional rights. I will never consent myself, as much as I admire this Union for the glories of the past, or the blessings of the present— as much as it has done for the people of these states—as much as it has done for civilization—as much as the hopes of the world hang upon it, I would never submit to aggression upon my rights to maintain it longer. . . . I will have equality for Georgia and for the citizens of Georgia, or I will look for new safeguards elsewhere.[20]

Stephens's arguments for the Union, in terms of the material prosperity it has engendered and the personal liberty it has provided its citizens, closely parallel those of Lincoln himself. His reference to "hopes of the world" echoes a theme of Washington, Jefferson, and Webster that will be repeated by Lincoln and that we associate with the greatest celebrations of union. Stephens too sees the American form of government as providing the vanguard for the progress of all humanity. Yet he will unhesitatingly put all this at risk if Georgia's "equality" is endangered.

And this equality has no other meaning than a guaranteed future for the institution of human slavery.

Lincoln's reaction to Stephens's speech is characteristic both in its brevity and in its epigrammatic summary of the entire conflict. The following letter to Stephens, dated December 22, 1860, is given in its entirety.

> Your obliging answer to my short note is just received, and for which please accept my thanks. I fully appreciate the present peril the country is in, and the weight of responsibility on me.
>
> Do the people of the South really entertain fears that a Republican administration would, *directly* or *indirectly*, interfere with their slaves, or with them, about their slaves? If they do, I wish to assure you, as once a friend, and still, I hope, not an enemy, that there is no cause for such fears.[21]
>
> The South would be in no more danger in this respect, than it was in the days of Washington. I suppose, however, this does not meet the case. You think slavery is *right* and ought to be extended; while we think it is *wrong* and ought to be restricted. That I suppose is the rub. It certainly is the only substantial difference between us.[22]

In the last three sentences of this letter, Lincoln repeats what he had written to Gilmore. He will repeat the thought again in his inaugural. Although his letter to Stephens is marked "For your eyes only," it must have been meant to strengthen Stephens's hand in the struggle against secession in Georgia. It therefore marks the uttermost extent to which Lincoln was willing to go to exert personal influence during this period of public silence. Yet he does not hesitate or compromise in identifying the central question in dispute, on which all lesser questions depend. He does this knowing, as the Cooper Institute speech demonstrates, that the one unforgivable sin, according to dominant Southern public opinion, was moral condemnation of slavery. And he knew that the idea of state rights, as encompassing the right of secession, was in the service of this opinion. He knew moreover that Stephens, although against the exercise of the right of secession, nonetheless believed completely in that right, just as he believed completely in the beneficence of the institution of slavery. If Stephens represented the most moderate and reasonable Southern leadership, as he did, Lincoln could have had no delusions as to the possibility of a peaceful resolution of the crisis.

∽

Historians have generally divided Lincoln's war policy into two distinct phases: that preceding the preliminary Emancipation Proclamation of September 22, 1862, and that following it. They have taken their bearings from Lincoln's public letter to Horace Greeley of August 22, 1862, whose theme is expressed in the words, "I would save the Union," and which goes on to say that whatever he does about slavery will be subordinated to this paramount and overriding policy.[23] That policy, Lincoln repeated, was simply and solely to preserve the Union, and neither to preserve nor to destroy slavery. Many critics have held that this proves that in the decisive moment, Lincoln subordinated morality (antislavery) to an amoral national interest (Union). But the Greeley letter is misunderstood unless it is read against the background of Lincoln's off-the-record letters of the winter of 1860–61.

Above all, it is necessary to understand the indissoluble unity of Lincoln's three permanent and unchanging goals: preserving the right of free elections, preserving the Union, and placing slavery in the course of ultimate extinction. These three ends were distinguishable in Lincoln's mind only as different aspects of one sovereign purpose, represented by the principles of the Declaration of Independence. We must understand that Northern opinion at the time was also, in many respects, a house divided against itself. Many Northerners would not fight for the Union if it meant the destruction of slavery. Others would not fight for the Union unless it did mean the destruction of slavery. Lincoln's task throughout the war was to combine these unwilling partners, and his public arguments reflected his own judgment as to where it was prudent to place the emphasis at any given moment. The comprehensive reasoning underlying these apparent differences was not grasped by many of Lincoln's contemporaries and has not been grasped by historians.

We have seen that Lincoln was, in his own words, "inflexible" in refusing any concession involving the extension of slavery. His opposition to slavery extension had been central to his candidacy, and he believed that the American people, acting by the constitutional majority, had elected him to put an end to it. The right of the people to act by means of such a majority was itself grounded in the principle of all popular government, the principle of human equality enshrined in the Declaration and the Gettysburg Address. The principle that justified the right of the people to rule themselves was the same principle that denounced slavery as morally wrong.

If the election of 1860 had put an end to slavery extension, Lincoln believed it had also, by that fact, placed slavery in the course of ultimate extinction. However, for reasons that were at once moral, political, and constitutional, the election had not authorized Lincoln, or the Republican Party, to interfere with slavery in states in which it was lawful. Lincoln was as unwavering in his refusal to go beyond what the people had constitutionally authorized as he was in his refusal to compromise what they had authorized. He would yield neither a jot nor a tittle of their mandate. But neither would he, by jot or tittle, exceed it. The mandate was a result of a constitutional process that lay at the heart of republican government,

government based upon the proposition that all men are created equal. When it came time to issue the Emancipation Proclamation, Lincoln did indeed feel obliged to justify an action that, on its face, appeared to go beyond the mandate as he had previously defined it. Yet a careful reading of his words will prove that, however much the circumstances in which he was compelled to act had changed, his every action flowed from adherence to an unchanging commitment to unchanging principles.

The Civil War is often represented as a struggle between state rights and national supremacy. But this is an error. The conflict was between two different conceptions of state rights and two different conceptions of what constituted the nation. The state governments formed in the period following July 4, 1776, were all formed upon the natural rights principles of the Declaration of Independence, as the bills of rights prefaced to most of the state constitutions proclaimed. The state rights that allegedly justified the ordinances of secession of 1860–61, and which served as the foundation of the Confederacy, had severed the connection with natural rights that had informed the generation of the Revolution. This great change in the conception of state rights had been mainly the work of John C. Calhoun, and we shall presently examine how he accomplished it. For now, we only observe that the divorce between state rights and natural rights was not a feature of Southern opinion alone. We must never forget that four deeply divided border slave states (not to mention deeply divided border free states) remained with the Union throughout the war and that without them the Union cause would have been hopeless.

∽

Lincoln left Springfield for Washington on February 11, 1861, the day before his fifty-second birthday. His route was east across Illinois, Indiana, and Ohio, into Pennsylvania. From there it jogged north from Pittsburgh to Buffalo, across New York State to Albany, then southward to New York City, through New Jersey, and back into Pennsylvania, to Philadelphia and Independence Hall. At that point it again jogged westward to the Pennsylvania capital at Harrisburg, and then again south through Baltimore to Washington. On this circuitous route Lincoln made nearly eighty stops, where he addressed great and excited crowds eager to see the president-elect. He addressed the Ohio legislature at Columbus, the mayor and citizens of Pittsburgh, the mayor and citizens of Buffalo, and the legislature of New York at Albany. He spoke at the Astor House in New York City and made separate addresses to the New Jersey Senate and the New Jersey General Assembly at Trenton. He made two speeches at Independence Hall, one of them a flag-raising ceremony. He made separate speeches to the governor and to the Pennsylvania General Assembly at Harrisburg. While in Philadelphia, he replied to a delegation from Wilmington, Delaware. But he made no speeches in the slave states of Delaware or Maryland. Of the major cities through which he passed, only at Baltimore, seething with Confederate sympathizers, did he fail to stop or make a public appearance.[24] On February 27, 1861, he replied to an address of welcome by the mayor of Washington. The following day he responded to a serenade that featured the U.S. Marine band playing, somewhat prematurely, "Hail to the Chief."

Lincoln's roundabout voyage from his Illinois home to the nation's capital was obviously calculated to gain the greatest possible public exposure. Since he had done no campaigning before the election, one might say that this was his "whistle-stop" crusade. Most important was simply showing himself to crowds of ordinary citizens. He did not stint his contacts with mayors, governors, and state legislatures, but he knew that it would not be long before he was seeing them, or at least many of them, in Washington. But for every one of the ordinary citizens who glimpsed him, however briefly, he knew there would be many others to whom the impression of his presence would be communicated. And that presence would tell them that he was one of them and belonged to them. In the hard days that he knew lay ahead, that would be the political asset that, above all others, he would need—and have.

What did he say on this fateful voyage? His first address was his leave-taking of his friends and neighbors in Springfield. In it, Lincoln transforms what might have been a merely conventional parting, a fleeting moment of change, into a glimpse of an eternal presence and a meditation upon the divine will. It will, in the end, serve as prologue to the Gettysburg Address and the second inaugural. In its simplicity, directness, and poignancy, in its biblical cadences, it is Lincoln's art in all its fullness. We give it here in its entirety.

No one, not in my situation, can appreciate my feelings of sadness at this parting. To this place, and the kindness of these people, I owe every thing. Here I have lived a quarter of a century, and have passed from a young to an old man. Here my children have been born, and one is buried. I now leave, not knowing when, or whether ever, I may return, with a task before me greater than that which rested upon Washington. Without the assistance of that Divine Being, who ever attended him, I cannot succeed. With that assistance I cannot fail. Trusting in Him, who can go with me, and remain with you and be every where for good, let us confidently hope that all will yet be well. To His care commending you, as I hope in your prayers you will commend me, I bid you an affectionate farewell.[25]

Historical commentary contains many reproaches of Lincoln for not grasping fully the gravity of the crisis or anticipating the lengths to which the South would go in defense of slavery and state rights. Nor did he, it has been said, appreciate the extent to which Southerners had become, in their own mind, a separate nation, determined to defend their independence as their forebears had done in the American Revolution. It is true that on his way to Washington, and in his inaugural, he kept repeating that there was no necessity for war or bloodshed and that there were no differences that could not be overcome by patience and forbearance. Much of what he said was dictated by the obligation to pursue every possible avenue of peace. He was under such obligation no matter what his private thoughts of the likelihood of success. He was under such obligation because he knew he could not lead a war for the Union unless it was believed that he had first exhausted every possible avenue of reconciliation. We have a window into his inner thoughts, however, in the remarkable statement that the task he faced was "greater than that which rested upon Washington."

〜

What did Lincoln tell the people as he traveled to take up the burden greater than had rested upon Washington? It is amusing that he devoted a major part of his speeches to explaining why he could not stop to make a speech. Here is a report of remarks at Thorntown and Lebanon, Indiana, from the Indianapolis *Daily Sentinel*, February 12, 1861. It conveys much of the down-to-earth way in which Lincoln spoke to the people, even as he was determined to avoid saying anything prematurely.

At Thorntown he was betrayed into an anecdote to illustrate a point, and the train started before he got to the place where the laugh came in, and the people were left to wonder what the meaning might be. He was apologizing for not making a speech. He had heard of a man who was a candidate for a country office, who owned a horse that he set great store by, but he was a slow animal and sure footed. He canvassed extensively with a good chance for the nomination. On the morning of the day of the convention, he mounted his favorite to go to the country seat, but in spite of whip and spur, his horse lagged on the road, biting at every bush, and when he arrived in the evening, the convention was over and he was defeated. So of him, if he stopped at every station to make a stump speech he would not arrive in Washington until the inauguration was over. The Thornton folks only heard the first part of the story, where the candidate was urging his steed to pass the juicy bushes. He laughed over the cutting short of his yarn, and when the train arrived in Lebanon he was jocularly told that some of the Thornton folks had followed the train on foot, and were panting outside to hear the conclusion of the story. He told it over good-humoredly to the crowd at Lebanon. Every station along the road had its crowd—all anxious to see the man whose election to the first office in the gift of a free people has been the cause (whether with reason or not) of the distracted state of the country.[26]

Of course the great crowds that turned out to salute Lincoln on his fateful trip were all anxious to know what he was going to do in response to the seven states that had seceded and the formation of a Confederate government. But just as the people were anxious to know what Lincoln was going to do, he was anxious to know what they were prepared to do, and to suffer, to uphold the policies that he might adopt. As we shall see, he could not decide upon his policies until he could form a reasoned judgment of what the people would support. A leader cannot decide in the abstract what policies he thinks reason and justice require without looking over his shoulder to see if he is being followed! The interaction between what was right in itself, what was constitutional, and what burden the people would accept was the constant theme of Lincoln's statesmanship.

In everything he said, Lincoln implied that the Union had to be preserved. What he said was intended to make everyone who heard him understand that the preservation of the Union was not a partisan policy. Lincoln's most frequent and characteristic utterance was the insistence that the respect being paid to him was not personal but as the representative of the nation. Here are some excerpts from his speech at Buffalo, New York, which may stand for many others like it:

> I am here to thank you briefly for this grand reception given to me, not person-ally, but as the representative of our great and beloved country. . . . We have not been met alone by those who assisted in giving the election to me . . . but by the whole population of the country through which we have passed. . . . Had the election fallen to any other of the distinguished candidates instead of myself . . . it would have been proper for all citizens to have greeted him as you now greet me. . . . I am unwilling . . . that I should be so meanly thought of, as to have it supposed for a moment that I regard these demonstrations as tendered to me personally. They should be tendered to no individual man. They are tendered to the country, to the institutions of the country, and to the perpetuity of the liber-ties of the country for which these institutions were made and created.[27]

Only at one point did Lincoln anticipate the arguments that he would make against secession. It will be remembered that President Buchanan had denied that any state had the constitutional right to withdraw from the Union and had at the same time denied that there was any constitutional power to coerce a state to remain in the Union. But Buchanan had not followed his argument to its conclu-sion: If a state could not secede, it could not be coerced for seceding. Coercion could, however, be applied lawfully to those who were unlawfully resisting the exe-cution of the Constitution and the laws of the United States. Lincoln at Indianapolis engaged in a little dissertation upon how the words "invasion" and "coercion" were being bandied about. Would it be coercion or invasion, he asked, for the government to hold or retake its own forts or collect the duties upon foreign imports? If the professed lovers of the Union regarded these things as coercion or invasion, then

> the means for the preservation of the Union . . . is of a very thin and airy character. If sick, they would consider the little pills of the homeopathist as already too large for them to swallow. In their view, the Union, as a family relation, would not be anything like a regular marriage at all, but only a sort of free-love arrangement, to be maintained by what that sect calls passionate attraction.[28]

The comparison of the Union to a marriage will reappear in the first inaugural.

Although the Civil War resulted from the question of the extension of slavery, as the crisis progressed, it was transformed into a difference concerning state rights. State rights and slavery extension were of course intertwined, since the followers of Calhoun insisted that, as a consequence of state rights, the citizen of any slave state had the right to carry his slave property into any U.S. territory and there receive all necessary protection from the United States. And as a necessary means to protect its constitutional rights *within* the Union, a state possessed the constitutional right to withdraw *from* the Union. After the Civil War began, Lincoln would find this to be the doctrinal core of the Confederate cause. At Indianapolis, he asked:

> What is the particular sacredness of a State? I speak not of that position which is given to a State in and by the Constitution of the United States, for that we all agree to—we abide by; but that position assumed, that a State can carry with it out of the Union that which it holds in sacredness by virtue of its connection with the Union. . . . If a State, in one instance, and a county in another, should be equal in extent of territory, and equal in number of people, wherein is that State any better than the county? Can a change of name change the right? . . . [W]here is the mysterious, original right, from principle, for a certain district of country with inhabitants, by merely being called a State, to play tyrant over all its own citizens, and deny the authority of everything greater than itself? I say I am deciding nothing, but simply giving something for you to reflect upon.[29]

The perfectly Socratic formulation of this disputed question should not mislead anyone into thinking it led merely to a doubt of any answer. Lincoln always recognized the possibility that sincere and reasonable human beings could reach opposite conclusions to such problems, but that did not release him from the ultimate obligation of making decisions with respect to them. Here Lincoln says he is deciding nothing, but that is because the moment for decision has not arrived. It is clear, however, that he is preparing the public mind for that moment of decision.

It is characteristic of Lincoln to address the principle of original right underlying American federalism. The comparison of the legal status of a state and of a county might appear at first to be defective, because a county is indisputably the legal creation of the state. Lincoln here anticipates his theory that the Union made the states, in opposition to the Calhounian theory that the states made the Union.[30] The thirteen colonies were fully functioning civil societies before the American Revolution. However, according to Madison, in an opinion in which Jefferson concurred, the Declaration of Independence was "the fundamental act of Union of these States."[31] With the Declaration the Continental Congress, acting in the name of "one people," transformed thirteen "United Colonies" into thirteen "free and independent States," which it said now possessed "full power to levy war, conclude peace, contract alliances," and in general to "do all other acts and things that independent states may of right do." But did they have the power to do these things individually and separately, or only as members of a Union that made them, with respect to the rest of the world, a single people with a single government? Jefferson Davis, following Calhoun, believed that the Declaration proclaimed, not one, but thirteen separate sovereignties, each as independent of the others as it was of Great Britain. Here was the alleged historical foundation of the state rights claimed in the secession crisis. That the claim was false is attested by the fact that none of the states had ever attempted individually to make war, conclude peace, or enter into alliances. They no more did any of these things than the counties of which they were composed.[32] They did these things only as members of a Union whose government acted for them. During the Revolution, Benjamin Franklin was reported to have said that the colonies had to hang together if they did not want to hang separately. The idea of any one of the states exercising the power either to make war or conclude peace separately from the others endangered the others as surely in 1860 as in 1775. At Indianapolis, Lincoln gave his first clear indication that he would not view the words "coercion" or "invasion" as his predecessor had done. The Union, as understood by Lincoln, was not a "free-love arrangement." It would be held together by reason no less than by passion.[33] As the Union created the states, and as a state created its counties, secession from the one was no less revolutionary than from the other.

~

Lincoln would come no closer than he did at Indianapolis to disclosing what measures he might announce in his inaugural address. However, in his speeches to the New Jersey Senate at Trenton and in Independence Hall in Philadelphia, he spoke some of the most memorable and revealing words of his life. If he did not say *how* he would save the Union, he indicated, as he would at Gettysburg, *why* the burden of world history was bound up with that saving. At Trenton, he begged the pardon of his audience for mentioning that

> away back in my childhood, the earliest days of my being able to read, I got hold of a small book, such a one as few of the younger members have ever seen— "Weem's Life of Washington." I remember all the accounts there given of the battle fields and struggles for the liberties of the country, and none fixed themselves upon my imagination so deeply as the struggle here at Trenton, New Jersey. The crossing of the river; the contest with the Hessians; the great hardships endured at that time, all fixed themselves on my memory more than any single Revolutionary event; and you all know, for you have all been boys, how these early impressions last longer than any others. I recollect thinking then, boy even though I was, that there must have been something more than common that those men struggled for. I am exceedingly anxious that that thing which they struggled for; that something even more than national independence; that something that held out a great promise to all the people of the world to all time to come—I am exceedingly anxious that this Union, the Constitution, and the liberties of the people shall be perpetuated in accordance with the original idea for which that struggle was made, and I shall be most happy indeed if I shall be a humble instrument in the hands of the Almighty, and of this, his almost chosen people, for perpetuating the object of that great struggle.[34]

What Lincoln recounts at the beginning of this passage resembles nothing so much as the effect upon a growing mind of the story of the Exodus. The qualification respecting "this his almost chosen people" does not reflect any reservations as to the providential character of American history but only Lincoln's care in not seeming in any way to contradict the Bible. The comparison of the emergence of the American people from the "Egypt" of the inequality of Europe's ancien régimes to the republican equality of the promised land, was something of a commonplace in the years when Lincoln was growing up. We might say that the story of the children of Israel and the story of the American Revolution combine into one symbolic form, representing in the end a universal experience, the story, not of Israel or of America, but of mankind in its mortal travail and its immortal destiny.

As the Trenton speech evoked memories of the crossing of the Delaware, so the speech in Independence Hall evoked the memory of the great document forged within its walls.

> I am filled with deep emotion at finding myself standing in this place, where were collected together the wisdom, the patriotism, the devotion to principle, from which sprang the institutions under which we live. You have kindly suggested to

me that in my hands is the task of restoring peace to our distracted country. I can say, sir, that all the political sentiments I entertain have been drawn, so far as I have been able to draw them, from the sentiments that originated in and were given to the world from this hall in which we stand. I have never had a feeling politically that did not spring from the sentiments embodied in the Declaration of Independence. I have often pondered over the dangers which were incurred by the men who assembled here and framed and adopted that Declaration of Independence. I have pondered over the toils that were endured by the officers and soldiers of the army that achieved that Independence. I have often inquired of myself what great principle or idea it was that kept this Confederacy so long together. It was not the mere matter of the separation of the Colonies from the motherland; but that sentiment in the Declaration of Independence which gave liberty, not alone to the people of this country, but hope to the world for all future time. It was that which gave promise that in due time the weights should be lifted from the shoulders of all men, and that all should have an equal chance. This is the sentiment embodied in that Declaration of Independence.[35]

At this point Lincoln asked, "Now, my friends, can this country be saved upon that basis?" And he made clear his conviction that the country could not be saved upon any other basis, any more than the children of Israel could have been be saved by the worship of the golden calf. The weight upon the shoulders of all men is an evocation of the great pack, the burden of sin, carried on the back of Christian in *Pilgrim's Progress*.[36] The escape from Egypt meant the ultimate release of all mankind from the bondage to false gods, and eventually the means of release from the burden of original sin. The story of Israel as the Lord's Suffering Servant, retold as the story of America, will find its final form in the second inaugural. There it will come as an explanation, within the framework of biblical teaching, of the terrible suffering of the war. In Philadelphia Lincoln says, "there is no need of bloodshed and war." In the second inaugural he will say that there was such a need. Of course, before the war began, Lincoln was under a conscientious obligation to deny its necessity in order to avert the war, if at all possible, consistently with his duty to the Union and the principles of the Declaration. Before the war began, neither he nor any man could know whether that was possible. In the end, he is compelled to say that the wisdom of God is not that of man.

In these two speeches, at Trenton and Philadelphia, Lincoln at once displays his inflexible purpose and his wish for peace. No one knew better than he that one of these would have to give way to the other. So far as it lay with him, the Union would not be surrendered, nor would that principle of the Union that gave promise to all humanity. These two speeches on the eve of his inauguration provide a lucid statement of his intentions, giving the lie to charges that would be made that in the war he subordinated the question of freedom to that of Union.

The two were always, in his mind, one and indivisible.

∼

We turn now to the text of the first inaugural itself, whose paragraphs we will number.[37] We cannot forbear mentioning that the overall theme of the speech is exactly what we would have expected of the author of the Lyceum speech of 1838, "The Perpetuation of Our Political Institutions." Then, Lincoln had warned of the growing tendency toward lawlessness, and had urged, as the only antidote thereto, "a reverence for the Constitution and the laws."[38] Now, as the constitutionally chosen representative of the laws, he will deliver a great sermon on why reverence for the Constitution and the laws is the only guide to safety in the present crisis.

If we are to understand this speech as Lincoln himself understood it, we must look out upon the crisis of March 4, 1861, with Lincoln's eyes, with all his certainty as to what was eternally true and right in man's relationship to man and to God, and yet with all his uncertainty as to whether force might be avoided. Above all, we must bear in mind that although all the issues of the Civil War were already drawn in the speeches, declarations, and manifestos of the opposing sides, no blow had yet been struck. Neither side knew how far the other was prepared to go to support its position with force or how far it could go to support its own position with force. Lincoln probably knew less of his side than Jefferson Davis of his, since the initiative in the crisis lay with the South and the very act of secession, although claimed to be lawful, was nonetheless an act of defiance, which no one would make who was not prepared to fight. Lincoln had to be firm but not belligerent. He had to command the most widespread support possible on the Union side, comprehending the border slave states as well as the free states, and reaching out as well to Unionists behind the Confederate lines. No political leader in all human history began his office in the midst of more profound difficulties nor a situation in which his leadership depended upon such contrary imperatives. The situation Winston Churchill confronted upon becoming prime minister in 1940 was more desperate. But in 1940, the threat of annihilation by Hitler simplified Churchill's task. While Hitler's appeasers remained where they had been, the British nation as a whole recognized that Churchill had told them the truth about Hitler all along and that he alone pointed to the path of survival. Lincoln at his inaugural in 1861 was in a position resembling rather that of Neville Chamberlain in 1938. All he had to do to escape the burden of responsibility was, Chamberlain-like, to accept either partition or a compromise formula for reunion. And the pressure to avoid war by allowing "our erring sisters to depart," like the pressure to compromise on the territorial question, was enormous. One must bear in mind that Northern opposition to the extension of slavery was hardly united in the desire, expressed by Lincoln, to place slavery in the course of ultimate extinction. It had much more to do with keeping the territories white. Race prejudice, as distinct from proslavery sentiment, was scarcely less in the North than in the South. Unifying the North to preserve the Union involved the most complex task of political leadership the world has ever witnessed.

No other political speech in history combines the timeless and the transient in such delicate equilibrium. In the balance between the necessities of action and of thought, of the imperatives of the time and of the timeless, it has no superior and perhaps no equal. Lincoln begins quietly.

[1] In compliance with a custom as old as the government itself, I appear before you to address you briefly, and to take, in your presence, the oath prescribed by the Constitution of the United States, to be taken by the President "before he enters on the execution of his office."

Lincoln combines "custom" and "old" in his first sentence, reminding us of the presumption of mankind in identifying the ancestral and the good, a presumption to which unqualified assent can never be given. The *novus ordo seclorum* introduced by the American Revolution represented a rejection of much of the wisdom that had been regarded as ancestral truth up until that moment. No constitution before that of 1787 had ever prohibited a religious test for office. No head of state before President Washington in 1790 had ever addressed Jews as equal fellow citizens. We have already quoted Washington declaring that the foundation of American government "was not laid in the gloomy age of ignorance and superstition, but at an epoch when the rights of mankind were better understood and more clearly defined, than at any former period."[39] Lincoln himself, in his Lyceum speech of 1838, had said, "We find ourselves under the government of a system of political institutions, conducing more essentially to the ends of civil and religious liberty, than any of which the history of former times tells us."[40] Lincoln will not appeal to custom simply, but to American custom, custom founded upon a better understanding of natural rights than has informed any government hitherto. But the existence of a government founded upon man's natural rights is compromised by the ultimate form of the denial of those rights, chattel slavery. The question now is whether it is fatally compromised.

Lincoln defers to *wise* custom. How wise, we will learn only later, when Lincoln turns the oath of office into a powerful means of preserving the very Constitution that enjoins the oath upon him. No president before him had ever discovered the reservoir of constitutional power contained within that presidential oath, the only one whose actual words are prescribed by the Constitution itself. Before the speech is over, Lincoln will have at least hinted at what that is.

[2] I do not consider it necessary, at present, for me to discuss those matters of administration about which there is no special anxiety or excitement.

The mention here of anxiety and excitement is the least excitable and anxious way in which the main subject of the address could be introduced. That now follows.

[3] Apprehension seems to exist among the people of the Southern States, that by the accession of a Republican Administration, their property, and their peace, and personal security, are to be endangered. There has never been any reasonable cause for such apprehension. Indeed, the most ample evidence to the contrary has all the while existed, and been open to inspection. It is found in nearly all the published speeches of him who now addresses you. I do but quote from one of those speeches when I declare that "I have no purpose, directly or indirectly, to interfere with the institution of slavery in the States where it exists. I believe I have no lawful right to do so, and I have no inclination to do so." Those who nominated and elected me did so with full knowledge that I had made this, and many similar declarations, and had never recanted them. And more than this, they placed in the platform, for my acceptance, and as a law to themselves, and to me, the clear and emphatic resolution which I now read:

> Resolved, That the maintenance inviolate of the rights of the States, and especially the right of each State to order and control its own domestic institutions according to its own judgment exclusively, is essential to that balance of power on which the perfection and endurance of our political fabric depend; and we denounce the lawless invasion by armed force of the soil of any State or Territory, no matter under what pretext, as among the gravest of crimes.

[4] I now reiterate these sentiments: and in doing so, I only press upon the public attention the most conclusive evidence of which the case is susceptible, that the property, peace, and security of no section are to be in anywise endangered by the now incoming Administration. I add too, that all the protection which, consistently with the Constitution and the laws, can be given, will be cheerfully given to all the States when lawfully demanded, for whatever cause—as cheerfully to one section, as to another.

The reference to a "lawless invasion" at the end of the Republican Party platform resolution in the third paragraph refers to John Brown's raid on Harper's Ferry in October 1859. In the Cooper Institute speech of February 1860, Lincoln repelled in much more vigorous language the Southern charge that Republicans were implicated in Brown's enterprise. We must bear in mind, from our review of Buchanan's last annual message to Congress, that the outgoing president had given credence to Southern fears of slave insurrections brought on by "anti-slavery agitation." The difficulty of Lincoln's position can be measured by the fact that his immediate predecessor, a Northern Democrat, had treated as altogether reasonable the fears that Lincoln says have no reasonable foundation.

Lincoln cites his often repeated declaration that he has no purpose to interfere with slavery in the states where it exists. But the Lincoln text most cited in the South was the House Divided speech, in which he expressed his belief in the "ultimate extinction" of slavery. It is true that Lincoln was always clear that he did not mean that, as a matter of Republican policy, anything more would be done to further that end than to limit the extension of slavery into the territories. That was all that would be necessary, he thought, for "the public mind" to rest in the belief in that "ultimate extinction."[41] Lincoln had also argued that this condition of the "public mind" was that of the Founding Fathers. But Lincoln's policy was no less anathema to the South because it did not envisage interference with slavery in the slave states. Lincoln had accurately portrayed the mind of the South in the Cooper Institute speech, saying that it had become immune to rational persuasion. What alone would serve to reassure Southerners of their security? "This, and this only: cease to call slavery *wrong*, and join them in calling it *right*. . . . The whole atmosphere must be disinfected from all taint of opposition to slavery, before they will cease to believe that all their troubles proceed from us."[42] Why then does Lincoln attempt to persuade the South now, when the passions he observed a year before had only intensified since the election? I think we can only conclude that Lincoln felt obliged to set forth to the world and to posterity the essential moderation of his position, without regard to its prospects of exerting any immediate influence. It certainly would not reverse the movement for secession where it had already occurred. But on March 4, 1861, eight of the fifteen slave states had not seceded.

The South was not as homogeneous as the Cooper Institute speech had implied. In general, proslavery feeling intensified as one progressed southwards. In the border slave states of Delaware, Maryland, Virginia, Kentucky, and Missouri, the bitter contests that were about to ensue between secessionists and unionists would be waged with a fair prospect of success on the part of the latter. Throughout the Appalachian regions of Virginia,[43] Kentucky, North Carolina, Tennessee, and even Georgia and Alabama, there were mountaineers who were fiercely anti-slavery. Even those who could not succeed in preventing their states from joining the Confederacy would provide a rearguard resistance behind the lines. During the war, 100,000 of them would migrate northwards to join the Union army. In his inaugural, Lincoln is calculating all the chances that might affect the fortunes of the Union cause, even as he poises on the brink and professes that there is no need for armed conflict.

When Lincoln speaks of the "protection . . . [that] will be cheerfully given . . . when lawfully demanded," he has in mind Article IV, section 4, of the Constitution, which reads in part, "The United States shall guarantee to every State in this Union a Republican Form of Government, and shall protect each of them against Invasion; and on Application of the Legislature, or of the Executive (when the Legislature cannot be convened) against domestic Violence." This section of the Constitution is of great importance in the political debates preceding the Civil War because of its ambiguity concerning the meaning of the guarantee of "a republican form of government." Since this is a constitutional guarantee, everyone who swears to uphold the Constitution swears to enforce it. But the Constitution nowhere defines what a republican form of government is. The question arose in the 1850s as to whether polygamy was compatible with such a form. Although it never assumed the political importance of the slavery question, the question of polygamy at the time of the Mormon war raised questions of equal philosophical magnitude concerning the limits imposed by the nature of republican government upon the freedom of an independent people to decide for themselves regarding their "domestic institutions." Certainly the laws governing marriage and the family were as "domestic" as those concerning master and servant. The first platform of the Republican Party, in 1856, denounced the "twin relics of barbarism, polygamy and slavery."[44] Jefferson, in his Bill for Proportioning Crimes and Punishment for Virginia in 1779, grouped "rape, sodomy, and bigamy" as felonies of equal heinousness.[45] During the Lincoln–Douglas debates, Lincoln trapped Douglas with the inconsistency of his doctrine of popular sovereignty, which presumably left the people of a territory or a state "perfectly free" to decide for themselves what their domestic institutions would be. Yet Douglas would not accept Utah either as territory or state unless polygamy was abolished.

It was clear to Lincoln, although not so clear to many of his contemporaries, that the "consent of the governed" could be rightfully exercised only within the boundaries of a moral law that gives consent its validity but whose validity does not depend upon consent. If a republican form of government is based upon the consent of the governed, as the seceding Southerners themselves insisted, how could the government of slaves be consistent with republicanism? How could anyone demand to be governed only with his own consent while denying to others even the slightest semblance of that right? On the other hand, if the United States guaranteed a republican form of government to each of the states, and if fifteen of the states receiving that guarantee had slavery among their domestic institutions, did not that necessarily imply that slavery was a republican institution? For the present, we note only that the protection due to each state "against domestic violence" was certainly understood to include protection against slave uprisings, as well as any other unlawful uprisings. And Lincoln shows that he is prepared to honor this constitutional commitment.

We should also bear in mind here that quite apart from the question of slavery, the principles of American federalism, grounded in the Declaration of Independence, require that the ordinary police powers of government reside in the states and in their localities, and not in the federal government. That is to say, the protection of life and property, which is the purpose of any government under the "laws of nature and of nature's God," must be entrusted to political authorities immediately responsible to those whose lives and property are to be protected. This means not only that the police power resides in the states rather than in the federal government but also that the states themselves delegate a necessary and sufficient portion of that power to local authorities responsible to the communities they serve. It is in the same sense according to nature that only the federal government can provide security to the Union as a whole against external dangers and that the federal government cannot provide security to individual communities within the Union. A federal police force or fire department cannot respond efficiently to the requirements of a local community, any more than a local government can respond to dangers from abroad. No one in Maine or Massachusetts, any more than someone in Alabama or Mississippi, would want to rely upon a federal police or fire department. Majority rule has its natural limits. Thus Lincoln did not expect the responsibility for the security of a Southern town, any more than for that of a Northern town, to be placed anywhere but in the hands of the townsmen themselves. The government of the slaves was looked upon as a matter of security by Southerners. Whether they ought to have looked upon it as they did, the principles of the Declaration made it a matter of right, and not only of prudence, that those immediately concerned be the rightful judges of what constituted their own security. Thus Lincoln was not merely abiding by a constitutional compromise when he said that he had no inclination to interfere with slavery in states where it was lawful.

[5] There is much controversy about the delivering up of fugitives from service or labor. The clause I now read is as plainly written in the Constitution as any other of its provisions: "No person held to service or labor in one State, under the laws thereof, escaping into another, shall, in consequence of any law or regulation therein, be discharged from such service or labor, but shall be delivered up on claim of the party to whom such service or labor may be due."

[6] It is scarcely to be questioned that this provision was intended by those who made it, for the reclaiming of what we call fugitive slaves; and the intention of the law-giver is the law. All members of Congress swear their support to the

whole Constitution—to this provision as much as to any other. To the proposition, then, that slaves whose cases come within the terms of this clause, "shall be delivered up," their oaths are unanimous. Now, if they would make the effort in good temper, could they not, with nearly equal unanimity, frame and pass a law, by means of which to keep good that unanimous oath?

Lincoln's reasons for fidelity to the fugitive slave clause of the Constitution resemble, but are not identical to, those for honoring the right of each state to order and control its own domestic institutions. In both instances it is the law of the Constitution, and fidelity to the Constitution is a sine qua non for the continued existence of the Union. But state rights, in the aforesaid sense relating to the rights of local self-government, are necessary in any government based upon the consent of the governed. The fugitive slave clause, however, was not among the provisions of the Articles of Confederation. Rendition of fugitives, whether runaway criminals or runaway slaves, depended entirely upon interstate comity under the Articles, because the government of the Articles could act only through the states. The government of the Constitution of 1787 was immeasurably more powerful because its laws were enforced by its own agents. Such a government, even if it could not interfere with slavery within a slave state, could interfere with the security of slave property if it acted in a hostile manner toward slavery when the slaves crossed state lines. The general assumption, which Lincoln shared, was that a government as powerful as the one established in the Constitution would not have been ratified without the fugitive slave clause. There was little in the record of the Constitutional Convention either to prove or disprove this contention.[46] It was cited as absolute historical fact by Southerners in the 1850s, and Lincoln seems at least to have been unwilling to dispute it. But Lincoln also believed that the strengthening of the government of the Union added enormously to the prosperity of the Union, which in turn strengthened the Union itself. In so doing, it made possible a federal government better able to contain the centrifugal forces of sectionalism. The concession to slavery in the fugitive slave clause was ultimately, he thought, in the interest of the slaves themselves, as the present crisis proved. The old government of the Articles would not have been able to present the obstacle to the expansion of slavery that Lincoln's election presented under the 1787 Constitution.

[7] There is some difference of opinion whether this clause should be enforced by national or by state authority; but surely that difference is not a very material one. If the slave is to be surrendered, it can be of little consequence to him, or to others, by which authority it is done. And should any one, in any case, be content that his oath shall go unkept, on a merely unsubstantial controversy as to *how* it shall be kept?

There is something anomalous about this discussion of the fugitive slave question. Southerners had complained bitterly about the alleged noncompliance of the free states with the fugitive slave law of 1850. We have already recounted the retaking of runaway slave Anthony Burns in Boston in 1854, utilizing a battery of United States artillery and four platoons of marines, supported by twenty-two companies of state militia.[47] The 1850 law could hardly have gone further in satisfying the legislative demands of the slaveholding South. Two proslavery presidents, Pierce and Buchanan, supported by the Taney Supreme Court, could scarcely have done more to enforce it. And Lincoln had always taken the position, outlined here, that he was bound by the fugitive slave clause. The question of whether this clause should be enforced by national or state authority was largely moot. Why then does Lincoln speak of framing and passing a new law?

[8] Again, in any law upon this subject, ought not all the safeguards of liberty known in civilized and humane jurisprudence to be introduced, so that a free man be not, in any case, surrendered as a slave? And might it not be well, at the same time, to provide by law for the enforcement of that clause in the Constitution which guarantees that "The citizens of each State shall be entitled to all privileges and immunities of citizens in the several States?"

We recall that Buchanan, in his last annual message, had condemned the personal liberty laws that had been passed by some twelve free states as "unconstitutional and obnoxious" and called for their repeal as a necessary step to save the Union. But where these laws conflicted with the enforcement of federal law, they were legal nullities. What good could result from their repeal, something over which Lincoln's government had no more control than Buchanan's? Again, Lincoln had answered this question in the Cooper Institute speech, when he said that nothing less would satisfy the proslavery demands than purging the free states of all taint of opposition to slavery. The personal liberty laws were galling to the South, even though they had no effect on slavery itself. Thus in paragraph 8 Lincoln is moving not to satisfy Southern discontents, as at first appears to be his purpose, but to satisfy the principal demands of the personal liberty laws of the free states. Lincoln implies that if a new fugitive slave law should be passed, it is because the 1850 law does not contain safeguards against a "free man" being surrendered as a slave.

It is also remarkable that Lincoln mentions the "privileges and immunities" clause of Article IV, section 2, of the Constitution. Having said that all members of Congress swear to support the whole Constitution, including the fugitive slave clause, he reminds them of another clause that, by the same token, they have also sworn to uphold. What exactly the privileges and immunities of Article IV were was largely a no man's land of constitutional law before the Civil War. In this context, however, Lincoln clearly implies that whatever they were, they applied to black citizens as well as white. Even in the midst of his attempt to be as conciliatory as possible toward his "dissatisfied fellow countrymen," Lincoln stands firmly by those provisions of the Constitution that require a color-blind application.

[9] I take the official oath today, with no mental reservations, and with no purpose to construe the Constitution or laws, by any hypercritical rules. And while I do not choose now to specify particular acts of Congress as proper to be enforced, I do suggest, that it will be much safer for all, both in official and private stations, to conform to, and abide by, all those acts which stand unrepealed, than to violate any of them, trusting to find impunity in having them held to be unconstitutional.

It is unusual for Lincoln to use a word as uncommon as "hypercritical." He is saying quite plainly, however, that he will interpret the Constitution and laws plainly and will not, by clever interpretations, discover meanings in them that any ordinary citizen would not recognize. It is not without significance that he says this immediately after quoting the privileges and immunities clause, which had in fact gone unenforced. But why does he suggest that it may be proper on his part to enforce some laws but not others? The explanation will come later in the speech, when he says that he will not attempt to enforce the law in those places where hostility to the government is so great as to make such enforcement impossible without bloodshed. He is also saying here what he said twenty-three years earlier, in the Lyceum speech, about the necessity of law-abidingness in a free society. If the people do not obey laws they have given themselves, they will have gone a long way toward proving that they cannot govern themselves. As the speech progresses, this will become its ever more dominant theme.

[10] It is seventy-two years since the first inauguration of a President under our national Constitution. During that period fifteen different and greatly distinguished citizens have, in succession, administered the executive branch of the government. They have conducted it through many perils; and, generally, with great success. Yet, with all this scope for precedent, I now enter upon the same task for the brief constitutional term of four years, under great and peculiar difficulty. A disruption of the Federal Union heretofore only menaced, is now formidably attempted.

Lincoln now approaches the theme of our first chapter. Can ballots in all cases succeed bullets as a means of preserving the people's rights? Was not the nation founded upon the exercise of the right of revolution? Did not Lincoln himself say in 1848, during the Mexican War and with reference to the Texan revolt against Mexico, that "Any people anywhere, being inclined and having the power, have the *right* to rise up, and shake off the existing government, and form a new one that suits them better. This is a most valuable,—a most sacred right—a right, which we hope and believe, is to liberate the world."[48] This sounds very much like the pre-1800 Jefferson, who saw the liberties of the people depending on the right of revolution rather than the right of free elections. In 1861, however, the South did not, by and large, appeal to the right of revolution. They chose rather to appeal to the doctrine of state rights, by which, as they understood it, secession was lawful under the Constitution. They chose to cast the Republicans and Lincoln in the role of lawbreakers and themselves in the role of the law-abiding. How could this be possible? The question will remain, however, whether the South *might* with reason have appealed to the right of revolution had it chosen to do so.

> [11] I hold, that in contemplation of universal law, and of the Constitution, the Union of these States is perpetual. Perpetuity is implied, if not expressed, in the fundamental law of all national governments. It is safe to assert that no government proper, ever had a provision in its organic law for its own termination. Continue to execute all the express provisions of our national Constitution, and the Union will endure forever—it being impossible to destroy it, except by some action not provided for in the instrument itself.

Lincoln here refers to the perpetuity implied in the fundamental law of all *national* governments. That the United States *is* a national government is for the moment assumed. What Lincoln says about this perpetuity is axiomatic. The Americans in 1776 terminated the authority of the British government in the thirteen colonies by revolutionary overthrow. The Texans did the same to the government of Mexico in 1836. But what happened in the replacement of the Articles of Confederation by the government of the Constitution of 1787? The Congress of the Confederation had authorized the convention to revise the Articles. Instead, it had scrapped them and called for an altogether new government. The old Congress submitted the new Constitution to the states for ratification, as called for, not in the Articles, but in the new Constitution itself. The government of the Articles ceased to exist when it was superseded by its own act, an act not "provided for in the instrument itself." The perpetuity implied in the Articles did not prevent this from happening, any more than it would have prevented a successful armed uprising. One might say that the thirteen states "seceded" from the Articles when they joined the Union under the Constitution, but what they did was sanctioned by the right of revolution rather than by any right under positive law. Lincoln has here delivered a legal truism, but one that provides a necessary foundation for the argument to follow.

[12] Again, if the United States be not a government proper, but an association of states in the nature of contract merely, can it, as a contract, be peaceably unmade, by less than all the parties who made it? One party to a contract may violate it—break it, so to speak; but does it not require all to lawfully rescind it?

Now Lincoln considers what follows from the hypothesis, which he of course rejects, that the United States is *not* a national government. He argues for the moment from the premises of his Calhounian or state-sovereignty opponents. Let us therefore recur to the compact or contract theory of political obligation, as it was in the minds of Jefferson and Madison at the time of the Revolution and of the Virginia and Kentucky Resolutions: Individual human beings in the state of nature are in precisely the same relationship to each other as "states" before they enter into a contractual relationship with other states. When individuals agree to form a political community, they do so by unanimous consent. At the same time, they unanimously consent to be governed by majority rule. The majority may then decide for all, but it may decide only those things entrusted to it for decision by the original contract. And as Madison said, it may decide only those things that may be decided *"rightfully."*[49] For example, a unanimous decision to establish a state church or to deny the free exercise of religion is beyond the *rightful* power of *any* majority. Likewise, as Lincoln declared in his debates with Douglas, to establish slavery in a U.S. territory was beyond the *rightful* power of any majority in that territory. By the same token it was beyond the rightful power of a territorial majority to establish polygamy among its domestic institutions. A majority, like an individual, may decide prudentially, or choose the lesser of two evils, when no better choice is possible.[50] But it cannot decide in principle, even unanimously, to establish a religion or to introduce polygamy or slavery.

Whatever the majority decides, within the boundaries of the commission arising from the original unanimous consent *and* within the boundaries of the moral law, binds all members of the community equally. Their purpose in agreeing to enter the political community can be served only by accepting the decisions of the majority as their own. While they have a right to resist decisions of the majority unauthorized by the original agreement, they must obey decisions that are so authorized. No one has the right, for example, to refuse to pay his taxes because he voted against the taxes in question, provided those taxes are to support a lawful purpose. One cannot "secede" from the political community because he does not want to pay taxes. Nor can he "secede" from his lawful obligations when his country is engaged in a just war because he did not agree with the decision to go to war.[51] In short, the social contract or compact, which underlies all political obligation, is an agreement of each to defend all and of all to defend each. One cannot accept the benefits of such an agreement while reserving the right to withdraw from it at will. If one man refuses to pay his taxes and is allowed to do so, then no one will pay taxes. Likewise, to concede to anyone the right to secede is de facto an agreement to dissolve the political community. This is the logic of Lincoln's argument, and we see that it asserts the perpetuity of union and the unlawfulness of secession, equally with respect to a national government and to an "association of states in the nature of contract merely."

[13] Descending from these general principles, we find the proposition that, in legal contemplation, the Union is perpetual, confirmed by the history of the Union itself. The Union is much older than the Constitution. It was formed in fact, by the Articles of Association in 1774. It was matured and continued by the Declaration of Independence in 1776. It was further matured and the faith of all the then thirteen States expressly plighted and engaged that it should be perpetual, by the Articles of Confederation in 1778. And finally, in 1787, one of the declared objects for ordaining and establishing the Constitution, was *"to form a more perfect Union."*

[14] But if destruction of the Union, by one, or by a part only, of the States, be lawfully possible, the Union is *less* perfect than before the Constitution, having lost the vital element of perpetuity.

[15] It follows from these views that no State, upon its own mere motion, can lawfully get out of the Union,—that *resolves* and *ordinances* to that effect are legally void; and that acts of violence, within any State or States, against the authority of the United States, are insurrectionary or revolutionary, according to circumstances.

In this history, Lincoln reasserts his view of the Union as a national government. Anticipating the metaphor of the Gettysburg Address, we may say that its prenatal history ("conceived in liberty") began in 1774 and that it was born in 1776. Lincoln ignores the Confederate contention that in 1776 the thirteen states declared their independence of each other, as well as of Great Britain. Since he is speaking before Fort Sumter, he does not think it proper to refute a contention that he still hopes will not control his "dissatisfied fellow-countrymen." The greatest difficulty with Lincoln's account is that it passes over the fact that the Constitution came into effect when nine states had ratified, "between the States so ratifying." The Southerners, as we saw in chapter 3, relied absolutely upon their interpretation of this fact to contend that the Union existed only upon the basis of the ratifications. They held that whatever Union existed under the Articles had been dissolved and a new one put in its place. But if, as Madison and Jefferson asserted in 1825, the Declaration of Independence was "the act of Union of these States," then neither the Articles nor the Constitution was ever in itself the sole or sufficient basis of union, and the abrogation of the Articles by the Constitution was not in itself an abrogation of the act of union of 1776.

[16] I therefore consider that, in view of the Constitution and the laws, the Union is unbroken; and, to the extent of my ability, I shall take care, as the Constitution itself expressly enjoins upon me, that the laws of the Union be faithfully executed in all the States. Doing this I deem to be only a simple duty on my part; and I shall perform it, so far as practicable, unless my rightful masters, the American people, shall withhold the requisite means, or, in some authoritative manner, direct the contrary. I trust this will not be regarded as a menace, but only as the declared purpose of the Union that it will constitutionally defend and maintain itself.

Unlike President Buchanan, who held that neither the president nor Congress had any constitutional power "to coerce a State into submission which is attempting to withdraw or has actually withdrawn" from the Union, Lincoln declares that all resolves and ordinances of secession are legally void and the Union unbroken. This meant that, as a state could not constitutionally withdraw from the Union, none had done so. A state, as state, could not secede, and hence could not be coerced. Secession in name is rebellion in fact, and the constitutional power to suppress rebellion was unquestionable. This declaration, more than anything else, presages what Lincoln will do to preserve the Union, and he trusts that it "will not be regarded as a menace." But how could it not be? The Confederate government and its supporters believed a theory of state rights that they identified with the essence of lawful self-government. Lincoln frames the issue in such a way as to make crystal clear that one side or the other will have to give way and that as president he has no intention of being on the yielding side.

Still, Lincoln is far from unambiguous in anticipating what measures he might take in the immediate or foreseeable future. He will, he says, perform his duty "so far as practicable." He does not know whether the American people will grant or withhold "the requisite means." Rebellions or invasions can be met only by armed force, and only Congress possessed the constitutional power to raise, support, and maintain armed forces. The Thirty-seventh Congress, elected in November 1860, before any states had seceded, would not normally have convened until December 1861. To wait that long would be tantamount to abandoning the Union. When he delivered his inaugural, Lincoln did not even know what the composition of this Congress would be. As explained by J. G. Randall and David Donald, Congress "would not have been in Republican control if the Southern states had stayed in the Union and preserved their membership. Counting members elected and 'to be elected,' the Republicans could muster only twenty-nine in the Senate as compared to thirty-seven for the opposition;

in the House the opposition could have mustered 129 to the Republicans' 108."[52] We recall that in his speech to the Georgia legislature in November 1860, Alexander Stephens had urged, as a compelling reason *not* to secede, that with the Southern members in their places, there would be a majority of four against Lincoln in the upper chamber. And on January 10, 1861, Andrew Johnson of Tennessee noted that if the Southern senators had all been present, the incoming administration would come into office "handcuffed."[53] Ironically, the more states that seceded and withdrew their members from Congress, the more Congress would be likely to fall under Republican control. The obverse of this, of course, was that the more states that seceded, the more difficult it would be to suppress the rebellion. Even among the representatives and senators from the loyal free states, especially the southern parts of Ohio, Indiana, and Illinois, there would be some with strong Confederate sympathies. Lincoln could not know in advance by what criteria the houses of Congress would judge the qualifications of their members, as the Constitution provided they should do. Nor could he know whether loyal members would take his position or Buchanan's with respect to the constitutional power to suppress the rebellion.

Since he first began to speak about the crisis, Lincoln had emphasized the ultimate authority of the people in determining their government and the policies it should pursue. But in what sense was there, at this moment, an American people? Does the defense of majority rule entitle the exclusion of those opposed to the majority that is ruling? Or does the defense of majority rule fail if those opposed to that defense are not counted in the electoral (and political) process? If some are to be excluded from the political process because of their opposition to the process itself, who is to determine who they are, and by what standard? In a nation as divided as the United States on the eve of the Civil War, who can qualify as *being* the people?

[17] In doing this there needs to be no bloodshed or violence; and there shall be none, unless it be forced upon the national authority. The power confided to me, will be used to hold, occupy, and possess the property, and places belonging to the government, and to collect the duties and imposts; but beyond what may be necessary for these objects, there will be no invasion—no using of force against, or among the people anywhere. Where hostility to the United States, in any interior locality, shall be so great and so universal, as to prevent competent resident citizens from holding federal offices, there will be no attempt to force obnoxious strangers among the people for that object. While the strict legal right may exist in the government to enforce the exercise of these offices, the attempt to do so would be so irritating, and so nearly impracticable with all, that I deem it better to forego, for the time, the uses of such offices.

[18] The mails, unless repelled, will continue to be furnished in all parts of the Union. So far as possible, the people everywhere shall have that sense of perfect security which is most favorable to calm thought and reflection. The course here indicated will be followed, unless current events, and experience, shall show a modification, or change, to be proper; and in every case and exigency, my best discretion will be exercised, according to circumstances actually existing, and with a view and a hope of a peaceful solution of the national troubles, and restoration of fraternal sympathies and affections.

We find the following paraphrase of the foregoing by a notable historian: "[Lincoln] would assert the Federal authority vigorously—but he would not exercise it. He would enforce the laws—where an enforcement mechanism existed. He would deliver the mails—unless repelled. He would collect the duties—offshore. He would hold the forts—at least the ones which Buchanan had held and which seemed capable of holding themselves."[54] This commentary certainly highlights the genuine ambiguity in Lincoln's text. But it hardly suggests the practical wisdom in that ambiguity. Of course Lincoln would not, because he could not, enforce the laws where no enforcement mechanism existed. Of course he would not, because he could not, deliver the mails where they were repelled. The questions remained: How could enforcement mechanisms be reinstated? And how could the repelling of the mails be itself repelled? In the end Lincoln answered these questions with the Union armies, and we surmise with some confidence that, in his own mind, he already knew here that that would be necessary. But at the moment of his inaugural there were no Union armies, and the seven-hundred-odd federal troops in the District of Columbia could have been swept away by almost any armed force that the seceded states might have put into the field against them. When we remember how militarily weak the Union government was at that moment, Lincoln's speech, notwithstanding its ambiguities, is remarkably bold. He makes no concession, either theoretical or practical, to the idea of any constitutional right of secession. Unlike Buchanan, he does not concede any constitutional obstruction to perpetuating one iota of the "strict legal rights" of the Union under the Constitution. Lincoln concedes nothing to the actual weakness of the moment. Instead he shows a magnanimous forbearance in the interest of "a peaceful solution of the national troubles," so far and so long as that solution is consistent with the claims of the unbroken Union. Otherwise, he reserves to the government any and every right to act in defense of the Union that experience and discretion may prove to be both possible and necessary.

[19] That there are persons in one section, or another, who seek to destroy the Union at all events, and are glad of any pretext to do so, I will neither affirm or

deny; but if there be such, I need address no word to them. To those, however, who really love the Union, may I not speak?

[20] Before entering upon so grave a matter as the destruction of our national fabric, with all its benefits, its memories, and its hopes, would it not be wise to ascertain precisely why we do it? Will you hazard so desperate a step, while there is any possibility that any portion of the ills you fly from have no real existence? Will you, while the certain ills you fly to, are greater than all the real ones you fly from? Will you risk the commission of so fearful a mistake?

Lincoln proposes something of a cost-benefit analysis, directed only to those "who really love the Union." There may be collateral benefits (or costs) in a man marrying the woman he loves, but accepting the benefits (or costs) is wise only if he really loves her. What makes the Union lovable, Lincoln had said most clearly in his speeches at Trenton and Philadelphia less than two weeks before. He will not now repeat what he said earlier about the Declaration of Independence. That will reappear, after Fort Sumter, in his July 4 message to Congress and again, most concisely, in the Gettysburg Address. Implicit in everything he says, however, is the thesis that the benefits of a free society cannot be long enjoyed by those who would arbitrarily deny them to others. Like fidelity in marriage, that is the one inescapable "cost" that the "benefit" of freedom entails. Hence the underlying question remains: Can those for whom slavery is a "positive good" or those who are indifferent to slavery love the Union as do those for whom the Union is the practical implementation of the principles of human freedom embodied in the Declaration?

The question of the ills one flies from or to echoes Hamlet's soliloquy.

> Who would these fardels bear,
> To grunt and sweat under a weary life?
> But that the dread of something after death
> In the undiscovered country from whose bourn
> No traveller return—puzzles the will;
> And makes us rather bear those ills we have,
> Than fly to others that we know not of.[55]

Unlike Hamlet, the secessionists are flying toward death, not away from it. They are flying not only toward civil war but also toward the reversal of those hopes of popular government that accompanied the Founding. The *novus ordo seclorum* rejected the divine right of kings because it rejected the idea of authority descending from above. Slavery, which denied any right of consent to the slave, represented the divine right of kings as much as any absolute monarch of the Old World. The South continued to appeal to the Declaration of Independence as justifying the withdrawal of their consent to be governed any longer in the Union without seeing any contradiction in the fact that they were withdrawing that consent in order to extend and perpetuate slavery.

Statesmen of the Old South proclaimed that the institution of slavery had grown and flourished, both politically and economically, in the generation preceding the Civil War—precisely during the period of mounting abolitionist agitation. Abolitionism had actually been counterproductive as far as the existing institution of slavery was concerned, and Lincoln assured the South that his election would make no difference to the existing institution. Alexander Stephens had admonished his fellow Georgians that in the event of a war, all the present prosperity of the South would be at risk, and in particular that a "vindictive decree of a universal emancipation . . . may reasonably be expected."[56] When Lincoln invited a comparison of the imaginary ills that the secessionists would fly from, compared with the certain ills they would fly to, he knew that the comparison had already been graphically made by Southern statesmen of high rank.

> [21] All profess to be content in the Union, if all constitutional rights can be maintained. Is it true, then, that any right, plainly written in the Constitution, has been denied? I think not. Happily the human mind is so constituted, that no party can reach to the audacity of doing this. Think, if you can, of a single instance in which a plainly written provision of the Constitution has ever been denied. If, by the mere force of numbers, a majority should deprive a minority of any clearly written constitutional right, it might, in a moral point of view, justify revolution—certainly would, if such right were a vital one. But such is not our case. All the vital rights of minorities, and of individuals, are so plainly assured to them, by affirmations and negations, guaranties and prohibitions, in the Constitution, that controversies never arise concerning them. But no organic law can ever be framed with a provision specifically applicable to every question which may occur in practical administration. No foresight can anticipate, nor any document of reasonable length contain express provisions for all possible questions. Shall fugitives from labor be surrendered by national or by State authority? The Constitution does not expressly say. *May* Congress prohibit slavery in the territories? The Constitution does not expressly say. *Must* Congress protect slavery in the territories? The Constitution does not expressly say.

All who really love the Union will necessarily be content if constitutional rights can be maintained. To the present day, devotees of the Confederate cause will argue, as we have seen Jefferson Davis argue (and as Alexander Stephens would argue most comprehensively in his postwar *Constitutional View*), that it was the South, and not the Union government under Lincoln, that was defending the Constitution of "the Fathers." These Confederate sympathizers have a hard time maintaining this argument in the light of Stephens's proclamation in his Cornerstone speech that the Confederate constitution, unlike that of the "old" Union, was based upon the newly discovered scientific truth that the Negro was not the equal of the white man. Nevertheless, the defense of the Confederate cause, even before the Civil War began, was mainly an identification of constitutionalism and state rights.[57]

Why does Lincoln make such a hyperbolic assertion as that "the human mind is so constituted" as to be incapable of "the audacity" of denying that a "plainly written" constitutional right has been denied? Lincoln knew perfectly well that there were no limits to the capacity of the human mind to deny what is true or affirm what is false. Clearly, he is bent upon impressing on his audience the distinction between what is plainly written and what is implied. Lincoln does not deny that there are implied constitutional rights. But he thinks that differences of opinion concerning these rights can and must be settled by the political process,[58] so long as the plainly written rights have been preserved in that process.

When Lincoln says that no one can point to a provision of the Constitution that is now being denied, he may have been thinking of such denial in terms of the Virginia and Kentucky Resolutions, which pointed to specific provisions of the First and Tenth Amendments as being transgressed by the Alien and Sedition Acts. In the present crisis, there had been no comparable violation alleged. Lincoln may also have had in mind the prohibitions upon the federal government in Article I, section 9, and the parallel prohibitions upon the states in Article I, section 10. For example, both the general government and the states are prohibited from passing ex post facto laws and bills of attainder, and certainly no one had had "the audacity" to say that any rights as plainly written as these had been violated.

Lincoln says that all the vital rights of minorities and individuals are plainly assured in the Constitution. But one may certainly question whether *some* implied rights were not vital. In a letter to Joshua Speed on August 24, 1855, Lincoln penned this magnificent passage:

> I am not a Know-Nothing. That is certain. How could I be? How can any one who abhors the oppression of negroes, be in favor of degrading classes of white people? Our progress in degeneracy appears to me to be pretty rapid. As a nation, we began by declaring that *"all men are created equal."* We now practically read it "all men are created equal, *except negroes.*" When the Know-Nothings get control, it will read "all men are created equal, except negroes, *and foreigners, and Catholics."* When it comes to this I should prefer emigrating to some country where they make no pretence of loving liberty—to Russia, for instance, where despotism can be taken pure, and without the base alloy of hypocrisy.[59]

The key to the then disputed questions of constitutional interpretation depended upon whether the "persons" mentioned in the Constitution, and particularly in the Fifth Amendment, are embraced without distinction by the proposition that all men are created equal. That is to say, the meaning of the Constitution in respect to its protection of private rights depended upon the understanding of the Declaration of Independence and its application to the Constitution. Whether Congress may prohibit or must protect slavery in the territories depended entirely upon whether the persons spoken of as being "held to service of labor" and "escaping" in Article IV, section 2, of the Constitution were, for constitutional purposes, primarily and essentially human beings or primarily and essentially chattels. Lincoln's letter to Speed shows that once Negroes are denied the rights of their humanity, there is no stopping point. Everyone's rights are at risk, and the question of whose rights are protected becomes a matter, not of right, but of power. Justice does indeed become nothing more than the interest of the stronger.

Lincoln says that if by mere force of numbers, a majority were to deny a minority a clearly written constitutional right, that would be a moral justification of revolution. Lincoln is thinking here of the right of revolution in the Declaration. In his mind also is the doctrine of the Declaration that justifies the altering or abolishing of governments only if they become destructive of "these ends." Voting can never legitimize despotism or tyranny.[60]

Lincoln implies, as does the compact theory upon which the Declaration itself is founded, that majority rule is for the sake of securing rights possessed equally by the majority and the minority. Whether anyone's rights to life, liberty, or property ought to be protected is not itself supposed to be subject to majority rule. Every elected official represents those who voted against him no less than those who voted for him. No majority can decide that any one or any number of those in the political minority, having committed no violation of criminal law, ought to be deprived of life, liberty, or property.

When a slave owner brings his slave property into a territory, is that slave property entitled to the same protection as any other form of property? Or is that slave, as a human person, entitled to the same liberty as any other human person? Which takes precedence, the character of chattel impressed upon the slave by the law of the slave state from whence he came or the character of a human person impressed upon him by "the laws of nature and of nature's God"? Within the antebellum debate, the laws of the slave states unquestionably took precedence over the laws of nature in the slave states themselves. Why should they not continue to do so in the territories? Lincoln's answer, given in all his speeches from 1854 on, was that the rights of every individual, of whatever race or nation or religion, were bound up in the mutual recognition of each other's humanity and that that humanity—and not their race or nationality or religion—was the foundation of their constitutional rights.

From the Southern point of view, the secession crisis is not about the rights of individuals or of minorities or of the economic interest groups out of which electoral majorities and minorities are compounded. For the South, minority rights are conceived only in terms of state rights. And although the alleged state right to carry slaves into the territories and to have them protected there as any other kind of property was certainly not "plainly written" in the Constitution, it came nonetheless, in the wake of the *Dred Scott* decision, to be regarded as if it had been so written. And as we shall see, Lincoln himself contributed to it becoming so regarded.

The question of the tyranny of the majority had been identified by the South with the tyranny of the federal government ever since that prologue to the Civil War, the nullification crisis. In 1833, South Carolina attempted to nullify the so-called Tariff of Abominations of 1828. John C. Calhoun, then vice president of the United States, was the anonymous author of South Carolina's "Exposition and Protest" of 1828.[61] In it he argued that the South, an exporter of agricultural products and an importer of industrial products, was compelled by the tariff to pay disproportionately high prices for what it bought. Still further, by limiting the access of foreign manufacturers to American markets, the tariff limited the ability of foreigners to buy Southern products. Thus Calhoun maintained that the tariff represented an arbitrary transfer of wealth from South to North.[62] The only assertedly constitutional defense against this alleged tyranny of the majority, known presently as the South Carolina doctrine, was that of nullification. By virtue of the reserved rights of the states, South Carolina could "nullify" the tariff within its borders. Of course, if South Carolina did not pay the duties, neither would any other state. This meant that the operation of the challenged law would be held in abeyance until a convention of the states, acting by a three-fourths majority (the same that would be required for an amendment), would decide upon its constitutionality. The Virginia and Kentucky Resolutions were hailed as the authoritative precedents for South Carolina, although James Madison vigorously denied it. It was Calhoun's writings, then and thereafter, that transformed the question of individual and minority rights into the question of state rights. It is reported that Jackson's proclamation against nullification was one of the small number of documents Lincoln had at hand as he drafted his inaugural. He well knew that in the sectional dispute Calhoun's disciples had sought to gain the moral high ground by identifying their cause with that of opposition to majority tyranny. And he knew that no theme loomed larger in the writings of the Founding Fathers, especially in the *Federalist*, than the necessity of preventing majority tyranny.

Lincoln now boldly faces the question, within the context of the present crisis, of the relationship of majority rule and minority rights. He begins by asking a series of questions that have arisen in the course of the "practical administration" of the federal government, questions that he says no constitution of reasonable length could possibly anticipate. Neither Lincoln nor his adversaries could have forgotten that he had already addressed these questions many times, most notably in his Cooper Institute speech. So he knew that they knew what his answers were. He does not now say how the questions should be answered but rather why the answers given in the election should be accepted, at least for the time being, as well by those who disagree as by those who agree with the results of that election. In fact, Lincoln had earlier in the inaugural responded to the first of these questions when he said that "If the slave is to be surrendered, it can be of but little consequence to him, or to others, by which authority it is done." But this is the only one of the questions upon which he and his adversaries could be said to agree. The next two questions—*may* Congress prohibit, or *must* Congress protect, slavery in the territories?—go to the heart of the crisis. Although among the secessionists the indignation expressed over the alleged nonenforcement of the fugitive slave clause was perhaps even greater than that expressed over the denial of their alleged rights in the territories, we know that that indignation was largely paranoid. But the stakes involved in the territorial questions, including the future balance of power between free and slave states, were quite real.

[22] From questions of this class spring all our constitutional controversies, and we divide upon them into majorities and minorities. If the minority will not acquiesce, the majority must, or the government must cease. There is no other alternative; for continuing the government, is acquiescence on one side or the other. If a minority, in such case, will secede rather than acquiesce, they make a precedent which, in turn, will divide and ruin them; for a minority of their own will secede from them, whenever a majority refuses to be controlled by such a minority. For instance, why may not any portion of a new confederacy, a year or two hence, arbitrarily secede again, precisely as portions of the present Union now claim to secede from it? All who cherish disunion sentiments, are now being educated to the exact temper of doing this. Is there such a perfect identity of interests among the States to compose a new Union, as to produce harmony only, and prevent renewed secession?

[23] Plainly, the central idea of secession, is the essence of anarchy. A majority, held in restraint by constitutional checks and limitations, and always changing easily, with deliberate changes of popular opinions and sentiments, is the only true sovereign of a free people. Whoever rejects it, does, of necessity, fly to anarchy or to despotism. Unanimity is impossible; the rule of a minority, as a permanent arrangement, is wholly inadmissible; so that, rejecting the majority principle, anarchy, or despotism in some form, is all that is left.

Never since Socrates has philosophy so certainly descended from the heavens into the affairs of mortal men. While addressing the immediate crisis, Lincoln is delivering a lecture to all men and all times on the essentials of free government. He is, we are tempted to say, the eternal political science professor addressing the eternal class. Starting from his premises, the mathematical character of his reasoning leaves no options except the ones to which he points. Ironically, the coincidence of philosophy and political power that Lincoln here represents only serves to underline the Platonic truth, which Lincoln learned from Shakespeare, that philosophy cannot cause the "evil in the cities" to cease and that politics is the realm of the tragic. In the presence of Lincoln's arguments, no sane person would have opted, as the South did, for secession, slavery, and war. Lincoln knew when he spoke these lines that they would have no effect upon the actions or passions of his antagonists. Were it possible for them to have been persuaded, tragedy might have been averted. But it was not possible, because slavery had engendered passions that were immune to reason. Lincoln knew this as well when he spoke as we do today. When he delivered his inaugural, there was yet a quiet moment before the storm, in which he had to vindicate his cause before God and man. The marching armies of North and South are yet a ghostly presence, as Lincoln records in heaven the reasons for peace. But he—and God—can hear their tread.

Still, we are faced with the question of why countless Southerners, many of whom were opposed to secession (like Alexander Stephens), and some of whom were even opposed to slavery (like Robert E. Lee), nonetheless accepted the decisions of their states for secession. They accepted Lincoln's reasoning about majority rule being the only alternative to despotism or anarchy. They held, however, that it applied to them only as citizens of their respective states, and not of the United States. Not only did they obediently go with their states out of the Union, but also they fought against the Union as if they had supported secession from the beginning. Why did they accept the decision of the majority in the one case but not in the other?

Lincoln's reasoning as to why the constitutional majority is the only alternative to anarchy or despotism has become so familiar to us that we must remind ourselves again how comparatively novel it was in 1861. We recall that in three of Jefferson's great compositions of the Founding period—the *Summary View*, the Declaration of Independence, and the Kentucky Resolutions—it was the right of revolution that appeared as the principal means of defending the rights of the people. Free election, as an alternative to revolution, was barely on the horizon. And in the Kentucky Resolutions, we recall, Jefferson invokes the right of revolution to protect the people even from their own elected representatives. It was only in consequence of the voting in 1800 that Jefferson was persuaded that elections could successfully replace revolution. He had discovered after the election that the divisions within the American people were not as great as he had believed before. "We are all republicans, we are all federalists" meant, we repeat, that not every difference of opinion is a difference of principle. But the corollary of this was that *some* differences of opinion *are* differences of principle. And it remains true that such differences, or some of them, cannot be resolved by the ballot box. Lincoln did say that if the majority votes to deprive a minority of any of its essential rights, it would morally justify revolution. And Lincoln, with Jefferson's reasoning in his mind, certainly did not regard that contingency as an impossibility. We have already noted that republican government is not viable where the community is divided by powerful religious differences, as were most of the nations of Europe before and after the Reformation. The prohibitions against religious tests for office and established religion and the guarantee of the free exercise of religion were necessary conditions for resolving political differences by the ballot box. But these written constitutional guarantees were not alone sufficient. It was necessary that the spirit of those guarantees of religious freedom become convictions in the minds of the American people, that they banish religious intolerance from their hearts and regard their fellow citizens of other faiths as their moral and political equals. No one would say that American history represents a perfect realization of that goal. But no one can deny that, in this respect, the American Founding has been a great success. It has not been as successful with respect to racial differences. However, the principles of the Founding are clear that the tyranny of the majority, no less than the tyranny of one or of a few, may justify revolution. Only when the purpose and therefore the limits of majority rule are recognized can the decisions of the majority gain acceptance. A free people is not merely one that is under no compulsion by an alien government. It is a people committed in its mind and conscience to the principles of freedom—of minority rights no less than majority rule. And Lincoln believed that the election of 1860, like that of 1800, had confirmed the commitment of a constitutional majority to the constitutional principles that were its own title deeds to rule. Those who rejected this decision of the ballot box rejected the reasons why any majority, whether within a state or within the nation, should rule.

The phrase "the central idea of secession" reminds us of a familiar expression used years earlier by Lincoln:

> Public opinion, on any subject, always has a "central idea" from which all its minor thoughts radiate. That "central idea" in our political public opinion at the beginning was, and until recently has continued to be, "the equality of men."
> . . . The late presidential election was a struggle, by one party, to discard that central idea, and to substitute for it the opposite idea that slavery is right, in the

abstract, the workings of which, as a central idea, may be the perpetuity of human slavery, and its extension to all countries and colors.[63]

The election of 1860 was seen on both sides as a contest over which "central idea" would prevail. But the two ideas were in radical opposition. The republican form of government differed in its essence according to which of these central ideas governed. This was what made the Union, at that moment, a "house divided." Alexander Stephens's Cornerstone speech was an authoritative pronouncement that the doctrine of racial inequality had replaced the Founding doctrine of equality.

Why the passions of Southerners were so profoundly enlisted on behalf of the new doctrine may be seen in two excerpts from the speeches of the philosopher–king of the Southern cause, John C. Calhoun. The first is from a speech in the Senate on February 19, 1847.

> I am a Southern man and a slaveholder—a kind and merciful one, I trust—and none the worse for being a slaveholder. I say, for one, I would rather meet any extremity upon earth than give up one inch of our equality—one inch of what belongs to us as members of this republic. What! acknowledged inferiority! The surrender of life is nothing to sinking down into acknowledged inferiority![64]

We perceive here that the attachment to "equality" has lost none of its Jeffersonian vigor. Now, however, it is an attribute of states, not of human persons. The citizens of the states derive their equality, and the dignity of that equality, not from their sovereignty as individual human persons under "the laws of nature and of nature's God," but from the constitutional equality of the states within the Union. And this state equality derives from the sovereignty of each state, a sovereignty that is sui generis, not derived from the citizens who compose it. It is a collective sovereignty, in the same sense that the sovereignty of Marx's proletariat is collective, and is in no way connected with antecedent rights of individuals. The sovereignty of the Union, by contrast, is not sui generis but derivative. Obedience to the laws of the Union is derivative from the decision of each state to join the Union. But obedience to the Union can be canceled by obedience to the state. Obedience to the state cannot be canceled by obedience to the Union.

As sovereign, each state is equal to every other state, both within and outside the Union. South Carolina is equal not only to New York and Massachusetts but also to Great Britain, France, and Spain. It is this equality of sovereignty that gives each state an equal constitutional right in the territories, which are the joint possession of the separate sovereigns that together make up the Union. Any denigration or denial of the equal rights of the slave states in the territories is therefore a denigration or denial of their sovereignty and of the equality intrinsic to that sovereignty. Just as our Revolutionary forebears regarded the stamp tax and the tea tax, however insignificant in themselves, as tantamount to slavery, so Calhoun thought it a fate worse than death to give up "one inch" of the rights of the slave states in the territories. That any such exclusion of slavery from the territories might be the result of the vote of a constitutional majority of the whole Union is, from this point of view, immaterial. In any conflict between state and Union, the constitutional majority of the state, not of the Union, is binding. We can see, therefore, why Lincoln's arguments would have no effect upon Calhoun's followers.

It is characteristic that Calhoun does not for a moment consider that the slaves too might object to "acknowledged inferiority."[65] Any objection on their part would carry no weight, since they are not a state or a part of a state and therefore do not participate in sovereignty. Again, Calhoun's doctrine is not one of individual rights, whether of whites or of blacks. And because he does not regard rights as connected with individuals, he does not recognize the right of revolution so central to Jefferson's (and Lincoln's) understanding of political right. The right of secession, as a constitutional right, functions as a replacement for both the right of revolution and the right of constitutional majority rule.

The inner dynamic of Calhoun's argument is most powerfully revealed by the following, from a Senate speech of August 12, 1849:

> "With us the two great divisions of society are not the rich and the poor, but white and black; and all the former, the poor as well as the rich, belong to the upper class, and are respected and treated as equals, if honest and industrious; and hence have a position and pride of character of which neither poverty nor misfortune can deprive them. [66]

In Calhoun's South, with its "two great divisions," there is no place for free Negroes. All blacks, whether by nature or by the curse of Canaan, are justly doomed to perpetual slavery. The inequality of black and white produces an otherwise unattainable equality between and among whites. Thus the "class struggle" that Calhoun, "the Marx of the master class," claimed to find in free society was avoided in the South. The distance between whites and blacks was so great that the distances between rich and poor whites became (or was imagined to become) infinitesimal by comparison. This also meant, of course, that the most intelligent black man was regarded as infinitely inferior to the most stupid white man, a psychological benefit that few white men were too stupid to claim. To be white in Calhoun's South meant to belong to an aristocracy, not of worth, but of birth—the very thing that Jefferson had declared must be abolished.[67] And Calhoun's South was no more prepared to yield its privileges to an election than was the

French aristocracy on the eve of the French Revolution. We see here why poor white Southerners, with little or no chance of ever owning slaves themselves, were bonded to the peculiar institution. Their own sense of personal dignity depended upon slavery.[68] Indeed, the lower classes of Southern white society were the most fanatical in the defense of slavery, because it was they, and not the rich slave owners, whose social status was threatened by emancipation. Herein is the mind of the South that fought the Civil War.

5

The Mind of Lincoln's Inaugural and the Argument and Action of the Debate That Shaped It—II

Lincoln turns next to the questions raised by *Dred Scott*. This case represented a challenge to everything he has said in his inaugural concerning the constitutional majority as the only true sovereign of a free people. By definition, such a majority operates within the boundaries of the Constitution, in which the rights of minorities are not placed at risk by the rule of the majority. Chief Justice Taney, in the opinion of the Court, had declared that the right to carry slave property into any U.S. territory and to be protected there in the ownership of that property was as much a constitutional right as freedom of speech or the free exercise of religion. It was therefore, Taney maintained, beyond the competence of any majority to deny or disparage. It is this precise point in constitutional interpretation that would give such force to the Confederate argument that they were defending and not assailing the Constitution and that Lincoln's election represented the tyranny of the numerical majority, as opposed to the constitutional majority. To this day, defenders of the Confederate cause maintain that Jefferson Davis's government was faithful to the Constitution of 1787 and that Lincoln's government aimed at its destruction.[1]

In order to comprehend fully what Lincoln says about *Dred Scott* in his inaugural, we must place before ourselves crucial passages of Taney's opinion in that fateful case. Here we must embark upon an extended detour from the text of Lincoln's inaugural, before returning to it at the point of his remarks about *Dred Scott*. We must recall that according to the House Divided speech, it was the conjunction of the Kansas–Nebraska Act of 1854 and the *Dred Scott* decision of 1857 that constituted the conspiracy to spread slavery throughout the nation. We must therefore review what Lincoln had said about the case and remind ourselves of its crucial role in the dynamics of the Lincoln–Douglas debates, the 1860 presidential campaign, and the crisis of secession.

In ruling that Negroes, whether free or slave, could not be or become citizens of the United States within the meaning of the Constitution, Taney wrote:

> It is difficult at this day to realize the state of public opinion in relation to that unfortunate race which prevailed in the civilized and enlightened portions of the world at the time of the Declaration of Independence, and when the Constitution of the United States was adopted. . . . They had for more than a century before been regarded as beings of an inferior order; and altogether unfit to associate with the white race, either in social or political relations; and so far inferior that they had no rights which the white man was bound to respect; and that the negro might justly and lawfully be reduced to slavery for his benefit. He was bought and sold, and treated as an ordinary article of merchandise and traffic, whenever a profit could be made by it. This opinion was at that time fixed and universal in the civilized portion of the white race. It was an axiom in morals as well as in politics, which no one thought of disputing or supposed to be open to dispute.[2]

Throughout his opinion, Taney maintains with overwhelming rhetorical force that the public opinion from which the Constitution was formed, and by which it was ratified, held Negroes to be so far inferior as not to belong, in any proper sense, to the human race. The bulk of his evidence has the purpose of supporting this thesis, although his interpretation of the evidence is as perverse as the thesis itself. For example, as Don E. Fehrenbacher points out in his magisterial book on *Dred Scott,* laws against intermarriage limited the freedom of whites no less than of blacks. In any case, such laws concerning marriage and the family have reference only to human beings. There are no laws against miscegenation with jackasses! Here is Fehrenbacher's assessment of the historical truthfulness of Taney's degradation of blacks:

> [T]he Chief Justice persisted in his refusal to regard free Negroes as a category of persons distinct from Negro slaves. Thus, in asserting that "the negro might justly and lawfully be reduced to slavery," he was talking about what could be done to blacks in Africa. Punishment for crime aside, free Negroes in the United States could not lawfully be hunted down and reduced to slavery in the African manner. In fact, some states defined the practice as kidnapping and made it punishable accordingly. Likewise, Taney was thinking of slaves when he declared that the Negro had no rights which the white man was bound to respect. Even then, the statement was not absolutely true, for slaves had some rights at law before 1789, and as a summary of the status of free Negroes in the 1780s it was plainly a falsehood. A list of the Negro's legal rights at that time would be at least as long as his legal disabilities. In some respects, such as property rights, a black man's status was superior to that of a married white woman, and it was certainly far above that of a slave. He could marry, enter into contracts, purchase real estate, bequeathe property, and, most pertinently, seek redress in the courts. The effect of Taney's statement was to place Negroes of the 1780s—even free Negroes—on

the same level as domestic animals. As "historical narrative," it was a gross perversion of the facts.[3]

One of the strangest features of Taney's opinion is his tacit disassociation of his personal belief from what he alleges to be the intent and meaning of the words of the Constitution. Thus he speaks of Negroes as an "unfortunate" and "unhappy" people, while the opinion he is characterizing regards them as simply "inferior" and reducible to slavery for their own benefit. Another strange feature is Taney's claim that it is difficult to imagine such a state of opinion as he attributes to the framers and ratifiers, when it was the very opinion that dominated all antiabolitionist political rhetoric at the time he was writing.

Taney asserts that the "fixed and universal" opinion of the Negroes "in the civilized portion of the white race" at the time of the Founding was such that Negroes stood outside the family of man. Every major conclusion concerning the meaning of the Constitution in the *Dred Scott* decision rests upon this proposition. Taney created a presumption in favor of the truthfulness of his assertions by a doctrine of constitutional interpretation that appears to be unexceptionable:

> No one, we presume, supposes that any change in public opinion or feeling in relation to this unfortunate race, in the civilized nations of Europe or in this country, should induce the court to give to the words of the Constitution a more liberal construction in their favor than they were intended to bear when the instrument was framed and adopted. Such an argument would be altogether inadmissible in any tribunal called on to interpret it. If any of its provisions are deemed unjust, there is a mode prescribed in the instrument itself by which it may be amended; but while it remains unaltered, it must be construed now as it was understood at the time of its adoption. It is not only the same in words, but the same in meaning, and delegates the same powers to the government, and reserves and secures the same rights and privileges to the citizen; and as long as it continues to exist in its present form, it speaks not only in the same words, but with the same meaning and intent with which it spoke when it came from the hands of its framers, and was voted on and adopted by the people of the United States. Any other rule of construction would abrogate the judicial character of this court, and make it the mere reflex of the popular opinion or passion of the day.

We have already quoted Madison, writing many years before to Henry Lee, endorsing the view that the Constitution should be interpreted in "the sense in which [it] was accepted and ratified by the nation" rather than "in the changeable meaning of the words composing it."[4] This opinion of the Father of the Constitution adds authority to Taney's statement of the responsibility of the judge to the text of the Constitution as it was understood by those who framed and ratified it. That authority is vitiated, however, by Taney's willful blindness to what

Madison (and nearly all his public contemporaries) said about the humanity of the Negro and about—in Madison's own words—the "barbarous policy [of the slave states] of considering as property a part of their human brethren."[5] Taney's self-proclaimed commitment to a jurisprudence of original intent is made a mockery by his repeated assertion of what is contrary to every recorded fact about that intent as it bears upon the question of the Negro's humanity.

Compounding this perversity, Taney's suggestion of the possibility of a "more liberal construction" in 1857 implies a public opinion that now recognizes that Negroes are members of the human race and therefore comprehended in the proposition that all men are created equal. It implies then that if the Fifth Amendment had been ratified in 1857, Negroes would be among the persons entitled to constitutional protection. But why did Taney suggest that opinion in the 1850s was favorable to the Negro race, when Jefferson Davis referred to them as "the degenerate sons of Ham," and when the dominant opinion in the South was that slavery was a positive good and held out a better possibility of happiness for slaves than freedom? Why does Taney represent the change in public opinion between the Founding period and the 1850s with respect to the humanity of the Negro as the exact opposite of what it was in fact?

Fehrenbacher says that "one must put aside the curious notion that Taney was at heart an anti-slavery man." This notion, he continues,

> rests almost entirely upon two actions taken nearly forty years before the *Dred Scott* decision. In 1818, he served as defense attorney for an abolitionist minister and in the process denounced slavery as an evil that must in time be "gradually wiped away." Beginning the same year, Taney emancipated his own slaves to the number of eight. Whatever moral conviction may have encouraged these actions, it does not appear again in his public record or his private correspondence. His attitude on the bench was consistently and solicitously proslavery. By 1857 he had become as fanatical in his determination to protect the institution as Garrison was in his determination to destroy it.[6]

Much of Taney's proslavery fanaticism in 1857 was clearly due to his hatred of abolitionism. He does not justify slavery itself, as did Calhoun, Davis, and Stephens, among others. But he is unequivocally committed to the political interests of the slave South. In *Dred Scott*, there seems to be no length to which he will not go to promote those interests. Yet there are residues of an opinion that jars with his dominant thesis.

Taney's contribution to the concatenation of causes leading to secession and war was immeasurable. It is not idle speculation to ask even whether the Civil War would have happened without his opinion in *Dred Scott*. Notwithstanding its massive defects in history and logic, it created an overwhelming presumption in favor of the most radical proslavery interpretation of the Constitution. Nothing could have done more to anticipate and to nullify in advance the argument in favor of majority rule set forth in Lincoln's inaugural. More than anything else, it accounted for the moral self-righteousness and moral indignation of the various declarations and manifestos of the seceding states in 1860–61. It gave an energy, a confidence, and an intransigence to the proslavery cause that ended—if it did end—only at Appomattox. There can be little doubt that that was Taney's intention, and from that perspective his opinion was a work of genius. Had Calhoun himself composed it, *Dred Scott* would have been more plausible (if not more accurate) in its statements of fact and tighter in its reasoning. But it is doubtful that Calhoun, even had he been chief justice, could at that moment have produced a greater political effect in invigorating the cause of slavery and state rights. As we shall see, Lincoln in his message to Congress of July 4, 1861, expressed the conviction that there would have been no secession had not public opinion in the South been persuaded that secession was a constitutional right. Taney's opinion gave a cutting edge to this idea that cannot be exaggerated.

The power of Taney's opinion derived largely from the fact that those who believed they had been vindicated by it were not in the least concerned with the truth of the alleged facts upon which it was based. For them, the authority of the chief justice and the Supreme Court, appointed by the Constitution itself (as they believed) to decide the questions at issue, was all that was needed to prove to themselves that they were in the right. How could it be imagined that the venerable chief justice would declare his unswerving allegiance to the true intent and meaning of the Constitution, as it came from the hands of the framers and ratifiers, and then construe it in a sense diametrically opposite? That, however, is what happened.

Notwithstanding the foregoing, Taney's 1818 speech to the jury in the Gruber case (as discussed at length in chapter 3) is of much greater consequence than Fehrenbacher implies. It casts a blinding light upon the disingenuousness of the central thesis of Taney's 1857 opinion and furnishes the most authoritative refutation possible of Taney's assertion that public opinion concerning the Negro had gone from less favorable to more favorable in the years since the adoption of the Constitution. As we have seen, Taney's speech in defense of Gruber is a perfect illustration of the antislavery convictions of Jefferson and the Founding generation generally and is exemplary of what Lincoln and the Republican Party stood for in 1857. While we cannot prove it, we are convinced that Taney in 1857 remembered every word of what he said in 1818.

A twice-told tale may be tedious, but the importance of what Taney said in 1818, as a hidden commentary on 1857, must justify it. In 1818, we recall, Taney gave it as his own opinion that "A hard necessity . . . compels us to endure the evil of slavery for a time. It was imposed on us by another nation, while we were yet in a state of colonial vassalage."[7] That the presence of slavery in the Founding was the result of necessity, that it represented compulsion and not moral choice, is the very opposite of what Taney would say in 1857. What happened between 1818 and 1857 was not that the facts changed but that as Taney reversed his position on slavery, he reversed history. In effect, and for all political purposes, he attributed the opinions of the generation of Jefferson Davis to that of Thomas Jefferson, and the opinions of the generation of Thomas Jefferson to that of Jefferson Davis. Not until Stalin rewrote the official Soviet account of the Bolshevik Revolution would history be so shamelessly altered to serve the ends of despotism.

The assertion of equality in the Declaration of Independence was the prop and pillar of the antislavery cause. One might epitomize everything Lincoln said between 1854 and 1861 as a demand for recognition of the Negro's human rights, as set forth in the Declaration. Thus in 1857 Taney took dead aim at the heart of the antislavery argument when he denied that Negroes were comprehended in the proposition of human equality in the Declaration. The memorable passages with which the Declaration begins, he wrote,

> would seem to embrace the whole human family, and if they were used in a similar instrument at this day, would be so understood. But it is too clear for dispute that the enslaved African race were not intended to be included, and formed no part of the people who framed and adopted this Declaration; for, if the language as understood in that day, would embrace them, the conduct of the distinguished men who framed the Declaration of Independence would have been utterly and flagrantly inconsistent with the principles they asserted; and instead of the sympathy of mankind, to which they so confidently appealed, they would have deserved and received universal rebuke and reprobation.

Taney speaks of the Declaration as *seeming* "to embrace the whole human family" and again includes the Negro within that family himself. He implies that by their true meaning, the words of the Declaration in fact do include Negroes, for no less a reason than that Negroes belong to the human family. But how was it possible for him to think that he understood the Declaration correctly while the Congress that adopted it did not? In 1776, after all, no one had ever heard of the "positive good" theory of slavery or of a "scientific" discovery of the inequality of the races.

How in civilized society does anyone identify others as belonging to the human family? Is it not that the species *Homo sapiens* is endowed with speech and reason, setting it apart from brute Creation? Do we not know that others are not beasts or gods by the same inductive reasoning by which we know ourselves to be neither the one nor the other? And do we not know that as we are not gods, we have no right to treat other human beings as beasts? Is it not a truth in epistemology as well as in metaphysics that black and white human beings are equally human, as much as black and white chairs are equally chairs? Every common noun—as a universal, as distinct from a particular—is an abstraction from sense perception. If "man" or "chair" had color, it would be a particular, not a universal. That is why "all men are created equal" cannot refer to the color of those encompassed by it. This is why, since the abolition of slavery and the adoption of the Thirteenth, Fourteenth, and Fifteenth Amendments, the Constitution as an uncompromised document of human government can be properly understood only as color-blind.

Taney in 1857 said that the meaning intrinsic to the proposition of human equality—that it encompassed the whole human family—could not have been the meaning of the men who adopted that proposition. Yet, he says, they were "high in literary acquirements." How was it possible for these educated and accomplished statesmen to say "all" when they meant only "some"? And if they meant "some" when they said "all," why did they not indicate which "some" of the "all" they meant? Taney's only explanation is that, had they meant what they said, their conduct would then have been "utterly and flagrantly inconsistent" with that meaning. What conduct did Taney think would have been consistent with the intrinsic meaning of the Declaration?

We recall once again that in his 1818 defense of Gruber, Taney saw no moral inconsistency in denouncing slavery as an evil and yet recognizing a necessity that compelled "us" to endure it "for a time." Morality only obligated those who recognized the evil of slavery to work for its removal as time and circumstances permitted. Did Taney not recall in 1857 what he recognized in 1818—that the immediate abolition of slavery in the wake of independence had not been possible? As we have written elsewhere, "It was not wonderful that a nation of slaveholders, upon declaring their independence, did not abolish slavery. What was wonderful—perhaps even miraculous—was that this nation of slaveholders, upon becoming independent, declared that all men are created equal, and thereby made the abolition of slavery a moral as well as a logical necessity." Certainly Taney knew in 1857 that the toleration of slavery "for a time" did not in any way imply a justification of it. He knew therefore that the public of the Founding period would never have thought anyone would deserve rebuke and reprobation who thought, spoke, and acted in 1776 or 1787 as Taney himself had thought, spoken, and acted in 1818.

How shocking it was for Taney to have denied in 1857 that "all men" in the Declaration included Negroes may be gathered from the following words of Lincoln during his joint debates with Douglas in 1858.

At Galesburg the other day, I said in answer to Judge Douglas, that three years ago there never had been a man, so far as I knew or believed, in the whole world, who had said that the Declaration of Independence did not include negroes in the term "all men." I reassert it today. I assert that Judge Douglas and all his friends may search the whole records of the country, and it will be a matter of great astonishment to me if they shall be able to find that one human being three years ago had ever uttered the astounding sentiment that the term "all men" in the Declaration did not include the negro. Do not let me be misunderstood. I know that more than three years ago there were men who, finding this assertion constantly in the way of their scheme to bring about the ascendancy and per-petuation of slavery, *denied the truth of it.* I know that Mr. Calhoun and all the politicians of his school denied the truth of the Declaration. I know that it ran along in the mouths of some Southern men for a period of years, ending at last in that shameful though rather forcible declaration of Pettit of Indiana, upon the floor of the Senate, that the Declaration of Independence was in that respect "a self-evident lie," rather than a self-evident truth. But I say . . . that three years ago there had never lived a man who had ventured to assail it in the sneaking way of pretending to believe it and then asserting it did not include the negro. I believe the first man who ever said it was Chief Justice Taney in the Dred Scott case, and the next to him was our friend Stephen A. Douglas. And now it has become the catch-word of the entire party.[8]

How indeed was it possible in 1857 to hold to such an obvious mendacity as that "all" in the Declaration really meant "some"? Besides the politically interest-ed motives of those who wished to defeat the Republicans and extend slavery, the answer, we believe, is to be found in large measure in a new and powerful con-ception of morality, which had been absent from the horizon in 1818. It is that of Kant's categorical imperative: *so act that the maxim of your will can become a uni-versal law.* According to Kant, a moral man is one who acts rightly as the cate-gorical imperative defines rightly, without any regard for consequences. Morality resides in the form of the will alone. An action is moral only insofar as it can be looked upon as legislating a moral universe called into being by the maxim that makes the will a good will. It has nothing whatever to do with the probable or even possible outcome of an action. For an action to be good, no consideration of its benefits or costs is permitted. Above all, morality has nothing to do with hap-piness, the end or ultimate purpose of all morality, both political and personal, according to the classical and Judeo-Christian tradition reflected in the Declara-tion of Independence. According to Kant, a moral man cannot lie even to a mur-derer as to the whereabouts of his prospective victim—not even if the latter is one's own child! Since one cannot conceive of a universe of liars (because it would immediately self-destruct), lying can never be justified. Likewise, according to Taney in *Dred Scott,* if the Founding Fathers believed slavery was wrong, that belief would have become the maxim of their will. They would have acted then and there to abolish slavery, without any regard to whether the attempt could succeed or to what the collateral consequences of the attempt might be. Since they did not act then and there to abolish slavery, and since they were moral men, it followed that they did not think slavery wrong and therefore that they could not have included Negroes in the proposition of human equality. So runs the reasoning underlying Taney's opinion.

We observe immediately, however, that according to Kant himself, we must always treat other human beings as ends in themselves and never as mere means. Kantian morality is that of rational beings whose reason enables them to distinguish other rational beings from beings that are subrational or subhuman. One can only lie, or tell the truth, to another rational being. The Founding Fathers could not—as they did not—fail to identify Negroes as human beings. Taney is doubly unjustified by a Kantian standard of moral consistency: first, because slavery (itself a living lie) can never be justified on Kantian grounds; and second, because it is irrational to mean "some" when you say "all."

According to Taney in 1857, the "fixed and universal" opinion of "the civilized portion of the white race" at the time of the Founding was that Negroes, whether free or slave, occupied an identical status with domestic animals, being "ordinary articles[s] of merchandise and traffic." But this opinion never existed— not in 1776, 1787, 1857, or at any other time. The Constitution, we remind ourselves, employs euphemisms in referring to slaves and slavery, never using the words themselves. Article IV, for instance, refers to "person[s] held to service or labor in one state, under the laws thereof, escaping into another." Here and elsewhere in the Constitution, slaves come into sight *only* as human persons. But the laws by which they were "held to service or labor" were obviously the laws of slave states, and these laws regarded them as chattel property. As chattels, they could be bought and sold like other chattels such as horses or hogs. But even in the slave states, their status was never merely and entirely that of chattels. As Lincoln pointed out, there were in the South several hundred thousand free Negroes, but no free horses or hogs. Nor were horses or hogs ever the children of their masters and owners, whereas many of the free Negroes were the offspring of those who emancipated them.

The definition of a chattel is that of a piece of movable property (as distinct from real property) without a rational will. Lacking the rational will possessed by all persons, a chattel such as a horse or a hog cannot be held responsible at law for any damages it may cause. Such damages are the responsibility of its owner. But there never was a time, even in the slave South, when slaves were not regarded as responsible for their actions under one or another provision of the penal code. Of course, it was difficult to find ways to punish someone with a deprivation of liberty when he had none to lose, or to fine someone who owned nothing that could be taken from him.[9] It was also difficult to punish a slave without in some way punishing his master by depriving the master of the slave's labor. Nevertheless, human chattels were always distinguished from other chattels, and that distinction always had reference to their human personality. By nature and reason, a person cannot be a chattel. The law of slavery was itself a self-contradiction. But contrary to Taney in *Dred Scott*, it was never unambiguous in regarding the Negro as a chattel.

Taney refers repeatedly to the opinion in the Founding period that Negroes were inferior "in the scale of created beings" as an opinion that was "fixed and universal in the civilized portion of the white race." We should note that Taney himself assumes a difference between the civilized and the uncivilized portions of the white race. That is to say, he assumes that there are qualitative differences within the place on the scale of created beings occupied by the white race itself. And this in turn implies nonracial criteria of civilization. In this, Taney agrees with the Declaration of Independence, which clearly assumes nonracial criteria for distinguishing civilization from barbarism and savagery. For instance, it accuses the king of Great Britain of "works of death, desolation, and tyranny . . . scarcely paralleled in the most barbarous ages, and totally unworthy of the Head of a civilized nation." And again: "He . . . has endeavored to bring on the inhabitants of our frontiers the merciless Indian savages, whose known rule of warfare is an undistinguished destruction of all ages, sexes, and conditions." But the heart of the Declaration's charges against the king is the design to reduce the colonies "under absolute despotism," which means nothing more nor less than enslaving them. As a general principle, to enslave other human beings gratuitously is itself the essence of barbarism. What then is civilization? Within the horizon of the Declaration, it is the recognition of the place of man's humanity in the scale of created beings, a place that is lower than that of God and higher than that of beasts. It recognizes that as man is not God, and as no man is marked out by God or nature to rule other human beings, the just powers of government are derived from the consent of the governed. It recognizes the moral necessity of the rule of law, of ruling and being ruled in turn. Yet slaves have no share in making the laws they live under, and masters do not live under the laws they make for their slaves. Slavery, in short, is the very negation of civilization.

The Declaration was a wartime document asserting the right to resist with force the barbarism of the British king and Parliament. The Declaration therefore concludes that it is the right of a civilized people not to be subjected to barbarism. The rights that belong to human beings as human beings demand mutual respect by fellow citizens and, ultimately, by the community of nations. It follows as well that those who do not respect the rights of others—whether they are common criminals, barbarians, or savages—may have to be governed despotically. It is notable that the barbarism and savagery referred to in the Declaration are those of white men and red men, not of black men. In fact, barbarism and savagery, like civilization, have no necessary relationship to the races into which the human race is subdivided. By the terms of the Declaration, the right to govern others despotically can be justified with respect to barbarians and savages if they threaten a civilized people's right to live in peace and freedom. It can never be justified on the basis of race or color, or by the mistaken identification of human beings with chattels. That is why the Republican Party platform of 1856 denounced "those twin relics of barbarism, polygamy and slavery."[10]

We noted above Taney's jurisprudential principle that the Constitution should be interpreted in accordance with the intent of those who framed and ratified it. That assumes, of course, that it is a civilized constitution. Yet Taney attributed to the framers and ratifiers a failure to recognize the Negro's humanity, a failure that would call into question the moral status of the Constitution itself. Someone who does not know another human being when he sees one and who would treat a human being as if he were a lower animal—as a beast of burden, or even as food—is by that fact alone disqualified as belonging to the civilized portion of mankind. To say, as Taney does, that those who adopted the Constitution assigned to Negroes a place below humanity is to assign to those who adopted the Constitution a place below civilization. According to Aristotle, as well as to common sense, a good man is a good citizen only under a good constitution. The primary moral obligation of a good man under a barbaric or savage constitution is to undermine its barbarism or savagery. Neither a judge nor anyone else can have a moral obligation to the laws of barbarism or savagery. It would then be impossible to justify a jurisprudence of original intent if the Constitution were actually based upon the opinion that the Negro was not a human being.[11] Taney's opinion amounts to declaring that a judge who knows that a Negro is human must pretend that he is not, in deference to a law that is founded upon barbaric ignorance. Was a judge in Nazi Germany under an obligation to the true intent of the laws of that regime, which held that Jews bore the same relationship to civilization as plague-bearing vermin? Or did not his duty as a human being oblige him to do whatever in him lay to undermine the laws of that despicable regime?

Taney's attempt in *Dred Scott* to justify the Founders as consistent in regarding blacks as subhuman chattels was impossible on four counts. First, had the Founders held such an opinion, they would not themselves have been civilized human beings. Second, it was never the case that slaves were regarded solely as chattels. Third, it was always true in the Founding era, as it was to Taney in 1818, that slavery depended upon positive law and that in its absence Negroes were possessed of the same natural rights as other human beings. Fourth, it was always recognized in the Founding era, as it was by Taney in 1818, that every free citizen of a slave society had a moral duty to work for the ending of slavery and to bring the positive law into harmony with the natural law.

One suspects that Taney was more cunning than ignorant in drawing, as he does, upon a Kantian conception of morality in assigning to the Founders the opinion that Negroes were subhuman. It is impossible to suppose that Taney was ignorant of the innumerable statements from the Founding era, not to mention his own of 1818, condemning slavery and recognizing the humanity of Negroes. He deliberately disregarded this evidence by assuming that it did not represent the Founders' real opinions. He assumed that it did not represent their real opinions by assuming that something like the maxims required by Kant's categorical imperative reveal men's true opinions. Based on this assumption, since the Founders did not act upon an abolitionist maxim, they could not have been genuinely antislavery. Strangely—or perhaps not strangely—this view of the Founding was shared in part by the abolitionists who were Taney's contemporaries and opposites. Unlike Taney, the abolitionists held that the Declaration of Independence included Negroes. Like Taney, however, they thought that this inclusion created an obligation for immediate abolition. Also like Taney, they thought that given this inclusion, the compromises with slavery in the Constitution brought "rebuke and reprobation" upon the heads of the framers and ratifiers. Hence the Garrisonians called the Constitution a "covenant with death and an agreement with Hell" and burned it at their meetings.[12] Their slogan was "No Union with slaveholders." It may also be recalled that in 1848 Henry David Thoreau had refused to pay a tax to Massachusetts on the ground that it would go to support the war with Mexico. He held that war to be a war to expand slavery and thought that Massachusetts should secede from the Union rather than support it. Barring that, Thoreau himself would secede from Massachusetts![13] We see from this that secession, the ultimate remedy of proslavery Southerners, had long been regarded by abolitionists as the ultimate *antislavery* remedy. The Kantianism of the abolitionists had a greater plausibility than Taney's, since it was at least based upon the recognition of the Negro's humanity. Yet its folly is equally evident, since the "secession" they advocated would only help slavery by emancipating the slave states from restraints arising from their union with the free states. In Kantian fashion, the abolitionists were more interested in the purity of their will than in the consequences of their actions.

Even as Thoreau was trying in 1848 to secede from Massachusetts, the Wilmot Proviso was passing the House of Representatives in Washington, with the assistance of the vote of an Illinois congressman named Abraham Lincoln. The Wilmot Proviso was the acorn from which the Republican Party would grow, and it foreshadowed the political means by which slavery would some day be destroyed. Attached to an appropriations bill for the prosecution of the war with

Mexico, the proviso declared that in any territory to be acquired from Mexico, slavery should be forever prohibited. It passed the House repeatedly but was always defeated in the Senate. In these votes, however, the "numerical majority" for the exclusion of slavery from U.S. territories, which came to its political fruition in Lincoln's election in 1860, was already visible. Had Thoreau's and Garrison's abolitionism prevailed, the slave South would have been freed from all the restraints arising from the free-soil movement in the Union under the Constitution. In the crisis of actual secession in 1860–61, the abolitionists' moral purity and practical folly were still alive and well, as when Horace Greeley said, "Let our erring sisters depart." It is almost as if abolitionism had been infiltrated and financed by proslavery agents! But one might also suspect that the Southern secessionists were financed by abolitionism as they catapulted slavery towards its destruction.

Taney's pseudo-Kantian attempt to infer the "true" meaning of the Declaration from the failure of the Founders to abolish slavery would have been merely ludicrous had it not been welcomed as supplying the constitutional justification for everything the proslavery South was demanding and, ultimately, for rejecting the results of the 1860 presidential election. There is no evidence that Taney or his following recognized the Kantianism of the test he applied to the Founding Fathers. But neither is there any evidence that in 1776 or 1787 anyone ever thought of applying such a test. The Declaration itself endorses the dictates of prudence, thereby endorsing a prudential morality that is the very antithesis of Kant's categorical imperative. Taney's Kantian test was, moreover, anachronistic, because Kant's *Foundations of the Metaphysics of Morals* was not published until 1785 and could have played no part in the American public opinion that ratified the Constitution. Yet German idealism in all its forms had come to possess a very great influence in the United States by 1857.[14]

The abolitionists represented extreme antislavery exactly parallel to Taney's extreme proslavery. Unlike Taney, they never doubted that the Declaration of Independence included Negroes. Like Taney, however, they were committed to a Kantian morality that ignored the role of prudence in the Declaration itself, and they denounced the compromises with slavery in the Constitution. The fact that such compromises may have been necessary to secure the adoption of the Constitution and that any possible alternative to the Constitution would have been vastly more favorable to slavery did not weigh with them. Their Kantian morality was one that no responsible statesman could ever adopt. In its later forms and transformations, its influence became, and still is, overwhelming. It is noteworthy, however, that abolitionism was always a marginal influence upon the antislavery movement in the North. Taney's opinion in *Dred Scott*, on the other hand, came to dominate and control the politics of the South.

As Lincoln's House Divided speech made clear, *Dred Scott* in 1857 was the sequel to the Kansas–Nebraska Act of 1854—which repealed the Missouri Compromise—and the conjunction of the two constituted a conspiracy to make slavery lawful nationwide. *Dred Scott* must not then be looked upon merely as judicial aggression. It emerged from the political process and was fostered by the dominance in the 1850s of proslavery Southerners who controlled the Senate, the presidency, and the Supreme Court. Ever since the Wilmot Proviso, the Southern oligarchy could see that the "numerical majority" in the House would eventually control the electoral college and that when that happened, their controlling influence within the political process would come to an end. *Dred Scott* was a convulsive effort of the slave power, while its power lasted, to cut off the slavery question from the political process and to place property in slaves upon a foundation that could not be threatened by elected majorities.

≈

Lincoln's 1857 response to *Dred Scott* is among his most remarkable dialectical tours de force. It is an answer to Douglas's endorsement of Taney's opinion, as well as to Taney himself. It presents in microcosm the differences that dominated the Lincoln–Douglas debates of 1858. In it, we can see the precise ways in which Lincoln later exploited these differences and how he shaped decisively the issues of the election of 1860 and of the crisis that followed upon it. Here is his characterization of the substance of Douglas's support for *Dred Scott*: "There is a natural disgust in the minds of nearly all white people, to the idea of an indiscriminate amalgamation of the white and black races; and Judge Douglas evidently is basing his chief hope, upon the chances of being able to appropriate the benefit of this disgust to himself." Public opinion in Illinois in the 1850s, which was fairly representative of public opinion throughout the free states of the North, held slavery and "amalgamation" in almost equal abhorrence. These were the defining parameters within which all debate was constrained. Douglas persistently identified Lincoln's and the Republicans' opposition to slavery as a cover for amalgamation. Lincoln just as persistently identified Douglas's opposition to amalgamation as a cover for slavery. This would be the core of each man's strategy in 1858. It is important to note, however, that Lincoln mentions the "natural disgust" for "amalgamation" only for the purpose of preventing Douglas from appropriating the benefit of it to the furthering of the cause of slavery.

If he can, by much drumming and repeating, fasten the odium of that idea upon his adversaries, he thinks he can struggle through the storm. He therefore clings to this hope, as a drowning man to the last plank. He makes an occasion for lugging it in from the opposition to the Dred Scott decision. He finds the Republicans insisting that the Declaration of Independence includes ALL men, black as well as white; and forthwith he boldly denies that it includes negroes at all, and proceeds to argue gravely that all who contend it does, do so only because they want to vote, and eat, and sleep, and marry with negroes! He will have it that they cannot be consistent else. Now I protest against that counterfeit logic which concludes that, because I do not want a black woman for a *slave* I must necessarily want her for a *wife*. I need not have her for either, I can just leave her alone. In some respects she is certainly not my equal; but in her natural right to eat the bread she earns with her own hands without asking leave of anyone else, she is my equal, and the equal of all others.[15]

Lincoln makes his obeisance to the dominant conviction of Negro inferiority when he says that the black woman is not his equal "in some respects." Here as elsewhere, Lincoln makes this disclaimer as a prologue to the affirmation of the equality of natural rights of all human beings. The equal natural right of black human beings to put into their mouths the bread that their hands have earned is repeated almost as a mantra or incantation throughout Lincoln's speeches in this period. It is an example of his peculiar felicity in reducing a great subject to a small compass, and one that cannot easily be misunderstood. The right is a natural right for the reason that the attachment of a given set of hands to a given mouth is natural. This right is at bottom the same as the one the colonies fought to defend in the Revolution when they declared that taxation without representation is tyranny. The amount of bread that the king and Parliament attempted to take from the mouths of the colonists without their consent was infinitesimal in comparison with the depredations of slavery. The colonists, because they were not slaves, were able to resist, and they fought to prevent ever becoming slaves. The right itself, however, belonged equally to all human beings, regardless of their power to enforce it. Lincoln by implication invokes Locke's idea of the natural right of property as originating in that with which a man mixes his labor. He will return to this idea in his first annual message to Congress, in December of 1861.

Lincoln extends his analysis as he turns to Taney's opinion in *Dred Scott.* Taney, he says,

admits that the language of the Declaration is broad enough to include the whole human family, but he and Judge Douglas argue that the authors of that instrument did not intend to include negroes, by the fact that they did not at once, actually place them on an equality with the whites. Now this grave argument comes to just nothing at all, by the other fact, they did not at once, *or ever afterwards,* actually place all white people on an equality with one or another. And this is the staple argument of both the Chief Justice and the Senator, for doing this obvious violence to the plain unmistakable language of the Declaration. I think the authors of that notable instrument intended to include *all* men, but they did not intend to declare all men equal *in all respects*. They did not mean to say all were equal in color, size, intellect, moral developments, or social capacity. They defined with tolerable distinctness in what respects they did consider all men created equal—equal in "certain inalienable rights, among which are life, liberty and the pursuit of happiness." This they said, and this they meant. They did not mean to assert the obvious untruth, that all were then actually enjoying that equality, nor yet, that they were about to confer it immediately upon them. In fact, they had no power to confer such a boon. They meant simply to declare the *right*, so that *enforcement* of it might follow as fast as circumstances should permit. They meant to set up a standard maxim for free society, which should be familiar to all, and revered by all; constantly looked to, constantly labored for, and even though never perfectly attained, constantly approximated, and thereby constantly spreading and deepening its influence, and augmenting the happiness and value of life to all people of all colors everywhere.

Lincoln continued, saying that the assertion that all men are created equal had no practical use in effecting our separation from Great Britain and that it was placed in the Declaration for future use: "Its authors meant it to be, thank God, it is now proving itself, a stumbling block to those who in after times might seek to turn a free people back into the hateful paths of despotism."[16]

This "standard maxim" passage, one of the most illuminating of Lincoln's life, has two characteristic functions: to promote good and to prevent evil. Lincoln makes the same distinction between equality of rights and equality of personal attributes that in chapter 3 we saw Henry Wilson make in his debate with Jefferson Davis on the floor of the Senate. No human being can confidently deny that he has a superior in all or some of the qualities that constitute humanity. Nor does any one believe that he has no inferior. But who will concede to his superior a right to govern him without his consent? And who cannot see that to deny his superior this right, he must deny the same right to himself? Here is the equality that the Declaration meant to affirm. How anyone's "color, size, intellect, moral developments, or social capacity" may redound to his advantage or disadvantage is an altogether separate question from that of ruling someone else, in the sense of coming between his hand and his mouth. The brain surgeon and the street sweeper may have very unequal rewards for their work. Yet each has the same right to put into his mouth the bread that his own hand has earned. The brain surgeon has no more right to take the street sweeper's wages than the street sweeper to take the brain surgeon's. Over and over again, Lincoln will argue that the alleged superiority of any man to another is no justification for denying the intrinsic connection between the fruits of a man's labor and the right to possess those fruits, be they great or little.

Lincoln rebuffs the Kantian (or pseudo-Kantian) argument that the Founders could not have understood all men to have equal natural rights because they did not actually legislate an equality of whites and blacks. Neither, he says, did they legislate an equality of all whites. We recall here Don Fehrenbacher's observation that in 1787, free black men had greater control over their own property than married white women. The civil and political rights acquired by women in the course of two centuries, as well as those acquired by blacks, are examples of the influence of the standard maxim contemplated by Lincoln. But in 1776 and 1787, the Fathers of the Republic had no more power to confer on women the rights they would one day acquire than they had to abolish slavery. Let us also note, however, that Lincoln in this speech cites Justice Curtis's dissenting opinion in *Dred Scott*, which notes that in five of the thirteen states that ratified the Constitution, there were Negro voters. Hence, contrary to Taney, the "We the people" who ordained the Constitution did indeed include blacks.[17]

As we have maintained in chapter 2, the characteristic understanding of political obligation from the end of the ancient city until the American Revolution was of a movement of authority from above—from God to emperor or king, and from him to his vassals and to their subjects. In its most abbreviated form it was called, as it was by Lincoln, the divine right of kings. In the Declaration of Independence this order is reversed: All legitimate authority is derived from the exercise of the rights with which every human soul has been equally endowed by its Creator. There is no intrinsic obligation to obey any authority to which one has not given consent. But recalling the wise words of Bourke Cockran that "men find it easier to accept a truth than to regulate their lives by it" and that "it took eighteen centuries for the religious beliefs of Christians to bear fruit in political institutions of freedom," we can see that it was no more possible that these institutions could bear their fruit immediately than that they should have been the immediate fruit of Christianity. Not only slavery, but all forms of arbitrary inequality were meant to be affected by the political institutions of freedom. The "standard maxim" would be the political truth whose progressive acceptance would set in motion a political process whereby equality of rights would be progressively realized. Since authority now originates in the people rather than in kings or privileged classes, the consent of the governed must attend this process. Once such political institutions of freedom as those established in 1787 were in existence, the movement toward greater equality of rights had to be accomplished in and through the constitutionally expressed consent of the governed. This meant that the citizens of the Republic would be constantly learning how to regulate their political lives by the truth to which they were committed. Patience in and with this process was required, not merely as a virtue in itself, but because arbitrary government or government outside the constitutionally appointed boundaries—

even in the ostensible interest of greater equality of rights—would negate its own end. As Lincoln said in his Lyceum speech, it would do no good to free the slaves by enslaving the free. But the critical and indispensable requirement is the acceptance of the truth of human equality itself. As long as this truth is the defining axiom of republican citizenship, its beneficence in the life of the people will continually spread and deepen. The Constitution is a vehicle of this influence. But like the body in relationship to the soul, however healthy in itself, it can serve no wise purpose apart from the health of the soul. And the health of the soul of the regime is defined in the Declaration of Independence. Taney's and Douglas's negation of the standard maxim meant nothing less than the reversal of the divine purpose of eighteen centuries in bringing forth the political institutions of freedom.

Lincoln's conception of the standard maxim is both teleological and prudential. It is teleological because it is oriented, as is the Declaration, toward the end of human happiness, which according to Aristotle is the ultimate end of all human action, whether individual or political. It is prudential because it measures the goodness of human actions, whether individual or political, by their consequences. The consequences, in turn, are judged by whether they advance or retard happiness. Perfect happiness or perfect justice is no more to be expected, in most circumstances, than perfect health. But both individuals and peoples can become happier or healthier, depending upon whether they act foolishly or wisely. In 1854 Lincoln remarked that he "would consent to any great evil, to avoid a greater one."[18] In the history of human civilization, slavery arose as an alternative to the killing of prisoners in war. In fact, killing only prisoners taken in battle came as an improvement upon killing whole populations of defeated cities.[19] That slavery itself was at one time a desirable alternative does not make it less evil. But neither does the fact of its being evil make it less desirable as an alternative. In the *Politics*, Aristotle has recommendations for the improvement of tyrannies. That does not mean that Aristotle recommends tyrannies. It means only that a moderated or improved tyranny may be better than a naked tyranny. Prudential morality is the antithesis of the morality implied by Kant's doctrine of the categorical imperative, a doctrine concerned with the form of the will of the moral agent, regardless of consequences. Yet Kantianism, in one or another of its versions, is assumed to be the true moral doctrine by many present-day commentators on American slavery, the intellectual heirs of Thoreau and Taney.

It is important to realize that Taney's and Douglas's interpretation of the Declaration negated not only its antislavery implications but also all those other implications of the doctrine of equality that have led over time to removing arbitrary inequalities in American life. It is also important to realize that these arbitrary inequalities are only of *rights*, not of *rewards*. Some latter-day critics of Lincoln wrongly attribute to him the leveling egalitarianism characteristic of twenti-eth-century socialism and welfare statism. In taking property from those who earn it and giving it to those who do not, in coming between the hand and the mouth of the producer or laborer, such egalitarianism reproduces the essential character-istic of slavery. Lincoln's doctrine of the relationship of capital and labor, which is elaborated in his first annual message to Congress, proposes no such thing. For Lincoln, the guarantee of *rights* means the guarantee that there shall be *no* inter-vention by law or government, so far as possible, between the work of any man's hand and his mouth.

By denying that Negroes were human beings under the Constitution, Taney's (and Douglas's) doctrine struck at the ground in human nature of the right of all human freedom and thus at the security of every man's freedom. It struck as well at the security of every man's property, because the root of all property is the nat-ural right of every man to own himself. For Lincoln, therefore, the entire antebel-lum debate came down to the question of whether the Negro was or was not a human being. If he was a human being, then he was included in the proposition that all men are created equal. If he was included in that proposition, then it was a law of nature antecedent to the Constitution that he ought to be free and that civil society had as its originating purpose the security of his freedom and of the fruits of his labor under law. Throughout the Lincoln–Douglas debates, this was the central idea from which everything else radiated. Lincoln was unrelenting in his tenacity in bringing the argument back to this point, again and again, in the face of Douglas's equal tenacity in denying its truth and its relevance.

∿

The Kansas–Nebraska Act of 1854 repealed the Missouri Compromise of 1820 and declared that the people of those territories should be "perfectly free to form and regulate their domestic institutions in their own way."[20] Whether the territory of Kansas (and ultimately the state of Kansas) became free or slave would depend presumably upon whether or not the settlers there wanted slavery among their domestic institutions. Accordingly, for the next two years, Kansas became the focal point of the intersectional struggle. But the attempt to ascer-tain the will of the settlers by "popular sovereignty" was virtually impossible. It was like asking Protestants and Catholics in sixteenth-century Europe to join in an election to decide whether they should be obliged by law to accept or reject transubstantiation. What happened, of course, was that slave staters and free staters rushed into the territory. Because of the proximity of the slave state of Missouri, proslavery immigrants had an initial advantage, and it was by means of this advantage that they attempted to fix slavery on the territory with the

Lecompton Constitution. As the slower but much larger population of free-state immigrants arrived, they refused to take part in elections previously arranged by their rivals. Each side claimed to be the lawful government and denounced whatever the other did as fraudulent.

Although Stephen Douglas was the mastermind of the Kansas–Nebraska Act, it represented the official policy of the Pierce administration and was endorsed in the 1856 Democratic platform and by the Democratic Party's successful presidential candidate of that year, James Buchanan. On March 4, 1857, Buchanan referred to the Kansas–Nebraska Act in his inaugural address as follows:

> What a happy conception then was it for Congress to apply this simple rule— that the will of the majority shall govern—to the settlement of the question of domestic slavery in the Territories! Congress is neither "to legislate slavery into any Territory or State, nor to exclude it therefrom, but to leave the people thereof perfectly free to form and regulate their domestic institutions in their own way, subject only to the Constitution of the United States." As a natural consequence, Congress has also prescribed that, when the Territory of Kansas shall be admitted as a State, it "shall be received into the Union, with or without slavery, as their constitution may prescribe at the time of their admission." A difference of opinion has arisen in regard to the point of time when the people of a Territory shall decide this question for themselves. This is, happily, a matter of but little practical importance. Besides, it is a judicial question, which legitimately belongs to the Supreme Court of the United States, before whom it is now pending, and will, it is understood, be speedily and finally settled. To their decision, in common with all good citizens, I shall cheerfully submit, whatever this may be.[21]

It is difficult to understand Buchanan's "happy" thought processes with regard to the Kansas–Nebraska Act. With a virtual civil war in Kansas in the immediate background, he says that the question of when the people of a territory might decide the issue of freedom or slavery is of "little practical importance." In fact the Supreme Court never addressed this question, because Taney's *Dred Scott* opinion not only denied that Congress could exclude slavery from a territory but also denied that the people of a territory could exclude it. As Lincoln would say, *Dred Scott* squatted "squatter sovereignty" (as he called Douglas's version of popular sovereignty) out of existence.[22] Buchanan's assertion that "all good citizens" should accept the forthcoming *Dred Scott* decision, "whatever [it] may be," would have been only a very bad joke if Buchanan were known to have a sense of humor. If anything, it was reminiscent of the Declaratory Act of 1766, wherein the British government asserted its right to bind the American colonies "in all cases whatsoever."

One of two letters attached as notes to the foregoing passage in Buchanan's inaugural is from Supreme Court Justice Catron:

> The Dred Scott case has been before the Judges several times since last Saturday, and I think you may safely say in your inaugural, "That the question involving the constitutionality of the Missouri Compromise line is presented to the appropriate tribunal to decide; to wit, to the Supreme Court of the United States. It is due to its high and independent character to suppose that it will decide & settle a controversy which has so long and seriously agitated the country, and which must ultimately be decided by the Supreme Court. And until the case now before it . . . presenting the direct question, is disposed of, I would deem it improper to express any opinion on the subject."[23]

Thus a member of the Supreme Court submitted to the president-elect a draft of the most important passage of his inaugural! Catron does not say in so many words that the Court will hold the Missouri Compromise line unconstitutional, but that is unquestionably what Buchanan was given to understand.

Not only Buchanan, but others—including Alexander Stephens, who was a cousin of Supreme Court Justice Daniel—were in correspondence with members of the Court. How many were privy to the effort to have the Court decide as it did is impossible to say. What is indubitable is that the proslavery political combination that placed Buchanan in the White House knew that a majority of the Supreme Court shared its political passion and would use its authority to place the interests of slavery beyond the control of electoral majorities. Lincoln's charge in the House Divided speech of a conspiracy to make slavery national was certainly well founded.

A retrospective glance at the electoral politics of the period preceding *Dred Scott* may be helpful here. The Kansas–Nebraska Act was passed by the Thirty-third Congress in May of 1854. The House contained 159 Democrats, 71 Whigs, and 4 "Others," while the Senate contained 38 Democrats and 22 Whigs. As a result of the elections in November of that year, the Thirty-fourth Congress had 108 Republicans, 83 Democrats, and 43 "Others" (remnants of the Whigs, plus Know-Nothings) in the House, and 40 Democrats and 15 Republicans in the Senate. Thus, in a matter of six months, the Kansas–Nebraska Act had brought into existence—out of nothing, so to speak—the largest single party in the House, organized primarily to prevent the extension of slavery into the territories. In the Senate, although the Republicans went from 0 to 15, the Democrats retained their majority with 40. In addition we should note that in 1856 the first Republican candidate for president, John Charles Fremont, received 1.3 million popular votes and 114 electoral votes, compared with 1.8 million popular and 174 electoral votes for Buchanan. The Whig–American candidate, Fillmore, received 874,000 popular votes but only 8 electoral votes. Buchanan was thus elected by a minority of the total votes cast, and it was clear that a fusion of Republican and Whig–American votes in 1860 could threaten the Democratic majority in the electoral college. From this we see the hard political reality governing the territorial question: With no chance of competing for the "numerical" majority in the House, and with a diminishing chance of retaining their majority in the electoral college, the slave states' only security for the future lay in keeping control of the Senate. This could be accomplished only by extending slavery into territories from which new states would be formed.

The Republican Party sprang up in the fall elections of 1854 like Athena, fully armed, from the head of Zeus. But the diminution of the ranks of the Democratic Party in the House was almost entirely a result of losses in the free states. This meant that most of the survivors of the Democratic electoral debacle of 1854 were Southerners, who would now, as never before, become dominant within the party. It meant that the defeated Northern Democrats would be bitter against the Kansas–Nebraska Act that had driven them from office and that many of them would be prepared to return to Congress as Republicans. David Potter's review of these developments is illuminating:

> When [the Kansas–Nebraska Act] came to the floor of the House in 1854, the Democrats held a triumphant majority, with 91 free state and 67 slave state members. Presumably, each group was large enough to command the respect of the other and to insist that all major policies should be based upon consensus. Sectional equilibrium thus seemed assured. But when Douglas and the [Pierce] administration decided to force the passage of the Kansas-Nebraska Act they weakened the northern wing, first by causing some northern members to quit the party, and second by exposing those who followed the party mandate to decimation by northern voters. . . . The whiphand tactics of Douglas in the Senate and Alexander H. Stephens in the House left some deep scars. But more serious in the long run was the fact that the northern Democrats were so badly defeated in the subsequent congressional elections that they could no longer hold their own against southern Democrats in the party caucuses. . . . In the elections of 1854, northern Democratic representation fell . . . from 91 to 25, while southern representation slipped only slightly, from 67 to 58. . . . In 1856 they rallied from their crushing post-Nebraska defeat, capturing 53 seats instead of 25, but in the counsels of the party, they were still outnumbered by 75 southerners, and in the Senate they were outnumbered within their own party, 25 to 12. In 1858 their strength declined again, and the Democrats in the House numbered 34 from the North and 68 from the South, while those in the Senate numbered 10 from the North and 27 from the South. This was the last Congress in which southerners sat until after Appomattox.[24]

The foregoing is indispensable for understanding the unity of Buchanan and Douglas on the eve of the former's inauguration and of Dred Scott, two days later. It is equally indispensable for understanding the pressures that brought about their split nine months later, which set the stage for the Lecompton controversy (in which Buchanan, but not Douglas, backed the Lecompton Constitution) and for the Lincoln–Douglas debates.

We need not enter the byzantine intricacies of the dispute over the Lecompton Constitution. Suffice it to say that it was drafted by a body that was legally elected as a technical matter, but in an election from which free-state Kansans had abstained. Regardless of whether they were justified in abstaining, Lecompton was not the authentic expression of the will of the people of Kansas that the Kansas–Nebraska Act had promised. Buchanan argued that admitting Kansas as a state would, once and for all, give the people of Kansas exclusive jurisdiction over their "domestic" institutions. But the Kansas–Nebraska Act had guaranteed popular sovereignty before, not after, statehood. To the nation, Kansas had become the symbolic center of the struggle over slavery in all the territories. For its part, the South felt that popular sovereignty was now irrelevant, since *Dred Scott* said that there was no constitutional power of any kind to exclude slavery from any territory. Still, it rallied behind Buchanan's effort to make Kansas a slave state.

Here is David Potter's summary of the struggle over Lecompton:

In many respects, this was 1854 all over again. Once again a newly elected president, with all the influence a new president commands, had been induced, because of his southern sympathies, to support a bill that was highly objectionable to the northern members of his own party. Once again, a party revolt followed, leading once again to a pitched political battle, famous in the annals of party warfare. Once again, the administration prevailed first in the Senate, but faced a longer and harder fight in the House. . . . Along with these similarities, there were two important differences. First, Stephen A. Douglas, previously the Senate floor leader for the administration, was now the floor leader for the opposition. The same tireless energy and the same matchless readiness and resourcefulness in debate which had carried Kansas–Nebraska to victory were now devoted to the defeat of Lecompton. Whereas Buchanan could not face the revolt of southerners if he opposed Lecompton, Douglas could not face the hostile response of Illinois and of the North generally if he supported it. Hence Congress presented a new spectacle. Day after day, Douglas voted on the same side with Chase and Wade and the men who had treated him in 1854 as if he were the Antichrist. Stranger political bedfellows no one had ever seen, but for a season it was seriously believed that Douglas might become a Republican. Some of the eastern Republicans, especially, took up the idea of supporting him and bringing him into the party. Henry Wilson believed Douglas would join the Republicans, and praised him as being "of more weight to our cause than any other ten men in the country." Horace Greeley, for all his professions of idealism, now declared: "The Republican standard is too high; we want something practical." His idea of practicality was to throw Republican support behind Douglas in the pending Illinois election. He called on Douglas in Washington, and his *Tribune* began to praise Douglas extravagantly. To the end of his life, he believed that it would have been sound Republican strategy to support Douglas. In Massachusetts, Nathaniel P. Banks urged the Illinois Republicans to "sustain" Douglas. In Washington as early as December 14, Douglas talked with Anson Burlingame and Schuyler Colfax about forming a great new party to oppose southern disunionists.[25]

This "season [when] it was seriously believed that Douglas might become a Republican" may have been the gravest of all the crises of the Union, surpassing even the Civil War itself. This was the moment when Lincoln's purpose, and everything it has come to represent in the life of America and the world, hung in the balance. Had the Illinois Republicans "sustained" Douglas, and had the Republican standard been lowered as Greeley desired, the contest between Lincoln and Douglas in 1858 would not have taken place.[26] The Declaration of Independence as the "sheet anchor of American republicanism" would have been abandoned, to be replaced by popular sovereignty. There would have been no Gettysburg Address to memorialize the Founding in the minds of American citizens. Lincoln's argument that the principles of the Declaration contained a promise to all men everywhere would have perished from the earth. What would have made the Union worth saving in such a case is hard to imagine.

The fight over Lecompton had been brutal. We might today compare the alliance of Douglas and the Republicans with that of Great Britain and the United States with the Soviet Union in the Second World War—an alliance based solely upon having Hitler as a common enemy. During the war against the Axis, and for some time afterwards, there were those who romanticized the wartime relationship with the USSR into one of true friendship and common principles. Those who thus deluded themselves could not see that Stalin's regime was no less a threat to human freedom than Hitler's, and they very nearly lost the freedom that had been saved from Hitler.[27] Similarly, in the spring of 1858, Lincoln was confronted with the powerful temptation of the eastern Republicans to turn the fortuitous circumstance of the anti-Lecompton alliance into something greater and more permanent. Defeating Lecompton was like defeating Hitler, and turning Republicans against Douglas was like turning the western alliance against Stalin. Nothing in Lincoln's life revealed his genius more completely than his campaign against Douglas, which not only ended the alliance of Douglas and the Republicans but also cut off Douglas's retreat into his former alliance with the South.

In defense of Douglas, and to understand his attractiveness to eastern Republicans in the spring of 1858, we can say that the character of his rhetoric was not theoretical but practical and that he was unperplexed by inconsistencies that might have puzzled a philosophic statesman. The great temptation of popular sovereignty was that it appeared, in the wake of Lecompton, as a means to keep slavery out of the territories without the danger of secession and civil war. Whereas Lincoln insisted upon polarizing the nation in a contest to decide whether slavery was a good or an evil, Douglas proposed to defuse the slavery question by confining it to the settlers in individual territories. "Popular sovereignty" was thus a policy that aimed to avoid disunion and civil war at the same time that it held forth the vision of a victorious coalition of Douglas supporters enjoying the abundant rewards of office. If only Republicans would abandon the intoxicating pleasure of self-righteousness attendant to the uncompromising insistence that slavery is morally evil and align themselves with Southerners willing to abandon the similarly intoxicating pleasure of insisting that slavery is a positive good, there would be many sober consolations. As the majority, they would have all the spoils of electoral victory, all the patronage and power, and all the government contracts to divide up. Never in the history of politics were there greater incentives, in terms of evils avoided and benefits gained, to "rise above principle."

If the Republican Party had welcomed Douglas, it would be fatuous to suppose that he would have become no more than a spear carrier in their ranks. If, at the behest of eastern Republicans, he had been unopposed in Illinois for reelection as senator in 1858, how could the party have opposed his nomination for president in 1860? And if Douglas represented a coalition of free-soil Democrats and Republicans—perhaps anticipating a Union Party under Lincoln in 1864—his election would have been virtually guaranteed, with a much larger margin of victory than Lincoln's. It is doubtful that the South would then have seceded, because, Lecompton notwithstanding, Douglas had never opposed slavery on moral grounds and had no objection to the indefinite extension of slavery under the banner of popular sovereignty. Suppose that, with Lincoln out of the way, Douglas had approached the South as the leader of an apparently irresistible free-soil coalition, with an offer to support territorial expansion in a southerly direction, beginning with Cuba. What might his reception have been? If Douglas had used the same words that Lincoln did in his inaugural in telling the South that it had no more to fear from him than it had from Washington, might he not have been believed? Douglas might well have pointed out that, with the exception of Kansas, popular sovereignty had in practice governed all the territories south of the Mason and Dixon Line and had invariably resulted in slave states.

Douglas was a radical Manifest Destiny man, with no assignable limits to his appetite for territorial expansion. When asked by Lincoln whether he favored the acquisition of territory without regard to its effect upon the slavery question, Douglas replied:

> I answer that whenever it becomes necessary, in our growth and progress to acquire more territory, that I am in favor of it. . . . I will leave the people free to do as they please, either to make it slave or free territory. . . . It is idle to tell me . . . that we have territory enough. . . . We have enough now for the present, but this is a young and a growing nation. It swarms as often as a hive of bees, and as new swarms are turned out each year, there must be hives in which they can gather and make their honey. . . . With our natural increase, growing with a rapidity unknown in any other part of the globe, with the tide of emigration that is fleeing despotism in the old world to seek a refuge in our own, there is a constant torrent pouring into this country that requires more land . . . and just as fast as our interests and our destiny require additional territory in the north, in the south, or on the islands of the ocean, I am for it.[28]

One of the notable features of the 1860 presidential election, as it actually came to be, was the call for the acquisition of Cuba by both the Douglas and the Breckinridge party platforms. Once Douglas had the Republicans in tow, he could have turned his attention to the South, pointing out that future territorial acquisitions, for example, in Mexico, the Caribbean, and Central America, would as certainly lead to slave states under the aegis of popular sovereignty as under the Calhoun–Taney formula of state sovereignty.

But was Douglas's position actually the compromise that those eastern Republicans thought it was? Douglas never looked to the ultimate extinction of slavery. He said that the Founding Fathers had made the nation half slave and half free, and he saw no reason why it should not continue such for all time. His expansionism was actually a form of imperialism, guided—like Hitler's—by a naked doctrine of racial inequality and racial domination. No advocate of slavery as a positive good was more convinced of the distinction between superior and inferior (or "dependent") races. The following is from Douglas's third joint debate with Lincoln, at Jonesboro:

> I hold that a negro is not and never ought to be a citizen of the United States. I hold that this government was made on the white basis, by white men, for the benefit of white men and their posterity forever, and should be administered by white men and none others. I do not believe that the Almighty made the negro capable of self-government. . . . Now I say to you, my fellow-citizens, that in my opinion the signers of the Declaration had no reference to the negro whatever when they declared all men to be created equal. They desired to express by that phrase, white men, men of European birth and European descent, and had no

reference either to the negro, the savage Indians, the Feejee, the Malay, or any other inferior and degraded race, when they spoke of the equality of men.

Douglas then repeats almost verbatim Taney's pseudo-Kantian hypothesis that if the Signers of the Declaration had meant to include Negroes, they would have been "bound, as honest men, that day and hour to have put their negroes on an equality with themselves."[29] But unlike Taney, who said that if the Declaration had been written in 1857 it would be understood to include the whole human family, implying that Negroes were part of such a family, Douglas denies any such relationship: "I do not question Mr. Lincoln's conscientious belief that the negro was made his equal, and hence is his brother, but for my own part I do not regard the negro as my equal, and positively deny that he is my brother or any kin to me whatever."[30]

The essence of popular sovereignty is revealed in the following comment by Douglas during the final joint debate at Alton: "We in Illinois . . . tried slavery, kept it up for twelve years, and finding that it was not profitable we abolished it for that reason."[31] Clearly wherever slavery or any form of racial domination was found profitable, however one defined profit, Douglas had no moral inhibitions against it. As he never tired of saying, he didn't care whether slavery was voted up or down, he cared only for the "sacred right" of the people to make that decision. What made the rights of only some men sacred, or why one should measure the rights of some by the interests of others, he never said, during the course of his debates with Lincoln in 1858 or at any other time.

In a passage that Lincoln took pains to make famous, Douglas illuminated the growing power in midcentury of the idea of the separate evolutionary origin of the different races of mankind by comparing the differences of blacks and whites to the differences between blacks and crocodiles. In any quarrel between the Negro and the crocodile, Douglas said, he was on the side of the Negro, but when it came to the Negro and the white man, he was on the side of the white man. According to Lincoln, this meant that "as the negro is to the white man, so is the crocodile to the negro; and as the negro may rightfully treat the crocodile as a beast or reptile, so the white man may rightfully treat the negro as a beast or reptile."[32] Not slavery as such, but the denial of human equality that the defense of slavery required, was the ultimate evil to Lincoln. That denial could justify many evils other than chattel slavery, as we have learned from the great tyrants of the twentieth century.

Neither Thrasymachus nor Machiavelli espoused more completely than Douglas the doctrine that "justice is the interest of the stronger." And no one since Socrates more resolutely opposed that doctrine than Lincoln. As we have said, the House Divided speech and Lincoln's subsequent tactics in the joint debates had the dual aim of destroying Douglas's political stature in the North and in the South. How Lincoln succeeded is a masterpiece of both tactical and strategic statesmanship and deserves study as much as any campaign of Caesar, Marlborough, or Napoleon. In the Civil War period, it resembles nothing so much as Stonewall Jackson's Valley Campaign, when Jackson immobilized three Union armies, each larger than his own, preventing them from reinforcing General McClellan on the peninsula, while he himself was able to join Robert E. Lee in time to assist in McClellan's defeat.

∽

There is a story, certainly apocryphal, that Lincoln rejected advice to moderate the radicalism of the House Divided speech because he had his sights set on 1860 more than on 1858. Clearly he was as thoroughly engrossed in the immediate contest with Douglas in 1858 as any man on a campaign has ever been. It is uncanny, however, that nearly every event of that campaign contributed directly to his nomination and election two years later. That Douglas actually won reelection to the Senate itself turned out a blessing, however well disguised, to Lincoln's cause. Had Douglas not been returned to the Senate, he almost certainly would not have become the Democratic candidate for president in 1860, and Lincoln's own importance as Douglas's nemesis would thereby have been discounted.

On November 2, 1858, "the voters of Illinois cast about 125,000 votes for the Republicans, 121,000 for the Douglas Democrats, and 5,000 for the Buchanan Democrats. When broken down by legislative districts, this balloting resulted in the election of forty-six Democratic legislators and forty-one Republicans. This result assured the reelection of Douglas by the legislature."[33] Thus while losing the election to the U.S. Senate in the Illinois legislature, Lincoln nonetheless demonstrated his ability to defeat Douglas in a presidential election, where only the statewide popular vote would count. In 1856 Buchanan had carried both Indiana and Illinois, and it was vital that the Republicans have a presidential candidate who could carry these states. This was a powerful point in Lincoln's favor in the nomination process of 1860.[34]

Even the defection of the eastern Republicans before the 1858 Lincoln–Douglas contest turned to Lincoln's advantage. Illinois Republicans reacted fiercely to the proposal to abandon their standard-bearer in favor of a Democrat they had been fighting against for years. Loyalty to Lincoln thus became a political passion, and although directed as much against the eastern Republicans as against Douglas, it was nonetheless to Lincoln's advantage, both in 1858 and 1860.

Finally, one must bear in mind that the contest between Lincoln and Douglas in 1858 became, in effect, the contest of 1860. It was augmented by the speeches of both men in Ohio in 1859, by Douglas's *Harper's* essay in September 1859, and by Lincoln's Cooper Institute speech in February 1860. The joint debates of 1858 were published in book form by Follett-Foster, of Columbus, Ohio (and included Lincoln's September 17, 1859, speech in Cincinnati), shortly before the Republican convention in Chicago. This and the publication in pamphlet form of the Cooper Institute speech constituted Lincoln's personal contribution to the presidential election campaign. Still, what was not fortuitous, and what proved decisive for 1860, was how Lincoln shaped the issues between himself and Douglas in the House Divided speech and in the long, hot, dusty campaign that followed.

∼

The focal point of Lincoln's strategy was, first, to identify Douglas with a conspiracy to extend slavery. By reminding his fellow Republicans, east as well as west, that the Republican Party came into existence in opposition to Douglas's Kansas–Nebraska Act, he revived the war between Douglas and the Republicans that had antedated the Lecompton fight. He reminded them that there would have been no Lecompton had not Douglas's bill repealed the Missouri Compromise and opened Kansas, not only to slavery, but also to armed conflict between proslavery and antislavery settlers. The alliance of Douglas and the Republicans on Lecompton, Lincoln pointed out, turned on a question of fact, not of principle. The fact was that Lecompton was not an authentic expression of the will of the people of Kansas. On that basis, Douglas and the Republicans agreed that Lecompton ought to be rejected. More important, however, Douglas and the Republicans remained at odds over the reasons *why* Kansas ought to become a free state. Douglas thought it should become a free state if, but only if, the people of the territory so desired it. Conversely, he held that it was only wrong to have slavery in Kansas if the people did not want it. For Lincoln, on the other hand, it was wrong to have slavery in Kansas or anywhere else because slavery was wrong. For Republicans to welcome Douglas into their party merely because popular sovereignty had proved an obstruction to Lecompton meant abandoning the moral ground of republican government. No more memorable words were pronounced in the debates than the following:

> [Judge Douglas] says he "don't care" whether [slavery] is voted up or voted down" in the territories. . . . Any man can say that who does not see anything wrong in slavery, but no man can logically say it who does see a wrong in it; because no man can logically say he don't care whether a wrong is voted up or

voted down. . . . He contends that whatever community wants slaves has a right to have them. So they have if it is not a wrong. But if it is a wrong, he cannot say people have a right to do wrong.[35]

We recall Jefferson's pronouncement in his first inaugural that for the will of the majority to be rightful it must be reasonable. Jefferson never held that the will of the majority was rightful because it was the will of the majority. Contrary to Douglas, none of the Founders ever regarded popular sovereignty merely as majority rule, or majority rule as a self-justifying principle.

In the political thought of Western civilization, Douglas's position is recognizable in the thesis that justice is the interest of the stronger. In a democracy, this would mean that justice is nothing other than the interest of the people who possess the franchise and who decide who shall form the government. In Book I of Plato's *Republic*, Thrasymachus sets forth this thesis in classic form. Socrates asks him what he means by saying that justice is the interest of the stronger

> "Don't you know," [Thrasymachus] said, "that some cities are ruled tyrannically, some democratically, and some aristocratically?"
> "Of course."
> "In each city, isn't the ruling group master?"
> "Certainly."
> "And each group sets down laws for its own advantage; a democracy sets down democratic laws; a tyranny, tyrannic laws; and the others do the same. And they declare that what they have set down—their own advantage—is just for the ruled, and the man who departs from it they punish as a breaker of the law and a doer of unjust deeds . . . so the man who reasons rightly concludes that everywhere justice is the same thing, the advantage of the stronger."[36]

Douglas had said that the people of Illinois had tried slavery and had abolished it because they decided it was not to their advantage. Had they decided it was to their advantage, they might have kept it. For Douglas, as for Thrasymachus, "the people" make the laws in a democracy and are therefore themselves the source of the distinction between just and unjust, right and wrong. Wherever the people make the laws and have the power to enforce the laws, they decide what is right and wrong. Wherever they do not hold the power, as in tyrannies or aristocracies, they do not hold this right. Those altogether without power, such as slaves, are for that reason altogether without right. In chapter 7 we will see that this is essentially the position of John C. Calhoun as well, in his *Disquisition on Government*.

Douglas tells the people that no other justification for slavery is necessary than their decision that it is in their interest. Like Thrasymachus—and the

Sophists generally—he presented himself as the people's servant, ready to procure for them whatever they wanted. By presenting himself as the slave of their desires, so to speak, he hoped that they would reciprocate by presenting him with their power. In this way the slave of the people becomes the master of the political regime. Thus slavery and despotism are linked in a democracy by the medium of that most insidious form of flattery that says that what the people want must be good because they want it, and that there is no wrong that does not become right by their wanting it.[37]

For Lincoln, as for Jefferson and for all genuine supporters of the principles of the Declaration of Independence, the distinction between right and wrong is antecedent to any form of government and is independent of any man's or any majority's will. The wrongness of slavery, Lincoln said,

> is the issue that will continue in this country when these poor tongues of Judge Douglas and myself shall be silent. It is the eternal struggle between these two principles—right and wrong—throughout the world. They are the two principles that have stood face to face from the beginning of time; and will ever continue to struggle. The one is the common right of humanity and the other the divine right of kings. It is the same principle in whatever shape it develops itself. It is the same spirit that says, "You work and toil and earn bread, and I'll eat it." No matter in what shape it comes, whether from the mouth of a king who seeks to bestride the people of his own race and live by the fruit of their labor, or from one race of men as an apology for enslaving another race, it is the same tyrannical principle.[38]

As Douglas could see no moral wrong in slavery, neither could he see that if there was no moral wrong in slavery, there could be no reasoned set of principles by which majority rule could be combined with minority rights. If the majority can enslave one minority, why not another, and another? If majorities swallow up minorities, one after another, the majority itself will become a minority—perhaps even a minority of one. The slippery slope to tyranny begins with the first exclusion of any class of persons within the community whose rights may be trampled. There must be, a priori, a firm foundation of minority rights as the very basis of majority rule. That foundation, which Lincoln presented as the only possible foundation for free government, was bound up with the proposition that all men are created equal.

It is notable that when Thrasymachus speaks of democracy, he implies that the "people" are a class apart from other classes that make up the community, and that each class, when it has a government of its own, has both the power and the right to exploit the other classes. Thus in a democracy the poor would have the right to divide up the property of the rich; and in an oligarchy the rich would have the right to grind the faces of the poor. In Douglas's political vocabulary, we find the distinction between superior and inferior races taking the place of rich and poor, but the effect is the same. Superiority and inferiority are defined by who holds power. Power defines the right. By the doctrine of equality as Lincoln understood it, by contrast, the "people" is not a class apart but the entire political community. No one is entitled to use power to deny or disparage the natural rights that all share alike as human beings and that are the foundation of their citizenship.

Underlying Douglas's position is the conviction that there is no objective criterion by which the different partisan claims to justice can themselves be measured and judged. It was Lincoln's position (as it was Jefferson's) that right and wrong have an objective existence, that they are knowable by human reason, and that they are binding upon the majority no less than the minority.

❧

As we have seen, Douglas followed Taney in the unprecedented denial that Negroes were included in the Declaration's proposition of equality. Both of them thereby converted the Declaration into an assertion of power rather than right. For them, the Declaration was made for the advantage of white Englishmen in America, who were declared to be equal to white Englishmen in England—a category, we recall, that Douglas eventually broadened to include white Europeans. According to Taney and Douglas, the American people in 1776 rejected the advantage that the British king and Parliament sought to gain at their expense, because they were equal to them. But from Taney's and Douglas's perspective, that equality proved to be only an equality in power, as manifest in the American victory in the war. The American assertion of right was merely an American assertion of self-interest backed by power and did not recognize any right possessed by "inferior or degraded races." This interpretation of the Declaration did not explain, however, why the Signers of the Declaration addressed their justification to a "candid world," a world largely made up of "inferior and degraded races."

In bringing the moral argument to the forefront, Lincoln effectively burned Douglas's bridges to the free-soil movement. By driving the pugnacious Douglas to counterattack the "black Republicans," Lincoln not only reclaimed the moral high ground but also preserved for himself a position of Republican leadership and ended the Republican dalliance with Douglas.

❧

In the House Divided speech Lincoln accused Douglas of being party to a conspiracy, with Presidents Pierce and Buchanan and Chief Justice Taney, to spread slavery not only to all the territories but also to all the states. Historians generally have doubted that Douglas was party to such a conspiracy, or indeed that there was any such a conspiracy. Lincoln, however, characterized the heart of Taney's *Dred Scott* opinion as follows: "Nothing in the Constitution or laws of any State can destroy a right distinctly and expressly affirmed in the Constitution of the United States; The right of property in a slave is distinctly and expressly affirmed in the Constitution of the United States; Therefore, nothing in the Constitution or laws of any State can destroy the right of property in a slave."[39] Lincoln said that no fault could be found in this reasoning. The fault lay rather in the premises. The right of property in a slave is *not* expressly affirmed in the Constitution. The fugitive slave clause provides security for a property right expressly affirmed only in the laws of the slave states, but such right had no existence outside of state law. *Dred Scott* applied the foregoing syllogism only to territories. But in itself, the syllogism applied no less to states, free as well as slave. Thus Douglas's unwavering support for *Dred Scott* made him a party to a doctrine that, if followed to its logical and political consequences, would make the nation all slave. Throughout the debates, Lincoln said that all that was necessary for this to occur was for a second *Dred Scott* decision to apply the foregoing logic to the states as the first had applied it to the territories. And all that was necessary for this second *Dred Scott* was for public opinion to accept the logic of the first. And Douglas, he said, was doing everything within his power to prepare public opinion for that acceptance: "In this and like communities [Lincoln declared] public sentiment is everything. With public sentiment nothing can fail; without it nothing can succeed. Consequently he who moulds public sentiment, goes deeper than he who enacts statutes or pronounces decisions. He makes statutes and decisions possible or impossible to be executed."[40]

Historians have taken insufficient notice that Douglas, in the heat of his fight against the Lecompton Constitution, had himself accused the Buchanan administration of intending to make slavery lawful in all the states, north as well as south. Lincoln brought this forward at the first joint debate at Ottawa and again at the second debate at Freeport.[41] At Ottawa he quoted at length from what Douglas had said in the Senate on March 22, 1858. This speech gives us a savor of the viciousness of the infighting between the northern and southern wings of the Democratic Party and is a powerful confirmation, by Douglas himself, of Lincoln's charge of a plot to spread slavery nationwide. It also shows how near Douglas came to becoming a Republican—or, conversely, how near the Republican Party came to being absorbed by Douglas.

In this 1858 Senate speech, Douglas was responding to an article in the *Washington Union*, which by the custom of the time was recognized as a mouthpiece of the Buchanan administration. The editor of the *Union*, not holding an official position, could say what the president or his cabinet did not at that moment wish to say openly, but which nonetheless represented their real intentions or ulterior motives. In the last two or three months, said Douglas (as quoted by Lincoln), the *Union* "has read me out of the Democratic Party every other day . . . using such terms as 'traitor,' 'renegade,' 'deserter,' and other kind and polite epithets of that nature." Douglas then characterized the *Union* article as advancing four propositions, while denouncing every man who questioned them "as an Abolitionist, a Free-Soiler, a fanatic." These four propositions were,

> first, that the primary object of all government at its original institution is the protection of person and property; second, that the Constitution of the United States declares that the citizens of each State shall be entitled to all the privileges and immunities of citizens in the several States; and that therefore thirdly, all State laws, whether organic or otherwise, which prohibit the citizens of one State from settling in another with their slave property, and especially declaring it forfeited, are direct violations of the original intention of the Government and Constitution of the United States; and fourth, that the emancipation of the slaves of the northern States was a gross outrage on the right of property, inasmuch as it was involuntarily done on the part of the owner.[42]

This, representing in naked form the most radical proslavery position imaginable, is what Stephen Douglas said was the true policy of the Buchanan administration. It is perhaps even better proof than the House Divided speech of the intention to make slavery lawful everywhere in the nation. In fact, according to the *Union*, slavery was at that moment lawful everywhere in the United States, and all laws or ordinances against it were unconstitutional. The *Union* was therefore advancing, in somewhat less condensed form, the conclusion of the syllogism Lincoln had extracted from Taney's opinion. Indeed, we can see in the *Union* the seeds of the secession crisis. It is Douglas, not Lincoln, who here delineates the minds of those prepared to issue an ultimatum to the free states: Either adopt our understanding of the "original intent" of the Constitution or we will leave the Union. It is a dramatic confirmation of Lincoln's thesis that a crisis had been reached and that the nation must now decide which path to follow. Douglas's speech repudiates the possibility enshrined in Douglas's own idea of popular sovereignty, that only local decisions on slavery were needed.

It is not likely that the *Union* articles represented an unqualified expression of Buchanan's own opinions, because they are inconsistent with the antisecession doctrine of his last annual message to Congress, which we discussed in chapter 3. They do, however, give substance to Buchanan's pronouncement that secession would come unless the free states repealed their personal liberty laws and that it would be the fault of northern antislavery agitation.

The first proposition advanced by the *Union*, concerning the primary object of government, would be unexceptionable if its authors had understood the meaning of their own words. It is in fact a condition of the social compact that presides at the institution of legitimate government that everyone recognize the equal natural right to life, liberty, and property of their fellow humans. There cannot then be slavery prior to the institution of government. Slavery can only arise from positive law after such institution. The second and third propositions are tainted by the same defect as the first. The "original intention" of any government arising from "the laws of nature and of nature's God" cannot be the protection of slave property, since slave property cannot be lawful prior to the institution of government. Hence only those "privileges and immunities" of citizenship that are consistent with such an "original intention" can be recognized across state lines, and the right of some humans to own other humans is not one of them. By the third proposition the *Union* is asserting, without waiting for a second *Dred Scott* decision, that slavery is lawful in every state, as well as every territory, of the United States. The fourth proposition, consistently with the third, denies that any state has or ever had the constitutional power to abolish slavery against the wishes of any slave owner.

These four propositions, Douglas noted (as noted by Lincoln), were advanced in the *Union* on November 17, 1857, and were followed on the very next day by the *Union*'s "adhesion" to Lecompton. Douglas then quoted from the *Union* of November 18, including in his quotation the following clause of the Lecompton constitution: "The right of property is before and higher than any constitutional sanction; and the right of the owner of a slave to such slave and its increase is the same and as inviolable as the right of the owner of any property whatever." Finally, Lincoln quotes Douglas as saying that "When I saw that article in the *Union* of the 17th of November, followed by the glorification of the Lecompton Constitution on the 18th of November, and this clause in the Constitution asserting the doctrine that a state has no right to prohibit slavery within its limits, I saw that there was a fatal blow being struck at the sovereignty of the States of this Union."[43]

This speech by Douglas closely resembles Lincoln's House Divided speech, but there are two notable differences. First, Douglas does not include himself in the conspiracy to strike a "fatal blow" at the Constitution. Second, Douglas charges a conspiracy against state sovereignty, not against free soil. Here is the very heart of the reason Lincoln declared that Douglas did not belong among the Republicans. Douglas does not admit, here or anywhere, any limitation upon the sovereignty of the states or territories to include or exclude slavery. Lincoln himself saw no legal limitations upon the states (although he did upon the territories), but he did see moral limitations, and he thought it was of the essence of Republican policy to be governed by them. For Douglas, popular sovereignty is an end in itself. But by the principles of the Declaration of Independence, popular sovereignty arises to secure natural rights—rights defined, not by positive law, but by natural law. Popular sovereignty was a means to these ends, not an end in itself.

In one sense, Lincoln had more in common with the *Washington Union* than with Douglas, in that he believed there was a right of property "before and higher than any constitutional sanction." For Douglas, there were no rights antecedent to government, no rights defining the ends of government and thereby limiting government. Of course, while Lincoln and the *Union* agreed upon an antecedent right of property, they differed as to its nature. For Lincoln (following the Founding Fathers), the origin of the right of property, antecedent to civil society, was the natural right of every man to own himself and thus to own the product of his labor. From that perspective, the *Union*'s idea of an antecedent right of property in slaves is a self-contradiction, since it denies the only possible foundation for antecedent property rights of any kind. As we shall see, in Calhounian constitutionalism, property in slaves is grounded in state sovereignty and state equality, not in any antecedent right. Thus even when he most appeared a hero to the eastern Republicans, Douglas was a better Calhounian than the champions of Lecompton.

It is of no little importance, in comprehending the dialectical dynamics that drove the nation to civil war, to see that the premise underlying the *Union* article and the pro-Lecompton cause—indeed, the entire proslavery cause—was that the right to own a slave, whether that right was antecedent to, or coextensive with, the Constitution, was not less than the right to own any kind of property whatever. The passage quoted from the Lecompton Constitution shows that its acceptance by Congress would have meant much more than the admission of Kansas as a slave state. It would have meant a ratification of the most radical of proslavery claims to the nationalization of slavery. These claims, from *Dred Scott* forward, were grounded upon Taney's declaration that under the Constitution the Negro, whether free or slave, was in effect a subhuman animal with "no rights which the white man was bound to respect."

Douglas would not repudiate one word of Taney's opinion. He not only accepted the subhuman constitutional status of the Negro asserted by Taney but also (unlike Taney) asserted it without qualification. For Douglas to accept what Taney said about the Negro as property, however, while insisting upon the sovereign authority of the territories or the states to deny slave property protection was a logical, moral, and ultimately a political impossibility. The nation would indeed have to become all slave if the conception of the Negro as a subhuman chattel prevailed. Lincoln pounded Douglas on this point remorselessly.

But I cannot shake Judge Douglas' teeth loose from the Dred Scott decision. Like some obstinate animal . . . that will hang on when he has once got his teeth fixed, you may cut off a leg, or you may tear away an arm, still he will not relax his hold. . . . He hangs on to the last, to the Dred Scott decision. These things show there is a purpose *strong as death and eternity* for which he adheres to this decision, and for which he will adhere to *all other decisions* of the same Court.[44]

As we have noted, Douglas's Senate speech against the *Washington Union* illuminated his extraordinary proximity in March 1858 to the Republican Party. To distinguish a conspiracy against state sovereignty from one against free soil required, at that moment, unusual perspicuity. Yet the doctrine of state sovereignty or state rights that Douglas was defending was, despite the circumstances of the moment, the mainstay of the proslavery cause. In its Calhounian and Taneyite form, this doctrine completely divorced state rights from natural rights. By his unqualified adhesion to *Dred Scott*, and especially to the status of the Negro as subhuman, Douglas's lot was in principle cast with the proslavery South, Lecompton to the contrary notwithstanding. Had southern leaders been less blinded by their demand for an unqualified endorsement of the moral rightness of slavery, they would have recognized that Douglas—by use of his free soil credentials gained from his successful fight against Lecompton—could gain for them what they sought, without secession and without civil war.

Lincoln was confident that in any straightforward national political contest between proslavery and antislavery, antislavery would win. But Douglas's "popular sovereignty" presented itself as a "practical" solution that both sides could live with. It had therefore a seductiveness that an unambiguous proslavery policy did not. The eastern Republicans had already shown their gullibility, and we have seen Lincoln respond. Now Lincoln had to make certain that the proslavery South did not see that Douglas's moral neutrality could serve their cause better than any endorsement of slavery as a "positive good."

Nearly everyone knows the famous "Freeport question," the second of the four "interrogatories" propounded by Lincoln to Douglas in the second of their joint debates: "Can the people of a United States Territory, in any lawful way, against the wish of any citizen of the United States, exclude slavery from its limits prior to the formation of a State Constitution?" According to the legend that grew up around the Lincoln–Douglas debates, this was a sudden and unexpected thrust that caught Douglas off guard, and from which he never recovered. In fact, as Douglas himself said, he had answered it many times before, and his response was well known. Lincoln's prowess lay not in asking the question but in his counterattack upon the answer. Here is Douglas's answer, as given at Freeport.

It matters not what way the Supreme Court may hereafter decide as to the abstract question whether slavery may or may not go into a territory under the constitution, the people have the lawful means to introduce it or exclude it as they please, for the reason that slavery cannot exist a day or an hour anywhere, unless it is supported by local police regulations. These police regulations can only be established by the local legislature, and if the people are opposed to slavery they will elect representatives to that body who will by unfriendly legislation effectually prevent the introduction of it into their midst. If, on the contrary, they are for it, their legislation will favor its extension. Hence no matter what the decision of the Supreme Court may be on that abstract question, still the right of the people to make a slave territory or a free territory is perfect and complete under the Nebraska bill.[45]

It is curious that Douglas refers to what the Supreme Court had already decided as what it might decide "hereafter." This may reflect the fact that Douglas had been a leader among those who, like Presidents Pierce and Buchanan, advocated a judicial resolution of the controversy over slavery in the territories and had become accustomed to speak of the Court's decision as forthcoming. No one had been more emphatic than Douglas in insisting that the Court was the authority whose decisions all good citizens were in conscience bound to accept as final. As an advocate of judicial resolution of this most political of all questions, Douglas had stood together with those who were confident that the Court, as then constituted, would render a thoroughly "Southern" decision, as indeed it did. Douglas almost certainly expected that the Court would, as it did, vindicate the repeal of the Missouri Compromise in the Kansas–Nebraska Act, by declaring the former unconstitutional. But he almost certainly did not expect the Court to say that neither Congress nor a territorial legislature had the constitutional power to prohibit slavery in a territory. And he most certainly did not expect the Court to declare that Congress possessed the power, "coupled with the duty," to protect the slave owner in his rights. As we have seen, this last component of Taney's opinion did as much damage to Douglas's "popular sovereignty" as to the Republican call for the restoration of the Missouri Compromise. Indeed, after the campaign of 1858 was over, it drove Douglas to compose a constitutional treatise, his *Harper's* essay of September 1859, in a vain attempt to find a theoretical ground by which to escape the self-contradiction that Lincoln ruthlessly exposed.[46] (For a commentary on Douglas's essay, see the appendix to this volume.)

Douglas could not retreat from his formal acceptance, given in advance, of the *Dred Scott* decision. So he sought a formula consistent with that acceptance that would nonetheless nullify that part of Taney's opinion incompatible with the "perfect freedom" of the people of Kansas to decide their own domestic institutions. He declared that the Court's opinion was merely "abstract" and that the right to hold slaves was dependent upon "friendly" or "unfriendly" legislation that only the local legislature could supply. That slavery cannot exist without friendly legislation, however, was simply not true. As Lincoln pointed out, Dred Scott himself had been held as a slave in both a free state and a free territory before returning to a slave state. And all the slave states, except for the original thirteen, had been formed from territories into which slavery had gone before there was "friendly" legislation.

The argument that the *Dred Scott* decision was merely "abstract" and that the people of a territory were "perfectly free" to ignore it is subject to powerful con-tradiction by Lincoln in a number of places, and never more so than in his con-cluding words at Alton, in the last joint debate.

The first thing I ask attention to is the fact that Judge Douglas constantly said, before the [*Dred Scott*] decision, that whether [the people of the Territories] could or not [exclude slavery], *was a question for the Supreme Court.* But after the Court has made the decision he virtually says it is *not* a question for the Supreme Court, but for the people. And how is it he tells us they can exclude it? He says it needs "police regulations," and that admits of "unfriendly legislation." . . . Let me take the gentleman who looks me in the face before me, and let us suppose that he is a member of the Territorial Legislature. The first thing he will do will be to swear that he will support the Constitution of the United States. His neigh-bor by his side in the Territory has slaves and needs Territorial legislation to enable him to enjoy that constitutional right. Can he withhold the legislation which his neighbor needs for the enjoyment of a right fixed in his favor in the Constitution of the United States which he has sworn to support? Can he with-hold it without violating his oath? Why this is a *monstrous* sort of talk about the Constitution of the United States! *There has never been as outlandish or lawless a doctrine from the mouth of any respectable man on earth.* I do not believe it is a con-stitutional right to hold slaves in a Territory of the United States. I believe the decision was improperly made and I go for reversing it. Judge Douglas is furious against those who go for reversing a decision. But he is for legislating it out of all force while the law itself stands. . . .

I suppose most of us, (I know it of myself), believe that the people of the Southern States are entitled to a Congressional fugitive slave law—that it is a right fixed in the Constitution. But it cannot be made available to them without Congressional legislation. In the Judge's language, it is a "barren right" which needs legislation before it can become efficient and valuable to the person to whom it is guaranteed. And as the right is constitutional I agree that the legisla-tion shall be granted to it—and that not that we like the institution of slavery. . . . Why then do I yield support to a fugitive slave law? Because I do not under-stand that the Constitution, which guarantees that right, can be supported with-out it. And if I believed that the right to hold a slave in a Territory was equally fixed in the Constitution with the right to reclaim fugitives, I should be bound to give it the legislation necessary to support it. . . . I say that no man can deny his obligation to give the necessary legislation to support slavery in a Territory, who believes it is a constitutional right to have it there. No man can, who does not give the Abolitionist an argument to deny the obligation enjoined by the Constitution to enact a fugitive slave law. Try it now. It is the strongest abolition argument ever made. I say if that Dred Scott decision is correct, then the right to hold slaves in a Territory is equally a constitutional right with the right of a slaveholder to have his runaway returned. No one can show the distinction between them. The one is express, so that we cannot deny it. The other is construed to be in the constitution, so that he who believes the decision to be correct believes in the right. And the man who argues that by unfriendly legislation, in spite of that constitutional right, slavery may be driven from the Territories, cannot avoid furnishing an argument by which Abolitionists may deny the obligation to return fugitives, and claim the power to pass laws unfriendly to the right of the slaveholder to reclaim his fugitive. I do not know how such an argument may strike a popular assembly like this, but I defy anybody to go before a body of men whose minds are educated to estimating evidence and reasoning, and show that there is an iota of difference between the constitutional right to reclaim a fugitive, and the constitutional right to hold a slave in a Territory, provided this Dred Scott decision is correct. I defy any man to make an argument that will justify unfriendly legislation to deprive a slaveholder of his right to hold his slave in a Territory, that will not equally, in all its length, breadth, and thickness furnish an argument for nullifying the fugitive slave law. Why there is not such an Abolitionist in the nation as Douglas, after all.[47]

We have quoted Lincoln at length here, because nearly all the threads of his arguments in the joint debates come together in this remarkable peroration. It is doubtful if Socratic rationalism ever appeared more powerfully in public utterance since the founder of political philosophy walked the streets of Athens. Douglas might accept *Dred Scott*, and with it slave codes for the territories, or he might oppose slave codes and reject *Dred Scott*. But he could not accept *Dred Scott* and reject the slave codes. The links in Lincoln's chain of argument were unbreakable. By exploiting as he did Douglas's refusal to reject *Dred Scott*, Lincoln burned Douglas's bridges to the Republican Party and the free soil movement. By exploiting as he did Douglas's refusal to accept the obligation under *Dred Scott* to protect the slave owner in his rights in the territories, Lincoln burned Douglas's bridges to the proslavery South. In truth, no one did more than Lincoln in fortifying the Deep South in its determination to insist upon slave codes as its price to remain in the Union.

Lincoln's argument was thus a contributing cause—perhaps the major contributing cause—to the action of the delegates of the Deep South in seceding from the Democratic national convention in Charleston in April 1860. This happened when the Douglas delegates, locked into Douglas's doctrine of popular sovereignty, refused to approve the demand for territorial slave codes. This split in the Democratic Party virtually assured Lincoln's election—and civil war.

Let us not, however, leave Lincoln's dialectical tour de force without seeing Douglas's rejoinder—to which, since Douglas had the closing argument in this last of their joint debates, Lincoln had no rebuttal.

> I hold that the people of a territory, like those of a state . . . have the right to decide for themselves whether slavery shall or shall not exist within their limits. The point upon which Chief Justice Taney expresses his opinion is simply this, that slaves being property, stand on an equal footing with other property, and consequently that the owner has the same right to carry that property into a territory that he has any other, subject to the same conditions. Suppose that one of your merchants was to take fifty or one hundred thousand dollars worth of liquors to Kansas. He has a right to go there under that decision, but when he gets there he finds the Maine liquor law in force, and what can he do with his property after he gets there? He cannot sell it, he cannot use it, it is subject to the local law, and that law is against him, and the best thing he can do with it is to bring it back into Missouri or Illinois and sell it.[48]

Douglas was a shrewd and skillful debater, and his response is persuasive on the surface. But Taney had said that the right to own slaves is "expressly affirmed" in the Constitution, something he did not say about any other form of property.[49] And Douglas simply ignored what Taney had said about Congress having the power, *coupled with the duty*, of protecting the slave owner (not the liquor owner) in his rights. It should also be kept in mind that it was commonly believed that prior to statehood, sovereignty in the territories, subject to the Constitution, was vested in Congress. Congress could, and frequently did, revise territorial laws. Hence it could repeal a "Maine liquor law" as well as any legislation unfriendly to slavery. But it could not, according to Taney's interpretation of the Constitution, repeal any territorial legislation *friendly* to slavery.

Lincoln attacked Douglas and Taney for dehumanizing the Negro and reducing him to a common (or uncommon) article of property. Douglas counterattacked, saying that if Lincoln was right that the Negro was equally entitled to all the rights mentioned in the Declaration of Independence, then the Negro must also be entitled to all the other rights, civil and political, that white men enjoyed. In a sense, the charges of self-contradiction of each man against the other were mirror images. We must then examine the validity of Douglas's charges.

In Chicago on July 10, 1858, before the joint debates, Lincoln said: "Let us discard all this quibbling about this man and the other man—this race and that race and the other race being inferior, and therefore must be placed in an inferior position. . . . Let us discard all these things, and unite as one people throughout this land, until we shall once more stand up declaring that all men are created equal."[50]

Yet at Charleston on September 18, in the fourth of the joint debates, he said: "I will say, then, that I am not, nor ever have been, in favor of bringing about in any way the social and political equality of the white and black races: that I am not, nor ever have been, in favor of making voters or jurors of negroes, nor of qualifying them to hold office, nor to intermarry with white people."[51] The opinions apparently implied in these two passages do indeed seem to express opposing views. Whether they are in actual contradiction remains to be seen. For a comprehensive view of the subject, we return to Lincoln's most comprehensive speech on this question, his Peoria speech of 1854. In it we find in its purest form the Socratic dialectic that is the powerful chord unifying all of Lincoln's speeches from 1854 until his election in 1860: "Equal justice to the south, it is said, requires us to consent to the extending of slavery to new countries. That is to say, inasmuch as you do not object to my taking my hog to Nebraska, therefore I must not object to you taking your slave. Now I admit this is perfectly logical, if there is no difference between hogs and negroes."[52] Here, three years before *Dred Scott*, Lincoln confronted the fundamental premise of that decision: that Negroes are so far inferior that they have no rights that white men are bound to respect and that therefore the right of property in slaves is no less inviolate than that in any other form of chattel property.

Was equating the Negro with the hog consistent with the experience accessible to every civilized human being as a civilized human being? Is not objective reality a necessary foundation of the law of a civilized people? Is law whatever a deluded or savage mentality wills it to be, or is there not a reason in nature that governs, or ought to govern, a civilized society? Lincoln continues:

> But while you thus require me to deny the humanity of the negro, I wish to ask whether you of the South yourselves, have ever been willing to do as much? It is kindly provided that of all those who come into the world, only a small percentage are natural tyrants. That percentage is no larger in the slave states than in the free. The great majority, south as well as north, have human sympathies, of which they can no more divest themselves than they can their sensibility to physical pain. These sympathies in the bosom of the southern people, manifest in many ways their sense of the wrong of slavery, and their consciousness that, after all, there is humanity in the negro. If they deny this, let me address them a few plain questions. In 1820 you joined the north, almost unanimously, in declaring the African slave trade piracy, and annexing to it the punishment of death. Why did you do this? If you did not feel that it was wrong, why did you join in providing that men should be hung for it? The practice was no more than bringing wild negroes from Africa, to sell to such as would buy them. But you never thought of hanging men for catching and selling wild horses, wild buffaloes or wild bears.

Lincoln next considers a phenomenon of which he obviously had had direct personal experience, but which might surprise someone unacquainted with the antebellum South.

> Again, you have amongst you a sneaking individual, of the class of native tyrants known as the "slave dealer." He watches your necessities, and crawls up to buy your slave, at a speculating price. If you cannot help it, you sell to him; but if you can help it, you drive him from your door. You despise him utterly. You do not recognize him as a friend, or even as an honest man. Your children must not play with his; they may rollick freely with the little negroes, but not with the "slave-dealer's" children. If you are obliged to deal with him, you try to get through the job without so much as touching him. It is common with you to join hands with the men you meet; but with the slave-dealer you avoid the ceremony—instinctively shrinking from the snaky contact. If he grows rich and retires from business, you still remember him, and still keep up the ban of non-intercourse upon him and his family. Now why is this? You do not so treat the man who deals in corn, cattle, or tobacco.[53]

Research on the economics of slavery in the antebellum south has shown that the peculiar institution was, as a whole, a highly profitable enterprise.[54] Essential to that overall profitability, however, was the sale of slaves from the older slave states, where they formed a labor surplus, to the newer ones, where there was a labor shortage. The economic dynamics of slavery required new territories from which new slave states might be formed to continue this pattern of general profitability. Among the most sensitive questions in antebellum politics was that of the right of Congress to regulate the trade in slaves between the states and territories. The Constitution quite plainly gives to Congress the power to regulate commerce "among the several states." But so adamant were Southerners that any interference with the slave trade was interference with the "domestic" institution of slavery itself that nothing much was ever done to employ this power.[55] Lincoln, concentrating all his efforts upon the territorial question, looked upon the domestic slave trade issue as a diversion. But we can see in the Southerners' loathing for the slave dealer how profound must have been their guilt because of their reliance upon the trade in human flesh. And such guilt could only intensify their defensiveness and aggressiveness on the question of slavery as a whole.

Lincoln reveals dialectically the moral impossibility of an opinion whose logical inconsistency is grounded in its inconsistency with nature. Lincoln knew perfectly well that human beings live all the time with both logical and moral inconsistencies. Like the Jefferson who said that he "trembled for his country," however, Lincoln believed that sooner or later a terrible price would have to be paid for this particular inconsistency. Here he is attempting to warn his fellow citizens of the South.

We may doubt Lincoln's assertion, however, that the great majority of Americans had human sympathies of which they could no more divest themselves than their sensibility to physical pain. Is feeling the pain of others, however diminished from the original, really an attribute of human nature? Lincoln admits that there are "natural tyrants" who do not possess this sympathy, although they do not lack sensibility to physical pain. What effect does this have on his argument? We know, as a matter of simple fact, that there are human beings who can take pleasure in committing terrible crimes of violence, who feel no compassion for their victims and no remorse for their crimes. Hitler was a hypochondriac and showered largess upon a quack doctor who supplied him with drugs. But he sent millions of innocent human beings to horrible extinction without a trace of guilt or regret. Lincoln of course knew, from the Declaration of Independence itself, that there were "merciless savages" whose sympathies, such as they were, did not extend outside their tribes.[56] Why then is sympathy, and not tyranny, a natural norm for mankind?

We note that Lincoln's generalization about the sympathy in the bosoms of the Southern people is not applied to mankind as a whole. Lincoln supplies abundant empirical evidence from the behavior of Southerners that it is true of them specifically. May not then this "sympathy" of Southern people, such as it was, have been a cultural and not a natural phenomenon? To answer this, we return to the distinction between the Negro and the hog and ask if that is natural or merely cultural. For barbarians or savages, whose perception of nature is governed by the myths or customs of the tribe, there is no distinction between culture and nature. That distinction is itself a consequence of civilization. More precisely, it is a consequence of what we call Western civilization, with its traditions both of reason and revelation. That civilization, symbolized by the Declaration of Independence, rests upon the recognition that while the manifestations of human nature may be infinite in their variety, nature itself is one and the same. Knowledge of human nature and recognition of the mutuality of rights and duties, antecedent in nature to civil society itself, is a condition of civilized existence. And the superiority of civilization to barbarism or savagery is not an arbitrary assertion of opinion but is evident to any human being who understands the difference between them—or, we might add, to anyone who understands that the superiority of humans to hogs no more depends upon the color of the humans than upon the color of the hogs.

All of this is implicit in the civility of Lincoln's dialectical address to his fellow citizens. Demonstrating to them that *his* conclusions are implicit in *their* premises is of the essence of Socratic method. As a method by which differences can be resolved by speech and reason, it is—like Socrates himself—perhaps the purest manifestation of what it means to be a civilized human being.

Lincoln did not appeal to the Declaration of Independence merely because it was our first and foremost founding document. It was, he said, the immortal emblem of man's humanity and the father of all moral principle because it incorporated a rational, nonarbitrary moral and political standard. The equality of man and man was a necessary inference from the inequality of man and beast—and of man and God. No one possessed of a civilized conscience can fail to feel this sympathy. The empirical evidence bears Lincoln out.

Let us consider again the relevance of insisting that human beings are equal to each other in the same sense that they are unequal to the lower orders of living beings. The admonition to "do unto others as we would have others do unto us" represents a moral standard for all mankind, a standard whose validity is in no way gainsaid by the fact that barbarians or savages do not understand or accept it. It is grounded both in the recognition by reason of the unity of the human species and the corresponding biblical recognition that God "hath made of one blood all the nations of men to dwell upon all the face of the earth."[57] Because of this Lincoln could say, "As I would not be a slave, so I would not be a master."[58] How did it come about, however, that someone like John C. Calhoun, who himself preferred death to the least acknowledgment of inequality, saw no moral reason not to enslave others? How is it that anyone who considered himself a good Christian, as Calhoun apparently did, could see no obligation not to impose slavery on others, if he himself preferred death to slavery? In fact, Calhoun could see *some* mutuality of rights and duties, believing that the master should be a good master for the same reason the slave should be a good slave. Underlying this conception of morality was a degradation of the Negro to a status below humanity, but not far enough below it to constitute a subhuman species. This was possible because the moral authority of the idea of nature, implied in the idea of permanent species, had itself been undermined. As we saw in chapter 2, this undermining came to a victorious conclusion in the understanding of evolution that held that species were no more than well-marked varieties. Some varieties were closer to the lower animals than others and therefore were not entitled to full consideration as human beings. The historical school, which by the 1850s had largely displaced the natural rights school of the Founding, had also given rise to the romantic movement of the mid-nineteenth century. It too repudiated natural right, because it repudiated "rationalism," insisting as it did that "the heart had its reasons which reason did not know."[59] Accordingly, Lincoln's Socratic reasoning was rejected, because the very idea of justification by reasoning had come to be rejected. History, not reason, decided that some should be masters and others should be slaves. This movement of Western thought, from the natural rights school to the historical school, culminated in the Nazi and the Communist regimes of the twentieth century. Their treatment of race or class enemies as subhuman represents a rebarbarization of mankind that is far more deadly than earlier barbarism, because it is armed with the instruments of modern science. The beginning of this process of rebarbarization is already visible in the Calhounian defense of slavery.

Lincoln's Socratic argument in the Peoria speech proceeded:

> And yet again, there are in the United States and territories, including the District of Columbia, 433,643 free blacks. At $500 per head they are worth over two hundred millions of dollars. How comes this vast amount of property to be running about without owners? We do not see free horses or free cattle running at large. How is this? All these free blacks are the descendants of slaves themselves, and they would be slaves now, but for *something* which has operated on their white owners, inducing them, at vast pecuniary sacrifices, to liberate them. What is that *something*? Is there any mistaking it? In all these cases it is your sense of justice and human sympathy, continually telling you that the poor negro has some natural right to himself—that those who deny it, and make mere merchandise of him, deserve kickings, contempt, and death.[60]

In Lincoln's speech on *Dred Scott*, a little less than three years after the Peoria speech, he addresses the topic that will take up so much of the joint debates of 1858—Douglas's horror "at the thought of the mixing of blood by the white and black races." Lincoln points out that of 405,751 mulattoes in the United States in 1850, only 56,649 were in the free states; and even these, he notes, came from the slave states "ready made up." These facts are meant to demonstrate that slavery is itself the principal cause of racial mixing. Douglas expresses a horror at miscegenation but ignores the "forced concubinage . . . that produces nine tenths of all mulattoes." But Lincoln has a further argument to make here, whose import has largely escaped the notice of commentators.

> The proportion of free mulattoes to free blacks—the only colored classes in the free states—is much greater in the slave than in the free states. It is worthy of note too, that among the free states those which make the colored man the nearest to equal the white, have proportionably the fewest mulattoes, the least of amalgamation. In New Hampshire, the State which goes the farthest toward equality between the races, there are just 184 mulattoes, while there are in Virginia . . . 79,775, being 23,126 more than in all the free States together.[61]

The most powerful of Douglas's arguments in 1858 were those appealing to race prejudice, and of these the most powerful were those based upon fear of miscegenation. Lincoln, in slyly pointing out that where there was the greatest equality there was the least miscegenation, drew from the premises of racial bigotry a forceful argument for racial equality. Here is a profound intimation of how little Lincoln actually shared the general opinions on race that dominated the political discourse of his time.

From the fact that the numbers of mulattoes and of free people of color in the slave states were roughly equal, it is probable that many if not most of those who had been emancipated were emancipated by their own fathers. We know as well that there were slave owners among the free Negroes of the antebellum South, although Lincoln himself makes no mention of it. That there should have been such is not too surprising, when we reflect that the fathers who emancipated their own children would also in many instances provide them with property and sometimes the means to buy (and unite) their own family members.[62]

We return to the Peoria speech and Lincoln's question of what that *something* was that told Southerners that the Negro has some natural right to himself—and that slave dealers deserved kickings, contempt, and death. We know that that something was also often founded upon consanguinity and that the horror of the slave dealer often reflected the fact that a slave owner might be forced to sell— and perhaps separately—his own children and their mother. At one point in the joint debates, when Lincoln went out of his way to ridicule Douglas's charge that he was promoting miscegenation, he said that he had "never seen to my knowledge a man, woman or child who was in favor of producing a perfect equality, social and political, between negroes and white men. I recollect of but one distinguished instance that I ever heard of so frequently as to be entirely satisfied of its correctness—and that is the case of Judge Douglas' old friend Col. Richard M. Johnson." Then Lincoln continued that he had "never had the least apprehension that I or my friends would marry negroes if there was no law to keep them from it, but as Judge Douglas and his friends seem to be in great apprehension that they might, I give him my most solemn pledge that I will to the very last stand by the law of this state, which forbids marrying of white people with negroes."[63] The transcript shows that these remarks were accompanied by roars of laughter and applause. But Lincoln was using this hilarity both to conceal and to reveal some serious thoughts.

Colonel Richard M. Johnson of Kentucky was a member of the U.S. House of Representatives from 1807 to 1819, a U.S. senator from 1819 to 1829, and a representative again from 1829 to 1837. From 1837 to 1841 he was vice president of the United States. He held a command in the War of 1812, while keeping his seat in Congress, and distinguished himself in a battle in which he was severely wounded. He was a strong supporter of, and closely associated with, Andrew Jackson. The *Dictionary of American Biography* notes laconically that Johnson never married but had two daughters by Julia Chinn, a mulatto slave who came to him in the distribution of his father's estate. These few words only hint that Julia Chinn presided over Johnson's domestic establishment and that neither she nor her daughters were counted among the servants. Nor does it hint at the great pains and expense Johnson took with his daughters' education. Both girls married white men, and both couples were deeded a part of Johnson's estate. As recounted by Johnson's biographer, "The provision Johnson made for his daughters, their husbands and his grandson, during his life, is all they received." The record of his estate in the Fayette County records says that it "was further proved that he left no widow, children, father or mother living." After his death there was no recognition in the laws of Kentucky of the family that he himself had recognized as his own by the laws of God and nature. How he felt about them may be seen by what he wrote to a close friend after the death of one of his daughters, Adaline, in 1836:

> I thank you and all who administered to that lovely and innocent child in her final painful hour. She was a source of inexhaustible happiness and comfort to me. She was mild and prudent. She was wise in her counsel beyond her years and obedient to every thought and every advice of mine. . . . She was a firm and great prop to my happiness here, but she is gone where sorrow and sighing can never disturb her peaceful and quiet blossom. She is happy, and has left me unhappy in mourning her loss.[64]

One can think only of King Lear, holding the dead body of Cordelia in his arms. Surely no parent ever felt the loss of a child more deeply or expressed his feelings more movingly than this. We can understand what Lincoln meant by Colonel Johnson representing the only case he had ever heard of someone believing in "perfect equality."

The race barrier that fell athwart Julia Chinn was lifted by Colonel Johnson from her daughters and their descendants. But it could far more easily have gone the other way. In its practical application, the barrier to legal marriage between the different races was often merely arbitrary. Some of the "best" families of the antebellum South, like Colonel Johnson's descendants, had Negro blood, a fact no less true because of the vigor with which it was usually denied. In *Pudd'nhead Wilson*, Mark Twain, a son of the antebellum South, spins a tale of "passing" in *both* directions: A change in the cradles results in a white infant being raised as a slave and a black infant being raised to become a master of slaves. Clearly that "something" of which Lincoln spoke that induced the liberation of slaves despite "vast pecuniary sacrifices" was often founded upon an even greater consanguinity than that of common humanity. We have previously pointed out that Taney's strongest evidence to prove the subhumanity of the Negro—the laws prohibiting intermarriage—actually proved the exact opposite. We also noted that such prohibitions fell upon whites no less than blacks. The case of Colonel Johnson, Julia Chinn, and their daughters, to which Lincoln points, reminds us not only of the logical contradiction inherent in the law of slavery but also of the pathos and tragedy inherent in that contradiction.

Lincoln then concludes his Socratic refutation of Southern demands in his Peoria speech as follows: "And now, why will you ask us to deny the humanity of the slave, and estimate him as the equal of the hog? Why ask us to do what you will not do yourselves? Why ask us to do for nothing, what two hundred millions of dollars could not induce you to do?"[65] The division in the divided house is not only that between free and slave states. It is also the division within the American soul, not limited to the proslavery party, which was at once committed to the equality and the inequality of the human species. When Lincoln asked why, if there were free blacks, there were no free horses or cattle, he evoked the memory of Jefferson's memorable expression "that the mass of mankind has not been born with saddles on their backs, nor a favored few booted and spurred ready to ride them." Lincoln's argument appeals beyond the changing intellectual fashions that masquerade as science, such as we saw in Alexander Stephens's Cornerstone speech, to the unmediated experience—open to anyone, anywhere, and at any time—that distinguishes hogs and horses from human beings. Lincoln's flawless reasoning is an eternal witness to the truth. But it is also a witness to the limits of reason in the face of such passions as animated the proslavery South.

In the Peoria speech, Lincoln turns from the reductio ad absurdum of the equation of slaves and hogs to a confrontation with Douglas's version of popular sovereignty. This doctrine attempted to preserve the divided house by preserving its division, leaving the people of the territories to decide for themselves whether to include slavery among their "domestic" institutions. Whether they voted slavery up or down, Douglas said, was no concern of his. The only "right" to be upheld was the right of the people in each state and territory to decide in a free and fair election. Lincoln answered:

> I trust I understand, and truly estimate the right of self-government. My faith in the proposition that each man should do precisely as he pleases with all that is exclusively his own, lies at the foundation of the sense of justice there is in me. I extend the principles to communities of men, as well as to individuals. I so extend it because it is politically wise as well as naturally just. . . . The doctrine of self-government is right—absolutely and eternally right—but it has no just application, as here attempted. Or perhaps I should rather say that whether it has such just application depends upon whether a negro is *not* or *is* a man. If he is *not* a man, why in that case, he who *is* a man may, as a matter of self-government, do just as he pleases with him. But if the negro *is* a man, is it not to that extent a total destruction of self-government to say that he too shall not govern *himself?* When the white man governs himself that is self-government; but when

he governs himself, and also governs *another* man, that is *more* than self-government—that is despotism. If the negro is a *man*, why then my ancient faith teaches me that "all men are created equal;" and that there can be no moral right in connection with one man's making a slave of another.[66]

Self-government is human government by majority rule. Douglas, like Jefferson Davis, located the right of majority rule in communities, while ignoring the question of why the majority has this right. Lincoln, like Madison and Jefferson, saw that the political rights of majorities are preceded by the equal natural rights of individuals and by the agreement of individuals to form a community for the better protection of those rights.

Although government by majority rule is not government by unanimity, it is preceded logically by unanimous consent to have majority rule. The question of what constitutes self-government turns decisively upon the nature of that unanimous consent. As we discussed in chapter 1, such consent implies a contract of each with all, and of all with each, to be governed by certain laws for the common good. It is irrational to suppose that anyone could be a party to such a contract who reserved to himself greater authority over others than those others are to have over him. It is against reason that anyone who attempted to make such a reservation—which is aptly expressed by Lincoln's characterization of slavery as "You work, I'll eat"—would be accepted by the other parties to the agreement. While governments do exist upon such premises, they are despotic and depend upon force or fraud rather than reason and free choice.

The unanimous consent that transforms individuals who are not fellow citizens into a political community is possible only when the consenting parties recognize each other as equals. As that recognition is a condition of the agreement that brings the political community into existence, it is prior to the contract. That "all men are created equal" refers, therefore, to what is antecedent to civil society. It is because of this equality in nature that equality before and under the law becomes a distinguishing feature of legitimate civil society. We must qualify this, however, by noting that the consenting parties, as in the case of contracts within civil society, must have reached the age of consent. Here the age of consent is that of nature, not positive law, although the positive law is itself a reflection of nature. Those who, through mental infirmity, lack the necessary degree of rationality, can no more wield the power of consent than small children. Human beings judged lacking this power of consent may also include those referred to in the Declaration of Independence as barbarian or savage. A barbarian or savage is precisely someone who does not recognize other human beings as possessed of the same nature or as being of the same species as himself. When Taney imputed to the Founding generation the belief that the Negro had no rights which white men were bound to respect, he represented them, whether he knew it or not, to be bar-barians. Jefferson characterized the essence of barbarism and savagery when he wrote of those who believed that some men were born with saddles on their backs, and others booted and spurred to ride them. That the varieties of human beings do not constitute separate species forms the consciousness of those who are civilized, and who are competent to contract with each other to form a political community. Civilized human beings who are not children or mentally retarded must be recognized, each by all and all by each, as equal contracting partners to the agreement that brings civil society and majority rule into being. Contrary to Douglas, no vote that does not rest upon these premises can be an authentic manifestation of self-government.

In constituting civil society, offices and ranks may be established, with differing powers and privileges. But these are justified only by their contribution to the safety and well being of the community. They are not justified as what is due to beings superior in nature. In their ability to serve the community, some may seem to be, or may actually be, superior. And recognition of that superiority may come in the form of election to office. But such recognition must come from those who are served. It is not bestowed by the superior on themselves.

Douglas's version of popular sovereignty is fundamentally defective. By authorizing the majority to decide for or against slavery, it authorizes the majority to decide a question that nature has decided a priori. In the political literature of the Founding, "born equal" and "created equal" mean one and the same thing. We do not choose to be born, and we do not choose to be born human beings. That by virtue of which we are able to choose, we are not able to choose. Because we are not able to choose our humanity, we are not free to ignore the humanity of others. That is the forbidden fruit! As the authority of the majority is itself derived from nature, it cannot call into question the authority of nature without calling into question its own authority.

As Lincoln's inaugural address—following the Declaration of Independence—makes abundantly clear, the authority of the majority ceases when it denies to a minority any of the fundamental rights implicit in the original unanimous consent upon which the majority's authority is based. At that point, the right of revolution replaces the majority as the arbiter of political differences. A vote for slavery is a vote to abrogate the initial understanding that brought society into existence. It is no more consistent with the principles of self-government than a vote to establish one religion and forbid the free exercise of any other. One cannot decide between Protestantism and Catholicism, or Christianity and Judaism, by a vote. In such an event, the decision of the majority has no rational claim to obedience. It could be enforced, if at all, only tyrannically, and it would be an invitation to rebellion and anarchy.

Lincoln continues in his Peoria speech:

Judge Douglas frequently, with bitter sarcasm and irony, paraphrases our argument by saying: "The white people of Nebraska are good enough to govern
themselves, *but they are not good enough to govern a few miserable negroes!!*" Well
I doubt not that the people of Nebraska are, and will continue to be as good as
the average of people elsewhere. I do not say the contrary. What I do say is, that
no man is good enough to govern another man, *without that other's consent.* I say
this is the leading principle—the sheet anchor of American republicanism. Our
Declaration of Independence says: "We hold these truths to be self-evident:
That all men are created equal; that they are endowed by their Creator with
certain inalienable rights, that among these are life, liberty, and the pursuit of
happiness. That to secure these rights, governments are instituted among men,
deriving their just powers from the consent of the governed." I have quoted so much
at this time merely to show that according to our ancient faith, the just powers
of government are derived from the consent of the governed. Now the relation
of masters and slaves is, *pro tanto,* a total violation of this principle. The master
not only governs the slave without his consent; but he governs him by a set of
rules altogether different from those which he prescribes for himself. Allow *all*
the governed an equal voice in the government, and that, and that only is self-
government.[67]

Here, in essence, is the meaning of the rule of law as it arises from the proposition that all men are created equal: Those who live under the law have an equal
right in the making of the law, and those who make the law have a corresponding
duty to live under the law. Then Lincoln adds the single most revealing utterance
of his life on the Declaration as a proposition of political right: "Allow *all* the governed an equal voice in the government, and that, and that only, is self-government." Although revealing, it is also delphic when placed in the context of his
other antebellum utterances, which seem to contradict such an unqualified commitment. Let us be clear, however, that Lincoln thought that the just powers of
government are derived from the consent of *all* the governed, with no exceptions.
Let us also be clear that Lincoln did not mean consent in any passive sense. He
meant, as he said, that it entailed an equal voice in the government. He meant
democracy in the fullest sense.

We remind the reader of Jefferson's question, addressed to the king in 1774:
"Can any one reason be assigned, why one hundred and sixty thousand electors
in the island of Great Britain, should give the law to four millions in the States of
America, every individual of whom is equal to every individual of them, in virtue,
in understanding, and in bodily strength?" And we must again remember Jefferson's query to his fellow countrymen some six years later: "And with what execration should the statesman be loaded, who, permitting one half the citizens thus

to trample on the rights of the other, transforms those into despots, and these into enemies."[68] In the first of these pronouncements, Jefferson ranks every American, man and woman, black and white, free and slave, as equal in right to every one of the aristocrats and privileged few of Great Britain. In the second, he refers to the slaves in Virginia as "one half the citizens." It is clear that Lincoln's "Allow *all* the governed an equal voice in the government" is founded squarely upon its Jeffersonian antecedents, which means that the slaves, as well as the free Negroes, are ultimately and in principle entitled to an equal share in the forming of the laws by which they are governed.

The very next sentence in the Peoria speech, however, is: "Let it not be said I am contending for the establishment of political and social equality between whites and blacks. I have already said the contrary." In successive sentences, Lincoln says that there is self-government only where all the governed have an equal voice in the government and that he is not contending for political and social equality for blacks. Concerning the latter, Lincoln refers to what he had "already said," which is this:

> What next? Free them, and make them politically and socially our equals? My own feelings will not admit of this; and if mine would, we well know that those of the great mass of white people will not. Whether this feeling accords with justice and sound judgment, is not the sole question, if indeed, it is any part of it. A universal feeling, whether well or ill founded, can not be safely disregarded.

This passage from the earlier part of the Peoria speech has a parallel near the end. In Judge Douglas's view, Lincoln says,

> the question of whether a new country shall be slave or free, is a matter of as utter indifference, as it is whether his neighbor shall plant his farm with tobacco or stock it with horned cattle. Now, whether this view is right or wrong, it is very certain that the great mass of mankind take a totally different view.—They consider slavery a great moral wrong; and their feeling against it, is not evanescent, but eternal. It lies at the very foundation of their sense of justice, and cannot be trifled with. It is a great and durable element of popular action, and I think no statesman can safely disregard it.[69]

Lincoln speaks in both of these passages of what a statesman cannot "safely disregard." In the first instance, it is a universal feeling against the political and social equality of races. In the second, it is an equally universal feeling that slavery is a great moral wrong. On the surface, this would appear to point to combining these two: abolish slavery and keep the former slaves as an underclass.[70] This combination is not a permissible choice, except as a temporary and transitional condition, because a nation founded upon human equality cannot justify holding any class as an under class. Either the just powers of government are derived from the consent of the governed or they are not. If they are, then it is essentially as unjust to govern former slaves (or their descendants) as it is to govern slaves without their consent. If there is a duty to move from slavery to freedom, there must also be a duty to move from political inequality to political equality. Lincoln says this many times in many places.[71] How and when such great transformations are to take place is an open question, and the answer must be given by prudence. There will be great dangers in the process. We recall once again that in the Lyceum speech of 1838, Lincoln warned against emancipating slaves at the expense of enslaving freemen. Those enjoying the rights flowing from the principle of consent must be made to understand that their own rights depend upon recognizing the equal rights of others. But they must be made to understand this. It cannot be imposed upon them. The example of Napoleon was never far removed: The dictates of equality, no less than those of inequality, can become the pretext for tyranny.

In the Peoria speech, as in all his speeches thereafter, until his inauguration as president, Lincoln tried to make his fellow citizens understand that by right, as opposed to power, the same principles applied to the slaves as to themselves. But here he is notably ambiguous as to his own feelings about political and social equality. First he says that his feelings do not admit of such equality and then that it does not matter whether his feelings do or not, because the great mass of white opinion does not. Of course the opinion he calls universal cannot, strictly speaking, be universal, if there may be dissenters. But a free society is governed by the majority, and any large majority may pass as universal, *because there is unanimous agreement to be governed by the majority.* And a statesman must be governed by such a majority, because the only alternatives are tyranny and anarchy.

Equality gives rise to consent, but the opinion informing consent may not be logically or morally consistent with equality. That all the governed who recognize the equal rights of others ought to have an equal voice in the government is indeed implied in the doctrine that all men are created equal. To demand full recognition of that right of participation, however, would be entirely reasonable only in a nation of philosophers. And as James Madison recognized in the forty-ninth *Federalist*, "a nation of philosophers is as little to be expected as the philosophical race of kings wished for by Plato."[72] Among the paradoxes of the American Founding is that it is based upon philosophic wisdom while denying to philosophers, or to anyone else, the right to rule without the consent of the governed. Authority in Plato's imaginary *Republic*, to which Madison refers, is based upon a "noble lie," a myth that tells the ruled that they have inferior natures (like Jefferson's saddles) and that their rulers have superior natures (like Jefferson's boots and spurs). This justifies ruling without the consent of the governed. But

Plato's *Republic* is imaginary precisely because, according to Plato himself, philosophers do not wish to rule, and anyone wishing to rule is not a philosopher. Anyone who asserts a right to rule on the basis of his claim to wisdom is accordingly condemned in advance as a charlatan by philosophy itself. In the world of philosophic reality, outside of philosophic poetry, the right to rule can be conceded only to those who gain the consent of the governed. This they must do by persuading their fellow citizens that they will rule for the common good and not for their own private advantage. Madison correctly understood the political teaching of the *Republic*: Philosopher–kings are not possible, and genuine philosophers will always prefer a regime of equality under the law. We recall that in 1792 Madison wrote of the republican form of government under the Constitution as one "deriving its energy from the will of society, and operating, by the reason of its measures, on the understanding and interest of the society. Such is the government for which philosophy has been searching and humanity been fighting from the most remote ages. Such are the republican governments which it is the glory of America to have invented, and her unrivalled happiness to possess."[73] This was what Hamilton meant in the first *Federalist* when he spoke of good government "from reflection and choice" as opposed to "accident and force."

We return to Lincoln's assertion that "the mass of mankind . . . consider slavery a great moral wrong." The contrast is striking that while the popular sentiment against social and political equality may *not* accord "with justice and sound judgment," the popular sentiment that regards slavery as a great moral wrong lies at the foundation of the people's sense of justice. This sense of justice is said to be "not evanescent but eternal" and therefore to be "great and durable." One reason for this is that no one, except that small class of "natural tyrants," has an interest in returning to the "divine right of kings" or any other mythical justification of human inequality. Is it not therefore a task of statesmanship to see that, in time, the people's durable and eternal sense of justice overcomes whatever is not in accordance with "justice and sound judgment"?

"It may be argued," Lincoln said in a speech in Chicago on July 10, 1858,

> that there are certain conditions that make necessities and impose them upon us, and to the extent that a necessity is imposed upon a man, he must submit to it. I think that was the condition in which we found ourselves when we established this government. We had slavery among us, we could not get our Constitution unless we permitted them to remain in slavery, we could not secure the good we did secure if we grasped for more, and having by necessity submitted to that much, it does not destroy the principle that is the charter of our liberties. Let that charter stand as our standard.[74]

By "necessities," Lincoln clearly referred to such opinions as may be inconsistent with "justice and sound judgment" but that may not be "safely disregarded" by a statesman. They may not be disregarded—that is to say, they may not justly be disregarded—because they constitute an element of that "consent of the governed" from which the "just powers of government" are derived. We must then consider that opinions unjust in themselves may nonetheless form a necessary element in the foundation of just government.

The American people, acting by assemblies elected for the sole purpose of expressing the sovereign authority of the people, ratified the Constitution of 1787. Because of this ratification, the just powers of the government of the United States were, except for the slaves, derived from the consent of the governed. The people of the United States, except the slaves, had exercised their sovereign right, according to the laws of nature, to institute a new government that seemed to them more likely to effect their safety and happiness. However, as we have seen Lincoln point out—quoting Justice Curtis's dissenting opinion in *Dred Scott*—free blacks were qualified in five states to vote on the ratification of the Constitution and presumably did vote in proportion to their numbers.[75] Hence "We the people," who ordained and established the Constitution, were both white and black. It was remarkable that blacks *had* been part of the process of ratification, the most solemn and authoritative legislative act of a free people. In this most important respect, there *had* been political equality of the races in the foundation of the Constitution. That Lincoln pointed to and approved this fact contradicts, to some extent, his declaration that he had never favored such political equality. But any attempts to abolish slavery at the time of the formation of the Constitution would only have had adverse consequences for freedom, including that of the slaves. Only the stronger Union, with the stronger central government, could have grappled with the problem of slavery, as eventually it did. And any attempt in 1858 to propose "perfect" social and political equality would have been as imprudent as demanding the abolition of slavery in 1787.

We may conclude then that Douglas was not entirely wrong, and that in one sense he was not wrong at all, in saying that Lincoln's commitment to the principles of the Declaration of Independence was a commitment to a perfect equality of rights between whites and blacks. When Lincoln at Charleston said, "I am not, nor ever have been, in favor of" the social and political equality of the races, he was careful to limit his declaration to the present and to the past. It may perhaps seem disingenuous that he did not say that he would never be for such equality. Lincoln had made it plain on other occasions, however, that "perfect" equality was the goal to be approximated, even if never reached. At the moment, approximation to that goal was possible only by waging political war to prevent the extension of slavery. That was the necessary and indispensable means by which to place slavery "in course of ultimate extinction." The "universal feeling" against the injustice of slavery had to be deployed in that war. At the same time, Lincoln had to prevent the feeling against social and political equality from undermining the feeling against slavery. Lincoln knew that among the motives in the free soil movement for keeping slavery out of Kansas was that of keeping out blacks, whether free or slave. Indeed, among the first acts of the free soil Topeka government was a measure excluding free Negroes. And Lincoln himself stated repeatedly that he wanted the territories for "free white men." In a desperately close political contest in which Douglas did not hesitate to use anti-Negro prejudice against freedom, Lincoln did not hesitate to turn that same prejudice against slavery.

We conclude that, Douglas to the contrary notwithstanding, there was no contradiction whatever between Lincoln's unqualified professions of belief in the doctrine of equality in the Declaration of Independence and his denials in 1858 of any intention to bring about a "perfect" social and political equality of the races.

～

We return now to Lincoln's first inaugural where we left it in the last chapter, at the point at which Lincoln addresses *Dred Scott* (and we resume numbering its paragraphs):

[24] I do not forget the position assumed by some, that constitutional questions are to be decided by the Supreme Court; nor do I deny that such decisions must be binding in any case, upon the parties to the suit, as to the object of that suit, while they are also entitled to very high respect and consideration in all parallel cases by all other departments of the government. And while it is obviously possible that such decision may be erroneous in any given case, still the evil effect following it, being limited to that particular case, with the chance that it may be over-ruled, and never become a precedent for other cases, can better be borne than could the evils of a different practice. At the same time, the candid citizen must confess that if the policy of the government upon vital questions, affecting the whole people, is to be irrevocably fixed by decisions of the Supreme Court, the instant they are made, in ordinary litigation between parties, in personal actions, the people will have ceased to be their own rulers, having to that extent practically resigned their government into the hands of that eminent tribunal. Nor is there in this view any assault upon the court or the judges. It is a duty from which they may not shrink, to decide cases properly brought before them; and it is no fault of theirs if others seek to turn their decisions to political purposes.

The most striking thing about this paragraph, and in particular its ending, is how it differs from nearly everything Lincoln has said hitherto about *Dred Scott*. In the House Divided speech, Chief Justice Taney was portrayed as an active participant in a conspiracy to extend slavery nationwide. That portion of the federal government controlled by proslavery throughout the 1850s, notably the presidency and the Senate, had shaped the political process toward a judi-cial resolution out of confidence in the partisanship of the Taney Court. Terri-torial legislation that Douglas steered through the Senate in 1850 provided that disputes concerning property rights in slaves might be appealed directly from the supreme courts of the territories to the Supreme Court of the United States. By that fact alone, Congress had injected the Court directly into the heart of the sectional controversy. Douglas, as we have seen, was committed to the doctrine of "popular sovereignty." But the commitment to the Supreme Court of the task of resolving the legal status of slavery in the territories left entirely unresolved how much jurisdiction the people of the territories really possessed. Before *Dred Scott* was announced, Douglas was a member in full standing of the chorus of Southerners and "doughfaces" (Northern men with Southern principles, the most prominent of whom were Presidents Pierce and Buchanan) who said that the territorial question was one for the Supreme Court to decide. It is possible, however, that no one outside the Court knew how far Taney would go to give constitutional standing to the most radical proslavery demands.

The assertion in *Dred Scott* that the only power of Congress over slavery in the territories was the power, "coupled with the duty," of protecting the slave owner in his rights, became in effect the heart of the Southern Democratic plat-form of 1860. The claimed right to a slave code for the territories was now iden-tified with the Constitution itself. Taney's opinion made it appear that the right to the secure possession of slave property in a territory enjoyed the same status as the free exercise of religion or freedom of speech and was beyond the power of any majority to deny or disparage. In defending property rights thus defined, the proslavery South now insisted that it was defending the boundaries that made a regime of majority rule and minority rights possible. It was axiomatic, they held, that neither the majority nor the minority could define each other's rights. The Constitution had established the Supreme Court as the arbiter between the two. If the antislavery majority refused to accept that arbitration, then it refused to accept the Constitution. That is how the South identified secession from the Union as a defense of the Constitution. And that is the argu-ment that Lincoln tried to defuse, so far as possible, in the foregoing passage of his inaugural.

Lincoln says that it is "obviously possible" that any given Supreme Court decision "may be erroneous." The error that dwarfed all others was the one that denied that the Negro had any rights that the white man was bound to respect. Consistent with this error was Taney's denial that the Declaration's proposition of human equality meant what it said. Here Taney was flatly denying the historical record and in the process was transforming American constitutionalism from its foundation in the "laws of nature and of nature's God" to that of the right of the stronger.

This paragraph in the inaugural on *Dred Scott* (which is not mentioned by name) is as little contentious as Lincoln can make it. Lincoln knew perfectly well that the majority cannot decide upon the rights of the minority. He had already declared that if the majority deprived the minority of any clearly written constitutional right, it would justify revolution. The First Amendment rights of religion, speech, etc., are clearly written. The right to hold slaves in territories, on the other hand, was inferred by an interpretation of the Constitution that was not sustained by the historical record to which the interpretation itself appealed. Yet Taney placed the latter right on the same footing as the former, which were literally enumerated in the Constitution. No government could be carried on if a constitutional majority could be denied the title deeds of office upon such a basis.

[25] One section of our country believes slavery is *right*, and ought to be extended, while the other believes it is *wrong*, and ought not to be extended. This is the only substantial dispute. The fugitive slave clause of the Constitution, and the law for the suppression of the foreign slave trade, are each as well enforced, perhaps, as any law can ever be in a community where the moral sense of the people imperfectly supports the law itself. The great body of the people abide by the dry legal obligation in both cases, and a few break over in each. This, I think, cannot be perfectly cured; and it would be worse in both cases *after* the separation of the sections, than before. The foreign slave trade, now imperfectly suppressed, would be ultimately revived without restriction, in one section; while fugitive slaves, now only partially surrendered, would not be surrendered at all, by the other.

The paragraph on *Dred Scott* dealt explicitly only with the question of the right of the Court to determine the policy of the political branches of government. Lincoln had in fact dealt earlier with the main issue in the case, when he spoke of the territorial question and said that as the Constitution did not expressly answer it, the people must. Now, without asperity, and without either diffidence or temerity, he simply and quietly defines the central issue in the sectional dispute upon which everything else depends: One side believes slavery is right, the other believes it is wrong. Nothing more is said here in support of the one opinion or in detraction of the other. Lincoln shows unbending firmness without any suggestion of self-righteousness. From here until the end, Lincoln will plead with his "dissatisfied fellow countrymen" to put aside their grievances in favor of a larger good. It is Lincoln's mission in these last paragraphs somehow to evoke that larger good in the presence of the difference concerning slavery.

Disunion, Lincoln points out, would only magnify the reasons for present dissatisfaction. Both the fugitive slave clause and the law for the suppression of the foreign slave trade are now imperfectly enforced, as is always the case when "the moral sense of the people imperfectly supports the law itself." If separation of the sections should become an accomplished fact, what is now imperfectly enforced would be perfectly unenforced. Lincoln seems to assume that all (or nearly all) of the slave states then in the Union would join a successful Confederacy, since slaves escaping from Confederate slave states to Union slave states (or vice versa) would in all probability have been returned. Some commentators have moreover doubted Lincoln's certainty that the foreign slave trade would have been revived. It is true that the Confederate government outlawed the foreign slave trade during the Civil War. But we should recall that Taney's opinion had said that "the negro might justly and lawfully be reduced to slavery for his benefit," notwithstanding the fact that at that time there was no lawful way that a free Negro could be reduced to slavery in any state or territory.[76] Nor since 1808 had there been a lawful way that a Negro could be enslaved in Africa for transport and sale in the United States. It should also be borne in mind that when Jefferson Davis's government outlawed the foreign slave trade, it did so because it hoped desperately for recognition by European governments, which had themselves banned the African slave trade. How a prosperous, peaceful, and independent Confederacy would have behaved in the course of supplying cotton to the world ever more abundantly with slave labor is another matter. Lincoln did well to advertise to the world the probability of the revival of that nefarious traffic.[77]

> [26] Physically speaking, we cannot separate. We cannot remove our respective sections from each other, nor build an impassable wall between them. A husband and wife may be divorced, and go out of the presence, and beyond the reach of each other; but the different parts of the country cannot do this. They cannot but remain face to face; and intercourse, either amicable or hostile, must continue between them. Is it possible, then, to make that intercourse more advantageous or more satisfactory, *after* separation than *before?* Can aliens make treaties easier than friends can make laws? Can treaties be more faithfully enforced between aliens than laws can among friends? Suppose you go to war, you cannot fight always; and when, after much loss on both sides, and no gain on either, you cease fighting, the identical old questions, as to terms of intercourse, are again upon you.

The dominant theme in the remaining paragraphs, as it was in Jefferson's inaugural, is friendship as the basis of union. A subdominant theme is the right of revolution, not as a threat to the Union, but as the basis of the friendship that formed the Union.

Not even in the *Federalist* is the utility of the friendship of union more concisely or forcefully presented than in the foregoing paragraph. Lincoln and his hearers knew that the countries of Europe—divided by language, religion, and ethnicity—had engaged over the centuries in interminable wars and had enjoyed only intermittent peace. They also knew that never before had any considerable part of mankind enjoyed the good fortune of the Americans in their physical separation from the ancient enmities of the Old World, in the limitless bounties of nature, in a common language, and above all in common institutions of political and religious freedom. Why should they not have a common government that would never go to war with itself? Why should not the wealth that Europe had poured into the support of monarchies and aristocracies and standing armies and wars instead enrich the free and peaceful life of the common man? One can sense, almost without reflection, why a Frenchman is not a German, a Russian, or an Englishman. But why are the French, Germans, and Russians, when they have emigrated to the United States, all equally Americans with those of English descent?

Lincoln's argument at this point has the same quasi-mathematical character as his demonstration that a constitutional majority is the only alternative to anarchy or tyranny. He compares the rupture of the Union to a divorce, but one in which husband and wife must continue to live together. He reminds us that marriage is the most intimate form of human friendship, as elsewhere he says that it must be distinguished from a "free-love arrangement" that depends upon "passionate attraction" merely. We are reminded as well of the Lyceum speech, in which Lincoln argued that passion had sustained the American Revolution but that the Union needed a firmer foundation in cold and sober reason.[78]

Lincoln asks whether aliens can make or enforce treaties more easily than friends can make or enforce laws. The question, put in this form, is rhetorical. Of course it is easier for friends to make laws. But can those who have become alienated continue to make laws as if they were still friends? Lincoln is calling for an effort by the alienated to overcome that alienation. He is pointing at a low but powerful form of friendship, that of utility. In this instance it is a common interest in returning fugitive slaves, on the one hand, and in suppressing the foreign slave trade, on the other. What is notable about this argument is that it makes no assumption of moral superiority on one side or the other. Lincoln does not say anything here that implies a weakening of his resolve to end the extension of slavery. But we must keep in mind that as he speaks, there are still more slave states *in* the Union than *out* of it. The presence of loyal slave states, now and in the war to come, was vital to the success of the antislavery cause no less than to that of union.

Having just asked whether aliens can make treaties more easily than friends can make laws, Lincoln now asks what utility there can be, either for friends or aliens, in trying to resolve differences by war. Again he makes no assumption of superiority. His argument, in fact, is much the same as that of pacifists through the ages: War does not solve problems. But Lincoln is no pacifist. He has made it clear that there will be no war unless the other side starts it. But he has also made it clear that the Union will defend itself if war ensues and that the decision by the American people against the extension of slavery can only be reversed by the American people themselves, through means as constitutional as those by which he had been elected president.

[27] This country, with its institutions, belongs to the people who inhabit it. Whenever they shall grow weary of the existing government, they can exercise their constitutional right of amending it, or their revolutionary right to dismember or overthrow it. I cannot be ignorant of the fact that many worthy and patriotic citizens are desirous of having the national Constitution amended. While I make no recommendation of amendments, I fully recognize the rightful authority of the people over the whole subject, to be exercised in either of the modes prescribed in the instrument itself; and I should under existing circumstances favor rather than oppose a fair opportunity being afforded the people to act upon it.

[28] I will venture to add that to me the Convention mode seems preferable, in that it allows amendments to originate with the people themselves, instead of only permitting them to take or reject propositions, originated by others, not especially chosen for the purpose, and which might not be precisely such as they would wish to either accept or refuse. I understand a proposed amendment to the Constitution, which amendment, however, I have not seen, has passed Congress, to the effect that the federal government shall never interfere with the domestic institutions of the States, including that of persons held to service. To avoid misconstruction of what I have said, I depart from my purpose not to speak of particular amendments, so far as to say that holding such a provision to now be implied constitutional law, I have no objection to its being made express and irrevocable.

Lincoln distinguishes between the constitutional right to amend the existing government and the revolutionary right to dismember or overthrow it. He does not recognize a constitutional right to dismember or overthrow it. This, however, was the right that the seceding states claimed, and it explains why they took great pains to deratify the Constitution through conventions identical in form to those by which they had ratified it. Lincoln does not here confront the claim of secession as a constitutional right, for he has not abandoned hope that the separation that has occurred will yet prove temporary. This question, however, will be central to his address to Congress on July 4, 1861, after the firing on Fort Sumter, when civil war had begun.

Lincoln is perfectly candid about the right of revolution, as indeed he must be, since at the center of everything he believes is the Declaration of Independence. The Declaration says that governments are instituted to secure the rights with which we have been endowed by our Creator and that "whenever any form of government becomes destructive of these ends it is the right of the people to alter or abolish it." In an 1848 speech in the House of Representatives on the Mexican War, Lincoln spoke of the boundary in dispute between Texas and Mexico. It was not fixed by treaty, he said, because no treaty existed. Texas and its boundary were the result of revolution. He then continued:

> Any people anywhere, being inclined and having the power, have the *right* to rise up and shake off the existing government, and form a new one that suits them better. This is a most valuable, a most sacred right—a right which, we hope and believe, is to liberate the world. Nor is this right confined to cases in which the whole people of an existing government may choose to exercise it. Any portion of such people that *can, may* revolutionize, and make their *own* of so much territory as they may inhabit. More than this, a majority of any portion of such people may revolutionize, putting down a *minority*, intermingled with, or near about them, who may oppose their movement. Such minority was precisely the case of the Tories of our own Revolution. It is a quality of revolutions not to go by old lines, or old laws; but to break up both, and make new ones.[79]

This passage has been cited as evidence that the seceding states had the same revolutionary right to separate from the Union as their ancestors had to separate from Great Britain. It has also been cited as evidence that according to Lincoln, inclination and power constitute *right*.

That the seceding states had the same right of revolution as their revolutionary ancestors is of course perfectly true, for the simple reason that everyone everywhere always has this right. But it follows as well that any people anywhere has the right to suppress a revolution that they believe would endanger their rights. The people of the North had a perfect right to suppress a Southern rebellion that, in their opinion, greatly endangered the security they enjoyed under the government of the Union.

The broad context of Lincoln's 1848 speech included the Latin American revolutions that had thrown off European colonial regimes, just as the North Americans (or Anglo-Americans) had done before them. Mere inclination and power, taken by themselves, would indeed provide an amoral justification for such revolutions. But Lincoln calls the right of revolution a *sacred* right, which implies that it is the God-given right of the Declaration of Independence and that it may be rightly exercised only under the conditions laid down in the complete doctrine of the Declaration.

Lincoln's implied reference is first of all to Mexico, in its revolution against Spain. But when he says that any portion of a people that can revolutionize, may revolutionize, he is referring to Texas's revolution against Mexico. And when he says that a majority of revolutionaries may put down a minority amongst themselves, he is referring to the majority of Texans who put down the Mexicans loyal to the Mexican government, just as the majority of Americans put down (or drove out) the Tories who were loyal to the British government.

Although Lincoln's 1848 speech is an attack upon President Polk for unjustly and illegally beginning the war with Mexico, it does not in any way question either the Texans' right to independence or their right to join the United States by congressional action under the Constitution. Elsewhere Lincoln refers to the Mexican government as one fluctuating between tyranny and anarchy, so that any portion of the people under that government certainly had a right to a better government if they had the power to establish it.

There is then no contradiction between Lincoln's justification of the right of revolution by either Mexicans or Texans and his denial of the right of secession in 1861. This is true for two reasons of the highest moment. First, the South did not claim secession as a revolutionary, but as a constitutional, right. Second, contrary to Southern claims, Lincoln was scrupulously concerned with the right of the states to the exclusive control of their domestic institutions. This reflected his conviction that such control involved the immediate physical security of the free inhabitants of the slave states. Thus it was not only a right secured to them by the Constitution but also a right whose endangerment would justify revolution. This explains Lincoln's endorsement of a constitutional amendment making "express and irrevocable" what was now "implied constitutional law." In this there was no concession to slavery whatever. The insistence upon local control of domestic institutions was required by the natural law of the Declaration of Independence no less than by the positive law of the Constitution.

[29] The Chief Magistrate derives all his authority from the people, and they have conferred none upon him to fix terms for the separation of the States. The people themselves can do this also if they choose; but the executive, as such, has nothing to do with it. His duty is to administer the present government, as it came to his hands, and to transmit it, unimpaired by him, to his successor.

We must keep firmly in mind the distinction between the natural right of revolution and the positive law of the Constitution. But it is no less important to understand their continuity. The authority of the American people in separating from Great Britain was derived from the laws of nature and of nature's God. They were authorized at the same time, and by the same source, to institute new government, which the Congress did in virtue of the fact that it was then acting for the thirteen united colonies in conducting the war against Great Britain. Subsequently the people instituted newer government under the Articles of Confederation. Later the Articles were replaced by the Constitution. However, as we discussed in chapter 3, the framers of the Constitution went beyond any authority they might have had from the Congress of the Articles in submitting an entirely new constitution to the people. Madison, in the forty-third *Federalist*, is explicit that the framers' authority was derived solely from that "transcendent law of nature and of nature's God, which declares that the safety and happiness of society are the objects at which all political institutions aim, and to which all such institutions must be sacrificed."[80] This law of nature is identical with the sanction for the right of revolution. Hence the Constitution, no less than our nation's independence, rests squarely upon the right of revolution.

In the earlier parts of his inaugural, Lincoln showed why his election was an authentic expression of the will of the people, exercised through the Constitution. He declared that in his election there had been no violation of minority rights. In short, there had been no law higher than that upon which Lincoln's government rested to justify altering or abolishing that government. In saying that he derives all his authority from the people, Lincoln is saying that he derives all his authority from *their* original right. Under a constitution formed by the principles of the Declaration of Independence, all political authority is a delegation from the people and is limited by the terms of that delegation. Throughout the war, Lincoln will take the greatest pains to prove in every instance that the authority he exercises, however extraordinary it may appear, is genuinely derived from the people by means of the Constitution and that he has exercised no authority originating in any will or purpose of his own. Here he says simply that the people may, if they wish, change the duties of his office. If they charge him with a different authentic mandate of office, he will obey that new mandate. But he himself cannot alter or abolish the people's constitutional mandate.

> [30] Why should there not be a patient confidence in the ultimate justice of the people? Is there any better or equal hope, in the world? In our present differences, is either party without faith of being in the right? If the Almighty Ruler of nations, with his eternal truth and justice, be on your side of the North, or on yours of the South, that truth, and that justice, will surely prevail, by the judgment of this great tribunal, the American people.

Here in the first inaugural we begin to hear the great themes of the second. The American people is a religious people, whose every thought and action presuppose a God who rules the world.[81] The Declaration of Independence ended by the

Signers pledging to each other their lives, fortunes, and sacred honor. They did so because they placed "a firm reliance upon the protection of Divine Providence." As they had with perfect sincerity appealed to "the Supreme Judge of the world" for the rectitude of their intentions, they were confident of that protection. And Divine Providence seems in truth to have protected them. No theme runs more consistently through Washington's later pronouncements than that the American Revolution was blessed by God's favor. Yet that favor was manifested in a war in which the victors were united in their defense of the principles of the Declaration. They did not—they could not—at once fulfill the promise of those principles. But as to the principles themselves, they were clear and united. Now, in 1861, the American people are divided by these principles.

Lincoln is expressing the hope that a belief in God's providence might lead to a peaceful resolution of differences. We remember that it is but threescore years since the first time in human history that a government was peacefully replaced by its bitterest rivals through a free election. In Locke's *Second Treatise of Government*, as in the Declaration of Independence, as in the entire political tradition of the West, "appeal to Heaven" meant an appeal to arms. Now Lincoln makes the appeal to heaven an appeal for patience and for peace.

One side in the country believes that slavery is right, the other that it is wrong. Lincoln here displays a kind of neutrality such as God might take toward his quarreling children. Yet Lincoln himself is a principal in this dispute. The "great tribunal" of the people speaks with the voice of God. But has it not already rendered judgment by electing Lincoln? What Lincoln is arguing for here is a judgment not so much upon slavery itself as upon the method of accommodation to the judgment already rendered. He has gone every last mile imaginable, except surrendering the principle of the election itself. That principle is God's own truth, and no one can ask God's providence in abandoning it.

No more than Pharaoh of old, however, will the hearts of those who are ready to fight for slavery be softened by the voice of God. Nor will those who are faithful be delivered from the terrible responsibility entailed upon them. God's eternal truth and justice will indeed finally prevail by the tribunal of the American people, but it will do so only by the agony of a great civil war. Lincoln's expression of hope on the eve of that war may now seem utopian. But there was no false optimism in Lincoln. If the war comes, his conscience and the nation's require that no one think that any possible avenue of peace has been neglected.

[31] By the frame of government under which we live, this same people have wisely given their public servants but little power for mischief; and have, with equal wisdom, provided for the return of that little to their own hands at very short intervals.

[32] While the people retain their virtue and vigilance, no administration, by any extreme of wickedness and folly, can very seriously injure the government in the short space of four years.

These two short paragraphs extend the meaning of "this great tribunal, the American people." The wisdom of the people, embodied in the Constitution, delegates only limited powers to the president, and for a limited time. No extreme of wickedness or folly can do great damage while the people retain their virtue and vigilance. Lincoln argues the effectiveness of the Constitution in limiting any possible damage from his own wickedness. There is further irony in the fact that, as Alexander Stephens pointed out in his antisecessionist speech to the Georgia legislature, Lincoln could not have appointed a single member of his cabinet without the consent of a Democratic Senate, had the Southern states kept their seats. The larger political fact of life, however, was that Lincoln's election marked the beginning of the end of slavery extension, and nothing seemed likely to reconcile the seceding states to the finality of this decision.

[33] My countrymen, one and all, think calmly and *well*, upon the whole subject. Nothing valuable can be lost by taking time. If there be an object to *hurry* any of you, in hot haste, to a step which you would never take *deliberately*, that object will be frustrated by taking time; but no good object can be frustrated by it. Such of you as are now dissatisfied, still have the old Constitution unimpaired, and, on the sensitive point, the laws of your own framing under it; while the administration will have no immediate power, if it would, to change either. If it were admitted that you who are dissatisfied, hold the right side in the dispute, there still is no single good reason for precipitate action. Intelligence, patriotism, Christianity, and a firm reliance on Him, who has never yet forsaken this favored land, are still competent to adjust, in the best way, all our present difficulty.

The Constitution is a complex organism, dividing power and checking and balancing the various elements that must collaborate in the process of government. It works in this way because the people, whose voice is said to be the voice of God, is not an undifferentiated mass or a mere plurality of numbers. The Constitution, adopted by the people, transforms the people by the discipline it imposes upon them. Lincoln hopes that the constitutional process of deliberation will somehow form a consensus out of the conflicting opinions now so strident. The entire inaugural has been testimony to the fact that there is no immediate danger, nor indeed any danger at all, that can justify precipitate action.

But precipitate action has already transpired. The process of secession began almost from the moment of Lincoln's election. And secession meant abandoning the deliberative processes of the Constitution, despite the secessionists' claim to be defending the Constitution by abandoning it. Lincoln's words here are consistent with the statement earlier in the inaugural that "the Union is unbroken." On the assumption that peace is still possible, Lincoln will appeal to the constitutional processes in which the seceded states are still at liberty to participate. In fact, as we have seen, all they need to confirm their security under the Constitution is merely to resume their seats in the Senate.

Lincoln calls upon "intelligence, patriotism, Christianity, and a firm reliance" upon God to solve "in the best way" the present difficulty. This is one of the very few times that Lincoln, who often and with unrivaled felicity invokes Scripture, mentions Christianity directly. Although he speaks once or twice of "the Savior," he never (so far as we know) pronounces the name of Jesus Christ. And he never himself professed the Christian (or any other) religion.[82] It is undoubtedly true that Lincoln has become the greatest interpreter of America's religious destiny in part because of his distance from any sectarian religious identification. Every church or synagogue can think of him as one of their own, because he scarcely ever spoke a word inconsistent with such an assumption. By belonging to none, he belonged to all. For these reasons his mention of Christianity here is particularly arresting.

Why does Lincoln speak both of Christianity and of reliance upon God? In this context, the latter refers to "this great tribunal, the American people." The former refers to the fact that the great majority of the American people are members of Christian churches. By the grace of religious freedom, the theological differences of Americans are not a cause of political alienation. Religious freedom under the Constitution, which blesses each church separately, allows all to come together in support of that Constitution. Lincoln knows that the churches themselves had begun to divide along sectional lines. But he hopes that Christian fellowship will yet work towards reconciliation.

There is another reason for Lincoln to speak of Christianity here. That is because he does not at this moment wish to speak of the Declaration of Independence. The doctrines of the Declaration had, in this crisis, become the cause of division, in much the same way that Christian doctrine had been the cause of division in the religious wars of Europe. Yet for Lincoln, as we saw at the end of chapter 2, the moral and political teaching of the Gospels had an apocalyptic fulfillment in the American Founding.

Throughout his speeches of the 1850s, Lincoln invoked the Declaration in a context that implied a perfectly nonsectarian Christianity. A notable example is the following, from a speech in Illinois in August 1858. According to Lincoln, the Founding Fathers' doctrine, embodied in the Declaration, was their majestic interpretation of the economy of the Universe. This was their lofty, wise, and noble understanding of the justice of the Creator to His creatures. . . . In their enlightened belief, nothing stamped with the Divine image and likeness was sent into the world to be trodden on, and degraded, and imbruted by its fellows. They grasped not only the whole race of man then living, but they reached forward and seized upon the farthest posterity. They erected a beacon to guide their children and their children's children, and the countless myriads who should inhabit the earth in other ages. Wise statesmen as they were, they knew the tendency of prosperity to breed tyrants, and so they established these great self-evident truths, that when in the distant future some man, some faction, some interest, should set up the doctrine that none but rich men, or none but white men, were entitled to life, liberty, and the pursuit of happiness, their posterity might look up again to the Declaration of Independence and take courage to renew the battle deeds which their fathers began—so that truth, and justice, and mercy, and all the humane and Christian virtues might not be extinguished from the land; so that no man would hereafter dare to limit and circumscribe the great principles on which the temple of liberty was being built.[83]

The Founding Fathers here are apostles of the justice of the Creator to his creatures, no less than those of the Gospels. Just as the doctrine of the Declaration flows from the Golden Rule ("As I would not be a slave, so I would not be a master"), so is the Golden Rule implied in the Declaration. That only certain classes of men should be entitled to the birthright of the whole great family of man is a denial of divine as well as natural law. The "humane and Christian virtues" not only correspond to each other, they are the same. We know, as Lincoln knew, that the defenders of slavery found in "the curse of Canaan" a biblical defense for their position. It is a measure of their differences that Lincoln found the antithesis in the proposition that we should do unto others as we would have others do unto us.[84]

The foregoing passage is one of the great anticipations of the Gettysburg Address. The "new birth of freedom" will reaffirm not only the principles of the Declaration of Independence but also the moral essence of the Gospels. It is in this sense that Lincoln speaks of Christianity in his inaugural.

[34] In *your* hands, my dissatisfied fellow countrymen, and not in *mine*, is the momentous issue of civil war. The government will not assail *you*. You can have no conflict, without being yourselves the aggressors. *You* have no oath, registered in Heaven, to destroy the government, while *I* shall have the most solemn one to "preserve, protect, and defend" it.

Lincoln reaffirms that there will be no war unless it is begun by others. He will not speak of "secession," because he denies that it is constitutionally possible.

Those who in their own minds have already become citizens of another country he insists upon calling his "dissatisfied fellow countrymen." He will have an oath, he says, registered in heaven, "to preserve, protect, and defend the Constitution," whereas they have no such oath to destroy the Union—notwithstanding the fact that the Confederate constitution, already in operation, required the identical oath of its president and a similar oath of all its other officials. Of course, if secession was not legally possible, then neither was an oath predicated upon it.

Lincoln has been adamant in refusing to abandon any of the claims of the Constitution and the Union. He remains equally adamant in refusing to initiate any use of force on behalf of those claims. The dilemma of Lincoln's inaugural is the simultaneous commitment to a peaceful resolution of the crisis and to the preservation of the Union. Here are the Scylla and Charybdis between which Lincoln must pilot his ship. The worst thing that could happen in the weeks ahead would be for the authorities in Charleston to have invited the Fort Sumter garrison to remain as their guests, for as long as they wished, and to have supplied them with all their needs. As time passed, and as the two governments lived side by side, it would have become extremely difficult, if not impossible, for Lincoln not to acquiesce in a peaceful separation. That kind of reasoning, however, was beyond the political mind of the proslavery South. As Lincoln said at Cooper Institute, nothing less than acceptance of the moral rightness of slavery could mollify them. They could no more avoid demanding recognition of their sovereignty in Charleston harbor than they could accept the leadership of Douglas in the 1860 election.

> [35] I am loth to close. We are not enemies, but friends. We must not be enemies. Though passion may have strained, it must not break our bonds of affection. The mystic chords of memory, stretching from every battle-field, and patriot grave, to every living heart and hearthstone, all over this broad land, will yet swell the chorus of the Union, when again touched, as surely they will be, by the better angels of our nature.

It seems almost impious to add commentary to such a peroration. And as in the Gettysburg Address, piety is what Lincoln here intended to arouse in us, no less than in those to whom he immediately addressed himself.

Throughout the 1850s, Lincoln, by his interpretation of the Declaration of Independence, transformed the Union of "the fathers" from one of blood to one of faith, as Jesus had done to Israel of old. Through faith, Abraham, Isaac, and Jacob became the ancestors not only of those, like Jesus himself, who were directly descended from them but also of everyone who accepted Jesus' teaching. Likewise, those who had come to America since the Revolution, or whose forebears had done so, were not related by blood to the men of the Revolution. But when they discovered that those men said, "We hold these truths to be self-evident, that all men are created equal" and that that assertion was "the father of all moral principle" in them, then—Lincoln said—they knew that they possessed the same inheritance "as though they were blood of the blood, and flesh of the flesh of the men who wrote that Declaration, and so they are."[85]

Lincoln appeals here to those all-powerful sentiments that have always bound men who feel the ties of kinship. That of course is the original meaning of patriotism, a meaning that survives all the changes of political life that have been wrought over the ages. The battlefield, the patriot grave, the heart and hearthstone evoke the ancient city and the lares and penates of the ancestors, who dwell as living presences within each household. In olden time, when a man went forth to fight for his city, he did so believing that he fought in defense of a partnership of the ancestors and of posterity, no less than of the living. Indeed, it was this partnership of the dead and of the unborn that constituted the living substance of citizenship. Lincoln can still appeal to his dissatisfied fellow citizens in the hope that the memory of a common inheritance will prove "better angels" than those driving secession and disunion.

But Lincoln's appeal was not to succeed. That appeal implied not only that French, Germans, Irish, and Norwegians belonged to the family of man but that black men did also. And so a different text proved prophetic for the event: "Do not think that I have come to bring peace on earth; I have come not to bring peace but a sword. For I have come to set a man against his father, and daughter against her mother, and daughter-in-law against her mother-in-law; and a man's foes will be those of his own household."[86] And so the war came.

6

July 4, 1861: Lincoln Tells Why the Union Must Be Preserved

On April 12, 1861, the Confederate batteries in Charleston harbor opened fire on the Union garrison at Fort Sumter. On April 14, the garrison surrendered. On April 15, Lincoln issued his proclamation calling into federal service 75,000 men of the militias of the several states. On April 19, he proclaimed a blockade of the seven states then in rebellion and summoned Congress into special session on July 4. On April 27, he added the states of Virginia and North Carolina to the blockade. Lincoln also suspended the writ of habeas corpus in Maryland. Troops from the North, marching through Baltimore for the relief of the nation's capital, had been assailed by Confederate sympathizers. Both soldiers and civilians had been killed—the first violent deaths of the war.

Lincoln had declared in his inaugural address that the government would not fire the first shots. He had not, however, declared how the government would react if shots were fired upon it. Although he had declared the Union perpetual and unbroken, what he declared was law, not fact. The Confederate government existed. What measures he would take to bring the facts into harmony with the law he did not say. It was already apparent that he had an entirely different conception of the constitutional role of the president than his predecessor. There was no suggestion in the inaugural that he would be unable to act until he had received instructions from Congress. Indeed, it was Congress that received its instructions from the president when, on July 4, he requested them to pass legislation ratifying the actions he had already taken. Lincoln's choosing July 4 to call Congress into session had, of course, great symbolic significance. But his postponing that session for nearly three months after Sumter meant presenting Congress, when it met, with accomplished facts. All the theoretical dilemmas and uncertainties that had plagued Buchanan, and that Lincoln himself had deliberately left unresolved in the inaugural, had been resolved by action before Congress met.

Lincoln's reaction to the attack on Fort Sumter was as electrifying as the attack itself. Here was no Hamlet-like indecision. In the several months since his election, the secessionists, by their actions and their words, had dominated the scene. They had done so without any certain sign that the government of the Union would find within itself the constitutional means of defending itself. Buchanan had said in effect that such means did not exist. Lincoln had implied that they did, while expressing the hope that peaceful reconciliation would obviate the necessity to discover what they were. Now Lincoln made it clear that, as the president was commanded by the Constitution to preserve the Constitution, he would regard as constitutional any means that he deemed indispensable to that end. In swift succession he issued commands that began to bring into existence the armies that would, first of all, defend the capital and the government and then subdue the rebellion. From the firing on Fort Sumter until Lee's surrender, Lincoln never hesitated for a single moment to do what seemed necessary to him to fulfill the obligation he understood had been imposed upon him by the constitutional oath.

Lincoln called the American people his "masters" and deferred only to them. He never confused "the people" with the advocates in his official family, Congress, or the organs of public opinion who raised their voices for his attention, thinking him too lenient or too harsh, too slow or too fast in his actions. Without public opinion polls, he knew far better than any present-day politician what the great mass of citizens thought and felt about unfolding events. And his actions were always timed to the beating of their hearts. Whenever Lincoln hesitated to act, it was to take whatever time was needed to be convinced of the wisest course. Although he proved peerless in sensing what measures the people would support and when they would support them, his greatest contribution to the final result was his ability to articulate the purposes of the war and to persuade those making terrible sacrifices why those sacrifices were worth making.

∽

If Fort Sumter represented the first great occasion for Lincoln to act, July 4, 1861, was his first great occasion to articulate the reasons for acting—to justify what he had already done and whatever else might become necessary to do to save the Union and the cause it represented.

To understand the past, it is necessary to attempt to see it as it appeared to those who lived it. No one today can narrate better than Lincoln did the facts that confronted him when he took office:[1] "[T]he functions of the Federal Government were found to be generally suspended within the several States of South Carolina, Georgia, Alabama, Mississippi, Louisiana, and Florida, excepting only those of the Post Office Department." Within those states, all federal property, both "movable and stationary . . . had been seized and [was] held in open hostility to this Government." The only exceptions were "Forts Pickens, Taylor, and Jefferson, on or near the Florida coast, and Fort Sumter in Charleston Harbor, South Carolina."

> The forts remaining in the possession of the Federal government in and near these States were either besieged or menaced by warlike preparations, and especially Fort Sumter. . . . A disproportionate share of the Federal muskets and rifles had somehow found their way into these States, and had been seized to be used against the Government. Accumulations of the public revenue, lying within them, had been seized for the same object. The Navy was scattered in distant seas, leaving but a very small part of it within the immediate reach of the Government. Officers of the Federal Army and Navy had resigned in great numbers; and of those resigning, a large proportion had taken up arms against the Government. Simultaneously, and in connection with all this, the purpose to sever the Federal Union was openly avowed. In accordance with this purpose, an ordinance had been adopted in each of these States, declaring the States, respectively, to be separated from the National Union. A formula for instituting a combined government of these States had been promulgated; and this illegal organization in the character of confederate States, was already invoking recognition, aid, and intervention, from foreign powers.

We pause here only to notice that Lincoln uses the word "confederate" in the lower case. From beginning to end, he held that secession was unlawful and that therefore all actions predicated upon it were unlawful.

Next Lincoln reviews his own inaugural address as a statement of his policy hitherto.

> Finding this condition of things, and believing it to be an imperative duty upon the incoming Executive to prevent, if possible, the consummation of such attempts to destroy the Federal Union, a choice of means to that end became indispensable. This choice was made, and was declared in the inaugural address. The policy chosen looked to the exhaustion of all peaceful measures, before a resort to any stronger ones. It sought only to hold the public places and property not already wrested from the Government, and to collect the revenue, relying for the rest on time, discussion, and the ballot box. It promised a continuance of the mails, at Government expense, to the very people who were resisting the Government; and it gave repeated pledges against any disturbance to any of the people, or any of their rights. Of all that which a President might constitutionally and justifiably do in such a case, everything was forborne, without which it was believed possible to keep the government on foot.

While the enemies of the Union had gone boldly forward in warlike preparations, seizing all the munitions and money belonging to the Union that came within their grasp, there had been no similar preparations on the Union side.[2]

On the 5th of March (the present incumbent's first full day in office) a letter of Major Anderson, commanding at Fort Sumter . . . was . . . placed in his hands. This letter expressed the professional opinion of the writer, that reinforcements could not be thrown into that fort within the time for his relief, rendered necessary by the limited supply of provisions, and with a view of holding possession of the same with a force of less than twenty thousand good and well disciplined men. . . . [But] no such sufficient force was then at the control of the Government, or could be raised and brought to the ground, within the time when the provisions in the fort would be exhausted. In a purely military point of view, this reduced the duty of the Administration . . . to the mere matter of getting the garrison safely out of the fort.

It was believed, however, that to so abandon that position, under the circumstances, would be utterly ruinous; that the *necessity* under which it was to be done would not be fully understood; that by many it would be construed as a part of a *voluntary* policy; that at home it would discourage the friends of the Union, embolden its adversaries, and go far to insure to the latter a recognition abroad; that in fact, it would be our national destruction consummated. This could not be allowed.

Lincoln next relates that an attempt was made to reinforce Fort Pickens, so that the evacuation of Sumter might appear to be a matter of military necessity, rather than voluntary. But the officer in command of the ship carrying the reinforcements, "acting upon some *quasi* armistice of the late Administration . . . had refused to land the troops." As a result, the crisis at Sumter would be reached long before the difficulties at Pickens could be overcome. Here is Lincoln's summing up.

They [the assailants of Sumter] knew that this Government desired to keep the garrison in the fort, not to assail them, but merely to maintain visible possession, and thus to preserve the Union from actual and immediate dissolution—trusting, as herein-before stated, to time, discussion, and the ballot box, for final adjustment; and they assailed and reduced the fort for precisely the reverse object—to drive out the visible authority of the Federal Union, and thus force it to immediate dissolution. That this was their object, the Executive well understood; and having said to them in the inaugural address, "You can have no conflict without being yourselves the aggressors," he took pains not only to keep this declaration good, but also to keep the case so free from the power of ingenious sophistry, as that the world should not be able to misunderstand it. By the affair at Fort Sumter, with its surrounding circumstances, that point was reached. Then and thereby the assailants of the Government began the conflict of arms, without a gun in sight or in expectancy to return their fire, save only the few in the fort, sent to that harbor years before for their own protection, and still ready to give that protection in whatever was lawful. In this act, discarding all else, they have forced upon the country the distinct issue: "immediate dissolution or blood."

It is impossible by comment to make Lincoln's account of the events culminating in the firing on Fort Sumter plainer or more intelligible. He follows with the first of many incomparable vindications of the cause of the Union, as the cause of mankind.

> And this issue embraces more than the fate of these United States. It presents to the whole family of man the question, whether a constitutional republic, or a democracy . . . can or cannot maintain its territorial integrity against its own domestic foes. It presents the question, whether discontented individuals, too few in numbers to control administration, according to organic law, in any case, can always, upon the pretenses made in this case, or on any other pretenses, or arbitrarily, without any pretense, break up their Government, and thus practically put an end to free government upon the earth.

Lincoln then poses the question with which we began this volume: "Is there, in all republics, this inherent and fatal weakness? Must a government, of necessity, be too strong for the liberties of its own people, or too weak to maintain its own existence?" And he concludes that "no choice was left but to call out the war power of the Government; and so to resist force employed for its destruction, by force for its preservation." We recall that Jefferson in his inaugural had also confronted the challenge that a republican government might be too weak to maintain itself. He had concluded that the republican form of government was "the strongest government on earth," in which "every man, at the call of the laws, would fly to the standard of the law, and meet invasions of the public order as his own personal concern."[3] But what was merely "theoretic and visionary" for Jefferson was intensely practical and real for Lincoln. Jefferson's election was accepted by his political enemies; Lincoln's was not. Lincoln has to test Jefferson's opinion that the people would fly to the standard of the people's government.

It will hardly have escaped the reader that we have here nearly all the themes of the Gettysburg Address. Lincoln will repeat throughout his July 4 message the theme that "discontented individuals" must not be permitted to break up a government that they cannot control through the political process. Nothing is said now explicitly about slavery, but the "issue . . . embraces the whole family of man." The question of whether republican government must alternate between anarchy and tyranny, the question so thoroughly defined in the inaugural, has now passed over from theory to practice.

In the next five paragraphs (of a total of forty) in the July 4 message, Lincoln describes the response to his call to arms. There were no troops from any slave state, with the exception of Delaware. The defection of Virginia is described in some detail, as well as the loyalty of that part of the state, later to become West Virginia, which for Lincoln *is* Virginia. Also described is the problem of the loyalty of the border slave states. Some in them would pursue a policy of "armed neutral-ity." This "would tie the hands of the Union men, and freely pass supplies from among them to the insurrectionists. . . . It would do for the disunionists that which of all things they most desire—feed them well and give them disunion without a struggle of their own." Lincoln in 1861, like Churchill in 1940, will not accept "compromise" that offers the delusion of escape from the harsh reality of the alter-natives of submitting to slavery or fighting for freedom.

Lincoln refers to his additional calls for volunteers and also "for large addi-tions to the regular Army and Navy": "These measures, whether strictly legal or not, were ventured upon under what appeared to be a popular demand and a pub-lic necessity, trusting then as now that Congress would readily ratify them. It is believed that nothing has been done beyond the constitutional competency of Congress." But can the president do whatever is not beyond the competency of *Congress?* The justification discovered in the combination of "popular demand" and "public necessity" would seem to constitute the very essence of that Cae-sarism against which Lincoln had warned in his Lyceum speech. Everything turns, however, upon whether this conjunction is brought about by "Caesar" himself or whether it is the consequence of circumstances that he himself deplores, but which he cannot escape. Buchanan placed all the responsibility for facing the cri-sis upon Congress. Lincoln will place upon Congress the responsibility to "ratify" the measures he has taken.

We must constantly remind ourselves of Lincoln's question of whether a republican government must of necessity "be too strong for the liberties of its people, or too weak to maintain its own existence." For Lincoln, the answer is clearly a resounding "No." It will follow, however, that in providing that answer in practice, he will be denounced from time to time, for being either too strong or too weak.

Soon after the first call for militia, it was considered a duty to authorize the commanding general in proper cases, according to his discretion, to suspend the privilege of the writ of *habeas corpus,* or, in other words, to arrest and detain, without resort to the ordinary processes and forms of laws, such individuals as he might deem dangerous to the public safety. This authority has purposely been exercised, but very sparingly. Nevertheless, the legality and propriety of what has been done under it, are questioned; and the attention of the country has been called to the proposition that one who is sworn to "take care that the laws be faithfully executed," should not himself violate them. Of course, some con-sideration was given to the questions of power, and propriety, before this matter was acted upon. The whole of the laws which were required to be faithfully exe-cuted were being resisted, and failing of execution in nearly one third of the States. Must they be allowed to finally fail of execution, even had it been per-fectly clear that by the use of the means necessary to their execution some sin-

gle law, made in such extreme tenderness of the citizens' liberty, that practically it relieves more of the guilty than of the innocent, should, to a very limited
extent, be violated? To state the question more directly, are all the laws *but one*
to go unexecuted, and the government itself go to pieces, lest that one be violated? Even in such a case, would not the official oath be broken if the government should be overthrown, when it was believed that disregarding the single
law would tend to preserve it?

We have here the first great test of whether there is in all republics that "inherent
and fatal weakness" of which Lincoln has spoken. In the present instance, Lincoln
is demonstrating the strength of his government. But he is scrupulous in his concern to prove that that strength is consistent with the rule of law and is not a pretext to undermine the liberties of the Constitution.

We notice, first of all, that Lincoln *assumes* that the right of self-preservation
must inhere in republics, no less than in other forms of government. That it
inheres even more rightfully in republics follows from the fact that, unlike other
forms of government, republics are grounded in the equal natural right of self-
preservation of each citizen. As we have seen repeatedly, the social compact or
contract arising from the primordial truth of human equality transfers to the government the exercise of the natural right to defend the life and liberty possessed
by every human person. And just as there is no assignable limit to what is permitted to individuals by the law of self-preservation in the state of nature, there
can be no assignable limit to what a government may do on behalf of those to
whose care that preservation has been entrusted.

Lincoln finds the formal presence of the right of self-preservation of the government in the presidential oath in Article II, section 1, of the Constitution,
whereby he is enjoined to "preserve, protect, and defend" the Constitution and in
the further injunction, in section 3, that he "take care that the laws be faithfully
executed." These texts, combined with what the laws of war conferred upon him
as commander in chief in time of war, will be a source of plenary constitutional
power for Lincoln. It cannot be emphasized too strongly, however, that it is *constitutional* power. And as we shall see, within the framework of the extraordinary
circumstances that have called it forth, it is not the less constitutional because it
is plenary.

It is an axiomatic premise of all written law, as explained by Aristotle, that if
circumstances arise in which the letter of the law negates the intention of the law-
giver, then the intention must be preferred to the letter. Lincoln here expounds
this premise with Euclidean clarity. Of course, Lincoln's and the Union's enemies
will charge him with lawlessness under any pretext whatever. In the present
instance, it is Lincoln's suspension of the writ of habeas corpus. Lincoln proceeds
to rebut this charge with a two-part answer. The first is that he would be justified

even if he had, as they charge, actually broken this one particular law. The second is that he denies having broken it.

Assuming that the letter of the Constitution enjoins Lincoln from suspending the writ, it is also true that that letter enjoins him to take care that the laws be faithfully executed. But he cannot execute any of the laws in one-third of the states. And the spread of the rebellion will prevent him from any or all of his efforts to fulfill the constitutional mandate. To prevent the rebellion from succeeding, the suspension of the writ is an indispensable means. Is it not certain that the failure of one law is to be preferred to a failure of all? Has Lincoln not proved this point with mathematical certainty?

Despite this proof, Lincoln next undertakes to prove that he has not, in fact, violated the constitutional provision concerning the suspension of the writ.

> The provision of the Constitution that "The privilege of the writ of *habeas corpus* shall not be suspended unless when, in cases of rebellion or invasion, the public safety may require it," is equivalent to a provision—is a provision—that such privilege may be suspended when, in cases of rebellion or invasion, the public safety *does* require it. It was decided that we have a case of rebellion, and that the public safety does require the qualified suspension of the privilege of the writ which was authorized to be made. Now it is insisted that Congress, and not the Executive, is vested with this power. But the Constitution itself is silent as to which, or who, is to exercise the power; and as the provision was plainly made for a dangerous emergency, it cannot be believed the framers of the instrument intended, that in every case the danger should run its course until Congress could be called together; the very assembling of which might be prevented, as was intended in this case, by the rebellion.

It is true that the clause dealing with habeas corpus is in Article I, which sets forth the powers of Congress, and not in Article II, which concerns the executive. But Lincoln has already shown that in construing any one provision of the Constitution in its relationship with other provisions with which it may appear to be in conflict, the dominating purpose of the Constitution, as distinct from its instrumental purposes, must provide the guide to its interpretation. There can hardly be any question but that the provision for suspending the writ of habeas corpus is placed in the Constitution to enable the government to provide for the public safety in the case of a rebellion. *Where* in the Constitution it is placed is wholly subordinate to why it is there at all. Lincoln's suspension of the writ is therefore lawful. Q.E.D.

∽

The foregoing argument, however conclusive in itself, rested upon the assumption that there was a *rebellion*. But the "rebels" denied this. Following the doctrine of John C. Calhoun, they believed that secession was a right *under the Constitution* and that their actions in withdrawing from the Union were lawful actions. They believed, therefore, that the Confederate States of America was a lawful government, entitled to recognition by the United States and by all other foreign governments. For that reason they, and their sympathizers within the Union, believed that Lincoln's suspension of the writ of habeas corpus, as well as all his other actions following Fort Sumter, was itself unlawful.

In his inaugural address, Lincoln had asserted that secession was "the essence of anarchy." A majority formed under the rules of the Constitution, with the clearly defined rights of minorities scrupulously observed, is "the only true sovereign of a free people." Whoever rejected this, he said, left only "anarchy or despotism" as alternatives. Underlying that argument, however, was the assumption that the Constitution was "the fundamental law of . . . a national government." It is true that in the inaugural Lincoln considered briefly the possibility that the "United States [was] not a government proper" but only "an association of States in the nature of contract merely." Appealing to the law of contracts, he denied that even then there could be a right of secession, since a contract can be broken by one of the parties but can be lawfully rescinded only by all. This argument was sufficient to assert the legal perpetuity of the Union. But it was not sufficient to justify the assertion that secession was rebellion. If today the United States unilaterally withdrew from "an association of states in the nature of contract merely"—for example, the United Nations—it might be a violation of international law, but Americans would not thereby become "rebels" against the authority of the United Nations. The primary obligation of American citizens to the laws of the United States would remain. The reason is that the United States today (thanks to Abraham Lincoln!) is a sovereign state, whereas the United Nations is not. Rebellion and treason consist in taking up arms against one's lawful sovereign. The Declaration of Independence, in proving that the king and Parliament of Great Britain had acted tyrannically, proved that, by the laws of nature and of nature's God, they had forfeited their lawful authority over the colonies. In appealing to natural law, the Founders appealed to the right of revolution, which is the rightful remedy, when it is possible, against tyranny. But the secessionists of 1861 denied that they were appealing to the right of revolution. They denied this because they denied that the United States had ever had the sovereign authority that Lincoln claimed for it as the "national government."

By the doctrine of John C. Calhoun, faithfully followed by both Jefferson Davis and Alexander Stephens, when the thirteen colonies became independent of Great Britain in 1776, they each became sovereign states, as independent of each other as of the British Crown. By this same doctrine, neither the Articles of

Confederation nor the Constitution impaired this sovereignty that resulted from the original act of independence. Thus to the secessionists in 1861, their lawful political obligation was primarily to their states. Whatever loyalty or obedience was owed to the Union, they believed, was derivative from that primary obligation. Citizens were morally bound by majority rule within their states, as that was defined by their state constitutions. They were morally bound to majority rule as defined by the U.S. Constitution only insofar as their state constitutions committed them to that obligation. We have seen that no less an adept in constitutionalism than Alexander Stephens, having delivered two powerful speeches opposing the secession of Georgia, nonetheless believed himself bound by the decision of the Georgia secession convention. By the theory of state rights prevailing in such conventions, secession, like nullification, was the constitutional means by which the states could protect the lawful rights of their citizens from aggression by hostile majorities in the larger community of the Union.

By July 4, 1861, secession had become the moral justification for a gigantic armed rebellion. For those in rebellion, the moral obligations arising from state sovereignty took precedence of their duties as American citizens under the Constitution. Here now is Lincoln's response.

> It might seem, at first thought, to be of little difference whether the present movement at the South be called "secession" or "rebellion." The movers, however, well understood the difference. At the beginning they knew they could never raise their treason to any respectable magnitude by any name which implies violation of law. They knew their people possessed as much of moral sense, as much of devotion to law and order, and as much pride in, and reverence for, the history and Government of their common country, as any other civilized and patriotic people. They knew they could make no advancement directly in the teeth of these strong and noble sentiments. Accordingly they commenced by an insidious debauching of the public mind. They invented an ingenious sophism, which, if conceded, was followed by perfectly logical steps, through all the incidents, to the complete destruction of the Union. The sophism itself is, that any state of the Union may, *consistently* with the national Constitution, and therefore *lawfully* and *peacefully*, withdraw from the Union, without the consent of the Union, or of any other state. The little disguise that the supposed right is to be exercised only for just cause, themselves to be the sole judge of its justice, is too thin to merit any notice.
>
> With rebellion thus sugar-coated, they have been drugging the public mind of their section for more than thirty years; and, until at length, they have brought many good men to a willingness to take up arms against the Government the day *after* some assemblage of men have enacted the farcical pretense of taking their State out of the Union, who could have been brought to no such thing the day *before*.

Lincoln's antislavery career prior to his inauguration had been dominated by his conflict with Douglas. That conflict, in turn, was dominated by the question of whether popular sovereignty, properly so called, encompassed the right of the people of a territory to vote for or against slavery. Douglas held that the people of a territory, or indeed any people, had such a right. The rightness or wrongness of slavery had no bearing on the question. The only right or wrong was whether the people were or were not given a fair chance to decide. But Douglas never faced or answered the question of whence came this right of a people. For Lincoln, on the other hand, the right of any people anywhere to govern themselves rested upon the same foundation as the condemnation of slavery. One could neither condone slavery without condemning popular government nor extol popular government without condemning slavery. The right of self-government of a people was not an ultimate principle but was derived from the equal right to liberty with which each human person was endowed by his Creator.

In his inaugural address, Lincoln was candid in recognizing that the foundation of all the sectional differences was the difference as to whether slavery was right or wrong. While he pleaded for time and patience to allow the political process to resolve this difference, he did not propose or even suggest that there could be a compromise of the difference itself. Now, however, events in Charleston harbor have ended the hope for a peaceful resolution of the sectional crisis. The question facing the nation is not whether the Union can be preserved peacefully but whether it can be preserved at all. The Union, by the electoral process, with the full participation of all the states, has voted to limit the extension of slavery. Hence there is no need or purpose at this moment to speak out on the immorality of slavery. The preservation of the Union will accomplish the antislavery ends for which Lincoln was elected. For this reason Lincoln can, at least for the present, drop his antislavery thesis. For parallel reasons, the South can drop its proslavery thesis. The war of ideas will now be joined over the question of the right of the Union versus the right of secession. But this is only a proxy war. The real issue remains that of slavery.

The "movers" of the "rebellion," Lincoln says, well understood the importance of placing the stamp of lawfulness upon their cause. And Lincoln knew that these movers, by joining the "consent of the governed"—that part of the Declaration they pretended to accept—with the requirement by the Constitution that it be ratified by conventions, had provided a plausible ground for their claim. Why could not the states constitutionally deratify, by the same procedure by which they had ratified? That the people of the South were law abiding and patriotic was what Lincoln took for granted in his inaugural appeal to the "better angels of our nature." But Lincoln's appeal had failed precisely because the enemies of the

Union had succeeded beforehand in identifying law and patriotism with the right of secession.[4]

Lincoln sees this process of seducing the public mind of the South as a conspiracy. We cannot help noticing that Lincoln patronizes a conspiracy theory here as he had done in the House Divided speech. In fact, this conspiracy, which began "more than thirty years" ago, is the origin and ground of the other, which went back only seven years. Taney's opinion in *Dred Scott* can be explained plausibly as one of the effects of the conspiracy that Lincoln denounces now. The conspiracy charged in the House Divided speech was attributed to Taney, Douglas, and Presidents Pierce and Buchanan. Lincoln names no one in the earlier conspiracy. But the period of "more than thirty years" carries us back to the nullification debate, which began in 1828 and came to a crisis and resolution in 1833. What was then called the South Carolina doctrine, justifying at first only nullification, became in the end the justification of secession. Its author was John C. Calhoun, whose political philosophy will be examined presently. For the moment, we observe only that the starting point of this philosophy is the rejection altogether of the doctrine of human equality in the Declaration of Independence.

Secession is now condemned by Lincoln not, as in the inaugural, for its inconsistency with majority rule but as the instrument for "drugging" the "public mind" of the South. This raises an important question as to the integrity of "this great tribunal, the American people," to whose "ultimate justice" Lincoln in his inaugural had asked the South to defer. Lincoln says that a great part of the mind of that tribunal had been drugged by the doctrine of secession. But did not President Buchanan, in his last annual message, denounce abolitionism for seducing the public mind of the free states? Which president, Buchanan or Lincoln, is to be believed? Who is to define for us what is a corrupted, and what an uncorrupted, public mind? Can voting decide such a question?

Lincoln pays tribute to the "strong and noble sentiments" of the people of the "seceded" states. They are honest, but they have been deceived by an "ingenious sophism." Lincoln pays tribute to the ingenuity that has led to such success. If the underlying premise is conceded, the destruction of the Union follows "by perfectly logical steps." Lincoln, as president and commander in chief, must save the Union from physical destruction. But first he must save it from ingenious sophistry. The salvation of the Union depends, first and foremost, upon the defeat of the Unjust Speech by the Just Speech, or the victory of philosophy over sophistry. Lincoln is perhaps the greatest of all exemplars of Socratic statesmanship.

This sophism derives much, perhaps the whole, of its currency from the assumption that there is some omnipotent and sacred supremacy pertaining to a *State*— to each State of our Federal Union. Our States have neither more nor less power than that reserved to them in the Union by the Constitution—no one of them ever having been a State *out* of the Union.

Lincoln next repeats and elaborates the argument in his inaugural when he declared that "The Union is much older than the Constitution."

> The original [states] passed into the Union even *before* they cast off their British colonial dependence; and the new ones each came into the Union directly from a condition of dependence, excepting Texas. And even Texas, in its temporary independence, was never designated a State. The new ones only took the designation of States on coming into the Union, while that name was first adopted for the old ones, in and by the Declaration of Independence. Therein the "United Colonies" were declared to be "free and independent States"; but, even then, the object plainly was not to declare their independence of one another, or of the Union; but directly the contrary, as their mutual pledge, and their mutual action, before, at the time, and afterwards, abundantly show. The express plighting of faith, by each and all of the original thirteen, in the Articles of Confederation, two years later, that the Union shall be perpetual, is most conclusive. Having never been States, either in substance or in name, outside of the Union, whence this magical omnipotence of "State rights," asserting a claim of power to lawfully destroy the Union itself?

Lincoln's assertion that the colonies passed into the Union before independence leaves unanswered the question of the nature of that union. Was it a union such as to make the citizens of the several colonies embryonic fellow citizens? We recall that Aristotle says that men may associate for common defense, as when they are joined together by a common enemy, or for trade, as by a customs union. Neither of these implies a government or citizenship in common.[5] Secession from such associations, whether just or unjust, would not be rebellion.

We observe that long before the Gettysburg Address, the Union for Lincoln had become a nation in which faith in a proposition had transformed aliens into friends and fellow citizens. But what if some of them repudiate the proposition? Are they morally bound by a faith they no longer hold? If the convictions that served as the moral foundation of political obligation are no longer believed, is the Union not already—and justly—dissolved by that very fact? This question only forces upon us the further question of whether a reasonable faith has been replaced by an unreasonable one. Does falsehood have the same moral claim as truth? Does a movement from civilization to barbarism have the same moral claim as one from barbarism to civilization? Is any claim to ultimate truth only a pretext to deny one side in the conflict its freedom to choose? In point of fact, both sides in 1861 (unlike Carl Becker in 1922) believed that their positions rested upon ultimate truth. And as in Lincoln's debate with Douglas, both sides appealed to the "original intent" of the Founding Fathers for justification.

Lincoln says that the new states took the name of states only by virtue of becoming members of the Union, and that even Texas, "in its temporary independence, was never designated a State." But during its "temporary independence" Texas *was* a "state" within the meaning of the law of nations. This reminds us that the word "state" has two distinct meanings, one in reference to a "separate and equal" station in that law of nations and another in reference to the constitutional law of the United States. A "state" by the law of nations can have whatever form of government it may have upon becoming independent. A "state" under the Constitution is guaranteed a republican form of government. It is this latter meaning that Lincoln assigns to it. In the sense claimed by secessionist theory, on the other hand, each of the thirteen colonies would have been free to choose any form of government, at which point they would indeed have become as legally distinct and politically independent of each other as of the British Crown.

Which sense of the word "state" is the correct one? To answer, we must consider what kind of union the colonies thought they were entering when first they formed it. The colonial assemblies that sent representatives to the Continental Congress were each elected by the people of their respective colonies. Until July 4, 1776, they remained nominally subject to the Crown, even though a year earlier the Congress had issued its Declaration of the Causes and Necessity of Taking Up Arms, asking the British Parliament to provide "evidence" that the "divine Author of our existence" intended for that body to "hold an absolute property in, and an unbounded power over," the American colonists. The plain meaning of this magnificent irony was that it is impossible for men who exercise their reason to believe that any one part of the human race has been marked out by God or nature as so superior to any other. No man is by nature, or by manifest declaration of God's will, the possessor or possession—the master or slave—of another. Whoever asserts such a right to such domination or possession is, in Congress's words from that same document, "rightfully resistible."[6]

The aforesaid manifesto, issued on July 6, 1775—the very first manifesto by the American people to the world—represented the religious consensus, no less than the political and philosophical consensus, that made possible the American Revolution. The following is from a sermon by the Reverend Samuel Cooper, a Protestant minister, preached on October 25, 1780, before Massachusetts governor John Hancock and both houses of the Massachusetts legislature, upon the occasion of the inauguration of that state's new constitution.

> We want not, indeed, a special revelation from heaven to teach us that men are born equal and free; that no man has a natural claim to domination over his

neighbors, nor one nation any such claim upon another; and that as government is only the administration of the affairs of a number of men combined for their own security and happiness, such a society have a right freely to determine by whom and in what manner their own affairs shall be administered. These are the plain dictates and common sense with which the common parent of men has informed the human bosom. It is, however, a satisfaction to observe such everlasting maxims of equity confirmed, and impressed upon the consciences of men, by the instructions, precepts, and examples given us in the sacred oracles; one internal mark of their divine original, and that they come from him "who hath made of one blood all nations to dwell upon the face of the earth," whose authority sanctifies only those governments that instead of oppressing any part of his family, vindicate the oppressed, and restrain and punish the oppressor.[7]

Because there is one "common parent," "all nations [that] dwell upon the face of the earth" are "of one blood." We see that God has "informed the human bosom" with the "plain dictates" of right reason, which represent the voice of God no less than do the "sacred oracles" of the Bible. However, these oracles confirm that God sanctifies only those governments that do not oppress "any part of his family" but rather "restrain and punish the oppressor." Here in 1780, in the midst of the Revolution, is the theme of the Battle Hymn of the Republic! We recall how Jefferson Davis founded the defense of slavery upon a preposterous interpretation of the story of Noah and his sons. We also saw Alexander Stephens claiming the authority of science for the proposition that Negroes were marked out as slaves by nature. In all this we see how far from the genuine Fathers of the Revolution were the leaders of the rebellion of 1861, who in defense of slavery had discovered a right of lawful secession.

The declaration of July 6, 1775, has been overshadowed by the Declaration of July 4, 1776. Yet the earlier declaration is the first testimony by Americans as to the nature of their identity as "one people." Thus it provides an invaluable gloss upon the later Declaration, telling us what kind of union it was that became independent. From the secessionist perspective, the colonies constituted no more than a league of independent nations, like the United Nations in World War II—united for common defense, but not common government. In fact, however, the leading feature of the union *before* independence was its denunciation of slavery. The binding moral purpose shared by all the colonies, in virtue of which their people may be said to have been fellow citizens of a common country, is expressed by the rejection of any claim of any man or men to hold a right of property in another.

At Darien, on the southern border of settled Georgia, a group of citizens met in January 1775 to align themselves with the rebellion against Great Britain. These Georgians, including slave owners, promulgated a set of resolutions specifying both British evils and American purposes. Consider that this was three months before Lexington and Concord, six months before the declaration of July 6, 1775, and eighteen months before the Declaration of Independence. These were ordinary citizens whose names have not come down to us. This is grassroots opinion of ordinary Americans from which Jefferson would draw his portrayal of "the American mind" in the Declaration. They resolved as follows:

> To show the world that we are not influenced by any contracted or interested motives, but general philanthropy for all mankind of whatever climate, language, or complexion, we hereby declare our disapprobation and abhorrence of the unnatural practice of slavery in America (however the uncultivated state of our country or other specious argument may plead for it), a practice founded in injustice and cruelty and highly dangerous to our liberties (as well as lives), debasing part of our fellow creatures below men and corrupting the virtues and morals of the rest, and which is laying the basis of the liberty we contend for (and which we pray the Almighty to continue to the latest posterity) upon a very wrong foundation. We therefore resolve at all times to use our uttermost endeavors for the manumission of our slaves in the Colony, for the most safe and equitable footing for the masters and themselves.[8]

Reading this, one can hardly doubt that the antislavery principles enunciated in the declaration of July 6, 1775, were meant to apply to American slavery, as to slavery anywhere. In 1776, the possibility did not exist in the American mind (or in the Georgian mind) that Georgians and their fellow Southerners might one day, in defense of the right to extend slavery, claim a lawful right to secede from the Union.

Lincoln says that the object of the Declaration of Independence was plainly *not* to declare the colonies independent of one another, as secessionism maintained. And indeed, there is no shred of evidence from the era of the Revolution itself that those who were making the Revolution were conscious of any such intention. Secessionist theory imputed to the historical past a consciousness based upon the logic inherent in their doctrine of state rights, a consciousness that the historical past could not have possessed because the theory upon which it was based had not yet been invented. One reason it had not been invented, as we may infer from Alexander Stephens's Cornerstone speech, is that the positive good theory of slavery had not yet been invented.

That the authentic history of the Revolution was what Lincoln asserted it to be is shown as well by the resolutions adopted by the Revolutionary colonial assemblies authorizing *union* as well as *independence*. Here are some examples: Connecticut, on June 14, 1776, instructed its delegates in Congress to "move and promote, as fast as may be convenient, a regular and permanent plan of union and confederation of the colonies." New Jersey, on June 21, called for "entering a confederation for union and common defense." Maryland, on June 28, in authorizing independence, also authorized "such further compact and confederation . . . as shall be necessary for securing the liberties of America." Most extraordinary is the resolution of the House of Representatives of New Hampshire, in which the instruction for independence and the instruction for union, given separately in the other cases, were combined into one. New Hampshire told its one delegate "to join with the other colonies in declaring the thirteen United colonies a free and independent state." Here the thirteen become one. *E pluribus unum.*

Consider now the language of the Georgia Colonial Congress, which exhorted their representatives to

> always keep in view the general utility, remembering that the great and righteous cause in which we are engaged is not provincial, but continental. We therefore, gentlemen, shall rely upon your patriotism, abilities, firmness, and integrity, to propose, join, and concur in all such measures as you shall think calculated for the common good, and to oppose all such as appear destructive.

We see the coordination of "patriotism" with the "common good," which is said to be "continental" and not "provincial." Can anyone find here any intention that the rights of a state should take precedence of those of the union of the states? In fact, all these resolutions are perfectly consistent with Madison's and Jefferson's characterization of the Declaration of Independence as "the fundamental act of Union of these States."[9]

We must notice, however, an important qualification in the aforesaid declarations. Rhode Island required that the greatest care be taken "to secure to this colony . . . its present established form, and all powers of government, so far as it related to its internal police and conduct of our own affairs, civil and religious." Virginia, in like manner, asked that "the power of forming government for, and the regulating of the internal concerns of each colony, be left to the respective Colonial Legislatures." Pennsylvania required that there be reserved "to the people of this colony, the sole and exclusive right of regulating the internal government and police of the same." And the same New Hampshire legislature that thought the colonies should declare themselves a single state nonetheless required that "the regulations of our internal police be under the direction of our own Assembly." The reservation to itself by each colony of its own "internal police" is the first formal manifestation of American federalism, and any account of the location of "sovereignty" within the system of government established by the Constitution of 1787 must certainly take it into account. In Article I, section 10, however, the Constitution lays a series of nine prohibitions upon the states. Every one of these prohibitions—for example, the denial of the right to coin money—is a denial of a power regarded as an attribute of sovereignty by international law. The states did indeed possess an exclusive jurisdiction with respect to the powers that are reserved to them by the Constitution. Thus they could, euphemistically, be called sovereign—but only in this limited sense.

Can the reservation of police powers to the states in any way justify secession as a legal right? It was perfectly consistent with this reservation that the Republican Party platform of 1860 acknowledged the "inviolate" right of each state "to order and control its own domestic institutions according to its own judgment exclusively." This was, as we saw, repeated in Lincoln's inaugural. But the same platform resolution declared that this right was "essential to that balance of power on which the perfection and endurance of our political fabric depend." This shows that the exclusive jurisdiction of a state over its "internal police" is a concept within the framework of union, one contributing to its "perfection and endurance," and not to its destruction.

We also recall that this exclusive jurisdiction was regarded by the Republicans in 1860 to be a conclusion from the principles of the Declaration of Independence. The idea of entrusting to a national police the security of persons and property in every locality is as inconsistent with those principles as allowing individual states to enter into treaties or alliances with foreign powers. Neither is consistent with the purpose of legitimate government to provide security of life and property from dangers foreign and domestic. But the idea of a right of secession in the service of the extension of slavery is consistent with no constitutional theory of the Founding Fathers whatever.

The Congress that declared independence and the army formed under its government and commanded by George Washington were both called Continental. The expectation from the outset was that the United States would expand from the original thirteen to an empire as large as, or larger than, any the world had seen. The greatest model in the minds of the Founders was certainly ancient Rome. But the Roman Empire under Augustus Caesar and his successors was a military despotism. An argument can be made, and often has been made, that under the "enlightened despotism" of the Caesars there was greater prosperity, more personal liberty, and greater security of property than had hitherto been known in the ancient world. Slavery, of course, was accepted in imperial no less than in republican Rome, as indeed it had been throughout antiquity. Whatever may be conceded to imperial Rome, however, would certainly not have sufficed for America's Founding Fathers. The limitations of freedom in the provinces of the Roman Empire of the Caesars are familiar to every reader of the New Testament. When Jesus said to render unto Caesar the things that were Caesar's, he was not protesting against taxation without representation. He knew perfectly well that any resistance to the tax-gatherers was the shortest and swiftest path to being crucified.

America's Founding Fathers denied entirely any unilateral right of "Caesar," or of any government whatever, to levy taxes unless the taxpayers were represented in it. They considered any taxation without representation, however small or apparently insignificant the tax itself, to be the beginning of an attempt to reduce them under absolute despotism and to be rightfully resistible. Caesarism, which became the ultimate origin of the idea of the divine right of kings, was accordingly anathema to Americans. The American Founders looked toward an empire of freedom unprecedented in human history. They meant to combine power greater than that of the Rome of the Caesars with freedom greater than that of the Roman republic or any other republic of antiquity. It meant to do this by innovations combining the principles of representation with the principles of federalism. It meant to do this, however, upon the foundation of the rights of man—a doctrine unknown to the ancient world, politically if not philosophically—as the only legitimate source of power or authority. In the Constitution, the rights of man are the foundation of the powers equally of the United States and of each of the states. This is proved, as Lincoln maintained, by the guarantee in the Constitution to every state of a republican form of government.

Federalism, however, as we discussed in chapter 3, was a familiar term that would have its meaning transformed by the Constitution. Madison would refer to the form of the new government as "nondescript," meaning that it had no model among governments past or present and that no familiar word accurately characterized the division of powers between the states individually and the United States. Hitherto, a federal system was "not a government proper, but an association of states in the nature of contract merely." It had been understood that a federal government could not be national and that a national government could not be federal. This would imply divided sovereignty, which John C. Calhoun denied was possible. From this Calhoun inferred that the United States under the Constitution remained *all* federal. In this he was in flat contradiction of Madison, who called the government established under the Constitution "partly federal, partly national."

The difficulty in understanding this division of the powers of government derives in part from the fact that an old word had been given new meaning. In the debate over ratification of the Constitution in 1787–88, the government that would perform *national* functions came to be called *federal*. This novel and contrary application of a familiar word arose from the fact that in the struggle for ratification the party in favor of the Constitution—the party that wished to transform the general government into a genuine or national government—called itself "federalist." The Federalists preempted the name properly belonging to their opponents as a political tactic, intending thereby to defuse the fears of those who saw danger to liberty in a government that was, even in part, genuinely national.[10] As we shall presently see, the conspiracy charged by Lincoln, to persuade the South of the lawfulness of secession, had its ground in Calhoun's reinterpretation of the Constitution as a vehicle for federalism as federalism had been understood *before* the Constitution.

Under the Articles of Confederation, the Congress possessed no powers of its own by which to execute its laws. Under the Constitution, the United States possessed lawful power to collect taxes and otherwise implement the powers committed to it by the Constitution. If nullification and secession came to be recognized as lawful powers of the states, then any state might arrest the operation of the laws of the United States at any time, as had been the condition under the Articles. By attempting to restore the old and obsolete meaning of "federal," Calhoun's doctrine would have had the effect of changing the government under the Constitution back into the very form it was intended to supersede.

Before the Constitution of 1787, the human race had experienced empire without liberty and liberty without empire, but never an empire of liberty. When the Constitution is seen in the light of the Northwest Ordinance of 1787, which became an essential part of the Constitution after being reenacted by the First Congress, it is clear that all states added to the Union would be perfectly equal, politically and legally, to the older states. There would be no discrimination among the states or among their citizens. Unlike Rome, which expanded by conquest and governed by force, there would be no distinction between capital and provinces or between center and periphery. Because of this, and because every state, and the people of every state, would participate equally in the process by which the United States exercised the powers delegated to it, there could be no place for a constitutional right of secession.

All contemporary documents of the Revolutionary period, including those that preceded Jefferson's *Summary View* of 1774, preclude any doubt that the argument for freedom was simultaneously an argument against slavery and that this twofold argument was the animating principle of union. Nor is there any doubt that this was a moral argument, binding upon man as man, and not only Englishmen merely. In virtue of this bond all Americans, and not only the Signers of the Declaration, pledged to each other their lives, fortunes, and sacred honor. This pledge became the moral principle of political union, the reason why the Congress could speak in 1776 in the name of "one people." It is why Jefferson and Madison in 1825 referred to the Declaration as the act in virtue of which Americans in the several states became fellow citizens in substance, even before they discovered the most appropriate political form by which to express that citizenship.

We return to Lincoln's July 4 message.

Much is said about the "sovereignty" of the States; but the word, even, is not in the national Constitution; nor, as is believed, in any of the State constitutions. What is "sovereignty" in the political sense of the term? Would it be far wrong to define it "A political community, without a political superior"? Tested by this, no one of our States, except Texas, ever was a sovereignty. And even Texas gave up the character on coming into the Union; by which act, she acknowledged the Constitution of the United States, and the laws and treaties in pursuance of the Constitution, to be, for her, the supreme law of the land. The States have their *status* in the Union, and they have no other legal *status*. If they break from this, they can only do so against law and by revolution. The Union, and not themselves separately, procured their independence and their liberty. By conquest or purchase, the Union gave each of them whatever of independence and liberty it has. The Union is older than any of the States, and, in fact, it created them as States. Originally some dependent colonies made the Union, and, in turn, the Union threw off their old dependence for them, and made them States, such as they are. Not one of them ever had a State constitution independent of the Union. Of course, it is not forgotten that all new States framed their constitutions before they entered the Union; nevertheless, dependent upon, and preparatory to, coming into the Union.

Lincoln says that the word "sovereignty" is not in the national or the state constitutions. But he has cited the Articles of Confederation as articles of perpetual union, and in the second of these articles he would have found the following: "Each State retains its sovereignty, freedom, and independence, and every power, jurisdiction and right, which is not expressly delegated to the United States, in Congress assembled."[11] The secessionist argument was that as each state was said in 1777 to *retain* its sovereignty, it must have possessed this sovereignty from the moment of independence in 1776. Taken by itself, this would be strong evidence indeed. But it cannot be taken by itself. In the first place, as Lincoln said, the reservation of sovereignty, interpreted as justifying secession, would be inconsistent with "perpetuity," not to mention the "more perfect Union" of the Preamble of the Constitution. John Quincy Adams held that the reservation of sovereignty in the Articles of Confederation represented a backsliding from the understanding of the relationship of the states to the Union that prevailed in the Congress at the time of the Declaration in 1776.[12] It is likely, however, that the sovereignty referred to was the "internal police" power that each colony reserved at the very moment it was urging the formation of a permanent union. Sovereignty in this sense would not in any way imply a legal right of secession.

The second of the Articles of Confederation distinguished "power, jurisdiction and right" that was "expressly delegated" from what was retained. But did not the United States, even under the Articles of Confederation, possess exclusive jurisdiction or sovereignty with respect to the "expressly delegated" powers?

Could it have been imagined that any state had a right in 1777 to make a separate peace with Great Britain? The very suggestion shows the absurdity of imputing sovereignty in any unqualified sense to the states that had joined in, and were joined together by, the Declaration of Independence. Whatever meaning may be assigned to the word "sovereignty" in the Articles, it can hardly have envisaged a right of a state to secede without regard to the interests of the other states. Moreover, in light of the antislavery arguments at the very forefront of the declarations of Congress of July 6, 1775, and July 4, 1776, it is simply inconceivable that a colony or a state possessed a sovereignty that could justify secession in the interest of promoting and extending slavery. Lincoln is always careful to concede that secession might be a revolutionary right, as distinct from a constitutional right. But the right of revolution can justly be invoked only in the interest of human freedom, not of slavery. Jefferson, in the *Notes on Virginia*, made plain that the slaves had a right of revolution, and not the masters. In any servile uprising, he said, God would be on the side of the slaves.[13] That is unquestionably why the Confederate States always insisted that secession was a constitutional, not a natural or revolutionary, right.

Whatever may be conceded to the sovereignty of the states mentioned in the Articles of Confederation, it cannot be assumed to have continued unaltered under the Constitution. The Constitution represents a radical reallocation of government powers within the framework of union, a reallocation authorized and sanctioned by the sovereignty inherent in that "one people" of all the states that had declared independence. It must also be remembered that the Constitution of 1787 rested upon a different foundation of authority than the Articles. The latter were ratified by the legislatures of the thirteen states, the former by conventions chosen to exercise sovereignty in its purest and most unqualified sense. As such, the Constitution authorized any delegation of powers whatever by the states to the United States that might have been judged most likely to effect their safety and happiness. Indeed, the ratification process by the states resembled exactly the process by which several individuals, in the state of nature, might agree to incorporate themselves into a civil society. In the state of nature, every individual is equally a sovereign, no one having more authority over another than the other has over him. In such a condition, each individual, although perfectly free from any superior authority, is also perfectly without the protection of government. To gain the protection necessary to secure his rights, the individual must agree with others to form a government. But it is only as the citizens obey the government that the government can protect the citizens. While the source of obligation is thus voluntary, there must be compulsory processes for securing the obedience of those subject to the law created by that voluntary agreement. In addition to a legislature, there must be an executive to carry out the laws and courts of law whose orders can be enforced. Under the Articles of Confederation, the states remained in a condition resembling that of individuals who voted to leave the state of nature and have a common government but with only a legislature and no judiciary or executive. In that sense, the states may indeed be said to have reserved their sovereignty. The Articles, one might say, resembled an unconsummated marriage. The states had created a government with no power to govern. Having then discovered how ineffectual this original contract or compact was, they had to negotiate another de novo, drawing from the font of their own plenary sovereignty the powers that would enable their government to fulfill its purpose.

By ratifying the Constitution, the states agreed that they would no longer be separate as they had been with respect to the laws of their common government. Yet that government would still not have jurisdiction over what from the beginning had been regarded as "internal police." The states would remain separate in all those matters with respect to which the Constitution did not delegate powers to the United States nor deny powers to them. Thus was created a system of government that has come to be called "dual federalism," but which might as well be called "dual sovereignty"—a system with no precedent in human history, but one that was essential to the empire of freedom the United States was destined to become.

The distinct and separate existence of the states is preserved not only by the Constitution's allocation of powers but also by the form of the government to which those powers are delegated. Each state is represented by two senators, chosen by the state legislature, and all the important "officers" of the executive branch must be approved by the Senate. Moreover the president is chosen by an electoral college, whose members are themselves chosen by the states. The president has the power to negotiate treaties, "by and with the advice and consent of the Senate," two-thirds of whose members must approve a treaty for it to become law. The fact that the treaty-making power is shared by the president with the branch of Congress that represents the states directly shows how "federal" the "national" government remains. We can see therein that the opposition between "national" and "federal" as hitherto understood does not fit the Constitution of 1787. It may thus be seen that the "sovereignty" of the powers of the United States and of the states is so intermingled and intertwined as to form a whole in which the sovereignty of the one cannot be discerned apart from that of the other. There is nothing anomalous in calling the United States a sovereign nation of sovereign states. But within such a compound whole, the idea of a lawful right of secession is an absurdity.

As discussed in chapter 3, the Constitution of 1787 became the government of the United States in virtue of the right of revolution proclaimed in the Declaration of Independence. It is impossible to understand the quarrel over the right of secession that Lincoln addresses on July 4, 1861—as it is impossible to understand either the American Revolution or the Civil War—without understanding the divergent interpretations of this doctrine of the Declaration as applied to the transformation of the Union from the Articles of Confederation to the Constitution. Let us then briefly return to this issue.

The Articles were drafted in the Congress that had issued the Declaration of Independence, the Congress that was the civil authority conducting the war against Great Britain under the generalship of George Washington. The Articles were ratified by the legislatures of all thirteen states. This was the only way the Articles could have been ratified in the midst of the war. "Consent" during the Revolution had to defer to the exigencies of self-preservation. The Constitution of 1787, on the other hand, was drafted in peacetime, by a convention that had been authorized by Congress to recommend revision of the Articles. The convention recommended instead their replacement by a government resting upon different principles and organizing its powers in an altogether different form. It had no authority from the existing government to proceed as it did. Fully aware of this, the convention deliberately set in motion a ratification process that would ground the Constitution on a more authoritative source than that of the government it intended to replace. In providing for a "more perfect Union," it transformed the Union itself. When a state ratified the Constitution of 1787, its people consented thereby to become, for certain specified purposes, fellow citizens subject to a common government. With respect to the powers of government entrusted to the United States—powers exclusive of the "internal police" of the states—these citizens now formed a single political community, acting and being acted upon without the intervention of state government authority.

The method of ratification called for by the Constitution was by conventions, that is, by bodies chosen for this one purpose alone. This represented a direct appeal to the natural or revolutionary right of a people to alter or abolish their existing government and to institute a new one. But this convention method of ratification provided secessionists in 1860-61 with what they claimed as justification: Every state that "seceded" was allegedly deratifying upon the same constitutional ground as the original ratification. We must accordingly ask why Lincoln denounced as a "farcical pretense" a procedure that appeared to be exactly the same as that by which the Constitution had superseded the Articles.

Article VII of the Constitution, as we have seen, provided that the new government would come into existence when nine of the thirteen states had ratified, but only "between the states so ratifying." The secessionists pointed to this as proof that the Union under the Constitution rested solely upon the acts of the states in their ratifying conventions. Might it not be said that the Constitution, in effect, authorized the nine to "secede" from the thirteen? After the formation of the new Union by the nine, would not the other four exist then as states outside the Union—something Lincoln denied was possible?

In the forty-third *Federalist*, Madison writes that this provision of Article VII

speaks for itself. The express authority of the people alone could give due valid-ity to the Constitution. To have required the unanimous ratification of the thir-teen States, would have subjected the essential interest of the whole to the caprice or corruption of a single member. It would have marked a want of fore-sight in the Convention which our own experience would have rendered inex-cusable.[14]

Madison speaks of the convention mode as the "express authority of the people." As noted above, this authority represents the purest exercise of political sover-eignty. Madison also speaks of the "essential interests of the whole," meaning thereby the essential interests of all thirteen states. However paradoxical it may seem, Madison still sees the "whole" Union as consisting of all thirteen states, even though there will be no "political relation" between the nine and the four.

The transformation of the Union from the Articles to the Constitution, Madison says, cannot be governed by rules set under the Articles. The imperfect authorization of the Articles themselves by the legislatures of the thirteen states makes this impossible. In the reconstitution of the Union different majorities will rule than have ruled hitherto, so majority rule itself must be reauthorized. The relationship of the states under the Articles was less that of a "government prop-er" than of "an association . . . in the nature of contract merely." The Congress might pass "laws," but enforcement was by the individual states acting by state majorities alone. Now, in the exercise of its delegated powers, the Congress will embody the will of a majority representing the people of all the states. It will be a majority formed by the Constitution itself (or by the people collectively through their adoption of the Constitution) to exercise the aforesaid delegated powers. This new form of majority rule required a return to the font of all authority for majority rule in unanimous consent.

The convention, obeying the logic of the compact theory, could not justly subject all thirteen states to the new government, with its different majorities, until all thirteen had ratified. But neither could it resign the fate of the whole Union to the recalcitrance of one or a few of the states. Under the Articles, if one state failed to pay its share of taxes, others might withhold theirs, bringing the whole government to a standstill. The very purpose of the Constitution was to prevent such minority rule, and so the adoption of the Constitution itself could not be subject to such a veto.

Madison then asks the "two questions of a very delicate nature" we noted in chapter 3, which go to the very heart of the questions Lincoln addressed in his July 4 message. By what right might the nine states "secede" from the Union of the thirteen under the Articles? And what relationship can subsist between the nine ratifying (or "seceding") states and the four nonratifying (or "nonseceding") states? Clearly, the difference between the numbers of states in 1787 and 1861 does not affect the question of principle we are exploring.

Madison says the first question is answered "by recurring to the absolute necessity of the case; to the great principle of self-preservation; to the transcendent law of nature and of nature's God, which declares that the safety and happiness of society are the objects at which all political institutions aim, and to which all such institutions must be sacrificed." Thus Madison appeals directly to the same law (or laws) of nature and of nature's God to which the colonies *unanimously* appealed in declaring independence from Great Britain in 1776. This is an appeal to what came to be called the right of revolution, which is also the sovereign source of the authority of all lawful governments.

Recalling the catalog of abuses and crimes charged against the British king and Parliament in 1776, in the midst of war, we must ask whether such a justification existed in peacetime for the action of the convention. The answer, we believe, must start from the inadequacy of the government of the Articles. For this, we refer to the incomparable presentation of the *Federalist* itself, particularly in numbers 1 through 10. We have already noted that the government of the Union depended upon the voluntary cooperation of each of the states individually to carry out the enactments of Congress, in this respect having laws without government. Thus the *intention* of the Articles that the Union be perpetual could not be fulfilled. We must then match the anarchy threatened by the Articles with the tyranny of the British as justifications of the exercise of the right of revolution. If the right of secession in 1860–61 is modeled upon the reaction to either of these, then it too must be an exercise of the right of revolution, rather than a right sanctioned by the law of the Constitution.

Madison says that it is the "safety and happiness of society" at which "all political institutions aim" and to which all may (or must) be sacrificed. "Safety and happiness," like "law[s] of nature," comes directly from the Declaration of Independence. Both come, moreover, from that passage in the Declaration concerning the right of the people to alter or abolish governments and institute new ones. It is noteworthy that in the Declaration itself, as well as in Madison's paraphrase, there are *two* paramount ends for which the right of revolution may be exercised: safety *and* happiness. In the beginning of the *Nicomachean Ethics*, the book that defines for his *Politics* the meaning of happiness, Aristotle asks whether such knowledge of happiness "[w]ill not . . . have a great influence on life? Shall we not, like archers who have a mark to aim at, be more likely to hit upon what is right?"[15] In Aristotle's *Politics*, safety and happiness are the alpha and omega of political life. Government comes into being, says Aristotle, for the sake of life, meaning thereby the security of life, liberty, and property. But it continues not merely for the sake of these things but for the sake of the good life. "Happiness" is Aristotle's word, as it is Jefferson's and Madison's, for the good life.[16] It is remarkable that Madison and Aristotle speak of the good as something at which legislators (and the teachers of legislators) must "aim." This means that the end or purpose of political institutions must not be merely idiosyncratic desires of individuals but a goal shared by the people as a people and that it must in some sense be knowable and rational. Life, liberty, and property are themselves ultimately desirable as means to a higher end and possess intrinsic worth only as they contribute to this higher end. The laws of nature define happiness, and especially its moral components, as much as they define self-preservation. As "safety" distinguishes one set of conditions for altering or abolishing political institutions, so "happiness" does another. The transcendent law of nature and of nature's God directs human action not for self-preservation alone but for self-preservation *in the service of happiness.*[17] This too is in accord with Aristotle, for whom the last end is the first principle of each of the things that come into being according to nature.

It is also noteworthy that Madison speaks of the law of nature as aiming at the good of "society." Although individual human rights are the core of the law of nature, they are comprehended by the good of society once individuals leave the state of nature and are transformed into a people. The "good people" of the Declaration could, as individuals, pledge to each other their lives, fortunes, and sacred honor, because their well-being as a people transcended any individual good. But a people's happiness can be destroyed internally by moral causes no less than externally by physical causes. We may recall that Jefferson's indictment of slavery in the *Notes on Virginia* was directed, first of all, against its effect upon the character of the slave owners. Injustice to the slaves injured the injurers no less than those they injured.[18] The enslavers were enslaved by slavery no less than the slaves. And both were thereby deprived of a measure of that happiness at which, by the laws of nature, all political institutions aim. So much for a right to secede in order to extend and perpetuate slavery.

We recall that Madison offers another justification for dissolving the Articles of Confederation without the unanimous consent of the parties to them, which may at first appear to offer a precedent or justification for secession in 1861. The fact that the Articles represented a "compact between independent sovereigns, founded on ordinary acts of legislative authority" is said by Madison to be "among the defects of the Confederation." We saw that such a premise was made plausible (although not more than plausible) by the language of the second article. On this basis, Madison asserts "that a breach of any one article is a breach of the whole treaty; and that a breach committed by either of the parties absolves the others; and authorizes them, if they please, to pronounce the treaty violated and void." But Lincoln, in his inaugural, argued from the same premises that the violation of a contract does not end or rescind the contract unless all parties agree to end or rescind it. Is there not a contradiction here between Lincoln and Madison as to when or how a contractual relationship may be rightfully dissolved?

What we have here is essentially an exercise in the law of torts. We start from a proposition upon which Madison and Lincoln are implicitly agreed: The party that violates a contract may not enjoy an advantage for having committed the violation; and, conversely, the injured parties are not to be prevented from seeking and finding a remedy. Madison, on his side, says that the states that had repeatedly and notoriously failed to fulfill their obligations under the Articles have no right to complain if nine states enter into a new Union that will be proof against such violations. This is especially the case if the ratifications of the nine are not by ordinary legislatures but by the people in their sovereign capacity. Lincoln is saying that the Union under the Constitution—Madison's Union—was formed to prevent the individual states from disrupting the government as they had done under the Articles. Hence individual states cannot claim a right to do under the Constitution what the Constitution was designed to prevent them from doing. Such was the claim to a constitutional right of secession. Nor can those individual states deny to the federal government the remedy of suppressing secession as rebellion. Lincoln's action in suppressing rebellion would then correspond to the action of the Constitutional Convention in "suppressing" the Articles. Thus there is no contradiction here between Madison's argument and Lincoln's.

We now return to the second of the queries propounded by Madison in the forty-third *Federalist* as to the relation between the nine ratifying and the four nonratifying states. As we recall from chapter 3, after remarking that the prospect of this question "being merely hypothetical, forbids an over-curious discussion of it," Madison says that although the nine and the four can have no "political relation," their "moral relations will remain uncancelled." The "claims of justice" between them, he says, "will be in force, and must be fulfilled," and the "rights of humanity must . . . be duly and mutually respected." Madison hopes that "considerations of common interest, and above all the remembrance of endearing scenes which are past, and the anticipation of a speedy triumph over the obstacles to re-union" will lead the sides to act with "MODERATION on one side, and PRUDENCE on the other." This passage is virtually an epitome of what we have seen Lincoln say in his inaugural on the same matter some seventy-four years later. The seceded states in 1861 stand in a relationship to the rest of the Union that is similar to the relationship between dissenting and assenting states after the government under the Constitution had begun. Madison's discussion of the relationship, like Lincoln's, concerns how the states will be reunited.

What Madison may have meant by forbidding an "over-curious" discussion of the relationship of assenting and dissenting states may be illuminated by what Lincoln said about reconstruction in his last public address, April 11, 1865.

> I have been shown a letter . . . in which the writer expresses regret that my mind has not seemed to be definitely fixed on the question whether the seceded States, so called, are in the Union or out of it. It would, perhaps, add astonishment to his regret, were he to learn that since I have found professed Union men endeavoring to make that question, I have purposely forborne any public expression upon it. As appears to me that question has not been, nor yet is, a practically material one, and that any discussion of it, while it thus remains practically immaterial, could have no effect other than the mischievous one of dividing our friends. As yet, whatever it may hereafter become, that question is bad, as the basis of a controversy, and good for nothing at all—a merely pernicious abstraction.

After the states in question have been restored to their "proper practical relation with the Union," Lincoln added, everyone can "innocently indulge his own opinion" as to whether, in acting to return them to that relation, he "brought the States from without, into the Union, or only gave them proper assistance, they never having been out of it."[19]

We are in the happy situation of being able innocently to indulge ourselves in what was a "pernicious abstraction" at the time Lincoln spoke those words. We know that Lincoln's consistent refusal to credit secession with any legal or constitutional status meant that he himself regarded the states as never having left the Union. Those who claimed to have taken the seceded states out of the Union were accordingly in rebellion against law and never represented the states in the only legal status they possessed, which was as members of the Union. However, given the intensity of the passions generated by four years of war, the radicals of Lincoln's own party in Congress wished to govern "the seceded States, so called" as conquered provinces outside the Union, like the territories acquired by conquest. The cooperation of these radicals was vital for any plan of reconstruction Lincoln could support. He would not therefore insist upon his own opinion to the detriment of the results he was seeking. At this point, practical reason demanded that he leave his own theory, however indispensable in other circumstances, to one side.

Madison's call for moderation and prudence is also a plea that theory not perplex practice. Obviously, the best solution of the question of the relation of the assenting to the dissenting states was for the dissenters to become assenters. That of course is what did happen, and the question did, therefore, prove "merely hypothetical," as Madison had hoped. But when eleven states of the Union in 1860–61 became "dissenters" by seceding, the question reasserted itself in a context in which there was little or no prospect of its becoming "merely hypothetical."

We return to the theory underlying the ratification of the Constitution. We have said that the ratifying conventions represented the authority and sovereignty of the people of the states far more than did the ratifications of the Articles by ordinary legislatures. The nine states required to ratify before the Constitution would take effect represented two-thirds of the thirteen, which could have been taken as a sufficient majority to bind all thirteen. But the supremacy clause of Article VI of the new Constitution transformed the government of the Union such that all laws and treaties made pursuant to the Constitution would be binding upon all state as well as federal officials, "any thing in the constitutions or laws of any State to the contrary notwithstanding." By reason of this clause, the Constitution asserted an authority or sovereignty over the constitutions and laws of the states that departed radically from the Articles. In light of this clause, it could not be plausibly maintained that the Union was "an association of States in the nature of contract merely" or that secession was a constitutional right.

The ratification had to be unanimous for exactly the same reason that individuals, in the state of nature, had to agree unanimously to form a political community before a government acting by the majority could exist. If some individuals present at the original formation of a political community do not agree to join, they are not part of it and remain nominally in the state of nature. They are neither subject to its laws nor entitled to the protection of its government. Formally and legally, this would be the position of the dissenting states in 1788. This is what Madison meant by saying there was no "political relation" between those and the assenting states. We must also note that these two categories of states are not both states in the same sense. Those dissenting are in a kind of limbo, suspended between the Union of the Articles and the Union of the Constitution. Notwithstanding any appearances to the contrary, however, these are not two different Unions, but the same Union in the process of growth and transition. And it remains true, as Lincoln said, that no state ever had any legal status outside the Union.

The interruption of the "political relation" between the assenting and dissenting states does not leave a mere vacuum. Even in the "pure" state of nature, there would be families, clans, or tribes with moral relations antecedent to the political. These would continue to link those who had become citizens of the new polity and those who had not.[20] Madison says the claims of justice must be fulfilled between noncitizens and citizens, no less than between fellow citizens. The rights of property and the obligation of contracts (which the Constitution says no state may impair), for example, are antecedent to the political community and intrinsically independent of it. In fact, the political community comes into existence in great measure to secure the rights of property and enforce the obligation of contract. Even if the property owner was a foreigner, which the citizens of the dissenting states would not be, there would be the same intrinsic obligation to respect his property and to pay him any outstanding debts.

The laws of civil society exist in large measure to enforce the obligation of contract, but that obligation, like the right of property from which it arises, is antecedent to all positive law. The free exercise of religion, also like the right of property, is a right inherent in man's nature or humanity. It is the glory of the Constitution that it attempts to make this right as valuable as possible. But respect for the right itself is what every human being owes to every other human being, whether or not it is recognized by the Constitution and the laws.

The foregoing are only some examples of what Madison had in mind when he spoke with such emphasis of the "rights of humanity" that "must in all cases be duly and mutually respected." It is because the Constitution is so preeminently devoted to securing these rights that it deserved to be ratified. But "the remembrance of the endearing scenes which are past" is an appeal to friendship arising from a shared history and an ancestry that is common to Americans as such. It is the same kind of appeal that Lincoln would make in the peroration of his first inaugural. Yet the ancestry shared by Americans is, as Lincoln has repeatedly said, not one of blood merely, but of a devotion to a universal principle. In Madison's peroration to the forty-third *Federalist*, "MODERATION . . . and PRUDENCE" take the place of "the better angels of our nature." But the meaning is the same.

What we learn here from Madison about the nature of the Union is that it is primarily moral and only secondarily political. The foundation of the political is laid in the "claims of justice" and the "rights of humanity." These claims and rights were inadequately or badly fulfilled or respected under the Articles. The Union of the Articles left the states in a relation that resembled that of sovereign nations under a treaty or of individuals in a state of nature. It is understandable that states or individuals would be reluctant to give up the freedom that is rightfully theirs in the state of nature, but prudence dictates that freedom can never be better exercised than when consenting to a government dedicated to making that freedom valuable.

Did the Constitution form such a government? Here we must bear in mind the implications of moderation as well as prudence. Both of these virtues demand that we not allow the best to become the enemy of the good. The Constitution made compromises, among them that with slavery. The moral basis of the Union, or of the friendship that arose from the Revolution—from "the endearing scenes which are past"—was inextricably bound up with the denunciation of slavery.

Indeed, the negation of slavery and the affirmation of freedom were ultimately a single phenomenon. The demand of the Americans that their right to freedom be recognized was a demand based upon the right of all men everywhere not to be slaves. The assertion of a right of secession was nothing less than an attempt to divorce that affirmation of freedom from that negation of slavery. It was an attempt to make the moderation of the Constitution in tolerating slavery into a right to extend and perpetuate it, as if slavery were something either morally neutral or positively good. We must ask, moreover, why the political leaders of the states that formed the Confederacy were so insistent upon secession as a *constitutional* right and so averse to claiming it as a *revolutionary* right. Confederate leaders, in their rhetoric, repeatedly compared their actions to those of the Americans of the Revolution. Yet they insisted, contrary to this comparison, that their withdrawal was constitutional and not revolutionary. Clearly the explanation of this was not only, as Lincoln said, because of the devotion of their people to law and order. It was also because an appeal to the laws of nature and of nature's God would constitute as much of a justification for their slaves to rise in rebellion against them as for them to rise in rebellion against the Union. Their revolutionary ancestors had openly recognized slavery as an evil—even if, in some respects, and for some limited time, a necessary evil. But for the leaders of the Confederacy, slavery had become a positive good. The right of secession, as a right of the states, and the positive good of slavery had become inextricably intertwined and interdependent.

Lincoln's July 4 message to Congress continues:

> Unquestionably the States have the powers and rights reserved to them in and by the national Constitution; but among these, surely, are not included all conceivable powers, however mischievous or destructive; but, at most, such only as were known to the world, at the time, as governmental powers; and certainly a power to destroy the government itself had never been known as a governmental—as a merely administrative power. This relative matter of national power and State rights, as a principle, is no other than the principle of *generality* and *locality*. Whatever concerns the whole should be confided to the whole—to the general government; while whatever concerns *only* the State should be left exclusively to the State. This is all there is of original principle about it. Whether the National Constitution, in defining boundaries between the two, has applied the principle with exact accuracy, is not to be questioned. We are all bound by that defining, without question.

We saw that colonial resolutions for independence in 1776 were combined with resolutions for permanent union that reserved the "internal police" of each colony (and state) to itself. This was the beginning of that unprecedented empire of liberty compounding the separate autonomy of the individual states with the combined autonomy—when safety and happiness could be secured only when the many acted as one—of the United States. The Articles failed, because identifying liberty only with the autonomy of the states became the path to anarchy, to the destruction of liberty no less than of empire.

How to define the boundaries between the parts and the whole was not perfectly known in 1787, in 1861, or at any time thereafter. Many of the elements of that definition are unambiguous (or nearly so), such as the prohibitions upon Congress in Article I, section 9, and upon the states in Article I, section 10. But the "necessary and proper" clause of Article I, section 8, leaves wide latitude for interpretation, a latitude in no wise diminished by the Tenth Amendment. The boundaries between the states individually and the United States resulting from such interpretation would have to be drawn and redrawn in and by the political process, but always recognizing the necessity of what the Republican Party platform of 1860 called "that balance of power on which the perfection and endurance of our political fabric depend." In that process there would be majorities and minorities, with satisfaction and dissatisfaction as the normal accompaniment of each electoral resolution. To claim that any minority might lawfully, constitutionally, and peacefully break up the government because of the dissatisfaction that is the routine concomitant of a free election is to deny the possibility of a regime combining empire and liberty.

Lincoln turns next, in Euclidean fashion, to demonstrating this claim's absurdity.

What is now combated, is the position that secession is consistent with the Constitution—is *lawful* and *peaceful*. It is not contended that there is any express law for it; and nothing should ever be implied as law which leads to unjust or absurd consequences. The nation purchased with money the countries out of which several of these States were formed. Is it just that they shall go off without leave and without refunding? The nation paid very large sums (in the aggregate, I believe, nearly a hundred millions) to relieve Florida of the aboriginal tribes: is it just that she shall now be off without consent, or without making any return? The nation is now in debt for money applied to the benefit of these so-called seceding States in common with the rest. Is it just either that creditors shall go unpaid, or the remaining States pay the whole? A part of the present national debt was contracted to pay the old debts of Texas. Is it just that she shall leave and pay no part of this herself? Again: if one State may secede, so may another; and when all shall have seceded, none is left to pay the debts. Is this quite just to creditors? Did we notify them of this sage view of ours when we borrowed their money? If we now recognize this doctrine by allowing the seceders to go in peace, it is difficult to see what we can do if others choose to go, or to extort terms upon which they will promise to remain.

Lincoln reminds us that "just" and "unjust" are not merely relative terms and that, as applied to the law of contracts, they are objective and not subjective. We can imagine Lincoln's adversaries saying (as in fact they did say) that the sums Lincoln here refers to were trivial, especially as compared with the cost of the war, and could be settled peacefully by mutual agreement. Once Lincoln recognized the Confederacy, commissioners could be appointed by both sides to negotiate an equitable division both of the public debt and of the territories. But the purpose of Lincoln's analysis is not to prove the fiscal irresponsibility of the Confederacy. It is to demonstrate the essential irrationality of the idea of secession as a constitutional right.

The notion that the Confederate States would voluntarily have assumed the obligations that were justly theirs as former members of the Union must be placed in the scales against the record of the states under the Articles of Confederation. There was no more urgent reason for calling the Constitutional Convention of 1787 than the bad financial credit, both at home and abroad, of the United States. This arose mainly from the delinquency of the individual states in paying their debts, whether to the United States or to private or foreign creditors. Even graver than the defaulting of the public debt was the states' practice of inflating their currencies to relieve debtors of the burden of repaying their debts at full value. This explains why Article I, section 10, of the Constitution prohibits any state from making "any thing but gold and silver coin a tender in payment of debts" or from passing any law "impairing the obligation of contracts." Under the Constitution, Congress alone has the power to "coin money and regulate the value thereof." The latter power has for millennia been regarded as a hallmark of sovereignty, and its denial to the states by the Constitution is among the strongest proofs that whatever sovereignty may have been claimed by the states under the Articles was extinguished by the ratification of the Constitution. It is true that the Confederate constitution retained these same restrictions upon the states. But the power of these restrictions is attenuated, if not entirely negated, if at the same time the states have the constitutional right to secede.

The Confederate constitution said nothing about the right of secession. Its preamble began as follows: "We the people of the Confederate States, *each State acting in its sovereign and independent character* . . . do ordain and establish this Constitution."[21] The italicized words constitute an addition to the text of the 1787 Constitution. In themselves, however, they do not constitute a ground of secession as a constitutional right, since they do not say whether the acts of ratification negate the idea of a right of lawful secession. Lincoln will not permit the Confederates the luxury of evading the consequences of the dilemma into which their doctrine has led them.

The seceders insist that our Constitution admits of secession. They have assumed to make a national constitution of their own, in which, of necessity, they have either *discarded* or *retained* the right of secession, as they insist it exists in ours. If they have discarded it, they admit that, on principle, it ought not to be in ours. If they have retained it, by their own construction of ours they show that to be consistent they must secede from one another whenever they shall find it the easiest way of settling their debts, or effecting any other selfish or unjust object. The principle itself is one of disintegration, and upon which no Government can possibly endure.

It is difficult to imagine Euclid proving more conclusively that one geometrical figure was equal or unequal to another. If the Confederate constitution did not admit secession as a constitutional right, the seceders could hardly claim it as a right under the Constitution of the Union. If it did, there would be no constitutional means of denying to any of the Confederate States the right to withdraw from their confederation whenever they might wish to do so and for whatever "selfish or unjust object."

Hamilton's plans for the funding of the national debt in Washington's administration depended absolutely upon the power of the national government to levy taxes upon the people of all the states, without any veto (or nullification) by any state government or authority. The credibility of this national taxing power, which was used promptly by Hamilton to pay off all the debts of the states, gave the United States a credit, both at home and abroad, that produced almost overnight a prosperity unprecedented in the annals of nations. Whether in practice the secession of 1861 would have led to a default of the debts to the Union of the seceding states is nothing to the purpose. The pressure to obtain recognition in 1861 might indeed have caused a temporary paroxysm of "fiscal responsibility." But the experience of the Articles proved that without the powers granted to the national government and denied to the states by the Constitution, an enduring guarantee of fiscal responsibility was not possible. A constitutional right of secession would simply negate the distribution of fiscal powers, whether in the federal Constitution of 1787 or the Confederate constitution of 1861.

If all the states, save one, should assert the power to drive that one out of the Union, it is presumed the whole class of seceder politicians would at once deny the power, and denounce the act as the greatest outrage upon State rights. But suppose that precisely the same act, instead of being called "driving the one out," should be called "the seceding of the others from that one"; it would be exactly what the seceders claim to do; unless, indeed, they make the point that the one, because it is a minority, may rightfully do what the others, because they are a majority, may not rightfully do. These politicians are subtle and profound on the rights of minorities. They are not partial to that power which made the Constitution, and speaks from the preamble, calling itself "We the People."

Again we see Lincoln's Euclidean rationalism. Why may not the many secede from (or expel) the one, if the one may secede from (or expel) the many? Moreover, if the Union could expel one of the states under the pretense of the doctrine of secession as a constitutional right, why could it not go to war with it or enslave it? The idea of an empire of liberty depends upon the absolute legal and political equality of the states within the Union. One of the restraints upon aggressive war by a government under the Constitution is the knowledge that, as in the wake of the Mexican War, territory acquired by conquest must eventually either be formed into states and admitted to the Union on a level of perfect equality or be granted independence.[22] But the legal equality of the states is only a reflection of the underlying principle of human equality from which the definition of republican government, or government by the consent of the governed, is drawn.

Lincoln knew, of course, that his opponents would say that what the one may do to the many, the many may not do to the one, because it would be an abuse of majority rule. Lincoln knew that the political theory of John C. Calhoun, with its doctrine of the concurrent majority, had attained great celebrity in both America and Europe. Calhoun's doctrine was then, as it still is, widely believed to be definitive on how minority rights are to be protected from majority tyranny. During the crisis of 1860–61, the right of secession was presented repeatedly as the means by which the constitutional majority defended itself against the numerical majority. The ultimate validity of this argument will be examined in chapter 7, in the context of a thorough exploration of Calhoun's theoretical writings. It is certainly Calhoun's disciples whom Lincoln had in mind when speaking of politicians who are "subtle and profound on the rights of minorities." Their defense of minority rights is, as we shall see, divorced from majority rule. When Lincoln invokes "We the people" as the power that made the Constitution, he invokes the theory that combines majority rule with minority rights. This is not a theory that justifies the unfettered rule of the numerical majority. On the contrary, the majority may rule only in the name of the rights of the individual, the rights belonging equally to majority and minority. The indissolubility of majority rule and minority rights, so lucidly and powerfully set forth in Lincoln's inaugural, and the indissolubility of the Union are inseparable. The great stumbling block to the full acceptance of this theory was that the connection of majority rule and minority rights can be found only in the natural and unalienable rights of individual human beings, which rights must belong to black as well as white human beings if they are to belong to any human beings.

The alleged right of secession, although ostensibly in the service of minorities, rested nonetheless upon the right of a majority within each state. Lincoln challenges the authenticity of this claim.

> It may well be questioned whether there is, today, a majority of legally qualified voters of any State, except perhaps South Carolina, in favor of disunion. There is much reason to believe that the Union men are the majority in many, if not in every other one, of the so-called seceded States. The contrary has not been demonstrated in any one of them. It is ventured to affirm this even of Virginia and Tennessee, for the result of an election held in military camps, where the bayonets are all on one side of the question voted upon, can scarcely be considered as demonstrating popular sentiment. At such an election, all that large class who are at once for the Union, and against coercion, would be coerced to vote against the Union.

When one thinks of how hard the South fought over the next four years, it is difficult to imagine today that public opinion did not support secession. But such hindsight may be misleading. The bloodletting had not begun, and communities close ranks after that has happened. Lincoln had no polls by which to measure popular opinion, and the divisions may in fact have been close to what he suggests. We must bear in mind that in the 1860 presidential election, Virginia, Tennessee, and Kentucky cast their electoral votes for the Bell–Everett ticket of the Constitutional Union Party, a party that had no other purpose than the preservation of the Union. In Virginia, Bell received 74,681 votes to Breckinridge's 74,323. Douglas, however, had received 16,290 votes. If one combines Bell's and Douglas's votes, one can say that 54 percent of Virginians had voted for pro-Union parties and only 44 percent for the secessionist party. The Virginia secession convention had adjourned without seceding before Sumter and reconvened after it to vote for secession. Unlike Douglas, who was unqualifiedly for both the Union and, if necessary, coercion against secession, the Bell–Everett ticket represented those who were for the Union and against coercion. We have already shown how Lincoln's inaugural was shaped very largely by his concern for the pro-Union/anti-coercionists in the border slave states. Whether and to what extent this anti-coercionist sentiment became secessionist after Sumter is difficult to say. What is certain, however, is that there were ten slave states in which no Republican votes, either popular or electoral, were counted in the presidential election of 1860 or in the election of conventions thereafter. On the subject of slavery, the states of the Confederacy had for the most part become closed societies in which neither free speech, free association, nor free participation in the political process was permitted. On many levels, Lincoln's questioning of the validity of a voting process that claimed a right to nullify the national elections is justified.

It may be affirmed, without extravagance, that the free institutions we enjoy have developed the powers and improved the condition of our whole people, beyond any example in the world. Of this we now have a striking and an impressive illustration. So large an army as the government has now on foot was never before known, without a soldier in it, but who has taken his place there of his own free choice. But more than this: there are many single regiments whose members, one and another, possess full practical knowledge of all the arts, sciences, professions, and whatever else, whether useful or elegant, is known in the world; and there is scarcely one from which there could not be selected a President, a Cabinet, a Congress, and perhaps a Court, abundantly competent to administer the Government itself.

The latter portion of this passage puts us in mind of the Gettysburg Address, in which Lincoln says that the world will little note nor long remember what he is saying. Whatever he says about single regiments supplying a cabinet, Congress, or Supreme Court, we may be permitted to doubt that any regiment, then or since, contained another Lincoln. Of course we do not know what hidden genius there may have been in the many brave men who died before there was any opportunity to demonstrate that genius. We do know, however, that the genius of a Lincoln, like that of a Shakespeare or a Plato, is rare in mankind. Certainly, under the influence of the free institutions of the American Founding, the American people had prospered "beyond any example in the world."

Lincoln's remark that so large an army had never been seen, in which every man had taken his place of his own free choice, reminds us of Jefferson's conviction, stated in his inaugural, that the people would fly to the standard of the law and meet invasions of the public order as their personal concern. But with the "ingenious sophism" of secession as a constitutional right, the public mind of the South had been drugged into believing that the anti-Unionists were defending the standard of the law.

Nor do I say this is not true also in the army of our late friends, now adversaries, in this contest; but if it is, so much better the reason why the Government which has conferred such benefits on both them and us should not be broken up. Whoever, in any section, proposes to abandon such a Government, would do well to consider, in deference to what principle it is that he does it; what better he is likely to get in its stead; whether the substitute will give, or be intended to give, so much good to the people? There are some foreshadowings on this subject. Our adversaries have adopted some declarations of independence, in which, unlike the good old one penned by Jefferson, they omit the words "all men are created equal." Why? They have adopted a temporary national constitution, in the preamble of which, unlike our good old one, signed by Washington, they omit "We the people," and substitute "We the deputies of the sovereign and independent

States." Why? Why this deliberate pressing out of view the rights of men and the authority of the people?

The drumbeat of the Gettysburg Address grows ever more insistent. We have already reviewed secessionist declarations and have seen the consent of the governed invoked without any recognition of the equality from which it is derived. Lincoln makes it clear that the great proposition, rightly understood, is the moral and logical foundation of all just government. As it is the unanimous consent of equals that transforms a number of individuals into a people, so also does that consent define the conditions under which a majority may rule. The deliberate pressing out of view of the rights of all human beings as human beings is a necessity for those who cannot or will not admit that their human chattels possess these human rights. Lincoln could hardly have said more at this point to identify the causes of union and of antislavery.

> This is essentially a people's contest. On the side of the Union, it is a struggle for maintaining in the world that form and substance of government whose leading object is to elevate the condition of men; to lift artificial weights from all shoulders; to clear the paths of laudable pursuit for all; to afford all an unfettered start, and a fair chance in the race of life. Yielding to partial and temporary departures, from necessity, this is the leading object of the Government for whose existence we contend.

Lincoln is constantly refining and perfecting the articulation of that "central idea" that will take its final form at Gettysburg. The proposition that all men are created equal can no more distinguish the color of those to whom it refers than can the Golden Rule propounded by Jesus. It is "the condition of men," not of one class only or one race only, that is to be ameliorated. The artificial weights or handicaps are to be lifted from "all shoulders." A "fair chance in the race of life" means that, so far as possible, merit should determine the outcome. And Lincoln refers here, as he has done so many times before, to the Constitution's compromises regarding slavery as "temporary," in accordance with the conviction of the House Divided speech that slavery must be placed in the course of ultimate extinction.

> I am most happy to believe that the plain people understand and appreciate this. It is worthy of note, that while in this Government's hour of trial, large numbers of those in the Army and Navy who have been favored with the offices have resigned and proved false to the hand which pampered them, not one common soldier or common sailor is known to have deserted his flag. Great honor is due those officers who remained true, despite the example of their treacherous associates; but the greatest honor, and most important fact of all, is the unanimous

firmness of the common soldiers and common sailors. To the last man, so far as known, they have successfully resisted the traitorous efforts of those whose commands, but an hour before, they obeyed as absolute law. This is the patriotic instinct of the plain people. They understand, without an argument, that destroying the Government which was made by Washington means no good to them.

Exactly two years to the day after Lincoln delivers this message, Lee will retreat from Gettysburg, in the aftermath of the greatest battle of the war. His retreat will be followed, some four months later, on November 19, 1863, by the dedication of the final resting place of those who died in that battle. The world has not failed to note or to remember what Lincoln said on that occasion; nor has it forgotten the sacrifices he memorialized.

In contrasting the loyalty of the common soldiers and sailors with the treachery of many of their officers, Lincoln does not speak of the treachery of the common soldiers and sailors of the rebel states. He has already said that the people of the South possessed as much moral sense and as much devotion to law and order as any other people. They were not traitors. But they had been deceived by false reasoning into believing that secession was lawful. Why had not the patriotic instinct of the plain people of the South been proof against deception? Lincoln implies that those with most to gain from a government dedicated to human equality understand instinctively that they have most to lose from its destruction. We must recall, however, what Calhoun described as the social function of the distinction of race in the slave states: It reduced to insignificance the social distance between whites, because of the great gulf that divided all whites from blacks. The ambition to rise in white society was thereby attenuated by the diminished distance between high and low within that society. If all whites were *born* superior to all blacks, advancement in the race of life did not depend upon individual effort. Thus there was no such incentive to the common white man of the slave states to better his condition as there was to the common man of the free states. To the contrary, the common white man of the South was attached to slavery for some of the same reasons that his Northern brethren were attached to freedom. That is why poor whites, with no slaves and little prospect of ever owning them, were nonetheless often attached to slavery with fierce devotion.

> Our popular government has often been called an experiment. Two points in it our people have already settled—the successful *establishing* and the successful *administering* of it. One still remains—its successful *maintenance* against a formidable internal attempt to overthrow it. It is now for them to demonstrate to the world, that those who can fairly carry an election, can also suppress a rebellion; that ballots are the rightful and peaceful successors of bullets; and that when ballots have fairly and constitutionally decided, there can be no successful appeal

back to bullets; that there can be no successful appeal except to ballots themselves, at succeeding elections. Such will be a great lesson of peace; teaching men that what they cannot take by an election, neither can they take it by a war; teaching all the folly of being the beginners of a war.

Here our wheel comes full circle, to the beginning of chapter 1. The election of 1800, we recall, was the first in human history in which a government was peacefully replaced by its bitterest political opponents on the basis of a free election by a whole people. Now that precedent must be defended against a massive attempt to turn back the course of human history from the reflection and choice of free elections to the perpetual alternation between tyranny and anarchy that had dominated the regimes of mankind hitherto.

Prior to the election of 1800, as we saw, the idea of free election replacing revolutionary violence as the guardian of the rights of the people was not firmly established even in the mind of Thomas Jefferson. In the Kentucky Resolutions, Jefferson had threatened revolutionary resistance to the Alien and Sedition Acts, despite the fact that the government that passed them had been fairly and constitutionally elected. Those measures, he thought, violated clearly written constitutional provisions and could lead to a change in the republican form of the government. If the majority thus misuses the power of office, then ballots may not indeed prove to be the rightful successors of bullets. In his inaugural, Lincoln was careful to take such exceptions into account and to deny that in the election of 1860 any such deprivation of the rights of any minority had taken place or had in any way been threatened.

Jefferson and Lincoln both understood that the process of resolving political differences peacefully by free elections was possible only within a system combining majority rule and minority rights, a system resting upon certain axiomatic premises. In Jefferson's words, "The republican is the only form of government which is not eternally at open or secret war with the rights of mankind."[23] The rights of mankind are such as are mentioned in the Declaration of Independence, as well as in many other documents of the American Founding. In introducing the measures that became known as the Bill of Rights, Madison declared that by enacting these measures, Congress would "expressly declare the great rights of mankind secured under this Constitution."[24] It is the security of the natural rights of mankind that establishes the authority of the Constitution and of the electoral process established by the Constitution. It is this that makes the form of the government republican. The rights of mankind are the foundation of the authority of the people, and no majority that infringes upon these rights can do so without disparaging that authority. Conversely, no majority that does not infringe upon these rights but performs the functions that majorities, and only majorities, can lawfully perform can be dispossessed of its offices and functions. The attempt to do so must be met with persuasion if possible, but if necessary by force. The American people, who first displayed to the world that form of government by which reflection and choice might replace accident and force, must in 1861 vindicate that form. Reflection tells us that in this crisis, reason and peace can be vindicated only by force.

> Lest there be some uneasiness in the minds of candid men, as to what is to be the course of the government, towards the Southern States, after the rebellion shall have been suppressed, the Executive deems it proper to say, it will be his purpose then, as ever, to be guided by the Constitution and the laws; and that he probably will have no different understanding of the powers and duties of the Federal government, relatively to the rights of the States and the people, under the Constitution, than that expressed in the inaugural address. He desires to preserve the Government, that it may be administered for all, as it was administered by the men who made it. Loyal citizens everywhere have the right to claim this of their Government; and the Government has no right to withhold or neglect it. It is not perceived that, in giving it, there is any coercion, any conquest, or any subjugation, in any just sense of those terms.

There is a notable caveat when Lincoln says that after the rebellion is suppressed, he will *probably* have no different understanding than that expressed in his inaugural of the relationship of the federal government to the states. In what ways Lincoln was bound by the pledges in his inaugural address occupied him greatly as the war went on. In the inaugural, he had announced his intention both to preserve the Union and to leave slavery in the slave states untouched. As events would have it, however, he had to choose between saving the Union and saving slavery. There is no intention on his part, he says, to engage in anything that might be justly denominated coercion, conquest, or subjugation. From Lincoln's perspective, the action of the federal government, like that of any police officer, is to defend the peace. To subdue a breaker of the peace is not to coerce but to prevent coercion. The essence of the peaceful rule of law in republican government is the uncontested assumption of office by those who have won elections. The use of force to uphold the law is the only means of *avoiding* conquest or subjugation as the basis of the government. Lincoln means nothing more, and will accept nothing less, than the preservation of the rule of law under the Constitution.

> The Constitution provides, and all the States have accepted the provision, that "The United States shall guaranty to every State in this Union a republican form of Government." But if a State may lawfully go out of the Union, having done

so, it may also discard a republican form of government; so that to prevent its going out is an indispensable means to the end of maintaining the guarantee mentioned; and when the end is lawful and obligatory, the indispensable means to it are also lawful and obligatory.

Lincoln returns one more time to the refutation of the claim that secession is lawful. The Constitution requires the United States to guarantee to every individual state a republican form of government. If a state may leave the Union lawfully, it would be possible for it lawfully to discard the republican form of its government. There cannot at once be the republican guarantee and the right of secession. Once again we see Lincoln's practice of the Socratic art.

It is notable that Lincoln, like the Constitution itself, does not define here what is a republican form of government. From the Peoria speech in 1854 onwards, Lincoln had demonstrated repeatedly and precisely how the principles of the Declaration of Independence had formed the "sheet anchor" of American republicanism. Lincoln's adversaries, as followers of John C. Calhoun, had rejected those principles in forming their own definition of republicanism. They had defined republican government in such a way as to make secession an indispensable attribute of constitutionalism in general, and an indispensable means of preserving their own constitutions in particular. The right of secession, they said, like that of nullification, was an instrument to compel the numerical majority to bow to the constitutional majority. The true constitutional majority, according to this dispensation, is the one in which questions dividing the majority and the minority are resolved, not by any numerical force majeure, nor even by free constitutional elections, but by a negotiated compromise resulting in a concurrence of the wills of the contending parties. This doctrine, promulgated by Calhoun, is what had "sugar coated" rebellion and drugged the public mind of the South "for more than thirty years." We will examine Calhoun's argument in all its plenitude in the next chapter.

Lincoln draws his July 4 message to a close.

It was with the deepest regret that the Executive found the duty of employing the war power in defense of the Government forced upon him. He could but perform his duty, or surrender the existence of the Government. No compromise by public servants could in this case be a cure; not that compromises are not often proper, but that no popular government can long survive a marked precedent, that those who carry an election can only save the government from immediate destruction by giving up the main point upon which the people gave the election. The people themselves, and not their servants, can safely reverse their own deliberate decision.

Lincoln, a man of peace, is leading a great people into a great war. He is explaining why there is no escape from the conclusion that force to destroy the Union can only be met by force for its preservation. Those who will be making the sacrifices of life and treasure must know that there is no alternative open to him except the one he is asking Congress to endorse and implement. We who are the beneficiaries of those sacrifices may reflect that in the more than 135 years since Lincoln wrote these words, national elections have come and gone in peaceful succession, whether in changing or continuing those in office. No wisdom of elected officials has been a greater good than the certainty that ballots would decide their election; and no folly of elected officials has canceled the good of that same certainty. This is not in any way to depreciate the importance of the distinction between wisdom and folly; it is only to recognize the wisdom of the sovereignty of the constitutional boundaries by which wisdom and folly may be examined and tested.

The United States had pioneered this new form of government as the world looked on with amazement and skepticism. The self-perpetuating rule of the few over the many, interrupted from time to time by revolutionary violence, had prevailed almost without exception from the beginning of time. Even the justly acclaimed Athenian democracy of the Periclean age involved no more than 10 percent of the population in the government and displayed all the turbulence and injustice of direct democracy denounced by Madison in the *Federalist*.[25] And of course Athens, like every other ancient city, was founded upon slavery. Calhoun and his followers pointed repeatedly to this in asserting that every high civilization had been, and always would be, based upon slavery. Lincoln liked to point out, however, that in the ancient world the slaves were almost all white.

The American experiment was an experiment for all the world. The conditions for its success had been more propitious here than they were likely ever to be at any other time or place. Its failure here would probably forever discourage any attempt to make the experiment again. This was all the more true because of the vested interests in all the ancien régimes in keeping the people under foot. Chattel slavery was only the most extreme form of ruling without the consent of the governed. That the government that claimed the greatest degree of responsibility of the government to the governed should also enforce its greatest denial was an internal contradiction that could not be indefinitely endured, if that government was to endure.

The principle of free elections could not be sustained, however, merely because Lincoln and his party were permitted to hold the offices to which they had been elected. Even today the question is asked, Why did Lincoln not seek a compromise with the secessionists? We must ask, in turn, What compromise could he or should he have sought? The political process, from the Mexican War onwards, had shaped the electorate toward a decision on the question of slavery in the territories. *Dred Scott* had represented a final and desperate attempt to make the right of property in slaves into a minority right beyond the reach of any majority. The inconsistency of such a claim with the very idea of government by the consent of the governed had been demonstrated by Lincoln (and others) over and over again. The 1860 election represented an unambiguous decision by the American people to cut the Gordian knot, to end once and for all the extension of slavery into any existing territory or any territories hereafter to be acquired. To say that the American people had no right to make that decision, or that they had no right to make that decision without the "concurrence" of the slave states, would make an absurdity of popular government.

> As a private citizen, the Executive could not have consented that these institutions shall perish; much less could he, in betrayal of so vast and so sacred a trust as these free people have confided to him. He felt that he had no moral right to shrink, or even to count the chances of his own life, in what might follow. In full view of his great responsibility, he has, so far, done what he has deemed his duty. You will now, according to your own judgment, perform yours. He sincerely hopes that your views and your action may so accord with his, as to assure all faithful citizens, who have been disturbed in their rights, of a certain and speedy restoration to them, under the Constitution and the laws.

Unlike his inaugural address, Lincoln has throughout the July 4 message referred to himself in the third person. In his annual message to Congress he will return to the first person. Why there is this grammatical shift is not clear. In his distinction between the "private citizen" and "the Executive," however, the difference between the person and the office comes into sharp focus. Private citizens ask their government to do for them what they cannot do for themselves, such as repelling invasion and subduing rebellion. As a citizen, Lincoln would have been one of many who had entrusted to his government the task of preserving the Constitution and the Union. The many can act as one, however, only by the medium of government, which is why civil society came originally into existence. As president or executive, Lincoln is the one to whom, above all others, their purpose has been entrusted. There is no escaping the burden of that trust—greater than that which rested upon Washington. As president, he has taken those actions that he deemed indispensably necessary. But the president cannot fulfill his duty unless Congress performs its duty in passing those laws and supplying those means without which he would be powerless.

It is also the case that the government cannot perform its duties unless the citizens obey its lawful commands. In the present crisis, disobedience to the Constitution and the laws has manifested itself in a peculiarly aggravating form. Lincoln, with an acuteness of intellect unsurpassed in any public forum, has refuted the contention that secession is anything other than rebellion. He has taken the greatest pains to prove, by an unbreakable chain of reasoning, that it is the enemy of peace, of law, of freedom, and of that property that all men have in their rights. The faithful citizens must now be supplied by their government with the lawful means of protecting and preserving those rights. Speech must now be followed by action, words by deeds.

Lincoln will end his message as the Declaration of Independence ended, by "appealing to the Supreme Judge of the World for the rectitude of our intentions" and by relying upon the "protection of Divine Providence": "And having thus chosen our course, without guile and with pure purpose, let us renew our trust in God, and go forward without fear, and with manly hearts."

7

Slavery, Secession, and State Rights: The Political Teaching of John C. Calhoun

Part I

Lincoln's refutation of secession as a constitutional right rested entirely upon the truth of the doctrine that the just powers of government are derived from the consent of the governed. That, according to Lincoln, was the "sheet anchor" of the republican form of government embodied in the Constitution and guaranteed by it to the states. "We the people" possessed the authority to ordain and establish the Constitution, because those who ratified it had been endowed by their Creator with certain unalienable rights. Those rights entitle any people to alter or abolish any government that does not secure those rights and institute a government that, in their judgment, will do so and thereby provide for their safety and happiness. Those rights were the reason or reasons informing the authority of "We the people" and the ground of the republican form of government. The moral rightness of republican government was moreover identical, in principle, with the moral wrongness of slavery. Republican government could not be right unless slavery was wrong.

The rights of man were both natural and divine. They possessed their authority from God and nature. They were knowable by the exercise of unassisted reason and were the heritage of all men everywhere. The fact that they were knowable did not mean, however, that they were known. Like other truths, they became known by the progress of the human mind. Jefferson wrote that "The equal rights of man, and the happiness of every individual, are now acknowledged to be the only legitimate objects of government."[1] But what was acknowledged when Jefferson wrote this in 1808 had not been acknowledged in what Washington called "the gloomy age of ignorance and superstition."[2] Nor did the progress that led out of that gloomy age prevent regress back into it. In the age of Carl Becker (and William Rehnquist, inter alia), as we have seen, it has become received wisdom that to affirm the rights of man has no greater foundation in truth than to deny them.

According to Alexander Stephens's Cornerstone speech in 1861, the natural rights philosophy of the Founding Fathers had by then been replaced in all scientifically enlightened minds by the doctrine of racial inequality. Stephens never expounded the new "science," but it may be assumed that a decisive contributor to that science was John C. Calhoun. There can be no doubt that it was Calhoun who had supplied the "ingenious sophism" that had "sugar coated" rebellion and brought the public mind of the South to believe that secession was a constitutional right.

To understand the sense in which the doctrines of Calhoun, on the one hand, and of Lincoln and the Founders, on the other, are directly antithetical, we take a step back to the penultimate crisis over slavery in the territories. That crisis was precipitated in 1846 when the Wilmot Proviso was introduced onto the floor of the House of Representatives. This proviso, we recall, declared that in any territory to be acquired from Mexico (whether by conquest or by purchase), slavery was to be forever prohibited. Although the proviso repeatedly passed the House, it was as often defeated in the Senate. Calhoun saw then what Jefferson Davis and others would later come to see, namely, that without the addition of more slave states, a succession of free states would eventually eliminate the Senate veto of antislavery legislation. At some point, then, the free states might possess the three-fourths majority to amend the Constitution to abolish slavery altogether, without the consent of any slave state. The "numerical" majority would ride roughshod over the "minority" interests of the slave states, which interests the Constitution would no longer be able to protect from the "tyranny of the majority." According to Calhoun's understanding of constitutionalism, the ending of the veto power of the slave states would mean the end of constitutional government. Here then are Calhoun's resolutions on the question of slavery in the territories, introduced in the Senate on February 19, 1847.

1. Resolved, That the territories of the United States belong to the several States composing this Union, and are held by them as their joint and common property.

2. Resolved, That Congress, as the joint agent and representative of the States of this Union, has no right to make any law, or do any act whatever, that shall directly, or by its effects, make any discrimination between the States of this Union, by which any of them shall be deprived of its full and equal right in any territory of the United States, acquired or to be acquired.

3. Resolved, That the enactment of any law, which should directly, or by its effects, deprive citizens of any of the States of this Union from emigrating, with their property, into any of the territories of the United States, will make such discrimination, and would, therefore, be a violation of the constitution and the rights of the States from which such citizens emigrated, and in derogation of that

perfect equality which belongs to them as members of this Union—and would tend directly to subvert the Union itself.

4. Resolved, That it is a fundamental principle in our political creed, that a people, in forming a constitution, have the unconditional right to form and adopt the government which they may think best calculated to secure their liberty, prosperity, happiness; and that, in conformity thereto, no other condition is imposed by the Federal Constitution on a State, in order to be admitted into this Union, except that its constitution shall be republican; and that the imposition of any other by Congress would not only be in violation of the constitution, but in direct conflict with the principle on which our political system rests.[3]

These resolutions are nearly identical with those offered by Jefferson Davis thirteen years later, as discussed in chapter 3. That there must be a "perfect equality" of the states in relationship to each other is and was perfectly true. If the United States, unlike all former empires, was to be an empire of freedom, then no discrimination between the older and newer states of the Union could be tolerated. The constitutional formulae by which each state took its place in the Senate and was represented in the House and in the electoral college remained identical for every state. What constitutional meaning beyond this was to be attributed to "perfect equality"?

The proposition that the territories belong to the states of the Union was of course also perfectly true, if for no other reason than that they belonged to the United States. However, on what principle were the states united? When the states ratified the Constitution, did they, in some sense and in some respects, by that fact unite themselves into a single political community? Calhoun's answer is no. Lincoln's, like Madison's, is yes. The Preamble to the Constitution says "We the people," not "We the people [or peoples] of the several States." As we shall see, Calhoun does not consider the legal or moral relevance of the Union antecedent to the Constitution, which was to be made *more perfect* by the Constitution. His Union springs de novo from the ratification process alone.

Calhoun's third resolution says that Congress may not make any law that discriminates against any state or deprives its citizens of a right in any territory equal to that of the citizens of any other state. This also by itself is unexceptionable. It does not, however, decide exactly what is meant by an equality of right or what constitutes invidious discrimination. It certainly does not consider whether slavery may not be invidious discrimination. Calhoun implies that the Union, or the Congress of the Union, can make no lawful judgment as to the lawfulness of the property that any citizen of any state might take with him into any U.S. territory. When Calhoun offered these resolutions, Mormon polygamy had not yet come to center stage. We have already seen that Stephen A. Douglas, in a masterly exhibition of evasiveness, did not and could not justify polygamy on the basis of popular sovereignty. Yet Calhoun, in his fourth resolution above, anticipating Douglas, says that a people in forming a constitution have the *unconditional* right to adopt whatever government they like best. Quite inconsistently, he then adds that the *only condition* limiting their freedom of choice is that the government be republican. That is like saying that we have an unconditional right to live until we die! And it begs the question of what constitutes a republican form of government. Surely it means more than a prohibition of titles of nobility. Both slavery and polygamy raised this question in a radical way.

From the foregoing we see that the issue dividing North and South, or the followers of Lincoln and those of Calhoun, is the question of what constitutes the republican form of government. Is slavery, as the negation of the consent of the governed, the negation of republicanism or an essential element thereof?

~

Calhoun's speech in the Senate on the Oregon bill, on June 27, 1848, is perhaps his most comprehensive exploration of the issues relating to slavery in the territories. He is categorical that unless a balance can be maintained between the slave and free states so that legislation in regard to the conflict of interests arising from this difference represents the "concurrent majority" of the states of the Union, the Union itself cannot be preserved. Near the end of the speech, he asks what a future historian of the decline and fall of the Union might think was the cause of its failure.

> If he should possess a philosophical turn of mind, and be disposed to look to more remote and recondite causes, he will trace it to a proposition which originated in a hypothetical truism, but which, as now expressed and now understood, is the most false and dangerous of all political errors. The proposition to which I allude, has become an axiom in the minds of a vast majority on both sides of the Atlantic, and is repeated daily from tongue to tongue, as an established and incontrovertible truth; it is that "all men are born free and equal."[4]

Here Calhoun demonstrates truly that the territorial crisis is ultimately an epiphenomenon of the profounder crisis concerning the relationship of republicanism to the doctrine of human equality. Here is Calhoun's challenge to the position Lincoln will maintain in the debates with Douglas. Here is the ultimate denial of that of which the Gettysburg Address is the ultimate affirmation.

We observe that the "proposition" Calhoun takes up at first is not from the Declaration of Independence but from the Massachusetts Bill of Rights, adopted in 1780. The principal architect of the Massachusetts constitution was John Adams, and he composed Article I, which includes the idea that "All men are born free and equal."[5] In 1776, Adams had been one of the committee entrusted by the Continental Congress with the preparation of the Declaration of Independence, which committee then chose Thomas Jefferson to be its draftsman. Whatever differences there may be between the statements of principle of Massachusetts in 1780 and the Continental Congress in 1776 are merely verbal. Each casts light upon the other. Here we note that according to Calhoun, a proposition that "originated in a hypothetical truism . . . as now expressed and now understood, is the most false and dangerous of all political errors." This error, he says, "has become an axiom in the minds of a vast majority." Despite the emphasis implied in "*now* expressed and *now* understood," there is nothing in what Calhoun says to distinguish the "vast majority" of the American public at the time of the American Founding from that of 1847. In Calhoun's thought, as in his disciples', it was the axiomatic premise of the American Revolution and of the Constitution that was "the most false and dangerous of all political errors." Therefore the ratification process upon which Calhoun lays such stress as an exercise of state sovereignty was itself conducted under the authority of that same error.

Calhoun continues his Oregon speech: "I am not afraid to attack error, however deeply it may be entrenched, or however widely extended, whenever it becomes my duty to do so, as I believe it to be on this subject and occasion." Here now is the locus classicus of Calhoun's fearless encounter with the dragon of human freedom and equality.

> Taking the proposition literally (it is in that sense it is understood), there is not a word of truth in it. It begins with "all men are born," which is utterly untrue. Men are not born. Infants are born. They grow to be men. And it concludes with asserting that they are born "free and equal,' which is not less false. They are not born free. While infants they are incapable of freedom, being destitute alike of the capacity of thinking and acting, without which there can be no freedom. Besides, they are necessarily born subject to their parents and remain so among all people, savage and civilized until the development of their intellect and physical capacity enables them to take care of themselves. They grow to all the freedom of which the condition in which they were born permits, by growing to be men. Nor is it less false that they are born "equal." They are not so in any sense in which it can be regarded; and thus, as I have asserted, there is not a word of truth in the whole proposition, as expressed and generally understood.

Calhoun's specious literalness imputes to the proposition in question meanings that could not possibly be more at variance with what the "vast majority" of Americans had always understood them to mean. One wonders whether this critique is meant seriously. But Calhoun was not given to comic parodies such as one sometimes finds in Socrates' interlocutors in Platonic dialogues.

The word "born" in the Massachusetts Bill of Rights obviously does not refer to the birth of individuals. Rather it is synonymous with "by nature." Of course we are infants, not adults, when we first make our appearance in the world. But the process by which we are conceived and generated is one and the same for everyone who has been or will be brought into the world. And this process determines that we will be human beings, not beasts of the field, and neither God nor angels. Our place in the order or economy of nature is thus decided for us by God and nature, and we have no part in the making of that decision. The intellectual recognition of this all-encompassing fact, with respect to which man has no freedom whatever, is the condition upon which genuine human freedom may be profitably exercised. It is in this respect that all men may be said to be born or created equal. Surely Calhoun must have known this.

That men are born equal means that they share a common nature and that this nature does not distinguish one human being from another in such a way as to say who is to rule and who is to be ruled. This has always been understood to refer to the relationship of adult human beings to each other and is in no way gainsaid by the dependence of children upon their parents. That the very young or the very old or the sick or the infirm may be dependent upon others in no way contradicts this assertion about the human species as such. The queen bee is marked out by nature for her function in the hive. Human queens (or kings) are not so marked. Their rule is conventional, not natural. As we have seen Jefferson say, human beings are not born with saddles on their backs, and others booted and spurred to ride them. These are facts accessible to everyone. They are truths that are self-evident.

Nothing is more revealing than Calhoun's assertion that human beings "grow to all the freedoms of which the condition in which they were born permits, by growing to be men." If the American Revolution meant anything at all, it meant that no man ought to be limited by the condition into which he is born. According to the doctrine of the Revolution as expressed by Jefferson, there was both a natural and an artificial aristocracy, the former based upon virtue and talents, the latter upon wealth and birth. "May we not even say," he wrote, "that that form of government is best that provides the most effectually for the pure selection of these natural aristoi into the offices of government?"[6] The American Revolution, taking its bearings from nature, meant to prevent the artificial or accidental circumstances of wealth or birth from confining the virtuous and talented, whatever their origins, to the circumstances into which they were born.

Calhoun continues:

> If we trace it back, we shall find the proposition [that "all men are born free and equal"] differently expressed in the Declaration of Independence. That asserts

that "all men are created equal." The form of expression, though less dangerous, is not less erroneous. All men are not created. According to the Bible, only two, a man and a woman, ever were, and of these one was pronounced subordinate to the other. All others have come into the world by being born, and in no sense, as I have shown, either free or equal.

This reading of the great Declaration is no less perverse than that of the Massachusetts Bill of Rights. "Created equal" does not refer to particular individuals but to that "great chain of being" by which the higher and lower natures are both linked to, and distinguished from, each other. Again: Human beings are neither beasts nor gods. Men may not, therefore, rule each other as they may rule beasts or as God may rule them. Thus the rule of law, or rule by the consent of the governed, is consistent with man's nature and with the laws of nature. Calhoun says that according to the Bible, only two human beings were ever created. But the Bible clearly means that in Adam and Eve, God created the human species and that in that sense each one of us is a creation of God. Calhoun says that in creating Adam and Eve, God pronounced one subordinate to the other. That is not true. God did not pronounce Eve's subordination at her creation. He did so only after she had eaten the forbidden fruit and given it to Adam to eat, and they had both been expelled from the Garden.

> But this form of expression, being less striking and popular, has given way to the present, and under the authority of a document put forth on so great an occasion, and leading to such important consequences, has spread far and wide, and fixed itself deeply in the public mind. It was inserted in our Declaration of Independence without any necessity. It made no necessary part of our justification for separating from the parent country, and declaring ourselves independent. Breach of our chartered privileges, and lawless encroachment on our acknowledged and well-established rights by the parent country, were the real causes, and of themselves sufficient, without resorting to any other, to justify the step. Nor had it any weight in constructing the governments which were substituted in the place of the colonial. They were formed of the old materials and on practical and well-established principles, borrowed for the most part from our own experience and that of the mother country, from which we sprang.

This must be considered one of the most influential passages in the documentary record of the American political tradition. A major element of present-day scholarship and political opinion has virtually swallowed whole Calhoun's assertion that the laws of nature and of nature's God played no role in framing and ratifying either the federal or state constitutions. It has done so largely because it has accepted Chief Justice Taney's assertion in *Dred Scott* that the Founding Fathers never meant to include the Negro in the proposition of human equality. Calhoun, however, did not supply the precedent for Taney; he thought the Declaration did include the Negro but that this was a foolish opinion that had no practical bearing.

On Calhoun's own testimony, the doctrine of equality was one to which nearly everyone in the Founding period subscribed. How then could it have had no weight in the construction of their governments? Not only Massachusetts but also Virginia and six other states had bills or declarations of rights that formed the prolegomena to their Revolutionary constitutions. As we saw in chapter 1, Virginia's constitution, adopted June 12, 1776—before either the Declaration of Independence or the Massachusetts constitution—declared that "all men are by nature equally free and independent, and have certain rights, of which, when they enter into a state of society, they cannot by any compact deprive or divest their posterity."[7] Far from having no weight in constructing the new governments, this doctrine of equality, according to the Virginia constitution, is the "basis and foundation" of government. The rights that men possess by nature define the purpose and limit the authority of any government rightly formed.

Calhoun says that the equality proposition made no necessary part of our justification in separating from Great Britain. In fact, we have seen that Lincoln says something similar in his speech on *Dred Scott*: "The assertion that 'all men are created equal' was of no practical use in effecting our separation from Great Britain; and it was placed in the Declaration, not for that, but for future use."[8] What Lincoln meant by this, however, was that the importance of the great proposition was even more prospective than retrospective. The colonists could have revolted, as Calhoun says, on the basis of their prescriptive rights. But they did so instead on the basis of their natural rights. They did so, according to Lincoln, because they meant to build a civil society on different principles than could be found in anything that preceded it. In the wake of Kansas–Nebraska and *Dred Scott*, Lincoln emphasized the role of the proposition in preventing the triumph of slavery. This agrees with what he would say in his July 4, 1861, message to Congress about the constitutional guarantee by the United States to each of the individual states of a republican form of government—a guarantee that would be nullified if a state could lawfully secede. It is also consistent with the necessity of defining the principles a republican government is meant to implement. We are reminded of the great thematic passage in the thirty-ninth *Federalist*, where Madison asks whether "the general form and aspect" of the government proposed by the Constitution "be strictly republican." "It is evident," he writes, "that no other form would be reconcilable with the genius of the people of America; with the fundamental principles of the revolution; or with that honorable determination, which animates every votary of freedom, to rest all our political experiments on the capacity of mankind for self-government." In defining a republican government, Madison says it is "essential . . . that it be derived from the great body of the society, not from any inconsiderable proportion, or of a favored class of it."[9] Clearly this is inferred from the premise "that all men are created equal." It is "mankind" or the human species as such, considered as part of the order of nature, whose capacity for self-government the American people are to demonstrate. To say then, as Calhoun does, that the great proposition was inserted in the Declaration "without any necessity" and that it had no weight in the construction of the governments that replaced the colonial governments, is—on the most charitable view—merely gratuitous.

It is somewhat surprising for us today that Calhoun thought the words of the Declaration "less striking and popular" than those of the Massachusetts constitution. Nevertheless, it is the former that Lincoln invoked in the Gettysburg Address, and it is their authority that caused the idea of human equality to spread so widely and to fix itself so deeply in the public mind. But there may have been a reason for Calhoun's particular animus against the Massachusetts version. In 1783 the Supreme Court of Massachusetts, in the *Quock Walker* case, held that slavery had been outlawed in Massachusetts by the first article of the 1780 constitution. This opinion, delivered by Chief Justice Cushing, read in part:

> As to the doctrine of slavery and the right of Christians to hold Africans in perpetual servitude, and sell and treat them as we do our horses and cattle, that (it is true) has been heretofore countenanced by the Province laws formerly. . . . But whatever sentiments have formerly prevailed in this particular . . . a different idea has taken place with the people of America, more favorable to the natural rights of mankind, and to that natural, innate desire of liberty, with which Heaven . . . has inspired all the human race. And upon this ground our Constitution of Government, by which the people of this Commonwealth have solemnly bound themselves, sets out with declaring that all men are born free and equal— and that every subject is entitled to liberty, and to have it guarded by the laws, as well as life and property—and in short is totally repugnant to the idea of being born slaves. This being the case, I think the idea of slavery is inconsistent with our own conduct and Constitution; and there can be no such thing as perpetual servitude of a rational creature, unless his liberty is forfeited by some criminal conduct or given up by personal consent or contract.[10]

One can only speculate whether Calhoun knew of this decision. It seems likely, however, that the presence of the doctrine of equality in a state constitution with direct application to the positive law regarding slavery—something that the Declaration of Independence by itself could not effect—made it peculiarly invidious to Calhoun. Although the similar provision in the Virginia constitution of 1776 did not have the same effect upon the status of slavery in that state, the *Quock Walker* case proves that the law in the Revolutionary era was not, as Calhoun claimed, being formed merely on "the old materials." Laws more favorable to the natural rights of mankind were transforming the nature and purpose of government.

Calhoun continues his assault upon the doctrine of the equal natural rights of mankind as follows:

> If the proposition be traced still further back, it will be found to have been adopted from certain writers in government who had attained much celebrity in the early settlement of these States, and with whose writings all the prominent actors in our revolution were familiar. Among these Locke and Sydney were prominent. But they expressed it very differently. According to their expression, "all men in the state of nature were free and equal." From this the others were derived; and it was this to which I referred when I called it a hypothetical truism. To understand why, will require some explanation.
>
> Man, for the purpose of reasoning, may be regarded in three different states: in a state of individuality; that is, living by himself apart from the rest of his species. In the social; that is, living in society, associated with others of his species. And in the political; that is, being under government. We may reason as to what would be his rights and duties in either, without taking into consideration whether he could exist in it or not. It is certain that in the first, the very supposition that he lived apart and separated from all others, would make him free and equal. No one in such a state could have the right to command or control another. Every man would be his own master, and might do just as he pleased. But it is equally clear, that man cannot exist in such a state; that he is by nature social, and that society is necessary, not only to the proper development of all his faculties, moral and intellectual, but to the very existence of his race. Such being the case, the state is a purely hypothetical one; and when we say all men are free and equal in it, we announce a merely hypothetical truism; that is, a truism resting on a mere supposition that cannot exist, and of course one of little or no practical value.

Here we confront the ultimate justification in Calhoun's own mind for rejecting the central idea from which radiate all the minor thoughts of the American Founding. Here is the foundation of the doctrine of state rights divorced from natural rights, which made it possible to believe that secession was a lawful right under the Constitution.

According to Calhoun, man in the state of nature is man living a solitary existence apart from the rest of his species. To say that man in such a state is free and equal is, of course, merely a truism. It is also a tautology, because in a solitary state there would be no one with respect to whom he might be unequal.[11] In short, it is saying nothing more than that in such a state, every man is equal to himself (as

412

in one equals one). But Calhoun's self-congratulatory cleverness is based upon an error that will prove to be both false and dangerous. Man as a solitary being by nature, and in the state of nature, is a thesis descended from Rousseau's *Discourse on the Origins and Foundation of Inequality among Men.* It is not to be found in Locke or Sydney, and there is no evidence that it entered in any way into the political thought of the Founding Fathers. Nor does it have any bearing on what they understood to be the meaning of man's natural freedom and equality. For Jefferson and the Continental Congress, what man is by nature, or in the state of nature, is in no way hypothetical. That there is no difference between man and man that would make one man the ruler by nature and the other his servant by nature is a truth open to empirical observation and confirmation by anyone, anywhere, and at any time. It is not something that can be discovered only in the state of nature. The state of nature is then an inference from what we see with our own eyes. Certainly if someone, especially in the "gloomy age of ignorance and superstition," observed kings and nobles and contrasted them with ploughmen in the field, he might be deceived into thinking that the differences in their attire corresponded to natural differences. But strip these kings and nobles and place them naked alongside naked ploughmen (something as easily accomplished by the imagination as by the senses), and one can immediately see that there is no natural difference making one the ruler of the other.

We recall that by the Declaratory Act of 1766, the king and Parliament of Great Britain claimed a right "to bind the people and colonies of America . . . in all cases whatsoever."[12] In principle, this was a claim of unlimited or despotic power. The Continental Congress resisted this claim not, as Calhoun alleges, on the basis of "chartered privileges." They did so, they said, because no one possessed of reason could believe that any portion of the human race had any such right of property or of unlimited dominion over any other portion of the human race. Locke expressed this in terms of "there being nothing more evident than that creatures of the same species and rank, promiscuously born to all the same advantages of nature, and the use of the same faculties, should also be equal one amongst another without subordination or subjection."[13] The Founders abbreviated this into "All men are created equal." Jefferson and the Continental Congress, no less than John Locke in seventeenth-century England, lived in a civil society in which, except in civil war, they recognized lawful authority. This did not prevent or inhibit them from recognizing that such authority arose, not from natural differences, but from a contractual process, a process of consent in which the purpose of government was recognized to be the protection and security of the equal rights of nature. In this sense, the state of nature was nothing other than the conceptual form of the understanding of what made government legitimate. It was equally the conceptual form of what made despotic or tyrannical government illegitimate and rightfully resistible. This understanding formed the consciousness of the Founders as civilized human beings and did not depend upon a recollection of a primitive past.

Calhoun is wrong not only about the state of nature representing a solitary existence but also about man's prepolitical social state:

> Nor is the social state of itself his natural state; for society can no more exist without government, in one form or another, than man without society. It is the political, then, which includes the social, that is his natural state. It is the one for which his Creator formed him, into which he is impelled irresistibly, and in which only his race can exist and all his faculties be fully developed.

Aristotle is the philosopher with whom the doctrine that man is by nature a political animal is primarily identified. According to Aristotle, it is indeed true that man's nature is fulfilled and fully revealed only in the perfection of political life. In Aristotle, however, one may distinguish the ontological order of being from the chronological order of becoming. The political community may be prior to the individual, the family, and the village in order of being, but the individual, the family, and the village are prior to the political community in order of becoming. Hence in a chronological or historical sense, a prepolitical social state exists for Aristotle no less than for Locke. Aristotle says that "the impulse to form a community of this kind [a political community] is in all men by nature; but the man who first united people in such a community was the greatest of benefactors."[14] Thus, according to Aristotle, the political community, although more natural than the family or the village in the ontological sense, nonetheless requires a deliberate act, antecedent to government, to come into existence. This conflicts starkly with Calhoun's assertion that man is "impelled irresistibly" into the political community.

It would be impossible to exaggerate the importance of this difference between Calhoun, on the one hand, and Aristotle, Locke, and the Founding Fathers, on the other. According to Calhoun, the transition from the prepolitical to the political is governed by necessity. The coming into being of the political community is entirely nonrational and does not require or permit any conscious choice or deliberation. In this respect, there would be no difference between the political community and the beehive or the anthill.

As we have seen repeatedly, it is a necessary corollary of the proposition of human equality that civil society properly so called—civil society that is not the result of force or fraud—is a voluntary association. It is constituted in its primordial ontological foundation by unanimous consent, and this consent sets the boundaries within which majority rule and minority rights can subsist together.

That all men are created equal means that when these boundaries are violated, the ultimate recourse is the natural right of the people "to alter or abolish" governments. Calhoun's theory, by denying that government arises from a voluntary agreement, denies the existence in any proper sense of this right of revolution. This denial is the ultimate reason why Calhoun's theory requires a right of secession. As we will see later, it also obliges him to invent his much acclaimed doctrine of the concurrent majority as a defense of minority rights.

Calhoun's Oregon speech continues:

> Such being the case, it follows that any, the worst form of government, is better than anarchy; and that individual liberty, or freedom, must be subordinate to whatever power may be necessary to protect society against anarchy within or destruction from without; for the safety and well-being of society is as paramount to individual liberty, as the safety and well-being of the race is to that of individuals; and in the same proportion, the power necessary for the safety of society is paramount to individual liberty. On the contrary, government has no right to control individual liberty beyond what is necessary to the safety and well-being of society. Such is the boundary which separates the power of government and the liberty of the citizen or subject in the political state, which, as I have shown, is the natural state of man—the only one in which his race can exist, and the one in which he is born, lives, and dies.

Calhoun asserts that the worst form of government, which is tyranny, is better than anarchy. One may ask, however, how he conceives of anarchy as possible in political communities, any more than in beehives or anthills, if men are impelled irresistibly to live under government. The state of nature, as Locke or the Founding Fathers conceived it, is full of "inconveniences," and no rational understanding of the human condition would not wish to replace it with government. But it is equally true that no rational understanding of the human condition would wish to replace the state of nature with tyranny. Why would anyone, except a would-be tyrant, wish to escape from anarchy into tyranny? Is it certain that the random violence of the state of nature is worse than the concentrated and purposeful violence of the tyrant?

Calhoun next asserts that in protecting society, the power of government is rightfully paramount to individual liberty. He adds to this that government has no right to control individuals beyond what is necessary for the safety of society. This leads to the obvious reflection that tyrants always identify the safety of society with their own safety, leaving little or no room for individual liberty. Calhoun, assuring us that tyranny is always better than anarchy, leaves no room for rightful action to overthrow a tyranny on behalf of individual liberty. However piously Calhoun may declaim in favor of the right of individual liberty in the absence of threats to the safety of society, he provides no rational ground to secure that right. In actual tyrannies, threats against the tyrant, whether real or invented, are never absent (or admitted to be absent). Accordingly, "the boundary which separates the power of government and the liberty of the citizen" has no one, except the government, to define it. Without the right of revolution, that boundary remains merely hypothetical.

We recall that for Jefferson in the *Summary View*, the right of revolution, and the threat to exercise that right, had throughout history been the only recourse of the people against the evils of tyranny. After 1776, free elections replaced the right of revolution as the ordinary means by which the rights of the people may be safeguarded. But throughout the literature of the Founding, and especially in the *Federalist*, there is a concern to prevent the tyranny of the majority as well as all other forms of tyranny. And in 1798 in the Kentucky Resolutions, Jefferson still saw the right of revolution and the threat of exercising it as necessary to the safety of the people even against the usurpations of a government they themselves had elected. One might even say that the victory of the Republicans in the election of 1800 came about because of the threats implied in the Virginia and Kentucky Resolutions. Thus the right of revolution becomes a permanent element in the electoral process, reminding both government and people that the majority loses its moral authority if it tramples upon the rights of the minority.[15]

The importance of the right of revolution is therefore missed if one thinks of it only in the negative sense. In the Declaration of Independence, the right to alter or abolish tyrannical government is at one and the same time the right to institute new and better government. In the bill of complaints against the king and Parliament, we find a veritable catalog of the essentials of government designed to protect the rights of the people, considered individually as well as collectively. The argument of the Declaration against tyranny and its argument for constitutional government are two sides of the same coin.

In the *Disquisition on Government*, to which we will turn presently, Calhoun maintains that all government is inherently tyrannical—a view that in itself, is not far from that of Jefferson. As society is necessary for the human individual, and government for society, so, according to Calhoun, must a constitution be superimposed upon government. The necessity of constitutionalism to prevent government from becoming tyrannical is also common ground between Calhoun, Jefferson, and the Founders generally. But we recall that Madison, in the forty-third *Federalist*, justified direct appeal to the people to ratify the proposed Constitution—in disregard of the existing constitution—on the authority of that same "transcendent law of nature and of nature's God" that had authorized the American Revolution. Here the acts of abolishing one government and instituting another are inseparable. By denying the right of revolution, Calhoun was denying the right to institute a nontyrannical government.

Calhoun has said that the political is the natural state of man, as it is the only state in which man can exist and in which man's faculties can be fully developed. There is no question that the political state, when it is nontyrannical, is more favorable to the safety and well-being of its citizens than any state of nature. But it is in contemplating the state of nature that we discover the principles by which we are instructed to form governments that secure us from both anarchy and tyranny and by which we are authorized to replace governments that fail to provide such security. Thus Locke:

> The state of nature has a law of nature to govern it, which obliges every one; and reason, which is that law, teaches all mankind who will but consult it that, being all equal and independent, no one ought to harm another in his life, health, liberty, or possessions. For men being all the workmanship of one omnipotent and infinitely wise Maker—all the servants of one sovereign Master, sent into the world by His order, and about His business—they are His property. . . . [S]haring all in one community of nature, there cannot be supposed any such subordination among us that may authorize us to destroy one another, as if we were made for one another's uses, as the inferior ranks of creatures are for ours. Every one, as he is bound to preserve himself . . . so by the like reason, when his own preservation comes not in competition, ought he, as much as he can, to preserve the rest of mankind, and may not, unless it be to do justice on an offender, take away or impair the life, or what tends to the preservation of the life, the liberty, health, limb, or goods of another.[16]

Instruction by the law of nature, which is reason, can take place anywhere and at any time, not only in the state of nature. Certainly the Founding Fathers thought they had consulted it when they made the Revolution and when they framed and ratified the Constitution.

Locke brings into focus that teaching of the Declaration of Independence that defines man's place in the universe in terms of his distance from God no less than his distance from the beast. Locke believes, with Hamlet, that God has "fix'd his canon 'gainst self-slaughter."[17] Self-preservation is not only the first law of nature but also an obligation imposed by God. According to Locke, it is both a right intrinsic to ourselves and a duty we owe to God to preserve our lives, liberties, and property. But it is also a duty, when our own preservation comes not into question, to do nothing to impair the life, liberty, or property of others. It is a dictate of prudence and self-interest to respect the lives and property of others, as we would have others respect our own. That human beings belong to God has as its correlate that they do not belong to anyone else. God's property right is exclusive unless he deeds it or otherwise transfers it to someone else. Hence the heavy irony in the Continental Congress's invitation to the king and Parliament of Great Britain, in the Declaration of the Causes and Necessity of Taking Up Arms in 1775, to produce evidence that God had invested them with such a right. Of course, it follows inexorably that the right of property in black slaves in America was no less against the laws of God and nature than the right claimed by the British government in the American colonies. This truth, which none of the Founding Fathers ever denied, is what made the state of nature anathema to Calhoun.

In Calhoun, there is no doctrine of individual rights apart from the positive law of any given community. He does not recognize any criterion outside the political process to which men can appeal to justify rebellion against tyranny. Of course rebellions and revolutions do occur. And if the slaves become masters, and the masters slaves, then (as before) everyone still occupies the status he deserves. Men's rights in any given society are a consequence of the structure of power in that society. In the final analysis, whatever men lack in power, they lack in right. Consider the following:

> [T]he quantum of power on the part of the government, and of liberty on that of individuals, instead of being equal in all cases, must necessarily be very unequal among different people, according to their different conditions. For just as in proportion as a people are ignorant, stupid, debased, corrupt, exposed to violence within and danger from without, the power necessary for government to possess, in order to preserve society against anarchy and destruction, becomes greater and greater, and individual liberty less and less, until the lowest condition is reached, when absolute and despotic power becomes necessary on the part of government, and individual liberty extinct. So, on the contrary, just as a people rise in the scale of intelligence, virtue, and patriotism, and the more perfectly they become acquainted with the nature of government, the ends for which it was ordered, and how it ought to be administered, and the less tendency to violence and disorder within, and danger from abroad, the power necessary for government becomes less and less, and individual liberty greater and greater. Instead then of all men having the same right to liberty and equality, as is claimed by those who hold that they are born free and equal, liberty is the noble and highest reward bestowed on mental and moral development, combined with favorable circumstances. Instead then of liberty and equality being born with man; instead of all men and all classes and descriptions being equally entitled to them, they are prizes to be won, and are in their most perfect state, not only the highest reward that can be bestowed on our race, but the most difficult to be won— and when won, the most difficult to be preserved.

Here is the beginning of Calhoun's forensic summation. What Calhoun says about the relationship of individual liberty and governmental power varying according to the different conditions of different peoples and about liberty and equality being the most difficult of all prizes to be won or preserved is entirely consistent with the doctrines of Jefferson and Lincoln. But far from refuting the premise that all men are born or created free and equal, these conclusions are in fact drawn from that premise.

The freedom and equality of rights propounded in the American Revolution were never understood to describe conditions belonging to or enjoyed by human beings without struggle or effort. They were not "entitlements" in the sense of gifts bestowed from above. They were rather like the land promised to Israel by God—if they could conquer it. When they were announced to the world, the American people were engaged in a great and desperate war. When the Signers of the Declaration pledged to each other their lives, fortunes, and sacred honor, they knew as well as Calhoun could ever imagine that they were seeking "the highest reward that can be bestowed on our race." That reward was measured precisely by the rights they enjoyed by the laws of reason and nature. When the king and Parliament of Great Britain declared their right to bind the colonies "in all cases whatsoever," they claimed in effect that the colonies were their property. The Continental Congress responded by denying that, under the laws of nature and of reason, any human being can be the property of another. They did not say that Parliament or barbarians or savages could not pass such a law or any other laws based upon force or fraud. What they said was that such laws do not bind any individual or people who have the force to resist them. There may be compulsions originating in force or fraud, as in the "gloomy age of ignorance and superstition." But these are not the compulsions of a civilized conscience, born of the recognition of "the just powers of government." Civilization means the recognition of right as distinct from force, fraud, or ignorance.

The principles of the Declaration can be implemented only to the extent that they are understood and embraced. We recall again Washington's pronouncement that the American governments were formed at a time when the rights of man were better understood than at any time hitherto. It is axiomatic then that free government is possible only in proportion to the degree of the enlightenment of its citizens. As Jefferson wrote, "If a nation expects to be ignorant and free in a state of civilization, it expects what never was and never will be."[18] Calhoun speaks of the necessity for a people to become more perfectly acquainted with "the nature of government, the ends for which it was ordered, and how it ought to be administered." It is precisely these purposes that are served by the doctrine of the state of nature and of the law of reason and nature inherent in it. We will discover Calhoun's alternative to this doctrine shortly in the *Disquisition*. In the Oregon speech he merely assumes its existence. But if knowledge of the nature of government instructs us that man is "impelled irresistibly" into government and that tyranny is always better than anarchy, we must wonder how that knowledge redounds to the benefit of the oppressed. On what principle do a people go about altering or abolishing a government that refuses to allow them the liberty to which they are entitled? If they are resisting enslavement, what do they say, to themselves or to a candid world, to prove that theirs is a just cause? We are reminded of Lincoln's Rev. Dr. Ross, sitting in the shade, considering in his mind whether Sambo, who is toiling in the burning sun, should go free or remain a slave.[19] Except for the moral armament of the law of reason and nature, those with the power to enslave others will always proclaim their right to do so.

Calhoun justly observes that as a people rises in the scale of virtue and intelligence, the power necessary for their government decreases, and the sphere of individual liberty increases. In the *Disquisition*, as we shall see, he praises republican government, much as Lincoln would do, precisely for encouraging individuals to rise by their own efforts in the scale of society. Yet he never contemplates the slaves being permitted by their own efforts to rise in that scale. If slavery was, as Calhoun and his followers sometimes maintained, a school of civilization, it was not a school from which the slaves were ever to graduate. In fact, it was a prison to which they and their posterity were to be committed forever. Calhoun seems to suppose that the "quantum" of power in any given government and the individual liberty (or lack thereof) of its citizens (or subjects) are always what they ought to be, collapsing the distinction between power and right or between the "is" and the "ought." The existing condition of free and slave is taken as evidence of that to which free and slave are entitled. If that evidence is to be accepted, however, the divine right of kings (in one or another of its versions) should have remained the prevailing form of political right.

To repeat: the very purpose of the idea of the state of nature is to provide a rationale by which to understand the nature of government and by which we are instructed in the difference between power and right. Free government has its beginning, whether chronological or ontological, in the unanimous consent enjoined by the law of nature and reason upon human beings who, being naturally equal in authority, transform themselves into a civil society with lawful government. Those so consenting must understand a priori the nature of government *and understand each other to understand it.* This mutual understanding—or equality—is identical to that implicit in any valid contract, in which each party knows what is expected from himself as well as what he expects from the other. The contract that forms civil society, an agreement of each with all and of all with each, both empowers and limits the rule of the majority. For example, it is contrary to reason and nature for government to have any power over the rights of conscience. Consequently, a man's religious opinions can have no more bearing upon his civil rights than his opinions in physics or geometry. It is this kind of limitation that the law of nature and reason imposes upon majority rule. Thus equality of civil and political rights becomes the operational foundation of constitutional majority rule and of the just powers of government. This law of reason and nature is ontologically antecedent to all positive law. It is therefore the vital formative and motivating element in the minds of citizens in any genuinely civil society *at any time* and does not belong merely to some remote period in the past. That is implied in the "frequent recurrence to fundamental principles" that was an axiomatic premise of the constitutionalism of the American Founding—the constitutionalism rejected by Calhoun.

When Washington spoke of the gloomy age of superstition, he certainly included (together with primitive peoples) the feudal order, in which inferior classes were subordinated as if they were inferior species. Washington, in common with all the Founding generation, also had in mind the religious wars of the sixteenth and seventeenth centuries, in which Protestants and Catholics slaughtered each other as mercilessly as the savages denounced in the Declaration of Independence. Religious fanaticism extinguished the perception of a common human nature. Such fanaticism, no less than tribal consciousness, can therefore make majority rule impossible, since it is against the law of reason and nature to think that the questions that divided Protestants and Catholics (or Christians, Jews, and Muslims) could be decided by a vote. The civil religion, by which everyone has by nature a right of self-preservation and a duty, under God, to respect that right in others, is therefore a necessary foundation of a government in which individual liberty will be respected and cultivated. It is true that the free exercise of religion will of necessity protect atheists no less than those of differing religious persuasions. As is evident from what we have quoted of Locke's argument, however, atheism of itself can offer no protection either to itself or to believers.[20]

A combination of majority rule and minority rights is then possible only in a state of enlightened civilization. But as John Stuart Mill wrote in his essay *On Liberty*,

Despotism is a legitimate mode of government in dealing with barbarians, provided the end be their improvement, and the means justified by actually effecting that end. Liberty as a principle has no application to any state of things anterior to the time when mankind have become capable of being improved by free and equal discussions.[21]

Recognition of the law of reason and nature, condensed into the proposition that all men are created equal, is the necessary condition for being capable of improvement through free and equal discussion. It implies that the moral universe is constituted by the whole family of man, as does the injunction to do unto others as we would have others do unto us. When human beings agree to form a civil society, therefore, they do so only with those with whom there is that mutual recognition and understanding. Civil societies are not formed by or with barbarians or savages. When the latter come into contact with the civilized in such a way that there must be a relationship of ruling and being ruled, the civilized may have to govern the uncivilized without their consent. Even extreme forms of despotism may be justified if they are necessary to stamp out such practices as human sacrifice or cannibalism. The uncivilized may not, however, be governed as if they were an inferior species, existing only for the convenience of the superior. The civilized must recognize the humanity of the uncivilized and the equal rights inherent in that humanity, in the same sense that adults recognize the humanity of children prior to their reaching the "age of consent." Properly understood, the age of consent, like the state of nature, is not merely chronological` but represents the intelligence and maturity that makes possible a valid contract between two rational beings. The mentally retarded or anyone who is non compos mentis is incapable of making a contract. For a will to be valid, the testator must be of sound mind, since senility no less than juvenility can deprive someone of the power of consent. Notwithstanding the fact that qualifications for voting and other privileges of citizenship have often been used disingenuously, a free society always has the inherent right to limit these privileges to those whose moral and intellectual qualifications are sanctioned by the laws of nature and of reason.

The doctrine of the state of nature, we repeat, presumes legitimate government to have its origin in a valid contract entered into by the maturely rational. Thus it enables us to discriminate, as Calhoun says we must, between the different levels of government appropriate for the different levels of civilization. Only if barbarians are taught that they have a birthright as human beings can they cease to be barbarians and rise in the scale of civilization. And only as they do so can they begin to aim at the ends inherent in their nature.

According to Calhoun in his Oregon speech, the difficulties in achieving or preserving the "high prizes" of liberty and equality have been vastly increased

by the dangerous error I have attempted to expose, that all men are born free and equal, as if those high qualities belonged to man without effort to acquire them, and to all equally alike, regardless of their intellectual or moral condition. The attempt to carry into practice this, the most dangerous of all political errors, and to bestow on all, without regard to their fitness either to acquire or maintain liberty, that unbounded and individual liberty supposed to belong to man in the hypothetical and misnamed state of nature, has done more to retard the cause of liberty and civilization, and is doing more at present, than all other causes combined. While it is powerful to pull down governments, it is still more powerful to prevent their construction on proper principles. It is the leading cause among those which have been overthrown, threatening thereby the quarter of the globe most advanced in progress and civilization with hopeless anarchy, to be followed by military despotism. Nor are we exempt from its disorganizing effects.

But again, no sane person has ever argued that any people would or could enjoy the equal rights to life, liberty, or property without effort or without regard to their intellectual or moral condition. The equality of man, as Lincoln repeatedly emphasized, is an equality of rights, not of rewards. It is an equal right to try for the honest rewards of life, unconfined by arbitrary and irrational restraints.

Calhoun views European history from the perspective of the Holy Alliance that defeated Napoleon in 1814 and that had ever since attempted vainly to restore the European order that had ruled before the French Revolution. That order was characterized by divine right monarchy and by the union of altar and throne. It was an order of inherited rank and privilege and of enforced conformity to established religions. It was an order in which there was a place for everyone but in which everyone was kept in his place. It was an order that could not survive the dynamics of nascent capitalism and industrial revolution. A new world was coming into being in which individual merit could not be permanently barred by the absurd and archaic privileged order of the ancien régime. In Europe, the demands of this new order were backed by the rising power of new wealth. But the logic of these demands, whether in Europe or America, was not limited to what might be conceded to such power. Hereditary privileges, whether of kings by divine right or hereditary aristocrats, were indefensible in the court of reason. So also was the enslavement of blacks in America.

In the conflict between the French Revolution and the ancien régime, Calhoun's loyalties are divided, but irrationally. He believed in a career open to talents—but for white men only. Every white man of the South, we recall, by birth and inheritance, had "a position and pride of character of which neither poverty nor misfortune [could] deprive him."[22] In Calhoun's version of the Holy Alliance, the defense of altar and throne was replaced by the defense of slavery, and the divine right of kings by state (or white) rights.

There is an old story that in Napoleon's armies, every corporal had a marshal's baton in his knapsack. In his commitment to merit without regard to inherited class distinctions, Napoleon was a true child of the French Revolution. Under Napoleon, careers were open to talents. But Napoleonic egalitarianism, unlike the American, was imposed from the top down. It was, if anything, more despotic than the monarchies that it replaced. It revived the Caesarism of the ancient Roman Empire in all its glory. Unlike the inherited titles of the European kings Napoleon drove from their thrones, Napoleon's title was the plebiscite. Napoleon's uncontrolled exercise of power, like Caesar's, was legitimated by the

423

uncontrolled sovereignty of the people he claimed to represent.

We recall that Lincoln in his Lyceum speech of 1838 had warned against the danger of "an Alexander, a Caesar, or a Napoleon," the great military geniuses who were also the great destroyers of republics. Those who belonged "to the family of the lion or the tribe of the eagle" will seek distinction, he said, "whether at the expense of emancipating slaves, or enslaving freemen."[23] Lincoln implied, long before the charge was made against him, that the emancipation of the slaves might be accomplished by the enslavement of the free. Every step of Lincoln's antislavery career was governed, on the one hand, by the necessity of the recognition of the Negro's humanity and of his right to life and liberty and, on the other, by the equal necessity to bring about that recognition by the consent of the governed. Lincoln was conscious, very early in his political career, of the possibility of a Napoleonic solution to the problem of slavery. But he did not think it was to the ultimate advantage of the slaves, any more than of the free, to be invited into a regime of equality presided over by a Napoleon. Lincoln, like Tocqueville, was aware that the indiscriminate appeal to the idea of equality could lead to oppression as well as to freedom. That is why we must take pains here to discriminate between the idea of equality that dominated the French Revolution as distinct from that which dominated the American.[24] We must see that in confounding the two, it is Calhoun who commits a most false and dangerous political error.

The French Revolution was dominated by a popularization of Rousseau's doctrine of the general will. In the *Social Contract*, that will was discoverable only in a political community of very small size—probably smaller than Aristotle's outsize limit of ten thousand citizens for a polity. Its citizens would have been formed by a great legislator, like a Moses, a Solon, or a Lycurgus. Because of the severe discipline of the laws, they would learn when voting always to ask, in their inward souls, whether a proposal was for the common good, rather than whether it would be good for them individually. And the decisions in these very small communities would be made in conditions of such intimacy that the minority could always believe that the will of the majority was really their own. In such a communal setting, and under such severe internal discipline, the question of minority rights would hardly arise. But as Rousseau's teaching was popularized and its stringent limitations passed over, the general will of the people expressed en masse became a sovereign that could brook no limitation.[25] Under such conditions it was easy for minority rights to come to be viewed as assaults upon majority rule and dissent to be equated with treason.

The idea of sovereignty in the American Revolution was fundamentally different. The role of the superhuman legislator is played by the laws of reason and nature. These laws imposed severe limits upon the authority of the people. The Constitution of 1787 was necessary to overcome the imbecility of the government of the Union under the Articles of Confederation, but the autonomy of the states, within their constitutionally circumscribed sphere, remained. Political parties arose in America, and to some extent they represented an informal centralization of what was constitutionally decentralized. The president, as head of a party, might exert an influence upon the members of his party in Congress (and out of Congress) that he could not exert merely by reason of his constitutional powers. This influence might wax and wane according to circumstances. But unlike the Jacobins and Napoleon, the president's inducements of persuasion were limited by law and did not include death, exile, or expropriation.

Napoleonic despotism could be regarded as "democratic" because it emanated from the general will as confirmed in the plebiscite. No such justification of despotism was possible in the American mind that had found its expression in the Declaration of Independence. The will of the majority was supreme, but only within its constitutionally defined domain. Slavery could be tolerated as a necessity and as an evil to be overcome, but it could never be justified. The same principles that condemned any other manifestation of majority tyranny condemned slavery. Calhoun could not see this.

An allusion to the Rousseauian (or Jacobin) idea of equality is made in the tenth *Federalist*, in the context of Madison's quest for a solution to the problem of faction—a problem that is peculiarly that of a free society: "There are two methods of curing the mischiefs of faction: the one by removing its causes; the other, by controlling its effects. There are again two methods of removing the causes of faction: the one by destroying the liberty essential to its existence; the other, by giving to every citizen the same opinions, the same passions, and the same interests." It is this second method of removing the causes of faction that corresponds to that of the French Revolution, as it does to the later revolutions of National Socialism and Marxist Communism. But this method is the profoundest of all destructions of liberty. Here is Madison's commentary:

> As long as the reason of man continues fallible, and he is at liberty to exercise it, different opinions will be formed. As long as the connection subsists between his reason and his self-love, his opinions and his passions will have a reciprocal influence on each other; and the former will be objects to which the latter will attach themselves. The diversity in the faculties of men, from which the rights of property originate, is not less an insuperable obstacle to a uniformity of interests. The protection of these faculties is the first object of government. . . . The latent causes of faction are thus sown in the nature of man.[26]

That the causes of faction are sown in human nature would be denied by Rousseau and later by Marx. They would say that the reciprocal influence of man's self-love and his reason, and the corruption of the latter by the former, has its origin not in nature but in private property. For Marx, the abolition of private property would cause the abolition of human selfishness. For Rousseau, the institution of the general will would accomplish the same end. For Madison, as for Locke, the origin of private property is to be found in human nature because it has its origin in the law of self-preservation. In acting to preserve himself and his family, man labors to produce food, clothing, and shelter. These acquisitions are as naturally his as the bodies and souls they are meant to sustain. Thus Lincoln's oft repeated maxim that every human being has the natural right to put into his mouth the bread that his own hand has earned, without the leave of anyone else.

The attempt to solve the problem of faction by giving to every citizen the same opinions, passions, and interests has attracted political speculators for more than two thousand years. In Plato's *Republic,* Socrates is represented as proposing the abolition of the family and private property to the end that the guardians have no private (or factional) interests to conflict with their devotion to the common good.[27] The guardians were not even supposed to know who their own children were, so that they would say mine and thine equally of all the women and children. Madison and Plato agree that the root of faction is private property and the root of private property is the family. However, to attempt to eliminate faction by abolishing property would be like abolishing air to prevent fire. In rejecting the communism of the *Republic,* Aristotle pointed out that it is not possible for men to remain indifferent to the women who bear their children or for men or women to be indifferent to the children who are really theirs.[28] Whether mistakenly or not, nature will prompt them to claim their own, and private families and private property will return. The collapse, sooner or later, of all communist regimes is testimony to the inexorable power of nature manifested in the family and private property.

The project of the French Jacobins, like their National Socialist and Marxist–Leninist successors, was to employ a combination of terror and propaganda in order to overcome human nature, so that the "citizens" would not only prefer the common good to their private good but would not even believe themselves to have any private good apart from the common good. There would be no recognition of any such "diversity in the faculties of men" that could constitute an "obstacle to a uniformity of interests." Rousseau taught that man was by nature good but had been corrupted by society, and the Jacobins thought that under the aegis of the general will, corruption would be overcome and goodness restored. Madison's toleration of faction and his nonutopian constitutionalism were unacceptable. Propaganda and terror took their place.

Nothing illustrates better the difference between the spirits of the French and American Revolutions than the following passage from Aristotle's *Politics:* "[I]f the poor take advantage of their greater numbers to divide up the property of the rich, is this not unjust? By Zeus, it may be said, it was done justly because it was done by the sovereign authority. Then what may be pronounced the extreme of injustice?"[29] According to the "democrats" as here presented, to divide the property of the rich is lawful if it is done by act of the sovereign people. If we think of the decree of the democracy as that of the general will, then we cannot think of any higher authority that can rightfully contradict or countermand it. If we consult the laws of nature and of reason, however, we can say with Locke and Madison that majority rule exists to protect property, not to confiscate it. Those who suffer arbitrary loss of property, whether from a thief or from a government, have a right to appeal for redress to the laws of nature and to the right of revolution.

Calhoun, we have seen, confounded Locke's state of nature with Rousseau's. According to Locke, the state of nature is prepolitical but not presocial. So far from being prerational, it is governed by the law of reason. So far from being a part only of a remote past, it is present in the consciousness of every citizen when he thinks of his rights and duties. In Rousseau, we find the state of nature in a distant prehistoric past. Man in that state is solitary, and hence both presocial and prerational. In Rousseau's state of nature, man is not recognizably distinct from nonhuman species. Language and reason are not natural but acquired.[30] What man possessed distinctively in the state of nature, what no other animal possessed, was freedom. That freedom became manifest when he began to rise above his nature and become recognizably human. In contemplating man in the state of nature, Rousseau discovered the distinction of his species to consist in freedom from the limitations that nature had imposed on all other species. Reason in man arose in response to a freedom antecedent to reason and was the servant of the passion for freedom. Henceforth the form of the will that enabled man to acquire reason would determine the form of reason. Thus Rousseau laid the foundation for Kant and Hegel and for German idealism generally—of which, as we shall see, Calhoun became an epigone.

Suffice it for the present to say that under the influence of Rousseau, rationality would be identified with the form of the will, rather than with an act of knowing intrinsic to the mind itself. Thus Calhoun's substitute for Lockean–Madisonian constitutionalism will be the concurrent majority, which is another formulation of the general will. We find then this ironic anomaly: Calhoun begins his diatribe against the state of nature doctrine of the Founding Fathers by mistakenly identifying it with Rousseau. But he himself will end as a disciple of the very doctrine he denounces. Here in the Oregon speech, however, he insists that all the turmoil, destruction, tyranny, and anarchy caused by the wars of the French Revolution and Napoleon are traceable to that same false and dangerous error that was at the heart of the American Revolution: the idea that all men are born free and equal. For some unexplained reason, Europe experienced the evils of this error before America, despite the fact that the American Revolution preceded the French. It is notable that Calhoun does not attribute any of the evils of the wars of the French Revolution to absolute monarchy, feudal privilege, or established religion. It is all laid at the door of the democratic impulse embodied in the idea of human equality.

> We now begin to experience the danger of admitting so great an error to have a place in the declaration of our independence. For a long time it lay dormant; but in the process of time it began to germinate, and produce its poisonous fruits. It had strong hold on the mind of Mr. Jefferson, the author of that document, which caused him to take an utterly false view of the subordinate relation of the black to the white race in the South; and to hold, in consequence, that the former, though utterly unqualified to possess liberty, were as fully entitled to both liberty and equality as the latter; and that to deprive them of it was unjust and immoral. To this error, his proposition to exclude slavery from the territory northwest of the Ohio may be traced, and to that of the ordinance of '87, and through it the deep and dangerous agitation which now threatens to ingulf, and will certainly ingulf, if not speedily settled, our political institutions, and involve the country in countless woes.

Here Calhoun's Oregon speech ends, predicting civil war and the dissolution of the Union if the equal right of slave states in the territories is not acknowledged and settled to their satisfaction. We may acknowledge the accuracy of Calhoun's foresight. But we should also recognize the element of self-fulfilling prophecy. Calhoun's doctrine went a long way toward bringing about the events he predicted. He, more than anyone else, propounded that "ingenious sophism" by which the public mind of the South was persuaded that secession was a constitutional right. And the sine qua non of that sophism was the alleged erroneousness of the doctrine of equality as set forth in both the Massachusetts constitution of 1780 and the Declaration of Independence. In the greater part of this speech, Calhoun has treated the Massachusetts formulation as if it was primary and that of the Declaration secondary, although this is the reverse of their chronological order. This chronology is largely irrelevant, however, since the number of documents of the Revolutionary and Founding era displaying the same idea is virtually limitless. Calhoun himself testified to this when he said that "it had become an axiom in the minds of a vast majority on both sides of the Atlantic . . . repeated daily from tongue to tongue as an established and incontrovertible truth." It is therefore absurd for Calhoun to place a particular responsibility upon Jefferson for its currency. It might indeed have had less currency if it had not been given place in the Declaration, but it would not have had that place had it not already enjoyed an overwhelming currency. The Declaration was the public manifesto of a whole people and was taken then as it has been ever since—except by the defenders of slavery—as an authentic expression of the mind of that people. The error, if such it was, was not peculiarly Jefferson's. In the premises, however, the most false and dangerous of all political errors was that of Calhoun himself in confounding Rousseau's state of nature with Locke's and the general will of the Jacobins with the laws of nature and of reason of the American Founders.

Part II

Calhoun's political science is founded upon his belief that he has successfully refuted the "central idea" of the Declaration of Independence. We have examined that alleged refutation as we believe Socrates or Lincoln would have examined it, and we have found it utterly devoid of any ground in reason. Yet Calhoun built an elaborate superstructure upon his conviction that his refutation was itself irrefutable. He is today widely regarded as an eminent contributor to the development of political science, even apart from the political uses of his doctrine in the antebellum period and the Civil War itself. It is an understatement to say that Calhoun's ideas have had a far greater currency than Lincoln's, not because of their intrinsic soundness, but because (as we saw in chapter 2) they fit within the framework of the historicism and positivism that have dominated the intellectual world of the West in the intervening years.

We saw in the Cornerstone speech that for Alexander Stephens it was a sufficient justification of slavery to say that it rested upon a scientific foundation, even though he never attempted to say of what that foundation consisted. For Stephens it was a sufficient refutation of the Founders' belief in human equality to say that it had become anachronistic. Hence Calhoun did not really need to disprove the proposition "that all men are created equal." All he needed to say, as many since him have discovered, was that his political science was more scientific than what preceded it. The widespread and uncontradicted opinion that the nonhuman natural sciences are progressive had created a presumption in favor of the view that anything called science is progressive. This in turn had created a presumption in favor of any claim that represented itself as proceeding from progressive scientific thought.[31]

∼

Calhoun's *Summae*, the testaments of his life and work and the legacy upon which the case for the Confederate cause may be said above all to rest, are his two posthumous works, *A Disquisition on Government* and *A Discourse on the*

Constitution and Government of the United States. Published in 1851, they fortified the convictions of the leaders of the Southern cause in the last decade before the Civil War and have remained the principal source of intellectual justification, as well as emotional conviction, for those who have remained faithful to that cause in all the time since Appomatox.[32] During the Civil War, these books convinced so notable a liberal as Lord Acton that the cause of the Confederacy was the cause of the defense of minority rights against majority tyranny. Even today, there are many who believe that Calhoun's is the classic formulation of the problem of minority rights in a constitutional republic or democracy and that his solution to the problem represents a progress in political science beyond that of the *Federalist.* Indeed, many say that it has not been surpassed by any subsequent work and that it remains the theoretical foundation of the constitutional defense of any minority against the tyranny of any majority. In this sense, one might call Calhoun the founding father of "interest group liberalism" in twentieth-century American political science. Calhoun's theoretical writings are a landmark in the transition from individual rights to group rights as the ground of constitutionalism and the rule of law. On the surface, it would appear paradoxical that this most famous advocate of the "positive good" theory of slavery is also the chief architect of what many believe to be the most sophisticated theory of the defense of minority rights. However, reflection upon the substitution of group interests for individual rights as the focus of constitutional protection will, we believe, dispel in the end any appearance of inconsistency.[33]

The extent of the actual influence on our political history of the ideas in Calhoun's two books is difficult to judge. But for Calhoun himself, they represented the telos, or end, that explained in systematic form the thought animating his speeches and writings from the nullification crisis (beginning with the "Exposition and Protest" of 1828) onward. To use Aristotle's terminology, although of Calhoun's works these may be the last in order of becoming, they are first in order of being, as they are intended to represent the perfection of the understanding that informed what had gone before. Lincoln notwithstanding, the *Disquisition* and the *Discourse* represent one of the most remarkable attempts—perhaps the most remarkable since Cicero composed his *Republic* and *Laws*—of a statesman at or near the center of great political events for over forty years to crown his career with a comprehensive theoretical and historical account of the informing principles of his political words and deeds.

As a philosopher–statesman, Calhoun was of course following the tradition of the Founding, in which Jefferson, Madison, Hamilton, Adams, and others were men in whom the conjunction of philosophic reflection and historical study had laid the foundation for political action. The Declaration of Independence itself affirms the unity of philosophy and statesmanship: It is on the authority of "the laws of nature and of nature's God" that the originating actions of the United States—separation from Great Britain and union with each other—are proclaimed and justified. These "laws of nature" are a discovery of political philosophy in a line of development that runs from Aristotle and Cicero through Thomas Aquinas, Hooker, and Locke to Jefferson. In Calhoun's writings, "laws of nature" do indeed appear; but they are laws of cause and effect. They are not prescriptive or normative, as in the political philosophy of the Declaration. Calhoun, in his self-understanding, is emphatically more scientifically "modern" than Jefferson. Calhoun believed that philosophy and science, represented in part by his own person, had progressed to a higher level than in the generation of the Founding Fathers. Theirs was a foundation upon which he proposed to build; but there was no Lincolnian veneration of "our fathers who brought forth this nation." Any presumption of authority is reserved for science and the improved understanding of nature, both human and nonhuman, that results from the progress of science. But Calhoun does appeal to the *practice* of the Founding even while rejecting its *theory*.[34] In this he reminds us of Machiavelli, who appealed to examples of renowned and admirable political actions drawn from the histories of ancient cities as models to be imitated, while rejecting the classical political philosophy that had hitherto been regarded as the proper ground for understanding those examples. This resemblance between Calhoun and Machiavelli is perhaps most evident in Calhoun's discussion of the Roman constitution.

~

All of Calhoun's politics, theory and practice, point to the doctrine of the concurrent majority as the constitutional principle that prevents tyranny and anarchy and that elevates the conduct of government with respect to justice and the common good. Within the framework of American constitutionalism, the principle of the concurrent majority depended upon the right of secession for its efficacy. Unless a state could threaten to secede, its right to arrest or nullify actions of the central government said to threaten minority rights would be barren. We saw in Lincoln's inaugural a lucid demonstration that secession could lead only to anarchy and that the rule of a constitutional majority was the only alternative either to anarchy or to tyranny. According to Calhoun, however, this alternative was itself the path to tyranny or anarchy, and the constitutional right of secession the only means to prevent them. There could not be a more direct opposition of views.

According to Calhoun, the excellence of any regime is to be measured by the degree to which it implements the principle of the concurrent majority. Its perfect implementation (were such a thing possible) would produce the best regime. But

431

its implementation in particular cases to the greatest degree that particular circumstances admit would produce the best possible regime in those circumstances. Stated in its simplest form, the concurrent majority gives to each minority entitled to consideration a veto over the action of the government. (What it is that entitles a minority to consideration is a question that we must leave to one side for the time being.) This means that in order to act, the majority must solicit and receive the acquiescence of each such minority. Thus it is prevented from acting in a way that any such minority believes is destructive of its vital interests. Calhoun thinks that a popular republic is the best foundation for the implementation of this principle.[35] But the principle operates the same way whether the ruler is a king, a nobility, or a patriciate. In such cases, it would be a minority soliciting the acquiescence of a majority or of other minorities. In a government of the concurrent majority, only the community of interests of majorities and minorities—which is what the common good is presumed to be—can therefore actually govern.

Calhoun's doctrine bears an obvious resemblance to Rousseau's general will. The ruling principle is a form of the will, not of reason. Nor is it a form of the will upon which reason has been impressed. In Rousseau's doctrine of the general will, justice is divorced from wisdom, or rather wisdom is itself divorced from understanding what is intrinsically right or good. By the Declaration of Independence, the just powers of government are derived from the consent of the governed. It is sometimes overlooked that, by this doctrine, consent can authorize only *just* powers. Unless the governed are enlightened such that they understand a priori the distinction between just and unjust powers, consent alone will not make a government legitimate. Except upon prudential grounds, the governed may not consent to what is intrinsically unjust, as Lincoln argued against Douglas. The reconciliation of conflicting interests must ultimately proceed from a conception of right that is independent of the interests themselves. But Rousseau introduced into political philosophy the idea that political justice is to be found in the form of the will, rather than in the reason that informs the will. More than anyone else, Rousseau is Calhoun's intellectual progenitor.

Kant's categorical imperative is the clearest example of the kind of influence that Rousseau brought to bear upon Calhoun: *So act that the maxim of your will may be a universal law.* By this rule, someone would be obliged to tell a would-be murderer the truth as to where to find his intended victim, because if everyone always lied, no one would be believed. Lying as a universal principle would be self-defeating. Lying under some circumstances but not others cannot be made into a universal law. By this dispensation, a prudent regard for the outcome of one's actions is inconsistent with morality. The fact that an imprudent disregard for the outcome of one's actions may be catastrophic is of no consequence. It is the form of the will, not the consequence of one's actions, that constitutes morality. The Declaration of Independence, on the other hand, with its Aristotelian emphasis upon the dictates of prudence, presupposes an exercise of the cognitive function of the mind as preceding and guiding the proper exercise of the will to a beneficial end or purpose.

Like the categorical imperative, Calhoun's concurrent majority is not related to any particular end or good. Like the categorical imperative, it generalizes the will of the constituent interests and in so doing makes them "rational." Each interest within society must solicit the agreement of every other interest, with the understanding that the government cannot act until all the competing interests have reached a consensus. In a simulacrum of Rousseau's general will, the will of all becomes the will of each. As we shall see, Calhoun attributes every political virtue and political good to this universalized or concurrent will. No attempt is ever made, however, to show that such a cause would have such effects.

~

On the surface, Calhoun's doctrine of the concurrent majority appears to correspond with the theory of checks and balances of American constitutionalism as set forth in the *Federalist*. Is there not, for example, a concurrent majority in the requirement of agreement between the two houses of the Congress for legislation to reach the president? Is there not a concurrent majority in the requirement of agreement between the president and Congress (with two-thirds in Congress being required to override the president's veto) for a bill to become a law? Is not the requirement of the "advice and consent" of three-fourths of the Senate for treaties at least a partial embodiment of the concurrent majority? Is not the requirement of Senate approval for the appointment of judges and of the principal executive and military officers an exemplification of the same idea? Is not judicial review another? Most dramatic of all expressions of concurrent majoritarianism are the methods of amending the Constitution. In light of these examples, we must ask why Calhoun rejected the arguments of the *Federalist* as constituting an adequate defense of minority rights.

Fundamental to the defense of the Constitution by the *Federalist* is the theory of the "extended republic" propounded in the famous tenth paper. This theory by itself says nothing about constitutional checks and balances. Rather it finds a defense against the tyranny of the majority in the much larger republic that would result from the closer union of the states. The "extended republic" provided an underlying substructure more favorable to republican freedom than could be found in the smaller republics of the states or in the even smaller republics of antiquity. Madison argued that the number and variety of "factions" in the whole

United States was such that it was much "less probable that a majority of the whole will have a common motive to invade the rights of other citizens." And even if such a motive were to exist, "it will be more difficult for all who feel it to discover their own strength, and to act in unison with each other."[36] As the variety of interests grows greater, and as their local situations are more widely separated, any ruling majority necessarily becomes more complex. To form such a majority, it becomes necessary to combine, and therefore to find common ground among, the interests of more and more minorities. Hence it becomes increasingly improbable that any majority will be destructive of minority rights or interests. Indeed, it becomes increasingly improbable that the composition of the majority coalition will differ so much from that of the minority, since both will be competing for many of the same minorities. Thus it becomes increasingly improbable that a majority will ever possess the motive to invade minority rights and injure minority interests. The element of "concurrence" as between the different interests is apparently to be found in the manner in which a majority is formed in an extended republic.

In order to understand the difference between the arguments of the *Federalist* and Calhoun concerning the problem of minority rights and majority rule, we must take notice of a phenomenon that rose to prominence in the interval from 1787 to 1850. That phenomenon is the political party. Political parties, in the sense in which we have come to understand the term, were not anticipated in the *Federalist*. The nature of party government is such that an extraconstitutional body, the political party, may strongly influence (if not actually control) the manner in which the constitutional organs will operate. It may, for example, extend its control over the constitutionally separated branches of government so as to undermine, if not nullify, that separation. The president, members of Congress, and perhaps even federal judges may, as fellow party members, be possessed of an overriding common interest and subject to a discipline unknown to the Constitution itself. Such interest and discipline may induce a cooperation between them of precisely the kind that separation of powers was supposed to prevent. When the Alien and Sedition Acts were passed in 1798, the presidency, both houses of Congress, and the federal courts were all in the hands of the Federalists. Hence the appeal to the states in the Virginia and Kentucky Resolutions.

Madison declares in the fifty-first *Federalist* that "the great security against a gradual concentration of the several powers in the same department ['the very definition of tyranny'] consists in giving to those who administer each department the necessary constitutional means and personal motives to resist encroachments of the others." He continues: "Ambition must be made to counteract ambition. The interest of the man must be connected with the constitutional rights of the place."[37] But suppose the "interest of the man" as a party leader or, for that matter, party follower is greater than his interest as a constitutional officeholder? If this happens, his "interest" is no longer a guardian of "the constitutional rights of [his] place." In the later course of American history, we have become familiar with the great urban political machines, such as Tammany Hall, in which the great "bosses," sometimes holding no offices of their own, hired and fired mayors, city commissioners, city councils, and municipal judges. Putting this in context, scholars of American government have found that within our federal system, constitutional separation of powers at the local level has been so extensive as to disperse political authority to the point that what began as the prevention of tyranny ended frequently in anarchy or near anarchy. Effective government at the local level would then have been impossible had not the political party informally aggregated the power legally dispersed. We tend to see the old-time big-city machines as the outcome of "corruption," as in certain senses they undoubtedly were. But the phenomenon of the informal or extraconstitutional aggregation of political power undermining separation of powers does not of itself imply venality.

As discussed in chapter 1, Madison and Jefferson founded the Republican Party in the 1790s in part to oppose the policies of Alexander Hamilton. They believed that the Bank of the United States, incorporated by legislation Hamilton had sponsored, was unconstitutional, because it was not authorized by any of the "enumerated" powers of Congress under Article I, section 8, of the Constitution. That clause, however, authorized not only enumerated powers but also those "necessary and proper" for carrying out the ones enumerated. Jefferson insisted that a power might be regarded as necessary and proper only when it was impossible for the enumerated power to be exercised without it. For Hamilton, on the other hand, a power became necessary and proper for the exercise of an enumerated power whenever it constituted a means expedient or convenient for that end. This famous quarrel, early in Washington's administration, contained the question, so pregnant for Calhoun, of whether the government might not add to the danger of majority tyranny by adding to the powers of government with the "liberal" mode of construction advocated by Hamilton, as opposed to the "strict" mode advocated by Jefferson and Madison. And this in turn engendered the hypothesis, making its appearance in the Kentucky and Virginia Resolutions, that nullification by states (whether individually or severally) was a necessary means of preventing such despotism.

Jefferson addressed this question energetically in the Kentucky Resolutions, above all in the dictum that "the government created by this compact [the Constitution] was not made the exclusive or final judge of the extent of the powers delegated to itself."[38] Whether rightly or wrongly, these resolutions were fateful in the development of Calhoun's political theory. For our present purposes, however, we observe that Jefferson and Madison saw the bank as an instrument by which Hamilton could distribute favors among the members of Congress and corrupt their independence. Congress might then become a pliant tool of the executive, and separation of powers a nullity. But the Republican Party, by the very means used to carry the election of 1800, itself became an instrument to exert discipline over its members and thereby overcome the constitutional separation of powers.[39] It was the Jacksonian revolution, however—in which Calhoun himself played such a conspicuous role—that brought into clearest view the possibility of the victor using the spoils of electoral conquest to reward members of the winning coalition with plunder dispersed by the federal treasury. Thus, as Calhoun saw it, government itself came to constitute the most dangerous of all factions and one that could not be controlled by any majoritarian electoral process. Every election, however fair, produced a victor or a victorious coalition. No matter how wide-ranging the consensus that produced the victory at the polls, the winners became a faction with an interest at odds with the community as a whole, for the taxing and spending powers of government could be used to take from the losers and reward the victors.[40] This is precisely the light in which the so-called Tariff of Abominations of 1828, which led to the nullification crisis of 1833, appeared to Calhoun.

Calhoun insists that we must take account of the faction created by the electoral process itself. We cannot, moreover, look to that process to cure a problem that is intrinsic to the process. The rewards and punishments at the disposal of the government will consolidate the ruling majority and thereby perpetuate it in power. Once a national political party gains control of the government, its patronage produces an interest common to all the factions that have joined together to form it. This interest is in addition to, and apart from, whatever interests they may have had prior to combining for the sake of carrying the election. The governing coalition can always reward its constituent members by plundering those who are outside it. Thus the political party will bring those who are widely separated in feeling and local circumstance to feel and act in unison. Because the members of all three departments of government will be brought within the framework of a single party, checks and balances will be progressively undermined. The extended republic, lending itself to party government even more than the smaller republics, is therefore more, rather than less, vulnerable to the tyranny of the majority it was designed to prevent. This is Calhoun's judgment in the *Disquisition* upon the political science of the *Federalist*, which leads to the concurrent majority as the only sufficient "remedy for the diseases most incident to republican government."

The foregoing analysis by Calhoun of the defects of the constitutional arrangements of the Founding, which we have presented in an impartial summary, has a plausibility that cannot be gainsaid. But it invites comparison with the similar analysis by Lincoln in his House Divided speech, when he charged a conspiracy embracing Presidents Pierce and Buchanan, Senator Douglas, and Chief Justice Taney. The breakdown of the separation of powers that Lincoln saw in 1858 was not, however, caused by any innate disposition to majority tyranny. What united this conspiracy was the defense of slavery. The passions engendered by slavery cut across party lines, as they cut across the constitutional separation of powers. And it was the anticipated loss of the political power that had hitherto protected the interests of slavery that animated the officeholders Lincoln cited. After 1850, the slavery question had swept the Southern Whigs into the Democratic Party, even as somewhat later it swept the Northern Whigs into the Republican Party. It was the collapse of the two-party system, not its fruition in a spoils system, that threatened to bring about the alleged tyranny of the majority. Nor was it any generalized temptation to plunder, as described theoretically in the *Disquisition*, but rather the specific and practical threat to slavery that prompted the Calhounites. In short, there was in slavery an interest that claimed a status unlike that claimed by any other interest. As we shall see, however, Calhoun's theory did not allow for any qualitative differentiation among interests.

To repeat, the tyranny threatened by Lincoln's Republican Party—the threat that Calhoun foresaw but did not live to see—was not due to any tyrannical tendency peculiar to majority rule. In the *Disquisition*, all interests are seen as inherently tyrannical in disposition as the result of an invariable law of nature. No qualitative distinctions between the ends or purposes of different interests are recognized by Calhoun's political science. This homogenization may appear as a necessity of the scientific method to which, as we shall see, Calhoun is committed. But this commitment, in turn, is a by-product of a denial of the cognitive reality of such qualitative distinctions. Qualities are in the eye of the beholder. Only quantities are real.

This is why nothing is said in the *Disquisition* about slavery. Slavery, like religion, proved to be an interest unlike manufacturing or agriculture in that it was not amenable to the political process. The Founding Fathers knew that government by majority rule was not possible where questions of religious belief might be put to a vote. For majority rule to become compatible with minority rights, sectarian religious differences had to be excluded from the political process. Differences over slavery proved to be every bit as intractable as differences over religion. Yet there proved to be no way to exclude differences over slavery from the political process, because the defense of slavery challenged the very ground of that process itself. Calhoun's theory, by denying any rational ground to the formation of governments, denied that slavery challenged this ground. His doctrine of the concurrent majority did not recognize differences concerning religion, slavery, or tariffs as qualitative differences, but as mere differences of interest.

They may differ in intensity, size, or other quantitative factors, but not in quality. Thus Calhoun was able to "solve" the problem represented by slavery by treating the proslavery interest of the slaveholders as an interest entitled to a constitutional veto. But he could do this only by denying that the slaves themselves might be a political minority.

It was not possible to remove slavery from the political agenda, as it was religion, because majority rule, even to the extent conceded by Calhoun, was possible only when it was combined with an idea of minority rights. And there had to be some nonarbitrary ground for minority rights, a ground independent of the will of the majority, if the majority was not to be permitted simply to swallow up the minority. Calhoun attempted to supply this ground by giving each minority a veto. But this presupposed that each such minority had an identity. This leaves us with the question, How does a minority acquire the identity that entitles it to the veto Calhoun demands for it?

As we have repeatedly noted, the political community from the perspective of the Founding is a voluntary community, and the consent that brings it into existence is unanimous. The majority is the practical surrogate for the whole. But the authority of the majority is limited to those purposes for which the voluntary consent of each individual was given a priori. The representatives chosen by majority vote are then understood to be the representatives of the minority no less than of the majority. It is this understanding of the nature of majority rule that is excluded a priori by Calhoun. Calhoun is compelled, therefore, to invent means by which the underlying unity of civil society is injected back into it as part of the political process. But while Calhoun denies any underlying nonarbitrary unity to civil society prior to the advent of the constitution or concurrent majority, he assumes this very unity or homogeneity in the minorities that are to be granted the veto.

In the political theory of the state of nature, it is assumed that the majority will be composed of differing minorities within itself. In the end, the indefeasible minority of which every majority and every minority is compounded is the individual. It is individual rights that are to be protected by government. These individuals will, in a free society, belong to many different groups and will at the same time belong to many different majorities and minorities. By the logic of his own theory, Calhoun would be required to grant each individual a veto upon every action of the government. That is to say, by denying unanimous consent in the foundation of civil society or the social contract, he would end by requiring unanimous consent to the action of the government. This absurdity is avoided only by restricting the concurrent majority to those groups or groupings that have the ability to endanger the self-preservation of the numerical majority so as to compel it to grant the veto power. A minority—or, as the case may be, a majority—

that may be held in subjection need not be granted a veto. That is, whether a group or grouping ought to be part of a concurrent majority would be decided by its success in impressing the numerical majority that the cost of excluding it is greater than the cost of including it. On such premises, there could be no such thing as noble failure or vulgar success. Thus it is not the natural right to self-preservation of every human individual that counts but only the rights of those groups, whether counted as majorities or minorities, that have the power to control their own destinies. Hence the slave states constituted a minority, but the slaves did not.

For Lincoln and the Founders, there was only one answer to the question of who ought to be counted among those whose consent was required for the just powers of government. That answer was given by "the laws of nature and of nature's God," whose premise was that "all men are created equal." On this foundation there might be differences within the political process on how to secure the rights to life, liberty, or property. But there could be no difference as to whether life, liberty, or property ought to be secure. Nor could there be differences as to *whose* rights were to be secured. In this regard, every single individual, and hence every minority, stood upon the same ground. To deprive one class of liberty and property would call into question the right to liberty and property of everyone else. If the majority can plunder one minority, why not another, or another? Yet Calhoun's *Disquisition* professed to be, and has been widely accepted as being, a defense of minority rights.

～

Calhoun begins the *Disquisition* as follows: "In order to have a clear and just conception of the nature and object of government, it is indispensable to understand correctly what that constitution or law of our nature is, in which government originates; or, to express it more fully and accurately—that law, without which government would not, and with which it must necessarily exist."[41] Calhoun writes in the modern tradition of Descartes, Hobbes, and Spinoza. He will attempt to give a clear and distinct account—an account at least quasi-mathematical in form. His premises will be inductions from experience so universal as to be undeniable. His conclusions will be contained in his premises and logically irresistible. Hence we must subject those premises to the most rigorous analysis, mindful that the conclusions cannot possess any greater validity than the premises.

Calhoun's beginning is to discover that law "without which government would not, and with which it must necessarily exist." Calhoun understands *necessity* in a sense both Euclidean and Newtonian, that is to say, in a sense embracing both form and matter. In this respect as in others, Calhoun's political science will stand in opposition to that of Aristotle, who declared politics to be an inexact science.[42] Although Calhoun will allow for something like prudence in the implementation of the constitutional principle of the concurrent majority, he will not allow any room for difference of opinion on the inescapable necessity for the concurrent majority itself. Calhoun's assertion of a "scientific" foundation for his statesmanship has no rival in his time until we encounter similar claims by his younger contemporary Karl Marx. Calhoun admits no possibility that either enlightenment or moral education can overcome the tendency of every government to despotism absent the veto power by the weaker over the action of the stronger party.[43] Similarly Marx believed that there was no possibility of overcoming the despotism of the property-owning classes except by the abolition of private property. Marx also makes this assertion upon the basis of what he believes to be scientific necessity—a causality, inherent in matter, that is transferred from matter to mind in and by the process of production itself. According to Calhoun, only the necessity of government, combined with the necessity of the stronger to conciliate the weaker party, can generate rationality and justice in the government. Necessity, not prudence or any of the moral virtues informed by prudence, governs the relationship between cause and effect in politics. Politics thus becomes, in effect, a branch of physics. What appear as prudence, wisdom, justice, and concern for the common good are all by-products of necessity. In and of themselves, they have no substantial meaning. Insofar as human virtue is believed to be a habit of doing what is right for its own sake—so that virtue may be said to be its own reward—it is an illusion. According to Calhoun, our understanding of the science of government, like that of astronomy, is to be found in laws that express the immutable relationships inherent in the objects of our study. That there are forces operating on the souls of men exactly as gravitation acts upon their bodies, and upon all bodies, is *the* axiomatic premise of Calhoun's political science. As this leaves no room for moral virtue as traditionally understood, so it leaves no room for human freedom as traditionally understood.

Calhoun is explicit concerning the modern scientific character of the *Disquisition*. Hence he does not recognize the Aristotelian distinction between the exact and inexact sciences or between the theoretical and practical sciences. Science is one and the same whatever its subject matter. Calhoun proposes a "law of our nature" by which government must necessarily exist. Without such a law, he says, it would be "as impossible to lay any solid foundation for the science of government, as it would be to lay one for that of astronomy, without a like understanding of that constitution or law of the material world, according to which the several bodies composing the solar system mutually act on each other, and by which they are kept in their respective spheres." The parallelism between the sciences of astronomy (or physics) and politics is neither doubted by Calhoun nor (in his mind) in need of any argument, much less proof. We may also note at the outset how the theory of the concurrent majority resembles that of the solar system, the majority and minority each like planets keeping their place by a system of mutual action and reaction. In considering what this law of nature may be that renders government necessary, Calhoun makes two crucial assumptions. First, he regards it "as an incontestable fact that man is so constituted as to be a social being. His inclinations and wants, physical and moral, irresistibly impel him to associate with his kind; and he has accordingly never been found, in any age or country, in any state other than the social." Second, he assumes it as "a fact not less incontestable that, while man is so constituted as to make the social state necessary to his exis-tence and the full development of his faculties, this state cannot exist without government. The assumption rests on universal experience. In no age or country has any society or community ever been found . . . without government."[44]

Why does Calhoun say that society cannot exist without government? We have noted that according to Aristotle, families, clans, and villages precede the political community in time. It may be true that prepolitical communities are not without government, but their government is not *political* government. Aristotle distinguishes political rule from other forms of rule—for example, that of a king, a despot, or the head of a household. Calhoun reduces the different forms of rule to a common denominator.[45] To understand this, we must examine attentively Calhoun's account of the dynamics of the human soul. The reason government is necessary, according to Calhoun, is

> found in the fact (not less incontestable than either of the others) that, while man is created for the social state, and is accordingly so formed as to feel what affects others, as well as what affects himself, he is, at the same time, so consti-tuted as to feel more intensely what affects him directly, than what affects him indirectly through others; or to express it differently, he is so constituted that his direct or individual affections are stronger than his sympathetic or social feelings.

It is this greater strength of the individual, or self-regarding, feelings, affections, or passions in relationship to the corresponding sympathetic or social ones that lays the "solid foundation for the science of government." Both the self-regarding and the other-regarding feelings, affections, or passions belong to man's nature. Man as man cannot be conceived or discovered without either the one or the other. And although society is grounded in the weaker, or other-regarding, feelings, it is nonetheless intrinsically of a higher order of importance than government: "It is the first in the order of things, and in the dignity of its object; that of society being primary—to preserve and perfect our race; and that of government secondary and subordinate, to preserve and perfect society. Both are however necessary to the existence and well-being of our race and equally of Divine ordination."[46] Calhoun concludes this passage by observing that he has intentionally avoided the expression "selfish" as applied to the "direct or individual affections." In this he is like Spinoza, who in his Ethics declares that he treats the different passions of the soul as he would meteorological phenomena, which are neither to be praised nor blamed, but only understood.[47] A mild and sunny day and a tropical hurricane are indifferently manifestations of the same causes or laws of nature. Had Calhoun been writing in a later generation, he would have declared himself to have carefully avoided making any "value judgments." His object is to characterize invariant facts about the "phenomena appertaining to our nature—constituted as it is," facts "as unquestionable as is that of gravitation, or any other phenomenon of the material world."[48] As we have already observed, Calhoun seeks "scientific" status for his treatise by treating all causes as forming a homogeneous system. Yet his elevation of society above government of itself constitutes a ranking of human ends, a ranking consistent only with heterogeneity.

Calhoun says that government exists to serve society, and society "to preserve and perfect our race," understood as "the full development of [man's] moral and intellectual faculties"—those faculties in virtue of which man himself surpasses "the level of brute creation" in "the scale of being."[49] Man's distinctive place in this scale is evidently connected with man's rational nature, and to speak of a scale of being implies a noetic grasp of the objective reality of being as such. Yet Calhoun never calls man the rational animal or connects (as does Aristotle) man's social nature with that rationality. His characterization of the moving causes of human behavior as arising from nature is limited to the two kinds of feelings and affections or passion. Yet the placing of man on the "scale of being" implies the possession of reason and the possibility of utilizing reason as a guide to "upward mobility" upon that scale. The distinction between man and beast seems not only to mark the human level as higher than the bestial but also to provide the ground of distinction within the human species of those who represent what is higher in man from what is lower. Calhoun—again, like Marx—believes, on the one hand, in a science based upon materialism and materialistic determinism, while, on the other hand, upholding freedom as an end. This freedom is apparently the result of the human mind or soul being emancipated by science from the determinism of that very matter that is the ground of science. Hence with respect to the end or goal of his science, man would appear to be for Calhoun—as he is for Aristotle and Jefferson—the being in between God and beast, partaking of both the lower and higher natures. As such, he would be under the injunctions of "the better angels of his nature" to cultivate the higher and to subordinate the lower. Calhoun requires, with respect to the ultimate end or purpose of his science, a typology of human character in which the praiseworthy is distinguished from the blameworthy, notwithstanding his original disavowal of moral judgment in the analysis of the passions (an anomaly no less characteristic of Spinoza). Yet Calhoun's science appears to be stultified, as is that of Spinoza and Marx, by the contradiction between the human world as no less part of the material world than is that of the brutes (no *imperium in imperio*) and man himself being elevated in a "scale of being" above the brutes. To repeat, that elevation is only possible if, contrary to Calhoun's axiomatic premises, there is a human potentiality for self-determination, a possibility of human freedom from determinism.

The human soul elevated in the scale of being will, according to Calhoun, control matter, including the matter of the human passions, by the discovery of scientific laws. Indeed, the principle of Calhoun's constitutionalism, the concurrent majority, is a device for overcoming the mechanistic outcome of the material determinism of the soul by superimposing upon natural causality that conquest of nature that is scientific human wisdom. Yet this would not be possible if the human soul were wholly determined by that matter in which it discovers those laws of nature.

Although he gives no indication of knowing it, Calhoun apparently accepts that dualism between mind and matter that characterizes modern philosophy from Descartes (who distinguished *res cogitans* and *res extensa*) onward and that culminated in Kant's distinction between phenomena and noumena, between the world of necessity (of matter) and the world of freedom (of mind). But Kant was perfectly clear that from the deterministic perspective of phenomena as such, there is no difference in rank between man and beast—that both are automata regulated by the motions and necessities of the laws of matter as described by science. It is within the parameters of Kantian phenomena that Calhoun proceeds to describe, in purely mechanistic terms, the operation of the self-regarding (or individual) and the other-regarding (or social) feelings or affections that move the human soul. As Calhoun characterizes the necessities that cause man to be a member of society and society to fall under government, it is feelings or affections alone, and not reason, that are the moving or controlling causes. From the premises that Calhoun sets forth a priori, nothing intrinsic to the soul could, by taking thought, change in any way the relationship of the social to the individual passions. Reason or science is something that observes phenomena but does not appear itself to be a phenomenon. On Calhoun's Kantian premises, ideas purporting to direct the passions are illusions. Reason can be no more than the handmaid of the passions. Human behavior results from the mechanisms of the passions, as the weather results from the causality inherent in matter, as manifested in the interaction of light, heat, air, water, etc. The passions do and must act in accordance with the laws Calhoun has specified, or those laws are themselves illusory.

～

Notwithstanding his apparent denial of the possibility of indeterminacy in the "laws of nature," Calhoun admits a qualification to what he has asserted concerning the self-regarding and the other-regarding passions.

> In asserting that our individual are stronger than our social feelings, it is not intended to deny that there are instances, growing out of peculiar relations—as that of a mother and her infant—or resulting from the force of education and habit over peculiar constitutions, in which the latter have overpowered the former; but these instances are few, and always regarded as something extraordinary. The deep impression they make, whenever they occur, is the strongest proof that they are regarded as exceptions to some general and well understood law of our nature; just as some of the minor powers of the material world are apparently to gravitation.[50]

By speaking of "apparent" exceptions to the law of gravitation, Calhoun surely means that there are no real exceptions. The penny falls faster than the feather because of the different action of the air upon them. In a vacuum, we know, they would both fall at the same rate. But for the social to overpower the individual affections is altogether different from the example of the penny and the feather. As Aristotle dryly observes, no matter how many times you throw a stone into the air, you do not accustom it to fly upwards. Calhoun has declared that the law of nature with respect to the passions of the soul is the same as the law of nature with respect to the gravity of bodies. In such a case, no education or habituation would be able to make the social stronger than the individual passions. In the best regimes of classical political philosophy, as in Rousseau's *Social Contract*, education and habituation are relied upon to dispose the souls of the citizens away from private advantage and toward the common good. Here Calhoun admits a possibility that calls into question the premise upon which the entire superstructure of his argument, and especially his doctrine of the concurrent majority, depends.

Calhoun sees the normal predominance of the individual to the social feelings to be a manifestation of "the great law of self-preservation which pervades all that feels, from man down to the lowest and most insignificant reptile or insect." He will grant that man's "social feelings may indeed, in a state of safety and abundance, combined with high intellectual and moral culture, acquire great expansion and force; but not so great as to overpower this all-pervading and essential law of animated existence."[51] But is it not clear that in the case of the mother and the infant, it is precisely the instinct of self-preservation that makes the mother prefer, if necessary, her infant's life to her own? Nor is it the human mother only, or even the human species alone, in which this phenomenon occurs. A cock robin will attack a cat that comes too near the nest where the hen is brooding. While there is much variation among the species in the way in which this end is pursued, there can be no doubt that in nature self-preservation relates more to the species than to the individual. Indeed, "self" and "other," in regard to self-preservation, are not what Calhoun finds them to be. It is certain that in the specific case Calhoun mentions, that of mother and child, the instinct attaching the one to the other is not that of one individual to another. As the instinct of self-preservation is primarily a species instinct, self and other in certain relationships merge and appear to become one. Hence while the strength of the instinct of self-preservation, both as to the individual and the species, varies from case to case, it is undeniably true (to use a characteristic Calhounian locution) that fathers as well as mothers usually prefer the preservation of their young to their own individual preservation.

It follows from this that among humans it is the family, rather than the individual, that seeks survival. Those feelings, whether of pleasure or of pain, that are founded in sense perception alone must remain indefeasibly individual. But the passions connected with these feelings, important as they are, are not the only passions, nor the strongest, in human life. Within the family the individual and the social feelings or passions are not as distinct or as separate as Calhoun would have us think. But it is human families or their representatives, rather than "abstract" human individuals, who found or institute political communities. The contrast between self and other that figures so largely in Calhoun's thought must be interpreted in the light of this fact. Plato (or Socrates) in the *Republic* attempted to annihilate the tension between self and other by transforming the city into a single family in which wives and children, as well as property, were held in common.[52] All would regard these things as equally their own. But Plato tacitly assumed that within the family, the eros of the family tended to dissolve the tension between "mine" and "thine." More generally, "eros" is that in nature, or in the nature of things, by which the preservation of the species is accomplished. But the consummation of eros is in union, in which separateness is overcome as preservation is accomplished.

We can approve of the passion with which parents seek advantages for their children when it leads to good character, achievement, and improvement in the children. We can regret it when the children are spoiled, benefit from nepotism, or receive preferment to which they are not entitled. But clearly the difference between the one case and the other is not to be found in a discrimination between passions labeled individual or self-regarding and passions labeled social or other-regarding. It is rather to be found in the reason that directs the passion. It is according to nature that a mother should prefer the interests of her own children to the interests of the children of others, even if she recognizes that the other children are superior in their human qualities. Nevertheless, it is equally natural for the mother who prefers her own inferior child to exert herself for the improvement of her child, wishing her child to be better rather than worse. We are never indifferent to the distinction between the good and our own, even when we prefer our own to the good. Calhoun has then substituted the distinction between the individual and the social feelings or passions for the distinction between one's own and the good. He has done so because "good" is not a scientific term in the new dispensation of science.

That this "scientific" substitution by Calhoun is not true to the phenomena as they really are is proved by reflection upon his own admitted "exceptions." It is impossible to classify the passions of the human soul on the basis of their being individual or social without regard to whether their objects are good or bad. Calhoun is quite right in refusing to attach the epithet "selfish" to the individual passions as such, since that pejorative is undeserved in many cases.[53] But there are certainly self-regarding passions that deserve to be called selfish because they are bad. Nor is it possible indiscriminately to call other-regarding passions good. Calhoun rightly observes that if the order of nature were reversed so that we were not attached by our passions and feelings primarily to ourselves in preference to others, "all individuality would be lost; and boundless and remediless disorder and confusion would ensue."

> For each, at the same moment intensely participating in all the conflicting emotions of those around him, would of course forget himself and all that concerned him immediately, in his officious intermeddling with the affairs of all others: which from his limited reason and faculties he could neither properly understand or manage. Such a state of things would, as far as we can see, lead to endless disorder and confusion, not less destructive to our race than a state of anarchy. It would besides be remediless—for government would be impossible . . . [since it would be] administered by those who, on the supposition, would have the greatest aversion for selfishness and the highest admiration for benevolence.

Calhoun sees the "infinite wisdom and goodness" of "the Creator of all" in the allocation of both the self-regarding and the other-regarding passions. The former direct "every class of animated being" to attend to itself first of all, the latter to cultivate that "social and political state" that is "adapted to develop the great capacities and faculties intellectual and moral."[54] Calhoun seems here to be saying that the self-regarding passions are actually the best vehicle for accomplishing many of the social concerns of mankind. He apparently means this in much the same way that Adam Smith does in saying that it is not from the benevolence of the butcher and the baker that we expect our daily meat and bread but from their self-interest. But Smith also understood that it was more than individual self-interest that led the butcher and baker to provide for their own families; that it was more than the interest of their families alone that led them to prefer their own country to other countries; and that it was the interest of mankind to prefer their own species to the lower orders of Creation. The inducement to cooperation between individuals is seldom, if ever, motivated exclusively by a passion that can be conceived entirely as "individual" or by a passion that can be conceived entirely as "social."

~

Here we must retrace our steps in following the analysis of the *Disquisition*. Calhoun's distinction between the individual and the social places him in the mainstream not only of modern "scientism" but also of modern individualism. To speak of the "individual" has become so commonplace that we seldom consider that the word itself is an adjective, not a noun. It is an adjective that implies a noun—the noun "human." In fact, however, we never see individual human beings. We see individual men, women, and children. Nor do we, when we look around us, see men, women, or children in the abstract. We see mothers and fathers, brothers and sisters, grandparents and grandchildren. We see fellow citizens and aliens of other nationalities. Our consciousness is formed, as we grow up, first of all by our families, by individuals linked to each other within generations, by generations, and through generations. Individualism tends to abstract, not only from the distinction between men and women, but also from all those relationships that arise from, and are constituted by, the phenomenon of "generation." The Gospels begin with Matthew, and Matthew begins with an account of the descent of Jesus from Abraham through forty-two generations. Jesus' purpose in life is identified as carrying out the purposes of those from whom he is descended. But this is only a particularly striking example of how mankind has always identified individuals by genealogy. The passions and feelings that arise from generation cannot be regarded as merely or simply individual, or merely or simply social. Modern times have certainly detached our consciousness from the relationship with the ancestral that characterized all earlier generations. And Calhoun can be seen contributing to that detachment. In the Civil War, however, both sides will claim the authority of "our fathers" (and of the Bible) for their cause.

Calhoun is then mistaken in seeing the passion of the mother for her child as an exception to what individuals feel. He does not see the instinct for self-preservation in light of the complex social fabric, beginning in the family, that governs the genesis and development of our perceptions of each other and the world. He does not see that the eros each individual possesses for himself may be

447

consummated in union with another. Hence he does not see the essential ambiguity of the distinction between the individual and the social arising from generation. He does not see, as Aristotle did, that the ontological priority of community to individuality is the foundation of all society and government. Only as one understands the priority of the partnership of male and female in the generation, nurture, and education of the young can one understand the relationship of individuality to community in the political order.

In the paragraph in which Calhoun deduces the necessity of government, he writes that the

> constitution of our nature which makes us feel more intensely what affects us directly than what affects us indirectly through others, necessarily leads to conflict between individuals. Each, in consequence, has a greater regard for his own safety or happiness than for the safety and happiness of others; and, where these come in opposition, is ready to sacrifice the interests of others to his own. And hence the tendency to a universal state of conflict, between individual and individual; accompanied by the connected passions of suspicion, jealousy, anger and revenge—followed by insolence, fraud, and cruelty—and if not prevented by some controlling power, ending in a state of universal discord and confusion, destructive of the social state and the ends for which it is ordained. This controlling power, wherever vested or by whomsoever exercised, is GOVERNMENT.[55]

This is a crucial step in the development of Calhoun's argument. This "greater regard" each "individual" is said to have "for his own safety or happiness" is cause of the further fact that whenever that safety and happiness is in opposition to the safety and happiness of others, the "individual" is always "ready to sacrifice the interests of others to his own." For the present, we pass over the fact that the preference of the mother for the life of her child is no mere exception to this rule. For Calhoun, this alleged "greater regard" of each individual for his own life and safety is the fons et origo, the sufficient cause, of that "law of our nature without which government would not exist, and with which its existence is necessary."

According to Calhoun, therefore, it is a "law of our nature" that without government, the condition of man would be that "universal state of conflict" that is otherwise known as the *bellum omnia contra omnes*. Hobbes's state of nature, in which life is "solitary, poor, nasty, brutish, and short," is plainly the condition toward which mankind is propelled by the passions that are the law of his nature, according to Calhoun's understanding no less than Hobbes's. Why then may we not simply regard Calhoun as Hobbesian? The answer lies in part in the fact that Hobbes infers, from the same alleged facts cited by Calhoun, that there is a "state of nature" in which all men as men are equal. They are equally threatened with violent death and thus have an equal interest in ending that threat. It is this equal interest that leads them to acknowledge each other's equal right to be free from this threat. And this equal right leads to the idea of a social compact or contract as the foundation of legitimate government. The equal right of all men to life and liberty is a foundation stone of Hobbes's political teaching, and this is anathema to Calhoun.

The Hobbesian idea of man's equality in the state of nature, transformed from its Hobbesian origins (in part by Locke and in part by the American reception of Locke), became the characteristic theory of the American Revolution. As we have seen, Calhoun rejected it altogether in the Oregon speech—as he will reject it again in the *Disquisition*. This rejection is the essential prolegomenon to his political theory, which denies any role to freedom or reason in the origins of society or government. By contrast, we return again to Madison's oft repeated maxim that "Of all free government, compact is the basis and the essence." We reiterate that by free government, Madison meant one in which the equal natural rights of man in the state of nature are the ground of equal civil and political rights within civil society. In the *Discourse*, as we shall see, Calhoun regards the Constitution as a compact—a voluntary association of the states. For Madison as for Lincoln, the compact between the states is neither more nor less a compact than that between individuals in the original formation of civil society. We have seen that the heart of Lincoln's argument against the right of secession is that it contravened the very purpose for which the "compact" of the Constitution was entered into when it was ratified by the states. Calhoun accordingly takes advantage of the idea of compact in the interest of nullification and secession but denies it any role in the formation of society or government. Compacts or contracts can be made only by persons who are, for the purposes of the contract, equal. In Calhoun's thought, the legal or artificial personalities of the states are equal, but natural human persons are not.

Calhoun's Hobbesianism thus stops short of Hobbes's rationalism and egalitarianism. Calhoun sees necessity and not reason leading man out of the pernicious condition into which the law of his nature is driving him. There is accordingly nothing voluntary in man's becoming a member of civil society. Legitimate civil society is not, therefore, a voluntary association of free and equal human beings, as the generation of the Founding Fathers believed.

∽

Calhoun confronts us, at every point and moment, with the role of necessity in the government of human behavior. In what may perhaps be the most revealing assertion of all, he says that government, "like breathing . . . is not permitted to depend on our volition." The same may be said of society. One wonders whether Calhoun understood that insofar as he was denying any freedom at all to the human will, he was in effect denying any inner difference between a free man and a slave or between the social nature of man and that of the bee or the ant. The comparison of the motions by which we become members of society and by which society falls under government to "breathing" reminds us that Calhoun calls a constitution an "organism." Yet he also appears, with breath-taking inconsistency, to exempt that organism called constitution from the necessity that determines both society and government.

> Very different is the case as to constitution. Instead of a matter of necessity, it is one of the most difficult tasks imposed on man to form a constitution worthy of the name. . . . Constitution is the contrivance of man, while government is of Divine ordination. Man is left to perfect what the wisdom of the Infinite ordained as necessary to preserve the race.[56]

In traditional moral theology, the fact that God leaves to man the perfection of his being means that the perfection of man's being depends upon his freedom. Creating man in his image, God endowed him with the metaphysical freedom of reason—of being capable of forming ideas and comparing ideas in order to make rational choices. Although God leaves man free to choose between right and wrong, however, he does not leave man free to decide for himself what is right or wrong. The moral commandments—for example, the second table of the Decalogue—are not "optional." Man can disobey the moral order, but he cannot change it for his convenience. George Washington, in his first inaugural address, declared that "the foundations of our national policy will be laid in the pure and immutable principles of private morality . . . since there is no truth more thoroughly established than that there exists in the economy and course of nature, an indissoluble union between virtue and happiness." And again: "[W]e ought to be no less persuaded that the propitious smiles of Heaven can never be expected on a nation that disregards the eternal rules of order and right, which Heaven itself has ordained."[57] The "immutable principles of private morality," the "indissoluble union between virtue and happiness," and the "eternal rules of order and right" are not of human invention. They are antecedent to government and constitution and serve as guidance to those engaged in framing constitutions and administering governments. These principles and rules, we might observe, are not different from "the laws of nature" that guided the actions and conscience of the Continental Congress on July 4, 1776. When Calhoun denies to human volition any role in the formation of society or government, he in effect denies any role to human reason. Prior to constitution, man in society is neither rational nor moral.

On Calhoun's premises, man must live under government *without* constitution before living under it *with* constitution. This impels us to ask how man, thus situated, can exercise that "human wisdom" by which a constitution can transform a government from despotic to nondespotic. Calhoun's examples, as we shall presently see, prove to be the result not of human wisdom but of chance. The *Disquisition* ends with an account of the Roman and British constitutions—the two most memorable and successful regimes (and empires) in history. However different in "their origin and character," both these constitutions, according to Calhoun, had as their object "to blend and harmonize the conflicting interests of the community; and the means [were also] the same, taking the sense of each class or portion through its appropriate organ, and considering the concurrent sense of all as the sense of the whole community." However, following his sketches of the constitutional histories of these two famous polities, Calhoun concludes that their constitutions "originated in a pressure, occasioned by conflicts of interests between hostile classes or orders, and were intended to meet the pressing exigencies of the occasion; neither party, it would seem, having any conception of the principles involved, or the consequences to follow, beyond the immediate objects in contemplation."[58] Thus the objects of the constitutions of Rome and Britain were never the objects of those engaged in causing the events from which the constitutions resulted. The examples of Rome and Britain, as described by Calhoun, contradict his assertion that constitution, as distinct from society and government, is a contrivance of human wisdom. Their constitutions are represented as the unintended and involuntary consequence of wholly accidental events. It is chance (or Providence), not art or human wisdom, that is the actual cause of the implementation of the principle of the concurrent majority.

It follows from Calhoun's account of the Roman and British constitutions that the principle of the concurrent majority, although itself inherently rational, has not hitherto been an attribute of human wisdom or reason. Until now, we may say, reason has been a by-product of unreason. This account is reminiscent of Hegel's "cunning of history," in which the dialectic of history moves mankind in a predestined path. This path, according to Hegel, is itself intrinsically rational. But the proximate cause of those human actions that achieve history's rational ends is not human art or reason but human passion. In this respect, too, we might bear in mind that Karl Marx was also an epigone of Hegel.

Calhoun's account of these constitutions also reminds us of Darwinism. The constitutional organisms that enabled Rome and Britain to survive, prosper, conquer, and rule were the unintended results of the struggle for survival of their constituent elements. The resolution of these struggles into the regimes compounded of these elements can be viewed as an event in evolutionary history as much as the history of any surviving biological species. The "right of nature," moreover, comes to have the same nonmoral meaning in both cases. In this, Calhoun and Darwin were anticipated by Spinoza when he wrote that the big fish eat the little fish with supreme natural right.[59] To succeed in surviving (and conquering) and having the right to survive (and conquer) are ultimately one and the same. That the means of surviving (and conquering) might be immoral would be a self-contradiction. Success is its own justification, and failure its own condemnation. Again, there is no such thing as base success or noble failure. By the same reasoning, of course, one can say that those who are slaves deserve to be slaves and that those who are masters deserve to be masters. From this perspective, Machiavelli's moral teaching is the true teaching, and Calhoun must certainly be numbered among his votaries.

Calhoun's teaching will prove to be one variety of the Social Darwinism that dominated the later nineteenth century. Like other forms of Social Darwinism (including Marxism), Calhoun's doctrine will exempt itself from the determinism that otherwise dominates the evolutionary or historical process. Calhoun, like the others, believes in progress and in the moral and intellectual superiority of the regime of the civilization of the later age. The conflict between civilization and barbarism, which in the past seemed to end in the triumph of barbarism (as in the case of the fall of the Roman Empire), can never do so again. Ours is the first civilization to be armed by genuine science—science that is practical and not contemplative, and whose knowledge is power. Calhoun's perspective resembles that of the hero of Churchill's novel, *Savrola*, when he declared that if the morals of civilization did not persuade the barbarians, its maxims surely would![60] *Savrola* was written in the 1890s, long before Hitler and Stalin proved that barbarism could also master science and impose its morals with its maxims.[61] We shall have further occasion to see that for Calhoun the idea of progress—the idea of the necessary but essentially involuntary improvement, moral as well as physical, of the human condition—is the tacit premise of his whole political science. For the present, we repeat only that in the examples of Rome and Britain there is nothing to exemplify the proposition that "organism" or constitution is a human contrivance. We can only suppose that Calhoun intends us to understand that the principle of the concurrent majority, now for the first time articulated by him as the latest and best fruit of modern science, can now for the first time become a matter of human wisdom and human art.[62]

≈

For Calhoun, the scientific explanation of political behavior in the *Disquisition* had superseded the Lockean self-understanding of the Founding Fathers. As we have seen, Calhoun rejects the role of human freedom in the formation of government, which freedom is central to the Founders' doctrine of the state of nature. The scientific character of the *Disquisition*, from which all its authority proceeds, is anchored in the invariant relationship of the passions of the human soul to human behavior. These passions are said to have a uniformity in their action equal to that of gravity upon bodies. Understanding the laws of nature, whether of matter or of mind, enables us to master nature, both nonhuman and human. Calhoun's science will enable us to conquer despotism even as other sciences of nature enable us to conquer famine or disease.

The true or scientific ground for resisting despotism by imposing such an "organism" or constitution on an existing government as will maximize freedom and advance the ends for which Providence has ordained government awaited the *Disquisition*. Calhoun does not deny that there has been progress up to this point. But that progress has been the outcome of history, in which chance, not art, has served the ends that are said to be divinely ordained for man. We are faced, however, with this question: How can Calhoun postulate necessity as the axiomatic premise of government while postulating freedom as the axiomatic premise of constitution? How can reason intervene to form a constitution when it could not intervene to form a government?

In the political theory of Karl Marx, another epigone of the historical school, history begins with the institution of private property (before that there is prehistory, not history properly so called) and progresses through a long series of dialectical/revolutionary changes. Each revolution results in a synthesis of the antecedent thesis and antithesis. That synthesis becomes the thesis of the next cycle of conflict and resolution. Finally, however, history comes to an end. The synthesis resulting from the conflict between bourgeoisie and proletariat is to be the final synthesis. With the abolition of private property (from which all class conflicts are said to originate) there can be no further antithesis. The proletariat becomes the whole human race, and all the means of production are owned by all. Marx's own doctrine, on its own premise, is the first doctrine that is not properly called "ideology," that is, it is the first doctrine that is not a rationalization of the interests of one or another form of class-structured society. Strictly speaking, Marx is (to himself) the first disinterested thinker, and hence the first genuine philosopher. But he is also, in a sense, the last, because in the classless society of the future there will be no such vocational distinction. Because there will be no class differences, all men will be equally disinterested in the quest for truth, which will be available to all indiscriminately. In this, Marx foresees not only an "end of history" but also a "leap into freedom." In this classless (and history-less) society of the future, the human mind will be free of any interested motives for believing one thing rather than another. It will accordingly see things as they "really are."[63] Marx would admit, nonetheless, that his teaching has as its one ulterior motive to promote that revolution that will lead to the abolition of all ulterior motives. Living at or near the "end of history," he claims to see the progress and process of history "as it really is." Marx's historiography is thus proclaimed to be scientific. A progressive history, operating through necessity, culminates in the abolition of necessity as the determining force in human life.

Calhoun's doctrine clearly parallels this. Looking back, Calhoun discovers how history has illuminated the conditions of human freedom and how it reveals the operation of the principle of the concurrent majority. This operation, whenever and wherever it arises, enlarges human freedom. But only now, when at last the process underlying such enlargement becomes self-conscious in the form of modern science, can it be deliberately employed to further (and perhaps finally) enlarge the scope of human freedom. Human freedom has hitherto been the accidental outcome of chance causes. Now it can become the purposeful consequence of deliberate and scientific employment. To compare these two means by which the concurrent majority is built into constitutions—by chance hitherto, by science henceforth—is like comparing monkeys with typewriters (in infinite time) to Shakespeare as alternative means of writing *Hamlet*. In this sense, the achievement of the *Disquisition*, and the possibility it offers for the enlargement of human freedom, is conceived as a "leap into freedom" equivalent to any prophesied by Karl Marx. Yet we remain perplexed, by Calhoun no less than by Marx, as to how the law governing the relationship between reason and passion in the human soul can be suspended in the soul of the scientist who discovers that law.

∾

According to Calhoun, in governments of the numerical majority, where the spoils of party victories are taken by plundering the defenseless minority, influence is gained by "falsehood, injustice, fraud, artifice, slander, and breach of faith." In the government of the concurrent majority, by contrast, rewards are given to "truth, justice, integrity [and] fidelity."[64] Yet we must always bear in mind that whether falsehood or truth predominates is the result of the operation of the identical law of our nature upon which Calhoun's political science is built. Hence a preference for truth or justice does not arise from devotion to truth or justice but from having one's preference for falsehood and injustice frustrated by the concurrent majority. That this is mere theoretical utopianism, however, is proved by Calhoun's own experience in the Jackson administration.

Having been elected vice president with Jackson, Calhoun lost out to Martin Van Buren in an administration riddled with byzantine intrigue. By the theory of the *Disquisition*, Van Buren and Calhoun should have been too busy plotting the plunder of their defeated political adversaries to plot to plunder each other. The theory of the concurrent majority assumed a homogeneity of interest in majorities and minorities, which the concurrent majority would channel but would not itself generate. In the Jacksonian period, however, the issues raised by the attempted rechartering of the Bank of the United States and South Carolina's attempted nullification of the Tariff of Abominations split the Jacksonian coalition. Different coalitions, which crossed party lines, attacked and defended the Bank. Other such coalitions arose on the question of the tariff, and still others to fight or defend South Carolina's attempt to nullify it. Where would the veto powers be located under such conditions that would produce the concurrent majority?

Notwithstanding the Jacksonian victories at the polls in 1828, 1832, and 1836, there were no such clearly defined majorities or minorities as the *Disquisition* envisaged. To be more precise, majorities and minorities differed from issue to issue. Someone who was in the majority on one question would be in the minority on another. The truth is, in the extended republic celebrated in the *Federalist*, there was no such uniformity of interest, within either majorities or minorities, as the theory of concurrent majoritarianism required. Calhoun's own political experience conformed much more closely to Madison's theory than to his own—with one great and notable exception. In the end, the only majority and minority for whom the concurrence theory fit were proslavery and antislavery. In class-structured societies like ancient Rome or feudal England, one can speak of homogeneous class interests that might exercise constitutional vetoes. But no such homogeneity of interests to which such vetoes might attach exists in an extended popular republic. Except for slavery (and race), there is no single instance in American history that comes to mind in which there have been the kind of consistently identifiable minorities or majorities within the nation—or even within the states—that might form a Calhounian constitution.

Calhoun asserts, but gives no reason to believe, that the rapacity of governments without the concurrent majority will be transformed into virtue by the concurrent majority, as if rapacity, denied one channel, cannot find it in another. Where the veto of the concurrent majority is in place, he says, "knowledge, wisdom, patriotism and virtue . . . [will] be most highly appreciated and assiduously cultivated." Furthermore,

> the good effects resulting [from the concurrent majority] extend to the whole community. For of all the causes which contribute to form the character of a people, those by which power, influence, and standing in the government are most certainly and readily obtained, are, by far, the most powerful. . . . Neither religion nor education can counteract the strong tendency of the numerical majority to corrupt and debase the people.[65]

Even if we concede to the concurrent majority the negative effect of preventing the tyranny of the numerical majority, what reason is there to expect from it the positive effects of "knowledge, wisdom, patriotism and virtue"? Calhoun seems to think that whatever prevents evil is at the same time the cause of good. But that is only partially true. Health is indeed a good. But, as Aristotle would say, it is only an instrumental good. Like wealth and freedom, it is ultimately good only for those who can use it for good purposes. A healthy criminal or a healthy tyrant will be better able to pursue a life of crime or tyranny. The prevention of disease enables us to pursue healthy activities, but health itself does not tell us what those activities are. Nor does it tell us whether to pursue only activities that are healthy. Is the man wise or foolish who rescues the child from the burning building? Or the soldier who saves his platoon by throwing himself on the grenade? On the other hand, some deliberately risk disease and death by their promiscuity. Is the distinction between noble and base pleasures merely conventional, or does it have a ground in nature and reason? If it is true that the numerical majority can plunder the minority within the community, why may not the concurrent majority plunder those outside the community? Calhoun celebrates the concurrent majoritarianism in the Roman constitution. But the veto granted to the plebs through the institution of the tribunes turned Rome from internal strife to foreign conquest. It resulted in Romans plundering non-Romans rather than Romans. Is civil society not to be distinguished from a band of robbers?

Calhoun is eminently Aristotelian in saying that nothing is more effectual in forming the character of a people than the means by which power and influence in government are obtained. But for Aristotle, "knowledge, wisdom, patriotism and virtue" are the result of a certain kind of education, an education aimed at an intrinsic good or a good according to nature, an education that distinguishes the good from the pleasant and the noble from the base. But such knowledge is not, nor can it be, the by-product of arrested evil-doing. An education in virtue cannot be merely a by-product of contingent causality. It must be deliberately pursued for its own sake. The good must be an object of a cognitive process in order to become the compass in the education of the passions. Only when the passions have been disciplined by reason can any government—or any individual—pursue the good. For Aristotle, the only concurrence that counts in the end is that of reason and passion.

Calhoun's belief in the benevolent effects of the concurrent majority depends at every point upon the mid-nineteenth-century belief in science and progress that he shared with John Stuart Mill no less than with Karl Marx. This was the belief, which we have seen expressed repeatedly, that the nonmoral progress of science and the moral progress of civilization are inevitably and inextricably linked. The concurrent majority would produce virtue because it was itself the result of the progress of science in the solution of the problem of human government. But this belief, whose origin was in Rousseau and whose perfection was in Hegel, did not survive Nietzsche's critique. That critique has been empirically borne out by the experience of both National Socialism and Communism, two regimes of utter depravity that, more than any others, claimed to be based upon Science and justified by History. Yet neither Nietzsche's critique nor the experience of twentieth-century totalitarianism was really necessary to demonstrate that scientific progress was as consistent with evil as with good. Calhoun's identification of the defense of minority rights with the defense of slavery had itself disproved the idea of progress.

∼

Notwithstanding the foregoing, Calhoun says things in the *Disquisition* about liberty and equality that are astonishing in their apparent agreement with the principles of a free society that we associate with Jefferson and Lincoln. Consider the following, regarding the error of "the opinion that liberty and equality are so intimately united that liberty cannot be perfect without perfect equality."

> That they are united to a certain extent, and that equality of citizens, in the eyes of the law, is essential to liberty in a popular government, is conceded. But to go further and make equality of *condition* essential to liberty would be to destroy both liberty and progress. The reason is that inequality of condition, while it is a necessary consequence of liberty, is at the same time indispensable to progress. In order to understand why this is so, it is necessary to bear in mind that the mainspring to progress is the desire of individuals to better their condition, and that the strongest impulse which can be given to it is to leave individuals free to exert themselves in the manner they may deem best for that purpose, as far at least as it can be done consistently with the ends for which the government is ordained, and to secure to all the fruits of their exertions. Now, as individuals differ greatly from each other in intelligence, sagacity, energy, perseverance, skill, habits of industry and economy, physical power, position, and opportunity—the necessary effect of leaving all free to exert themselves to better their condition must be a corresponding inequality between those who may possess these advantages in a high degree and those who may be deficient in them. The only means by which this result can be prevented are either to impose such restrictions on the exertions of those who may possess them in a high degree as will place them on a level with those who do not, or to deprive them of the fruits of their exertions. But to impose such restrictions on them would be destructive of liberty, while to deprive them of the fruit of their exertions would be to destroy the desire of bettering their condition. It is indeed this inequality of condition between the front and rear ranks, in the march of progress, which gives so strong an impulse to the former to maintain their position, and the latter to press forward into their

files. This gives to progress its greatest impulse. To force the front rank back to the rear or attempt to push forward the rear into line with the front, by the interposition of government, would put an end to the impulse and effectually arrest the march of progress.[66]

One can hear in this passage the very accents of Adam Smith. Much of it could be taken as a manifesto of late-twentieth-century conservatism, such as might have appeared in a speech of Barry Goldwater or Ronald Reagan. And we are reminded once again that in the tenth *Federalist*, Madison declared it to be "the first object of government" to protect "the different and unequal faculties of acquiring property." By this Madison meant that there should be *equal* protection of *unequal* abilities. This equal protection of unequal abilities would result, from Madison's premises no less than from Calhoun's, in inequalities of *condition*, meaning especially thereby inequalities of wealth and property. As Madison puts it, "the most common and durable source of factions has been the various and unequal distribution of property."[67] While people differ in mathematical, musical, artistic, and athletic abilities, it is the faculties that lead to different kinds and amounts of property that drive the political process.

According to Calhoun, and also to Madison and Lincoln (and Adam Smith), the mainspring to progress is the desire of individuals to better their condition. The American Founding recognized this as an attribute of the nature of man and adopted the principle that in this respect, as well as others, all men are created equal. Other societies, contrary to nature, have confined men to fixed or inherited status derived from families, clans, tribes, religions, or socioeconomic classes. A free society abolishes merely conventional or inherited status as the basis for the acquisition or possession of property.

According to Calhoun, progress depends above all on two things: leaving individuals free to exert themselves in the manner they may deem best, and securing to all the fruits of their exertions. Today this is familiar free market doctrine. Calhoun does not say so, but his words certainly imply a natural right, as Lincoln would say, for each human person to put into his mouth the bread that his hands have earned. Calhoun does not say so, because this would also imply a right of each human person to own himself. It is certainly true, as Calhoun says, that giving free reign to inequalities of character and ability will result in inequalities with respect to wealth. But it is equally true that the possession of the lesser rewards of those who may deserve less should be as inviolate as the possession of the larger rewards of the more deserving. If there is to be sanctity to the property of the rich, there cannot be less sanctity to the property of the poor, and most especially to each human being's ownership of himself. If, as Aristotle says, the poor ought not, by the power of their numbers, divide the property of the rich, neither should the rich use the power of their wealth to oppress the poor. It is this conclusion from Calhoun's premises that Lincoln, but not Calhoun, would draw.

Calhoun says that the greatest impulse to progress comes from the impulse of the rear file to press forward and that of the front to stay ahead. Every attempt by government to interpose artificial barriers to fix the status of individuals, whether to keep the poor from becoming rich or the rich from becoming poor, will "effectually arrest the march of progress." By this Calhoun condemns, as much as any other American, the Old World regimes of inherited wealth, inherited status, inherited political power, and inherited privileges. These regimes were structured so that the lower classes, however able and industrious, would remain below, and the upper classes, however lazy and incompetent, would remain above. One of the main socioeconomic features of American society, from the Founding period until today, is the fluidity of socioeconomic classes. While inequality of wealth has remained remarkably constant—as indeed it should have done, given the natural inequality of the faculties of acquiring property—membership in the different classes constituted by wealth has remained remarkably changeable. The same persons or families do not remain either rich or poor. The top 1 percent may have nearly the same proportion of the wealth of society year in and year out, but the same persons do not constitute that top percent. Similar observations are in order for each successive percentile, down to the very bottom. The flow between the classes is at least as notable as their inequality. But again, there has been one great and notable exception to these general observations, which we note by repeating the following from Calhoun's Oregon speech: "With us [of the South], the two great divisions of society are not the rich and the poor, but white and black; and all the former, the poor as well as the rich, belong to the upper class, and are respected and treated as equals, if honest and industrious, and hence have a position and pride of character of which neither poverty nor misfortune can deprive them."[68]

One can only wonder how the same mind could have held within itself both the praise of the principles of free society in the *Disquisition* and this celebration of unmerited elevation and unmerited degradation in the Oregon speech. If all whites enjoy upper-class status without regard to their "intelligence, sagacity, energy," etc., then the motives that would lead them to contribute to the progress of society are, to say the least, greatly attenuated. Far worse, however, is the fate of those who are degraded because of their color and who cannot ascend by any exertions of their own despite whatever virtues and talents they might possess. Calhoun says that all whites belong to the upper class if they are honest and industrious. But it is difficult to imagine that any whites, with the barely possible exception of convicted criminals or the mentally defective, would ever lose status to blacks. The "equality" enjoyed by whites in the South is celebrated elsewhere by Calhoun as lessening, if not avoiding entirely, the class struggle between capital and labor that he (like Karl Marx) saw threatening the stability of free society in the industrializing North.

~

It is true that in the *Disquisition* Calhoun had prefaced his praise of the principle of liberty with the following qualification:

> [I]t is a great and dangerous error to suppose that all people are equally entitled to liberty. It is a reward to be earned, not a blessing to be gratuitously lavished on all alike—a reward for the intelligent, the patriotic, the virtuous and deserving and not a boon to be bestowed on a people too ignorant, degraded, and vicious to be capable either of appreciating or enjoying it. Nor is it any disparagement of liberty that such is and ought to be the case. . . . A reward more appropriate than liberty could not be conferred on the deserving, nor punishment inflicted on the undeserving more just than to be subject to lawless and despotic rule. This dispensation seems to be the result of some fixed law; and every effort to disturb or defeat it, by attempting to elevate a people in the scale of liberty above the point to which they are entitled to rise, must ever prove abortive and end in disappointment.[69]

Let us recall that the Declaration of Independence, no less than Calhoun, speaks of "barbarous ages" and "merciless Indian savages." But these distinctions in the Declaration, as for the Founders in general, depend upon an understanding of civilization grounded in the natural rights of mankind. That a people may not be qualified for the exercise of liberty does not mean that they are not human or that there is no moral obligation due to their humanity. It means only that they are not now what the Declaration calls a "civilized nation." Those who do not know of the rights with which they have been endowed by their Creator can hardly profit from their exercise or be expected to show consideration to others as possessed of the same rights. For these reasons it may be said that they are not entitled to liberty. But as we have seen John Stuart Mill suggest (in agreement with the Declaration), it is in the interest of civilized mankind that barbarians become qualified for freedom, rather than being fixed in their dependence for the same reason it is in the interest of parents that their children grow up.

Calhoun speaks of the intelligent and virtuous who are deserving of liberty and of the ignorant and degraded who are not. He says that liberty is a reward to be earned. But he does not say how it is to be earned. There is a sense in which it may be true, as Calhoun says, that every attempt to elevate a people in the scale of liberty above the point to which they are entitled must prove abortive. But this cannot justify declaring that any effort by any particular people to elevate itself must prove abortive. Why should there not be a desire of peoples, as of individuals, to better themselves? And why may this not be true even of black slaves, as it was of the children of Israel in Egypt?

One cannot concede the humanity of the black man without conceding the necessity for ultimate emancipation. Without such a policy, the only alternative, as we recall from Jefferson in the *Notes on Virginia*, was a servile war, in which the position of masters and slaves might be reversed. The "Almighty has no attribute which can take side with us in such a contest," Jefferson added.[70] No such thought seems ever to have crossed Calhoun's mind. For him, Science has guaranteed the victory of civilization over barbarism, and the record of that victory is History. This combination of Science and History is also called Progress, which is irreversible, and which certifies that those who are free and those who are enslaved deserve their conditions. But does not Calhoun's whole argument in the *Disquisition* contradict his distinction between those deserving and those undeserving of liberty? Does not any majority or any minority possessing the power of government act tyrannically unless compelled to act otherwise by the concurrent veto? By his own account, Calhoun's virtuous and deserving become virtuous and deserving only under the compulsion of that veto. How can he tell whether a people is enslaved because it is ignorant and degraded, or ignorant and degraded because enslaved?

Calhoun, unlike Mill and the Declaration, implies no obligation on the part of the civilized to provide for the improvement of those said to be barbarians. Indeed, it is difficult to see how, on Calhoun's premises, those who have become civilized by the action of the concurrent veto will act benevolently towards anyone who does not possess the veto. Calhoun does not recognize any common interest growing out of a common humanity. The only common interest he recognizes is that caused by the joint possession of the veto power. What meaning can there be to "deserve" or, for that matter, to "virtue," when all behavior is grounded in one or another form of compulsion? In Calhoun's worldview, right is founded on might, as it was in "the gloomy age of ignorance and superstition" decried by Washington.

～

Calhoun, we repeat, sees the tyranny of the numerical majority precisely as a vehicle by which government interposes to keep some undeservedly privileged and others undeservedly disadvantaged. As an example of what Calhoun means, one thinks of the tariff of 1828 and of Calhoun's "Exposition and Protest" directed against it. Calhoun made a skillful argument that a majority had in effect used the tariff as a means of confiscating a large measure of the wealth of one section of the United States and transferring it to another. But Calhoun's argument, however skillful, could not conceal the fact that the tariff had its origins in the circumstances leading to the War of 1812, in which Calhoun himself had been one of the "war-hawks." He, like Henry Clay, had been one of those who thought they might use American grievances against Britain as a pretext to take Canada. The grievances in question related mainly to Britain's interference, during its wars with Napoleon, with America's rights as a neutral party to freedom of commerce on the high seas. But those engaged in that commerce, who were mainly New Englanders, found it sufficiently profitable despite British interference and did not welcome Jefferson's embargo or the policies pursued by Madison, ending in war. There was even at the time a movement to break off a New England federation from the Union, the first great threat of secession in American history. But New Englanders were gradually mollified, as they transferred their capital from shipping to manufacturing. Republicans, among them Calhoun, recognized that these "infant industries" were the result, not of the free economic decisions of individuals, but of compulsions arising from the foreign policies of Jefferson and Madison. Such policies justified a political remedy, namely, protective tariffs. The tariff of 1828 was the latest in a series. South Carolina argued plausibly that the circumstances that justified the original tariff no longer justified its continuance. That may have been true, but politics had created vested interests, whose nature is to claim privileges long after their original justification has passed.[71] But just as the tariff had mollified New Englanders before, a reduction of the tariff was able to mollify South Carolina in 1833. In both cases, the political system followed a course of shifting coalitions of heterogeneous majorities, as had been anticipated by Madison. There was no such tyranny of a homogeneous majority as Calhoun's argument attempted to conjure. There was never such a homogeneous majority in American politics, except that arising from slavery. Yet the whole theory of the concurrent majority is predicated upon such homogeneity.

We conclude our critique of Calhoun's *Disquisition* by observing that nothing in it justifies a different conception of the republican form of government than the one to which Lincoln subscribed. Nor does anything in it justify rejecting Lincoln's view of secession as incompatible with the constitutional guarantee of a republican form of government to every state of the Union.

Part III

A *Discourse on the Constitution and Government of the United States* is a massive work of some 396 pages in the Cralle edition. This compares with the 107 pages of the *Disquisition,* itself a bulky work if one considers not only the number but also the density of its pages. As the reader will expect, the *Discourse* culminates with a demonstration that only if the principle of the concurrent majority is brought to bear upon the question of slavery in the territories—with the slave states having the veto power—can the United States be saved from tyranny, anarchy, or war. Calhoun's prophecy at the end of the *Discourse* incorporates earlier expressions of this thesis in his Oregon speech of 1848, as well as passages from his last Senate speech, on the admission of California, on March 4, 1850.

The first part of the *Discourse* is a resolute attempt to assert that the government of the United States is wholly and entirely federal. This assertion is accompanied by an uncompromising insistence that a federal regime is one in which an undivided sovereignty remains in the states individually. At the center of this undertaking is the absolute denial that the Constitution is or can be, as Madison had said in the thirty-ninth *Federalist,* "partly federal, partly national." It would not be amiss to characterize the *Discourse* as a whole as an attempt to replace the *Federalist* as the authoritative commentary on the Constitution. For our purposes, it will not be necessary to examine critically more of the *Discourse* than its fundamental premises, as Calhoun's rigidly deductive method lives or dies with those premises, from which everything else follows.

The undivided sovereignty of the states is the keystone upon which everything else in the *Discourse* depends. It is the indispensable constitutional and theoretical foundation for discovering in the states that legal and political interest that is to be defended by the concurrent veto. And the veto power, we recall from the *Disquisition,* is the power that is presumed to compel the compromises that result in a common good. The question of how to identify an "interest" entitled to the veto was not addressed in the *Disquisition.* Nor did Calhoun consider that those who had interests to protect with a veto were sometimes divided within themselves as to which interests to protect. To Calhoun, the possibility of divided sovereignty implied that the people of each state formed part of a national constituency for some purposes, while remaining separate and discrete for other purposes. This in turn implied that the people of a state, belonging simultaneously to two different communities, could be so divided within themselves as to nullify their ability to cast the veto upon which the Calhounian constitution depended. In 1860–61, when the states that would form the Confederacy "seceded," they did so by majority vote in their respective conventions. Notwithstanding the minorities that voted against secession, most members of the conventions (and their followers outside the conventions) believed themselves bound by the vote of the state majority. Interestingly, there was little or no talk in the seceding states of a concurrent veto by the pro-union minorities. Here the absolute rule of the numerical majority prevailed.[72]

As we have seen, Alexander Stephens, after leading the antisecessionist party in the Georgia convention, felt altogether bound by the vote to secede. Like Rousseau's citizen in the *Social Contract*, he discovered his "real" will in what the majority willed, not in what he himself had willed before the vote was taken. When Georgia joined the Confederacy, he gave his loyalty without reserve to the Confederate cause, becoming Jefferson Davis's vice president. It was as a disciple of Calhoun that he believed he owed his loyalty primarily to the people of Georgia, acting by its majority. His former obligation to the people of the United States, acting by its majority, was altogether derivative from his obligation to the people of Georgia. It was derivative from the fact that Georgia had ratified the Constitution. Georgia placed him under obligations to the Constitution. But Georgia remained the judge of the extent of those obligations, including those arising from the supremacy clause in Article VI of the Constitution.

Calhoun's theory required that the definitions of "federal" and "federalism" remain unchanged from what they had been before the adoption of the Constitution of 1787. As a matter of historical fact, however, the transformation of the meanings of these words had begun in the process by which American independence was declared in 1776. It began, as we have previously demonstrated, in the resolutions of the colonial assemblies for independence and union. The resolutions for union were accompanied by reservations of the "internal police" power to the individual colonies. Dual sovereignty or dual federalism was thus implicit in the mode by which the Declaration of Independence itself came to be authorized. We have seen that Jefferson and Madison, in 1825, called the Declaration "the act of union of these states." It was the common understanding of the Revolutionary generation that the separation of the thirteen colonies from Great Britain and union with each other were accomplished simultaneously. State sovereignty was from the outset an aspect of federalism within the framework of union. What was implicit in the Declaration, and only imperfectly embodied in the Articles of Confederation, became fully explicit in the more perfect union of the Constitution. This more perfect union could itself be called a more competent exercise in the allocation of the powers of sovereignty.

The writing identified above all others with the advocacy of the ratification of the Constitution is the *Federalist*. The authors of that notable treatise advocated a central government with powers beyond anything previously recognized as belonging to a federal system. Clearly, new wine was being poured into the old bottle of federalism. We are reminded again, moreover, that by calling themselves and their party "federalists," these partisans of a quasi-national federalism denied the name of federalist to their political opponents. Denied their "real" name, the opponents of the Constitution became known instead as *anti*federalists. This rhetorical transformation gave the partisans of the Constitution an advantage in the contest over ratification that may well have supplied the margin of victory.[73]

Calhoun's *Discourse* is a resolute denial that any such change in the meaning of the word "federal" had taken place and an equally resolute effort to interpret the Constitution in light of the concept of federalism that prevailed before the American experience had begun its transformation. Opposition to the Constitution in the ratification struggle was based upon the fact or opinion that all extensive regimes or empires in history had been governed despotically. Free government was identified with republics small enough for citizen participation. A free empire was looked upon as a contradiction in terms. The framers of the Constitution were frank in asserting that their enterprise was unprecedented—that it represented a *novus ordo seclorum*. In 1835 Madison referred to the form of government of the Constitution as a "nondescript," meaning thereby that it did not have a name provided by any previous theory and that it could be characterized only by reference to its own provisions.[74] In the thirty-ninth *Federalist*, Madison summarized the objections that embodied the position Calhoun would occupy as follows:

> "But it was not sufficient," say the adversaries of the proposed Constitution, "for the convention to adhere to the republican form. They ought, with equal care, to have preserved the *federal* form, which regards the Union as a *Confederacy* of sovereign states; instead of which, they have framed a *national* government which regards the Union as a *consolidation* of the States."[75]

According to Calhoun, what the adversaries of the Constitution wished is what the framers actually did. But Madison and the other framers believed that the device of representation had been either unknown or little understood by the political science of the past. Representation had already extended the range of popular government to states such as New York and Virginia, which were far more extensive than any past republic. Now the aggregation of counties into states could be replicated by the aggregation of states into a Union with a common government for common purposes. By the judicious use of representation, the republican form might become compatible with a regime as extensive as, or even more extensive than, past empires, with power in the service of freedom beyond anything known hitherto.

We earlier noted that Madison, in the *Federalist*, believed that the greater variety of interests comprised in the majority of an extended republic would minimize, if not prevent, the formation of a despotic majority. We have seen that, except with respect to the single question of slavery in the territories, Calhoun's prediction of a majority faction being formed by the very nature of the political process was not borne out. Thus experience supported the Madisonian argument that republicanism, so far from being subverted by its extended size, would by this fact be freed from the "instability, injustice, and confusion" in "the public councils" justly ascribed to it in the past.[76]

We recall that the second of the Articles of Confederation declared that "Each State retains its sovereignty, freedom, and independence, and every power, jurisdiction, and right, which is not by this Confederation expressly delegated to the United States in Congress assembled."[77] Calhoun assumes, with some plausibility, that this article affirms state sovereignty in its most uncompromising form. Yet even here there is ambiguity concerning whether expressly delegated powers, jurisdictions, and rights do not in some ways qualify state sovereignty, freedom, and independence. Calhoun also ignores the fact, later emphasized by Lincoln, that the Articles affirm that "the Union shall be perpetual." If state sovereignty implied a right of secession, how could the Union be perpetual? Is not retained sovereignty defined by the "internal police" power mentioned in the resolutions leading to independence?

On the side of undiluted state sovereignty was the fact that under the Articles of Confederation, the central government did not possess any instrumentalities of its own but depended entirely upon the governments of the states to carry out the measures adopted by Congress. As we have discussed previously, while the division of sovereignty may have begun, in theory, with the Declaration of Independence, it was not practically implemented by the Articles. The Congress of the Articles did not constitute a government in the accepted sense of the term, as is shown by the fact that it had no executive or judicial branches. Taxes were requisitions laid upon the states, but the Congress itself could not collect them. By Calhoun's theory, however, South Carolina in 1833 remained as much the arbiter of whether taxes levied by Congress might be collected within its precincts as it had been in 1783. In its nullification of the tariff of 1828, South Carolina claimed a lawful right to refuse to allow the federal customs to be collected within its boundaries. From a right to nullify to a right to secede was but a short step. From this perspective, state sovereignty really was unchanged from what it had been under the Articles.

Here is how Calhoun develops this theme:

> The Government of the United States was formed by the Constitution of the United States;—and ours is a democratic, federal republic. It is democratic, in contradistinction to aristocracy and monarchy. It excludes classes, orders, and all artificial distinctions. To guard against their introduction, the constitution prohibits the granting of any title of nobility by the United States, or by any State.

Calhoun's language is thoroughly within the tradition of the Founders. How he can reconcile the exclusion of classes and all artificial distinctions here with his pronouncement of racial classes in the Oregon speech, we can only conjecture. One supposes that for Calhoun, the distinction between black and white is not artificial. The aforesaid government, he continues,

> is federal as well as democratic. . . . It is federal, because it is the government of States united in a political union, in contradistinction to a government of individuals socially united; that is, by what is usually called a social compact. To express it more concisely, it is federal and not national because it is the government of a community of States, and not the government of a single State or nation.

Calhoun will repeat, with ever greater insistence, that the terms "federal" and "national" are exclusive of each other and that they cannot be combined in any proportions into any whole.

> The whole system is indeed democratic throughout. It has for its fundamental principle the great cardinal maxim, that the people are the source of all power; that the governments of the several states and of the United States were created by them, and for them; that the powers conferred on them are not surrendered, but delegated; and as such are held in trust, and not absolutely; and can be rightfully exercised only in furtherance of the objects for which they were delegated.[78]

It is difficult to imagine anything in the foregoing to which Jefferson, Madison, or Lincoln could take the slightest exception. If we look at the Revolutionary state constitutions, we find similar assertions of the authority of the people and of the doctrine of delegated and limited powers. However, in the case of Massachusetts, to take one example, such assertions are preceded by, and founded upon, the assertion that "all men are born free and equal." As we have seen, Calhoun in his Oregon speech called this the "most false and dangerous of all political errors." What are inferences from principle in these state constitutions (and in the Declaration of Independence) become free-standing principles, needing no justification, in the doctrine of Calhoun. Why a government should be democratic and why it should be limited to delegated and revocable powers are questions Calhoun neither asks nor answers. He takes all assertions of natural rights in the Founding as if they were assertions of prescriptive rights. If we look back to the *Disquisition*, however, we would be told that history or fate decides all questions of constitutional authority, just as it decides who should be enslaved and who should be free. Calhoun appeals to the facts resulting from the Revolution but ignores the theory.

467

When Calhoun speaks of "Individuals socially united . . . by what is usually called a social compact," he is compelled to explain facts by the theory he rejects. A social compact, we know, is possible only between individuals who acknowledge each other as equal in the rights that government is instituted to protect. Those rights must be antecedent to the social compact, which is to say that they are natural rights, which natural rights become thereby the foundation of the rights of positive law. For Calhoun, the governments of the states have arisen from "individuals socially united," whereas the government of the United States has arisen not from individuals but from the states. But cannot the individuals of the separate states also be "socially united" by reason of the fact that they agree to have a common government? Is not a social compact one by which a people agree to have a common government? Calhoun says no.

> That it [the Constitution] is federal and not national, we have the high authority of the convention which framed it. General Washington, as its organ, in his letter submitting the plan to the consideration of the Congress of the then Confederacy, calls it, in one place,—"the general government of the union;" and in another,—"the federal government of these States."[79]

In the end, the authority of the argument of the entire *Discourse* depends upon Calhoun's claim of the authority of the letter by which Washington transmitted the Constitution to the Congress. But Calhoun assigns to Washington's words a meaning that they clearly did not have. He assumes that for Washington, as for himself, "federal" can only mean "not national." That is to say, he assumes that Washington agrees with him that the Constitution described by Madison in the thirty-ninth Federalist as "partly federal, partly national" is impossible. It is instructive therefore to consider what Washington actually said:

> It is obviously impracticable in *the federal government of these states* to secure all rights of independent sovereignty to each, and yet provide for the interest and safety of all—Individuals entering into society, must give up a share of liberty to preserve the rest.[80]

We have italicized the words cited by Calhoun to highlight the fact that the sentence in which they occur, taken as a whole, says the exact opposite of what Calhoun imputes to it. The Constitution, says Washington, cannot secure all rights of independent sovereignty to the states individually if it is to provide for the interest and safety of all together.

Washington compares the action of the states in ratifying the Constitution to the action of "individuals entering into society." If individuals enter society, they must enter from somewhere. Washington assumes, as a matter of course, that very state of nature that Calhoun ridicules. Washington also assumes that the aforesaid entrance is voluntary and therefore that civil society is a voluntary association. Nothing could more directly contradict Calhoun's assertion that membership in society and government is as involuntary as breathing.

If Calhoun's theory of the indivisibility of sovereignty were true, it would follow that the states, in giving up some rights of sovereignty, as Washington says they must, would cease altogether to be sovereign. But clearly Washington, like Madison, thought that the new Constitution, in dividing the powers of government between the states individually and the United States, also divided the sovereignty from which these powers were derived.

In contemplating the generation from the social compact of "the just powers of government," we must bear in mind, as Calhoun himself says, that these powers "are not surrendered, but delegated; and, as such are held in trust . . . and can be rightfully exercised only in furtherance of the objects for which they were delegated." Here is Calhoun's version of the doctrine of limited government and the rule of law. But as Dr. Johnson would say, it is a doctrine "on stilts," because it is based upon a denial of the individual rights in the state of nature that are its foundation. According to the Declaration of Independence, the unrightful exercise of these powers may be resisted by what came to be known as the natural right of revolution. As we have seen, however, Calhoun recognizes no such right.

If the powers of government are "not surrendered but delegated," to whom does Calhoun think the unsurrendered powers belong? If government is only a trustee, who is the principal? By what means is the trustee held to his trust? Washington assumed that the process by which powers are transferred from individual states to the United States exactly parallels that by which powers are at first transferred from individuals in the state of nature to civil society. It is notable that in neither case are all powers surrendered or delegated by the principal to the trustee. For example, to no government are the rights of conscience surrendered. Thus all governments are limited governments in one sense or another, and the state governments are governments of delegated powers no less than is the government of the United States. The Constitution is therefore a compact or contract among the people of the several states, in the same way that the state constitutions are compacts or contracts among the people of those states. The people of the several states become one people with respect to those functions of government delegated to the common government. It will be this government with respect to which they will be fellow citizens. They are therefore bound in loyalty and conscience by the constitutional decisions of the constitutional majority of the federal union, just as much as they are bound to obey the constitutional decisions of a constitutional majority within their individual states with respect to the exercise of the just powers of the state governments. There would then be no constitutional process by which a state majority could lawfully nullify the acts of, or secede from, the federal union and its government, so long as that government acted within the boundaries of its delegated powers.

Washington, in his letter of transmittal, had these further words: "In all our deliberations . . . we kept steadily in our view that which appears to us the greatest interest of every true American, the consolidation of our Union, in which is involved our prosperity, felicity, perhaps our national existence." And he concluded with the hope and belief that the Constitution "may promote the lasting welfare of that country so dear to us all, and secure her freedom and happiness."[81] Clearly, for Washington, a "true American" is one who sees himself above all as a citizen of one "country." The word "country," like "nation" (as in the Gettysburg Address), implies the highest object of political loyalty. It is impossible to imagine the true Americans to whom Washington refers being anything but "socially united," that is, fellow citizens in the full sense.

To those who, like Calhoun, identified constitutionalism with state sovereignty, no word was more anathema than "consolidation." Yet Washington, without the least hesitation, called ratification consolidation and explicitly meant by it the surrender of some of the individual rights of sovereignty. Calhoun recognizes the danger here as follows: "It is a strong expression; but as strong as it is, it certainly was not intended to imply the destruction of the union, as it is supposed to do by the advocates of a national government."[82] Calhoun assumes that any change in the meaning of "federal" would destroy the union, not perfect it. But Washington expressly says the opposite: The greater perfection of the union depends upon the subtraction of some of the sovereign powers of the states and their transfer to the government of the Union. And Calhoun does not even try to pretend that Washington's "country dear to us all" referred to anything but the United States, as distinct from Virginia or any other state named individually.

Washington's letter in 1787 is no less an appeal to union than Lincoln's in 1861. It is no less an appeal to "the better angels of our nature." It is difficult to imagine a document more directly opposed to Calhoun's doctrine of separate, individual state sovereignty.

∾

Lincoln left Springfield for Washington on February 11, 1861, with a task greater than that which rested upon Washington. He was the truest heir of Washington, because of both the clarity of his understanding and the strength of his character. The attempts to diminish the cause of Lincoln in the American mind, in Lincoln's lifetime and in our own, have been substantially identical. Calhoun's heirs have dominated the academy and by a shallow and permissive historicism and relativism have subjected "the laws of nature and of nature's God" to scorn and contempt. They have done so by propaganda appealing to the basest passions, and reason has been in retreat. Nonetheless, "truth is great and will prevail, unless deprived of her natural weapons, free argument and debate, errors ceasing to be dangerous when it is permitted freely to contradict them." We must then take up the weapons of truth and go forth to battle once again for the cause of Father Abraham, of Union, and of Freedom, as in the olden time.

Appendix

"The Dividing Line between Federal and Local Authority: Popular Sovereignty in the Territories"—A Commentary

As 1860 drew near, Stephen A. Douglas was without doubt the most popular Democrat in the free states. Yet as events were to prove, he was essentially a man without a party, because he represented a policy and a principle that were being ground into dust between the upper and the nether millstones of proslavery and antislavery. The disaster that struck at the Democratic convention in Charleston in April 1860, dividing the Democrats into two parties and dooming their nominees to defeat, was the ineluctable outcome of the antebellum debate, and in particular of the Lincoln–Douglas debates. Perhaps there has never in political history been a time when the logic of events followed so closely the logic of argument. In the last analysis, Douglas failed in deed because he failed in speech to justify his compromise position.

Lincoln, in his letter to Alexander Stephens of December 22, 1860, summed up the difference between North and South as follows: "You think slavery is *right*, and ought to be extended; while we think it is *wrong* and ought to be restricted."[1] In his inaugural address Lincoln would use almost identical words. If there was no middle ground between those who thought slavery right and those who thought it wrong, one side or the other would have to yield or the decision would be made by force.

At some point after his joint debates with Lincoln, Douglas came to the realization that Lincoln's sustained critique of his version of popular sovereignty had made him vulnerable to the charge with which Lincoln would end his speech at Cooper Institute: "Let us be diverted by none of those sophistical contrivances such as groping for some middle ground between the right and the wrong, vain as the search for a man who should be neither a living man nor a dead man—such as a policy of 'don't care' on a question about which all true men do care."[2] Lincoln's antislavery policy was supported by the doctrine of human equality in the Declaration of Independence. The proslavery policy was supported by the denial of the truth of the Declaration's "laws of nature and of nature's God" and the assertion that, by the genuine laws of God and nature, slavery was the best possible condition for Negroes. Douglas had to prove that there was a constitutionally principled reason why Congress ought to ignore the question of the rightness or wrongness of slavery, leaving the issue of slavery in the territories to the people of each territory alone. For Douglas, moral right consisted in having the people of each territory or state decide the question for themselves, rather than in what the people decided. Popular sovereignty was itself neutral as to the rightness or wrongness of slavery, and only a policy of such neutrality could avert secession and civil war.

Douglas's *Harper's* essay, "The Dividing Line between Federal and Local Authority: Popular Sovereignty in the Territories," was an attempt to provide a broad historical and philosophical foundation for this policy.[3] It was the last—and perhaps the only—serious attempt to find that middle ground whose existence Lincoln denied. Don E. Fehrenbacher has written that "its publication may have been the most important political act of the year [1859] in the United States."[4] Certainly no understanding of the 1860 election campaign is possible without a careful reading and analysis of this essay, which was Douglas's principal contribution to that campaign.[5]

~

The *Harper's* essay expresses its thesis by subsuming the distinction between state and territory under the word "local." According to Douglas, there was not any fundamental difference between a state and a territory with respect to the right to internal self-government. By drawing a distinction between the right of Congress (or of any lawful government) to *confer* powers and its right to *exercise* powers, he denied the relevance of the fact that a territorial government (unlike a state government) was a legal creation of Congress. Once powers were conferred, he argued, the sovereignty inherent in the exercise of such powers belonged to those upon whom they were conferred.

> Congress may confer upon the judicial department all the judicial powers and functions of the Territory, without having the right to hear and determine a cause, or render a judgment, or to revise or annul any decision made by the courts so established by Congress. Congress may also confer upon the legislative department of the Territory certain legislative powers which it can not itself exercise. . . . The powers which Congress may thus *confer* but can not *exercise*, are such as relate to the domestic affairs and internal polity of the Territory, and do not affect the general welfare of the Republic.[6]

According to Douglas, no matter what the legal instrumentalities by which the legislative power of a territory is called into existence, once it exists, it possesses the exclusive right of legislation with respect to its domestic polity, and any interference with that right is both legally and morally wrong. The only qualification he would admit would be that it is subject to the restrictions of the Constitution (e.g., no bills of attainder, ex post facto laws, patents of nobility, etc.).

What Douglas's argument omits, however, is as important as what it includes. Here is the comment of President Buchanan's attorney general, Jeremiah Black:

> A Territorial government is merely provisional and temporary. It is created by Congress for the necessary preservation of order and the purposes of police. The powers conferred upon it are expressed in the organic act, which is the charter of its existence, and which may be changed and repealed at the pleasure of Congress. In most of those acts the power has been expressly reserved to Congress of revising the Territorial laws, and the power to repeal them exists without such reservation. This was asserted in the case of Kansas by the most distinguished Senators in Congress of 1856. The President appoints the Governor, judges, and all other officers whose appointment is not otherwise provided for, directly or indirectly, by Congress. Even the expenses of the Territorial government are paid out of the federal treasury. The truth is, they have no attribute of sovereignty about them.[7]

However much Black and the Buchanan administration represented the proslavery persuasion on the territorial question, what Black says here was also Lincoln's and the Republican Party's opinion concerning the dependent and contingent status of territorial governments. An organized territory was a state in *statu nascendi*. It was to the state it would become what the child is to the adult. The supervisory power of Congress corresponds to that of a parent before a child reaches the age of consent. Douglas's task was somehow to prove, notwithstanding the foregoing, that there was an element of sovereignty in territorial majorities sufficient to justify what he called popular sovereignty.

Douglas attempted to ground this conception of sovereignty in the history of the American Revolution. He drew an exact parallel between the local authority of the colonies within the British Empire and the local authority of states and territories within the Constitution. And he characterized the entire Revolution as a defense of local against central authority.

> [The American Colonists] conceded the right of the Imperial government to make all laws and perform all acts concerning the Colonies, which were in their nature *Imperial* and not *Colonial*—which affected the general welfare of the Empire, and did not interfere with the "internal polity" of the Colonies. . . . [I]n general they recognized the right of the Imperial government of Great Britain to exercise all the powers and authority which, under our federal Constitution, are

delegated by the people of the several states to the government of the United States.

Recognizing and conceding to the Imperial government all these powers—*including the right to institute governments for the Colonies,* by granting charters . . . the Colonies emphatically denied that the Imperial government had any rightful authority to impose taxes upon them without their consent, or to interfere with their internal polity; claiming that it was the birthright of all Englishmen—inalienable when formed into a political community—to exercise and enjoy all the rights, privileges, and immunities of self-government in respect to all matters and things which were Local and not General. . . .

Thus it appears that our fathers of the Revolution were contending, not for Independence in the first instance, but for the inestimable right of Local Self-Government . . . the right of every distinct community—dependent Colonies, Territories, and Provinces, as well as sovereign States—to make their own local laws, form their own domestic institutions, and manage their own internal affairs in their own way.[8]

The central idea in the *Harper's* essay, and indeed in all of Douglas's political thought, is his assertion that the birthright of all Englishmen (or white Americans) was "inalienable when formed into a political community." In the many documents of the Revolution, and especially the Declaration of Independence, inalienable (or unalienable) rights and natural rights are one and the same. Douglas does not speak of natural rights, yet he assigns to popular sovereignty the inalienability that can properly belong only to a right that is natural. Why such a right should have been the birthright of Englishmen or white Americans particularly, he does not say. Nor does he ever say what rights, if any, Englishmen or white Americans possessed *before* they were formed into a political community.

That the doctrine of the American Revolution was one of inalienable rights is undoubtedly true. However, rights can be and are inalienable only because they are natural. And natural rights belong to human beings in virtue of their humanity. Rights that are inalienable and natural are antecedent to the formation of political communities. They belong to human beings *in* political communities only because they belong to human beings *apart* from political communities. Human beings are formed by nature. No one chooses to be a human being, any more than he chooses to be born. Political communities are formed by the voluntary actions of human beings, not by nature. Yet nature supplies the nonarbitrary moral ground by which it is decided that political communities are despotic or free. That ground is the consent of the governed, or what Lincoln called the sheet anchor of republicanism. And that is itself the necessary inference from the proposition that all men are created equal.

It is only in virtue of the equal natural rights of mankind that free governments have the rights that they assert. And they deny the foundation of their own rights whenever they deny that others possess the same natural rights. Nowhere in the documents of the American Revolution is it said that rights are inalienable *only* "when [the people are] formed into a political community."

It is undeniable that "our fathers of the Revolution" were contending for local self-government, but they were so contending because of the sovereignty inhering in them in virtue of their natural rights. That sovereignty could not be justly exercised in the denial of the natural right to freedom of other human beings. It could not, in short, be exercised except within boundaries prescribed by the equal rights of other human beings. A vote for slavery would not be an exercise of an inalienable right. It would be a denial of its existence.

Douglas compares the pre-Revolutionary division between local and central authority in the British Empire with the division between local and central authority under the Constitution. In so doing he overlooks the fact that unlike the colonies in the empire, the states under the Constitution participate equally in the central government. There is therefore a presumption, with respect to the government under the Constitution, of a political process in which all parties participate to decide how the line between central and local authority is to be drawn.[9] This presumption could not be made with respect to the British Empire.

In pursuance of his thesis, Douglas quotes from Tucker's Appendix to Blackstone:

> The following extract from a petition to the Throne, presented by the House of Burgesses of Virginia, April 1, 1772, will show the sense of the people of Virginia on the subject of slavery at that period: "The importation of slaves into the colony from the coast of Africa hath long been considered a trade of great inhumanity; and under its present encouragement [by the Crown] we have too much reason to fear will endanger the very existence of your Majesty's American dominions."

Douglas exclaims:

> Mark the ominous words! Virginia tells the King of England in 1772, four years prior to the Declaration of Independence, that his Majesty's American dominions are in danger: Not because of the Stamp duties—not because of the tax on Tea—not because of his attempts to collect revenue in America! These have since been deemed sufficient to justify rebellion and revolution. But none of these are referred to by Virginia in her address to the Throne—there being another wrong which, in magnitude and enormity, so far exceeded these and all other causes of complaint that the very existence of his Majesty's American dominions depended upon it. That wrong consisted in forcing African slavery upon a dependent Colony without her own consent, and in opposition to the wishes of her own people![10]

Now it is true that the burgesses protested against the use of the powers of the Crown to prevent Virginia from outlawing the importation of slaves into their colony. Douglas takes this as evidence that in their understanding, popular sovereignty gave them the exclusive right to legislate for themselves upon the subject of slavery. But the reason they gave was not the reason he assigns to them. They considered it "a trade of great inhumanity." It was a denial of the rights of the enslaved, not the denial of their own rights, that was paramount in their petition.

It is true that the "existence" of Virginia was in a peculiar way threatened by the denial of its petition. That is because the very injustice of slavery made the slaves a danger. In the famous passage on the slave trade that was deleted from Jefferson's draft of the Declaration of Independence, Jefferson wrote that the king

> has waged cruel war against human nature itself, violating its most sacred rights of life and liberty in the persons of a distant people who never offended him, captivating and carrying them into slavery in another hemisphere, or to incur miserable death in their transportation thither. This piratical warfare, the opprobrium of INFIDEL powers, is the warfare of the CHRISTIAN King of Great Britain. Determined to keep open market where MEN should be bought and sold, he has prostituted his negative for suppressing every legislative attempt to prohibit or restrain this execrable commerce. And that this assemblage of horrors might want no fact of distinguished die, he is now exciting those very people to rise in arms among us, and to purchase that liberty of which he has deprived them, by murdering the people on whom he also obtruded them: thus paying off former crimes committed against the LIBERTIES of one people with crimes which he urged them to commit against the LIVES of another.[11]

Jefferson was never more seized by divine fire than when he penned these lines, and it remains a matter of profound regret that they did not remain in the text. They would have made impossible the perversity of Taney's and Douglas's misrepresentations of the Declaration. The passage was deleted because of South Carolina and Rhode Island, the one because they wanted to continue importing slaves, the other because they wanted to continue transporting them. These were matters of economic self-interest, not of right. But the Declaration had to be unanimous, and for the sake of that unanimity the passage on the slave trade was deleted.

These deleted lines remain, however, an authentic gloss upon the Virginia petition of 1772 and completely discredit Douglas's interpretation of that petition in his *Harper's* essay. Certainly Virginia regarded the use of the royal negative as an infringement of their natural right of self-government. But the same right that Virginians claimed for themselves belonged to the victims of the slave trade. A consequence of the importation of slaves into Virginia, as the Virginians foresaw, was a threat to their self-preservation such as actually arose in the Revolution. And the right of self-preservation, the first law of nature, certainly implied that no power of government inconsistent with that right could safely be placed elsewhere than in the hands of those whose selves were to be preserved. That is why the police power of government within the federal system of the Constitution has always placed the primary responsibility for the security of life and property with the states. As we have seen, this priority was never challenged—indeed, it was always insisted upon—by Lincoln and the Republican Party.

Slaves are by nature the enemies of those who enslave them. This is why the introduction of slavery is against the interest of the slaveholders themselves. The examples of popular sovereignty within the several colonies in the Revolutionary period cited by Douglas justify the exclusion of slavery and the regulation of slavery where it already exists. They do not justify the importation of slaves from Africa or the importation of slaves from slave states into territories hitherto uncontaminated by slavery.

It is unnecessary to recount Douglas's examples of the assertion by other colonies of the right to control slavery and the slave trade within their boundaries. While asserting their right of self-government, they nowhere denied the "inhuman" immorality of slavery itself. The same is true of the resolutions by the several colonies mentioned by Douglas authorizing the Declaration of Independence. These resolutions authorized both independence and union and declared that within the government of the union to be formed, each state was to be sovereign over its own "internal polity." In these resolutions we find the earliest enunciation of the federalism enshrined in the Constitution of 1787, and especially in the Tenth Amendment. But all this is merely carrying coals to Newcastle. No one in 1859 was contesting the right of "local" self-government. The only question was whether that included the right to extend slavery—a question that Douglas simply ignores.

Douglas discovers the paradigm of territorial popular sovereignty in congressional legislation, under the Articles of Confederation, for the government of the lands ceded to the United States by Virginia in March 1784. These lands, subsequently known as the Northwest Territory, were the first territory possessed by the United States, as distinct from any one of the states. Here is how Douglas appraises the 1784 plan for its temporary government.

> It was the first plan of government for the Territories ever adopted in the United States. It was drawn by the author of the Declaration of Independence, and revised and adopted by those who shaped the issues which produced the Revolution, and formed the foundations upon which our whole system of governments rests. It was not intended to be either local or temporary in its character, but was designed to apply to all "territory ceded or to be ceded," and to be universal in its

application and eternal in its duration, wherever and whenever we might have
territory requiring a government.

Douglas further observes that "this Jeffersonian Plan for the government of the
Territories—this 'Charter of Compact'—'these fundamental conditions,' which
were declared to be 'unalterable' without the consent of the people of 'the particular State [Territory] within which such alteration is proposed to be made,' stood
on the Statute Book when the Convention assembled at Philadelphia in 1787."[12]
The "Jeffersonian Plan" of 1784 was indeed of historic importance, and that it recognized a right of local self-government may be granted. But that right was not
unconditional. The "fundamental conditions" mentioned above are said to be
"unalterable" without the consent of the Congress, on the one hand, and of the
people of the territory (here called state), on the other. While it is true that Congress cannot make any alteration of these conditions without the consent of the
people concerned, neither can the people make such an alteration without the
consent of Congress. This was not quite the "perfect freedom" asserted by Douglas as popular sovereignty.

What is most remarkable about Jefferson's plan is that it establishes the principle that as new states are added to the Union, they will be constitutionally equal
in all respects to the original thirteen and to each other. The United States, unlike
any empire of the past, would be an empire of equality and freedom. It would not
govern subject provinces, like Rome, or dependent colonies, like Great Britain.
All states, old as well as new, would retain their independence with respect to
their internal polity. But they would also share equally with the other states in the
general or federal government in matters of common concern to the Union as a
whole. In the British Empire from which the thirteen colonies separated, the
colonies had no share in the government of the empire itself. Nor was there, as we
have already observed, any shared political process to resolve differences as to
how the line between central and local authority should be drawn.

What reason could there have been in Jefferson's mind for the legal equality
of the states within the Union other than the legal equality of the individual citizens within their respective states and within the several states? What foundation was there for the equality of citizens other than the natural equality of man,
proclaimed not only in the Declaration of Independence but also in the declarations prefatory to most of the original state constitutions themselves? Virginia's
constitution, for example, proclaims "That all men are by nature equally free and
independent," and Massachusetts's that "All men are born free and equal."[13] That
natural equality is the foundation for the equal right of self-government of all distinct political communities. And that right is incompatible with moral indifference as to whether slavery should be voted up or down.

We need not repeat the four articles that formed the "charter of compact" for both the temporary and permanent territorial governments under Jefferson's plan. There was another, however, that Douglas notices as follows: "The fifth article, which relates to the prohibition of slavery after the year 1800, having been rejected by Congress, never became a part of the Jeffersonian Plan of Government for the Territories, as adopted April 23, 1784."[14] Here is that fifth article, as it appears in Jefferson's text: "That after the year 1800 of the Christian era, there shall be neither slavery nor involuntary servitude in any of the said states, otherwise than in the punishment of crimes whereof the party shall have been convicted to have been personally guilty."[15] With this provision excised, could the plan still be properly called Jeffersonian? Here is what Jefferson himself had to say, in 1786, about the failure of this article:

> There were ten states present; six voted unanimously for it, three against it, and one was divided; and seven votes being requisite to decide the proposition affirmatively, it was lost. The voice of a single individual of the State which was divided, or of one of those which were of the negative, would have prevented this abominable crime from spreading itself over the new country. Thus we see the fate of millions unborn hanging on the tongue of one man, and heaven was silent in that awful moment! But it is to be hoped it will not always be silent, and that the friends to the rights of human nature will in the end prevail.[16]

One would hardly have guessed from Douglas's brief mention of the fifth article what popular sovereignty meant to Jefferson. Could it have been a right to spread an "abominable crime" over "new country"? While this passage from Jefferson reveals the profoundest source of Lincoln's stand on the territorial question, it illuminates the depth of the chasm that separated Douglas's thought from Jefferson's—even as Douglas cited Jefferson as his authority.

Midway in his *Harper's* essay, Douglas writes:

> Let us pause at this point for a moment, and inquire whether it be just to those illustrious patriots and sages who formed the Constitution of the United States, to assume that they intended to confer upon Congress that unlimited and arbitrary power over the people of American Territories, which they had resisted with their blood when claimed by the British Parliament over British Colonies in America? Did they confer upon Congress the right to bind the people of the American Territories in all cases whatsoever, after having fought the battles of the Revolution against a "Preamble" declaring the rights of Parliament "to bind the colonies in all cases whatsoever"?[17]

It is merely rhetorical deception, however, for Douglas to equate the right of Congress to exclude slavery from the territories with the right to bind them "in all cases whatsoever." Douglas also never mentions that the 1784 plan for the North-west Territory, which he cites and quotes at some length, was never implement-ed.[18] In July 1787, the 1784 measure was replaced by the Northwest Ordinance, which was reenacted in 1789 by the first Congress under the new Constitution. As Lincoln pointed out in his Cooper Institute speech, sixteen of the thirty-nine Signers of the Constitution were in that first Congress, which passed the Ordi-nance by voice vote, presumably unanimously, before it was signed into law by President Washington. Douglas's claim to represent the views of those "illustrious patriots and sages" dissolves into thin air.

In 1787 Thomas Jefferson was in Paris, but his hope that heaven would "not always be silent" and that "the friends to the rights of human nature [would] in the end prevail" was accordingly realized. Article 6 of the Northwest Ordinance declared that "There shall be neither slavery nor involuntary servitude in the said Territory, otherwise than in the punishment of crimes whereof the party shall have been duly convicted."[19] This was not understood to be a denial of popular sover-eignty. On the contrary, it was understood to be a confirmation of the principle that no man has the right to govern another without the other's consent, which is the true foundation of popular sovereignty.

Douglas's greatest difficulty in composing his *Harper's* article was in reconcil-ing the Supreme Court's opinion in *Dred Scott* with his assertion that the people of a territory had the ultimate right to include or exclude slavery from their domestic institutions. In the joint debates, Lincoln had declared that the essence of *Dred Scott* was compressed into the assertion that "The right of property in a slave is distinctly and expressly affirmed in the Constitution." If this were true, Lincoln argued, then slave owners had the same constitutional right to federal protection in the territories that they had (under Article IV) to the return of their runaways. Lincoln also paraphrased the supremacy clause of Article VI as requir-ing that "Nothing in the Constitution or laws of any State can destroy a right dis-tinctly and expressly affirmed in the Constitution of the United States." If the right of property in a slave was "distinctly and expressly affirmed in the Constitu-tion," slavery would be lawful in all the states as well as all the territories. How could Douglas defend the Court's assertion of the constitutional status of the right of property in a slave and yet repel these inferences, which were being drawn by both Lincoln and the proslavery South?

In Lincoln's third question to Douglas in their second joint debate, at Freeport, he asked if Douglas would support a Supreme Court decision that held "that States cannot exclude slavery from their limits." Douglas's reply, in part, was:

I am amazed that Lincoln should ask such a question. . . . Mr. Lincoln's object is to cast an imputation upon the Supreme Court. He knows that there never was but one man in America, claiming any degree of intelligence or decency, who ever for a moment pretended such a thing. It is true that the Washington *Union*, in an article published on the 17th of last December, did put forth that doctrine and I denounced the article on the floor of the Senate. . . . [Mr. Lincoln] casts an imputation upon the Supreme Court of the United States by supposing that they would violate the Constitution of the United States. I tell him that such a thing is not possible. It would be an act of moral treason that no man on the bench would ever descend to.[20]

Douglas blustered in response but never answered the question. Nevertheless, he enabled us to answer on his behalf. Douglas was certain beyond any doubt that a decision that states cannot exclude slavery from their limits would be unconstitutional. So certain was he of this that if the Court had ever reached such a decision, he would have denounced it as moral treason. In short, he would have acted exactly as the Republicans did about *Dred Scott*.

The central idea of the *Dred Scott* opinion was that the Negro was so far inferior that he had no rights that the white man was bound to respect. If this was accepted as true, then it certainly seemed to follow that there could be no constitutional distinction between slave property and any other form of chattel property. There could then be no reason, if someone from a free state could emigrate to Kansas with his hog, why someone from a slave state could not emigrate with his slave. Lincoln and Jefferson Davis agreed that if *Dred Scott* was right in its premises, as Douglas no less than Davis said it was, then Congress had no lawful power to exclude slavery from Kansas. But if slavery was in Kansas lawfully, why was it not entitled to the protection of law? As Lincoln asked—and as the proslavery South asked as well—how could slavery be lawfully driven from a place it had a lawful right to go? As we recall from chapter 5, Douglas asserted at Freeport that the Court's decision regarding the right to hold slaves in the territories was merely "abstract" and that in practice that right was dependent upon "friendly" or "unfriendly" legislation that only the local legislature could supply. But how can a property right "expressly affirmed" by the Constitution be merely "abstract"?

In his *Harper's* essay, Douglas attributes to President Buchanan the same "morally treasonous" view that he had denounced Lincoln for even suggesting might be held by the Supreme Court—the view that under *Dred Scott*, slavery would become lawful nationwide.

If the proposition be true, that the Constitution establishes slavery in the Territories beyond the power of the people legally to control it, another result, no less startling, and from which there is no escape, must inevitably follow. The

Constitution is uniform "everywhere within the dominions of the United States"—is the same in Pennsylvania as in Kansas—and if it be true, as stated by the President in a Special Message to Congress, "that slavery exists in Kansas by virtue of the Constitution of the United States," and that "Kansas is there-fore at this moment as much a slave State as Georgia or South Carolina," why does it not exist in Pennsylvania by virtue of the same Constitution? If it be said that Pennsylvania is a sovereign State, and therefore has a right to regulate the slavery question within her own limits to suit herself, it must be borne in mind that the sovereignty of Pennsylvania, like that of every other State, is limited by the Constitution, which provides that: "This Constitution, and all laws of the United States which shall be made in pursuance thereof . . . shall be the *supreme law of the land*, and the judges in every State shall be bound thereby, *anything in the Constitution or laws of any State to the contrary notwithstanding*."... The question recurs then, if the Constitution does establish slavery in Kansas or any other Territory beyond the power of the people to control it by law, how can the conclusion be resisted that slavery is established in like manner and by the same authority in all the States of the Union?[21]

Lincoln, whether in the House Divided speech or at Freeport, never stated his case more forcefully.

How then can Douglas reconcile Taney's *Dred Scott* decision with "popular sovereignty"? He attempts to do so by an ingenious "strict constructionist" inter-pretation of the fugitive slave clause. He quotes Taney as follows:

[T]he Constitution recognizes the right of property of the master in the slave and makes no distinction between that description of property and other property owned by a citizen. . . . And the government in express terms is pledged to pro-tect it in all future time, *if the slave escapes from his owner*. And no word can be found in the Constitution which gives Congress a *greater* power over slave prop-erty, or which entitles property of that kind to *less* protection than property of any other description. The only power conferred is the power coupled with the duty of guarding and protecting the owner in his rights.[22]

Taney invokes the fugitive slave clause, first, to show that slaves are recognized by the Constitution as property as defined by state law; and, second, to assert that Congress has no right to do whatever might lessen the security of that property or to omit doing whatever might be necessary to make it secure. In fact, Taney is asserting that no constitutional discrimination can be made between slave prop-erty and other property, while at one and the same time making just such dis-crimination. How could he not do so? There is no clause in the Constitution call-ing for the protection of any other kind of property. There is no fugitive horse clause in the Constitution. If horses are stolen, it is because there are horse thieves who are not horses! They are dealt with in the ordinary course of the administration of criminal justice. When slaves are stolen, it is the slaves stealing themselves.[23] It is impossible to resist the conclusion, not only that slave property is different from any other kind, but also that the Constitution recognizes that fact in the fugitive slave clause. Clearly, the Constitution in that clause is offering an extraordinary form of protection to an extraordinary form of property.

After quoting the text of the fugitive slave clause, Douglas writes:

> Thus it will be seen that a slave, within the meaning of the Constitution, is "a person held to service or labor in one State, *under the laws thereof*"—not under the Constitution of the United States . . . nor by virtue of any Federal authority whatsoever. . . . It will be observed that the term "State" is used in this provision . . . in the same sense in which it was used by Mr. Jefferson in his plan for establishing governments for the new States in the territory ceded and to be ceded to the United States. . . . In this sense the word "States" is used in the clause providing for the rendition of fugitive slaves, applicable to all political communities under the authority of the United States, including Territories as well as the several States of the Union. Under any other construction the right of the owner to recover his slave would be restricted to the *States* of the Union, leaving the Territories a secure place of refuge for all fugitives.[24]

At this point Douglas might have mentioned that the Northwest Ordinance, in the same Article 6 that said there should never be slavery in that territory, also provided for the rendition of fugitives from the slave states. Douglas is certainly right in saying that the absence of the word "territory" in the fugitive slave clause could not possibly have meant that territories might become sanctuaries for runaway slaves. But could not the territories become sanctuaries for slaves running away from their masters *in the territories* if the local legislatures adopted antislavery legislation such as Douglas asserted it was their right to adopt? This is Douglas's thesis—that runaway slaves can be lawfully returned to their masters under federal authority when they escape from their masters in slave states but not when they escape from their masters in territories.

Let us examine Douglas's thesis with great seriousness, since it offered the only constitutional interpretation that was not antislavery and yet denied the proslavery demand for congressional protection of slavery in the territories. In doing so, we must ask what it was that slave owners wanted in terms of protection in the territories. What was it, other than to have their slaves returned to them, should they escape? If the government is pledged to return a slave who runs away *to* a territory, why is it not pledged to return a slave who runs away *in* a territory?

Is it not clear that Douglas's argument turns against him? The right to own a slave is a right only under the law of the slave state—the local law, as Douglas would have it. Under *Dred Scott*, however, that state law, with all its attributes of state (or local) popular sovereignty, followed the slave owner into the territory. Under *Dred Scott* it is *because* the law of South Carolina invested the owner with the right of property in his slave that the same slave belongs to him in the territory of Kansas. That is what Taney affirmed, what Douglas accepted, and what Lincoln and the Republicans denied. At this point, however, Douglas tried to limit the effect of *Dred Scott* by resorting to his a priori thesis of an "inalienable" legislative power of any people "formed into a political community." According to Douglas, slavery became as much a "local" institution in Kansas as it had been in South Carolina. However, if the local sovereignty of South Carolina followed a South Carolinian to Kansas, why did not that same local sovereignty provide the legal basis to have his slave returned to him if the slave ran away? Did not *Dred Scott* make the ownership of the slave and the right to have him returned aspects of a single indissoluble right?

The reason Taney gave that the owner had the same right to own a slave in Kansas that he had in South Carolina was the sovereignty of South Carolina law, which adhered to him in Kansas until Kansas became a state. It was because of this extraterritorial power attributed in *Dred Scott* to state sovereignty, a power Douglas accepted, that led to declaring the Missouri Compromise void. How could the right to own a slave conferred by the law of South Carolina follow the owner all the way *to* Kansas, but not the right to have his slave returned to him if the slave ran away *in* Kansas? When the slave owner was in South Carolina, South Carolina law would return the runaway, as long as he was in South Carolina. If he ran away to another slave state, the law of that state would return him. If he ran away to a free state or to a federal territory, the federal fugitive slave law would come into operation. All these legal remedies were at the disposal of the South Carolina slave owner as long as he remained in South Carolina. If the same slave owner emigrated to Kansas, he would, according to both Taney and Douglas, still possess the right he had in South Carolina to own the slave. But he would not, according to Douglas, retain the right to have the slave returned if he ran away.

Douglas's doctrine of popular sovereignty was compromised at the outset by claiming that it possessed attributes of "inalienable" sovereignty while admitting that it was "subject to the Constitution." It was further compromised by the fact that Douglas had thoughtlessly committed himself, long before *Dred Scott*, to the unqualified authority of the Supreme Court to define what "subject to the Constitution" means. If he wished intellectual consistency for "popular sovereignty," he could have argued that the right to own slaves in Kansas, or in any territory, had to originate in the territorial legislature. He could have argued that the territorial legislature had to authorize slavery *before* a slave owner went there. In that case, he would have had to deny that South Carolina law left the borders of South Carolina and that there was any such thing as an "abstract" right to carry slaves into territories.

It was impossible to divorce theory from practice. Once Douglas admitted the extraterritorial force of state sovereignty in carrying the legal right to own a slave from South Carolina to Kansas, he had no ground upon which to deny to that slave property the same legal protection in Kansas that it enjoyed in South Carolina. In the end, the strongest argument he could make against a slave code for Kansas was his demonstration of the terrible truth that the principles of *Dred Scott*, carried logically forward, did indeed mean that Pennsylvania, no less than Kansas, had become a slave state. But that was neither more nor less than what Lincoln had contended in the House Divided speech.

Notes

Preface

1. It may of course have cross-references to other works of Aristotle.

Chapter 1

1. Abraham Lincoln, *The Collected Works of Abraham Lincoln*, ed. Roy P. Basler (New Brunswick, N.J.: Rutgers University Press, 1953), vol. IV, p. 426.

2. Lincoln, *Collected Works*, vol. IV, p. 433. Consider also the following excerpt from "Notes on Nullification," in *The Writings of James Madison*, ed. Gaillard Hunt (New York: G. P. Putnam's Sons, 1900), vol. 4, p. 599: "It is painful to be obliged to notice such a sophism. . . . Because an unconstitutional law is no law, it is alleged that it may be constitutionally disobeyed by all who think it unconstitutional. It makes no distinction . . . between a case of a law *confessedly* unconstitutional and a case turning on a *doubtful and divided opinion* as to the meaning of the Constitution. . . . And can it be seriously and deliberately maintained that every individual or every subordinate authority or every party to a compact has a right to take for granted that its construction is the infallible one. . . . Such a doctrine must be seen at once to be subversive of all constitutions, laws and all compacts." The use of the word "sophism" by Madison in just the same sense that Lincoln used it is striking. We will encounter much more evidence of Madison as Lincoln's preeminent predecessor in confronting the "South Carolina doctrines."

3. Present-day acceptance of this idea is nominal. The decline of Marxism–Leninism has led (for the time being at least) to the decline of the pejorative characterization of free elections in the West as "bourgeois." Many intellectuals, however, continue to insist that genuine human freedom (let alone free elections!) is possible only after the abolition of private property.

4. In *The Road to Disunion: Secessionists at Bay, 1776–1854* (New York: Oxford University Press, 1990), p. 147, William W. Freehling writes: "In the most important political contest in the early republic, the election of 1800, the three-fifths clause probably turned what might otherwise have been the Age of Adams into the Age of Jefferson. In an Electoral College where the three-fifths clause gave Southerners 14 extra electors, the Republicans' Thomas Jefferson defeated the Federalists' John Adams, 73-65. Jefferson swept the South's extra electors, 12-2. If no three-fifths clause had existed and House apportionment had been based strictly on white numbers, Adams would have likely squeaked by, 63-61." Certainly no irony in history can be greater than that the first free popular election to

change the government of a nation depended upon the margin of victory provided by the representation given to slavery.

5. Letter to Henry Lee, May 8, 1825, in Thomas Jefferson, *Writings*, ed. Merrill D. Peterson (New York: Library of America, 1984), p. 1500.

6. "Between sixty and one hundred thousand Loyalists, many of them wealthier and more established men, fled the country to Canada or England. Indeed, the American Revolution produced a proportionately greater exodus than the Jacobin repression during the French Revolution. Moreover, nearly as much property was confiscated in America as in France. But the guillotine did not take over the American Revolution, and that alone makes all the difference." Martin Diamond, Winston Mills Fisk, and Herbert Garfinkel, *The Democratic Republic: An Introduction to American National Government* (Chicago: Rand McNally, 1966), p. 16.

7. Declaratory Act, March 18, 1766, in *Documents of American History*, ed. Henry Steele Commager (New York: Appleton-Century-Crofts, 1948), p. 60.

8. "Burke and the United States Constitution," *The Intercollegiate Review*, Winter 1985–86, p. 6.

9. *U.S. News and World Report*, June 11, 1990. This pronouncement is consistent with what Boorstin has been writing for nearly fifty years. See, e.g., *The Genius of American Politics* (Chicago: University of Chicago Press, 1953), and the present writer's critique in "Theory and Practice in American Politics," chap. 6 of *Equality and Liberty* (Claremont, Calif.: Claremont Institute, 1999; originally published by Oxford University Press, 1965).

10. Jefferson, *A Summary View of the Rights of British America*, in *Writings*, p. 105.

11. Jefferson, *Summary View*, in *Writings*, p. 107.

12. Jefferson, *Summary View*, in *Writings*, pp. 105–106. Emphasis added.

13. See also Alexander Hamilton in the first *Federalist*: "It has frequently been observed that it seems to have been reserved to the people of this country, by their conduct and example, to decide the important question, whether societies of men are really capable or not of establishing good government from reflection and choice, or whether they are forever destined to depend for their political institutions on accident and force. If there be any truth in the remark, the crisis at which we are arrived may with propriety be regarded as the era in which the decision is to be made; and a wrong election of the part we shall act may, in this view, deserve to be considered as the general misfortune of mankind." *The Federalist Papers*, ed. Clinton Rossiter, with a new introduction and notes by Charles R. Kesler (New York: Mentor Books, 1999), p. 1.

Although Hamilton is usually thought of as an unreserved admirer of the British constitution, the sentiments in this passage are hardly consistent with that view. Certainly there was never anything comparable to the ratification process, a process of rational deliberation, in the formation of the British constitution. If the latter displayed many of the features of a free constitution, those features were themselves the outcome of "accident and force" rather than "reflection and choice."

The use of the term "choice" here is the most celebrated in American political literature. However, its antecedent use in the *Summary View* reveals its roots in Revolutionary doctrine. The natural right of emigration is the right to exercise one's reason in choosing where one thinks one ought to live. The ratification of the Constitution is the exercise of the same faculty in deciding what form of government will best "promote public happiness."

14. Jefferson, Letter to Judge Spencer Roane, in *Writings*, p. 1426. Emphasis added.

15. Jefferson, *Summary View*, in *Writings*, p. 121.

16. Lincoln, *Collected Works*, vol. IV, p. 270.

17. First Inaugural Address, April 30, 1789, in *George Washington: A Collection*, ed. W. B. Allen (Indianapolis: Liberty Classics, 1988), p. 460.

18. Cf. Justice Iredell, in *Calder v. Bull*, 3 U.S. 386 (1798): "[P]rovidence never can intend to promote the prosperity of any country by bad means."

19. "For it is possible that the many, though not individually superior, yet when they come together may be better, not individually, but collectively." Aristotle, *Politics*, 1281 b 1 ff.

20. Jefferson, *Summary View*, in *Writings*, p. 106.

21. Aristotle, *Politics*, 1269 a 3.

22. Lincoln, To Henry L. Pierce and Others, April 6, 1859, *Collected Works*, vol. III, p. 376.

23. On March 4, 1825, the Board of Visitors of the University of Virginia adopted a set of resolutions that had been hammered out in correspondence between Jefferson and Madison. It embodied the "*norma docendi*" for the Law Faculty of the new university. They affirmed, inter alia, "that on the distinctive principles of the government of our State, and of that of the United States, the best guides are to be found in 1. The Declaration of Independence, *as the fundamental act of union of these States. . . .*" Jefferson, *Writings*, p. 479. Emphasis added.

24. Jefferson, *Summary View*, in *Writings*, pp. 106–107.

25. See note 23 above.

26. That the American Revolution was, in a decisive sense, an intra-Whig debate is developed brilliantly by Stephen A. Cambone in "Noble Sentiments and Manly Eloquence: The First Continental Congress and the Decision for Independence," Ph.D. diss., Claremont Graduate School, 1982.

27. Lincoln, Speech in U.S. House of Representatives, January 12, 1848, *Collected Works*, vol. I, p. 438.

28. On Lincoln's familiarity with Shakespeare's English histories, see his letter to J. H. Hackett, August 17, 1863, in *Collected Works*, vol. VI, p. 392. This letter will be discussed in chap. 2.

29. *King John*, act III, scene 1.

30. The historical ambiguity of the doctrine of tyrannicide is repeated within the American context in the fact that both sides in the Civil War believed they were fighting against tyranny. John Wilkes Booth, when he leaped onto the stage of Ford's Theatre, cried out "Sic semper tyrannis," which was and is the motto of the State of Virginia.

31. John Milton in *Areopagitica*, the great tract for the liberty of unlicensed printing, says, "I mean not tolerated popery." John Locke's *Letters on Toleration* similarly exempts Catholics from its otherwise general doctrine. But Jefferson's Virginia Statute of Religious Liberty makes no exceptions. In its American setting, religious toleration, as a right, becomes for the first time unconditional. As Washington said in his immortal letter to the Newport Synagogue in 1790, "It is now no more that toleration is spoken of as if it were by

the indulgence of one class of people that another enjoyed the exercise of their inherent natural rights." *George Washington: A Collection*, p. 548.

32. "The error seems not sufficiently eradicated, that the operations of the mind, as well as the acts of the body, are subject to the coercion of the laws. But our rulers can have authority over such natural rights only as we have submitted to them. The rights of conscience we never submitted, we could not submit. We are answerable for them to our God." Jefferson, *Notes on the State of Virginia*, Query XVII, in *Writings*, p. 285. This applies to the people as rulers no less than to kings.

33. "Act Erecting a High Court of Justice for the Trial of Charles I," in *Select Documents of English Constitutional History*, ed. George Burton Adams and H. Morse Stephens (New York: Macmillan, 1901), pp. 389, 393.

34. Jefferson, *Summary View*, in *Writings*, p. 108.

35. Jefferson, *Notes on Virginia*, Query XIII, in *Writings*, p. 245.

36. Jefferson, *Summary View*, in *Writings*, pp. 111–112. Emphasis added.

37. Lincoln, *Collected Works*, vol. II, pp. 405–406; vol. I, p. 48.

38. Jefferson, *Notes on Virginia*, Query XVIII, in *Writings*, p. 288.

39. Jefferson, *Summary View*, in *Writings*, pp. 115–116.

40. Jefferson, *Summary View*, in *Writings*, pp. 112, 117.

41. Jefferson, Letter to Jean Nicolas de Meunier, June 26, 1786, in *Writings*, p. 592.

42. Lincoln, Speech at Peoria, Illinois, October 16, 1854, *Collected Works*, vol. II, p. 249.

43. Compare John C. Calhoun, Speech of June 27, 1848, in *The Works of John C. Calhoun*, ed. Richard K. Cralle (New York: D. Appleton, 1854) vol. 4, p. 508: "It [the proposition 'that all men are created equal'] . . . made no necessary part of our justification in separating from the parent country. Breach of our chartered privileges, and lawless encroachment on our acknowledged and well-established rights by the parent country, were the real causes." We will have occasion later to discuss Calhoun's views in detail. We note here his rejection of Jefferson's view in 1774 on "chartered privileges" as repositories of the rights of the Americans in their clash with the British crown and Parliament.

44. Jefferson, *Summary View*, in *Writings*, p. 119.

45. Jefferson, *Summary View*, in *Writings*, pp. 121–122.

46. Jefferson, First Inaugural Address, March 4, 1801, in *Writings*, p. 494.

47. This summary of the Petition is taken from the *Encyclopedia Britannica*, 15th ed., s.v. "Charles I."

48. *Encyclopedia Britannica*, 15th ed., s.v. "Charles I."

49. Jefferson, To William Stephens Smith, November 13, 1784, in *The Papers of Thomas Jefferson*, ed. Julian P. Boyd (Princeton, N.J.: Princeton University Press, 1950), vol. 12, p. 356.

50. Jefferson, To James Madison, January 30, 1787, in *Writings*, p. 882.

51. Jefferson, To Abigail Adams, February 22, 1787, in *Papers*, vol. 11, p. 174.

52. Jefferson, To William Stephens Smith, November 13, 1787, in *Papers*, vol. 12, p. 355.

53. *Documents of American History*, p. 159.

54. *Documents of American History*, p. 157.

55. George Anastaplo, in *The Constitution of 1787: A Commentary* (Baltimore: Johns

Hopkins University Press, 1989), p. 207, writes: "The 'in pursuance' language . . . looks more to the source of formal adequacy of a purported law of the United States than to its 'constitutionality.' This language is more likely to mean 'following upon' or 'made after this Constitution is adopted' than it is to mean 'in conformity to the Constitution' in the sense used today to denote 'constitutionality.'" On its face, this is eminently plausible. But when Hamilton and Jefferson squared off in 1791 on the question of the bank, they were already using the idea of "constitutionality" (and hence "in pursuance") in the present-day sense. Our view of "in pursuance" was of course introduced into constitutional jurisprudence by Chief Justice John Marshall in *Marbury v. Madison*. But Marshall was anticipated, in principle, by Justice Samuel Chase, in *Calder v. Bull:* "An act of the legislature (for I cannot call it a law), contrary to the great first principles of the social compact, cannot be considered a rightful exercise of legislative authority. The obligation of a law, in governments established on express compact, and on republican principles, must be determined by the nature of the power on which it is founded" (3 U.S. 386, [1798]). Chase was a signer of the Declaration of Independence, and "the great first principles of the social compact" refers unquestionably to the principles of the Declaration. Interpreting the "pursuance" clause to refer to constitutionality seems reasonable if one understands the principles of the Declaration to be the principles of the Constitution. In doing so, one must of course distinguish those parts of the Constitution that follow from its principles and those that are compromises dictated by "necessity."

Chase in 1798 was as much a Federalist as Jefferson and Madison were Republicans. That his use of "compact" is exactly the same as theirs in the Kentucky and Virginia Resolutions is impressive evidence of its ubiquity and authority.

56. The following memorable dinner table conversation, in 1791, was related by Jefferson in *The Anas*, in *Writings*, p. 671: "After the cloth was removed . . . conversation . . . was led to the British constitution, on which Mr. Adams observed, 'Purge that constitution of its corruption, and give its popular branch equality of representation, and it would be the most perfect ever devised by the wit of man.' Hamilton paused and said, 'Purge it of its corruption, and give its popular branch equality of representation, and it would become an *impracticable* government.'" The question of the praiseworthiness of the British constitution aside, Hamilton's remark is shrewd and perceptive. The necessity for corruption arose from the fact that the King was the executive head of the government and his ministers were responsible to him, although they could not govern effectively without a majority in both houses of Parliament. Corruption became then one of the means whereby the King sought to obtain parliamentary support for his policies. When the Prime Minister and his cabinet became the true executive, as they are today, and became responsible to the popularly elected House of Commons rather than the King, party discipline, founded upon an electoral majority, replaced corruption as the vehicle of executive government.

57. This charge is made in the Virginia Resolutions, December 24, 1798: "and so . . . consolidate the states, by degrees, into one sovereignty, the obvious tendency and inevitable consequence of which would be to transform the present republican system of the United States into an absolute, or, at best, mixed monarchy." *Documents of American History*, p. 182.

58. Consider Aristotle, *Politics*, III, 1279 17–22: "It is clear then that those constitutions that aim at the common advantage are rightly framed according to the just simply; while those that aim at the advantage of the rulers are deviations and departures from right constitutions. They are despotic, while a *polis* is a community of free men."

59. Jefferson, *Summary View*, in *Writings*, p. 121.

60. Lincoln, *Collected Works*, vol. IV, p. 270.

61. In reply to Douglas's query whether he stood "pledged against the admission of a new state into the Union, with such constitution as the people of that state may think fit to make," Lincoln in the Second Joint Debate on August 27, 1858, replied: "I state to you very frankly that I would be exceedingly sorry ever to be put in a position of having to pass upon that question. I should be exceedingly glad to know that there would never be another slave state admitted into the Union; but I must add, that if slavery shall be kept out of the territories during the territorial existence of any one given territory, and then the people shall, having a fair chance and a clear field, when they come to adopt the constitution, do such an extraordinary thing as to adopt a slave constitution, uninfluenced by the actual presence of the institution among them, I see no alternative, if we own the country, but to admit them into the Union." *Collected Works*, vol. III, p. 41.

62. Judicial review is not the same as judicial supremacy. The states that seceded in 1860–61 agreed with the Supreme Court's *Dred Scott* decision, but they did not regard the Court's authority in constitutional matters as higher than their own authority to nullify or to secede. This has been obscured by the fact that from 1857 on, the arguments for state rights and judicial supremacy coincided. They coincided because the *Dred Scott* decision, which found that Congress had the duty to protect the slaveholders' property in the Territories, represented the strongest justification, in the minds of proslavery Southerners, for their demand for a slave code for the Territories. Their insistence on a slave code as a constitutional right gave strength to their belief that if they were denied the slave code, they had a right to secede.

Civil disobedience is another mode of resistance to government usurpation. It is to be distinguished from the right of revolution since it is a civil, not a natural, right. It arises as a necessary inference from the distinction between constitutional and statute law. In some instances, it may be an aspect of judicial review, since one must sometimes disobey a law before one can ask a court to rule upon its constitutionality. It is also, in some of its manifestations, an aspect of state rights, since a state, like an individual, can challenge a statute of Congress in the courts only in a case in which it refuses to obey the statute.

63. *Documents of American History*, pp. 178–179.

64. See note 8 above. Emphasis added.

65. *Documents of American History*, p. 181. Emphasis added.

66. "[A]ll power in just and free governments is derived from compact." "Sovereignty," in *Writings of James Madison*, vol. 9, p. 569.

67. "But where is the philosophy or statesmanship which assumes that you can quiet that disturbing element [slavery] in our society which has disturbed us for more than half a century. . . . I say where is the philosophy or statesmanship based on the assumption that we are to quit talking about it. . . . I ask you if it is not a false philosophy? Is it not a false statesmanship that undertakes to build up a system of policy upon the basis of caring noth-

ing about *the very thing that everybody does care the most about?"* Lincoln, Seventh Debate, Alton, Illinois. October 15, 1858, *Collected Works*, vol. III, p. 311.

68. Virginia Resolutions, December 24, 1798, in *Documents of American History*, p. 182.

69, James Madison, *The Virginia Report of 1799–1800 and Other Documents*, ed. Leonard W. Levy (New York: Da Capo Press, 1970), p. 196.

70. *Documents of American History*, p. 107.

71. *The Jeffersonian Cyclopedia*, ed. John P. Foley (New York: Funk & Wagnalls, 1900), no. 7621. References to the *Cyclopedia* are given to entry, not page number.

72. Jefferson, Letter to Major John Cartwright, June 5, 1824, in *Writings*, p. 1494.

73. *Writings of James Madison*, vol. 4, pp. 569, 573.

74. *Writings of James Madison*, vol. 4, p. 570.

75. We note only briefly that "prior" can refer either to the order of being or to the order of becoming. For example, according to Aristotle the family is prior to the polis in order of becoming, but the polis is prior to the family in order of being. Again, the acorn is prior to the oak tree in order of becoming, but the oak tree is prior to the acorn in order of being. The priority of the state of nature includes both these senses of the concept.

76. Aristotle, *Politics*, III, 1276 a 5 ff. By Aristotle's understanding, the change from the Weimar Republic to the Third Reich changed the identity of the German political community. Being German would, for him, have been far less important than being republican or being Nazi. Unfortunately, it was not so to the Germans! For them, Germany was the fundamental reality, and the form of their government was incidental by comparison. In the American Revolution, by contrast, as the Tories migrated to Canada, being American meant necessarily being republican. Only the sovereignty of the people, under the auspices of the compact, has the authority to act on behalf of the whole community to secure natural rights. Although prudence might, in the light of contingent circumstances, dictate a choice among nondespotic forms of government, only republican government is inherently and intrinsically in accord with the social compact.

77. *The Mind of the Founder: Sources of the Political Thought of James Madison*, ed. Marvin Meyers (Hanover, N.H.:University Press of New England, 1981), pp. 245–246. The clarity with which Madison propounds what will become the constitutional doctrine of the British Empire over a century later shows how profoundly the American Revolution transformed the British government. This is the very reverse of the usual view of the relationship of British and American constitutionalism.

78. Legislative supremacy means popular sovereignty, as it emerges from the social compact of individuals. This legislative power is less a governmental than a constitution-making power. Under the Constitution of 1787, the supreme legislative power is not Congress but the ratifying conventions, as expressions of the constituent will of the people. The legislative powers of Congress are derivative and are limited by the legislative power exercised by the people in framing and ratifying the Constitution.

79. This does not mean that there cannot be an unconstitutional amendment. A number of provisions of the Constitution imply its unamendability in certain respects. Article I, section 9 forbade Congress to prohibit the importation of slaves before 1808. Article V declared that "no amendment shall be made" before 1808 to change this. The Constitution also declares that no state may, without its consent, be deprived of its equal

suffrage in the Senate and that no new state may be formed within the jurisdiction of any existing state, or by the junction of two or more states or parts of states, without the consent of the states and of Congress. Can these provisions be amended? We are confronted here with a terra incognita of constitutional law. The purely legal question is, "Can the people, in their sovereign capacity, bind themselves or their successors?" The underlying philosophical question is, "Can the people, in their sovereign capacity, enact laws inconsistent with the purposes for which, and by reason of which, they are sovereign?" In the Lincoln–Douglas debates, Lincoln answered this question in the negative, when he said that the people of a territory had no right to vote for slavery, since there was no such thing as a right to do wrong. Douglas said that he didn't care whether slavery was voted up or down, so long as the people's right to decide was preserved. Was there such an objective knowledge of right and wrong as Lincoln supposed, a knowledge binding their actions as sovereign? Jefferson had said as much in the *Summary View*: "The great principles of right and wrong are legible to every reader." This is really what the Civil War was about.

80. The philosophical foundation of the Kentucky and Virginia Resolutions is such as to authorize a citizen of any state to declare null and void any act of his state that in his conscientious opinion usurps authority not delegated to it by his state's constitutional compact. On such a foundation Henry David Thoreau claimed in 1846 to have "seceded" from Massachusetts, which was supporting a war with Mexico that Thoreau judged to be a war to extend slavery and therefore to be unconstitutional and immoral. Thoreau the abolitionist thus set the example that was later followed by proslavery Southern secessionists.

Civil disobedience, the right of a state to nullify or secede, and judicial review are different manifestations of the same right, because they are manifestations of the compact (or contract) theory of government, itself grounded in the proposition "that all men are created equal." As we contemplate the multiplying grounds upon which resistance to governmental acts may be justified by the compact theory, we wonder less at Lincoln finding himself forced to ask, as noted in the epigraph to this chapter, whether republics are inherently unable to maintain their existence.

The compact theory, which makes every individual the ultimate judge of his obligations under the Constitution, obviously resembles the Protestant belief that each individual believer is the ultimate authority for determining the meaning and obligation of the Bible. If each individual is free to determine whether the compact has been violated, however, the question arises how different his situation is from the state of nature. But as the Declaration of Independence makes clear, the incentives that lead someone out of the state of nature also operate to prevent him from willfully or gratuitously undermining the authority of a government that is not bent on tyranny.

A government based upon the compact theory, no less than the religion of Protestant Christianity, would be a formula for anarchy without an authoritative tradition in which the individual contemplates the constitutional or biblical text. We must read the Kentucky and Virginia Resolutions, then, not only in the light of their protests, but also in the light of their attempt to shape such an authoritative tradition.

81. Lincoln's "Address Before the Young Men's Lyceum of Springfield, Illinois," January 27, 1838, is directed especially to the problem of lawlessness in a popular government. The tendency to resistance inherent in the principles of the regime, and with it the tendency to anarchy, is a tendency Lincoln attempts to overcome by having "reverence for the

laws . . . become the *political religion* of the nation" *Collected Works*, vol. I, pp. 108–115. Lincoln urges his fellow citizens to obey even bad laws until they can be repealed, "if not too intolerable." Thus even in his utmost appeal to law-abidingness, Lincoln recognizes the right of resistance.

82. "Sovereignty," in *Writings of James Madison*, vol. 9, p. 570. Madison, to go to the "bottom" or the common sense of his subject, reverts to the language of Locke's *Second Treatise of Government*, just as Jefferson did in composing the Declaration. Consider the following from chap. II, para. 4 of the *Second Treatise of Government*: "To understand political power right and derive it from its original, we must consider what state all men are naturally in, and that is, a state of perfect freedom to order their actions, and dispose of their possessions and persons as they think fit within the bounds of the law of nature, without asking leave, or depending upon the will of any other man. A state also of equality, wherein all the power and jurisdiction is reciprocal, no one having more than another: there being nothing more evident, than that creatures of the same species and rank promiscuously born to all the same advantages of nature, and the use of the same faculties, should also be equal one amongst another without subordination or subjection."

83. This distinction runs throughout human life and society. When we are sick, we wish to be governed not by our equals but by the wise. For this reason we go to a doctor. Similar considerations govern our patronage of architects, engineers, professional pilots, and so on. But although we wish to be governed by the wise, that wish is contingent upon the expectation of such government arising through the medium of consent. That is to say, we want to know not only that the doctor is wiser than we are in the matter of our health but also that he has an *interest* in healing us. We rely upon our fees for that. We also rely upon criminal laws that make it a felony for him to injure us and civil laws that enable us to sue him for malpractice. In short, any acknowledged form of human superiority is entitled to rule only by the medium of consent designed to secure the interest of the rulers in the well-being of the ruled. See the present writer's "Equality, Liberty, Wisdom, Morality, and Consent in the Idea of Political Freedom," in *Interpretation*, January 1987, pp. 3–28.

84. "Sovereignty," in *Writings of James Madison*, pp. 570–571.

85. Jefferson, First Inaugural, in *Writings*, pp. 492–493.

86. This is what the seceding states would accuse the free states of attempting to do in 1860–61. Lincoln's policy of placing slavery "in course of ultimate extinction" was viewed not only as violating property rights without compensation but also as endangering the lives of the white population of the slave states. The slaughter of whites by blacks both in Haiti and in Santo Domingo was never far from the mind of the white antebellum South.

87. Jefferson, *Notes on Virginia*, Query XVII, in *Writings*, p. 285.

88. *Documents of American History*, p. 125.

89. Jefferson, *Notes on Virginia*, Query XVII, in *Writings*, p. 285.

90. Jefferson, First Inaugural, in *Writings*, p. 494.

91. Jefferson, *Notes on Virginia*, Query XVIII, in *Writings*, p. 289.

92. Matthew 7:12 RSV. All biblical citations are to this version.

93. Consider Locke's *Second Treatise of Government*, chap. 2, para. 5: "This equality of men by nature, the judicious Hooker looks upon as so evident in itself, and beyond all question, that he makes it the foundation of that obligation to mutual love amongst men, on

which he builds the duties they owe one another, and from whence he derives the great maxims of justice and charity." In many sermons of the Revolutionary period, the intrinsic harmony between natural law and the ethics of the Gospel was understood in exactly this light.

94. Churchill uses this quote in his *History of the English Speaking Peoples* (New York: Dodd, Mead, 1957), vol. 3, p. 251.

95. Compare the following from Lincoln's first inaugural: "A majority held in restraint by constitutional checks and limitations, and always changing easily with deliberate changes of popular opinion and sentiments, is the only true sovereign of a free people. . . . Unanimity is impossible; the rule of a minority, as a permanent arrangement, is wholly inadmissible; so that, rejecting the majority principle, *anarchy or despotism* in some form is all that is left." *Collected Works*, vol. IV, p. 268 (emphasis added). In contrast, here is Jefferson Davis, in his Message to the Confederate Congress, April 29, 1861: "[S]o utterly have the principles of the Constitution been corrupted in the Northern mind that, in the inaugural address delivered by President Lincoln in March last, he asserts as an axiom, which he plainly deems to be undeniable, that the theory of the Constitution requires that in all cases the majority shall govern" *Documents of American History*, p. 370. Davis ignores what Lincoln, echoing Jefferson, says about the restraints necessary to make majority rule legitimate.

96. *Documents of American History*, pp. 103, 107.

97. "A desire for some legitimate form of judicial activism runs strong and deep in our culture, a tradition that can be called 'Madisonian.' We continue to believe there are some things no majority should be allowed to do to us, no matter how democratically it may decide to do them. A Madisonian system assumes that . . . there are some aspects of life a majority should not control, that coercion in such matters is tyranny, a violation of the individual's natural rights. Clearly, the definition of natural rights cannot be left to either the majority or the minority. In the popular understanding upon which the power of the Supreme Court rests, it is the function of the Court to resolve this dilemma by giving content to the concept of natural rights in case by case interpretation of the Constitution." Robert Bork, "The Supreme Court Needs a New Philosophy," in *Fortune*, December 1968, p. 170. Unfortunately, Judge Bork later abandoned the idea of a constitutional status for natural rights. Of course, the idea of natural rights was Madisonian only because it was American and Madison was an American. It united "all American whigs"—that is to say, all Americans whose sentiments were expressed by the Declaration of Independence. But Bork does not consider that Madison himself, in the Virginia Resolutions, assigns the function of "giving content to the concept of natural rights," not to the Supreme Court, but to the states.

98. Lincoln, Message to Congress, July 4, 1861, *Collected Works*, p. 439.

99. This ability of a minority to exert compulsion on the majority was, in effect, what Henry David Thoreau advocated in his essay "Civil Disobedience": "A minority is powerless when it conforms to the majority; it is not even a minority then; but it is irresistible when it clogs by its whole weight." *Walden and Civil Disobedience*, ed. Owen Thomas (New York: W. W. Norton, 1966), p. 233.

100. Jefferson, Letter to Edward Carrington, August 4, 1787, in *Papers*, vol. 11, p. 678.

101. Locke, *Second Treatise of Government*, chap. 2, para. 13.

102. *Federalist Papers*, no. 10, pp. 46–47.

103. *Federalist Papers*, no. 47, p. 269.

104. *Federalist Papers*, no. 48, p. 279.

105. *Federalist Papers*, no. 10, p. 48.

106. *Federalist Papers*, no. 14, p. 68.

107. *Federalist Papers*, no. 51, pp. 291–292.

108. *Federalist Papers*, no. 45, p. 259.

109. *Federalist Papers*, no. 46, p. 265.

110. *Federalist Papers*, no. 46, p. 266.

111. Madison alludes to *Federalist* 46 in his "Report of 1799–1800": "It cannot be forgotten that, amongst the arguments addressed to those who apprehended danger to liberty from the establishment of the general government over so great a country, the appeal was emphatically made to the intermediate existence of the state governments between the people and that government, to the vigilance with which they would descry the first symptoms of usurpation, and to the promptitude with which they would sound the alarm. This argument was probably not without its effect, and if it was proper then to recommend the establishment of a constitution, it must be proper now to assist in its interpretation." *Mind of the Founder*, p. 272.

112. "This policy of supplying, by opposite and rival interests, the defect of better motives, might be traced through the whole system of human affairs, private as well as public. We see it particularly displayed in all the subordinate distributions of power; where the constant aim is to divide and arrange the several offices in such a manner as that each may be a check on the other; that the private interest of every individual may be a sentinel over the public rights. These inventions of prudence cannot be less requisite in the distribution of the supreme powers of the state." Madison, *Federalist Papers*, no. 51, p. 290. Compare Lincoln, Speech on the Sub-Treasury, December 26, 1839, *Collected Works*, vol. I, p. 167: "We . . . do not say, nor need we say . . . that bank officers are more honest than government officers. . . . What we do say is that the *interest* of the Sub-Treasurer is *against his duty*—while the *interest* of the bank is *on the side of its duty*. . . . It is for this reason, then, that we say a bank is the more secure. It is because of that admirable feature in the bank system, which places the *interest* and the *duty* of the depository both on one side, whereas that feature can never enter into the Sub-Treasury system. By the latter, the *interest* of the individuals keeping the public money, will wage an eternal war with their *duty*, and in very many instances must be victorious."

113. Madison's implied criticism of the *Federalist* in the Virginia Resolutions anticipates in principle the more radical critique of the same text in Calhoun's *Discourse on the Constitution and Government of the United States*.

114. Virginia Resolutions, December 24, 1798, in *Documents of American History*, p. 182.

115. We see here foreshadowed the "preferred freedoms" doctrine of the Supreme Court of later years.

116. *Documents of American History*, p. 182.

117. Kentucky Resolutions, November 16, 1798, in *Documents of American History*, pp. 181–182.

118. *Documents of American History*, p. 183.

119. *Mind of the Founder,* p. 270.
120. *Federalist Papers,* no. 43, p. 247.
121. Jefferson, First Inaugural, in *Writings,* p. 492.
122. Jefferson, First Inaugural, in *Writings,* pp. 492–493.
123. Jefferson, First Inaugural, in *Writings,* p. 493.
124. Aristotle, *Nicomachean Ethics,* 1155 a 17–29.
125. Aristotle, *Nicomachean Ethics,* 1155 a 17–29.
126. *Federalist Papers,* no. 10, pp. 45, 52.
127. Jefferson, First Inaugural, in *Writings,* p. 493.
128. The ending of the tenth *Federalist* is matched by the ending of the fifty-first: "And happily for the *republican cause,* the practicable sphere may be carried to a very great extent, by a judicious modification and mixture of the *federal principle.*" *Federalist Papers,* p. 293. This parallel was pointed out to me by Professor Colleen Sheehan.
129. Henry Adams, *History of the United States during the Administration of Jefferson and Madison* (Englewood Cliffs, N.J.: Prentice Hall, 1963), p. 21.
130. Jefferson, First Inaugural, in *Writings,* p. 493.
131. In the election of 1800, Jefferson and Burr received 73 electoral votes each, while Adams received 65. (Before the Twelfth Amendment, each elector cast votes for two persons for president, the runner-up becoming vice president.) Because each Republican elector cast his two votes for Jefferson and Burr, they each received the same number, which is why the choice between them had to be made in the House of Representatives. In 1804, however, subsequent to the Twelfth Amendment, with electoral college ballots being cast separately for president and vice president, Jefferson received 162 votes, to 14 for Charles C. Pinckney.
132. *Jeffersonian Cyclopedia,* no. 7331.
133. Jefferson, First Inaugural, in *Writings,* p. 493.
134. See note 91 above.
135. See note 41 above.
136. Lincoln, Eulogy of Henry Clay, July 6, 1852, *Collected Works,* vol. II, p. 130.
137. *Jeffersonian Cyclopedia,* no. 7987.
138. Lincoln, *Collected Works,* vol. III, p. 315.
139. Jefferson, Virginia Statute of Religious Liberty, January 16, 1786, in *Documents in American History,* p. 126.

Chapter 2

1. Aristotle, *Politics,* 1260 b 27–37. The writers in question are Plato, Phaleas, and Hippodamus.
2. Cf. "A social science that cannot speak of tyranny with the same confidence with which medicine speaks, for example, of cancer, cannot understand social phenomena as what they are." Leo Strauss, "Restatement on Xenophon's *Hiero,*" in *On Tyranny* (New York: Free Press, 1963), p. 189. See also Strauss's *What Is Political Philosophy? And Other Studies* (New York: Free Press, 1959), p. 95.

It is fair to point out, moreover, that in this respect John C. Calhoun was no less Aristotelian than Lincoln. Consider the following: "There are diseases of the body politic, as well as our natural bodies, that never stop of themselves. Abolition is one of them. If left to itself, it will pass through all its stages, from the first agitation, until it ends in emancipation and the destruction of the government." Speech in the Senate, August 12, 1849, in *The Works of John C. Calhoun*, vol. 4, p. 516. Abolitionism is the political disease in Calhoun's diagnosis, as slavery is in Lincoln's. In chap. 7, however, we will demonstrate that Calhoun is unable, from the nonnormative "scientific" perspective of his political theory, to speak *consistently* of health and disease in the body politic.

3. George Fort Milton, *The Eve of Conflict: Stephen A. Douglas and the Needless War* (Boston: Houghton Mifflin, 1934). As the authoritative work on Douglas, it has been replaced by Robert W. Johannsen, *Stephen A. Douglas* (New York: Oxford Press, 1973). Although as nearly definitive as a biography can be, Johannsen's work falls squarely into the historical school of Carl Becker, which we will discuss presently.

4. The "revisionist" movement in American historical scholarship, typified by J. G. Randall, Avery Craven, and George Fort Milton, decried equally the irrational posturing (as they thought it) of abolitionists and of positive good advocates of slavery. From their point of view, Lincoln was not different from either of these deplorable extremes, in that he insisted upon the primary political importance of slavery as a moral issue. Douglas's popular-sovereignty doctrine commended itself to them precisely because it sought to defuse the slavery question by denying its importance as a moral issue, thereby making it an issue only in local, not in national, politics.

Allen Nevins, in *The Emergence of Lincoln* (New York: Scribner, 1950), is an exception to this "revisionism," but only superficially. He sided with Lincoln rather than Douglas. But he thought that the institution of slavery was wrong because it was anachronistic, differing in this from Lincoln, who held slavery anachronistic because it was wrong. Nevins was convinced that the great trends of nineteenth-century thought and institutions were irreversibly on the side of freedom. He never seems to have entertained the possibility that these great trends might have culminated as much in the regimes of Hitler and Stalin (both neo-Darwinists) as in liberal democracies. Like Tocqueville, Lincoln, in the critique of Napoleon in his Lyceum speech, anticipated this possibility as early as 1838. Lincoln saw no ultimate guarantee of freedom in the allegedly impersonal laws of history or progress. He saw such a guarantee only in fidelity to the "abstract truth" embodied in the Declaration of Independence, a truth that was independent of history.

5. Abraham Lincoln, *The Collected Works of Abraham Lincoln*, ed. Roy P. Basler (New Brunswick, N.J.: Rutgers University Press, 1953), vol. IV, p. 160.

6. Consider the following excerpt from an interview with Shelby Foote, perhaps the greatest military historian of the Civil War: "Q. Why did Americans kill each other in such great numbers? A. Basically, it was a failure on our part to find a way not to fight that war. It was because we failed to do the thing we really have a genius for, which is compromise. Americans like to think of themselves as uncompromising. But our true genius is for compromise. Our whole government's founded on it. And it failed." *The Civil War: An Illustrated History*, by Geoffrey C. Ward, with Ric Burns and Ken Burns (New York: Knopf, 1990), p. 264. All political compromise presupposes an end that the compromisers share and that is more important to them than what they are asked to sacrifice in compromising.

How can Foote think that our government is founded on compromise, when it came into existence in a war in which the thirteen colonies declared principles which they said could not be compromised? ("The God who gave us life, gave us liberty at the same time: the hand of force may destroy, but cannot disjoin them.") It is the thesis of the Gettysburg Address, to which (like the Declaration of Independence) Foote seems never to have given a moment's notice, that the principles at stake in the Civil War were the same as those at stake in the Revolution.

7. Garry Wills's *Inventing America: Jefferson's Declaration of Independence* (New York: Doubleday, 1978) was a conscious attempt to overthrow Becker's authority. In his first chapter, Wills wrote that "Becker's little book, over a half a century old, remains for most scholars the beginning and the end of investigation into the *ideas* of the Declaration. As such, it has been the most broadly influential." In his attempt to discredit Becker, Wills contends, wildly and inaccurately, that Francis Hutcheson, and not John Locke, was the most important source for Jefferson in drafting the Declaration. Wills's book, although enjoying a brief vogue, has been so discredited as to fortify Becker's authority. See "Inventing the Past: Garry Wills' *Inventing America* and the Pathology of Ideological Scholarship," in the present writer's *American Conservatism and the American Founding* (Durham, N.C.: Carolina Academic Press, 1984), pp. 76–109.

8. Garry Wills, in *Lincoln at Gettysburg* (New York: Simon & Schuster, 1992), the sequel to his book on the Declaration of Independence, calls the Gettysburg Address a "giant (if benign) swindle." The only reason for calling the swindle benign is that, according to Wills, Lincoln's rhetoric has been so powerful and has persuaded so many people that the attempt to reverse its effects would be hopeless. But the truth is almost the opposite. The literature on the Civil War and on the idea of human equality that guided Abraham Lincoln is dominated by the Becker thesis. While Becker was too much of a gentleman to have called the Gettysburg Address a swindle, Lincoln's belief in "an abstract truth, applicable to all men and all times" was certainly, according to Becker, a fallacy. Wills does not point to a single writer, including himself, who has been persuaded by Lincoln that it is *not* a fallacy.

9. This is the view of Irving Kristol, a man widely recognized for his pretensions as an interpreter of the American political tradition: "[T]he American people seem never to have been torn by conflicting interpretations of the American political tradition, though scholars may be. Even our very bloody Civil War had surprisingly little effect on the course of American history. If one were to write an American history textbook with the chapter on the Civil War dropped out, to be replaced by a single sentence to the effect that slavery was abolished by constitutional amendment in 1865, very little in subsequent chapters, as now written, would need revision." One would think from this either that the Civil War had been fought entirely by scholars or that the differences concerning slavery were not real differences! Kristol continues: "The Civil War had even less effect on the American political tradition, since there never really was a distinctively Southern political tradition, nor did the war give rise to one. A textbook in American intellectual history could safely ignore the Civil War, were it not for the fact that one feels it to be almost sacrilegious that so much suffering should be so barren of consequence. The Civil War was and is a most memorable event—but not any kind of turning point in American history." "On the Char-

acter of the American Political Order," in *The Promise of American Politics*, ed. Robert L. Utley Jr. (Lanham, Md.: University Press of America, 1989), pp. 3–4.

More recently, Kristol has delivered himself of the opinion that "the authors of the Constitution . . . were for the most part not particularly interested in religion. I am not aware that any of them ever wrote anything worth reading on religion, especially Jefferson, who wrote nothing worth reading on religion or almost anything else." *The Spirit of the Constitution*, eds. Robert A. Goldwin and Robert A Licht (Washington, D.C.: AEI Press, 1990), p. 81. Jefferson was not, strictly speaking, an author of the Constitution. But what is notable is Kristol's patronizing contempt, not so much for the author of the Declaration of Independence and the Virginia Statute of Religious Liberty, as for the political thought of the American Founding as a whole. This contempt is consistent, however, with what he says about the intellectual insignificance of the differences that led to the Civil War. According to Kristol, only someone completely deluded could have written, as Lincoln did in 1859, that "The principles of Jefferson are the definitions and axioms of free society."

10. Hermann Rauschning, *The Voice of Destruction* (New York: Putnam, 1940), p. 69. This quotation is taken from the balance of the sentence quoted in the epigraph to this chapter. Consider in this connection M. E. Bradford, "The Heresy of Equality," *Modern Age*, Winter 1976. Reprinted in *Modern Age: The First Twenty-five Years, A Selection*, ed. George Panichas (New York: Liberty Press, 1988). Bradford writes: "Equality as a moral or political imperative, pursued as an end in itself—Equality with a capital 'E'—is the antonym of every legitimate conservative principle. Contrary to most Liberals, new and old, it is nothing less than sophistry to distinguish between equality of opportunity (equal starts in the 'race of life') and equality of condition (equal results). . . . And there is no man equal to any other. . . . Not *intellectually or physically or economically or even morally. Not equal!* Such, of course, is the genuinely self-evident proposition." Of course, the Declaration of Independence only asserts that human beings are equal in respect to certain rights, rights in virtue of which they may not be governed legitimately without their own consent. Bradford blusters against equality in irrelevant aspects, but it is clear that he does not think that men are equal even in that fundamental sense. Bradford and Hitler agree with the Lincoln of the House Divided speech, that America, on the eve of the Civil War, stood at a divide between "a great new social order based upon slavery and inequality" and one based upon the principles of the Declaration. They only disagree with Lincoln as to which choice ought to have been made. All three differ with Irving Kristol (see note 13 above), who denies that there were any fundamental alternatives present on the eve of the Civil War!

11. For brevity, let me call these successors to the earlier revisionists the disciples, whether direct or indirect, of David Brion Davis, the most notable academic writer on slavery of the last half century. Davis's many books include *The Problem of Slavery in Western Culture* (1966), *The Problem of Slavery in the Age of Revolution* (1975), and *Slavery and Human Progress* (1984). These books are great resources of information on the subject of slavery, written from an abolitionist viewpoint. But they are utterly condescending towards those historical figures, like Jefferson or Lincoln, who actually confronted the problems Davis describes.

12. As the revisionist historiography that elevated compromise over principle has been replaced by its radicalized offspring, the historiography of commitment over compromise, we find both abolitionism and proslavery perspectives in the ascendant. The latter, of

course, is muted because it is out of harmony with dominant public opinion. However, the existence of a journal, *The Southern Partisan*, is indicative of a small but lively school that is as loyal to the cause of the Confederacy as their opposites are loyal to the cause of abolitionism. Its members' testament remains the 1931 collection of essays entitled *I'll Take My Stand: The South and the Agrarian Tradition*. Slavery is still openly defended in the pages of the *Partisan*, although not in the pages of the more widely read *Chronicles of Culture*, notwithstanding the fact that many of the same persons write for both.

13. Lincoln, *Collected Works*, vol. II, p. 270.

14. A monument to this point of view may be found in William W. Freehling, *The Road to Disunion: Secessionists at Bay, 1776–1854* (New York: Oxford University Press, 1990) (see note 4 to chap. 1). Freehling's contempt for Jefferson is remarkable for its uncontrolled virulence. Consider the following: "The most dominating Southerner as late as 1860 was not Jefferson Davis . . . or any other Founding Father of the southern nation. . . . The master who mattered most had been buried at Monticello a third of a century before slaveholders rose in rebellion. . . . The history of southern extremism from Jefferson's day to Jefferson Davis' could be summed up as one long, losing campaign to extinguish Monticello's master's vision in more northern sections of the south. Recent historical wisdom makes these fire-eaters' concern unfathomable. Jefferson's way of awakening to the problem of slavery is currently seen as hypocrisy personified. . . . Against this latter-day standard of realism, the Calhouns who stewed about Jefferson become unrealistic abstractionists." The followers of Calhoun are derided for taking Jefferson seriously, notwithstanding the fact, admitted by Freehling, that it was Jefferson's ideas (above all in the person of Abraham Lincoln) that were the driving force in the movement that was about to destroy slavery. That the Gettysburg Address is the culminating vindication of the master of Monticello's vision is altogether beyond Freehling's horizon.

Freehling also writes that "Jefferson was not an epic figure in 1776 because he made the revolution happen. Events would have occurred the same way had he never lived. Nor did Jefferson, as author of the Declaration of Independence, create a new intellectual design. Instead he luminously expressed pre-existing American beliefs." One can hardly imagine a more gratuitous (and unhistorical) assertion than that the events of the Revolutionary period would have happened "the same way" without Jefferson! Of course, Jefferson himself asserted, in his famous letter to Henry Lee, May 8, 1825, that the purpose of the Declaration was "not to find out new principles, or new arguments, never before thought of, not merely to say things which had never been said before; but to place before mankind the common sense of the subject, in terms so plain and firm as to command their assent, and to justify ourselves in the independent stand we are compelled to take. Neither aiming at originality of principle or sentiment, nor yet copied from any particular and previous writing, it was intended to be an expression of the American mind, and to give to that expression the proper tone and spirit called for by the occasion. All its authority rests then on the harmonizing sentiments of the day, whether expressed in conversation, in letters, printed essays, or in the elementary books of public right, as Aristotle, Cicero, Locke, Sidney, etc." Thomas Jefferson, *Writings*, ed. Merrill D. Peterson (New York: Library of America, 1984), p. 1501. Freehling ignores Jefferson's own explanation of his purpose in drafting the Declaration, as well as Lincoln's evaluation, in his letter to H. L. Pierce and others, on Jefferson's birthday in 1859 (see the epigraph at the head of this chapter).

Freehling's abolitionist revisionism is notable for its conscious alienation from the past it purports to explain. Freehling's "past" becomes "unfathomable" when the actors in it appear to think differently from himself!

15. See Carl Becker, *The Declaration of Independence: A Study in the History of Political Ideas* (New York: Harcourt, Brace, 1922), pp. 273–279.

16. Lincoln, Letter to Pierce and Others, April 6, 1859, *Collected Works*, vol. III, p. 376.

17. Leo Strauss, *Natural Right and History* (Chicago: University of Chicago Press, 1953), pp. 1–2. These words were written several years before the publication date of the book. As Strauss's research assistant, I had transcribed them.

18. The original texts for the attack on the natural rights philosophy were supplied by Edmund Burke's writings on the French Revolution. Burke's rhetorical apostrophes concerning Marie Antoinette undoubtedly supplied the romantic movement with a great impulse. Whether this fairly represented Burke's Whig constitutionalism may well be doubted. Burke did support the American cause in 1775.

19. Becker, *Declaration of Independence*, pp. 265–266.

20. The classic disputation in our time between natural right and historical right is the exchange between Leo Strauss and Alexander Kojeve in *On Tyranny*, ed. Victor Gourevitch and Michael S. Roth (New York: Free Press, 1991), pp. 133–213. It might be argued that Darwinian evolution constitutes proof that nature is a changing, and not a permanent, reality. We will discuss that possibility below.

21. Becker, *Declaration of Independence*, p. 275.

22. It is fair to note, however, that the Declaration of Independence would be both appealed to, and rejected by, both proslavery secessionists and abolitionists. The secessionists appealed to the Declaration when they claimed the right to reject a government that allegedly no longer commanded the consent of the governed; but they denounced the constitutional restraints upon slavery arising from the commitment to equality. The abolitionists appealed to the Declaration to denounce the legitimacy of slavery; but they denounced the constitutional restraints arising from the commitment to consent.

23. Letter to Henry Lee, in *Letters and Other Writings of James Madison* (Philadelphia: J. B. Lippincott, 1865), pp. 441–442.

24. William Rehnquist, "The Notion of a Living Constitution," *Texas Law Review*, May 1976, vol. 54, pp. 693–706. This is the revised text of the ninth annual Will E. Orgain Lecture, delivered at the University of Texas Law School on March 12, 1976. It was reprinted in 1981 and 1985.

25. Rehnquist, "Living Constitution."

26. Chief Justice Rehnquist, in the passages cited, is even closer in his position to Calhoun than was Chief Justice Taney in 1857. In his *Dred Scott* decision of that year, Taney credited the Declaration of Independence with constitutional standing but denied that it included Negroes in the "all men" who are said to be "created equal." Rehnquist denies the Declaration any constitutional standing whatever.

27. See note 75 in chap. 1.

28. "Similarly, the things which are just, not by nature, but by human enactment, are not everywhere the same, since constitutions (i.e., forms of government) are also not the same, though there is but one which is everywhere by nature the best." Aristotle, *Nicomachean Ethics*, 1135 a 2–4.

29. John C. Calhoun, A *Disquisition on Government*, in *Union and Liberty: The Political Philosophy of John C. Calhoun*, ed. Ross M. Lence (Indianapolis: Liberty Fund, 1992), pp. 65–66.

30. Marx's *Communist Manifesto* was published in 1848. Calhoun's *Disquisition on Government* and *Discourse on the Constitution and Government of the United States* were published posthumously in 1851 but were probably being composed at the same time as the *Manifesto*. In their striking resemblance to one another, they represent equal and opposite reactions to the same intellectual influences.

31. Both Machiavelli and Spinoza note that men prayed not to be inundated by floods, until they learned that building dikes and dams is more effective than prayer!

32. Calhoun, A *Disquisition on Government*, in *Union and Liberty*, p. 6.

33. Hegel's and Marx's praise of classical philosophers for embodying the highest form of consciousness possible in their times is sincere but patronizing, since they assumed that such philosophers were necessarily prevented by their times from knowing what their limitations were—limitations presumably absent from the consciousness of Hegel and Marx.

34. Becker, *Declaration of Independence*, pp. 274–275.

35. Becker, *Declaration of Independence*, p. 276. There was never a more fashionable or influential epigone of Darwinism than Supreme Court Justice Oliver Wendell Holmes Jr. Holmes's rejection of natural law, cited by Chief Justice Rehnquist as the authority for his own opinions on this subject, is entirely Darwinian.

36. Becker, *Declaration of Independence*, p. 277.

37. Becker, *Declaration of Independence*, p. xvi.

38. Becker, *Declaration of Independence*, p. xvi.

39. Becker, *Declaration of Independence*, p. 274.

40. Becker, *Declaration of Independence*, p. xiv.

41. Speech in the House of Commons, June 4, 1940, in Winston S. Churchill, *Blood Sweat and Tears* (New York: G. P. Putnam's Sons, 1941), p. 297.

42. In the *Gorgias* as well as the *Republic*, which we have previously discussed, Socrates maintains the thesis that it is better to be the victim of a tyrant than to be a tyrant. These dialogues stand at the headwaters of the tradition so gloriously consummated in the Declaration of Independence.

43. Becker, *Declaration of Independence*, pp. 278–279.

44. Churchill in his *Marlborough* recounts how historians had for over seventy years accepted without question the authenticity of a letter, first featured in Macaulay's *History of England*, that attributed treason to Marlborough in secretly informing the French of an impending English attack on Camaret Bay. Yet Churchill was able to establish beyond any reasonable doubt that the supposed letter was a forgery. "The historians," he wrote, "like sheep, followed each other through the gates of error."

45. *Vetustas pro lege semper habetur* is the legal maxim cited by Edmund Burke and referred to by Leo Strauss. *Natural Right and History*, p. 83.

46. *The Federalist Papers*, ed. Clinton Rossiter, with a new introduction and notes by Charles R. Kesler (New York: Mentor Books, 1999), p. 1.

47. Lincoln, Speech on the Dred Scott Decision, June 26, 1857, *Collected Works*, vol. II, p. 406.

48. Aristotle, *Nicomachean Ethics*, 1134 b 25.

49. See Leo Strauss, "The Origin of the Idea of Natural Right," chap. III of *Natural Right and History*.

50. That a stone thrown upwards within a space vehicle beyond gravitational sphere behaves differently than one at the earth's surface does not affect the argument. An astronaut could no more habituate the stone to fall downwards than someone on Earth could habituate it not to do so.

51. *Documents of American History*, ed. Henry Steele Commager (New York: Appleton-Century-Crofts, 1948), p. 126.

52. "I have sworn upon the altar of God eternal hostility against every form of tyranny over the mind of man." Jefferson, Letter to Dr. Benjamin Rush, September 23, 1800, in *Writings*, p. 1082.

53. *Documents of American History*, p. 173.

54. Although breathing itself is involuntary, it may be either healthy or unhealthy (as in the case of someone who smokes or who works in an unhealthy atmosphere), and the possession of health (or its opposite) may be the result of good or bad habits.

Here we would also note that in the generation after Pascal, David Hume argued that all causality can be regarded as nothing but a custom of the mind of the observer. That a stone always falls back after being thrown upwards does not, according to Hume, mean that there is a cause called nature that makes the stone do so. All we can properly say, by Hume's account, is that we see a sequence of facts. But we never see anything connecting these facts. What we call a "cause" (including "nature") is nothing other than the custom of the mind in making an observation. By contrast, when we say that the three angles of the triangle equal two right angles, we really know the connection between our premises and our conclusions. According to Hume, all reasoning is either moral or demonstrative. The latter contains its conclusions in its premises. It would be possible, on Humian premises, to call nature a "first custom."

I surmise that it is partly because of Hume's influence that Becker cited Pascal. This reflects the radical skepticism characteristic of Becker's generation. But this skepticism, which still governs most academic thinking, ends in destroying itself. It is sufficient for our present purposes to note that the existence of nature in the sense used by Aristotle, Jefferson, or Lincoln is not more doubtful than belief in our own actual existence or identities as individual human beings. Any attempt to prove to someone else that you exist must always assume that you exist, as a condition of proving it. But this is exactly what is meant by a self-evident truth. Those who deny the existence of self-evident truths on the ground that they cannot be proved must deny the existence of everything that is known by inductive reasoning, beginning with themselves.

55. "[I]n a certain manner virtue, when it obtains resources, has in fact very great power to use force, and the stronger party always possesses superiority in something that is good, so that it is thought that force cannot be devoid of goodness, but that the dispute is merely about the justice of the matter (for it is due to the one party holding that the justification of authority is good will, while the other identifies justice with the mere rule of the stronger)" Aristotle, *Politics* 1255 a 16–21. To reduce a complex text to a simple dictum, Aristotle is saying here that other things being equal, the party that has virtue on its side will be stronger. Heaven does not help those who do not help themselves, but a reasoned confidence in the justice of one's cause is an advantage in battle.

Consider also the peroration of Lincoln's Cooper Institute speech, February 27, 1860, in *Collected Works*, vol. III, p. 550: "Neither let us be slandered from our duty by false accusations against us, nor frightened from it by menaces of destruction to the Government nor of dungeons to ourselves. LET US HAVE FAITH THAT RIGHT MAKES MIGHT, AND IN THAT FAITH, LET US, TO THE END, DARE TO DO OUR DUTY AS WE UNDERSTAND IT." (Capitals in original.)

56. Lincoln, *Collected Works*, vol. II, p. 222.

57. See Churchill's account in *A Roving Commission: The Story of My Early Life* (New York: Charles Scribner's Sons, 1930) of how as a child he resisted being sent to school. Like a fugitive slave, he took to the woods.

58. The classical discussion of this question is in Book I of Aristotle's *Politics*, 1253 b 15–1255 a 2.

59. To be a member of the species *Homo sapiens* means to be possessed, not of right reason, but of reason. Only those possessed of reason can reason either rightly *or* wrongly.

60. "For nature, as we declare, does nothing in vain . . . but speech (*logos*) is designed to indicate the advantageous and the harmful, and also the just and the unjust. For it is the special property of man, in distinction from all other animals, that he alone has perception of good and bad and just and unjust and the other moral qualities, and it is partnership in these that makes a household and a political community." Aristotle, *Politics*, 1253 a 10–19. The Aristotelian conception of nature, and its logical and moral embodiment in the idea of species, is fundamental to the doctrine of the Declaration. Its denial is equally fundamental to Becker's relativism and positivism—and to the proslavery argument, although Becker himself was not proslavery.

61. That the antislavery argument was politically "interested" was what the advocates of the "needless war" thesis maintained. Of course, they also thought that the "ultimate extinction" of slavery was needless.

62. Lincoln, Letter to the editor of the Illinois *Gazette*, August 11, 1846, in *Collected Works*, vol. I, p. 382.

63. "Since then the present inquiry does not aim at theoretical knowledge like the others (for we are inquiring not in order to know what virtue is, but in order to become good, since otherwise our inquiry would have been of no use), we must examine the nature of actions, namely, how we ought to do them" Aristotle, *Nicomachean Ethics*, 1103 b 26 ff.

64. Lincoln. *Collected Works*, vol. II, p. 278.

65. Lincoln. *Collected Works*, vol. II, p. 500.

66. Jefferson, Letter to Roger Weightman, June 24, 1826, in *Writings*, p. 1517.

67. Algernon Sidney, *Discourses Concerning Government*, ed. Thomas G. West (Indianapolis: Liberty Classics, 1990), pp. 510–511.

68. This phrase is almost certainly the antecedent of "We hold these truths to be self-evident."

69. *Documents of American History*, p. 92.

70. Quoted in "Rumbold's Dying Speech, 1685, and Jefferson's Last Words on Democracy, 1826," in Douglass Adair, *Fame and the Founding Fathers: Essays by Douglass Adair*, ed. Trevor Colbourn (New York: W. W. Norton, 1974), p. 200.

71. The borrower may be driven by his "necessities" in agreeing with the conditions

of the loan. He may look upon his action as choosing the lesser evil, rather than the greater good. But it is a choice nonetheless, and therefore in the decisive respect voluntary.

72. "The Inspiration of the Declaration," in Calvin Coolidge, *Foundations of the Republic* (New York: Scribner's, 1926), p. 447. Coolidge's speech is remarkable for upholding a thesis that is the exact opposite of Carl Becker's. But Becker expressed the intellectual consensus within our elite universities and continues to be the leading authority on the Declaration to this day. What President Coolidge had to say on this topic, although said with great eloquence and closely approximating the sentiments of Lincoln, is today virtually unknown. From this fact we may infer how great are the obstacles to the "unfinished work" of the Gettysburg Address.

73. Coolidge, "Inspiration of the Declaration," in *Foundations of the Republic*, p. 453.

74. Jefferson, *Notes on the State of Virginia*, Query XIII, in *Writings*, p. 245.

75. Caesarism has been the charge against Lincoln from his perennial critics, beginning with John Wilkes Booth.

76. It is in this context that one must view Hobbes's famous dictum that tyranny is merely monarchy "misliked."

77. "Spirit of Governments," February 20, 1792, in *The Mind of the Founder: Sources of the Political Thought of James Madison*, p. 184.

78. Lincoln, Address before the Young Men's Lyceum, Springfield, Illinois, January 17, 1838, in *Collected Works*, vol. I, p. 113.

79. See note 1 in chap. 1.

80. Jefferson, Kentucky Resolutions, in *Writings*, p. 454.

81. It should be remembered that Athenian democracy in the age of Pericles subsisted, not only on a base of slave labor, but also on the tribute exacted by Athens from the subject cities in her empire. It was this tribute that paid the wages of the demos when it attended the assemblies. Without it, the poor could not have afforded the leisure to leave their occupations to participate in government.

82. *Documents of American History*, p. 97.

83. *Federalist Papers*, no. 10, p. 47.

84. In this, the perspective of the Declaration is in agreement with Thomas Aquinas's conception of the natural law as the rational creature's participation in the eternal law, the law by which God governs the universe. The Declaration also assumes the existence of an eternal law when it speaks of an appeal to "the supreme judge of the world" and of "the protection of divine Providence." The voice of right reason in the natural law, therefore, is as much the voice of God as is divine revelation. Also, since every member of the human species has the potentiality to participate in the natural law, in this decisive respect, all men are created equal.

85. Winston Churchill, "Consistency in Politics," in *Thoughts and Adventures* (London: Butterworth, 1932), p. 39.

86. Thomas Babington Macaulay, *The History of England* (London: J. M. Dent, 1927) vol. II, pp. 279–280.

87. Lincoln, Letter to J. H. Hackett, August 17, 1863, in *Collected Works*, vol. VI, p. 392.

88. Act I, scene 7 of *Macbeth*, in which Lady Macbeth persuades her husband to commit murder, is obviously a reenactment of the temptation and fall in *Genesis*, and Lin-

coln must have read it as such. In his political theology, slavery was the forbidden fruit in the American Garden of Eden.

89. *Henry V,* act IV, scene 1. We note in passing the "Nuremberg" defense: Everyone except Hitler was merely obeying orders, and Hitler was dead! Bates's piety, however, required him to look upon the king as God's representative, which of course created a presumption (falsely certified by the archbishop of Canterbury) in favor of the justice of the king's cause.

90. *Henry V,* act IV, scene 1. The king's argument bears a striking resemblance to that of the Grand Inquisitor in Dostoyevsky's *Brothers Karamazov.*

91. Lincoln, Speech at Chicago, July 10, 1858, in *Collected Works,* vol. II, p. 500.

92. *Henry V,* act IV, scene 3.

93. In act II, scene 2, the king parleys with three of his highest-ranking advisers in terms of seeming intimacy and confidence, only to suddenly turn on them and accuse them—justly, as the chorus has already informed us—of high treason and order their execution. No one will outmaster Henry in treachery! Evidently he had spies who forewarned him of an impending attempt at assassination. We recall that Richard was assassinated in prison at the instigation of Henry's father. Apparently father and son are equally adept at assassinating and at not being assassinated. We are reminded also of Henry IV's supreme act of treachery, in act IV, scene 2 of *Henry IV, Part II.* Prince John of Lancaster, the then Prince Hal's younger brother, encounters the rebel army. These rebels had helped Bolingbroke redress his grievances against Richard but broke with him because of his seizing the crown, since he was not next in line of succession. Prince John promises the rebels' leaders a redress of all their grievances if they will lay down their arms. They do so and are immediately arrested, to be executed for high treason. Both these scenes represent Machiavellianism of the purest water.

94. *Henry V,* act IV, scene 8.

95. *Richard II,* act III, scene 2.

96. In this, Henry expects no more than what God allowed to King David, God's favorite sinner in the Old Testament.

97. This notwithstanding the numerous present-day society of Ricardians, who claim that Shakespeare is the villain for misrepresenting their hero. It is nothing to our purpose to enter into this dispute.

98. Fustel de Coulanges, *The Ancient City,* (Baltimore: Johns Hopkins University Press, 1980; published originally in 1864), pp. 353–354.

99. We think of our Capitol and our Senate and Publius's authorship of the *Federalist,* among the innumerable evidences of this relationship.

100. De Coulanges, *Ancient City,* (Baltimore: Johns Hopkins University Press, 1980; published originally in 1864), pp. 356, 358.

101. This is not to say that the United States was not augmented by war, notably by the war with Mexico. But the territory thus added was lightly peopled. The other major antebellum territorial acquisitions—the Louisiana Purchase, Florida, and the Gadsden Purchase—were cash transactions. The United States has added *people,* as distinct from land, almost entirely by natural increase and immigration.

102. Consider the following exchange in Shakespeare's *Antony and Cleopatra,* act IV, scene 3: "First Soldier: Peace, I say! What should this mean? Second Soldier: Tis the god

Hercules, whom Antony loved, Now leaves him." This is Shakespeare's way of marking the end of the ancient hero and of the ancient world. Antony's pursuit of Cleopatra is the pursuit of private pleasure rather than public duty. The god's leaving Antony represents the fact that Antony has already deserted the god. He is no longer a Roman but a citizen of the world (an oxymoron!), for whom duty and honor have no meaning.

103. I once saw a cartoon of two monks walking together in their cloister. One says to the other, "And when it comes to humility, we're tops!" One might call this proof of the invincibility of nature. In the same context, one might compare the contest between Coriolanus and Aufidius with that between Harry Hotspur and Prince Hal (later Henry V) in *Henry IV, Part 1*. Hotspur's desire for the warrior's honor above all things is, so to speak, the Christian shadow of the pagan Coriolanus. It is a desire for honor for its own sake, divorced from any desire to elevate his country or its cause. It is true that Hotspur has undertaken what he deems the just cause, first supporting Bolingbroke against Richard, and later Mortimer against Bolingbroke. But these are mere occasions for him to seek honor, and he is not politically involved in them. They pale beside Coriolanus's desire to embody Roman superiority and his insistence on the unequivocal identification of himself and Rome. Hotspur's defeat by Prince Hal means that all his honors are transferred to his conqueror, but that conqueror is not interested in the honor thus acquired. Prince Hal is his father's son, interested in the crown, the symbol of divine election, rather than honor as a sign of personal or civic excellence. Coriolanus wishes to be regarded as himself a god. King Henry V's universe is one in which the throne of heaven is fully occupied. It is for this reason that Henry, after Agincourt, insists that the honor of victory is God's alone.

104. We saw an echo of this in *Henry V*, when the king, the night before Agincourt, asked "the God of battles" to nerve his soldiers' arms and take from them the sense of fear. One assumes that the God of battles was the Christian God, although it is difficult to imagine a Christian justification for this identification.

105. Matthew 22:15–22.

106. Patrick Henry, Speech in the House of Burgesses, Williamsburg, Virginia, May 29, 1765, in *The World's Famous Orations*, ed. William Jennings Bryan (New York: Funk & Wagnalls, 1906), p. 62, note 1.

107. One might also contend that the peculiar characteristics of the Jews, as seen by the prophets, were the result of their not infrequent rebellions against those laws. In either case, God's legislation for a particular people could not be conceived in universal terms— as were, for example, the "laws of nature and of nature's God."

108. Over the centuries, local custom took on the force of law, in practice limiting the authority of kings and emperors. It is well to remember that the same King John who, according to Shakespeare, defied the pope by claiming to rule by divine right, was compelled by his subjects (in Magna Carta) to accept limitations upon his royal authority. But these rights of subjects were established by ancient custom, *not* by any original authority vested in the people. They were seen as self-limitations of royal authority, in the same sense in which the God of the Bible is seen as limited by his promises to Abraham, Noah, etc.

109. Romans 13:1–2.

110. Romans 13:3–4.

111. 1 Peter 2:13–17.

112. One might say that the person of Nero represented the negation of the person of Jesus.

113. Written between 1309 and 1313. All quotations are taken from *Dante: Monarchy and Three Political Letters,* translated by Donald Nicholl (New York: Noonday Press, 1954).

114. The "laws of nature and of nature's God" refers to the legislative function, the "supreme judge of the world" to the judicial function, and the "protection of Divine Providence" to the executive function. The first scholar to observe this "separation of powers" within the government of the universe was George Anastaplo, in "The Declaration of Independence," *St. Louis University Law Journal,* no. 9, 1965, p. 390.

115. See note 82 above.

116. *Documents of American History,* p. 181.

117. *Federalist Papers,* no. 47, p. 269. This definition of tyranny did not, of course, apply to God's government of the universe. Every reader of *Paradise Lost,* however, knows how difficult it was for that stubborn republican, John Milton, to portray God's monarchical government in heaven in sympathetic terms.

118. "But again [practical wisdom] is not *supreme* over philosophic wisdom, i.e. over the superior part of us, any more than the art of medicine is over health; for it does not use it but provides for its coming into being; it issues orders then for its sake, but not to it." Aristotle, *Nicomachean Ethics,* 1145 a 6–10.

119. Also, if Lucrece, the nemesis of the Tarquins, had been Christian, she would not have committed suicide This is made clear in Shakespeare's epic poem, *The Rape of Lucrece.* Tarquin gives Lucrece the alternative of submitting to him, in which case he will keep her infamy secret, or refusing him, in which case he will kill her and lie to the world that she has betrayed her husband. In the event, she cares more for her reputation of virtue than virtue itself. Of course, she redeems her fallen virtue by committing suicide. As a Christian, she could neither have submitted nor committed suicide. It was her suicide that propelled the events that led to the formation of the republican regime, and Coriolanus won his first fame in the fight against the Tarquins. I am indebted for this analysis to Michael Platt, *Rome and Romans According to Shakespeare* (Salzburg: Institut für Englishe Sprache und Literatur, Universität Salzburg, 1976).

120. This is exactly what we see happen in *Henry V,* in the corrupt bargain of the king and the archbishop of Canterbury.

121. Mark 3:31–35.

122. Lincoln, *Collected Works,* vol. II, p. 499.

123. M. E. Bradford, "The Heresy of Equality," *Modern Age,* Winter 1976. Reprinted in *Modern Age: The First Twenty-five Years,* ed. George Panichas (New York: Liberty Press, 1988), p. 287.

124. Speech delivered in New York City on November 24, 1910, at the dedication of a monument to Orestes Brownson, quoted in James McGurrin, *Bourke Cockran* (New York: Scribner's, 1948), pp. 307–308.

Chapter 3

1. Of course slavery also existed in parts of Africa and Asia. The "untouchables" in Hindu India also lived in the most abject degradation. While the living conditions of American slaves, as productive workers in a flourishing economy, compared favorably with those of working classes in many other parts of the world, the fixity of their status was not thereby diminished. What was peculiarly aggravating was that they were slaves in what was otherwise a land of freedom.

2. This is true, notwithstanding the fact that it took some time for the provisions of the First Amendment to make their way into the state constitutions. The intention of the Framers is, however, indicated by the fact that religious freedom—along with the exclusion of slavery—was required in the Northwest Territory by the Northwest Ordinance, adopted by the first Congress in 1789.

3. *Abraham Lincoln: His Speeches and Writings*, ed. Roy P. Basler (Cleveland: World Publishing, 1946), p. 427. This is Basler's one-volume selection of Lincoln's writings and contains some items not in *Collected Works*.

4. Speech at Jackson, July 6, 1859, in *Jefferson Davis, Constitutionalist: His Letters, Papers, and Speeches*, ed. Dunbar Rowland (Jackson: Mississippi Department of Archives and History, 1923), vol. IV, pp. 71–72.

5. See note 36 in chap. 1.

6. Acts 17:26.

7. See, e.g., Daniel T. Reff, *Disease, Depopulation, and Culture Change in Northwestern New Spain, 1518–1764* (Salt Lake City: University of Utah Press, 1991).

8. Thomas Jefferson, *Notes on the State of Virginia*, Query XIV, in *Writings*, ed. Merrill D. Peterson (New York: Library of America, 1984), p. 269.

9. *Jefferson Davis, Constitutionalist*, vol. IV, p. 72.

10. Jefferson, *Notes on Virginia*, Query XIV, in *Writings*, pp. 267–268.

11. *Jefferson Davis, Constitutionalist*, vol. IV, p. 72.

12. See note 41 in chap. 1.

13. That the political foundation of the civil rights movement of our time was laid in the Negro churches is indicated by the name of the Southern Christian Leadership Conference and its most famous protagonist, the Reverend Martin Luther King Jr.

14. *Jefferson Davis, Constitutionalist*, vol. IV, pp. 72–73.

15. We remind the reader of Dante's argument for universal and absolute monarchy, as discussed in chap. 2. We see no reason to doubt Dante's sincerity in making this argument, as absurd as it was. Yet it is clear that his paramount goal was to defeat the papal party and return to Florence, and his argument was subordinate to that end. It would have been a necessary argument for him to make, in the circumstances, whether he believed in it or not.

16. Since the beginning of my study of the Lincoln–Douglas debates in 1946, I have become deeply convinced of this, even as I am persuaded that this reason escaped even Jefferson and Lincoln.

17. Abraham Lincoln, *Speeches and Writings, 1832–1858*, ed. Don E. Fehrenbacher

(New York: Library of America, 1989), pp. 685–686. The triple exclamation points are apparently in Lincoln's manuscript.

18. *Jefferson Davis, Constitutionalist*, vol. IV, p. 71.

19. For such analysis, see chap. XVII of the present writer's *Crisis of the House Divided* (Chicago: University of Chicago Press, 1982; originally published in 1959).

20. *The Federalist Papers*, ed. Clinton Rossiter, with a new introduction and notes by Charles R. Kesler (New York: Mentor Books, 1999), p. 47.

21. *Federalist Papers*, p. 290.

22. See note 69 in chap. 2.

23. Abraham Lincoln, Speech at Peoria, Illinois, October 16, 1854; To William Kellogg, December 11, 1860; and To John D. Defrees, December 18, 1860, in *The Collected Works of Abraham Lincoln*, ed. Roy P. Basler (New Brunswick, N.J.: Rutgers University Press, 1953), vol. II, p. 270; vol. IV, pp. 150, 155.

24. Lincoln, *Collected Works*, vol. IV, p. 439.

25. All quotations from Buchanan in this section are from his Fourth Annual Message to Congress, December 3, 1860, in *The Works of James Buchanan*, ed. John Bassett Moore (New York: Antiquarian Press, 1960), vol. XI, pp. 7–54.

26. Lincoln, Address at Cooper Institute, New York City, February 27, 1860, in *Collected Works*, vol. III, pp. 547–548.

27. Buchanan cites the fact that "In 1835, pictorial handbills and inflammatory appeals were circulated extensively throughout the South, of a character to excite the passions of the slaves, and, in the language of General Jackson, 'to stimulate them to insurrection and produce all the horrors of servile war.'" He fails to mention that 1835 was nearly twenty years before the formation of the Republican Party and that in the interim the slave states had virtually sealed off all access by the slaves to any contact with abolitionist literature. Whatever danger there might have been from the "inflammatory appeals" of 1835 had long since ended.

28. Lincoln, Speech at Hartford, Connecticut, March 5, 1860, in *Collected Works*, vol. IV, p. 8.

29. Lincoln, *Collected Works*, vol. III, pp. 539–541.

30. Unless it be Neville Chamberlain's waving Hitler's scribble in the air in 1938 and saying he brought "peace in our time" from Munich.

31. The Republican Platform of 1860, in *National Party Platforms, 1840–1972*, compiled by Donald Bruce Johnson and Kirk H. Porter (Urbana: University of Illinois Press, 1973), p. 32.

32. The furor could be said to have dated from the Wilmot Proviso of 1848, but there was a brief hiatus after the Compromise of 1850, a hiatus that ended in 1854 with the Kansas–Nebraska Act.

33. *Federalist Papers*, p. 247.

34. On Southerners who fought for the Union cause, see Richard Nelson Current, *Lincoln's Loyalists: Union Soldiers from the Confederacy* (Boston: Northeastern University Press, 1992).

35. The Kansas–Nebraska Act, in *Documents of American History*, ed. Henry Steele Commager (New York: Appleton-Century-Crofts, 1948), p. 332.

36. Dred Scott was held in Minnesota, a territory formed from the Louisiana Pur-

chase of 1803, from which slavery had been excluded by the Missouri Compromise. The case did not arise from the legislation of 1850, which dealt with territories formed from the conquests of the Mexican War of 1846–48. But the idea of having the Supreme Court decide the status of slavery in the territories was embodied in the 1850 legislation. It reflected the continuing inability of Congress to come to any conclusion on that subject.

37. Democratic Platform of 1856, in *National Party Platforms*, p. 25.

38. We may think more charitably of nullification if we think of it as an alternative to judicial review. Nothing could have been more disastrous than the attempt by the Supreme Court, in *Dred Scott*, to settle the nation's differences over slavery by judicial fiat.

39. Lincoln, First Inaugural, in *Collected Works*, vol. IV, p. 264.

40. Articles of Confederation, March 1, 1781, in *Documents of American History*, p. 114.

41. *Federalist Papers*, p. 247.

42. Willmoore Kendall, a faithful Confederate, would call the states declaring independence a "baker's dozen." See Kendall and George W. Carey, *Basic Symbols of the American Political Tradition* (Baton Rouge: Louisiana State University Press, 1970), p. 90. Although the Declaration was issued by the thirteen united states of America, Calhounites would say that they were united only in declaring their separate independence!

43. *Documents of American History*, p. 111.

44. Calhoun's 1848 speech on the Oregon Bill—in *Union and Liberty*, pp. 539–570—asserted that the American Revolution was caused solely by British violations of the colonists' prescriptive rights under the British constitution, implying a constitutional right of secession very similar to what was claimed by the American South in 1860–61. Of course, it is also the case that for Calhoun all right was positive right. Natural right, including the natural right of revolution, did not exist for him.

45. For pioneering work on this topic, see "The Federalist's View of Federalism," a 1961 essay by Martin Diamond. It is reprinted in *As Far as Republican Principles Will Admit: Essays by Martin Diamond*, ed. William A. Schambra (Washington, D.C.: American Enterprise Institute Press, 1992).

46. Among the many ironies of Calhoun's conception of undivided sovereignty was the fact that his own idea of the concurrent majority implied, not dual, but multiple sovereignty.

47. We must note, however, that Buchanan's acceptance of Madison's conception of sovereignty here is stultified by his acceptance of Calhoun's conception elsewhere, especially as it appeared in Taney's opinion in *Dred Scott*.

48. We will discuss further and supply passages from these resolutions in chap. 6.

49. See note 23 in chap. 1.

50. *Federalist Papers*, p. 248.

51. See note 84 in chap. 1.

52. Article V of the Constitution imposes two limitations upon the amending power. One of them—that no state may be deprived of its equal representation in the Senate without its consent—remains to this day. This limitation upon the power of even three-fourths of the states reflects the fact that the essential elements of the unanimous consent underlying all free government cannot be breached. Reflection will teach us that there are many

other unmentioned limitations—for example, that represented by the guarantee to every state of a republican form of government.

53. In *Ableman v. Booth*, 62 U.S. 506 (1859).

54. *Documents of American History*, p. 342.

55. Unless otherwise noted, all quotations from Davis in this section are from his Farewell Address to the U.S. Senate, January 21, 1861, in *The Papers of Jefferson Davis* (Baton Rouge: Louisiana State University Press, 1971), vol. VII, pp. 18–23.

56. Relations of State Resolutions, May 8, 1860, in *Jefferson Davis, Constitutionalist*, vol. IV, p. 251.

57. Relations of State Resolutions, in *Jefferson Davis, Constitutionalist*, vol. IV, p. 251.

58. See note 39 in chap. 1.

59. See note 124 in chap. 2.

60. The reference in Article IV, section 2, to persons "held to service or labor in one state . . . escaping into another" would include white indentured servants as well as slaves. Certainly the number of indentured servants was very small by 1861, but it would require only one of them to destroy the assumption that the article referred only to chattel slaves. When Benjamin Franklin as a young man ran away from Boston to Philadelphia, he was escaping from his indentured servitude to his brother.

61. Although free Negroes counted as five-fifths, not three-fifths, they would nonetheless belong to Davis's "lower caste."

62. Speech on the Oregon Bill, 1848, in *Union and Liberty*, pp. 569–570.

63. Alexander Stephens, Speech in the State Convention of Georgia, January 1861, in *The Political History of the United States of America during the Great Rebellion, 1860–1865*, ed. Edward McPherson (New York: Da Capo Press, 1992), pp. 25–26.

64. (Lord) John Emerich Edward Dalberg Acton, "Political Causes of the American Revolution," in *Essays in Freedom and Power*, selected with an introduction by Gertrude Himmelfarb (Boston: Beacon Press, 1948).

65. The passage from Psalms is quoted by Jesus in Matthew 21:42: "Jesus said to them, 'Have you never read in the scriptures: The very stone that the builders rejected has become the head of the corner.'" In Acts 4:11, Peter, speaking of Jesus, says "This is the stone which was rejected by you builders, but which has become the head of the corner." And again, in 1 Peter 2:6–7: "For it stands in scripture, 'Behold, I am laying in Zion a stone, a cornerstone chosen and precious, and he who believes in him will not be put to shame.' To you therefore who believe, he is precious, but for those who do not believe, 'The very stone which the builders rejected has become the head of the corner.'"

66. The Cornerstone Speech, March 21, 1861, in *Alexander H. Stephens in Public and Private with Letters and Speeches* (Philadelphia: National Publishing, 1866), p. 721.

67. Relations of State Resolutions, in *Jefferson Davis, Constitutionalist*, vol. IV, p. 251.

68. *Documents of American History*, p. 342.

69. This is also how the Confederates of our time have argued. See *Basic Symbols of the American Political Tradition* (cited in note 43 above) and M. E. Bradford, *A Better Guide than Reason: Federalists and Anti-Federalists* (New Brunswick, N.J.: Transaction, 1994).

70. *Documents of American History*, p. 342.

71. For detailed refutation of Taney on this point, see Don E. Fehrenbacher, *The Dred*

Scott Case: Its Significance in American Law and Politics (New York: Oxford University Press, 1978), pp. 339–364, 388, 674–675. We will return to the topic in chap. 5.

72. Lincoln, Speech at Springfield, Illinois, June 26, 1857, in *Collected Works*, vol. II, p. 404.

73. This trial was apparently not known to Lincoln. It is mentioned by Fehrenbacher in *The Dred Scott Case* but not marshaled in the evidence he presents to refute Taney on the change in opinion concerning the humanity of Negroes between the Founding and 1857.

74. Clement Eaton, *Freedom of Thought in the Old South* (Durham, N.C.: Duke University Press, 1940), p. 131.

75. I am indebted to Dr. John West for calling to my attention Taney's arguments in the Gruber case, found in Eaton, *Freedom of Thought*.

76. Consider also these remarks of Senator James H. Hammond of South Carolina in 1858, speaking of the rise of abolitionism in the North after the emancipation of the slaves in Great Britain's West Indian colonies in 1833–34: "And what then was the state of opinion in the South? Washington had emancipated his slaves. Jefferson had bitterly denounced the system, and had done all that he could to destroy it. Our Clays, Marshalls, Crawfords and many other prominent Southern men, had led off in the colonization scheme. The inevitable effect in the South was that she believed slavery to be an evil—weakness—disgraceful—*nay, a sin*. She shrunk from the discussion of it. . . . But a few bold spirits took the question up: they compelled the South to investigate it anew and thoroughly, and what is the result? Why it would be difficult to find a Southern man who feels the system to be the slightest burden on his conscience; who does not, in fact, regard it as an equal advantage to the master and the slave elevating both, [in] wealth, strength and power. . . . The rock of Gibraltar does not stand so firm on its basis as our slave system. For a quarter of a century it has borne the brunt of a hurricane. . . . And how stands it now? Why, in this very quarter of a century our slaves have doubled in numbers and each slave has more than doubled in value. The very negro who as a prime laborer would have brought $400 in 1828, would now, with thirty more years upon him, sell for $800." *Political History*, p. 26. Hammond was famous as the author of the "mudsill" theory of slave labor, to which Lincoln gave a thorough reply in his speech to the Wisconsin State Agricultural Fair, in Milwaukee, September 30, 1859. The present selection confirms the testimony of both Stephens and the Taney of 1818 as to the state of Southern opinion on slavery in the generation of the Founding. It also testifies, in opposition to both Buchanan and Davis, to the fact that the slave South had not suffered but in fact had prospered since the rise of abolitionism in the North.

77. *Stephens in Public and Private*, pp. 721–722.

78. *George Washington: A Collection*, ed. W. B. Allen (Indianapolis: Liberty Classics, 1988), p. 240.

79. *Stephens in Public and Private*, p. 722.

80. Darwin himself held antislavery views.

81. Relations of State Resolutions, in *Jefferson Davis, Constitutionalist*, vol. IV, p. 253.

82. Remarks on the Bill for the Benefit of School in the District of Columbia, April 12, 1860, in *Jefferson Davis, Constitutionalist*, vol. IV, p. 231.

83. See note 8 above.

84. *Jefferson Davis, Constitutionalist,* vol. IV, p. 234.

85. Wilson speaks of the "mental and physical" inequality of the black and white races. One thinks of the dominance in our time of black athletes in nearly all sports in which they have been allowed to compete. Have the obstacles to mental competition been removed to the same extent as the physical? Have there been anything like the *incentives* to mental competition comparable to the physical?

86. The foregoing sentences are paraphrased from editorial comments by Henry Steele Commager in *Documents of American History,* p. 372.

87. *South Carolina Secedes,* ed. John Amasa May and John Reynolds Faunt (Columbia: University of South Carolina Press, 1960), pp. 88–89.

88. *South Carolina Secedes,* pp. 76–77.

89. *South Carolina Secedes,* pp. 76–77.

90. This account of the case of Anthony Burns is paraphrased from James M. McPherson, *Battle Cry of Freedom* (New York: Oxford University Press, 1988), pp. 119–120. McPherson says that the cost to the federal government to secure Burns's return was $100,000, which he estimates to be equal to $2 million in 1987 currency. The use of federal troops to enforce the fugitive slave law in 1854 in Boston resembles remarkably the use of federal troops to integrate Central High School in Little Rock in 1956.

91. *South Carolina Secedes,* p. 80.

92. Possibly the breakdown was because of feuds between neighbors, something not uncommon in the antebellum South. Again, we refer our readers to *Huckleberry Finn.*

93. Stanley W. Campbell, *The Slave Catchers: Enforcement of the Fugitive Slave Law, 1850–1860* (Chapel Hill: University of North Carolina Press, 1970).

94. McPherson, *Battle Cry of Freedom,* p. 237.

95. These losses could easily have been compensated, if relief had been sought. But the inflammatory value of the fugitive slave question outweighed any such considerations. Moreover the Southern strict constructionists would have rebelled at the suggestion that the Constitution delegated any authority to the federal government to appropriate money for such a purpose. When in 1862 Lincoln submitted a plan to Congress to assist slave states in programs of compensated emancipation, he presented it in the form of a series of constitutional amendments, authorizing the federal government to appropriate money for this purpose.

96. See note 78 above for these quotations from Senator Hammond.

97. *South Carolina Secedes,* p. 80.

98. Inaugural Address of the President of the Provisional Government, February 18, 1861, in *Jefferson Davis, Constitutionalist,* vol. V, pp. 49–50.

Chapter 4

1. This is a lesson that present-day Americans should recognize readily from the war in Vietnam. No two enemies in all history were more unevenly matched than North Vietnam and the United States. It is also true that no anti-Vietnam-war violence even approached the draft riots of 1863 in New York.

2. Aristotle, *Nicomachean Ethics*, 1181 a 14.

3. Leo Strauss often pointed out that Xenophon, the pupil of Socrates, could rule both gentlemen and nongentlemen, whereas Proxenus, the pupil of the Sophist Gorgias, could rule only gentlemen. See, e.g., Xenophon's *Anabasis* II.vi.16. Nothing illustrates the differences of the two conceptions of rule better than the story of the Missouri farmer who hit his mule over the head with a two-by-four "in order to get his attention."

4. We do, however, refer our readers to "The Political Philosophy of a Young Whig," chaps. IX and X of the present writer's *Crisis of the House Divided* (Chicago: University of Chicago Press, 1982; originally published in 1959).

5. Actually this speech had been given at Springfield several weeks earlier. But the printed text comes from Peoria and contains additions to the Springfield version.

6. Lincoln, Speech at Hartford, Connecticut, March 5, 1860, in *The Collected Works of Abraham Lincoln*, ed. Roy P. Basler (New Brunswick, N.J.: Rutgers University Press, 1953), vol. IV, pp. 10–11.

7. This speech—or the report of it—does not follow the line of argument of the Cooper Institute speech. It is, rather, an attack on Douglas's attempt to evade his own popular sovereignty argument in dealing with polygamy in Utah. Lincoln is merciless in skewering Douglas's inconsistency.

8. Perhaps the classic account is Roy F. Nichols, *The Disruption of American Democracy* (New York: Free Press, 1967).

9. The Democratic (Breckinridge Faction) Platform of 1860, in *National Party Platforms, 1840–1972*, compiled by Donald Bruce Johnson and Kirk H. Porter (Urbana: University of Illinois Press, 1973), p. 31.

10. *Documents of American History*, ed. Henry Steele Commager (New York: Appleton-Century-Crofts, 1948), p. 345.

11. Lincoln, Speech at Hartford, Connecticut, March 5, 1860, in *Collected Works*, vol. IV, p. 9.

12. Resolution 8 of the Republican platform of 1860 read as follows: "That the normal condition of all the territory of the United States is that of freedom; That, as our Republican fathers, when they had abolished slavery in all our national territory, ordained that 'no person should be deprived of life, liberty, or property without due process of law,' it becomes our duty, by legislation, whenever such legislation is necessary, to maintain this provision of the Constitution against all attempts to violate it; and we deny the authority of Congress, of a territorial legislature, or of any individual, to give legal existence to slavery in any territory of the United States." *National Party Platforms*, p. 32.

13. See esp. Lincoln's First Annual Message to Congress, December 3, 1961, in *Collected Works*, vol. V, pp. 35–53.

14. Crittenden Peace Resolutions, December 18, 1860, in *Documents of American History*, p. 370.

15. Lincoln, *Collected Works*, vol. IV, pp. 175–176.

16. We say "especially" because the convention mode, as Lincoln says in his inaugural, originates with the people themselves.

17. Lincoln, To John A. Gilmer, December 15, 1860, in *Collected Works*, vol. IV, pp. 151–152.

18. Lincoln, *Collected Works*, vol. IV, p. 146.

19. Speech against Secession, November 14, 1860, in *Alexander H. Stephens in Public and Private with Letters and Speeches* (Philadelphia: National Publishing, 1866), p. 695.

20. Speech against Secession, in *Stephens in Public and Private*, pp. 696–698.

21. In a letter to John D. Defrees, on December 18, 1860, Lincoln inquired whether Stephens would "go into the cabinet." He was apparently under consideration as secretary of the navy. *Collected Works*, vol. IV, p. 155.

22. Lincoln, *Collected Works*, vol. IV, p. 160.

23. Lincoln, *Collected Works*, vol. V, pp. 388–389.

24. It is needless here to say anything about Lincoln's midnight trip (allegedly but not really in disguise) through Baltimore. The ridicule he received for this in the press stung him, and he always regretted it. Nevertheless it was the prudent thing to do. Many Baltimoreans would have assassinated him if they could have done so, and the Union might have come to an end then and there. It should be remembered that the first casualties of the Civil War were in Baltimore.

25. Lincoln, Farewell Address at Springfield, February 11, 1861, in *Collected Works*, vol. IV, p. 190.

26. Lincoln, *Collected Works*, vol. IV, pp. 192–193.

27. Lincoln, Speech at Buffalo, New York, February 16, 1861, in *Collected Works*, vol. IV, p. 220.

28. Lincoln, Speech from the Balcony of the Bates House, Indianapolis, Indiana, February 11, 1861, in *Collected Works*, vol. IV, p. 195.

29. Lincoln, *Collected Works*, pp. 195–196.

30. In 1981 President Ronald Reagan, in his inaugural address, declared that the states had made the Union, showing that Calhounianism, even at the highest levels, was still alive and well. I am confident that Reagan, a native of Illinois, had no idea that he was contradicting Lincoln. His entourage, from which the speech emerged, like the conservative movement generally, was, however, filled with disciples of Calhoun.

31. *The Writings of James Madison*, ed. Gaillard Hunt (New York: G. P. Putnam's Sons, 1900), vol. 9, pp. 219–220.

32. Washington took Lincoln's view of the relationships of county to state and state to nation even *before* the adoption of the Constitution of 1787: "We are known by no other character among nations than as the United States; Massachusetts or Virginia is no better defined, nor any more thought of by foreign powers than the County of Worcester in Massachusetts is by Virginia, or Glouster County in Virginia by Massachusetts (respectable as they are); and yet these counties, with as much propriety, might oppose themselves to the laws of the state in which they are, as an individual state can oppose itself to the federal government, by which it is, or ought to be bound." Letter to Reverend William Gordon, July 8, 1783, in *George Washington: A Collection*, ed. W. B. Allen (Indianapolis: Liberty Classics, 1988), p. 258.

33. On Lincoln's earlier consideration of the relationship of reason and passion in the future of the Union, see his Address to the Young Men's Lyceum of Springfield, January 27, 1838, in *Collected Works*, vol. I, pp. 108–115; also chapter IX of the present writer's *Crisis of the House Divided*.

34. Lincoln, Address to the New Jersey Senate, Trenton, February 21, 1861, in *Collected Works*, vol. IV, pp. 235–236.

35. Lincoln, Speech in Independence Hall, Philadelphia, February 22, 1861, in *Collected Works*, vol. IV, p. 240.

36. Perhaps the best-known book, next to the Bible, in Protestant America.

37. All quotations from this speech in the remainder of this chapter and chap. 5 are taken from the First Inaugural Address—Final Text, March 4, 1861, in *Collected Works*, vol. IV, pp. 262–271. We have numbered the paragraphs as they occur in this text, but the numbers are not in the printed text itself.

38. Lincoln, *Collected Works*, vol. I, p. 115.

39. See notes 31 in chap. 1 and 79 in chap. 3.

40. Lincoln, *Collected Works*, vol. I, p. 108.

41. Lincoln, House Divided Speech, Springfield, Illinois, June 16, 1858, in *Collected Works*, vol. II, p. 461.

42. Lincoln, *Collected Works*, vol. III, pp. 547–548.

43. Especially that part of Virginia that became West Virginia (by seceding from secession) during the war.

44. *National Party Platforms*, p. 31.

45. Thomas Jefferson, A Bill for Proportioning Crimes and Punishments, in *Writings*, ed. Merrill D. Peterson (New York: Library of America, 1984), pp. 355–356.

46. See Don E. Fehrenbacher, *The Dred Scott Case: Its Significance in American Law and Politics* (New York: Oxford University Press, 1978), pp. 24–27.

47. This enforcement of federal law reminds one today of nothing so much as President Eisenhower's deployment of federal troops in Little Rock, Arkansas, in 1956, to enforce a desegregation order of a federal court. This transformation of the federal government from an enforcer of slavery to an enforcer of freedom is a direct legacy of the policy we are now interpreting.

48. Lincoln, Speech in the U.S. House of Representatives, January 12, 1848, in *Collected Works*, vol. I, p. 438.

49. See note 84 in chap. 1.

50. Thomas Aquinas gives an explanation along these lines of the polygamy that prevailed among the patriarchs of the Old Testament. *Summa Theologica*, trans. Fathers of the English Dominican Province (Allen, Texas: Christian Classics, 1981), vol. IV, pp. 2806–2810.

51. I leave out of this argument the claims of the conscientious objector, which have been recognized throughout American history.

52. J. G. Randall and David Donald, *The Civil War and Reconstruction* (Boston: Heath, 1961), p. 169.

53. Randall and Donald, *Civil War and Reconstruction*, p. 169.

54. David Potter, *Lincoln and His Party in the Secession Crisis* (New Haven: Yale University Press, 1942), p. 329.

55. *Hamlet*, act III, scene 1.

56. See note 64 in chap. 3.

57. There is, however, an inner connection between the Southern version of state rights and slavery, which remains to be fully articulated.

58. As were the differences between Jefferson and Hamilton on the constitutionality

of the Bank of the United States and later differences concerning the constitutionality of a protective tariff, etc.

59. Lincoln, *Collected Works*, vol. II, p. 323. Lincoln mentions Catholics in this letter because at the time they were particular objects of intolerance. There is no question but that any and every invidious discrimination on the basis of religion was equally abhorrent to him.

60. Since Napoleon, the plebiscite has been the resource of tyrants to claim democratic (or republican) legitimacy for their regimes. Lincoln will contend that the convention mode, by which the Constitution was adopted, no more than the plebiscite, could bestow legitimacy upon the secessionist conventions. Means otherwise good do not remain good when they serve bad ends.

61. *Union and Liberty: The Political Philosophy of John C. Calhoun*, ed. Ross M. Lence (Indianapolis: Liberty Fund, 1992), pp. 313–365. Calhoun conceived of his role in this controversy on the model of Jefferson, who was also vice president when he anonymously drafted the Kentucky Resolutions.

62. The infamous "forty bale" theory held that of every hundred bales of cotton sold abroad, forty represented the value transferred from the sellers of cotton to Northern manufacturers.

63. Lincoln, Speech at a Republican Banquet, Chicago, December 10, 1856, in *Collected Works*, vol. II, p. 385.

64. *Union and Liberty*, p. 520.

65. Why the slaves are not entitled to consideration will become clearer when we examine the argument of Calhoun's *Disquisition*. The mind-set of the Old South is, however, rendered to perfection by the following exchange in chap. 32 of *Huckleberry Finn*:

> "We blowed out a cylinder head."
>
> "Good gracious! anybody hurt?"
>
> "No'm. Killed a nigger."
>
> "Well, it's lucky; because sometimes people do get hurt."

The interlocutor is Aunt Sally, a paragon of womanly human sympathies and virtues. Mark Twain captures brilliantly, without unkindness, that unconscious sense of racial difference that amounts to a difference of species.

66. Calhoun, Speech on the Oregon Bill, June 27, 1848, in *Union and Liberty*, p. 564.

67. "For I agree with you that there is a natural aristocracy among men. The grounds of this are virtue and talents. . . . There is also an artificial aristocracy, founded on wealth and birth . . . [which] is a mischievous ingredient in government, and provision should be made to prevent its ascendancy." Jefferson, Letter to John Adams, October 28, 1813, in *Writings*, pp. 1305–1306. We should note that the racial attitude described by Calhoun did not end with slavery. On the contrary, it dominated the Jim Crow South—and not the South alone—more completely than it ever dominated Calhoun's South. This was due to the complete ascendancy in Western thought of social Darwinism—one version of which resulted in Marxism, and another in Naziism.

68. It is fair to note, however, that the great race riots in New York City in 1863 to protest the draft were also motivated by opposition to the Emancipation Proclamation. New York City's large Irish population, then at the bottom of the socioeconomic ladder of

free society, saw itself as about to be degraded by emancipation in much the same way as poor whites in the Confederate ranks.

Chapter 5

1. E.g., Willmoore Kendall, Garry Wills, M. E. Bradford, Thomas Fleming, and James McClellan. Consider McClellan's assertion that "the armies of Lee and Jackson were the real defenders of the Constitution and the principles of liberty, self-determination, and republicanism embodied in the Declaration of Independence." "Defending the High Ground: The Legacy of M. E. Bradford," in *Intercollegiate Review*, Spring 1994, p. 43.

2. Unless otherwise noted, all quotes from Taney in this chapter are from his *Dred Scott* decision, in *Documents of American History*, ed. Henry Steele Commager (New York: Appleton-Century-Crofts, 1948), pp. 339–345.

3. Don E. Fehrenbacher, *The Dred Scott Case: Its Significance in American Law and Politics* (New York: Oxford University Press, 1978), p. 349.

4. See note 23 in chap. 2.

5. *The Federalist Papers*, ed. Clinton Rossiter, with a new introduction and notes by Charles R. Kesler (New York: Mentor Books, 1999), no. 54, p. 306.

6. Fehrenbacher, *Dred Scott Case*, p. 560 n.

7. See note 75 in chap. 3.

8. Abraham Lincoln, Seventh Debate, Alton, Illinois, October 15, 1858, in *The Collected Works of Abraham Lincoln*, ed. Roy P. Basler (New Brunswick, N.J.: Rutgers University Press, 1953), vol. III, pp. 301–302.

9. In practice slaves were often allowed to have some money and own some things. In law, however, everything belonged to their owners.

10. See note 44 in chap. 4.

11. We should note that Taney's view of the Founding is prevalent today among so-called liberals, who deny the authority of "original intent" jurisprudence precisely because they deny—with Taney—that the Declaration of Independence included Negroes in "all men."

12. Isaiah 28:15.

13. Thoreau's thoughts on this subject are immortalized in his essay "Civil Disobedience." Also see the present writer's "Reflections on Thoreau and Lincoln: Civil Disobedience in the American Tradition," in *The Conditions of Freedom* (Baltimore: Johns Hopkins University Press, 1975), pp. 124–148.

14. The transcendental movement in New England, which inspired much of the abolitionism there, was wholly an offshoot of German philosophy. As we shall see, Calhoun was influenced decisively by Rousseau—the inspiration for Kant—and by Hegel.

15. Lincoln, Speech at Springfield, June 26, 1857, in *Collected Works*, vol. II, p. 405.

16. Lincoln, Speech at Springfield, in *Collected Works*, pp. 405–406.

17. Lincoln, Speech at Springfield, in *Collected Works*, p. 403.

18. See note 13 in chap. 2.

19. Witness the fate of the inhabitants of Jericho in Joshua 6:21: "And then they

utterly destroyed all in the city, both men and women, young and old, oxen, sheep, and asses, with the edge of the sword." The Romans did the same to the Carthaginians. The Athenians killed all the Melians defeated in battle and carried the women and children into slavery.

20. The Kansas–Nebraska Act, May 30, 1854, in *Documents of American History*, p. 332.

21. *The Works of James Buchanan*, ed. John Bassett Moore (New York: Antiquarian Press, 1960), vol. X, pp. 105–107.

22. "Squatters" referred to the settlers who went into a territory before Congress had opened it to immigration. They would try to create a presumption of ownership of the land they were on and prevent anyone else from claiming a legal title to it when such became available. Some of the legendary land battles of the old West concerned attempts of legal owners to take possession of property from squatters.

23. *Works of James Buchanan*, vol. X, pp. 105–107. The second attached letter, from Supreme Court Justice Grier, was along the same lines.

24. David Potter, *The Impending Crisis* (New York: Harper & Row, 1976), pp. 238–239.

25. Potter, *Impending Crisis*, pp. 320–321.

26. On December 28, 1857, Lincoln wrote to Lyman Trumbull: "What does the New York Tribune mean by its constant eulogizing, and admiring, and magnifying of Douglas? . . . Have they concluded that the republican cause, generally, can be best promoted by sacrificing us here in Illinois? If so we would like to know it soon; it will save us a great deal of labor to surrender at once. As yet I have heard of no republican here going over to Douglas; but if the Tribune continues to din his praises into the ears of its five or ten thousand republican readers in Illinois, it is more than can be hoped that all will stand firm." *Collected Works*, vol. II, p. 430.

27. Stalin's regime was the greater threat of the two, because, unlike Hitler's, it pretended not to hold democracy in contempt. Rather it represented itself as a higher form of democracy than that of the capitalistic countries. Because of this Stalin, unlike Hitler, had many dupes and allies to promote his cause from within the free societies. There are notable resemblances between the delusive character of the communist simulacrum of democracy and that of Douglas's simulacrum of popular sovereignty.

28. Douglas's Reply, Second Debate at Freeport, Illinois, August 27, 1858, in *The Collected Works of Abraham Lincoln*, vol. III, pp. 54–55.

29. Douglas' Speech, Third Debate at Jonesboro, Illinois, September 15, 1858, *Collected Works*, pp. 112–113.

30. Douglas' Speech, First Debate at Ottawa, Illinois, August 21, 1858, in *Collected Works*, p. 10.

31. Douglas' Speech, Seventh Debate at Alton, Illinois, October 15, 1858, in *Collected Works*, p. 297. Douglas is here denying that the prohibition of slavery in the Northwest Ordinance had, as Lincoln maintained, kept slavery out of Illinois.

32. Lincoln, Speech at Cincinnati, Ohio, September 17, 1859, in *Collected Works*, pp. 445–446.

33. Potter, *Impending Crisis*, pp. 354–355.

34. The candidacy for the Republican presidential nomination in 1860 of New York-

er William Seward really foundered on the fact that he would not be needed to carry New York, given that Fremont had carried that state for the Republicans by a large margin in 1856.

35. Lincoln, Seventh Debate at Alton, Illinois, October 15, 1858, in *Collected Works*, vol. III, p. 315.

36. *The Republic of Plato*, trans. Allan Bloom (New York: Basic Books, 1968), p. 16.

37. These sentences embody the teaching of the Sophists as presented in Plato's dialogues—especially the *Protagoras* and the *Gorgias*. This is also the position, we would remind the reader, of Chief Justice Rehnquist in "The Notion of a Living Constitution" (see note 24 in chap. 2).

38. Lincoln, in *Collected Works*, vol. III, p. 315.

39. Lincoln, Fifth Debate at Galesburg, Illinois, October 7, 1858, in *Collected Works*, p. 231.

40. Lincoln, First Debate at Ottawa, Illinois, August 21, 1858, in *Collected Works*, p. 27.

41. At Freeport he did not repeat the verbatim reading from the text of Douglas's Senate speech alleging this intention of Buchanan. He did, however, hand the text to the reporters.

42. Lincoln quoting Douglas's Senate speech of March 22, 1858, in *Collected Works*, vol. III, pp. 24–25.

43. Lincoln quoting Douglas's Senate speech, in *Collected Works*, pp. 25–26.

44. Lincoln's Reply, in *Collected Works*, pp. 28–29.

45. Lincoln, Second Debate at Freeport, Illinois, August 27, 1858, in *Collected Works*, pp. 43, 51–52.

46. Douglas's *Harper's* essay, "The Dividing Line between Federal and Local Authority: Popular Sovereignty in the Territories," is discussed in full in the appendix to this chapter.

47. Lincoln, *Collected Works*, vol. III, pp. 317–318.

48. Lincoln, *Collected Works*, p. 324.

49. There was no "fugitive whiskey" clause in the Constitution!

50. Lincoln, *Collected Works*, vol. II, p. 501.

51. Lincoln, *Collected Works*, vol. III, p. 145.

52. Lincoln, Speech at Peoria, Illinois, October 16, 1854, in *Collected Works*, vol. II, p. 264.

53. Lincoln, *Collected Works*, vol. II, p. 264.

54. See Alfred H. Conrad and John Meyer, "The Economics of Slavery in the Ante-Bellum South," *Journal of Political Economy*, April 1958; Robert Fogel and Stanley Engerman, *Time on the Cross: Evidence and Methods—A Supplement* (Boston: Little, Brown, 1974); and Robert W. Fogel, *Without Consent or Contract* (New York: W. W. Norton, 1990).

55. Regulation of the interstate trade in slaves, especially to bring about more humane and hygienic conditions in their transportation and sale, was the topic of many petitions to Congress by abolitionists and others.

56. Lincoln himself had been a captain of militia in the Black Hawk war. He certainly knew that some tribes tortured their prisoners—prolonging the torture as long as

possible, because of the amusement it provided—before putting them to death. Lincoln, however, also prevented his men from lynching a lone Indian who strayed into their lines.

57. Acts 17:26.

58. See note 3 in chap. 3.

59. *The Provincial Letters of Blaise Pascal*, trans. Thomas McCree (London: J. M. Dent, 1904), p. 277. This aphorism became a favorite of the defenders of slavery. The late M. E. Bradford, a rugged and unbending defender of the cause of the antebellum South, entitled one of his books *A Better Guide than Reason*. The title was taken from John Dickinson, who did not in the least mean by it what Bradford meant. For Dickinson the "better guide" was what Aristotle meant by practical wisdom, which could be gained only by experience, as distinct from theoretical reason, which could be entirely abstract. Bradford, echoing Jefferson Davis, insisted that he knew from the inherited wisdom of "our fathers" that slavery was a positive good. He hated Lincoln because he gave reasons against slavery, as much as because of the reasons he gave.

60. Lincoln, *Collected Works*, vol. II, p. 265.

61. Lincoln, Speech at Springfield, June 26, 1857, in *Collected Works*, vol. II, p. 408.

62. There were also some few successful black businessmen who bought slaves. Again, these were usually family members.

63. Lincoln, Fourth Debate at Charleston, Illinois, September 18, 1868, in *Collected Works*, vol. III, p. 146.

64. Leland Winfield Meyer, *The Life and Times of Colonel Richard M. Johnson of Kentucky* (New York: AMS Press, 1967), pp. 322–323.

65. Lincoln, *Collected Works*, vol. II, p. 265.

66. Lincoln, *Collected Works*, pp. 265–266.

67. Lincoln, *Collected Works*, pp. 265–266.

68. See notes 36 and 38 in chap. 1.

69. Lincoln, *Collected Works*, vol. II, pp. 256, 281–282.

70. "What then? Free them all, and keep them among us as underlings? Is it quite certain that this betters their condition?" Lincoln, *Collected Works*, pp. 255–256. Lincoln thus anticipates what happened after the end of Reconstruction. For nearly three quarters of a century, Jim Crow imposed on free Negroes a regime in many respects harsher than slavery. The persons of slaves received a certain protection from the fact that they were valuable property, a protection that was stripped from them after they were free.

71. Most notably in the "standard maxim" passage of his speech on *Dred Scott* (see note 16 above). But consider also: "It is said in one of the admonitions of the Lord, 'As your father in Heaven is perfect, be ye also perfect.' The Saviour, I suppose, did not expect that any human creature could be as perfect as the Father in Heaven; but he said, 'As your Father in Heaven is perfect, be ye also perfect.' He set that up as a standard, and he who did most towards reaching that standard, attained the highest degree of moral perfection. So I say in relation to the principle that all men are created equal, let it be as nearly reached as we can." Lincoln, Speech at Chicago, July 10, 1858, *Collected Works*, vol. II, p. 501

72. *Federalist Papers*, p. 283.

73. See note 77 in chap. 2.

74. Lincoln, *Collected Works*, vol. II, p. 501.

75. See note 17 above.

76. One might ask, however, whether Dred Scott had not actually become free by reason of his residence in Illinois. Was he not reenslaved when he returned to Missouri?

77. One should remember, however, that there were also economic disincentives to the importation of slaves. Domestic "producers" of slaves looked upon cheap foreign imports the same way domestic producers of anything else looked upon such imports.

78. See note 25 in chap. 4; see also Lincoln, *Collected Works*, vol. 1, p. 115.

79. Lincoln, Speech in the U.S. House of Representatives, January 12, 1848, in *Collected Works*, vol. I, pp. 438–439.

80. See note 34 in chap. 3.

81. The last paragraph of Article XIII of the Articles of Confederation begins: "And whereas it hath pleased the Great Governor of the world to incline the hearts of the legislatures we represent. . . ." *Documents of American History*, p. 115.

82. We have in mind his speeches, messages, and letters. There are those who have asserted that in private conversations he acknowledged the orthodox Christian belief concerning Jesus. But these remain unauthenticated.

83. Lincoln, Speech at Lewistown, Illinois, August 17, 1858, in *Collected Works*, vol. II, pp. 546–547.

84. Lincoln's Old Testament text, to which we shall return, was Genesis 3:19: "In the sweat of your face you shall eat bread."

85. See note 122 in chap. 2.

86. Matthew 10:34–36.

Chapter 6

1. Unless otherwise noted, all quotations from Lincoln in this chapter are from his Message to Congress in Special Session, July 4, 1861, in *The Collected Works of Abraham Lincoln*, ed. Roy P. Basler (New Brunswick, N.J.: Rutgers University Press, 1953), vol. IV, pp. 421–441. In this message, we can see what a great political historian Lincoln might have been had he survived to write of the Civil War, as Churchill did of World War II.

2. According to an apocryphal tale of World War II, after Churchill finished his "We will fight on the beaches" speech on June 4, 1940, he put his hand over the microphone and said, "And we shall hit them over the head with beer bottles, because that's all we have." The disproportion in military preparedness and power between the Confederate and Union governments when Lincoln was inaugurated may be compared to that between Hitler's and Churchill's governments when the latter became prime minister. A comparison of their predecessors, Buchanan and Chamberlain, is also warranted.

3. See note 133 in chap. 1.

4. In May 1995, a letter to the *Wall Street Journal* by someone identifying himself as the president of the Southern League—with members, he said, in thirty-seven states—asserted that the foundation of all our liberties under the Constitution was the right of secession!

5. Aristotle, *Politics*, 1280 b 24–34.

6. See note 69 in chap. 2.

7. "A Sermon on the Day of the Commencement of the Constitution," in *Political Sermons of the American Founding Era*, ed. Ellis Sandoz (Indianapolis: Liberty Press, 1991), p. 637.

8. *The Revolutionary Records of the State of Georgia*, ed. Allen D. Candler (Atlanta: Franklin-Turner, 1908), vol. I, pp. 41–42.

9. See note 23 in chap. 1.

10. See note 46 in chap. 3.

11. Articles of Confederation, March 1, 1781, in *Documents of American History*, ed. Henry Steele Commager (New York: Appleton-Century-Crofts, 1948), p. 111.

12. John Quincy Adams, *Jubilee of the Constitution: A Discourse Delivered at the Request of the New York Historical Society* (New York: Samuel Colman, 1839), pp. 19–31.

13. See note 91 in chap. 1.

14. All quotations from Madison in this section are from *The Federalist Papers*, ed. Clinton Rossiter, with a new introduction and notes by Charles R. Kesler (New York: Mentor Books, 1999), no. 43, pp. 247–248.

15. Aristotle, *Nicomachean Ethics* 1094 a 23–25.

16. "Eudaimonia" is the Greek word for which the standard translation is happiness. Literally, it means to have a good "daimon," a divine power overseeing your good fortune. This popular understanding is replaced in the *Nicomachean Ethics* by a precise philosophical understanding.

17. Nothing more directly contradicts the view that the philosophic origins of the Founding are Hobbesian. For Hobbes the law of nature directs us only to avoid violent death. Hobbes's nature has nothing whatever to do with happiness.

18. This of course was the thesis of both Plato's *Republic* and his *Gorgias*. How Macbeth's crime destroyed all possibility of happiness *for him* (and Lady Macbeth) is also the theme of Lincoln's favorite play (see note 87 in chap. 2).

19. Lincoln, *Collected Works*, vol. VIII, pp. 402–403.

20. We may think of immigrants to the United States who become citizens and their relatives who remained in the "old country."

21. The Constitution of the Confederate States of America, March 11, 1861, in *Documents of American History*, p. 376.

22. In the aftermath of the war with Spain, both Cuba and the Philippines were granted independence. Puerto Rico remains a territory. Guam, the Virgin Islands, and some other anomalies do not affect the main argument.

23. See note 132 in chap. 1.

24. *The Mind of the Founder: Sources of the Political Thought of James Madison*, ed. Marvin Meyers (Hanover, N.H.:University Press of New England, 1981), p. 162.

25. *Federalist Papers*, no. 63, p. 352.

Chapter 7

1. See note 71 in chap. 1.

2. See note 79 in chap. 3.

3. John C. Calhoun, Speech on the Slave Question, February 19, 1847, in *Union and Liberty: The Political Philosophy of John C. Calhoun*, ed. Ross M. Lence (Indianapolis: Liberty Fund, 1992), p. 521.

4. Unless otherwise noted, all quotations from Calhoun in this section are from his Speech on the Oregon Bill, June 27, 1848, in *Union and Liberty*, pp. 565–570.

5. See note 97 in chap. 1.

6. Thomas Jefferson, Letter to John Adams, October 28, 1813, in *Writings*, ed. Merrill D. Peterson (New York: Library of America, 1984), p. 1306.

7. See note 96 in chap. 1.

8. Abraham Lincoln, *The Collected Works of Abraham Lincoln*, ed. Roy P. Basler (New Brunswick, N.J.: Rutgers University Press, 1953), vol. II, p. 406.

9. *The Federalist Papers*, ed. Clinton Rossiter, with a new introduction and notes by Charles R. Kesler (New York: Mentor Books, 1999), no. 39, pp. 208–209.

10. *Documents of American History*, ed. Henry Steele Commager (New York: Appleton-Century-Crofts, 1948), p. 110. I am indebted to Philip Jaffa for bringing the *Quock Walker* case to my attention.

11. "Solitary" here and elsewhere does not, as it cannot, mean apart from the family. No individual could exist if he did not have a mother and father who protected and nurtured him.

12. See note 7 in chap. 1.

13. See note 82 in chap. 1.

14. Aristotle, *Politics* 1253 a 30–32.

15. The campaign of civil disobedience led by Martin Luther King Jr., although featuring nonviolent resistance, with its constant appeal to human equality was at the same time a reminder of the revolutionary foundations of the Constitution.

16. John Locke, *Second Treatise of Government*, chap. II, para. 6.

17. *Hamlet*, act I, scene 2.

18. To Colonel Charles Yancey, January 6, 1816, in *The Writings of Thomas Jefferson*, ed. Andrew Lipscomb (Washington, D.C.: Thomas Jefferson Memorial Association, 1904), vol. XIV, p. 384.

19. See note 18 in chap. 3.

20. From the experience of the twentieth century, we know that fanatical atheism (e.g., that of Communism) can be as baneful as religious fanaticism. The "quiet atheism" of the premodern variety was neither a threat nor a support to the civil order. It was not a support as it cannot make respect for the rights of others a duty.

21. John Stuart Mill, *On Liberty* (New York: W. W. Norton, 1975), p. 11.

22. See note 66 in chap. 4.

23. *Collected Works*, vol. I, p. 114.

24. Tocqueville himself, for all his genius, did not make it clear that there were two different ideas of equality, one of Lockean and the other of Rousseauian origin. It was the latter that could and did lead to tyranny. It was the former that incorporated the consent of the governed into a constitutionalism designed to prevent the tyranny of the majority no less than of the minority.

25. It should be noted, however, that the Jacobins, in deference to Rousseau's actual teaching, divided France into 10,000 "communes." These were the repositories of legal

sovereignty. But the real government was the Committee of Public Safety and the party apparatus under its control. This pattern was reduplicated in the Bolshevik Revolution, whose slogan under Lenin was "all power to the soviets." The Central Committee of the Communist Party centralized all power in its own hands, and the soviets actually had none. Napoleon took over a regime that had been theoretically decentralized but actually completely centralized. The same may be said of the regimes of Lenin and Stalin.

26. *Federalist Papers*, no. 10, p. 46.

27. Among the predecessors of Plato's *Republic* is Aristophanes' *Assembly of Women*, an excruciatingly comical (and raunchy) enactment of an attempt to establish a communist regime.

28. Aristotle, *Politics*, 1261 a 10 ff.

29. *Politics*, 1281 a 15–18.

30. Rousseau's account of the state of nature is far more agreeable to the theory of evolution than that of Hobbes or Locke. According to some interpretations, Rousseau gave the first great impulse to the doctrine that came to fruition in Darwin. Only Locke's theory, however, is consonant with the Bible.

31. "[E]ven the highest lawcourt in the land is more likely to defer to the contentions of social science than to the Ten Commandments as the words of the living God." Leo Strauss, *The City and Man* (Chicago: University of Chicago Press, 1977), p.1. Strauss had reference to Chief Justice Earl Warren's opinion in *Brown v. Board of Education* (1954), which inferred from Kenneth Clark's famous doll tests that segregation caused psychological harm to black schoolchildren. Actually the tests proved nothing of the kind, and Warren had little interest in what they did prove. Like Alexander Stephens, it was sufficient for him to cite "science" as supporting his own opinion of what the Constitution ought to mean. Had he cared to refute "separate but equal" with the true intent and meaning of the Fourteenth Amendment, it was readily available to him in Justice Harlan's dissenting opinion in *Plessy v. Ferguson* (1896). "Science" was merely a means of justifying a preconceived opinion, unhampered by the Constitution itself. And Warren (or anyone else) could have found "scientific" support for any other preconceived opinion.

32. In the December 1996 issue of *Southern Partisan*, the lead article was entitled "Why the South Was Right." The alleged rightness of the South is discovered entirely from within the texts of Calhoun's *Disquisition* and *Discourse*. The author identifies justice with state rights, and state rights are divorced from natural rights. There is nothing to set this article apart from hundreds of others that have preceded it. What is interesting is that the argument of defenders of the Confederate cause has not changed since the Civil War, and Calhoun remains their unchallenged intellectual progenitor.

33. It is no accident that the civil rights movement, ever since the passage of the great Civil Rights Acts of 1964 and 1965, has been based almost entirely upon the idea of group as opposed to individual rights. As a theoretical concept, "black power" is no different from the "white power" espoused by Calhoun.

34. Jefferson Davis, like Calhoun, took the example of the Founding Fathers as slaveholders to be authoritative while ignoring their antislavery pronouncements.

35. See John C. Calhoun, *A Disquisition on Government*, in *Union and Liberty*, p. 13: "Such an organism . . . as will furnish the means by which resistance may be systematically and peaceably made on the part of the ruled to oppression and abuse of power on the

part of the rulers is the first and indispensable step toward *forming* a constitutional government. And this can only be effected by or through the right of suffrage—the right on the part of the ruled to choose their rulers at proper intervals and to hold them thereby responsible for their conduct—the responsibility of the rulers to the ruled through the right of suffrage is the indispensable *foundation* of a constitutional government." But unlike the Founders and Lincoln, who see the inconsistency between the principle of a popular republic and slavery, the "scientific" Calhoun does not.

36. *Federalist Papers*, no. 10, p. 51.

37. *Federalist Papers*, no. 51, pp. 289–290.

38. See note 63 in chap. 1.

39. Jefferson, in both the Louisiana Purchase and in the embargo, construed enumerated powers in a manner altogether Hamiltonian. Madison, having opposed the first Bank of the United States as unconstitutional, as president signed into law the charter of the Second Bank of the United States.

40. "The apportionment of taxes on the various descriptions of property is an act which seems to require the most exact impartiality; yet there is, perhaps, no legislative act in which greater opportunity and temptation are given to the predominant party to trample on the rules of justice." Madison, *Federalist Papers*, no. 10, p. 48. It should be noted, however, that for Madison the "rules of justice" are knowable apart from the political process.

41. Calhoun, *Disquisition on Government*, in *Union and Liberty*, p. 5.

42. Aristotle, *Nicomachean Ethics*, 1094 b 11 ff.

43. "If the impulse and the opportunity [for the oppression of one faction by another] be suffered to coincide, we well know that neither moral nor religious motives can be relied on as an adequate control." Madison, *Federalist Papers*, no. 10, p. 49. We must notice the resemblances between Madison and Calhoun to gain a firm grasp upon their differences.

44. Calhoun, *Disquisition on Government*, in *Union and Liberty*, pp. 5–6.

45. This is what Aristotle, in the *Politics*, accuses Plato (or Socrates) of doing in the *Republic*. See *Politics*, 1261 a 10–24.

46. Calhoun, *Disquisition on Government*, in *Union and Liberty*, pp. 5–6, 8.

47. Calhoun's reference to "Divine ordination" also implies Spinoza's God, who is essentially the necessity uniting cause and effect.

48. Calhoun, *Disquisition on Government*, in *Union and Liberty*, p. 6.

49. Calhoun, *Disquisition on Government*, in *Union and Liberty*, pp. 5, 8.

50. Calhoun, *Disquisition on Government*, in *Union and Liberty*, pp. 6–7.

51. Calhoun, *Disquisition on Government*, in *Union and Liberty*, p. 7.

52. Communism in the *Republic* refers explicitly only to the class of the guardians. Its application to the lower class as well, according to Aristotle, is an insoluble problem. See *Politics*, 1264 a 11 ff.

53. For instance, a selfish desire to receive recognition for any great and praiseworthy accomplishment would be an element of the virtue of magnanimity as described by Aristotle in Book IV of the *Nicomachean Ethics*.

54. Calhoun, *Disquisition on Government*, in *Union and Liberty*, pp. 8–9. Cf. *The Buttercup Factor*, by Henry Cecil.

55. Calhoun, *Disquisition on Government*, in *Union and Liberty*, p. 7.

56. Calhoun, *Disquisition on Government*, in *Union and Liberty*, p. 10.

57. *George Washington: A Collection*, ed. W. B. Allen (Indianapolis: Liberty Classics, 1988), p. 462.

58. Calhoun, *Disquisition on Government*, in *Union and Liberty*, pp. 68, 76.

59. Benedict de Spinoza, "Political Treatise," in *The Political Works* (Oxford: Clarendon Press, 1958), chap. 2.6, p. 271.

60. That is to say, machine guns! Also see Mark Twain's *Connecticut Yankee in King Arthur's Court* for a mordant reflection on the relative merits of nineteenth-century scientific and democratic civilization (with its machine guns) and medieval superstition and barbarism.

61. Winston Churchill observed in the early 1920s that the theory and practice of Bolshevism had been perfected millions of years ago—in the society of the white ant. By then he had realized that the "progress" attributed to modern science was as consistent with the destruction as with the perfection of man's humanity. "Mass Effects in Modern Life," in *Thoughts and Adventures* (London: Odhams Press, 1948), p. 195.

62. Comparing Calhounism to Darwinism, we are struck by the popularity of the idea of eugenics among some Darwinians (e.g., George Bernard Shaw). Natural selection has been a matter of chance hitherto. Now it can become a conscious application of scientific reason. Eugenics, of course, lay at the heart of Hitler's program for race purification and improvement.

63. See "The German Ideology," in *The Marx-Engels Reader*, ed. Robert C. Tucker (New York: W. W. Norton, 1978), p. 154. One is struck by the similarity of expression to Saint Paul in 1 Corinthians 13:12: "[N]ow we see as through a glass darkly, but then face to face." The "end of history" can only be understood as a replacement for the messianic promises of either the Old or the New Testament.

64. Calhoun, *Disquisition on Government*, in *Union and Liberty*, pp. 38–39.

65. Calhoun, *Disquisition on Government*, in *Union and Liberty*, pp. 39–40.

66. Calhoun, *Disquisition on Government*, in *Union and Liberty*, pp. 43–44.

67. *Federalist Papers*, no. 10, pp. 46–47.

68. See note 66 in chap. 4.

69. Calhoun, *Disquisition on Government*, in *Union and Liberty*, pp. 42–43.

70. See note 91 in chap. 1.

71. The unusually high rates in the Tariff of Abominations were the result more of political miscalculation than of evil intent. The Southerners believed that by raising rates in committee beyond the point that would command a majority on the floor of the House, they could defeat the whole bill. But they judged wrongly and were hoist by their own petard. Calhoun's attempt to portray a sectional alliance designed to plunder the South was altogether an illusion. As such, it commanded little support outside South Carolina. The South Carolina doctrines, forged in the nullification controversy, returned, however, many times more powerful in 1860, when the issue was slavery.

72. Calhoun does assert that the internal constitution of South Carolina represented a balance of power between the low country or tidewater counties and the up-country counties, with each having a veto upon the other. This, he claimed, was what made the

state so well governed and harmonious. But he saw no such distinction in 1833 between unionists and nullifiers.

73. See note 46 in chap. 3.

74. "Notes on Nullification," in *The Writings of James Madison*, ed. Gaillard Hunt (New York: G. P. Putnam's Sons, 1900), p. 601.

75. *Federalist Papers*, p. 210.

76. *Federalist Papers*, no. 10, p. 45.

77. See note 44 in chap. 3.

78. Calhoun, A *Discourse on the Constitution and Government of the United States*, in *Union and Liberty*, pp. 81–82.

79. Calhoun, *Discourse on the Constitution*, in *Union and Liberty*, pp. 81–82.

80. George Washington, Letter to the President of the Continental Congress, September 17, 1787, in *Writings*, ed. John Rhodehamel (New York: Library of America, 1997), p. 654.

81. Washington, Letter to the President, in: *Writings*, p. 654.

82. Calhoun, *Discourse on the Constitution*, in *Union and Liberty*, p. 98.

Appendix

The only reprinting of Douglas's *Harper's* essay is in *In the Name of the People: Speeches and Writings of Lincoln and Douglas in the Ohio Campaign of 1859*, ed. Harry V. Jaffa and Robert W. Johannsen (Columbus: Ohio State University Press, 1959), pp. 58–125.

1. See note 5 in chap. 2.

2. Abraham Lincoln, Address at Cooper Institute, New York City, February 27, 1860, in *The Collected Works of Abraham Lincoln*, ed. Roy P. Basler (New Brunswick, N.J.: Rutgers University Press, 1953), vol. II, p. 550.

3. Concerning Douglas's preparations, Robert W. Johannsen writes: "It was no secret . . . that Douglas had been studying early American history in an attempt to find historical precedents for popular sovereignty. Like so many others, both in his day and ours, Douglas was convinced that his position would be unassailable if he could trace it back to the Founding Fathers. During the year Douglas withdrew from the Library of Congress such standard works as *The Federalist*, Jonathan Elliott's *Debates*, and the first six volumes of George Bancroft's *History of the United States*, in addition to a number of other books, including histories of several of the American colonies. To George Bancroft, America's most distinguished historian, he appealed for additional help. . . . Answering almost immediately, [Bancroft] sent the Senator copies of colonial documents bearing upon the subject of slavery." "Stephen A. Douglas, *Harper's Magazine*, and Popular Sovereignty," *Mississippi Valley Historical Review*, vol. 45, 1958–59, pp. 613–614.

4. Don E. Fehrenbacher, *The Dred Scott Case: Its Significance in American Law and Politics* (New York: Oxford University Press, 1978), p. 515.

5. In the four-way presidential election of 1860, Douglas received the second highest number of popular votes: 1,375,157 (29.3 percent) to Lincoln's 1,866,452 (39.8 percent).

6. *In the Name of the People*, p. 65.

7. "Observations on Senator Douglas' Views of Popular Sovereignty" was originally published in the *Washington Constitution* on September 10, 1859. At first anonymous, Black's authorship soon became known. The article is reprinted in *In the Name of the People*, pp. 187–188.

8. *In the Name of the People*, pp. 66–68.

9. We use the word "presumption" advisedly. In our comments on Jefferson's Kentucky Resolutions in chap. 1, we observed that he asserted the right of revolution even against an elected government. And Lincoln in his inaugural conceded that if his government or any government violated the constitutional rights of the minority, the violation would justify rebellion.

10. *In the Name of the People*, p. 70.

11. Thomas Jefferson, *Writings*, ed. Merrill D. Peterson (New York: Library of America, 1984), p. 22. Consider also the following from James Otis, *The Rights of the British Colonies* (1764), in *Pamphlets of the American Revolution*, ed. Bernard Bailyn (Cambridge: Harvard University Press, 1965), p. 439: "The Colonists are by the law of nature free born, as indeed all men are, white or black. No better reasons can be given, for enslaving those of any color than such as baron Montesquieu has humorously given, as the foundation of that cruel slavery exercised over the poor Ethiopians; which threatens one day to reduce both Europe and America to the ignorance and barbarity of the darkest ages. Does it follow that tis right to enslave a man because he is black? Will short curled hair like wool, instead of christian hair, as tis called by those whose hearts are as hard as the nether millstone, help the argument? Can any logical inference in favor of slavery, be drawn from a flat nose, a long or short face? Nothing better can be said of a trade that is the most shocking violation of the law of nature. . . . It is a clear truth, that those who every day barter away other men's liberty will soon care little for their own." Here is an exact parallel to Jefferson's deleted stricture, written eleven years before the Declaration of Independence. That it was published in Boston proves that natural rights, under the laws of nature, were the common coin of Revolutionary America. It is difficult to imagine more biting sarcasm than Otis's reference to "christian hair." Even Lincoln, in 1858, would not have ventured upon anything so bold.

12. *In the Name of the People*, p. 80.

13. See note 97 in chap. 1. Such declarations are part of the most recent state constitutions as well. For example, Hawaii: "All persons are free by nature and are equal in their inherent and inalienable rights." And Alaska: "This constitution is dedicated to the principles that all persons have a natural right to life, liberty, the pursuit of happiness, and the enjoyment of the rewards of their own industry."

14. *In the Name of the People*, p. 81.

15. Jefferson, Report on Government for Western Territory, March 1, 1784, in *Writings*, p. 377.

16. Letter to Jean Nicolas de Meunier, June 26, 1786, in *Writings*, p. 592.

17. *In the Name of the People*, p. 91.

18. Douglas mentions the Northwest Ordinance in passing later in the essay. But he never acknowledges the fact that it, and not the 1784 plan, became the paradigm for all future territorial governments.

19. *Documents of American History*, ed. Henry Steele Commager (New York: Appleton-Century-Crofts, 1948), p. 173.

20. Douglas' Speech, Second Debate, Freeport, Illinois, August 27, 1858, in *Collected Works*, vol. 3, pp. 53–54.

21. *In the Name of the People*, pp. 101–103.

22. *In the Name of the People*, pp. 113–114.

23. We know from *Huckleberry Finn*, of course, that the most degraded character in the antebellum South was the "nigger stealer." Unlike a horse thief, however, he did not steal slaves in order to sell them for his own profit.

24. *In the Name of the People*, p. 114.

Index

About the Author

Harry V. Jaffa is the Henry Salvatori Research Professor of Political Philosophy Emeritus at Claremont McKenna College and Claremont Graduate University and a Distinguished Fellow of the Claremont Institute. He is the author of ten books and coauthor of, or contributor to, numerous other publications; he also wrote Barry Goldwater's acceptance speech at the 1964 Republican National Convention. He has received fellowships from the Ford, Rockefeller, Guggenheim, and Earhart Foundations and was the founding president of the Winston S. Churchill Association. He holds a B.A. from Yale and a Ph.D. from the New School for Social Research.

P.158
P.104
P.164

$54.46